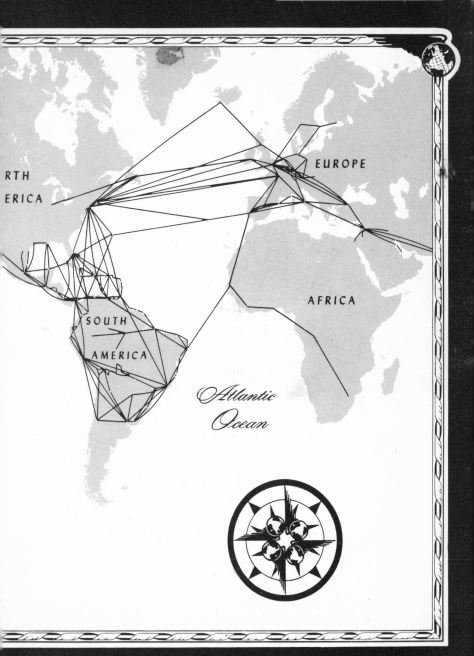

*THE COMPLETE ROUND-THE-WORLD COOKBOOK*

# THE COMPLETE
# ROUND-THE-WORLD
# COOKBOOK

*Recipes gathered by*
*Pan American World Airways*
*from the 84 countries they serve,*
*with food and travel comments by*

# MYRA WALDO

*with illustrations*

*Doubleday & Company, Inc., Garden City, New York*

*BIBLIOGRAPHICAL NOTE*

First published October 21, 1954
Reprinted October 25, 1954
Reprinted February 4, 1955
Reprinted December 2, 1955
Reprinted March 29, 1957

Library of Congress Catalog Card Number 54-10769

*BON VOYAGE AND BON APPÉTIT—*

*on this trip around the world to all those who love travel and fine food.*

# INTRODUCTION

Brillat-Savarin, PHYSIOLOGIE DU GOÛT:
*"In compelling man to eat that he may live, Nature gives him an appetite to invite him, and pleasure to reward him."*

The past few years have seen a tremendous awakening of interest in foreign foods and cookery. While the exact reason for this is not known, it undoubtedly includes such varying factors as the exposure of American G.I.s to a wide assortment of different cooking styles, the increasing number of Americans always on the move and touring in foreign countries, and, inevitably, the gradual maturity of our own country, gastronomically speaking.

The recipes in this book were gathered, for the most part, by Pan American World Airways. Pan American agents in each of the more than eighty countries and territories served by the air line were requested to furnish recipes for local food specialties, eating and drinking customs, and other culinary information. The recipes came from all possible sources, including hotels, restaurants, local gourmet groups, and private citizens. Many of the recipes were in weights and measurements of the particular country, and these were converted into our normal usage. In certain other cases the dishes were not to the American taste or called for ingredients not normally available to us, and these were discarded.

The recipes were tested, and in only a very few instances was it found necessary to make some small changes in order to make them more acceptable to the American palate. In the interest of reproducing the cuisine of the various countries with the greatest possible accuracy, this was done only where it was found to be unavoidable. In general it may be said that where any dish is found to vary from the traditional method of preparation it is because the dish required ingredients not readily available to the American housewife, or was unwarrantedly difficult to prepare, or was not in accordance with American taste by reason of excessive sweetness, spiciness, and so forth.

The editor has taken a certain amount of liberty in the spelling of the names of certain foreign dishes in the interest of greater simplicity. In addition there is almost always a degree of regional variance within the particular country involved as to the preparation of the dish itself as well as to the spelling and pronunciation of its name. This is particularly noticeable in those countries whose languages do not have Romanic backgrounds. Further, the translations supplied for many of the dishes are intentionally not always literal or exact, since many such translations would fail to explain the nature of the dish. The classic Dutch preparation called *Filosoof* literally means "Philosopher"; if this were supplied as the translation it would not mean nearly so much as "Dutch Meat and Potato Pie." Most philosophers are hard to digest, but this particular meat and potato pie is delicious.

Occasionally it may be noted that a given dish is listed under a country other than the one in which the reader believes it should be placed. In certain groups of countries the food is quite similar; thus, in order not to repeat dishes and in the interest of a better balanced book, various other local specialties are substituted.

It is the intention of this book to make it possible for the reader to prepare complete dinners as served in any of the countries concerned. The book offers in order within each country selections of recipes for appetizers, soups, fish, meat, vegetables, desserts, etc. There are large numbers of casserole and stew preparations which represent complete meals in one dish. Therefore it is not necessary to prepare all of the dishes to reproduce the foreign flavor of a given country at your own dinner table or at a party.

This book will not teach the reader how to cook. It has been assumed that such fundamentals of food preparation as the washing of vegetables, fruits, and poultry, etc., are known. In that vein, the simple everyday steps have been either merely mentioned or purposely omitted. Nevertheless, it is believed that any person who follows the instructions may prepare any of the recipes in this book.

Of course the opinions and comments expressed in the book are those of the author and do not necessarily represent those of Pan American World Airways. Many descriptive chapters herein refer to United States citizens as "Americans." The other peoples of North and South America also believe that they are Americans, as indeed they are. On the other hand, it has been found that no other word describes the people of this country so well, and we are called Americans all over the globe. Further, it is extremely cumbersome to refer to ourselves as United Statesians, or even as North Americans, because Mexicans, for example, rightly consider themselves North Americans. It is hoped that this explanation will satisfy those who object to the use of the word "American" on the grounds of inaccuracy or unwarranted monopoly.

To those who find that many of the recipes contain onions, garlic, dried peppers, rice, and similar ingredients, it can only be said that the recipes represent the local cookery customs of the country involved. It is also true that in many countries vegetables and salads are not served as separate courses, and therefore these omissions may be noted. The reader's attention is invited to the back of the book, which contains cooking hints and terms, tables of weights and measurements, etc., a gourmets' glossary, and sources of foreign ingredients in the United States.

The editor wishes to thank all of those who have helped by supplying information for this book: the Voice of America, Radio Free Europe, Mr. Chyz of the Common Council for American Unity, the various foreign consulates, and of course most particularly Pan American World Airways' agents all over the world. Very special thanks are due to Harold Laird and Gerald Whitted of Pan American.

The world of travel, the observation of the life and ways of others, the spirit of inquiry, the willingness to eat what others eat, and fundamentally and primarily the maintaining of an open mind on all subjects is the surest way for us to learn something about the rest of the world. Whether we wanted it or not, world leadership has come to the United States. We can no longer sit back and let the world think what it will of us, nor can we fail to learn as much as possible about our neighbors who inhabit the globe. In this atomic age our neighbors *are* the Patagonians, the Zulus, and the people next door.

Myra Waldo

# CONTENTS

# ASIA

# THE PACIFIC

# NORTH AMERICA

# THE ATLANTIC AND THE CARIBBEAN

# SOUTH AMERICA

## COOKING HINTS

## SOURCES OF FOREIGN INGREDIENTS

## INDEX

*All recipes serve six
but are easily adaptable
to other numbers*

# EUROPE

Austria

Belgium and Luxembourg

Czechoslovakia

Denmark

England, Wales, and Northern Ireland

Finland

France

Germany

Holland (The Netherlands)

Hungary

Ireland

Italy

Norway

Poland

Portugal

Russia

Scotland

Spain

Sweden

Switzerland

Ukraine

Yugoslavia

## AUSTRIA

A glance at a map of Europe will indicate Austria's central location on the continent. Unfortunately it isn't always profitable to occupy the center of the stage, because struggles and power politics have raged across Austria's soil for many centuries. The policies of the land-hungry Hapsburgs have ultimately made Austria a shadow of its former greatness. Like all good-natured people who would rather play with clarinets than with cannons, who would prefer to waltz than to march, they have been taken advantage of by their neighbors. Nevertheless, something of old Austria remains alive today; to re-create the atmosphere of yesterday, you should be in your best clothes, in your gayest mood, a glass of champagne in your hand and with "The Blue Danube" playing on your phonograph. If some of the music seems to be in a minor key or to have a slightly melancholy air, that cannot be helped.

The Pan American plane on which you are traveling arrives at Tulln Airbase, the airport for Vienna. Shortly after your arrival, you'll want to join in Austria's favorite sport—eating. The country is filled with people who love to eat and consider it an important part of life. Anything in the nature of a drugstore lunch, American style, would be beyond their understanding. On arising, a cup of coffee with a piece of bread or flaky pastry is the rule, but this is followed about 10:30 A.M. with a second breakfast. Lunch is usually eaten about 1 P.M., and then most good Austrians look forward to their favorite repast of the day, *Jause*, or tea. The tea is much more likely to be coffee, but what of that? Coffee is immensely popular in the Austrian capital of Vienna, and coffeehouses are places for social gathering. Since everyone has been fasting since lunch (a good three hours ago!) most people will have sandwiches and many rich cakes and pastries. The Viennese, not satisfied with merely a plain cup of coffee, order it in many different fashions. The overwhelming favorite (although this has not been clearly proven by a 3 to 1 poll of doctors) is *Kaffee mit Schlagobers*, which can only be translated as coffee with whipped cream owing to the unfortunate limitations imposed by the English language. This is a very cold and pale description for a gleaming white cup filled with freshly brewed hot coffee, hidden by foamy mountains of rich, fluffy, cumulus clouds of whipped cream. It's all so *gemütlich,* so agreeable! *Gemütlich* also loses in the translation; there is no English equivalent for it.

Dinner is in the evening about 7:30 to 8:00 P.M., and this in turn is followed by a midnight snack consisting of cheese, dark bread, cold meats, and beer. Those who are still hungry have a few pieces of pastry or other low-calorie foods—it is so long until breakfast! Visitors to Austria who are not on guard will probably gain weight, but they will also have a wonderful time in the process. Life can be *schön,* life can be beautiful.

Austria's cuisine has an international flavor because it has so many neighbors. Although it has its own national cuisine, the country has borrowed freely from those who surround it—it's a small return for what has been taken from them. These dishes include Italian *pastas,* Hungarian *paprikas* and *gulyas,* German sausages and beer, and French Cuisine.

Most people have heard of Austria's famous *Wiener Schnitzel,* or the Viennese method of treating veal; others know of the strudels and of the *Sacher Torte,* both rich desserts. In addition the country has such things as *Brennsuppe,* a brown soup; *Nockerl,* very delicious dumplings; and also the *Schönbrunner lunch,* a satisfying ham and vegetable pie. The most popular single dish is boiled beef, prepared in many different ways and using dozens of different cuts of beef. These do not exhaust the possibilities but are merely intended to suggest some of the country's fine dishes. Much of the food is built around such varying ingredients as goose fat, thick soups, dumplings, whipped cream, and the nation's fine potato dishes. Everything is strictly non-fattening.

Beer is exceptional here, and many of the brews are world-renowned. Hard liquor is not important nationally, but the so-called international bars serve scotch and rye. Austrian wines, though extremely satisfying, are not quite equal to the French competition. Few Austrian wines are shipped to the United States; this is unfortunate in view of the excellence of Gumpoldskirchner, which twists the tongue on first pronunciation and several glasses later. Beer gardens, German style, are replaced in Austria by wine gardens. To see a relaxed Austria and to know the people, a visit to a wine garden on a fine summer evening is recommended: music by Mozart, wine from Austria's vineyards, and the most lighthearted, charming people in the world.

## BROWN SOUP

BRENNSUPPE

| | |
|---|---|
| 4 tablespoons butter | 1 cup red wine |
| 4 onions, sliced thin | 2 eggs |
| 3 tablespoons flour | 3 tablespoons heavy cream |
| 6 cups stock or 2 cans consommé and 2½ cans water | 2 tablespoons chopped parsley |
| | 1 teaspoon chopped chives |

Melt the butter in a deep saucepan. Add the onions and sauté until very brown, about 15 minutes, stirring frequently. Sprinkle with the flour and stir well. Gradually add the stock, stirring constantly until the boiling point is reached. Add the wine and cook over low heat for 1 hour. Correct seasoning.

Beat together in a bowl the eggs, cream, parsley, and chives. Gradually add 1 cup of the hot soup, stirring constantly to prevent curdling. Return to the saucepan, mixing well. Heat thoroughly but do not allow to boil.

## SOUR CREAM SOUP

### STEIRISCHE SUPPE

6 cups stock or 2 cans consommé and
  2½ cans water
½ teaspoon pepper
½ teaspoon salt
1 teaspoon cumin seed

1 tablespoon flour
1 cup sour cream
1 cup heavy sweet cream
4 boiled potatoes, peeled and cubed

Combine the stock, pepper, salt, and cumin seed in a saucepan. Boil for 10 minutes. In a bowl mix the flour and sour cream to a smooth paste. Add 1 cup of the stock gradually, beating constantly. Return to the stock in the saucepan and beat well. Add the sweet cream and potatoes. Cook over low heat for 10 minutes but do not allow to boil. Correct seasoning. Serve hot.

## PAPRIKA FISH

### PAPRIKA FISCH

 2 teaspoons salt
1½ tablespoons paprika
 6 fish fillets

4 tablespoons melted butter
1 tablespoon flour
½ cup light cream

Combine the salt and paprika and rub into the fillets thoroughly. Place them in a buttered baking dish and pour the melted butter over them. Bake in a 375° oven for 25 minutes, or until fish is browned. Remove the fillets carefully and place them on a platter in a warm place.

Mix the flour and cream together until smooth, and add to the butter in the baking dish, stirring constantly. If the dish cannot be placed over direct heat, use an asbestos pad. Cook until the mixture reaches the boiling point and for 3 minutes longer. Pour the sauce over the fish. Serve hot, with buttered small, boiled potatoes sprinkled with parsley.

# VEAL CUTLET, VIENNA STYLE

WIENER SCHNITZEL

½ cup flour
1 teaspoon salt
½ teaspoon pepper
2½ pounds veal steaks, pounded thin
   and cut into 6 pieces

2 eggs, beaten
¾ cup bread crumbs
¼ pound butter
3 tablespoons lemon juice
3 tablespoons chopped parsley

Combine the flour, salt, and pepper. Dip the veal in the mixture. Then dip each piece in the beaten egg and then in the bread crumbs. Melt half the butter in a large frying pan and place the veal in it. Cook over low heat until tender and well browned on both sides, about 15 minutes. Remove the veal and place on a platter in a warm place. Brown the remaining butter in the frying pan. Add the lemon juice and parsley and stir well. Pour over the veal and serve.

# VEGETABLE AND HAM PIE

SCHÖNBRUNNER LUNCH

¼ pound butter
6 egg yolks
½ cup sour cream
4 tablespoons flour
6 egg whites
¾ cup grated Parmesan cheese

¼ pound ham, coarsely chopped
½ cup cooked green peas
2 cups cooked cauliflower, broken in
   small pieces
1 cup sautéed mushrooms, sliced

Cream the butter in a bowl and add the egg yolks, sour cream, and 2 tablespoons of the flour. Beat well. Beat the egg whites until stiff but not dry. Fold in the remaining flour and 2 tablespoons of the Parmesan cheese. Fold into the first mixture gently. Pour half of the mixture into a buttered casserole. Spread evenly with the chopped ham and sprinkle with 2 tablespoons of the cheese. Spread with the peas and sprinkle with 2 additional tablespoons of cheese. Spread with the cauliflower and sprinkle with an additional 2 tablespoons of cheese. Spread with the mushrooms and sprinkle with the remaining cheese. Spread the remaining half of the egg mixture on top.

Do not preheat oven. Place the casserole in a cold oven and set the gauge at 350°, then bake for 45 minutes, or until set firmly and browned on top. Do not overbake. Serve hot, as promptly as possible, directly from the casserole.

## CHICKEN PAPRIKA

PAPRIKA HÜHNER

2 3½-pound frying chickens, disjointed
2 teaspoons salt
1 teaspoon pepper
4 tablespoons butter

6 onions, peeled and sliced thin
1½ tablespoons paprika (sweet)
½ pint sour cream

Wash and dry the chicken. Season with salt and pepper, rubbing in well, both inside and out. Melt the butter in a heavy saucepan. Add the sliced onions and the paprika, and cook for 3 minutes, stirring constantly. Add the chicken and brown over high heat. Lower the heat and cover the pan. Cook for 30 minutes, stirring occasionally. Add a little water if the pan becomes too dry. Add the sour cream, stir well, and let simmer for 15 minutes. Serve with *Nockerl*, the popular dumplings of the Austrians. (See recipe in this section.) Pour a little of the sauce over the dumplings.

## POTATOES WITH MUSTARD SAUCE

SENF KARTOFFELN

6 large potatoes, unpeeled
6 tablespoons butter
3 tablespoons chopped onion
3 tablespoons flour

1½ cups stock or 1½ cups hot water
  and 2 bouillon cubes
¾ teaspoon salt
½ teaspoon pepper
¼ cup prepared mustard
¼ cup bread crumbs

Scrub the potatoes well. Place in a saucepan and cover with water. Boil until tender, about 30 minutes. Drain, peel, and cut into ½-inch slices.

While the potatoes are cooking, melt half of the butter in a saucepan. Add the onions and sauté for 5 minutes, stirring frequently. Add the flour and mix well until light brown in color. Add the stock, salt, and pepper, stirring constantly until the boiling point is reached. Cook over low heat for 10 minutes. Strain. Add the mustard, mixing well.

Arrange the potatoes in a buttered pie plate in uniform rows, with each slice of potato resting on the adjacent slice. Pour the strained sauce over the potato slices. Sprinkle with the bread crumbs and dot with the remaining butter. Bake in a 375° oven for 15 minutes, or until delicately browned on top.

## NOODLES AND CABBAGE

KRAUT FLECKERL

1 large head cabbage
1 tablespoon salt
½ pound butter

2 teaspoons sugar
½ teaspoon pepper
2 8-ounce packages broad noodles

Wash the cabbage and cut it as fine as possible, discarding all imperfect leaves and the core. Place the shredded cabbage in a bowl and add the salt, mixing well. Allow to stand for at least 1 hour, preferably 2 hours. Rinse and drain well, squeezing out all the liquid. Melt half the butter in a saucepan. Add the cabbage, sugar, and pepper. Cook over low heat for 1½ hours, or until browned, stirring frequently. Add the remaining butter at intervals until all has been used. Correct seasoning.

Break the noodles in half, so that each piece is flat. Boil in salted water for 8 minutes. Drain well. Add to the cabbage and stir together until mixed. Heat for a few minutes. Serve with roast meats or poultry.

## DUMPLINGS, AUSTRIAN STYLE

NOCKERL

¼ pound butter
4 eggs

1¾ cups sifted flour
½ teaspoon salt

Cream the butter until light and fluffy. Add the eggs one at a time, beating well after each addition. Sift the flour and salt together, and add to the previous mixture. Mix well and shape into a long, thin roll. Set aside for 15 minutes. Break off very small pieces and drop into either boiling, salted water or boiling soup. Remove the *Nockerl* as they come to the top, which should be in about 3 minutes. Place in a colander to drain. Serve hot, in place of potatoes, with any dish having a gravy. Pour some of the gravy over the *Nockerl*. If desired, the boiled *Nockerl* may be fried in butter and served in this fashion.

## EMPEROR'S DESSERT OMELET

KAISERSCHMARREN

4 egg yolks
2 cups flour
2 cups milk

4 tablespoons sugar
2 tablespoons melted butter
4 egg whites

Beat the egg yolks in a bowl until light. Add the flour and milk, beating until very smooth. Add the sugar and butter, and mix again. Beat the egg whites until stiff but not dry and fold them into the previous mixture gently. Pour half of the mixture into a hot, well-buttered frying pan, and fry until light brown on both sides. Turn out onto a hot plate and pull into small shreds with two forks. Sprinkle generously with sugar. Repeat with the remaining mixture. Serve hot. If desired, *Kaiserschmarren* may be served with jam.

## SACHER'S CHOCOLATE CAKE

SACHER TORTE

5 ounces sweet chocolate
1 tablespoon water
¾ cup butter
6 egg yolks, beaten

1 cup powdered sugar
6 egg whites
1¼ cups sifted cake flour

Break the chocolate into small pieces and place in the top of a double boiler with the tablespoon of water. Cook over hot water until the chocolate melts. Add the butter and stir until melted. Add the beaten egg yolks, beating constantly. Add the sugar and beat steadily until well mixed. Cool for 10 minutes. Beat the egg whites until stiff but not dry. Fold in the chocolate mixture and the flour alternately, thoroughly but gently. Preheat oven to 325°. Butter an 8-inch-square pan and dust with flour. Pour the mixture into it. Bake for 30 minutes, or until a cake tester comes out clean. Remove from the pan and allow to cool. Now prepare:

⅓ cup apricot jam
3 ounces unsweetened chocolate
¾ cup confectioners' sugar
2 tablespoons hot water

1 egg
1 egg yolk
5 tablespoons butter

Put the jam in a cup and place it in hot water. Stir until melted. Spread on top of the cake and allow to set, about 20 minutes. Melt the chocolate over hot water. Remove from the heat, add the sugar and water, and beat until well blended. Add the egg, beating briskly. Add the egg yolk and continue to beat. Add the butter, a tablespoon at a time, beating steadily. Spread on top of the cake. Cool. Cut into oblong pieces to serve.

## BELGIUM AND LUXEMBOURG

Belgium is a rather small country, but it has a distinctive national cuisine. Many dishes are so old that their origins are lost in antiquity. The visitor will find Belgian food among the finest in the world, similar to that of

France but with certain important limitations. The quality and manner of preparation are not unlike the French cuisine in many respects. In Brussels, for example, there are so many excellent and renowned restaurants that listing them would be impossible. However, a selected few might include the Chantraine, La Couronne, Le Mail, and Le Lion d'Or.

Beer is the national drink of the country, usually a darker type than is customary in the United States. Wines are quite important, particularly to city folk, but they are almost all French imports. A few good cordials are produced, but the favorite after-dinner beverage is probably brandy. Coffee with a chicory base is also a national choice.

Soups are popular favorites, and the classic soup of the country is the *waterzooï*, made with either chicken or fish. Almost a complete meal in itself, many fainthearted tourists fail to get past this famous dish, but hearty Belgian diners often continue through several more courses. In the meat group, *boeuf à la flamande*, made with beer, is one of the accepted classic preparations in the world of gourmets. Many dishes popular in France, Holland, and Luxembourg are also eaten in Belgium, just as Belgian food is popular in these neighboring countries.

Since Belgium is on the North Sea, all sorts of seafood are enjoyed by the nation. A tourist sight that should not be missed is a visit to the local fish market on the water front. Herrings, shrimp, oysters, mussels, and fresh fish of all sorts have a deep-sea flavor that will surprise the visitor accustomed only to frozen or iced fish.

The nation has two great food specialties which it exports to countries prepared to pay a large price for a desired delicacy. These are the famous Belgian endive, the pale, bitter leaf that is considered the finest of all salad material, and the equally famous black Belgian grapes, which are fabulous in both size and price. Both are important delicacies the world over.

Although rich desserts, such as the *tarte liégeoise*, are appreciated, the usual meal ends with cheese, and with fruit in season. Soufflés and other fancy desserts are growing in popularity in the larger cities, but the country people still prefer to end their meals with cheese.

If Belgium is small, Luxembourg is tiny by world standards. With only 999 square miles of territory, this grand duchy unbelievably still exists in a world of power politics. The food is of the highest quality and very reasonable in price. The meals are memorable, but the Luxembourger does not fuss with his average fare in the same way that his neighbor, the Frenchman, does.

Luxembourg is truly like a little girl's fairyland, with ruined castles, palaces, cathedrals, moats, and fortresses. It is a wonderful place for a visit, particularly if night clubs are not on your list. Beer and wines are good here, especially the Moselle, which is locally produced.

## CHERRY SOUP

SOUPE AUX CERISES

| | |
|---|---|
| 1 pound cherries, pitted | 6½ cups water |
| ¼ cup sugar | 3 tablespoons cornstarch |

Combine the cherries, sugar, and 6 cups of the water in a saucepan. Bring to a boil. Cover and cook over low heat for 1 hour. Mix the cornstarch and remaining ½ cup of water to a smooth paste. Add to the cherries, mixing constantly. Bring to a boil, reduce heat, and cook for 2 minutes. Serve warm but not hot.

## CHICKEN SOUP

WATERZOOÏ DE POULET

| | |
|---|---|
| 2 2-pound broilers | 2 teaspoons salt |
| Chicken livers, gizzards, hearts, feet, veal bones | ½ teaspoon pepper |
| | 1 lemon, peeled and sliced thin |
| 6 cups water | 2 cups white wine |
| 2 parsley roots | 4 tablespoons butter |
| 3 sprigs parsley | ½ cup bread crumbs |
| 2 stalks celery | |

Clean the chickens carefully, singeing the skin to remove all pinfeathers. Combine the chicken livers, gizzards, hearts, and feet and the veal bones in a saucepan. Add the water, parsley roots, parsley, celery, salt, pepper, and lemon. Bring to a boil and skim the top thoroughly. Cover and cook over low heat for 2 hours. Strain.

Place the chickens in a casserole. Pour the soup stock and the white wine over them. Add the butter. Cover and cook over low heat for 45 minutes, or until tender. Remove the chickens and cut into serving pieces. Add the bread crumbs to the soup. Return the chickens to the soup and stir well. Serve hot, directly from the casserole, placing a piece of chicken in each soup plate and pouring the soup over it.

## BROWN FISH

POISSON BRUN

| | |
|---|---|
| 6 mackerel fillets | 2 tablespoons flour |
| Head, skin, and bones of fish | 2 tablespoons chopped parsley |
| 1 onion | 1 clove garlic, minced |
| 2 teaspoons salt | ⅛ teaspoon chervil |
| 1 teaspoon pepper | ⅛ teaspoon sage |
| 3 cups water | 1 tablespoon grated lemon rind |
| ¼ pound butter | ½ cup burgundy or other red wine |

Combine the head, skin, and bones of the mackerels with the onion, salt, pepper, and water in a saucepan. Bring to a boil and cook over medium heat for 45 minutes. Strain. Melt the butter in a skillet. Add the flour and stir until very smooth. Add the fish stock, stirring constantly until the boiling point is reached. Place the mackerel fillets in the sauce and add the parsley, garlic, chervil, sage, lemon rind, and wine. Cook over low heat for 20 minutes. Correct seasoning. Place under the broiler for 1 minute to brown the top.

## BEEFSTEAK, FLEMISH STYLE

BOEUF À LA FLAMANDE

| | |
|---|---|
| 4 tablespoons butter | 2 tablespoons vinegar |
| 6 onions, sliced | 2 teaspoons salt |
| 4 pounds beef, about 1 inch thick, cut into 12 pieces | ½ teaspoon pepper |
| | 1 teaspoon sugar |
| 2 tablespoons flour | 3 tablespoons chopped parsley |
| 1 cup water | 2 bay leaves |
| 2 cups beer | ½ teaspoon thyme |

Melt the butter in a saucepan or casserole. Add the onions and sauté until brown, stirring frequently. Remove the onions and set aside. Brown the beef on both sides and remove. Sprinkle the flour on the pan juices and mix until smooth. Add the water, stirring constantly. Return the onions and beef to the saucepan. Add the beer, vinegar, salt, pepper, sugar, parsley, bay leaves, and thyme. Cover and cook over low heat for 2 hours. Serve hot with boiled potatoes.

## PURÉE OF BRUSSELS SPROUTS

PURÉE DES CHOUX DE BRUXELLES

| | |
|---|---|
| 2 pounds brussels sprouts | 1 tablespoon meat extract |
| 4 tablespoons butter | 1 cup water |
| 1 tablespoon flour | 2 egg yolks, beaten |
| | ¼ cup cream |

Boil the sprouts in salted water for 10 minutes. Drain well. Melt the butter, add the sprouts, and toss gently for 2 minutes. Sprinkle the flour on them, add the meat extract and the cup of water, mixing well. Cover and cook over low heat for 15 minutes. Force the sprouts through a sieve. Beat the egg yolks and cream together in a bowl. Gradually stir in the puréed sprouts. Correct seasoning. Heat but do not allow to boil.

## CARROTS, FLEMISH STYLE

CAROTTES À LA FLAMANDE

3 tablespoons butter
12 small carrots, scraped
1 teaspoon salt

¼ teaspoon pepper
1 teaspoon sugar
¼ cup heavy cream.

Melt the butter in a heavy saucepan. Add the carrots, salt, pepper, and sugar. Cover and cook over low heat for 20 minutes, or until tender. Add the cream, stir, and cook 2 minutes longer.


## FRUIT TART, LIÉGE STYLE

TARTE LIÉGEOISE

1 cup flour
¼ teaspoon salt
2 teaspoons sugar

4 tablespoons butter
1 egg yolk
1 tablespoon cold water

Sift the flour, salt, and sugar together into a bowl. Cut in the butter with a pastry blender or two knives. Combine the egg yolk and water and add to the previous mixture, tossing lightly with a fork until a ball of dough is formed. Preheat oven to 375°.

Roll out the dough about ⅛ inch thick on a lightly floured surface. Line a 9-inch pie plate with the dough and prick in several places with a fork. Cover with a piece of wax paper and pour some beans or rice on the paper to keep the dough down. Bake in a 375° oven for 15 minutes, or until lightly browned. Discard the beans or rice. Now prepare the filling:

3 egg yolks
1 teaspoon flour
⅛ teaspoon salt
1 cup scalded milk, cooled
4 tablespoons sugar

1 tablespoon brandy
1 cup heavy cream, whipped
2 cups blueberries or seedless grapes
¼ cup melted raspberry jelly

Beat the egg yolks, flour, and salt together in the top of a double boiler. Gradually add the milk, beating constantly for 2 minutes. Place over hot water and stir with a wooden spoon until the mixture begins to thicken. Remove from the heat and place pan in cold water. Stir until the mixture becomes cool and thick. Add the brandy. If the mixture is not completely smooth, force it through a sieve. Fold in 4 tablespoons of the whipped cream. Spread half of the custard on the bottom of the tart shell. Combine the fruit and jelly and pour half of the mixture on the custard. Cover with the remaining custard, then add the remaining fruit and jelly.

Cover with the remaining whipped cream. If desired, the whipped cream may be forced through a pastry tube for additional effect. Chill for 2 hours.

*CZECHOSLOVAKIA*

This is a country where fine food and its preparation are given serious consideration. In any event that was the situation before the war. Everywhere the people consumed vast quantities of good food accompanied by heroic beakers of one of the world's finest beers, the *Plzeňské pivo,* the Pilsener beer of Czechoslovakia. Many beer drinkers consider Pilsener the finest beer in the world, but a certain amount of difference of opinion on the subject, supported by national partisanship, makes an ultimate decision rather difficult. The country also produces local wines and some fairly good brandies, but beer is unquestionably the national beverage.

The Czechs like fresh-water fish dishes, of which *ryba na cerno,* or fish made with a black sauce, is one of the best. It has many ingredients, and the resulting flavor is superb. Undoubtedly the favorite main dishes are those made with pork or goose. These are inevitably served with sauerkraut and dumplings, but the meat or poultry is treated in a variety of ways. A favorite Czech manner of handling sauerkraut is to serve it hot with caraway seeds. Pork products are prepared in countless manners, but the favorite of all is sausage in one shape or another. No other country has such a variety, and sausages really constitute a cult among the Czechs. People will argue fiercely the relative merits of one pork butcher as against another across the street. The most famous of Czech ways with ham is undoubtedly the renowned Prague-style ham, which is canned and shipped all over the world.

25

The one feature of Czechoslovakian food that cannot be dismissed lightly is the matter of the ever present *knedlíky*, or dumplings. This is not to be taken humorously, for the local dumplings are very light indeed. These come in every conceivable size and shape, round and small, egg-shaped, nut-shaped, heavy, light, doughy, spongy, rich, unsweet, and so on endlessly. To date, no one has come up with a triangular one, but it is always possible. They are served in soups, with meats or poultry, and of course there is a tremendous array of desserts built around sweet *knedlíky*. The only possible limit is the imagination of the maker. Housewives treasure dumpling recipes and refuse to trade them with their best friends; discussions rage endlessly as to which housewife makes better *knedlíky*. A good *knedlíky* recipe is regarded as part of every young girl's dowry.

This is not to indicate that the local cuisine is completely dependent upon pork sausages, beer, and dumplings. There are also famous rabbit, chicken, and game dishes, and above all the Czech way with goose is unsurpassed. Of all vegetables, probably the only one that appeals to the people is the mushroom in its many varieties, a fondness shared with their Polish neighbors.

*Hovězí maso* is another important part of the local cooking style; it is similar to the French *pot au feu,* a type of boiled beef in the pot. Various sauces are served with it, recalling the Austrian ways with boiled beef. Thus, while the cuisine resembles those of neighboring countries, it retains its own individuality even when borrowing from them.

## BEER SOUP

PIVNÍ POLÉVKA

| | |
|---|---|
| 1 quart beer | 1 tablespoon butter |
| 1 quart water | 3 egg yolks |
| 2 tablespoons sugar | 1 cup heavy cream |

Combine the beer and water in a saucepan. Bring to a boil and add the sugar and butter. Cook over low heat for 30 minutes. Beat the egg yolks in a bowl. Add the cream and again beat well. Very gradually add the beer mixture to the egg and cream mixture, beating constantly to prevent curdling. Pour the mixture back into the saucepan and heat again but do not allow to boil.

# FISH IN BLACK SAUCE

RYBA NA CERNO

2 cups water
1 cup vinegar
2 onions, sliced
2 sprigs parsley
1 stalk celery
2 cloves garlic, minced
2 bay leaves
⅛ teaspoon thyme
2 tablespoons pickling spice
½ teaspoon powdered ginger
6 slices (¾ inch thick) pike, white-fish, carp
1 pound prunes, presoaked

¾ cup water
2 cups beer
2 tablespoons lemon rind
4 slices rye bread, cut into small cubes
6 gingersnaps
½ cup seedless raisins
½ cup almonds, sliced
2 tablespoons lemon juice
¼ cup sugar
2 tablespoons butter
2 tablespoons flour

Combine in a saucepan the 2 cups of water, vinegar, onions, parsley, celery, garlic, bay leaves, thyme, pickling spices, and ginger. Bring to a boil and cook over medium heat for 30 minutes. Add the fish and cook 30 minutes longer.

Cook the prunes in ¾ cup of water until soft, about 25 minutes. Drain, reserving the juice. Remove the pits and chop the prunes very finely. Return the chopped prunes to the juice, and add the beer, lemon rind, bread cubes, gingersnaps, raisins, almonds, lemon juice, and sugar and mix well. Cook over medium heat for 10 minutes. Place the fish on a platter, reserving the stock.

In a separate saucepan melt the butter and add the flour, stirring constantly until brown. Gradually add the fish stock to this saucepan, stirring constantly until the boiling point is reached. Add the prune and beer mixture and stir well. Cook for 5 minutes. Pour the sauce over the fish and serve.

*Note: Although the quantity of fish listed in this recipe will serve 6, it may be increased to serve up to 12 merely by adding additional slices of fish. It will not be necessary to increase the quantity specified for any other ingredient, since the sauce will be sufficient to serve 12.*

## GOOSE WITH APPLE STUFFING

HUSA S JABLKOVOU NÁDIVKOU

10- to 12-pound goose
3 teaspoons salt
1 teaspoon pepper
2 teaspoons caraway seeds
3 cups sliced apples

2 tablespoons water
1 cup bread crumbs
1 small onion, minced
⅛ teaspoon cayenne pepper

Wash the goose and carefully remove any remaining feathers. Dry thoroughly. Combine the salt, pepper, and caraway seeds and rub into the skin and inside of the goose. This is best done at least 8 hours before using, to allow the seasoning to be absorbed.

Place the sliced apples in a saucepan with the water. Cook over low heat until very soft, about 20 minutes. Mash the apples with a fork and add the bread crumbs, minced onion, and cayenne pepper. Mix well. Stuff the goose with the apple mixture and fasten the opening with skewers or with thread. Roast in a shallow pan in a 350° oven for 3 hours. Pour off the fat as it accumulates. At the end of 2 hours, carefully pour over the skin 1 cup of ice water. Baste a few times during the final hour of roasting. The skin should be crisp and brown when the goose is completed.

## STEWED MUSHROOMS

DUŠENÉ HOUBY

2 pounds mushrooms
4 tablespoons butter
3 tablespoons chopped parsley
½ teaspoon salt

2 teaspoons caraway seeds
1 tablespoon flour
1 teaspoon vinegar
3 tablespoons sour cream

Wash the mushrooms thoroughly under cold water. Drain. Peel them, if the skin is heavy, and slice. Melt the butter in a saucepan and add the mushrooms, parsley, salt, and caraway seeds. Sauté lightly for 15 minutes. Add the flour and mix well until smooth. Add the vinegar and sour cream. Cook 15 minutes longer, stirring occasionally. Serve as a vegetable or on slices of buttered toast.

## FARINA DUMPLINGS

KRUPIČNÉ KNEDLÍKY

2 eggs
1 egg yolk
½ cup melted butter

1 teaspoon salt
½ cup farina
¼ cup bread crumbs

Beat the eggs and the yolk in a bowl. Add 2 tablespoons melted butter, the salt and farina. Mix well. Set aside for 1 hour. Drop by the teaspoon into boiling salted water. Boil for 30 minutes. Drain well but carefully. Serve with remaining melted butter and bread crumbs.

## POTATO NOODLES

BRAMBOROVÉNUDLE

4 large potatoes, unpeeled
3 cups water
2 teaspoons salt

2 tablespoons flour
3 eggs
4 tablespoons butter

Place the unpeeled potatoes in a saucepan with the water and cook until soft. Peel them while hot and mash in a bowl. Add the salt, flour, and eggs. Mix well and knead into a dough. If the mixture is too thin to roll, add a very little additional flour. Place on a lightly floured board and roll as thin as possible. Cut into strips about ¼ inch wide by about 4 inches in length.

Butter a baking dish and place the strips of dough in it, preferably in a crisscross arrangement. Dot the top of the noodles with little pieces of butter. Bake in a 375° oven for 30 minutes, or until browned on top. Serve with meat or poultry dishes.

## POPPY SEED CAKE

MAKOVÝ DORT

½ pound poppy seeds
8 egg yolks
1¼ cups sugar
¼ cup seedless raisins

1 teaspoon grated lemon rind
1 teaspoon cinnamon
8 egg whites

Grind the poppy seeds thoroughly in a food chopper or grinder and set aside. Beat the egg yolks in a bowl until thick. Gradually add the sugar, a tablespoon at a time, until well blended and very thick. Add the raisins, lemon rind, cinnamon, and ground poppy seeds. Mix well. Preheat oven to 325°. Beat the egg whites until stiff but not dry, and fold them gently and carefully into the previous mixture.

Butter a spring-form pan and dust with a little flour. Pour the mixture into it. Bake in a 325° oven for 50 minutes, or until a cake tester comes out clean. Cool, then carefully remove the spring form. The cake may be served with whipped cream on top. It will keep fresh and moist for several days.

## DENMARK

Denmark has a cuisine similar to its Scandinavian neighbors', but with many unusual variations and local specialties. The vast selection of appetizers known in Sweden as *smörgåsbord* exists in a different form in Denmark, where it is called *smørrebrød*. Instead of being placed in bowls and on platters, the appetizers are made into individual open-faced sandwiches with one slice of bread. The eating of these delightful sandwich-appetizers has assumed an importance in Denmark which can only be understood by a person who has visited the country.

Most Danes begin their day with a light breakfast in the European fashion. The children have the same meal, but usually some sort of porridge is added. Lunch, eaten about one in the afternoon, is the *smørrebrød*. A description of the *smørrebrød* custom follows in the recipe section, but this is a meager outline of the possibilities. For example, a Copenhagen restaurant called Davidsen's serves about 200 different varieties of sandwiches from its yard-long menu! There are many other excellent eating places in Copenhagen, such as the Wivex, De 7 smaa Hjem (The Seven Small Homes), the Nimb, and others.

Dinner is about six or seven in the evening and consists primarily of a meat dish and dessert. It is customary to pass both the main course and the dessert several times.

Denmark has numerous food specialties: shrimp (which are of a unique delicacy of taste), butter (often thought to be just about the finest in the world), and of course the world-renowned Danish pastry. In Denmark this pastry has a lightness and flakiness that will astonish those who believe they have ever previously eaten this confection. The recipe for the pastry as it is made in Denmark follows in the recipe section. Although it may seem to be troublesome to prepare and to consist of many steps, the results will warrant the time and energy expended.

Danish drinking habits are interesting. It is customary for a host to lift his glass and say, "Welcome," with everyone present being expected to drink; if a guest wishes to take a drink he must raise his glass, greet the other guests, every person present must drink, and so on. The entire ceremony must be repeated with each sip from a glass of liquor. This has been known to be very trying to young ladies of limited capacity.

Wines are served only on holidays and important dates. Danish beer is particularly good and is really the national drink. *Snaps,* a very potent drink, is served ice-cold with *smørrebrød.* Cherry Heering, a delicate cherry brandy, is the favorite after-dinner drink.

Denmark is a land of abundance, filled with good things to eat. The people fancy themselves as among the leading gastronomes of Europe, although they are hotly disputed by the French and the Belgians. No matter, for whoever wins the contest, visitors will find much to enjoy at a Danish table. Under no circumstances should a tourist miss the delicious fish, fresh or smoked, and the shellfish, which may be described only by that hackneyed and moth-eaten word, fabulous! The oysters, shrimp, and lobsters of Denmark are worth the trip to Europe in the opinion of many gourmets.

## OPEN SANDWICHES

### SMØRREBRØD

Open-faced sandwiches—that is, on one slice of bread—are a Danish cult, a phenomenon, and a way of life almost impossible to describe. *Smørrebrød* is eaten by almost everyone in Denmark for lunch every single day. The reason for their popularity is easily understood, once they have been seen and tasted.

The Danes are great believers in exciting as well as satisfying the appetite, and thus the preparation of the open-faced sandwiches follows a tradition. First, the bread should be very thinly sliced, not so thickly as it is normally supplied to us by commercial bakeries. If possible, obtain unsliced bread and cut thin slices by hand, using a knife with a serrated edge. Try not to use just plain white bread. Instead, try whole-grain, sour rye, pumpernickel, or other unusual types of bread.

Next, spread very small amounts of butter (preferably sweet butter if available) on each slice of bread; when whipped butter is obtainable, it should be used. If meat sandwiches are planned, mix a little mustard in with the butter and spread the bread with the mixture.

Now we come to the question of eye appeal. If hard-cooked eggs are used, slice them as thin and as uniform as you can. Spread the egg slices on the buttered bread as evenly as possible, in two or three equal rows.

Place a sardine diagonally across the sandwich. Place a paper-thin slice of lemon over the sardine.

Shrimp are definitely the most popular single type of *smørrebrød*. Use the smallest cooked shrimp you can obtain and place them evenly on the buttered bread, so that each shrimp rests on the one behind it. The main thing to remember is that the shrimp should be arranged as carefully as possible to create an even pattern. Place 1 teaspoon of mayonnaise in the center of the sandwich and sprinkle a little parsley on top.

Place a slice of crisp, washed and dried lettuce on the buttered bread and put a piece of cold, cooked fish on the lettuce. Cut a paper-thin slice of lemon. Hold a piece of paper over one half of the lemon slice and sprinkle with paprika. Now cover the side that has the paprika on it and sprinkle minced parsley on the other side. Place the decorated lemon slice on top of the fish. (When using pieces of cold fish, make sure that there are no bones in the fish.)

For meat sandwiches, cut away any possible fat. Place the meat so that it hangs over the sides of the bread. If desired, prepare a special butter by melting 4 tablespoons of butter and, when cool, combining it with 2 tablespoons of grated horseradish.

Cheese sandwiches may be imaginatively prepared too. If Swiss cheese is used, have the edges hang over the sides of the bread; this is the type of sandwich in which the bread should be spread with mustard butter. Cheese may be combined with slices of meat or with lettuce.

These delicious and appealing sandwiches may be served for lunch or late suppers. The bread should not be sliced thick, regardless of when it is served. If several different types of open-faced sandwiches are served, the fish sandwiches should be served first, followed by the meat, and lastly the cheese.


## BROWN CABBAGE SOUP

BRUNKAALSSUPPE

3 pounds cabbage  
½ pound butter  
2 tablespoons sugar  

9 cups stock or 3 cans consommé and 3 cans water  
1 teaspoon salt  
½ teaspoon black pepper  

Shred the cabbage finely. Melt the butter in a saucepan and add the cabbage. Stir the cabbage frequently so that it is coated with the butter. Sprinkle the sugar over it and sauté over very low heat for 45 minutes, stirring occasionally. If the cabbage has not browned completely at the end of this time, increase the heat and cook for an additional 1 or 2 minutes, stirring constantly. Add the stock, salt, and pepper. Cover and cook over low heat for 2 hours.

## MINCED FISH AND ONION SAUCE

FISKEFARS AND LØGSOVS

| | |
|---|---|
| 3 pounds cod or pike fillets | 2 teaspoons salt |
| ¼ cup butter, softened | ½ teaspoon white pepper |
| 2 eggs, beaten | ½ cup heavy cream |
| 2 tablespoons potato flour | |

Wash and dry the fillets. Grind or chop very fine in a food mill or chopper. Add the softened butter and beat together with the ground fish until thoroughly blended. Add the beaten eggs, the potato flour, salt, and white pepper and mix well. Correct seasoning. Preheat oven to 350°.

Whip the cream until stiff. Fold into the fish mixture. Butter a 7- or 9-inch ring mold carefully. Pour the mixture into the mold and cover it. If you do not have a pot cover sufficiently large, use a piece of aluminum foil. Place the mold in a pan of hot water. Bake in a 350° oven for 50 minutes. Meanwhile prepare the following sauce:

| | |
|---|---|
| ¼ pound butter | 1½ cups cream, scalded |
| 2 onions, chopped fine | 1 teaspoon salt |
| 3 tablespoons flour | ¼ teaspoon pepper |

Melt the butter in a saucepan. Add the chopped onions and cook over low heat about 10 minutes, or until golden brown. Stir occasionally to prevent the onions from burning. Add the flour, stirring constantly until smooth. Add the scalded cream and continue stirring until the boiling point is reached. Add the salt and pepper and stir again.

Run a knife around the edge of the mold, tap the sides gently, and unmold the fish onto a platter. Serve with the sauce in a separate dish.

## ROAST PORK WITH APPLES AND PRUNES

STEGT SUINEKAM MED AEBLER OG SVEDSKER

| | |
|---|---|
| 1 pound prunes, pitted | 6-pound loin of pork or 2 racks spareribs |
| 1 cup water | 1 teaspoon salt |
| 6 apples | ½ teaspoon pepper |

Place the prunes in a saucepan with the water and bring to a boil. Remove from the heat and allow to soak for 5 minutes. Peel and core the apples and cut them into ¼-inch slices. Place them in the saucepan with the prunes.

If a loin of pork is used, ask your butcher to prepare it as a crown. If spareribs are used, have them cracked in the middle of each strip. Combine the salt and pepper and rub it into the meat. Place the pork in a roasting pan.

Drain the water from the prunes and apples. If the crown of pork is used, fill the center with this mixture and cover with a piece of aluminum foil. If spareribs have been selected, place half of the prune and apple mixture on each of the two strips of spareribs. Fold the spareribs over, at the places where the ribs have been cracked in the middle. Fasten with skewers. Roast in a 350° oven for 25 minutes per pound. Add small amounts of hot water to the pan if it becomes too dry.

About 15 minutes before the pork is done, prepare the following sauce:

3 tablespoons pan drippings
2 tablespoons flour

1 cup stock or 1 cup hot water and
1 bouillon cube
¼ cup milk, scalded

Carefully remove 3 tablespoons of drippings from the roasting pan and put it in a small saucepan. Add the flour, stirring constantly until the mixture is smooth. Slowly add the stock, stirring steadily, and then the scalded milk, again stirring well. Allow the mixture to reach the boiling point and remove from the heat. Serve separately in a sauceboat.

## SPAGHETTI WITH SWEETBREADS

SPAGHETTI MED BRISLER

3 pairs calves' sweetbreads
2 cups water
2 tablespoons vinegar
2 teaspoons salt
1 bay leaf
1 onion

¼ pound butter
2 tablespoons flour
½ cup heavy cream
2 cups sliced mushrooms
1 8-ounce package thin spaghetti

Wash the sweetbreads carefully and soak in cold water for ½ hour. Drain thoroughly. Combine the sweetbreads, water, vinegar, salt, bay leaf, and onion in a saucepan. Cook over medium heat for 15 minutes. Drain but reserve 1 cup of the stock. Remove the membrane from the sweetbreads and cut into small cubes.

Melt half the butter in a saucepan. Add the flour, stirring until smooth. Gradually add the reserved stock and the cream, stirring constantly until the boiling point is reached. Cook over low heat for 5 minutes, stirring occasionally. Melt the remaining butter in a frying pan. Add the mushrooms and sauté for 10 minutes, stirring frequently. Combine the sweetbreads, sauce, and mushrooms and mix well. Correct seasoning. Place over low heat.

Cook the spaghetti in boiling, salted water for 10 to 12 minutes. Drain thoroughly and rinse with cold water. Put the spaghetti on a platter, our the sauce over it, and serve immediately.

## POTATOES, DANISH STYLE

KARTOFLER

3 tablespoons butter
1 onion, sliced
6 cold boiled potatoes, peeled
2 teaspoons sugar

2 teaspoons vinegar
1 teaspoon salt
¼ teaspoon pepper

Melt the butter in a large frying pan. Add the sliced onion and sauté for 5 minutes, stirring occasionally. Slice the potatoes and add to the onion. Sauté for 5 minutes, turning the potatoes over to brown on both sides. Add the sugar, vinegar, salt, and pepper and mix. Cook 5 minutes longer.

## RED CABBAGE

AADKAAL

3 pounds red cabbage
¼ cup butter
4 tablespoons vinegar
½ cup water

2 tablespoons currant jelly
1 tablespoon sugar
1 teaspoon salt

Wash the cabbage thoroughly, discarding the core and all imperfect leaves. Cut or shred into thin strips. Drain well. Melt the butter in a deep saucepan. Add the cabbage and toss it around with a large spoon so that it becomes evenly coated with butter. Add the vinegar and water. Cover and cook over low heat for 1½ hours. Add the jelly, sugar, and salt and mix well. Cook for 20 minutes. Correct seasoning. This dish is best prepared a day in advance and then reheated.

## RICE FRITTERS

RISENGRYNSKLATTER

1½ cups rice
1 cup water
2 quarts milk
1 teaspoon salt
2 eggs, beaten
¼ cup flour

¼ cup currants
¼ cup chopped almonds
2 teaspoons cinnamon
1 teaspoon grated lemon rind
  Butter for frying

Wash the rice carefully in several changes of water. Place in a saucepan with the cup of water and bring to a boil. Drain thoroughly. In a separate saucepan boil the milk. Gradually add the rice, stirring constantly until the mixture reaches the boiling point. Add the salt and then cover the saucepan. Cook over low heat for 1 hour. Remove from the heat and let cool for 15 minutes. Add the beaten eggs, mixing well. Add the flour, and again mix well. Add the currants, almonds, cinnamon, and lemon rind.

Melt butter in a frying pan and form pancakes by dropping 1 tablespoon of the rice mixture into the pan. If it is too runny, add a little more flour. Brown on both sides. Serve hot, with jelly on the side.

## DANISH PASTRY

DANSK KAGE

1 cake or package yeast
1¼ cups milk, scalded and cooled
¼ cup sugar
2½ cups sifted flour
¼ cup melted butter

2 eggs, beaten
½ teaspoon salt
½ pound sweet butter
½ cup melted butter

Place the yeast in a bowl. Add the cooled milk and dissolve the yeast. Add the sugar and ½ cup of the flour. Cover and allow to rise for 30 minutes in a warm place.

In a separate bowl place the melted butter, beaten eggs, and salt and mix well. Add the remaining flour alternately with the yeast mixture. Knead the dough on a floured surface for about 5 to 10 minutes, until smooth in texture and elastic. If the dough is too spongy, add a very little more sifted flour. Place in a bowl, cover with a cloth, and put in a warm place to rise for about ¾ to 1 hour, or until double in bulk. When risen, roll out about ¼ inch thick on a floured surface. Break ¼ pound of the butter into small pieces and place them in the center of the dough. Fold the sides of the dough over, wrap in wax paper, and place in the refrigerator for 30 minutes.

Remove from refrigerator. On a floured surface, roll the dough ½ inch thick. Break the remaining ¼ pound of sweet butter into small pieces and again place in the center of the dough. Fold the sides of the dough over again, wrap in wax paper, and return to the refrigerator for 30 minutes. Remove once again, roll out again ½ inch thick, fold over again. Wrap in wax paper and return to the refrigerator for 30 minutes. Remove from refrigerator, place in a bowl, cover, and allow to rise for 45 minutes in a warm place. Roll ¼ inch thick on a floured surface. Preheat oven to 425°. Cut into 4-inch squares and fill with either of the following mixtures:

| FILLING 1 | FILLING 2 |
|---|---|
| 1 cup chopped nuts | 1 cup cottage cheese |
| ¼ cup sugar | 1 egg yolk, beaten |
| 2 teaspoons cinnamon | ¼ cup sugar |
| | ½ teaspoon vanilla |

For either filling, combine the ingredients and place a portion in the center of each square of dough. Fold the dough over in any desired shape. Brush with a little melted butter. Place on a buttered baking sheet. Bake in a 425° oven for 20 minutes. Makes about 30–36 pastries.

*Note: If desired, use only part of the dough, keeping the balance in the refrigerator. It will keep about a week.*

## ENGLAND, WALES, AND NORTHERN IRELAND

What can possibly be said about England's food that hasn't been said before? It has been criticized by almost every foreign visitor as lacking in imagination, deficient in preparation, and always as unexciting. The statement is true. But, like many other generalizations, it is true only as far as it goes. England *does* have good food, though many scoffers would have you believe otherwise. It should also be remembered that England is an island and is not self-sufficient. It must of necessity import the largest proportion of its food—staples, not merely luxuries. If fruits and green salads are rarities it is because most of these items must be imported.

France is separated from England only by the few miles that make up the English Channel, but a million light-years separate the cuisines of France and England. It has been previously said but it is worth repeating that France is a land of one religion and a hundred sauces, whereas England has one sauce and a hundred religions. Both statements are incorrect, because France has a thousand sauces, and England doesn't have a hundred religions. The ultimate insult in France is to tell a cook that he is fit to cook only for the English. *Tiens! Alors!*

For their own protection, visitors to England should understand British food habits. Breakfast is the best meal of all, with delicious and substantial local specialties such as kippers, hot cereals, broiled ham or bacon, and the like. Lunch, at about 1 P.M., and dinner, served late in the evening, are the meals that bring forth those hollow groans from the tourists. They find the fish and meat dull and the desserts impossibly sweet, and as for the vegetables, there are only two words for them—brussels sprouts. The time to stoke up is at teatime, in the late afternoon. The British have many delicious cakes, delicate sandwiches, and tea specialties such as bath buns and crumpets. Crumpets are really good, in spite of all the P. G. Wodehouse-style jokes about them. Scones are often served, but these are probably Scotch in origin. The visitor to England can eat well, if only he will learn to emphasize breakfast and tea rather than lunch and dinner. If you get hungry between times there's always fish and chips, England's answer to the American hot dog. This favorite dish of all classes of people is nothing more or less than slices of fish, deep-fat fried, with potato chips.

Despite all of the above, good food is to be had in England, usually at a price. This is particularly true at London's better hotels such as the Grosvenor House, the Berkeley, and the Dorchester. The small Caprice Restaurant has London's best food, but it is French. Manetta's and Hatchett's are other popular London restaurants, but many people go to Soho, a part of London where the majority of the city's foreign restaurants are found. The Soho restaurants offer good value, but the meals are definitely not British.

No discussion of John Bull's food should omit England's contribution in the way of dairy products. Devonshire cream, thick and rich, is a treat. Cheeses are a British tradition and are among the finest in the world. Those with an international reputation include Cheshire, Stilton, and Cheddar cheeses.

Everyone knows about the famous pubs of England—the workingmen's clubs. Here it is that one finds the famous beers of the country in a variety that will startle the beer drinker from the States. There is stout (a powerful black brew), bitter ale (made with an extra quantity of hops), old ale, lager, and many more. The Briton likes to order a combination of two beers, and this is known as " 'alf and 'alf." Bourbon and rye are little known here, but scotch whisky is much appreciated, though somewhat short in supply. A much more traditional drink is English-style gin, known as London gin in certain parts of the world. It is a high-quality drink, made from barley and juniper berries. Gin is served straight, with Italian vermouth (shortened to "gin and it"), with quinine water (known as "gin and tonic"), or in various other ways.

Coffee is not the national drink of the country as any tourist will immediately tell you. The British must distrust coffee—why else would they treat it so badly? It is not true that coffee in Britain is undrinkable, it merely takes a good deal of practice to learn to swallow it. Tea is the drink here, and tourists are cautioned not to vary from the norm. Properly made tea tastes much better than anyone ever thought it could, and the varieties of tea used by the English far exceed our own limited taste and knowledge on the subject. In any event, don't order coffee in England.

## GIN AND IT

3 jiggers Italian vermouth              6 jiggers gin

Gently pour the vermouth and gin into a glass pitcher or other receptacle. Stir but do not shake. Do not add any ice. Pour into cocktail glasses and serve at room temperature. If desired, before pouring the liquor into a glass, a piece of lemon peel may be rubbed around the edges.

## STAR GAZY PIE

| | |
|---|---|
| 4 tablespoons butter | 2 tablespoons tarragon vinegar |
| 4 mackerel fillets | 4 egg yolks |
| 1¼ cups bread crumbs | 4 slices bacon, half cooked |
| 3 tablespoons chopped parsley | 1 cup sifted flour |
| ½ teaspoon thyme | ½ teaspoon salt |
| ½ teaspoon marjoram | ⅓ cup shortening |
| 1 teaspoon salt | 3 tablespoons water |
| ½ teaspoon pepper | |

Melt the butter in a skillet. Brown the mackerel on both sides. Butter a casserole and sprinkle it with half of the bread crumbs, making sure that the bottom is heavily coated. Combine the parsley, thyme, marjoram, salt, and pepper. Arrange a layer of mackerel, top with the remaining bread crumbs, and sprinkle with the parsley mixture. Beat the vinegar and egg yolks together and add to the casserole. Arrange the bacon slices on top.

Sift the flour and salt together into a bowl. Cut in the shortening with a pastry blender or two knives until the consistency of coarse sand. Add the water, tossing lightly with a fork until a ball of dough is formed. Roll out on a lightly floured surface and place on top of the casserole, sealing the edges. Prick with a fork in a few places. Bake in a 325° oven for 1¾ hours. Serve hot or cold, directly from the casserole.

## LANCASHIRE HOT POT

4 tablespoons butter
6 loin or shoulder lamb chops
3 teaspoons salt
1 teaspoon pepper
6 potatoes, peeled and sliced

4 onions
1 cup sliced mushrooms
½ cup string beans, cut in half
1 cup stock or canned consommé
½ cup light cream

Melt 2 tablespoons of the butter in a skillet. Brown the chops well on both sides. Arrange the chops on the bottom of a casserole. Sprinkle with 1 teaspoon of the salt and ½ teaspoon of the pepper. Place half the potatoes on the chops in a layer. Add successive layers of onions, mushrooms, and string beans. Combine the stock, cream, and remaining salt and pepper. Pour over the vegetables. Arrange the remaining potatoes in an even, overlapping design. Dot with the remaining butter. Cover the casserole and bake in a 350° oven for 2½ hours. Remove the cover and bake for 20 minutes, or until potatoes brown on top. Serve hot, directly from the casserole.

## BUBBLE AND SQUEAK

4 teaspoons salt
2 teaspoons pepper
12 slices cold roast beef or 1 cold chicken, sliced

4 tablespoons butter
1 boiled cabbage, chopped fine
½ teaspoon nutmeg
2 tablespoons vinegar

Mix together 2 teaspoons of salt and 1 teaspoon of pepper. Sprinkle it over the beef or chicken. Melt 2 tablespoons of the butter in a skillet. Brown the slices of beef or chicken on both sides. Remove and set aside in a warm place. Melt the remaining butter in the skillet and add the cabbage, remaining salt, remaining pepper, and nutmeg. Cook over medium heat, stirring constantly, until the cabbage is lightly browned. Sprinkle the vinegar over it and cook 1 minute longer. Serve with the meat or chicken.

## EXETER STEW

3 tablespoons shortening
2 onions, chopped
1 cup flour
2 cups stock or 1 can consommé and ½ cup water
2½ pounds top round (or similar cut), in 6 pieces
2 tablespoons vinegar
2½ teaspoons salt
½ teaspoon pepper
½ teaspoon thyme
¾ teaspoon baking powder
1 tablespoon chopped parsley
¼ teaspoon marjoram
Dash of cayenne pepper
3 tablespoons butter
2 tablespoons ice water

Melt the shortening in a skillet. Add the onions and sauté for 10 minutes, stirring frequently. Add 3 tablespoons of the flour, stirring until smooth. Gradually add the stock, stirring constantly until the boiling point is reached. Place the meat in a heavy saucepan and sprinkle with the vinegar. Add the previously prepared sauce, 2 teaspoons of the salt, pepper, and thyme and mix together. Cover and cook over low heat for 2 hours.

Sift the baking powder, remaining flour, and remaining salt together into a bowl. Add the parsley, marjoram, and cayenne pepper and stir. Cut in the butter with a pastry blender or two knives until well blended. Add the ice water and toss lightly until a ball of dough is formed. Shape into 6 balls and drop into the saucepan. Cover and cook over low heat for 35 minutes. Arrange the meat on a platter, with the dumplings around it. Pour the sauce over all and serve.

## YORKSHIRE SALAD

3 tablespoons molasses
6 tablespoons vinegar
½ teaspoon black pepper
2 heads lettuce, shredded
3 scallions (green onions), sliced fine

Combine the molasses, vinegar, and pepper in a bowl and mix well. Combine the lettuce and scallions and mix well together. Pour the dressing over it. Toss until the lettuce is well coated with the dressing. Serve cool but not ice cold.

## YORKSHIRE PUDDING

2 cups sifted flour
1 teaspoon salt
1 cup light cream
1 cup milk
4 eggs, beaten
1 cup beef drippings

Sift the flour and salt into a bowl. Gradually add the cream and milk, beating well. Add the eggs, beating vigorously. Cover and place in the refrigerator for 1 hour. Heat the drippings in an 8-inch square pan. Beat the batter for 1 minute and pour into the pan. Bake in a 425° oven for 15 minutes. Reduce oven temperature to 350° and bake for 15 minutes, or until the pudding is crisp and brown.

*Note: Yorkshire pudding is the traditional accompaniment to roast beef. No recipe is given for roast beef since it is cooked in the usual manner. The drippings called for in this recipe may be obtained from the pan in which the meat is roasted.*

## CRUMPETS

2 cakes or packages yeast
½ cup lukewarm water
2 eggs
1½ cups lukewarm milk

2 tablespoons melted butter
½ teaspoon salt
1 teaspoon sugar
3 cups sifted flour

Dissolve the yeast in the water. Allow to soften for 5 minutes. Beat the eggs, add the milk, butter, salt, and sugar. Add the yeast mixture and the flour, beating until smooth and well blended. Cover and set aside in a warm place for 15 minutes. Preheat oven to 400°. Fill buttered muffin tins about half full. Bake in a 400° oven for 15 minutes. Serve hot with plenty of melted butter and raspberry jam.

## MARLBOROUGH PUDDING

1 cup flour
¼ teaspoon salt
⅓ cup shortening
4 tablespoons milk
4 tablespoons butter
1 cup sugar

4 eggs
2 tablespoons lemon juice
1 tablespoon grated lemon rind
¼ teaspoon nutmeg
2 cups applesauce
1 cup heavy cream

Sift the flour and salt into a bowl. Cut in the shortening with a pastry blender or two knives until the consistency of coarse sand. Add the milk, tossing lightly with a fork until a ball of dough is formed. Wrap in wax paper and place in the refrigerator, while preparing the filling.

Cream the butter, add the sugar, and beat well together. Add the eggs and beat until light and fluffy. Add the lemon juice, lemon rind, nutmeg, applesauce, and cream. Mix well. Preheat oven to 350°.

Roll out the dough about ⅛ inch thick on a lightly floured surface. Place in a buttered 11-inch pie plate. Pour the filling into it. Bake in a 350° oven for 45 minutes, or until delicately browned and firm in texture. Serve hot or cold. If desired, whipped cream may be served with this pudding.

## TIPSY PUDDING

4 eggs
½ cup sugar

1 cup sifted flour
¾ cup rum

Beat the eggs in a bowl. Gradually add the sugar, beating until thick and light. Add the flour, mixing lightly until well blended. Preheat oven to 350°. Butter 6 custard cups and dust lightly with sugar. Divide the mixture evenly among the cups. Bake in a 350° oven for 20 minutes or until set and lightly browned. Pour 2 tablespoons of rum on each pudding. Serve cold.

*Note: This old English pudding is served on Pan American World Airways' flight to England.*

## SEED CAKE

5 eggs
2 teaspoons water
1 teaspoon orange extract
1 cup sugar

2 teaspoons caraway seeds
1¼ cups sifted cake flour
2 tablespoons grated lemon rind
½ cup confectioners' sugar

Beat the eggs in a bowl. Place the bowl over hot water and continue beating until thick and lemon-colored. Add the water, orange extract, sugar, and caraway seeds. Beat with a rotary beater (still over hot water) for 10 minutes. Remove from hot water. Preheat oven to 350°. Sift the flour and combine with the lemon rind. Fold into the egg mixture thoroughly. Butter a 12-inch loaf pan or an angel-cake pan and dust lightly with flour. Pour the batter into it. Sprinkle the top with confectioners' sugar. Bake in a 350° oven for 50 minutes, or until a cake tester comes out clean.

## CHICKEN LIVER AND ANCHOVY SAVOURY

4 tablespoons butter
6 chicken livers
½ teaspoon pepper
2 anchovy fillets

½ cup stock or ½ cup hot water and
   1 chicken bouillon cube
3 slices buttered toast, edges
   trimmed, and cut in half
2 tablespoons bread crumbs
2 tablespoons grated Parmesan cheese

Melt the butter in a skillet. Sauté the chicken livers in it. Chop the livers with the pepper and anchovy fillets until well blended. Return the mixture to the skillet and add the stock. Cook over medium heat for 5 minutes, stirring frequently. Place the mixture on the toast. Sprinkle with the bread crumbs and cheese. Place under the broiler for 1 minute to brown. Serve hot.

*Note: Savouries occupy a unique position in England. They are served at the conclusion of a meal, after dessert.*

## FINLAND

Most Americans know Finland as the only country that repaid loans made during World War I, but it is more than a country that respects its obligations. Its citizens are only stolid outwardly, for they are actually a warm and friendly people. The land they inhabit has a rude climate, at least during the winter, but the summers are very pleasant, with an invigorating, pine-laden freshness. The country has a considerable coastline facing the Gulfs of Bothnia and Finland, with thousands of beautiful lakes, unspoiled forest land, and exhilarating scenery.

Both fresh-water and ocean fish are important in the food habits of the people. Fish of all types are caught, but sardines and fresh-water salmon are particularly appreciated. Fish cakes and fish puddings are typical seafood treatments in the Finnish cuisine. Unbelievable quantities of herring are eaten; many Finns buy it by the barrel, and it is served in countless ways. Actually herring is a staple food and many people eat it almost every day of their lives.

Here, as in the Scandinavian countries, the long table laden with appetizers is an institution, but instead of being called *smörgåsbord* as it is in Sweden, it is known as the tongue-twisting *voileipäpöytä*. The change in name works no appreciable change in the flavor of the various smoked fish, meats, and cheeses. Soups are frequently served, as might be expected in a normally cold climate. Fruit and pea soups and fish chowders are typical, but *kurkkukeitto* (cucumber soup) is an interesting and unusual dish. Dumplings and other garnishes for soup are almost standard in Finland.

All of the usual meats, prepared in the usual fashions, are eaten, but meat stews are especially liked. Game birds such as grouse, hazel hens, and wild ducks are unusual treats for the visitor but commonplace for the Finns. Also available are bear, elk, and venison. A national dish is the *piirakka*, a pastry dough filled with meat or fish.

The people are very fond of nuts, and a tasty nut steak (*pähkinä-paisti*) makes an excellent Lenten dish. Although the summer growing season is a brief one, the vegetables do quite well because it is light almost twenty-four hours a day from late May to July. Wild mushrooms, found in Finland's beautiful forests, are great treats to everyone, and mushroom-gathering parties are common occurrences.

Desserts are not complicated. Tourists see Finnish pancakes most often; these are usually served with lingonberries, something like our cranberries. Rice desserts are also popular, but these are not unusual except that Finland's fine native berries are often used in them. These include strawberries, raspberries, and cloudberries, which resemble raspberries. The recipe for *mansikkatorttu* (strawberry cake) is extremely good.

Many delicious cordials are made from the fruits and berries of the country, such as *mesimarja*, distilled from the brambleberry of Finland's arctic region, and also *lakka*, the product of the cloudberry.

## PICKLED HERRING

ETIKKASILKAT

| | |
|---|---|
| 4 salt herring | ¼ cup sugar |
| 3 onions, sliced | 2 tablespoons pickling spices |
| ½ cup hot water | 2 bay leaves |
| 1½ cups vinegar | |

Wash the herring thoroughly. Place in a bowl with water to cover, and allow to soak for 24 hours. The water should be changed frequently, but at least twice. Drain, and cut off the heads of the herring. Cut each fish into 4 pieces. Place in a large jar or other container which can be covered. Add the sliced onions.

Combine the water, vinegar, sugar, pickling spices, and bay leaves. Stir until the sugar is dissolved. Pour over the herring. Cover and marinate in the refrigerator for at least 24 hours. Serve cold. This dish may be accompanied by boiled potatoes over which melted butter and parsley have been poured.

## INDIVIDUAL CABBAGE PIES

KAALIPIIRAKKA

2 cups flour
1¼ teaspoons salt
¾ cup shortening
2 egg yolks
2 tablespoons cold water

¼ pound butter
5 cups finely shredded cabbage
  (about 1 large head)
2 teaspoons sugar

Sift the flour and ¼ teaspoon of the salt together in a bowl. Cut in the shortening with a pastry blender or two knives until it is the consistency of corn meal. Beat the egg yolks and water together and add to the flour, tossing lightly with a fork until a ball of dough is formed. Wrap in wax paper and place in the refrigerator while preparing the cabbage.

Melt the butter in a saucepan and add the shredded cabbage. Cook over low heat for 1 hour, stirring occasionally. Add remaining salt and the sugar and continue cooking over medium heat until the cabbage is delicately browned, about 5 minutes, stirring frequently. Set aside to cool for 30 minutes. Preheat oven to 375°.

Roll the dough ⅛ inch thick on a lightly floured surface. Cut out 4-inch circles. Place 1 tablespoon of the cabbage mixture in the center of each circle of dough. Fold over the edges and seal with a little water or egg white. Place on a lightly greased baking sheet. Bake in a 375° oven for 20 minutes, or until golden brown.

## CUCUMBER SOUP

KURKKUKEITTO

¼ pound butter
1 small onion, chopped
4 cucumbers, peeled and sliced
3 tablespoons flour
6 cups chicken stock or 2 cans chicken
  consommé and 2½ cans water

¼ teaspoon pepper
2 egg yolks
1 tablespoon sherry
1 cup light cream
3 tablespoons chopped parsley

Melt the butter in a saucepan. Add the onion and cucumbers. Cook over low heat for 10 minutes, stirring frequently. Do not allow the onion or cucumbers to brown. Sprinkle the flour over them and mix well. Gradually add the stock, stirring constantly until the boiling point is reached. Add the pepper and cook over low heat for 10 minutes, stirring occasionally. Force the mixture through a sieve.

Beat the egg yolks, sherry, and cream in a bowl. Gradually add the soup, stirring constantly to prevent curdling. The soup may be served hot or cold. If it is to be served hot, return the soup to the saucepan and re-heat, but do not allow it to boil. Correct seasoning. Sprinkle with parsley and serve. If the soup is to be served cold, correct seasoning and place in the refrigerator. Sprinkle with parsley before serving.

## CHICKEN LIVERS WITH APPLES

KANANMAKSAA OMENIEN KANSSA

¼ pound butter
6 apples, peeled, cored, and cut into
   sixths
4 tablespoons sugar
1½ pounds chicken livers
1½ teaspoons salt
1½ teaspoons pepper

¼ cup stock or ¼ bouillon cube
   dissolved in ¼ cup hot water
1½ tablespoons cornstarch
1 cup apple juice
2 tablespoons currant jelly
1 tablespoon lemon juice

Melt half the butter in a skillet. Add the apples and sprinkle them with the sugar. Cook over low heat for 10 minutes, or until the apples are soft. Turn them frequently but do not break the slices.

Melt the remaining butter in a skillet. Add the chicken livers and sauté for 5 minutes. Sprinkle with the salt and pepper. Add the stock and cook over medium heat for 5 minutes.

Mix the cornstarch and 2 tablespoons of the apple juice together in a cup to form a smooth paste. Combine this mixture with the remainder of the apple juice and add the currant jelly and lemon juice. Place the mixture in a saucepan and cook over low heat, stirring constantly, until the mixture thickens. Place the apples on a serving dish. Arrange the chicken livers over them. Serve the sauce separately.

## RICE AND NUT STEAK

PÄHKINÄ-PAISTI

1 cup bread crumbs
1½ cups heavy cream
⅓ cup melted butter
2 cups cooked rice
1 cup ground nuts

1 teaspoon salt
¼ teaspoon pepper
3 eggs, well beaten
1 egg yolk

Soak the bread crumbs in the cream for 5 minutes. Add butter, rice, nuts, salt, pepper, and eggs and beat well. Pour into a buttered 10-inch loaf pan. Brush the top thoroughly with the egg yolk. Bake in a 350° oven for 1 hour. Cut into ¾-inch slices and serve.

## BAKED MUSHROOMS

### SIENIMUREKE

6 tablespoons butter
2 onions, chopped fine
1 cup milk
1 cup light cream
2 cups bread crumbs

2 pounds mushrooms, chopped fine
2 teaspoons salt
½ teaspoon pepper
3 eggs, well beaten

Melt the butter in a saucepan. Add the onions and sauté for 10 minutes, stirring frequently. Combine the milk, cream, and bread crumbs. Set aside for 10 minutes. Combine the sautéed onions, bread-crumb mixture, mushrooms, salt, pepper, and eggs. Mix well. Pour into a buttered 10-inch loaf pan. Bake in a 350° oven for 1 hour. Pour a little melted butter over the mushrooms and serve.

## FINNISH PANCAKES

### SUOMALAINEN PANNUKAKKU

1 cup sifted flour
1½ cups milk
2 egg yolks
3 tablespoons sugar

½ teaspoon salt
1 tablespoon melted butter
2 egg whites
4 tablespoons butter

Sift the flour into a bowl. Add the milk and mix until smooth. Set aside for 30 minutes. Beat the egg yolks, sugar, and salt together. Add to the flour mixture, together with the melted butter, and mix thoroughly. Beat the egg whites until stiff but not dry, and fold them into the previous mixture carefully. Melt half the butter in a frying pan or griddle. When the butter is hot, drop the batter into it by the tablespoon to form small pancakes. Bake over medium heat until browned on both sides. Continue until all the batter is used up, using additional butter as required.

If desired, very thin slices of peeled apple may be placed in each tiny pancake while it is baking. Serve with preserved lingonberries. (These are available in cans or jars.) Cooked whole-cranberry sauce may be used as a substitute.

## STRAWBERRY TART

### MANSIKKATORTTU

5 egg yolks
¾ cup sugar
3 cups crushed strawberries, fresh or
frozen

1 cup lady-finger crumbs or bread
crumbs
1 teaspoon vanilla extract
5 egg whites
Whipped cream

Beat the egg yolks in a bowl. Add the sugar and beat until light and fluffy. Add the strawberries; if frozen berries are used, drain slightly. Add the crumbs and vanilla extract and mix together thoroughly. Beat the egg whites until stiff but not dry. Fold into the strawberry mixture carefully. Preheat oven to 375°. Butter a glass or pottery baking dish and dust lightly with sugar. Pour the mixture into it. Bake in a 375° oven for 35 minutes, or until firm. Serve cold with whipped cream. If desired, a few sliced strawberries may be placed in the whipped cream.

*FRANCE*

France holds a unique place in the hearts of gourmets. To speak of French food is to speak of the world of food. If it is true that every country gets the food it deserves, certainly France deserves the finest food. In no other country do the pleasures of the table occupy such an important position, become the subject of so much conversation, and constitute so important a part of the national character. Tips about restaurants are considered as important as tips about the stock market. A Frenchman demands the best, will refuse anything else, and thus by elimination France has the greatest restaurants, chefs, and food, and French cooking has become the accepted and classic cuisine of the world.

The French are serious eaters. Breakfast is completely unimportant, consisting almost inevitably of coffee with a *brioche* or a *croissant,* little masterpieces of pastry. A businessman's quick lunch may take two or more hours, consist of four or five courses, a bottle or two of wine, followed by a brandy or several. While eating his dinner, a true son of France will often be planning next day's lunch or that of the day after.

French specialties? It would be necessary to list the thousands of dishes that make up the cuisine of the entire world. French cooking has made itself felt in almost every metropolitan community in the world, and French menus are known wherever civilization exists. There are two general styles of French cooking: the *bourgeoise* (middle-class) and the *haute cuisine* (high cuisine). The former is the home style of the average person, the way it is prepared by the peasants and by ordinary folk even in the large cities. The *haute cuisine* is the classic and traditional style of the great chefs, employing the famous sauces, elaborate rituals, and attention to detail that constitute the essence of French cooking. Of course French food may also be subdivided regionally, but in France there is a tremendous difference in this regard as compared with our own country. It is not unusual for volatile arguments to take place between Frenchmen concerning the excellence of one regional dish over another, whereas in our country the differences are really trivial. These discussions are conducted with a seriousness that most Americans would find difficult to comprehend.

France has so many unique food specialties that any listing would have to be inadequate and incomplete, but here are a few: truffles (a mysterious tuberlike growth used to flavor many dishes), *bar-le-duc* (the finest of all currant jellies), *bouillabaisse* (a Mediterranean fish soup), *pâté de foie gras* (goose livers ground to a fine paste), *fraises des bois* (tiny wild strawberries), *agneau pré sale* (lamb grown on salt marshes and possessing a unique flavor), and *escargots* (snails). Many of these specialties exist because Frenchmen are willing to forgo mass production of food in favor of excellence of quality. For example, veal is slaughtered at the age of six weeks in order to present the gourmet with snow-white meat and a more delicate flavor. Chickens, particularly those from Bresse, are hand-fed and not permitted to exercise, in order to preserve their succulence and tenderness.

Almost 250 varieties of cheese are produced in France, but comparatively few have reached this country. Everyone knows Port Salut, Pont Lévêque, Roquefort, Brie, Camembert; but not many people are familiar with the fine local cheeses produced in very small quantities and generally unavailable outside of France.

The drinking of wine occupies a unique position in France. Just as the gourmet's food is a matter of the utmost importance, so is the selection of the proper wine with his meal. But the average Frenchman does not worry too much about vintage wines or about what wine with what food, so long as wine is available. Most Frenchmen will not eat a meal unless it is accompanied by wine, even *vin ordinaire*—ordinary wine, either red or white. While many tourists concern themselves unduly with vintage years, the average Frenchman recognizes only two primary rules: white wine with fish or chicken, red wine with meats.

Champagne stands alone in the world of wines. It is the undisputed king in the eyes of the world. The bubbles that delight so many people are the result of many years of constant effort and attention, since the fermentation is produced individually in each bottle. To visit the great caves of Epernay or Rheims where the wines are made is one of the truly great tourist experiences of a visit to France.

But France is also the land of many other wines, including the red types, the whites, and the pinks (*rosés*). In addition there are many liqueurs, such as Chartreuse, Grand Marnier, and the different types of brandy. Almost without exception, the wine and liquor producers welcome visitors and will be pleased to show them through their establishments, often with complimentary tastings of their various products.

Paris is the center of the world of French restaurants. Many of these are frankly designed to attract tourists, specializing more in glamor, high prices, and décor than fine food. Parisians shake their heads mournfully and say that such places have "gone American." Others have resisted temptation, often at a substantial loss, and continue to serve the great dishes that have made their country the byword for fine food.

Paris has its great and famous restaurants, some of which are listed with no attempt to differentiate among them: Maxim's (which caters for Pan American's de luxe flights), Drouant, Grand Vefour, Café de Paris, Pharamond, Lapérouse (still one of the greatest of all), Rotisserie Périgourdine, Tour d'Argent, Cabaret, Crémaillère, Joseph, Lasserre, and San Francisco, this last famous even in Paris for Italian food. Unfortunately these are all expensive, but Paris is filled with excellent moderate-priced establishments.

Even Parisians are usually willing to admit that the best food in the country is obtainable farther south, in the vicinity of Lyon, the heart of the food-producing area of France. Just a little farther south is the town of Vienne, home of what is undoubtedly the most famous and superb restaurant in all the world, the Pyramide. But wherever one goes in France, in the cities or in the villages, there are good and often great restaurants serving what may only be called inspired food.

## VERMOUTH CASSIS

3 jiggers Crème de Cassis, black currant, or blackberry syrup
6 large jiggers French vermouth
12 ice cubes

Mix the vermouth and Crème de Cassis and pour into tall highball glasses. Place 2 ice cubes in each glass. Fill each glass with carbonated water and stir lightly.

## ANCHOVY HORS D'OEUVRE

ANCHOÏADE

2 tins anchovy fillets
2 cloves garlic, minced
1 teaspoon lemon juice

1 tablespoon olive or salad oil
3 slices bread

Place the anchovies and the oil in which they were prepared in a bowl with the minced garlic. Mash with a fork until they are soft. Add the lemon juice and oil and mix well. Trim the crusts from the bread and cut each piece in half lengthwise. Spread the mixture on the 6 pieces of bread and place under a broiler for a few minutes until thoroughly heated.

This dish is usually served as an appetizer or hors d'oeuvre. To serve as a first course, fry the bread slices in some butter or oil before spreading with the anchovy mixture. Then place on a buttered baking sheet and put under the broiler until heated.

## ONIONS WITH RAISINS

OIGNONS À LA MONÉGASQUE

⅓ cup tarragon vinegar
1 cup water
2 tablespoons white wine
4 tablespoons olive oil
2 tablespoons tomato paste
⅓ cup seedless raisins

1 tablespoon sugar
1 teaspoon salt
¼ teaspoon pepper
2 tablespoons chopped parsley
1 bay leaf
1 pound small white onions, peeled

Combine the vinegar, water, wine, oil, tomato paste, raisins, sugar, salt, pepper, parsley, and bay leaf in a saucepan. Mix well. Add the onions. Bring to a boil. Cover and cook over low heat for 25 minutes, or until the onions are done. Cool, then chill in the refrigerator. Serve as an hors d'oeuvre.

## CHICKEN LIVER SPREAD

PÂTÉ DE FOIE DE VOLAILLE

1 pound chicken livers
1 onion
¾ cup rendered chicken fat or melted butter
4 tablespoons grated onion
2 teaspoons salt

½ teaspoon pepper
¼ teaspoon mace
1½ teaspoons dry mustard
⅛ teaspoon anchovy paste
1 tablespoon brandy

Wash the livers carefully, removing any discolored areas. Place them in a saucepan with the onion and water to cover. Bring to a boil, cover, and cook over low heat for 20 minutes. Drain completely and discard the onion. Grind the livers in a food chopper three times, or until very smooth. Add the chicken fat, grated onion, salt, pepper, mace, mustard, anchovy paste, and brandy. Mix together until completely smooth. Place the pâté in a mold or other attractive dish, pressing it down until fairly firm. Chill for at least 3 hours. If in a mold, turn out onto a plate. Slice the pâté about ¼ to ½ inch thick and serve with crusty French bread. Freshly ground pepper may be sprinkled on top. This is delicious as a cocktail spread.

## ONION SOUP

### SOUPE À L'OIGNON

⅓ cup butter
5 onions, sliced thin
2 tablespoons flour
7 cups stock or 3 cans beef consommé and 2 cans water
½ teaspoon pepper

6 slices white toast (French, if possible)
6 thin slices Gruyère or Swiss cheese
4 tablespoons grated Gruyère or
   Swiss cheese

Melt the butter in a heavy saucepan. Add the onions and sauté over very low heat until brown. Stir frequently. Add the flour and mix until smooth. Add the stock gradually, stirring constantly. Add the pepper. Cover and cook over low heat for 30 minutes. Correct seasoning. Put a slice of toast in each soup plate or individual tureen. Place a slice of cheese on the bread and pour the soup over it. Place under the broiler for 1 minute to melt the cheese, if desired. Sprinkle with grated cheese and serve.

## PEA SOUP

### POTAGE ST. GERMAIN

2 cups green split peas
5 cups water
6 tablespoons butter
1 carrot, sliced
1 onion, sliced
3 tablespoons chopped cooked ham

1 cup stock or 1 can consommé
1 cup light cream
1 teaspoon salt
⅛ teaspoon pepper
½ teaspoon sugar

Wash the peas carefully and soak in water overnight, at least 12 hours. Drain. Place the peas in a saucepan and add the 5 cups of water. Bring to a boil, then skim the top carefully.

53

Melt 2 tablespoons of the butter and add the carrot and onion. Sauté for 5 minutes over low heat, then add to the peas. Add the ham, cover, and cook for 1½ hours. Certain varieties of peas may require a little additional cooking time. Force the mixture through a sieve or place in an electric blender. The mixture should be very smooth. Return to the saucepan and add the stock, cream, salt, pepper, sugar, and the remaining butter. Heat thoroughly. If the resulting soup is too thick, it may be thinned by adding a small quantity of stock or milk. Serve with croutons.

## LEEK AND CHEESE SOUP

SOUPE AU POIREAU ET AU FROMAGE

8 leeks
1 onion, chopped
6 tablespoons butter
6 cups stock or 2 cans consommé and
   2½ cans water
1 quart boiling water

1 cup uncooked macaroni
1 tablespoon salt
2 cloves garlic
1 cup grated Swiss cheese
1 cup white wine

Wash the leeks thoroughly to remove any possible sand. Slice thin, using all of the white part and about half of the green portion. Combine with the chopped onion. Melt the butter in a deep saucepan and add the leek and onion mixture. Cook over low heat, stirring occasionally, for 10 minutes. Do not allow the leeks or onions to brown. Add the stock, cover, and cook for 45 minutes.

In a separate saucepan boil the water. Break the macaroni into small pieces and add to the water, together with the salt and garlic. Boil until the macaroni is tender, about 15 minutes. Drain. Add to the leek mixture and continue cooking over very low heat while preparing the cheese mixture.

Place the cheese in the top of a double boiler over hot water and add the wine. Stir frequently until the cheese melts. Pour the soup into individual plates and add 2 tablespoons of the cheese mixture to each portion.

## MARSEILLE FISH SOUP

BOUILLABAISSE MARSEILLAISE

½ cup olive oil
3 onions, chopped fine
5 tomatoes, peeled and chopped
2 cloves garlic, minced
1 bay leaf
1 teaspoon salt
1 teaspoon saffron

½ teaspoon pepper
3 pounds assorted fish (at least 3 different varieties)
2 quarts boiling water
1 lobster, cut in small pieces
1 pound shrimp, shelled and cleaned
1 cup white wine

This dish requires certain fish that are obtainable only in France. However, even with substitutes, you will find it excellent and unique.

In a large casserole heat the oil. Add the onions, tomatoes, and garlic. Cook over low heat for 5 minutes, stirring occasionally. Add the bay leaf, salt, saffron, pepper, fish, and boiling water. The more different kinds of fish you have, the better the results will be. Add the lobster and cook for 10 minutes. Add the shrimp and wine, stir gently so as not to break up the fish, and cook for 10 more minutes. Correct the seasoning, bearing in mind that the dish should be fairly spicy.

Prepare individual soup plates for each person. Place pieces of fish, lobster, and shrimp in each plate, and pour the soup on top. Serve with toasted French bread.

## PIKE BALLS WITH SHRIMP SAUCE

QUENELLES DE BROCHET

4 eggs
¾ cup flour
½ pound butter
1 cup milk

1 pike (about 2½ pounds) or other freshwater fish
1 teaspoon salt
¼ teaspoon pepper

Beat 2 of the eggs and add the flour, 2 tablespoons of the butter, and the milk. Cook over low heat, stirring constantly until thick. Set aside to cool.

Remove the fish from the bones or have the fish filleted by the fish dealer, reserving the skin and head for the sauce. Put the fish through a food mill or chopper twice. Cream the remaining butter and combine it with the ground fish. Add the egg and flour mixture, salt, pepper, and the remaining 2 eggs. Blend all the ingredients well. It is essential that the mixture be extremely smooth.

Flour a board or other surface. Taking about 1 tablespoon of the fish mixture, roll it into the shape of a small sausage, about 2 inches long.

55

Continue until all of the mixture is used up. Butter a shallow pan and place the *quenelles* in it. Add just enough boiling water to cover. Cook over very low heat for 15 minutes; do not allow the water to boil. Drain carefully, so as not to break the *quenelles*. Although they may be served with melted butter, they are traditionally served with Sauce Nantua, prepared as follows:

| | |
|---|---|
| 1 onion, sliced | 2 tablespoons butter |
| 3 cups water | 2 tablespoons flour |
| 2 teaspoons salt | ¼ cup heavy cream, scalded |
| ½ teaspoon pepper | ¾ cup chopped cooked shrimp |
| Fish head and skin | |

Place the onion, water, salt, pepper, fish head and skin (previously reserved) in a saucepan. Bring to a boil and cook over medium heat for 45 minutes. Strain, reserving 1½ cups of stock. Melt the butter in a saucepan, add the flour, and make a smooth paste. Gradually add the stock and cream, stirring constantly until the boiling point is reached. Cook for 10 minutes, stirring occasionally. Add the shrimp, and correct the seasoning. Place the *quenelles* in this sauce and simmer over very low heat for 5 minutes.

## FISH WITH BREAD SAUCE

POISSON À LA RESERVE DE BEAULIEU

| | |
|---|---|
| 6 fillets of trout, red snapper, or sole | 8 slices white bread, trimmed |
| Fish heads and skin | ½ pound butter |
| 2 cups water | 2 egg yolks |
| 3 teaspoons salt | 2 teaspoons chopped chives |
| ¼ cup white wine | |

Combine the fish heads and skin with the water and 1 teaspoon of the salt in a saucepan. Boil for 30 minutes, or until only ½ cup of stock remains. Place the fish flat on a buttered baking dish. Sprinkle with the remaining salt. Pour the stock and wine over it. Soak the bread in boiling water, then squeeze dry. Cream the butter and add the egg yolks, chives, and bread, blending well. Spread this mixture about ½ inch thick over the fish. Bake in a 375° oven for 20 minutes, or until browned on top. Serve at once. Do not accompany this dish with lemon slices.

*Note: When prepared at the Restaurant La Reserve de Beaulieu, it is made with the renowned Mediterranean fish, the loup, or wolf fish.*

## FILLET OF SOLE WITH LOBSTER SAUCE

FILET DE SOLE À L'AMÉRICAINE

4 tablespoons olive oil
1 lobster, cut in eighths, in the shell
1 tablespoon butter
1 clove garlic, minced
3 shallots, chopped
¼ cup brandy
1½ cups white wine
½ cup water

4 tomatoes, peeled, seeded, and chopped
2 teaspoons salt
½ teaspoon tarragon
Dash of cayenne pepper
6 fillets of sole
2 tablespoons chopped parsley

Heat the olive oil in a saucepan. Add the lobster and cook over high heat until it turns red. Add the butter, garlic, and shallots. Cook over low heat for 2 minutes. Add brandy and set it aflame. Let burn a few seconds. Add 1 cup of the wine, the water, tomatoes, 1 teaspoon of the salt, tarragon, and cayenne pepper. Cover and cook over low heat for 20 minutes. Strain the sauce. Remove the lobster meat from the shells and cut into ¼-inch cubes. Return to the sauce. Cook over very low heat while preparing the fillets.

Place the fillets in a buttered skillet. Sprinkle with the remaining salt and add the remaining wine. Cover with buttered wax paper and cook over low heat (without boiling) for 15 minutes. Place the fillets on a platter. Combine the sauces and pour over the fish. Sprinkle with parsley.

*Note: The above dish is served on Pan American World Airways' "President Special" flights to Europe.*

## BEEF, BURGUNDY STYLE

BOEUF BOURGUIGNON

4 pounds beef (cross rib or bottom round)
⅓ cup flour
2 teaspoons salt
¼ teaspoon pepper
6 tablespoons butter
3 tablespoons brandy
3 medium onions, sliced
3 carrots, sliced

3 sprigs parsley
2 bay leaves
Dash of thyme
1 clove garlic, minced
3 cups dry red wine
3 slices bacon, half cooked
1 cup fresh or canned sliced mushrooms
1 tablespoon tomato paste

Cut the meat into 1½-inch cubes. Combine the flour with the salt and pepper and coat each cube of meat with the mixture. Melt 4 tablespoons of the butter in a heavy saucepan or casserole. Add the meat and brown on all sides over very high heat. Pour the brandy over the meat and set it aflame.

In a separate pan melt the remaining 2 tablespoons of butter and sauté the onions and carrots for 5 minutes. Add to the meat. Add the parsley, bay leaves, thyme, and garlic and stir. Add the red wine and just enough water to cover the meat. Add the bacon, cover, and cook over low heat for 2½ hours. Add the mushrooms and tomato paste and stir well. Cook 30 minutes longer.

## FILLET OF BEEF WITH TRUFFLE SAUCE

FILET MIGNON ROSSINI

¼ pound butter
6 beef fillets
1½ teaspoons salt
½ teaspoon pepper

4 black truffles, sliced thin
½ cup brandy
1 cup beef stock or 1 cup canned beef consommé

Melt 2 tablespoons of the butter in a skillet. Place the fillets in it and cook over high heat for 3 minutes on each side or to desired degree of rareness. Sprinkle with salt and pepper. Keep warm.

Combine the truffles, brandy, and stock in a saucepan. Bring to a boil and cook over high heat until liquid is reduced by half. Add the remaining butter, stirring until melted. Pour over the fillets and serve.

*Note: This dish is served on Pan American World Airways' "President Special" flights.*

## VEAL AND MUSHROOMS

VEAU AUX CHAMPIGNONS

½ pound butter
3 onions, sliced thin
2 tablespoons flour
1 cup chicken stock or 1 cup canned consommé
½ cup milk
1 teaspoon salt

⅛ teaspoon pepper
2 egg yolks
3 tablespoons heavy cream
24 mushrooms, stems removed
12 slices veal (¼ inch thick)
1 3-oz. can pâté de foie gras

Melt half the butter in a saucepan. Add the onions and cook over very low heat for 15 minutes; do not allow them to brown. Sprinkle with the flour and mix well. Gradually add the stock and milk, stirring constantly until the boiling point is reached. Add the salt and pepper. Cover and cook over very low heat for 40 minutes, stirring occasionally. Force the mixture through a sieve. Beat the egg yolks and cream together in a bowl. Gradually add the sauce, beating constantly to prevent curdling. Reheat but do not allow to boil.

Melt 4 tablespoons of the butter in a skillet. Add the mushrooms and sauté for 5 minutes, stirring occasionally. Melt the remaining 4 tablespoons of butter in a skillet. Add the veal slices and sauté for 5 minutes on each side. Spread the pâté de foie gras on 6 of the veal slices and cover with the remaining 6 slices.

Place the veal in an ovenproof dish that may be brought to the table. Arrange the mushrooms around the meat and pour the sauce over it. Place under the broiler until delicately browned, about 5 minutes. Serve directly from the dish.

## CHICKEN IN THE POT

POULE AU POT

| | |
|---|---|
| 5- to 6-pound chicken | 2 egg yolks |
| Gizzard and liver | 2 egg whites |
| ¼ pound ham | 1 pound short ribs of beef |
| 2 tablespoons butter | 3 quarts water |
| 1 onion, chopped | 3 carrots, peeled and sliced |
| 1¼ cups bread crumbs | 1 bay leaf |
| ¼ cup light cream | 1 onion |
| 2 tablespoons chopped parsley | 3 sprigs parsley |
| 4 teaspoons salt | ¼ teaspoon thyme |
| 1 teaspoon pepper | 1 cup rice |

Wash and dry the chicken. Chop the gizzard, liver, and ham or grind in a food chopper. Melt the butter in a skillet. Add the onion and sauté for 5 minutes. Place the bread crumbs in a bowl and moisten with the cream. Add the sautéed onion, the ham mixture, parsley, 1 teaspoon of salt, ½ teaspoon of pepper, and the egg yolks. Mix well. Beat the egg whites until stiff but not dry and fold into the bread-crumb mixture. Stuff the chicken and carefully fasten the opening with skewers or thread. Truss.

Place the beef and water in a large heavy saucepan. Bring to a boil. Add the chicken, carrots, bay leaf, onion, parsley, thyme, and the remaining salt and pepper. Cover and cook over low heat for 3 hours, or until meats are tender. About 30 minutes before the cooking time is up, transfer 3 cups of the soup to another saucepan. Wash the rice in warm water and add. Cover and cook over low heat 20 minutes. The soup is usually served as a separate course, together with the carrots. The meats are served with the rice.

## CHICKEN IN WHITE WINE WITH DUMPLINGS

POULET NIVERNAIS

4 teaspoons salt
1 teaspoon pepper
2 3-pound chickens, disjointed
⅓ cup butter
2 cloves
12 small white onions
12 mushroom caps
3 carrots, peeled and sliced
1 clove garlic, minced
½ teaspoon marjoram
¼ teaspoon thyme

4 sprigs parsley
1 bay leaf
1¼ cups white wine
½ teaspoon saffron
2 tablespoons hot water
1½ cups sour cream, scalded
1½ cups sifted flour
2½ teaspoons baking powder
2 eggs, beaten
⅓ cup milk

Combine 3 teaspoons of the salt with the pepper and rub it into the chicken. Melt the butter in a casserole or Dutch oven. Brown the chicken in it on all sides. Place the cloves in an onion and add to the chicken with the remaining onions, mushrooms, carrots, garlic, marjoram, thyme, parsley, bay leaf, and wine. Cover. Bake in a 375° oven for 1 hour. Remove the casserole from the oven and place over low direct heat. Dissolve the saffron in the hot water. Add to the chicken. Add the sour cream. Mix lightly. Correct seasoning.

Sift the flour, baking powder, and remaining salt into a bowl. Combine with the eggs and milk, mixing well until smooth. Bring the contents of the casserole to a boil. Drop teaspoons of the mixture around the edge. Cover and cook over low heat 15 minutes. Do not lift the cover during this period.

## ROAST DUCK WITH CHERRIES

CANARD À LA MONTMORENCY

5- to 6-pound duck
2 teaspoons salt
½ teaspoon pepper
1 cup white wine
2 tablespoons sugar
2 tablespoons vinegar
1 tablespoon butter
2 tablespoons flour

1 cup stock or 1 cup boiling water
  and 1 bouillon cube
½ cup orange juice
3 tablespoons grated orange rind
2 tablespoons lemon juice
1 tablespoon grated lemon rind
1 No. 2 can bing cherries
2 tablespoons brandy.

Clean the duck carefully. Combine the salt and pepper and rub into the duck. If possible, season the duck a day ahead of time. Roast in a 475° oven for 20 minutes. Drain the fat thoroughly. Pour the wine over the duck and reduce the oven temperature to 350°. Continue roasting for an additional 1½ hours, or until tender. Meanwhile prepare the sauce as follows:

Place the sugar and vinegar in a saucepan, and cook over low heat, stirring occasionally, until the sauce becomes dark brown in color. In a separate saucepan melt the butter, add the flour, and make a smooth paste. Gradually add the stock, stirring constantly until the boiling point is reached. Cook over very low heat for 10 minutes, stirring occasionally. Add the orange juice and rind, lemon juice and rind, 1 cup of cherry juice, and the brandy, stirring constantly while adding these ingredients. Add the sugar and vinegar mixture, stirring constantly. Add ¼ cup of pan drippings to the sauce but first be sure to skim off the fat. Cook for 15 minutes over low heat, then add the whole cherries, but do not add any additional juice from the can. Allow the sauce to simmer while carving the duck. Pour a little of the sauce on top of the pieces of duck and serve the remainder in a sauceboat.

*Note: One duck will serve about 6 with rather small portions. If you are serving an elaborate meal with many courses, one duck may be sufficient. However, if the duck course constitutes the main part of the meal, it will be necessary to roast two somewhat smaller ducks. There is sufficient sauce in the recipe to accompany two ducks.*

## BAKED MUSHROOMS

CHAMPIGNONS AU GRATIN

| | |
|---|---|
| 1 clove garlic, minced | 2 tablespoons wine vinegar |
| 1 onion, grated | 1½ pounds mushrooms, washed and |
| 2 tablespoons chopped parsley | sliced |
| ⅛ teaspoon basil | ¼ pound butter |
| 1 teaspoon salt | ½ cup bread crumbs |
| ¼ teaspoon pepper | 1 tablespoon grated Parmesan cheese |
| ⅓ cup olive oil | |

Combine the garlic, onion, parsley, basil, salt, pepper, oil, and vinegar in a bowl. Add the mushrooms and allow to marinate for 3 hours, basting frequently. Drain. Melt half the butter in a skillet. Add the mushrooms, and cook over high heat for 1 minute. Reduce the heat to low and cook for 10 minutes, stirring frequently. Butter a baking dish very well and place the mushrooms in it. Sprinkle the bread crumbs and Parmesan cheese on top and dot with the remaining butter. Place under the broiler until browned.

## POTATOES IN CREAM

GRATIN DAUPHINOIS

6 potatoes, peeled and sliced very thin
2 teaspoons salt
¾ teaspoon pepper

½ teaspoon nutmeg
1 cup light cream
3 tablespoons butter

Arrange layers of potatoes sprinkled with salt, pepper, and nutmeg in a buttered baking dish. Pour the cream over the top and dot with butter. Bake in a 300° oven for 1 hour, or until the cream is absorbed and the top lightly browned.

## GREEN SALAD

SALADE VERTE

1 cup olive oil
¼ cup wine or tarragon vinegar
1 teaspoon salt
¼ teaspoon black pepper

1 clove garlic, crushed
1 head romaine lettuce
2 endive
1 head escarole

Combine the olive oil, vinegar, salt, pepper, and garlic in a bowl. Beat vigorously with a rotary beater, or place the ingredients in a bottle and shake vigorously. Chill. Wash, drain, and chill the lettuce, endive, and escarole. Tear, do not cut, the lettuce into 2-inch pieces. Cut the endive into ½-inch pieces. Tear the escarole into small pieces. Combine the greens in a salad bowl. Add the dressing just before serving and toss lightly.

Note: Any combination of green vegetables may be used with this simple classic dressing.

## DESSERT PANCAKES

CRÊPES

1¼ cups sifted flour
1 teaspoon salt
2 eggs, beaten

1 cup milk
1 tablespoon salad oil
4 tablespoons butter

Combine the flour and salt. Gradually add the eggs and the milk, beating steadily until the mixture is smooth and completely free of lumps. Add the oil and beat 1 minute longer. Chill for 2 hours. Place a small piece of butter in a 6-inch frying pan and when it begins to bubble pour 2 tablespoons of the batter into it, and turn from side to side, to spread the batter evenly and thinly. Cook over very low heat for 1 minute, then turn over and cook for about 30 seconds. Remove carefully to a plate. Repeat the process until the batter is used up. Be very careful not to tear the pancakes when removing them from the pan. With a little practice it is possible to work with two frying pans at the same time.

The pancakes may be filled with jam or jelly, and then rolled up. Serve about 3 to a portion. They may also be served with the following *Suzette* sauce:

| | |
|---|---|
| 3 tablespoons sugar | 2 teaspoons grated lemon rind |
| 4 tablespoons butter | ¼ cup curaçao or Grand Marnier |
| ¾ cup orange juice | ¼ cup brandy |
| 2 tablespoons grated orange rind | |

Cream the sugar and butter together. Place in a skillet and add the orange juice and orange and lemon rind. Cook over very low heat until the sugar is completely melted, stirring occasionally. Add the liqueur. Fold each pancake in half then fold again so as to bring the opposite corners together, forming a pie-shaped wedge. Carefully place each folded pancake in the sauce and heat thoroughly. Place the pancakes and sauce in a serving dish. Heat the brandy, set it afire, then pour it over the pancakes and serve flaming.

## CHOCOLATE MOUSSE

MOUSSE AU CHOCOLAT

| | |
|---|---|
| 2 tablespoons brewed coffee, cooled | ¼ cup sugar |
| 3 ounces sweet chocolate | 4 egg whites |
| 4 egg yolks | 1½ cups heavy cream |

Combine the coffee and the chocolate in the top of a double boiler. Place over hot water until the chocolate is completely melted. Remove from the heat and set aside to cool for 15 minutes.

Beat the yolks until light in color. Add the sugar and continue beating until light and fluffy. Add the cooled chocolate and mix well. Beat the whites until stiff but not dry and fold them slowly and carefully into the chocolate mixture. Whip the cream and gently fold it into the mixture. Pour into unbuttered individual dishes or into a 2-quart mold. Chill at least 4 hours.

## LIQUEUR SOUFFLÉ

SOUFFLÉ AUX LIQUEURS

4 tablespoons butter
4 tablespoons flour
1½ cups light cream, scalded
⅓ cup sugar

5 egg yolks
½ cup brandy or fruit cordial
10 ladyfingers
6 egg whites

Melt the butter in a saucepan. Add the flour and mix to a smooth paste. Gradually add the cream, stirring constantly until the boiling point is reached. Add the sugar and cook over low heat for 5 minutes, stirring frequently. Let cool for 5 minutes. Beat the egg yolks in a bowl. Gradually add the cream mixture, beating constantly. Add half the brandy. Cool for 10 minutes. Preheat oven to 350°. Soak the ladyfingers in the remaining brandy. Beat the egg whites until stiff but not dry and fold into the cream mixture. Butter a 2-quart soufflé dish and dust lightly with sugar. Pour half the soufflé mixture into it. Drain the ladyfingers and arrange them over it; cover with remaining soufflé. Bake in a 350° oven for 30 minutes. Serve at once.

*Note: A soufflé must be served and eaten immediately when it is ready. A delay of a few minutes is enough to allow the soufflé to fall. Have your guests waiting for the soufflé, because it will not wait for them.*

## CHERRY DESSERT

CLAFOUTIS AUX CERISES

3 eggs
2 cups milk, scalded and cooled
1 cup light cream, scalded and cooled
⅔ cup sifted flour
⅔ cup confectioners' sugar

¾ teaspoon salt
1 pound pitted sweet cherries or 2½ cups canned bing cherries, drained
½ teaspoon almond extract

Beat the eggs in a bowl. Add the milk and cream, beating well. Sift the flour, confectioners' sugar, and salt into a bowl. Gradually add the egg mixture, beating constantly until smooth. Add the cherries and almond extract and mix lightly. Preheat oven to 375°. Pour the batter into a 2- or 3-quart buttered soufflé dish or casserole. Bake in a 375° oven for 35 minutes, or until set and lightly browned on top. Serve hot or cold, sprinkled with confectioners' sugar.

*GERMANY*

Although France and Germany are neighbors, their cuisines are as far apart as the poles. The French style of cooking may have become the accepted standard of the world, but it has made practically no progress whatsoever in Germany, nor is it likely that it ever will. Though both nations are extremely fond of good food, the differences in tastes are decisive.

The problem is exemplified in the national drinking habits. Though Germany produces and consumes some fine wines, the country is known primarily as a land of beer drinkers. In France, although beer is popular, wine is by all odds the drink of the country. Where lies the distinction between the two countries? It is suggested that the difference is so basic that any discussion must take into account the nationalistic differences in character. As a generalization, the French are given to that which is light and bright, whether in art, decoration, music, or food. The Germans are sober and grave; their expression in any form is more than likely to be serious, ponderous, and cautious. German buildings are stolid, German art is weighty, and inevitably their approach to any problem is stolid and thoughtful.

The two countries definitely express their national characteristics in their food. German food is always substantial; seldom does one encounter a dish that could possibly be described as frivolous, as is the case with a considerable number of French dishes. A Frenchman may work for hours to create a bit of fluff or pastry to tempt the appetite; a German chef would seldom waste his time unless the results were material. Even German desserts are substantial enough to constitute a light meal for an American. This is a land of outdoor people, of mountain climbers, skiers, and hikers; it is also a country where people usually come to the table seeking hearty fare. However, German cookery is not necessarily limited to plain dishes; it has one of the very few important cuisines of the world, with numerous noteworthy and outstanding dishes.

Germany has made a distinct impression on the food of the United States, although the full effect is little realized here. Our national favorite, the "hot dog," is definitely traceable to the German sausage. Sauerkraut, to be sure, is distinctly German. When frankfurters (from Frankfurt, Germany) are combined with sauerkraut, it is easy to see that the favorite snack of millions of Americans is a direct descendant of German ancestors. Our second popular favorite is the hamburger, a chopped meat specialty reputed to have originated in Hamburg, Germany. And there can be no argument about the nationality of beer or the nationality of those who brought it to its present stage of popularity in the United States.

Not popular in our country but a national favorite in Germany is the famous *Aalsuppe* (eel soup), which is much better than it sounds. Cold and hot beer soups are immensely popular there, and are easily duplicated although they represent something of an acquired taste. Fruit soups are good but often too sweet for American tastes, except as light lunches. Another great German favorite is herring, prepared in bewildering variety and particularly esteemed when served with beer.

*Sauerbraten*, a sour pickled beef dish, is well known here. Goose stuffed with apples and onions is a national dish; chicken livers are also prepared with the same accompaniments. Sauerkraut is so important to some Germans that it is eaten two or even three times a day. It is served in diversified styles, hot or cold, with wine, with caraway seeds, with apples, etc. Dumplings, a part of almost every meal, are prepared in countless fashions; potatoes are of nearly equal importance.

A special section could be devoted to a discussion of the world-famous German *Delikatessen* (delicate eating). The word itself has moved into the English language almost intact as delicatessen. It includes the entire range of smoked and pickled meats, sausages, liverwurst, potato salad, pickles, and the like. Cheeses that have emigrated to our own country include Münster, Limburger, and Tilsiter; some of these have become naturalized, or have taken out first citizenship papers.

There is one style of German cooking called "sweet and sour" which has made little headway in this country, except in the area surrounding Milwaukee and in the Pennsylvania Dutch region near Lancaster. Since these areas were predominantly settled by Germans, this is not surprising. This style consists in combining in one sauce both sweet ingredients (fruit, sugar) and sour stuffs (vinegar, lemon juice). Meats, vegetables, and other dishes are prepared in the sweet and sour style.

Space limitations prevent any serious discussion of other great specialties, such as Westphalian ham, potato pancakes, mountain trout, and noodle dishes. Since the war, good food has returned to Germany, and most of the prewar food specialties are now available. In Berlin excellent meals are to be had at the Hotel Kempinski restaurants and at many other fine spots. In Frankfurt, at the Restaurent zum Kaiserkeller and the Grillroom Frankfurter Hof.

Most American visitors admire German beers but are not too fond of the German style of serving them at room temperature. The recent influx of G.I.s has encouraged some chilling of beer, but the custom is not yet widespread. Beer drinking is about two thousand years old in the region we call Germany today, and customs are not quickly changed. All German beer is of high quality in this land of beer connoisseurs, but some brews are exceptional, Munich being particularly renowned in this respect. The vineyards of Germany produce, among others, the Rhine and Moselle wines which are highly regarded by wine drinkers the world over. Germans drink enormous amounts of wine, which may come as a surprise to those who believe that only beer is important to the people.

## APPLE AND BREAD SOUP

APFELBROTSUPPE

8 large cooking apples, peeled and sliced
2 quarts water
6 slices pumpernickel bread
3 tablespoons sugar
¼ cup currants or seedless raisins
⅛ teaspoon cinnamon
3 tablespoons lemon juice
1 tablespoon grated lemon rind

Combine the apples and water in a saucepan. Soak the pumpernickel in water, then squeeze dry. Add to the apples. Cook over medium heat for 20 minutes, or until apples are very soft. Force the apple mixture through a sieve. Return the purée to the saucepan and reheat. Add the sugar, currants, and cinnamon. Cook over medium heat for 10 minutes. Add the lemon juice and rind. Cook 5 minutes longer. Serve very hot.

## FISH WITH CARAWAY SEED CABBAGE

FISCHE MIT KÜMMELKRAUT

¼ pound butter
1 medium head cabbage, shredded
4 potatoes, sliced thin
2 tablespoons caraway seeds
3 teaspoons salt
1 cup boiling water
¾ teaspoon pepper
6 slices pike, whitefish, or halibut

Melt the butter in a deep saucepan. Add the cabbage, potatoes, caraway seeds, 2 teaspoons of the salt, and boiling water. Cook over medium heat for 25 minutes. Stir well. Sprinkle the pepper and the remaining salt on

67

the fish slices. Place the fish slices on top of the cabbage and do not stir. Cover and cook over low heat for 35 minutes, or until fish is done. Correct seasoning. Serve carefully so as not to break up the slices of fish.


## MEAT BALLS IN CAPER SAUCE

KLOPSE

4 tablespoons butter
3 onions, chopped
6 slices white bread
1 cup light cream
1½ pounds beef, ground
½ pound veal, ground
½ pound pork, ground
4 anchovy fillets
3 eggs
2 teaspoons salt

1 teaspoon pepper
½ cup ice water
3 cups boiling water
¼ teaspoon marjoram
3 sprigs parsley
3 stalks celery
2 tablespoons flour
2 tablespoons lemon juice
¼ cup capers, drained

Melt 2 tablespoons of the butter in a skillet and add the onions. Sauté for 10 minutes, stirring occasionally. Soak the bread in cream for 10 minutes. Press the excess liquid from it. Grind the bread with the sautéed onions, ground beef, veal, and pork and the anchovies in a food chopper. Add the eggs, 1 teaspoon of the salt, ½ teaspoon of the pepper, and the ice water. Mix together and shape into 2-inch balls. Combine in a deep saucepan the boiling water, remaining salt and pepper, marjoram, parsley, and celery. Drop the meat balls into it and boil for 20 minutes.

Melt the remaining butter in a saucepan. Add the flour and mix to smooth paste. Strain the liquid in which the meat balls were cooked, and add, stirring constantly until the boiling point is reached. Cook over low heat for 5 minutes. Add the lemon juice and capers and stir well. Place the meat balls on a platter and pour the sauce over them.


## BROWNED, MARINATED BEEF

SAUERBRATEN

2 cups vinegar
2 teaspoons salt
10 peppercorns
3 cloves
2 bay leaves
2 onions, chopped

2 carrots, sliced
4 to 6 pounds beef (top round, breast, or other desired cut)
3 tablespoons butter
1½ cups boiling water
½ pint sour cream

Combine in a saucepan the vinegar, salt, peppercorns, bay leaves, onions, and carrots and bring to a boil. Remove from heat and cool for 30 minutes. Place the beef in a bowl and pour the previous mixture over it. Marinate for 3–5 days in the refrigerator, turning the meat several times. Baste occasionally.

Drain the meat, reserving the marinade, and dry with paper towels. Melt the butter in a heavy cast-iron pot or Dutch oven. Brown the meat on all sides, then add the marinade and the boiling water and cook over low heat for 3 hours, or until the meat is tender. Add the sour cream, stirring constantly, and simmer for 15 minutes. Slice and serve with the gravy. Potato pancakes (see recipe in this section) are usually served with *Sauerbraten*.

## PORK SAUSAGES IN BEER, BERLIN STYLE

BRATWURST IN BIER, BERLINER ART

| | |
|---|---|
| 2 cups boiling water | 6 peppercorns |
| 18 pork sausages | ½ teaspoon salt |
| 1 tablespoon butter | 2 cups beer |
| 4 onions, sliced | 2 tablespoons water |
| 1 bay leaf | 3 tablespoons potato flour |

Pour the boiling water over the sausages; drain and dry them. Melt the butter in a skillet. Add the sausages and brown on all sides. Remove the sausages from the pan and pour off all but 2 tablespoons of the fat. Add the onions; sauté 10 minutes. Return the sausages to the pan and add the bay leaf, peppercorns, salt, and beer. Cook over low heat 20 minutes. Mix the water and potato flour to a smooth paste and add to the sausages, stirring constantly until the boiling point is reached. Cook over low heat 5 minutes. Serve with mashed potatoes.

## STEAK WITH PINEAPPLE AND CHERRIES

RINDFLEISCH MIT ANANAS UND KIRSCHEN

| | |
|---|---|
| ¼ pound butter | 1 onion |
| 1 fresh pineapple, peeled and cut into strips, or 1 No. 2 can sliced pineapple, drained | 1¼ teaspoons salt |
| | Dash of cayenne pepper |
| | 2 cups milk |
| 1 cup canned sour red cherries, drained | 1 cup bread crumbs |
| | 6 slices toast, trimmed |
| 1 cup port wine | 6 individual fillets mignon, 1 inch thick |
| 2 cloves | |

Melt 1 tablespoon of the butter in a saucepan. Add the pineapple and cherries and simmer until glazed, about 20 minutes. While the fruit is simmering, place the cloves in the onion. Combine the onion, ¼ teaspoon of the salt, cayenne pepper, and milk in a saucepan. Bring to a boil and cook over medium heat for 5 minutes. Strain. Add the bread crumbs, stirring constantly until thick and smooth. Add this mixture to the fruit and mix well. Simmer over low heat while preparing the fillets.

Melt half of the remaining butter in a saucepan and place the toast in it. Fry for 30 seconds on each side. Remove and set aside. Melt the remaining butter in the same saucepan and place the fillets in it. Fry for 3 or more minutes on each side, depending on the degree of rareness desired. Place the toast on individual plates or a large platter. Put a fillet on top of each slice of toast and pour the sauce on top.

## BAKED APPLES STUFFED WITH LIVER

ÄPFEL MIT LEBERFÜLLE

6 large apples
½ pound chicken livers
⅛ teaspoon thyme

½ teaspoon salt
2 tablespoons butter
½ cup cider

Wash and core the apples carefully. Scoop out the interiors of the apples but do not discard. Grind the scooped-out apple pulp with the chicken livers. Add the thyme and salt and mix well. Stuff the apples with the mixture and dot the tops with butter. Preheat oven to 350°. Place the apples in a well-buttered baking dish. Pour the cider over the apples. Bake in a 350° oven for 35 minutes, or until apples are tender. Serve as an accompaniment to roast turkey or chicken.

## PIGS' KNUCKLES WITH SAUERKRAUT AND PEAS-PUDDING

EISBEIN MIT SAUERKRAUT UND ERBSEN PUREE

1 cup dried yellow peas
6 pounds pickled pigs' knuckles
2 bay leaves
8 peppercorns
2 eggs, beaten
2 tablespoons potato flour

2 teaspoons salt
½ teaspoon pepper
2 tablespoons lard or butter
3 onions, sliced
2 pounds sauerkraut, drained
3 slices bacon, cooked and crumbled

Soak the peas overnight in water to cover. Drain and again cover with water, boil until tender, about 1 hour. Drain and set aside. Soak the pigs' knuckles for 3 hours. Drain, cover with water, add the bay leaves and peppercorns. Boil 3 hours, or until tender.

Combine the peas, eggs, potato flour, salt, and pepper in a bowl. Pour into a buttered baking dish. Bake in a 375° oven for 30 minutes.

Melt the lard in a saucepan and add the onions. Sauté for 10 minutes, stirring occasionally. Remove 2 tablespoons of the onion and set aside. Add the sauerkraut, and cook over low heat for 15 minutes. Place the sauerkraut on a large platter. Drain the pigs' knuckles carefully and place them over the sauerkraut. Sprinkle the reserved sautéed onions and crumbled bacon on top of the peas-pudding. Serve together, with the peas-pudding in individual dishes.

## LOIN OF VEAL STEAK

KALBSRÜCKENSTEAK KEMPINSKI

| | |
|---|---|
| ¼ pound butter | 1 cup heavy cream |
| ½ cup finely chopped mushrooms | 1 teaspoon salt |
| 3 onions, chopped | ¼ teaspoon pepper |
| 4 tablespoons flour | 6 loin of veal steaks |
| 2 cups stock or 1 can consommé and | 3 kidneys (optional) |
| ½ can water | ¼ cup grated Parmesan cheese |

Melt 1 tablespoon of the butter in a saucepan. Add the mushrooms and sauté for 5 minutes. Set aside. Place the onions in a saucepan, cover with water, and bring to a boil. Cook for 5 minutes. Drain. Melt 1 tablespoon of the butter in a saucepan; add the onions, and cook over low heat for 10 minutes but do not allow to brown. Set aside. Melt 3 tablespoons of the butter in a saucepan, add the flour, and mix to a smooth paste. Add the stock, cream, salt, and pepper, stirring constantly until the boiling point is reached. Cook over low heat for 15 minutes, stirring occasionally. Combine with the onions. Correct seasoning.

Melt the remaining butter in a skillet. Add the veal steaks and fry until brown on both sides. Remove the steaks. Cut the kidneys in half and brown on all sides. Arrange the veal in a buttered baking dish. Put a piece of kidney on each piece of veal and top with 1 tablespoon of mushrooms. Pour the sauce over it. Sprinkle with the Parmesan cheese. Bake in a 350° oven for 30 minutes, or until brown on top. Serve hot.

## POTATO PANCAKES

KARTOFFELPUFFER

4 medium raw potatoes, grated
1 cup cooked, mashed potatoes
1 egg
1 egg yolk

1 teaspoon salt
½ teaspoon pepper
Fat or butter for frying

Press the liquid from the grated potatoes and discard. Combine the grated potatoes with the mashed potatoes, egg, egg yolk, salt, and pepper. Shape into desired size pancakes and fry until brown and crisp on both sides. The pancakes are often served with *Sauerbraten* (see recipe in this section) or other substantial meat dishes, or as a luncheon dish together with applesauce.

## BAKED STUFFED POTATOES

GEFÜLLTE KARTOFFELN

6 large potatoes
¼ pound cooked ham, chopped
1 onion, chopped
1 egg, beaten

½ cup sour cream
1 cup stock or 1 cup hot water and 1 bouillon cube

Scrub and dry the potatoes. Bake in a 400° oven for 45 minutes. Place each potato on its side and cut off the top quarter lengthwise. Remove the pulp carefully but reserve the skins of the larger part of each potato. Mash the pulp and combine with the ham, onion, egg, and sour cream. Correct seasoning. Stuff the potato shells with the mixture. Place in a buttered baking dish and pour the stock over and around the potatoes. Cover and bake in a 350° oven for 20 minutes. Serve hot.

## PLUM DUMPLINGS

ZWETSCHGENKNÖDEL

3 medium potatoes, boiled and cooled
⅓ cup flour
½ cup potato flour
½ teaspoon salt
1 egg, beaten

12 small blue plums, pitted
12 small cubes sugar
¼ pound butter, melted
3 tablespoons bread crumbs

Peel the potatoes and put them through a ricer or sieve, or mash them until very smooth. Add the flour, potato flour, salt, and egg. Mix until a dough is formed. Place on a lightly floured surface and shape the dough into a long roll, about the shape of a rolling pin. Cut into 12 pieces, as evenly as possible.

Place a cube of sugar in the center of each plum. Press each plum into a piece of dough, making sure that the plum is completely covered. Cook in rapidly boiling, salted water for 10 minutes. Drain well. Pour melted butter over the dumplings and sprinkle with the bread crumbs.

*Note: This recipe provides for 12 dumplings, or 2 per person. If served as a dessert, or as an accompaniment to a main course, it will probably be sufficient. However, for healthy appetites, it may be advisable to double this recipe.*

## SWEET PASTRY

MÜRBETEIG

2 cups sifted flour
⅛ teaspoon salt
½ cup sugar
½ pound butter
1 egg

1 tablespoon cold water
3 tablespoons heavy cream
½ cup blanched walnuts or almonds, chopped fine

Sift the flour, salt, and 2 tablespoons of the sugar into a bowl. Add the butter, using one hand to blend until smooth. Make a hollow in the center of the mixture and place the egg and water in it. Mix all together until a dough is formed. Wrap in wax paper and place in the refrigerator for at least 2 hours, overnight if possible.

METHOD 1: Roll out about ¼ inch thick on a lightly floured surface. Cut with a cooky cutter into desired shapes, brush with the cream, sprinkle with the remaining sugar and the chopped nuts. Place on a baking sheet. Bake in a 375° oven for 15 minutes, or until lightly browned.

METHOD 2: Roll out about ¼ inch thick on a lightly floured surface. Place in an unbuttered pie plate or baking sheet. Place rows of thinly sliced fruits, such as apples or peaches, on the dough. Sprinkle remaining sugar and the chopped nuts on top. Bake in a 375° oven for 40 minutes.

*Note: Mürbeteig is the basic dessert pastry of Germany. It can be used in countless ways to make sweet pastries.*

## HOLLAND (THE NETHERLANDS)

Only an hour after your Pan American plane lands at Schiphol Airport you will find yourself in Amsterdam, the capital. In that short hour it is possible to see enough of the Old World charm of the country to understand why tourists always find Holland a delight. It is an immaculate land, filled with canals, windmills, picturesque buildings, not a few wooden shoes, and a multitude of flowers, particularly tulips. These last are seen at their best during the month beginning about April 15 of each year at Haarlem. Holland sometimes looks like the stage setting for a road-company Schubert operetta.

The wealth of Holland goes back to its early colonial days, when fearless explorers and settlers hacked out the nation's claims in the new worlds. Dutch travelers, businessmen, and government officials have brought back to their small country the wealth and flavors of faraway places, especially those of the islands of Indonesia. Ginger, cinnamon, nutmeg, and curry are recognized examples of spices accepted in Holland. Cinnamon is used with considerable abandon by the Dutch, often in dishes where its use might well be questioned.

Hollanders who can afford it often eat six or more times daily. Breakfast is a real meal, usually based upon a hot cereal made of groats. Coffee and possibly some cake is the rule at eleven o'clock. Lunch is about 1 P.M. and dinner as early as six-thirty, but most people require a hearty tea at about four-thirty plus the addition of some small sandwiches and little cakes. Before retiring for the night, a large cup of cocoa and any cold meats or leftover cake are consumed. Apparently the ladies of Holland are not yet counting their calories, for the well-rounded female figure divine is still the Dutch ideal.

Seafood is one of the pivot points of the local cuisine. Such delicacies of the sea as shrimp, lobster, eel, mussels, the famous Zeeland oysters, and the herring are commonplaces of the table. Herring is particularly appreciated, as it is in the Scandinavian countries, and is served in almost every conceivable fashion. You may not believe it, but there is a little Dutch rhyme that may be paraphrased as "A herring a day keeps the doctor away!"

Substantial soups are the rule, and no Hollander considers a soup worth while unless it is rich and filling. Meat dishes also follow this pattern; instead of plain roast or broiled meat, they are often supplemented with garnishes, as typified by the recipes for *heete bliksem* (pork chops with apples) or *gevulde kalfsborst* (stuffed breast of veal). If a dish is good, the Dutch cook prefers to make it better by making it richer or more fattening. Also popular throughout the land are the well-known rice-table dishes of Indonesia; recipes for those East Indian specialties will be found in the Indonesian section.

Holland beers are famous all over the world, and the same is true of Dutch gin, *jenever*. Many people at first do not like its dry taste, but initiates proclaim it the world's best, providing it is chilled within an inch of its life. There are no locally produced wines, but after-dinner cordials are excellent, particularly those made by Bols, and the orange *curaçao* is probably the best of these; Advocaat is an apéritif made with eggs and liquor.

Dutch chocolates are exported everywhere, and the coffee candy known as *hopjes* is the standard confection. Of course no discussion about Holland and its food would be complete without mentioning the two outstanding cheeses of the nation, the rich, creamy Edam and the equally excellent Gouda. No gourmet in Holland fails to nibble at one of these cheeses at the conclusion of a substantial Dutch meal.

## CARROT SOUP

PEENSOEP

| | |
|---|---|
| 4 tablespoons butter | 2 quarts stock or 3 cans consommé |
| 6 carrots, sliced | and 3 cans water |
| 1 onion, chopped | 3 tablespoons farina |
| 1 cup sliced celery root (optional) | ½ teaspoon pepper |
| | Dash of nutmeg |
| | 2 tablespoons chopped parsley |

Melt the butter in a saucepan. Add the carrots, onion, and celery root. Sauté for 15 minutes, stirring frequently. Add the stock and stir. Cover and cook over low heat for 45 minutes. Force the soup and vegetables through a fine sieve or place in an electric blender. Return the soup to the saucepan. Add the farina, pepper, and nutmeg, stirring constantly. Cook over low heat for 20 minutes. Correct seasoning. Sprinkle parsley on each portion before serving.

## FISH CAKES

### VISCHKOEKJES

8 slices white bread, trimmed
1½ cups milk
1 pound fish fillets
½ pound butter
2 eggs, beaten

2 teaspoons salt
1 teaspoon pepper
¼ teaspoon nutmeg
3 tablespoons chopped parsley

Soak the bread in the milk for 10 minutes. Mash until very smooth. Grind the fish twice in a food chopper and place in a bowl. Cream half of the butter until soft, and add to the fish, together with the bread, eggs, salt, pepper, nutmeg, and parsley. Mix well. Shape into small croquettes. If the mixture is too loose, a little cracker meal may be added. Melt the remaining butter in a frying pan. Fry the fish cakes over low heat until browned on both sides. Serve with small boiled potatoes.

## PORK CHOPS WITH APPLES

### HEETE BLIKSEM

5 potatoes, peeled and cubed
2 onions, diced
5 apples, peeled and cubed
4 cups stock or 2 cans consommé
  and 1 can water

2 teaspoons pepper (see Note)
2 teaspoons salt
6 pork chops, 1 inch thick
12 pork sausages

Combine the potatoes, onions, apples, and stock in a saucepan. Cook over medium heat for 45 minutes, or until the liquid is absorbed. Sprinkle 1 teaspoon of the pepper and the salt on the pork chops. Heat a skillet. Add the chops and fry until tender and well browned on both sides, about 30 minutes. In a separate frying pan, fry the sausages until browned. Drain well. Add the remaining pepper to the potato and apple mixture and stir. Form into a mound in the center of a platter. Arrange the pork chops and sausages around it.

*Note: This dish is called* heete bliksem *in Holland, which may be translated as "hot lightning." The pepper suggested in this recipe is comparatively little by Dutch standards but quite high by ours.*

## STUFFED BREAST OF VEAL

GEVULDE KALFSBORST

½ pound beef, ground
1 egg, beaten
4 teaspoons salt
2 teaspoons pepper
2 tablespoons chopped parsley
6 gherkins

2 hard-cooked eggs
1 breast of veal (with pocket for stuffing)
4 tablespoons butter
3 onions, sliced

Mix the ground beef, egg, 1½ teaspoons of the salt, ¾ teaspoon of the pepper, and the parsley together. Divide the mixture in half and shape each half to fit the pocket in the veal. On one of the halves arrange the gherkins and eggs. Cover with the remaining half. Place in the veal pocket and fasten the opening with skewers or toothpicks. Sprinkle the remaining salt and pepper on the veal. Melt the butter in a roasting pan. Place the veal in it, with the onions arranged around the meat. Roast in a 350° oven for 3 hours, or until the veal is brown and tender. Baste frequently. Slice carefully between the ribs and serve.

*Note: If breast of veal is not available, thin veal steaks may be used. The stuffing should be placed on top of the veal, then rolled up and fastened.*

## HOT CURRIED SLAW

KERRY KOOL SLA

2 cups stock or 1 can consommé and ½ can water
1 bay leaf
1 clove garlic
4- to 5-pound head cabbage, shredded
2 cloves
1 onion

3 teaspoons salt
1 teaspoon pepper
4 tablespoons butter
3 tablespoons flour
1½ cups cream
1 tablespoon curry powder
¼ cup ground nuts or bread crumbs

Combine the stock, bay leaf, garlic, and shredded cabbage in a saucepan. Place the cloves in the onion and add to the cabbage, together with 2 teaspoons of the salt and the pepper. Cook over medium heat for 10 minutes, stirring occasionally. Drain, discarding the bay leaf, garlic, and onion. Butter a baking dish and place the cabbage in it.

Melt the butter in a saucepan. Add the flour, stirring until smooth. Gradually add the cream, stirring constantly until the boiling point is reached. Place ½ cup of this sauce in a cup and add the curry powder, mixing until smooth. Return to the saucepan, stirring well. Add the remaining salt. Cook over low heat for 5 minutes, stirring frequently. Pour the sauce over the cabbage in the baking dish. Sprinkle either ground nuts or bread crumbs on top. Bake in a 425° oven for 15 minutes. Serve hot. This dish is particularly good with roast meats.

## DUTCH MEAT AND POTATO PIE

FILOSOOF

6 potatoes, peeled and quartered
½ cup light cream
¼ pound butter
3 teaspoons salt
½ teaspoon nutmeg
3 onions, chopped
3 cups diced, cooked meat

¾ cup stock or leftover gravy, or ½ bouillon cube dissolved in ¾ cup boiling water
1 bay leaf
1 teaspoon pepper
⅛ teaspoon ground cloves
¼ cup bread crumbs

Cook the potatoes in boiling water until tender. Drain well and mash. Add the cream, 3 tablespoons of the butter, 2 teaspoons of the salt, and the nutmeg. Beat until light and fluffy. Melt 3 tablespoons of the butter in a saucepan. Add the onions and sauté for 10 minutes, stirring frequently. Add the meat, stock, bay leaf, pepper, cloves, and remaining salt. Cover and cook over low heat for 15 minutes.

In a buttered casserole or baking dish, arrange layers of potatoes and the meat mixture. Start and end with the potatoes. Sprinkle the top with bread crumbs. Dot with the remaining butter. Bake in a 425° oven for 20 minutes, or until brown on top.

## BAKED ENDIVE

LOFSCHOTEL

6 endive or 6 small bunches celery
6 slices ham
6 hard-cooked eggs, halved

½ cup melted butter
¼ teaspoon nutmeg

If celery is used, cut off the leaves, but each bunch should remain whole. Boil the endive in salted water for 10 minutes, or until tender. Drain. Wrap a slice of ham around each endive and place in a buttered baking dish. Arrange the eggs around the endive and add the melted butter. Sprinkle the nutmeg on top. Bake in a 400° oven for 10 minutes.

## RAISIN PANCAKES

DRIE IN DE PAN

½ cake or package yeast
½ cup lukewarm milk
¾ cup sifted flour

½ teaspoon salt
3 tablespoons seedless raisins
4 tablespoons butter

Soften the yeast in ¼ cup of the lukewarm milk for 5 minutes. Stir until smooth. Sift the flour and salt into a bowl. Add the yeast mixture and mix well. Add the balance of the milk and beat well. Cover and place the bowl in a pan of warm water. Allow to rise for 1 hour. Wash and dry the raisins. If they are not very fresh and plump, soak them in hot water for 15 minutes. Add the raisins to the batter, mixing lightly.

Melt half of the butter in a frying pan. Drop a tablespoon of batter at a time into the pan, to form small pancakes. Bake over low heat until brown and well done on both sides. Serve sprinkled with sugar.

## CHOCOLATE LAYER CAKE

CHOCOLADE TAART

2 tablespoons butter
3 ounces unsweetened chocolate
4 eggs
2 cups sugar

2½ cups sifted flour
4 teaspoons baking powder
1 cup milk

Place the butter and chocolate in a saucepan over hot water. Stir until melted and smooth. Cool for 10 minutes. Beat the eggs in a bowl. Add the sugar, beating steadily until light and fluffy. Add the melted chocolate and mix well. Sift the flour and baking powder together. Add the milk and flour mixture alternately to the chocolate mixture, beating thoroughly after each addition. Preheat oven to 350°. Butter two 9-inch layer-cake pans and dust lightly with flour. Pour the batter into the tins as equally as possible. Bake in a 350° oven for 30 minutes, or until a tester comes out clean. Cool for 15 minutes and turn out. Now prepare:

¼ cup sugar
2½ tablespoons cocoa (Dutch style, if possible)
1 tablespoon cornstarch

1 cup milk
1 teaspoon vanilla extract
2 cups heavy cream, whipped

Combine the sugar, cocoa, and cornstarch in the top of a double boiler. Gradually add the milk, stirring constantly until smooth. Cook over hot water over medium heat, stirring constantly until the mixture is thick. Add the vanilla. Cool for 30 minutes. Add ⅛ cup of the cocoa mixture to the whipped cream and stir lightly but thoroughly. Spread the remaining cocoa mixture between the layers. Cover the cake with the whipped cream. If desired, sprinkle a little shaved chocolate on top of the cake.

### HUNGARY

Although once a part of the great monarchy of Austria-Hungary of pre-World War I days, Hungary has gone its own separate way. Just as Austria has always turned toward the west, Hungary has faced the east, and to this day its cuisine has always evidenced more or less a *magyar*, or Mongoloid, influence. While Vienna danced to Strauss waltzes, the people of Budapest preferred the wild gypsy music, unrestrained, unfettered. In its cuisine Austria has always been conservative, classic, and correct. In Hungary the food habits again indicate the character of the people, for caution has been abandoned, and unusual and exciting tastes and colors greet the diner.

The mere mention of Hungary means "goulash" to most people for it is the one particular dish that Hungary has exported to the world. Actually the word itself is a corruption from the Hungarian term, *gulyás*, but goulash it is and always will be to the average person. This dish is usually made of chicken or beef, plentifully laden with Hungary's favorite condiment, paprika, sweet or hot. The sweet paprika is a mild, beautiful shade of red which adds greatly to the taste and eye appeal of the dish, without burning the lips or palate. Unless it is used in unwarranted quantities, paprika can be a most satisfactory addition to the kitchen shelf. So fond are Hungarians of their beloved paprika that they make a paprika cheese, the *liptói*. Rather similar to the *gulyás* are two close relations, the *paprikás* and the *tokány*. For general purposes, it may be said that the meat in *tokány* is usually cut into smaller pieces than in the *gulyás*, and some vegetables are added. The *paprikás* dishes are similar but as a rule sour cream is used in preparing them.

Among Hungary's unique foods are the famous *Balaton fogas*, a variety of lake fish unlike any other known variety. Before the war tourists always made a point of having a *fogas* in one of Hungary's many fine restaurants. Another unique creation is the renowned "red bacon" of the peasantry. It is made by dipping extremely fat pieces of bacon into paprika. The coloring soaks into the bacon and creates the red effect. Bacon prepared this way has a rather interesting flavor but it is not recommended that it be eaten in the peasant fashion—raw!

Noodles, dumplings, and other doughy materials have been developed to a state of perfection closely resembling the Italian standard. These are used in soup, with meat and poultry, with desserts, in almost endless and inconceivable ways. Particularly good are the noodles with melted butter and poppy seeds; also the dumplings enclosing pitted fresh plums and covered with buttered bread crumbs. Strudels are high in popularity and are made with any filling that strikes the baker's fancy, such as cheese, *mohn* (poppy seed), cherries, nuts, and jams. While somewhat difficult to make, they are spectacular. Of course the national dessert of the country is undoubtedly the *dobos torta,* a very tricky cake to make. This many-layered confection of chocolate and caramel has been acclaimed by pastry fanciers throughout the world.

Hungarians are always acclaimed as gourmets, and they are undoubtedly very fond of good living. Part of their search for the better things of life has led to the development of unique liquors and brandies, mostly fruit-based. The best of these cordials is probably put out under the Zwack label, and these include some fine plum brandies.

The Tokay wine of the nation is unique in quality and acceptance and well deserves the position of honor it holds with knowing wine drinkers. Even Frenchmen who look condescendingly upon the wines of other countries have been heard to admit that Hungary possesses a fine wine in the Tokay. The very best of these is made from grapes that have been allowed to become overripe upon the vines. When the grapes have lost all their moisture and are shrunken and dried out, they are harvested. These raisins are known as the *formint,* which is carefully blended with normally harvested grapes. It is of interest to note that many Tokay "Essence" wines command fabulous prices in the world market, particularly in view of the fact that they are customarily sold in smaller than average bottles.

## GOULASH SOUP

### GULYÁSLEVES

| | |
|---|---|
| 1 pound beef | 1 teaspoon pepper |
| 1 pound pork | 2 green peppers, diced |
| 1 pound lamb | 2 tomatoes, diced |
| ½ pound ham | 6 cups boiling water |
| 3 tablespoons butter, lard, or chicken fat | 4 potatoes, peeled and cut into cubes |
| 6 onions, chopped | ½ pound smoked sausage (Hungarian or German type, if available) |
| 2 tablespoons paprika | |

Cut the beef, pork, and lamb into 1-inch cubes. Cut the ham into ¼-inch cubes. Melt the butter in a large saucepan. Add the chopped onions and the cubed meats and cook over high heat until brown, stirring frequently. Add the paprika and pepper and cook over low heat for 30 minutes, stirring occasionally. Add the green peppers, tomatoes, and water. Continue cooking for 1 hour. Add the potatoes and cook 30 minutes longer.

While the soup is cooking, cut the sausage into ½-inch slices and boil in a saucepan for 10 minutes. Drain and add to the soup immediately. Correct seasoning. No salt has been provided in this recipe because certain sausages have a great deal of salt. If necessary, add some now.

## BEAN SOUP AND DUMPLINGS

BABLEVES CSIPETKÉVEL

| | |
|---|---|
| 1 cup dried white beans | 2 teaspoons salt |
| 2 quarts stock or 3 cans consommé and 5 cans water | ½ teaspoon pepper |
| | 1 teaspoon paprika |
| 2 carrots, sliced | 1 egg |
| 1 parsnip, sliced | 2 tablespoons water |
| 4 tablespoons butter | 3 frankfurters (Hungarian style, if |
| 2 onions, chopped | available), sliced |
| 1¼ cups sifted flour | |

Soak the beans overnight in water to cover. Drain. Place the beans in a saucepan with the stock, carrots, and parsnip. Cook over low heat for 2 hours. Remove 1 cup of the beans and force them through a sieve. Return the purée to the soup. Melt the butter in a saucepan. Add the onions and sauté until brown, stirring frequently. Sprinkle 2 tablespoons of the flour over them, stirring until smooth. Gradually add 1 cup of the soup, stirring constantly. Return the contents of the saucepan to the soup. Add the salt, pepper, and paprika. Cook over low heat for 1 hour.

Meanwhile, sift the remaining flour into a bowl. Make a well or depression in the center and add the egg and water. Mix to a smooth paste. Knead until the dough does not stick to the fingers. Roll out very thin on a lightly floured surface and allow to remain there for 45 minutes. Pinch off small pieces of the dough and drop them into the boiling soup. Cook until they float. Fry the frankfurter slices for 5 minutes. Drain. Add them to the soup. Serve hot.

## FISH, HUNGARIAN STYLE

SÜLLÖ

6 fillets of sole or 6 slices salmon
Head, skin, and bones of fish
3 teaspoons salt
1 teaspoon pepper
½ cup boiling water
¼ pound butter

6 onions, chopped
2 teaspoons paprika
2 cups water
2 tablespoons melted butter
2 tablespoons flour
1 pint sour cream

Wash and dry the fish but reserve the head, skin, and bones. Place the fish in a buttered baking dish. Sprinkle with 1½ teaspoons of the salt and ½ teaspoon pepper. Add the boiling water. Bake in a 375° oven for 35 minutes.

Melt the ¼ pound of butter in a deep saucepan and add the chopped onions. Sauté until brown, about 10 minutes, stirring frequently. Add the remaining salt and pepper, the paprika, water, and the fish head, skin, and bones. Boil for 30 minutes. Strain. Combine the melted butter and flour in a saucepan and stir until smooth. Gradually add the fish stock, stirring constantly until the boiling point is reached. Cook over low heat for 10 minutes. Add the sour cream, beating well. Pour over the fish and serve.

## HUNGARIAN GOULASH

GULYÁS

6 tablespoons butter
5 onions, chopped
2 tablespoons Hungarian paprika
2 teaspoons salt
½ teaspoon pepper

3 pounds beef (cross rib, chuck, etc.)
1 can tomato sauce
1 clove garlic, minced (optional)
½ cup sour cream

Melt 4 tablespoons of the butter in a heavy saucepan. Add the onions and sauté for 15 minutes, stirring frequently. Remove the onions and set them aside. Combine the paprika, salt and pepper. Cut the meat into 2-inch cubes and roll in the mixture. Melt the remaining butter in the saucepan. Add the meat and brown well on all sides. Return the onions to the saucepan. Add the tomato sauce and garlic and stir. Cover and cook over low heat for 3 hours, stirring occasionally. Add the sour cream and stir. Heat but do not allow the mixture to boil. Serve hot with boiled *nokedli* (see recipe in this section).

## BRAISED STEAK, HUNGARIAN STYLE

ESTERHÁZY ROSTÉLYOS

⅓ cup flour
1½ teaspoons salt
¾ teaspoon pepper
6 individual steaks, about 1 inch thick
3 slices bacon, chopped
4 tablespoons butter
2 carrots, chopped

2 stalks celery, chopped
½ cup sliced mushrooms
3 tablespoons chopped parsley
1 bay leaf
½ cup water
1 cup sour cream
2 tablespoons capers, drained

Mix the flour, salt, and pepper together. Dip the steaks in it, coating well. Fry the bacon in a large skillet until half done. Drain the fat from the pan. Add the butter and brown the steaks on both sides over high heat. Add the carrots, celery, mushrooms, and parsley and cook over high heat for 2 minutes. Add the bay leaf and water. Cover and cook over low heat for 30 minutes, or until the steaks are tender. Remove the bay leaf and force the gravy and vegetables through a sieve. Return to the saucepan. Correct seasoning. Add the sour cream and capers, stirring constantly. Cook over low heat for 3 minutes. Serve hot.

## DUMPLINGS

NOKEDLI

3 cups sifted flour
1 teaspoon salt
2 eggs
¾ cup water

1 tablespoon melted butter
2 quarts boiling, lightly salted water
¼ cup melted butter

Sift the flour and salt into a bowl. Beat the eggs in a separate bowl; add the ¾ cup water and the butter and mix. Combine the egg mixture with the flour, beating constantly until smooth.

Have the boiling, salted water in a deep saucepan and drop the batter by teaspoons into the water. The dumplings will come to the surface as they are done. Remove immediately. Drain well and pour the melted butter over them. They may be eaten in place of potatoes with a meat course, or serve with Hungarian *gulyás* (see recipe in this section), pouring the *gulyás* sauce over the *nokedli*.

## NUT STRUDEL

DIÓSRÉTES

2½ cups sifted flour
½ teaspoon salt
1 egg
2 tablespoons salad oil
⅔ cup warm water
½ cup melted butter
4 egg yolks

⅓ cup sugar
2 cups ground nuts
1 tablespoon grated lemon rind
2 tablespoons lemon juice
½ cup seedless raisins (optional)
4 egg whites
¼ cup bread crumbs

Sift the flour and salt into a bowl. Make a well in the center and put the egg and oil in it. Work the flour into it gradually, adding enough warm water to make a soft dough. Knead it well and pick it up and slap it down on a board several times. Continue until the dough loses its stickiness, about 10 minutes. Form into a ball and dust with a little flour. Cover with a warmed bowl and allow to remain for 45 minutes.

Spread a fresh tablecloth on a large table. Sprinkle the cloth freely with flour and roll the dough as thin as possible. Brush the dough with a little of the melted butter. Flour the hands and begin stretching the dough from underneath, using the backs of the hands, not the fingers. Go around the table slowly at least several times, gently pulling the dough toward you until it is as thin as possible, almost transparent. Brush the dough again with some of the melted butter.

Beat the egg yolks well. Add the sugar, beating until light and creamy. Add the nuts, lemon rind and juice, and the raisins. Beat the egg whites until stiff and fold into the mixture. Sprinkle the dough with the bread crumbs. Spread the nut mixture evenly over about one third of the dough on one of the long sides of the table. Lift up the tablecloth and slowly and carefully roll the dough over as for a jelly roll. Preheat oven to 400°. Butter or oil a baking sheet. Transfer the strudel carefully. Brush with the remaining butter. Bake in a 400° oven for 35 minutes, or until brown on top. Cut into slices while hot. Serve hot or cold.

## APPLE CAKE

ALMA TORTA

2 cups sifted flour
Dash of salt
¾ pound butter (sweet, if available)
½ cup ice water
1½ tablespoons vinegar

½ cup sugar
2 tablespoons cinnamon
¼ cup melted butter
5 large apples, peeled, quartered, and sliced thin

85

Sift the flour and salt together into a bowl. Add the butter and, using one hand, blend the ingredients together. Combine the ice water and vinegar and add. Continue mixing until well blended. Form into a ball, place in a bowl, and cover. Store in the refrigerator overnight. Remove the dough from the refrigerator 15 minutes before using. Preheat oven to 375°. Roll out the dough as thin as possible on a lightly floured surface. If the dough should tear, patch it with additional thin pieces of dough.

Place the dough on an unbuttered cooky sheet, approximately 10 by 16 inches. Arrange the apple slices on the dough in rows as uniformly and evenly as possible. Sprinkle the sugar and cinnamon on top. Pour the melted butter over the apples. Bake in a 375° oven for 25 minutes, or until delicately brown on top. Cut into squares or strips. Serve with whipped cream.

*IRELAND*

Ireland, which has made famous the wearing of the green, is also a land of green. Visitors are always surprised at the lush carpet of color that covers everything: it is as if Ireland were one big garden dedicated to the production of cholorophyll. Surrounded by the sea, it is a country of considerable interest to the tourist.

Fisheries play an important part in the life of the people, and much of the Irish diet is based upon the fisherman's catch. Herring, particularly, is one fruit (what a word to describe herring!) of the sea that is eaten regularly; halibut, cod, and haddock, as well, are of prime importance. The country also is proud of its trout and the world-famous salmon, both fresh and smoked. Fish soups are well made and deservedly popular.

Irish beef is exceptional, and the young, Irish lamb is also of high quality. But it is the locally cured hams and bacon that are the pride of the countryside. They are now being exported extensively, and one taste of these pork products will convince any skeptic. Poultry and game, too, are in the top category.

Everyone knows of Ireland's fondness for the potato, but comparatively few know of colcannon, made of potatoes and cabbage, or of Irish potato cakes. A favorite Irish way of handling vegetables is to boil cabbage, potatoes, and onions together with meat. Salads and greens are becoming more important but are still comparatively rare except during the summer season.

A staple food is porridge, which the country people eat almost every day of their lives. The coarse, full-grain oatmeal is so nourishing and filling that a pot of it is kept cooking all day long over the farmer's fire. An unusual Irish item is carrageen, a moss collected along the shore and used as the basis for sweet desserts and milk puddings. Coffee is much appreciated here, but tea has a strong traditional hold upon the people, and if you stop at an Irish country cottage you will almost always be offered tea rather than coffee.

Irish whisky has its adherents, for there are those who find it superior to scotch. It resembles scotch whisky but is not so thick or so smoky as that liquor. The world-renowned Guinness stout, an extremely rich dark beer, is produced here. Many people prefer to drink stout half and half— that is, mixed with ordinary beer in order to cut its heavy body.

Good food is easily obtained in Ireland, and at prices that please those who have unwillingly become accustomed to high prices. Fine meals are to be had in Dublin at the Royal Hibernian and the Gresham hotels. Jammet's Restaurant is famous, as are the Unicorn and Bailey's. Ireland does not have night clubs but it does have pubs such as the Abbey Bar and the Buttery. Here you should try Celtic coffee made of hot, black coffee and Irish whisky, topped with a dollop of whipped cream.

Just a passing word about a rather weak, ineffectual drink called *poteen*, or tiny pot. It is said that the little Irish leprechauns distill a liquor from potatoes high up in the hills, and according to their own secret formula. Very little of this innocuous beverage reaches the outside world.

## IRISH WHISKY HIGHBALL

6 jiggers Irish whisky                    Ginger ale
6 thin pieces lemon peel

Place 2 ice cubes in each highball glass. Add 1 jigger Irish whisky and 1 piece of lemon peel. Fill each glass with ginger ale.

## IRISH POTATO SOUP

7 cups water                              1 clove
6 medium potatoes, peeled and sliced      ½ cup milk, scalded
2 onions, sliced                          ½ cup cream, scalded
1 carrot, sliced                          1½ teaspoons salt
½ teaspoon thyme                          ½ teaspoon pepper
1 bay leaf

Boil the water in a saucepan. Add the potatoes, onions, carrot, thyme, bay leaf, and clove. Cook over low heat for 45 minutes. Force the mixture through a sieve. Add the milk, cream, salt, and pepper. Cook over low heat for 10 minutes. Correct seasoning. Serve hot.

## SALMON LOAF PUDDING

2 cups milk, scalded
1 cup rice, half-cooked and drained
2 tablespoons grated onion
2 teaspoons salt
1 teaspoon pepper
½ teaspoon sugar

2 tablespoons lemon juice
1½ cups cooked, canned, or smoked
   salmon, flaked
3 tablespoons chopped parsley
3 eggs
½ cup melted butter

Combine the milk, rice, onion, salt, pepper, sugar, lemon juice, salmon, and parsley in a bowl. Mix well. Correct seasoning, depending upon the type of salmon used. Beat the eggs well and add to the previous mixture, stirring thoroughly. Pour into a buttered casserole or baking dish. Bake in a 350° oven for 35 minutes, or until firm and brown on top. Pour the melted butter on top. Serve hot or cold.

## IRISH-STYLE CABBAGE AND POTATOES

COLCANNON

6 boiled potatoes
¼ pound butter, melted
1½ teaspoons salt

½ teaspoon pepper
1 onion, chopped fine
1 small head cabbage, boiled

Peel and mash the potatoes with half of the butter and the salt, pepper, and onion. Mix well together. Chop the cabbage coarsely. Add to the previous mixture and mix lightly but thoroughly. Heat in a buttered pan but do not allow the mixture to brown. Serve very hot. Heap in a mound. Make a well in the center and pour the remaining melted butter in it.

## IRISH STEW

6 large potatoes, peeled and cut into
   1½-inch cubes
2 teaspoons salt
½ teaspoon pepper

6 large onions, sliced
3 pounds boneless lamb, cut into 1-
   inch cubes
1 cup water

In a heavy saucepan place a layer of potatoes and sprinkle with a little of the salt and pepper. Add a layer of onions, and again season. Place a layer of lamb on top and season. Repeat until all of the ingredients are used up; the top layer should consist of potatoes. Pour the water over it and cover. Bring to a boil and cook over low heat for 1½ hours, or until the lamb is tender.

*Note: This recipe is an authentic one for an Irish stew. In certain localities carrots, celery, and tomatoes are added in additional layers.*

## POTATO CAKES

4 boiled potatoes
2 teaspoons salt
½ cup sifted flour

1 teaspoon baking powder
4 tablespoons melted butter
⅓ cup milk

Mash the potatoes. Add the salt, flour, and baking powder and mix well. Add the melted butter and milk and knead lightly. The dough should be soft enough to roll. Roll out ½ inch thick on a lightly floured surface. Cut into rounds with a cooky cutter. Bake on a hot griddle or lightly greased frying pan for 5 minutes on each side. Shake the griddle occasionally to prevent burning the cakes.

## TREACLE BREAD

2 cups flour
1 teaspoon baking soda
¼ cup sugar
¼ teaspoon salt

3 tablespoons butter
1 tablespoon molasses
¼ cup buttermilk

Sift the flour, baking soda, sugar, and salt into a bowl. Work in the butter with the hand until well blended. Add the molasses and buttermilk. Knead until quite smooth. Preheat oven to 350°. Roll out ½ inch thick on a lightly floured surface. Cut out with a round cooky cutter. Place on a buttered and floured cooky sheet. Bake in a 350° oven for 20 minutes, or until lightly browned. Serve hot or cold with plenty of butter.

## PANCAKES

### FADGES

1 cup milk
⅓ cup butter

½ teaspoon salt
3 cups whole wheat flour

Boil the milk and butter together in a saucepan. Sift the salt and flour into a bowl. Add the milk mixture, beating well. Roll out about ¾ inch thick on a lightly floured surface. Cut into 2-inch squares. Place on a lightly greased griddle. Bake over very low heat for 1¼ hours, turning frequently. Be sure that the heat is as low as possible. Serve with butter and jelly.

## CHOCOLATE POTATO CAKE

½ pound butter
2 cups sugar
4 eggs, beaten
3 ounces unsweetened chocolate, melted
1 cup cold mashed potatoes

1 teaspoon cinnamon
¼ teaspoon nutmeg
2 cups sifted flour
1 teaspoon baking soda
1 cup sour milk
1 cup coarsely chopped nuts

Cream the butter. Add the sugar gradually, beating until light and fluffy. Add the eggs and beat well. Add the chocolate, potatoes, cinnamon, and nutmeg. Preheat oven to 350°. Sift the flour and baking soda together and add to the chocolate mixture alternately with the sour milk. Beat well. Add the nuts, mixing lightly. Pour into a deep 9-inch buttered baking or spring-form pan. Bake in a 350° oven for 45 minutes, or until a cake tester comes out clean. Cool in the pan, then turn out.

## ITALY

The word "cuisine" is used to describe a style of cooking. Seldom is the word employed in its most limited sense, that of a truly individual and nationalistic manner of preparing food. Certainly the word may be used in all honesty to describe the food of Italy, for here is a truly great cuisine.

Many Americans, particularly those who are not fond of garlic, mistakenly believe that all Italian food is based on tomatoes and garlic. In certain parts of Italy, particularly in the north, rice is a much more important and popular food than spaghetti, though one would hardly know this by eating the typical food served in Italian restaurants in the United States. The reason for this apparent contradiction is readily explained. Most Italian immigrants to our shores have come from the south of Italy, and from Sicily and Sardinia, rather from the north. The southerners have brought with them their own style of cooking, which is based on olive oil, garlic, spices, tomatoes, and spaghetti. The northern preference for butter, rice, and the use of little or no garlic is scarcely known in this country.

Italians love good food and spend long hours eating their meals and drinking their wines. They seldom drink hard liquor, but almost every meal is taken with wine, most of which is comparatively inexpensive and of modest quality. Breakfast is a simple repast, usually coffee and hot milk with a crust of bread. The midday meal is fairly substantial, and of course the evening meal is very important, at least for city dwellers. It is eaten at a late hour and is as elaborate as the means of the family permit.

Seafoods of all kinds are a regular part of Italian food. Shellfish, in particular, are looked upon as great delicacies, which indeed they are in Italy. The people eat many things that are unattractive to Americans educated only to canned tuna fish but are really not so exotic when they are tasted. Squid in its ink and baby octopus are examples of what is exotic to Lincoln, Nebraska, but very ordinary to Naples, Italy. Best of all are the seafood soups of the small fishing villages, where the seafood practically leaps out of the fisherman's basket into the oil of the casserole. Surely the old proverb that fish live in water and die in oil holds true in the Mediterranean area.

Vegetables and salads are of great importance and are served at almost every lunch and dinner. To most Italians, it is the *pasta asciutta,* or dry dough, that makes the meal. This term refers to the various spaghettis, macaronis, and other starchy products that have become an accepted part of our own American eating habits. But the Italian people do not limit themselves to one or two varieties as we do, for there are dozens and dozens of different *pastas.* From the extremely thin strands, such as *vermicelli* (little worms) and *capellini d'angelo* (angel's hair), to the enormous varieties that are stuffed with meat and cheese, from the tiniest bits of dough used for baby foods to the most beautiful shell forms, the world of *pasta asciutta* is a wide one. To accompany this range of shapes and sizes, there is an equal variation in color for sauces to accompany these pastes, including white, yellow, green, and red mixtures.

Italian cheeses are excellent. Those known to us include the increasingly popular Bel Paese, Gorgonzola, Mozzarella, Provolone, and Ricotta. Worthy of mention are the comparatively little-known Caciocavallo, Lodigiano, and Robiolino.

Except on festive occasions, rich desserts and fancy cakes are little known. The custom is to end most meals with fresh fruit and cheese, eaten together. Coffee, black as a starless night, is the usual finish to a meal. *Caffé espresso,* made by forcing steam through finely pulverized coffee, is the favorite method of preparation.

Almost the only strong drink that the people like is the rather crude grape liquor, *grappa,* beloved of the G.I.s during the war. Wines are

Italy's pride. *Chianti* is so much a part of the American concept of Italy that when an American tourist in that country orders wine without specifying the type, he will automatically be served with Chianti. But Chianti is only one of Italy's wines, and there are others deserving of notice. Among the red wines there are Barbera, Bardolino, Barolo, Nebbiolo, and Valpolicella. The whites include Est! Est! Est! (certainly the most fascinating name in the world for a wine), Frascati, Lachryma Christi (the Tears of Christ), Marsala, Orvieto, and Zucco. Asti Spumante, a sparkling wine, is delightful.

Most travelers regard Italian food as one of the high points of their trip. Famous restaurants in Rome include Hosteria dell'Orso, Capriccio's, and Alfredo's, which is almost exclusively a tourist restaurant. No two people agree as to Rome's best eating places, and many consider Biblioteca del Valle and Passetto's to be the finest. In Venice the famous restaurant is La Colomba, which specializes in seafood.

## STUFFED PEPPERS

PEPERONE RIPIENO

6 red or green peppers
3 cups bread crumbs
6 anchovies, chopped

½ cup chopped ripe olives
2 tablespoons minced capers
6 tablespoons olive oil

Slice the tops off the peppers and remove the seeds carefully. Mix together the bread crumbs, anchovies, olives, and capers. Stuff the peppers with this mixture. Place the peppers on an oiled baking pan. Pour 1 tablespoon of the olive oil on each pepper. Bake in a 350° oven for 35 minutes.

Serve hot or cold. The peppers may be used as the center of an Italian antipasto. Place slices of Italian salami and ham, olives, pimentos, celery, tuna fish, radishes, and other similar ingredients around it.

## ANCHOVY AND RICE SOUP

MINESTRA ALLA CAPUCINA

3 tablespoons butter
1 onion, chopped
4 anchovies, mashed
1½ cups cooked rice

7 cups stock or 3 cans consommé
  and 2 cans water
Grated Parmesan cheese

Melt the butter in a saucepan. Add the onion and sauté for 10 minutes, stirring frequently. Add the anchovies, rice, and stock. Cook over medium heat for 30 minutes, or until the soup has a custardlike consistency. Correct seasoning. Serve with grated Parmesan cheese.

## VEGETABLE SOUP, ITALIAN STYLE

MINESTRA ALLA GENOVESE CON PESTO

½ pound fresh or ½ package frozen string beans, French style
3 potatoes, peeled and sliced
3 tomatoes, peeled and sliced
2½ quarts water
½ pound vermicelli or very fine spaghetti
1 tablespoon salt

½ teaspoon pepper
1 clove garlic, minced
⅛ teaspoon thyme
⅛ teaspoon basil
2 tablespoons tomato paste
3 tablespoons olive oil
½ cup grated Parmesan cheese

Combine the string beans, potatoes, tomatoes, and water in a saucepan. Cook over medium heat for 15 minutes. Add the vermicelli, salt, and pepper. Cook 12 minutes longer. Mix the garlic, thyme, basil, and tomato paste in a bowl. Add the oil, drop by drop, mixing steadily. When the mixture is smooth, add to the soup very gradually, stirring constantly. Serve very hot, sprinkled with the grated cheese.

## FRESH GREENS SOUP

ZUPPA D'ERBE

1 large head lettuce
2 cups sorrel or spinach, fresh or frozen
2 stalks celery, diced
6 scallions (green onions), chopped
6 cups stock or 2 cans chicken consommé and 2½ cans water

1½ teaspoons salt
3 tablespoons butter
6 slices toast (French-style bread, if available)
¼ cup grated Parmesan cheese

Wash the lettuce and sorrel thoroughly. Drain. Tear the lettuce leaves into small pieces. Remove the stems from the sorrel and chop coarsely. Combine the lettuce and sorrel in a saucepan. Add the celery, scallions, stock, salt, and butter. Cook over medium heat for 30 minutes, stirring occasionally. Correct seasoning. If desired, the soup and vegetables may be forced through a sieve or puréed in an electric blender. Place a slice of toast in each soup plate. Pour the soup over it and sprinkle with the Parmesan cheese.

93

## SHRIMP IN WINE SAUCE

SCAMPI NELLA SALSA DI VINO

2 pounds shrimp, shelled
and cleaned
½ cup flour
½ cup olive oil
½ cup dry white wine
2 teaspoons tomato paste
4 tablespoons warm water

1 teaspoon salt
½ teaspoon pepper
Dash of cayenne pepper
1 tablespoon chopped parsley
1 scallion (green onion), chopped
2 teaspoons lemon juice

Wash and drain the shrimp. Roll them in the flour. Heat the olive oil in a skillet. Add the shrimp and brown on both sides. Drain the oil but reserve it. Add the wine to the shrimp and cook over low heat until the wine is absorbed.

Combine the reserved olive oil, tomato paste, water, salt, pepper, and cayenne pepper in a saucepan. Cook over low heat for 5 minutes. Pour this sauce over the shrimp, add the parsley and scallion, and cook for 5 minutes. Remove from the pan, add the lemon juice, and serve.


## FISH, SARDINIAN STYLE

PESCE AL USO SARDO

½ cup olive oil
1 clove garlic, minced
2 onions, chopped
1 carrot, grated
6 slices fish (sea bass, tuna, or other
firm-meated fish)
4 anchovies, minced
1 cup sliced mushrooms
1 bay leaf
1 teaspoon orégano

1 tablespoon tomato paste
1 teaspoon salt
½ teaspoon pepper
1 cup white wine
½ cup stock or ½ bouillon cube dissolved in ½ cup hot water
2 egg yolks
1 tablespoon heavy cream
1 tablespoon lemon juice

Heat the olive oil in a frying pan. Add the garlic, onions, and carrots and sauté for 10 minutes, stirring frequently. Add fish and brown well on both sides. Add the anchovies, mushrooms, bay leaf, orégano, tomato paste, salt, pepper, wine, and stock. Stir gently and cook over medium heat for 30 minutes, or until the fish is tender.

Place the fish on a platter. Force the fish sauce and vegetables through a sieve. Beat the egg yolks, cream, and lemon juice in a bowl. Gradually add the puréed mixture, beating constantly to prevent curdling. Reheat this mixture, stirring constantly, but no not allow it to boil. Pour over the fish and serve.

# FISH, HOME STYLE

PESCI ALLA CASALINGA

3 tablespoons butter
2 tablespoons olive oil
3 onions, chopped
2 cloves garlic, minced
½ cup chopped mushrooms
¼ cup capers, drained
3 tablespoons chopped parsley
¼ cup ground almonds

1 tablespoon flour
½ cup stock or ½ bouillon cube
   dissolved in ½ cup hot water
¼ teaspoon orégano
3 teaspoons salt
¾ teaspoon pepper
6 slices bass, trout, or any other
   mild-flavored, white-meat fish

Combine the butter and olive oil in a large skillet. Add the onions and garlic and sauté for 10 minutes, stirring frequently. Add the mushrooms, capers, parsley, almonds, flour, stock, orégano, 1 teaspoon of the salt, and ¼ teaspoon of the pepper. Mix well. Cook over low heat for 10 minutes, stirring occasionally.

Combine the remaining salt and 1 teaspoon of pepper and sprinkle on the fish slices. Carefully place the slices on top of the vegetable mixture. Cover and cook over medium heat for 35 minutes. If desired, the fish may be baked, uncovered, in a 400° oven for 35 minutes. Serve immediately.

# VEAL WITH TUNA FISH SAUCE

VITELLO TONNATO

3 pounds rolled shoulder or leg of
   veal
1 clove
1 onion
1 bay leaf
4 sprigs parsley
2 carrots
2 stalks celery

6 whole peppercorns
1½ teaspoons salt
2 7-ounce cans tuna fish
8 anchovy fillets
2 tablespoons lemon juice
1 cup olive oil
2 teaspoons capers

Place the veal in a large saucepan. Add water to cover. Place the clove in the onion, and add, together with the bay leaf, parsley, carrots, celery, peppercorns, and salt. Cover and cook over medium heat for 1¾ hours, or until the veal is tender. Drain well, discarding the vegetables. Place the veal in a large pottery or glass bowl; do not use a metal bowl.

Drain the tuna fish and anchovies. Mash them together until they form a smooth paste; it may be advisable to force them through a sieve. Add the lemon juice. Add the olive oil gradually, beating well. Add the capers and stir. Pour the sauce over the veal and allow to marinate for at least 12 hours in the refrigerator.

Remove the veal from the marinade. Using a very sharp carving knife, cut the thinnest possible slices of veal. Spread the sauce over the veal as evenly as possible. Serve cold either as an appetizer or as a main course. If desired, decorate each portion with a slice of tomato and several ripe olives.

## FILLET OF BEEF WITH MARSALA

### FILETTO AL MARSALA

2½ teaspoons salt
1 teaspoon pepper
¼ teaspoon thyme
3-pound fillet of beef
4 tablespoons butter
2 onions, chopped
1 carrot, sliced

¼ pound ham, chopped
2 tablespoons flour
1 cup stock or 1 bouillon cube dissolved in 1 cup hot water
1 cup Marsala (or other sweet red wine)
2 tablespoons chopped parsley

Combine the salt, pepper, and thyme. Rub into the meat thoroughly. Melt butter in a heavy pot or a Dutch oven, over direct heat. Add the meat and onions, and brown the meat on all sides. Add the carrot and ham. Sprinkle the flour on top of the meat and add the stock to the pan.

Place the meat in a 350° oven and roast for 1 hour, basting occasionally. Remove the gravy, vegetables, and ham from the pan, and force through a sieve. Add the wine and combine with the puréed gravy. Pour over the meat. Continue roasting for 15 minutes, for rare meat, or 20 minutes for medium, 30 minutes for well done. Baste occasionally. Slice the meat and pour gravy over the slices.

## BEEF AND HAM ROLLS

### BRACIOLE

¼ cup dried mushrooms (Italian style, if possible)
¾ cup boiling water
6 slices sirloin steak, about 2 by 5 inches, ¼ inch thick
6 slices prosciutto (a spicy, smoked ham may be substituted)
½ teaspoon orégano
2 teaspoons salt

1 teaspoon pepper
¼ cup olive oil
1 tablespoon butter
2 cloves garlic, minced
2 onions, chopped
2 carrots, sliced
1½ cups canned tomatoes, strained (Italian type, if possible)

Wash the mushrooms thoroughly. Add the boiling water and soak for 30 minutes. Have the steak pounded as thin as possible by the butcher, or pound it with a mallet or the flat side of a kitchen knife. Place a slice of ham on each piece of steak. Sprinkle a little orégano on the ham. Roll the meat up carefully and tie at each end with thread. Sprinkle the salt and pepper on the outside of the steak, and rub in.

Heat the olive oil and butter in a saucepan. Add the garlic, onions, and carrots, and the meat rolls. Brown the meat well on all sides. Slice the mushrooms fine, reserving the water. Add the mushrooms, the mushroom water, and the tomatoes and mix well together. Cover and cook over low heat for 1½ hours, stirring occasionally. Serve with spaghetti or egg noodles.

## LAMB, ROMAN STYLE

AGNÈLLO AL USO ROMANO

1 tablespoon olive oil
5-pound leg of lamb
1 teaspoon salt
1 teaspoon freshly ground black pepper
1 clove garlic, minced

1 teaspoon rosemary
2 teaspoons flour
½ cup wine vinegar
½ cup water
2 anchovies, chopped

Heat the olive oil in a roasting pan or Dutch oven. Add the lamb and brown well on all sides over high heat. Add the salt, pepper, garlic, and rosemary and continue browning for 10 minutes. Sprinkle the lamb with flour and press it into the meat with a wooden spoon. Add the vinegar and water. Cover and cook over low heat for 2 hours, or until tender, adding a little water if necessary. Mix the anchovies with a little of the gravy and return to the sauce in the pan. Cook 1 minute longer.

## CHICKEN LIVERS AND CORN MEAL

POLENTA

1½ quarts boiling water
2 teaspoons salt
3 cups corn meal
¼ pound butter
3 slices bacon, diced

10 chicken livers, diced
⅛ teaspoon pepper
1½ cups stock or 1 bouillon cube dissolved in 1½ cups hot water

Combine the boiling water and salt in a large saucepan. Add the corn meal very gradually, stirring constantly to prevent lumps. Cook for 30 minutes, stirring occasionally. Melt the butter in a saucepan. Add the bacon, chicken livers, and peppers and sauté for 5 minutes, stirring frequently. Add the stock and cook 10 minutes longer. Correct seasoning. Place the corn meal in a large dish and pour the chicken-liver sauce over it.

## CHICKEN IN WHITE WINE

POLLO AL VINO BIANCO

2 teaspoons salt
1 teaspoon pepper
1 tablespoon flour
2 2½-pound chickens, disjointed
4 tablespoons olive oil
2 onions, chopped
1 cup white wine
1 tablespoon tomato paste

1 cup stock or 1 bouillon cube dissolved in 1 cup hot water
3 anchovies, mashed fine
¾ cup wine vinegar
2 cloves garlic, minced
1 tablespoon capers, drained
3 tablespoons chopped sweet pickles
2 tablespoons chopped parsley

Combine the salt, pepper, and flour. Rub into the chicken as thoroughly as possible. Heat the olive oil in a casserole or skillet. Add the onions and sauté for 5 minutes, stirring frequently. Add the chickens and brown well on all sides. Add the wine and cook over high heat for 5 minutes. Mix the tomato paste and stock together and add, stirring well. Reduce heat to medium, cover, and cook for 45 minutes, or until chickens are tender.

In a small saucepan, bring the vinegar to a boil and cook over high heat for 2 minutes. Add the garlic, capers, pickles, and parsley and cook over low heat for 1 minute only. Pour over the chicken. Serve hot.

## PEAS AND RICE

RISI E BISI

2 tablespoons olive oil
⅓ cup butter
1 slice bacon, cut in pieces
1 onion, chopped fine
2 pounds fresh or 1 package frozen peas

4 cups stock or 2 cans consommé and 1 can water
1 cup rice
1 teaspoon salt
⅛ teaspoon pepper
2 tablespoons grated Parmesan cheese

Place the olive oil, butter, bacon, and onion in a saucepan and sauté for 5 minutes, stirring frequently. Add the peas and cook for 5 minutes. Add the stock and stir. Bring to a boil and add the rice. Cook for about 20 minutes, or until the rice is tender. Add the salt, pepper, and cheese and mix well. Serve hot.

*Note: This is a famous Italian rice dish. Since it is so rich and substantial, it should not be served when either a thick soup or spaghetti is a part of the meal.*

## CELERY, PARMIGIANA STYLE

SEDANI ALLA PARMIGIANA

3 bunches celery
3 tablespoons butter
½ cup stock or ½ bouillon cube dissolved in ½ cup hot water
¼ cup chopped ham

* 1 teaspoon salt
¼ teaspoon pepper
¼ cup grated Parmesan cheese
¼ cup grated Gruyère or American cheese

Wash the celery thoroughly and remove the leaves. Cut into slices ½ inch thick. Melt the butter in a skillet. Add the celery and sauté for 5 minutes, stirring gently so as not to break up the slices. Add the stock, ham, salt, and pepper. Cover and cook over medium heat for 15 minutes. Drain carefully. Place the celery in a buttered baking dish. Sprinkle the grated cheeses on top. Bake in a 425° oven for 15 minutes, or until the cheese is delicately browned.

## TOMATO SAUCE FOR SPAGHETTI

SALSA DI POMODORO

¼ cup olive oil
3 onions, chopped
3 cloves garlic, minced
3 tablespoons chopped parsley
2 No. 2½ cans Italian-style tomatoes
3 tablespoons white wine

2 teaspoons salt
½ teaspoon pepper
1 teaspoon orégano
¼ cup chopped spinach (optional)
¼ cup chopped mushrooms (optional)

Heat the olive oil in a saucepan. Add the onions and garlic and sauté for 10 minutes, stirring frequently. Add the parsley, tomatoes, wine, salt, pepper, and orégano. Stir well. Cover and cook over low heat for 2 hours. Add the spinach and mushrooms. Cover and cook over low heat for 2 hours. Force the mixture through a sieve. Correct seasoning. Serve over spaghetti or other Italian macaroni. A glass of Chianti, Barbera, or Bardolino wine is excellent with this sauce.

*Note: The sauce improves with flavor as it cooks. If possible, make the sauce the day before it is used, and reheat before serving.*

## ANCHOVY SAUCE FOR SPAGHETTI

SALSA DI ACCIUGHE

½ cup olive oil
¼ pound butter
1 can anchovy fillets, undrained

8 cloves garlic, sliced
2 tablespoons chopped parsley

Combine the olive oil and butter in a saucepan. Cook over low heat until the butter melts. Mash the anchovies very fine. Add, with the oil from the can and the garlic, to the saucepan. Cook over medium heat for 1 minute, stirring constantly, or until garlic browns. Do not allow the garlic to burn. Add the parsley, stir well, and serve. The sauce may be poured over spaghetti. It may also be used as a dip or sauce for artichokes and broccoli.

*Note: This sauce may be changed into the classic* bagna cauda *sauce by adding 1 sliced truffle to the mixture when the anchovies are added.*

## NOODLES WITH WALNUTS

GNOCCHI ALLA GRANERESE

| | |
|---|---|
| 1 cup ground walnuts | 2 teaspoons salt |
| 1 clove garlic, minced | ½ teaspoon pepper |
| 1 pound Ricotta or cottage cheese | 1 pound broad noodles |
| 1 cup grated Parmesan cheese | |

Roll or pound the walnuts and garlic on a board or in a mortar until a paste is formed. Place in a large bowl. Add the Ricotta and Parmesan cheeses, salt, and pepper. Mix well. Boil the noodles in salted water until tender, about 10 minutes. Drain. Add to the walnut mixture and toss lightly with two forks until the noodles are well coated. Place on a heated platter and serve.

## BAKED STUFFED NOODLES

LASAGNE

| | |
|---|---|
| 2 Italian sausages (sweet), chopped | 1 pound lasagne, cooked (or use the broadest noodles available) |
| 1 onion, chopped fine | |
| 2 cloves garlic, minced | 2 tablespoons water |
| 1 No. 2½ can Italian-style tomatoes | 1 pound Ricotta or creamed cottage cheese |
| ½ cup boiling water | |
| ¼ teaspoon basil | ½ cup grated Parmesan cheese |
| 2 tablespoons chopped parsley | |

Fry the sausages in a saucepan for 3 minutes. Drain off the fat. Add the onions and garlic and sauté for 10 minutes, stirring frequently, or until the onions are browned. Add the tomatoes, water, and basil and stir. Cover and cook over low heat for 3 hours, stirring occasionally. Correct seasoning and add the parsley.

Place a layer of lasagne on the bottom of a buttered baking dish or casserole. Pour a little of the sauce over it. Mix the water and Ricotta cheese together and spread some of it over the sauce. Sprinkle with some of the Parmesan cheese. Repeat the procedure until all of the ingredients are used up, ending with the Ricotta and Parmesan cheeses on top. Bake in a 350° oven for 25 minutes. Serve hot, directly from the dish.

## POTATO BALLS

### GNOCCHI

3 pounds potatoes (about 8 large potatoes)
2 egg yolks, beaten
2 tablespoons salt

1 cup sifted flour
Boiling water
⅓ cup grated Parmesan cheese
¼ cup melted butter

Boil and mash the potatoes. Add the egg yolks and 2 teaspoons of the salt, beating well. Add the flour gradually, adding just enough so that a dough is formed; it may not be necessary to add all of the flour. Knead the dough until very smooth. Break off pieces and roll out ¾ inch in diameter and about 1½ inches long.

Add the remaining salt to a large saucepan of boiling water. Drop the *gnocchi* into it, about 10 at a time. When they come to the surface, remove them immediately, drain, and keep warm. Continue until all of the *gnocchi* have been cooked. Place the *gnocchi* in a serving dish and sprinkle with Parmesan cheese and melted butter. If desired, serve with a little hot tomato sauce.

## TOMATO PIE

### PIZZE

1 cake or package yeast
1 cup lukewarm water
3¼ cups sifted flour
¼ teaspoon salt
2 tablespoons shortening
½ cup olive oil

1½ cups canned tomatoes, drained
1 small can anchovy fillets
½ pound sliced Mozzarella cheese
½ teaspoon salt
½ teaspoon pepper
¾ teaspoon orégano

Soak the yeast in the water for 5 minutes. Sift the flour and salt onto a board. Make a well in the center and pour the yeast mixture into it. Add the shortening to the well and mix the flour into it gradually. Knead until smooth and elastic. Form into a ball and place in a bowl. Cover and put in a warm place to rise for 2 hours.

Preheat oven to 400°. Divide the dough into two equal parts. Stretch each part to fit into two 10- or 12-inch round pans. Place the *pizze* dough on the bottoms and trim the edges. Sprinkle with ¼ cup of the olive oil.

Spread with the tomatoes and arrange the anchovies and cheese on top. Sprinkle with the salt, pepper, orégano, and remaining oil. Bake in a 400° oven for 25 minutes. Cut into pie-shaped wedges and serve hot.

*Note: There are many different variations of* pizze, *which are also known as* pizza. *Salami, cheese, ham, etc., may be used.*

## GREEN SALAD

INSALATA VERDE

½ cup chopped green pepper
½ cup chopped red pepper
2 teaspoons chopped parsley
½ cup chopped fresh tomatoes
2 tablespoons chopped celery
2 scallions (green onions), sliced
6 radishes, chopped

1 teaspoon chopped anchovies
2 tablespoons capers
½ teaspoon salt
¼ teaspoon pepper
3 tablespoons wine vinegar
½ cup olive oil

Combine the green pepper, red pepper, parsley, tomatoes, celery, scallions, radishes, anchovies, capers, salt, and pepper in a bowl. Add the vinegar, mixing lightly. Add the olive oil very gradually, mixing thoroughly. Chill and serve.

## ALMOND SPONGECAKE

BOCCA DI DAMA

5 egg yolks
5 tablespoons sugar
3 tablespoons sifted flour
3 tablespoons ground almonds
2 teaspoons grated lemon rind

5 egg whites
1 cup heavy cream
¼ cup confectioners' sugar
¼ cup sliced toasted almonds

Beat the egg yolks in the top of a double boiler. Add 4 tablespoons sugar, beating well. Place over hot water and beat with a rotary beater for 5–10 minutes. Remove from heat. Combine the flour, almonds, lemon rind, and remaining sugar; add to the yolk mixture. Preheat oven to 300°. Beat the egg whites until stiff but not dry. Fold them into the previous mixture carefully. Butter a 9-inch layer-cake pan and dust lightly with flour. Pour mixture into it. Bake in a 300° oven for 35 minutes, or until a cake tester comes out clean. Allow to cool in the pan.

Whip the cream and add the confectioners' sugar. Cover the cake with it and sprinkle the sliced almonds on top. The cake is also very good with fruits instead of the sliced almonds.

## NUT TART

TORTA DI NOCI

1¼ cups ground walnuts
¾ cup sugar
⅓ cup unsweetened cocoa
4 egg yolks, beaten

1 teaspoon vanilla extract
1 teaspoon grated lemon rind
4 egg whites
2 tablespoons bread crumbs

Combine the walnuts, sugar, and cocoa in a bowl. Gradually add the egg yolks, beating well. Add the vanilla extract and lemon rind and mix well. Preheat oven to 350°. Beat the egg whites until stiff but not dry and fold them into the mixture carefully. Butter a 9-inch glass baking dish and dust with the bread crumbs. Pour the mixture into it. Bake in a 350° oven for 30 minutes, or until a cake tester comes out clean. The tart may be served hot or cold. When eaten hot, the texture is somewhat like that of a soufflé.

*NORWAY*

Norway and Alaska have in common the fact that they are in similar latitudes, but differ in that Alaska has warmer winters and Norway has milder summers. At least this is true for the two cities of Oslo, Norway, and Juneau, Alaska.

Pan American planes land at Fornebu Airport, rather a long ride from Oslo, but one that will immediately give the visitor an opportunity to learn something of the country.

This is a tourist land and it is becoming more so with each successive year. Filled with scenery that may honestly be described as awe-inspiring, populated with sturdy, resourceful people, Norway attracts more and more tourists. The *fjords,* the coastal chasms of the western part of the country, and the North Cape, the land of the Lapps, are must-sees for every visitor. From May until September, Norway has practically no darkness at all; in the northern portion of the country it is not only light but quite bright every hour of the day. It requires an effort to go to bed with the sun shining, even though your watch tells you it is after midnight, but it is a wonderful experience.

The very things that make Norway so exciting for the visitor, such as the mountains, the scenery, and the rugged countryside, also militate to the nation's disadvantage, for only a small part of the land, estimated to be as little as three per cent, is suitable for agriculture. By force of circumstances, the people have turned to grazing cattle and to the sea for their food.

Herring is the principal fish, though cod and mackerel are almost equally important. Herring is eaten fresh, dried, smoked, salted, spiced, pickled, and even made into *sildegryn* (herring soup)! There are apparently no dishes calling for whipped cream and herring, but there are several made with sour cream. In a country where fish is such an important part of the diet, it is understandable that the Norwegians should excel in fish cookery. To the housewife's way of thinking, fresh fish must be really fresh, and she will often buy her fish only from the boat from which it was actually caught, particularly at the renowned Bergen market. Smoked fish is much appreciated here; a local specialty is an overripe fish dish, *rakørret-raketrout,* or salted trout kept for a month or longer until it is ripe. To those who would turn up their nose, it is only necessary to remind them of our fine cheeses, kept until they have reached the desired state of moldiness—pardon, ripeness.

Although most of the usual meat dishes are eaten with appreciation, Norway has for the intrepid eater more unusual fare, such as elk, bear, and especially reindeer steak (*rensdyrstek*), all of which are eaten fresh, dried, and salted. Grouse, elk, and hare are other common game sources.

Breads follow the Scandinavian pattern, and the *flattbröd,* wafer-thin, is unusually good. Dairy products are excellent and the local cheeses outstanding. *Gjetost,* the chocolate-colored goat's milk cheese, and *gammelost,* made of fermented cow's milk, may be singled out for comment. Desserts follow the Swedish style, although there are exceptions.

Norwegians drink a considerable quantity of hard liquor; a little too much, by their own admission. The favorite is *dram,* similar to *snaps* in Sweden. Beer is very good, and the local fruit wines, *fruktvin,* are worth trying.

There is much good food to be had in Norway, particularly in the restaurants of Oslo. The Kongen and Dronningen restaurants are the apparent leaders, but the Speilen and Telle are both high on any list for fine meals.

## LIVER LOAF

LEVERPOSTEI

1½ pounds calf or beef liver
¼ pound salt pork
2 anchovy fillets
3 eggs, beaten
2 tablespoons milk

1 cup bread crumbs
2 tablespoons grated onion
2 teaspoons salt
½ teaspoon pepper

Wash the liver carefully and remove any membranes. Grind it 3 times with the salt pork and anchovies. Place in a bowl and add the eggs, milk, bread crumbs, grated onion, salt, and pepper. Mix until very smooth. Preheat oven to 350°. Butter a 9-inch loaf pan and pour the mixture into it. If desired, the pan may be lined with very thin slices of salt pork. Place the loaf pan in a pan of hot water. Bake in a 350° oven for 1½ hours. Let the pan cool for a while at room temperature, then place it in the refrigerator to chill. Cut into ½-inch slices and serve cold as an appetizer with thin slices of buttered rye or pumpernickel bread.

## HERRING SOUP

SILDEGRYN

½ cup dried yellow peas
½ cup barley
3½ quarts water
1 turnip, sliced
1 carrot, sliced
1 onion, chopped

¼ teaspoon salt
½ teaspoon pepper
3 potatoes, peeled and diced
¼ teaspoon thyme
2 salt herring, filleted and sliced
　½ inch thick

Soak the peas overnight in water to cover, if a presoaked variety is not used. Drain well. Combine the peas, barley, and water in a saucepan. Cook over medium heat for 45 minutes. Add the turnip, carrot, onion, salt, and pepper. Cover and cook for 45 minutes. Add the potatoes and thyme and stir well. Cook for 25 minutes. Add the herring slices and cook 5 minutes longer. Correct seasoning. Serve hot.

## CREAM OF TAPIOCA SOUP

FLØTESUPPE

1 cup pearl tapioca
2 quarts water
¼ cup coarsely chopped almonds
2 tablespoons seedless raisins
2 teaspoons grated lemon rind

½ cup white wine
1 egg yolk
1 cup heavy cream
½ teaspoon salt
1 tablespoon sugar

Wash the tapioca and combine with the water in a saucepan. Cover and cook over low heat for 3 hours. Add the almonds, raisins, lemon rind, and white wine. Cook 30 minutes longer. Beat the egg yolk in a bowl. Add the cream, salt, and sugar. Gradually add 2 cups of the soup to the bowl, beating constantly to prevent curdling. Return the contents of the bowl to the balance of the soup, beating constantly. Do not allow the soup to boil after the egg is added. Serve hot.

## ROAST FRESH HAM

**SKINNESTEK**

| | |
|---|---|
| 1½ tablespoons salt | 1½ cups boiling water |
| 1½ teaspoons pepper | 2 tablespoons butter |
| 1 teaspoon nutmeg | 2 tablespoons flour |
| 1 fresh ham | ½ teaspoon dry mustard |

Combine the salt, pepper, and nutmeg; rub into the ham thoroughly. Score the fat in several places with a knife. Place the ham in a roasting pan. Roast in a 450° oven for 30 minutes. Add the boiling water, reduce the oven temperature to 350°, and roast 25 minutes a pound.

Remove the gravy from the pan and skim off all the fat. Add water if necessary to make 1½ cups of gravy. Melt the butter in a saucepan. Add the flour and mustard, stirring until smooth. Add the gravy, stirring constantly until the boiling point is reached. Cook over low heat for 5 minutes. Correct seasoning. Carve the ham and serve the gravy separately.

## CAULIFLOWER WITH SHRIMP SAUCE

**BLOMKÅL MED REKESOS**

| | |
|---|---|
| 3 tablespoons butter | 1 cup coarsely chopped cooked |
| 1 cup bread crumbs | shrimp |
| 1½ cups milk | 1 tablespoon brandy |
| 1 teaspoon salt | 1 whole cauliflower |
| 1 teaspoon sugar | |

Melt the butter in a saucepan. Add the bread crumbs, mixing well. Add the milk, stirring constantly until the boiling point is reached. Add the salt, sugar, and shrimp and cook over low heat for 5 minutes. Remove from heat and add the brandy. Place a whole head of firm cauliflower in a large saucepan of boiling, salted water. Cook for 20–25 minutes but do not allow to overcook. Place the sauce over low heat and allow to thicken for 2 minutes. Drain the cauliflower completely and place on a serving platter. Pour the sauce over it and serve at once.

## RAW POTATO DUMPLINGS

KUMLER

| | |
|---|---|
| 6 large potatoes, peeled | 2 tablespoons flour |
| 1 teaspoon salt | ¼ pound pork, diced |
| ⅛ teaspoon thyme | 6 cups stock or 2 cans consommé and |
| ⅓ cup cracker meal | 2½ cans water |

Grate the potatoes into a bowl. Add the salt and thyme and stir. Add the cracker meal and flour and mix well. The mixture should be fairly stiff; add a little more cracker meal if necessary. Wet the palms of the hands and form the mixture into 1-inch balls. Press a cube or two of pork into the center of each ball and roll in the hands so that the pork is completely covered. Place the stock in a saucepan and bring it to a boil. Drop the dumplings into it and cook over low heat for 1 hour. Serve with soup, boiled meats, or sausages.

## CHRISTMAS CAKE

JULEKAKE

| | |
|---|---|
| 2 cakes or packages yeast | ¼ cup melted butter |
| ½ cup sugar | ¼ pound butter |
| 1⅛ cups lukewarm milk | ¾ cup chopped candied fruit |
| 3¾ cups sifted flour | ¼ cup seedless raisins |
| ½ teaspoon ground cardamom seeds | |

Place the yeast in a bowl with 1 tablespoon of the sugar and ¼ cup of the milk. Mix until smooth. Add 3 tablespoons of the flour and mix again. Cover and allow to rise in a warm place for 20 minutes. Combine the remaining sugar, remaining flour, and the cardamom seeds in a bowl. Add the melted butter and the remaining milk. Mix well and add the yeast mixture, again mixing well. Cover and allow to rise in a warm place for 30 minutes.

Cut the butter into small dots and knead into the dough. Place the dough on a lightly floured surface and knead steadily for 5 minutes. Add the candied fruit and the raisins and knead until they are well distributed. Butter two 12-inch loaf pans and dust lightly with flour. Divide the dough in half, shape into loaves, and place in the pans. Brush the top of each loaf with a little milk. Cover with a cloth and allow to rise for 20 minutes. Preheat oven to 375°. Bake in a 375° oven for 35 minutes, or until lightly browned.

## BUTTER MERINGUE CAKE

### TÅRTA

½ pound butter
2½ cups sugar
6 egg yolks
¾ cup sifted flour
2 teaspoons baking powder

⅔ cup milk
2 teaspoons vanilla extract
8 egg whites
¾ cup ground walnuts
1½ cups heavy cream

Cream the butter well. Add 1 cup of the sugar and continue creaming until light and fluffy. Add the egg yolks and beat well. Sift the flour and baking powder together and add to the butter mixture alternately with the milk. Beat well. Add the vanilla and mix lightly. Butter two 9-inch layer-cake pans. (Use pans with removable or slip bottoms, or spring-form pans, if possible.) Dust lightly with flour. Divide the mixture evenly and place half in each pan. Preheat oven to 325°.

Beat the egg whites until stiff but not dry. Gradually add the remaining sugar, beating well. Spread this mixture on top of the cake batter to within 1½ inches of the outside edges of the pans. Sprinkle with the walnuts. Bake in a 325° oven for 40 minutes. Cool for 1 hour.

Whip the cream. Remove the layers from the tin, meringue side up. Spread the whipped cream on top of the meringue and put layers together, meringue sides up. Sprinkle a few walnuts on top, if desired.

*POLAND*

Poland, which has seen so much unhappiness in the past centuries, is filled with many conflicting ways of life. Surrounded by two larger and more powerful neighbors, Russia to the east and Germany to the west, the nation has never been at peace with itself or with the world for any great length of time.

Since Poland was once part of Russia, the Russian influence on Polish food is strongly felt. The great beet soup of Poland, its *barszcz,* is a first cousin to Russia's *borscht,* although there are differences. Poles, however, are great individualists, and there are many talented amateur cooks and chefs in Poland; most Poles fancy themselves as gourmets, and possibly they are correct in their belief. Certainly it cannot be denied that they evince great interest in food, and Polish food is well recognized for its fine qualities.

The cuisine of the country is largely based upon the following: freshwater fish, ham and pork, sour cream, dark breads, mushrooms, cucumbers, game dishes, sauerkraut, noodles and dumplings, rich cakes, and buckwheat groats, *kasza,* as they are called in Poland.

A great national favorite is the mushroom, of which the Poles are excessively fond. For the most part these fungi grow wild in Poland's forests, are gathered by the peasants and brought to the markets, fresh and moist. Dried mushrooms find their way into homes all over the globe. Cucumbers are also enormously popular and are prepared in many ways, often with sour cream.

The people's reason for loving such growing things of the fields and forests as cucumbers, radishes, scallions, and mushrooms is not hard to discern. Winter in Poland bears little resemblance to our own. In America, snowplows immediately clear the roads, television breaks the monotony for the few people who are snowbound, and those who can, go to Florida for two weeks. In Poland, when winter begins the people are forced into a state of semihibernation. Snow covers the landscape, there is little sun, and Florida is a long way off. When spring comes and the earth permits the tender green shoots to emerge, the people rejoice in a way that we, who live around the corner from a supermarket that has strawberries in February, will find hard to comprehend.

Because of these cold winters the people are interested in solid and substantial fare rather than in delicacies which would tempt a jaded palate. That is not to say that Polish food is not exciting or stimulating to the appetite, because it certainly is that. However, it does mean that much of the cuisine is based upon filling and satisfying ingredients.

By the same token, Poles are very fond of rich desserts, particularly cakes. *Babka,* more or less the national cake, is made of a yeast dough, often filled with many kinds of candied fruits, raisins and nuts, and covered with a sugar glaze.

To correct one misunderstanding about Polish drinking habits: they do not drink *vodka,* as you might have thought previously; they drink *woudka.* There's a great difference, for the Polish drink has a *w* instead of a *v,* and somehow a *u* sneaked in. It must be admitted that, other than the difference in spelling, both drinks taste exactly the same. The people prefer coffee to tea (when they can afford it), and beer to wine.

## BEET SOUP

### BARSZCZ

½ cup dried lima beans
8 large beets, peeled and halved
2 pounds stewing beef, cut into
  2-inch cubes
  (Beef bones if available)
1 cup canned tomatoes

3 quarts water
1 head cabbage, shredded
1 apple, peeled and quartered
2 teaspoons salt
1 teaspoon pepper
Sour cream

Wash the beans carefully. Soak in water to cover overnight. Cook in the same water until tender, about 2 hours. Drain and set aside. Combine the beets, meat, tomatoes, and water in a deep saucepan. Bring to a boil and skim the top. Cook over medium heat for 1½ hours. Add the cabbage, apple, salt, and pepper. Cook for 30 minutes. Add the lima beans. Correct seasoning. Cook for 15 minutes. Grate the beets and return to the saucepan. Serve very hot, with a tablespoon of sour cream and a few pieces of meat in each plate.

## PIKE, POLISH STYLE

### SANDACZ

3 onions, sliced
1 carrot, sliced thin
1 slice lemon
2 cups water
2 teaspoons salt
1 teaspoon pepper

6 slices (2 inches thick) pike or other
  fresh-water, white-meat fish
2 tablespoons salt butter
4 hard-cooked eggs, chopped
3 tablespoons lemon juice

In a large saucepan place the onions, carrot, lemon, water, salt, pepper, and fish. Bring to a boil. Cook over medium heat for 40 minutes. Melt the butter in a separate saucepan and add the chopped eggs and lemon juice. Cook for 2 minutes. Arrange the fish on a platter and pour the egg sauce over it.

## SAUERKRAUT WITH PORK

### KAPUSTA Z WIEPRZOWINA

2 tablespoons salad oil or butter
3 pounds spareribs, cut into individual pieces, or 6 pork chops
2 onions, coarsely chopped
2 cloves garlic, minced
1 teaspoon salt
½ teaspoon pepper

1 bay leaf
1½ cups boiling water
1 pound sauerkraut
1 apple, peeled and chopped
2 tablespoons barley
1 teaspoon caraway seeds

Heat the oil in a large saucepan and add the pork. Cook over high heat, turning the meat frequently until it is brown on all sides. Add the onions and garlic, and cook over medium heat until the onions and garlic are browned. Add the salt, pepper, bay leaf, and water and cook for 30 minutes, stirring occasionally. Add the sauerkraut and its liquid, apple, barley, and caraway seeds and mix well. Continue cooking for 1 hour, or until meat is tender. Correct seasoning. Remove the bay leaf. Serve the pork and sauerkraut together.

## STUFFED DOUGH POCKETS

### USZKA

2 cups sifted flour
1 teaspoon salt
2 eggs, beaten
⅓ cup water

2 tablespoons butter
1 onion, chopped
1 pound mushrooms, chopped
¼ teaspoon pepper

Sift the flour and ½ teaspoon of the salt into a bowl. Combine the eggs and water and add, mixing well. Knead until smooth, cover, and set aside while preparing the filling.

Melt the butter in a skillet. Add the onion, mushrooms, pepper, and remaining salt. Sauté for 10 minutes, stirring frequently. Cook over high heat for 1 minute to evaporate any remaining liquid. Cool for 15 minutes.

Roll out the dough ⅛ inch thick on a lightly floured surface. Cut into 3-inch squares. Place a tablespoon of the mushroom mixture in the center and fold over the dough, sealing the edges carefully. Cook in boiling salted water for 12 minutes. Drain well. If desired, after the *uszka* are boiled, they may be fried in butter.

## POTATO DUMPLINGS

### KARTOFLANE KLUSKI

1 cup cold mashed potatoes
3 eggs, beaten
1 teaspoon salt
1 cup sifted flour

½ teaspoon baking powder
3 slices white bread
¼ cup butter

Place the mashed potatoes in a bowl. Add the beaten eggs and the salt. Beat well. Add the flour and baking powder and again beat well. Cut the bread into small cubes. Melt the butter in a saucepan, and brown the cubes of bread on all sides.

Take a heaping tablespoon of the potato mixture and wrap it around several fried cubes of bread, forming them into 2-inch balls. Place them carefully in boiling, salted water. Cover and cook for 15 minutes. Drain well. Serve with meat dishes.

## POLISH COFFEECAKE

### BABKA

¼ pound butter
½ cup sugar
1 teaspoon salt
3 egg yolks, beaten
1 cake or package yeast
¼ cup milk, scalded and cooled
2 tablespoons grated lemon rind

½ cup seedless raisins
2 cups sifted flour
½ cup milk
3 tablespoons crushed zwieback
  crumbs
1 tablespoon cinnamon
3 tablespoons chopped almonds

Cream the butter, then add the sugar. Continue creaming until well blended. Add the salt and egg yolks and beat. Place the yeast in the ¼ cup cooled milk and stir until dissolved. Add to the previous mixture. Add the lemon rind and raisins and stir well. Gradually add the flour and the ½ cup milk alternately, beating well after each addition. Turn out onto a lightly floured surface and knead the dough until it becomes elastic and does not stick to the fingers. Place it in a bowl, cover, and put in a warm place to rise for 1 hour. At the end of this time punch the dough down firmly, re-cover, and allow to rise for 2 hours longer.

Butter a 12-inch loaf pan and dust with the zwieback crumbs. Place the dough in the pan, brush with a little milk, and sprinkle with the cinnamon and almonds. Bake in a 350° oven for 30 minutes.

## PORTUGAL

This comparatively small but resolute nation, facing upon the Atlantic Ocean, draws its livelihood primarily from the sea. Thus you would expect the cuisine of the country to be based upon seafood. The visitor expects to see fish, his mind accepts the possibility of seeing tremendous quantities of fish, and he anticipates eating all sorts of delectable fish dishes. The realization is here greater than any possible anticipation, for the mind cannot cope with the enormous catches made by the fishermen; a visit to the fishing docks may often be described as stupefying.

Shellfish are prepared in hundreds of different ways, but oysters and crabs are notably of the highest rank. Oysters from Portugal are highly regarded in France, that land of forty million gourmets. Any possible excess in the population of France over forty million is undoubtedly composed of infants under one year of age and visiting Americans.

For those who have not examined the mark of origin on a can of sardines in recent months, it should also be pointed out that this is the home base of that amazingly fertile fish, which reproduces itself by the billions. The Portuguese prefer them fresh or dried rather than canned. Another pillar of the local cuisine is the humble cod, the *bacalhau*. Soups and chowders are often made of seafood and are uniformly excellent.

But it must not be assumed that seafood is the sum total of all that is noteworthy in Portugal. There are excellent meat dishes of which *iscas* (calf's liver) and *carne de vinha* (spicy pickled meat) are merely representative examples. Many desserts are rich, sticky pastries of astronomical caloric value. The local fruits are often superb; also recommended are the Portuguese cheeses, the best of which are made from ewe's milk, such as *evora, serra,* and *azeitão.*

Most people remark how close a resemblance Portuguese food bears to that of its neighbor, Spain, but the Portuguese version is likely to have garlic in it, which is used much more sparingly next door. French influence on the local cuisine is also strong, but actually, and somewhat irrationally, the food seems closer to that of Italy than any other country, especially in the use of garlic, oil, tomatoes, and onions. In fact the French expression *à la portugaise* means that those ingredients appear in a given dish.

Until recently the Portuguese people strongly criticized their own port wine. Their objection was based upon the fact that, before being marketed, the wine received many additives: about twenty per cent brandy, artificial red coloring, and elderberries were introduced into the product. A good deal of substandard wine was shipped out of the country only to run into additional adverse criticism. At the present time Portuguese legislation prohibits many of these practices and the great name of port is slowly regaining its former eminence. Formerly the bulk of this wine was shipped to Britain, where it was highly regarded. In recent years the British palate has changed and the demand has dwindled somewhat; Portuguese wine merchants are finding it extremely difficult to locate a substitute market.

Tawny and ruby port are the best known, but one of the most interesting types is the so-called "crusted" port, in which a sort of crusted deposit forms on the inside of the bottle. Madeira is well thought of by experts but has found a rather small audience in the competitive world market. It is available both as a dry wine, suitable for use before dinner, and also in a sweet type for desserts or after-dinner consumption. The best known of these are the Sercial and the Malvasia.

## GREEN SOUP

### CALDO VERDE

2½ quarts water
4 tablespoons olive oil
4 potatoes, peeled and diced
2 teaspoons salt

½ teaspoon pepper
2 pounds kale or 1 pound spinach
   and 1 pound cabbage

Combine the water, olive oil, and potatoes in a saucepan. Cook over medium heat for 30 minutes. Force the potatoes through a sieve or mash them as fine as possible. Return them to the liquid in the saucepan. Add salt and pepper and cook over low heat for 1 hour. Wash the kale (or the spinach and cabbage if they are substituted for the kale) and remove the tough fibers. Shred finely and drain well. Add to the potato mixture and cook over medium heat for 15 minutes, stirring occasionally. Correct seasoning. Serve hot or cold.

## PORTUGUESE FISH SOUP

### SOPA À PORTUGUESA

3 tablespoons olive oil
3 fillets of sole or other white-meat
   fish
1 pound shrimp, peeled and cleaned
6 cups water
6 sprigs parsley
½ teaspoon basil
6 white onions

5 slices bread, trimmed
6 hard-cooked egg yolks, mashed
1 cup ground almonds
2 teaspoons salt
1 teaspoon pepper
6 slices toast (French bread, if possible)

Heat the olive oil in a frying pan. Add the fillets and brown on both sides. Set aside. Combine the shrimp, water, parsley, basil, and onions in a saucepan. Cook over medium heat for 10 minutes. Add the fried fillets, bread, and egg yolks. Cook over medium heat for 15 minutes. Force the mixture through a sieve and return it to the saucepan. Add the almonds, salt, and pepper. Cook over low heat, stirring constantly, until hot, but do not allow the mixture to boil. Place a slice of toast in each soup plate and pour the soup over it. The result is so thick that it might well be considered as a stew but it is an old Portuguese soup recipe.

## CODFISH, PORTUGUESE STYLE

BACALHAU À GOMES DE SÁ

2 pounds dried codfish
6 potatoes
1½ cups olive oil
3 onions, sliced
4 cloves garlic, minced

1 teaspoon pepper
½ cup white wine
6 hard-cooked eggs
¼ cup chopped parsley

Wash the fish thoroughly, in several changes of water. Soak the fish overnight in water to cover. Drain well. Add fresh water to cover. Cook over medium heat for 20 minutes. Drain, reserving the liquid. Remove the skin and bones carefully. Shred the fish coarsely. Cook the unpeeled potatoes in the fish stock until tender, about 30 minutes. Peel and slice thin.

Heat the olive oil in a frying pan. Add the onions and garlic and sauté for 5 minutes. Add the fish and potatoes. Cook over high heat for 2 minutes, stirring constantly. Add the pepper and white wine and stir. Place the mixture in a buttered baking dish or casserole. Bake in a 425° oven for 15 minutes. Chop 3 of the eggs coarsely and slice the other 3. Garnish with the eggs and parsley. Serve directly from the baking dish or casserole.

## CALF'S LIVER IN WINE

ISCAS

12 thin slices calf's liver
2 cloves garlic, minced
1 teaspoon salt
½ teaspoon pepper

1 bay leaf
1 cup white wine
¼ cup olive oil

Wash the liver carefully. Combine the garlic, salt, pepper, bay leaf, and wine in a bowl. Add the liver and marinate overnight in the refrigerator. Baste occasionally. Heat the olive oil in a frying pan until it smokes. Add the liver slices and wine mixture all at once. Stir gently, but constantly for 5 minutes. Serve immediately.

## TRIPE, OPORTO FASHION

TRIPAS À MODA DO PORTO

2 cups white beans
2 pounds tripe
1½ quarts water
2 chicken breasts, removed from bone and cubed
½ pound ham, cubed

½ pound sausage (Portuguese or Spanish type, if possible), sliced
2 tablespoons olive oil
3 onions, chopped
4 tomatoes, peeled and chopped
2 teaspoons salt
1 teaspoon pepper

Soak beans in water to cover overnight. Drain. Add fresh water to cover. Cook over medium heat until tender, about 1½ hours. Drain. Cut the tripe into small pieces and combine in a large saucepan with the water. Cook over medium heat 2 hours. Add the chicken, ham, and sausage and cook over low heat 1 hour longer. Drain, reserving the stock.

Heat olive oil in a saucepan. Add the onions and sauté for 10 minutes, stirring frequently. Add the tomatoes, beans, cooked meat, 2 cups of the stock, salt, and pepper. Stir well and cook over low heat for 30 minutes. Correct seasoning and add a little more stock if necessary. The dish should have the consistency of a thick stew. Serve hot.

## SPICY PICKLED MEAT

CARNE DE VINHA

2 cups vinegar
1 tablespoon salt
½ teaspoon thyme
1 teaspoon dried ground chili peppers
3 cloves garlic, minced

2 bay leaves
3 cloves
3 pounds boneless pork
2 tablespoons olive oil
6 slices stale bread

Combine the vinegar, salt, thyme, chili peppers, garlic, bay leaves, and cloves in a large bowl. Place the pork in it and baste for 5 minutes. Marinate in the refrigerator for 2 days. Turn the pork several times.

Place the pork and marinade in a saucepan, cover, and cook over medium heat for 45 minutes. Drain the pork but reserve the marinade. Heat the olive oil in a frying pan and brown the pork in it on all sides. Fry for at least 35 minutes, or until the pork is tender. If desired, the pork may be roasted in a 450° oven for 40 minutes. Dip the bread in the marinade and fry in the oil in which the pork was browned. Fry until the bread is browned on both sides. Slice the pork and serve it with the fried bread slices.

## STUFFED CAPON

GALUIHA RECHIADA

7-pound capon
1½ tablespoons salt
2 teaspoons pepper
3 cups white wine
¼ pound butter
4 onions, chopped
½ teaspoon nutmeg

1 teaspoon cinnamon
2 cups bread crumbs
1½ cups sliced green olives
6 hard-cooked eggs, coarsely
   chopped
1 teaspoon vinegar
½ cup milk, scalded

Wash and dry the capon, reserving the gizzard and liver. Combine 1 tablespoon of the salt and 1½ teaspoons of the pepper and rub it into the capon inside and out. Place the capon in a large bowl or pan and pour the wine over it. Marinate overnight in the refrigerator. Baste occasionally.

Place the gizzard in a saucepan with water to cover and boil for 30 minutes. Add the liver and boil 10 minutes longer. Drain. Cut up the gizzard and liver finely. Melt the butter in a skillet. Add the onions and sauté for 10 minutes, stirring frequently. Combine the sautéed onions with the nutmeg, cinnamon, remaining salt and pepper, bread crumbs, olives, eggs, vinegar, milk, and the gizzard and liver. Mix well.

Drain the capon but reserve the wine. Stuff the capon with the previous mixture, fastening the opening with skewers or with thread, or cover with a piece of aluminum foil. Roast the capon in a 350° oven for 25 minutes per pound. Add 1 cup of the reserved wine after the first 30 minutes of roasting time. Baste frequently, adding more wine if required.

## FRIED BREAD DESSERT

RABANADAS

3 cups milk
⅓ cup honey
⅓ cup sugar
2 tablespoons grated lemon rind
½ cinnamon stick (optional)
⅛ teaspoon salt

12 slices French bread (½ inch thick)
   or 6 slices white bread, cut in half
4 eggs, beaten
1 cup salad oil
¼ cup confectioners' sugar
¼ cup cinnamon

Combine the milk, honey, sugar, lemon rind, cinnamon stick, and salt in a saucepan. Bring to a boil and cook over low heat for 1 hour. Remove from the heat. Dip the bread slices in this mixture and then in the beaten eggs. Heat ½ cup of the oil in a frying pan. Fry the bread in it until light brown on both sides. Add additional oil as required. Cool the fried bread for 30 minutes. Serve with the confectioners' sugar and cinnamon.

117

## MERINGUE IN CUSTARD

LEITE CREME CON FARÓFIAS

| | |
|---|---|
| 2 cups milk | 1 cup sugar |
| 1½ cups light cream | 3 egg yolks |
| 2 teaspoons vanilla extract | 2 tablespoons cornstarch |
| 3 egg whites | 1 teaspoon cinnamon |

Combine the milk, cream, and vanilla in a saucepan and bring to a boil slowly over low heat. Beat the egg whites until stiff but not dry. Add ½ cup of the sugar gradually, beating well. Drop a tablespoon of the egg whites into the boiling milk mixture. Turn continuously with a fork until firm. Remove each meringue carefully and drain. Continue until all of the egg whites are used up. Reserve the milk.

Beat the egg yolks, cornstarch, and remaining sugar in a saucepan. Gradually add the reserved milk, stirring constantly until the boiling point is reached. Pour the mixture into a large serving bowl and place the meringues carefully on top. Sprinkle with the cinnamon. Chill for at least 2 hours. This dessert may be served hot, but if so desired, it is advisable to pour the hot milk mixture into individual dishes and place the meringues on top of each portion.

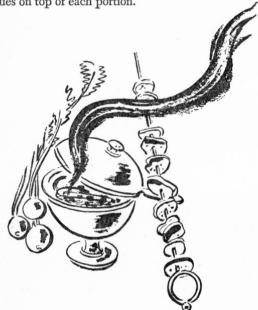

*RUSSIA*

It is difficult to consider the food and eating habits of Russia, because there is the unresolved question of whether to discuss the problem as of today or yesterday. Certainly it will be agreed that the excessively lavish meals of the czarist regime are gone, and that the native cuisine has been greatly simplified. However, recent visitors to Russia have attested to the fact that state banquets honoring diplomats or distinguished persons are almost as lavish as ever, though food in such quantity and quality is unavailable to the general public.

*Vodka* is the national drink. It is taken straight for the most part, accompanied by herring or some other appetizer. Most foreigners think of *vodka* as a clear white liquid, usually about 100 proof. There is, however, a red variety known as *riabinovka,* and a more or less yellowish type called *zubrovka. Vodka* should be taken in tiny glasses and never tasted or sipped. The correct procedure is to throw the fiery liquid to the back of the throat and hope for the best.

The Russians are fond of *zakuska* (appetizers). Probably the popular favorite is herring, but caviar would undoubtedly be the national choice except for its price and scarcity. It is now too expensive for all but a few.

The French, recognized as the leading gourmets of the world, have proclaimed that Russia's contribution to the world of serious eaters—that is connoisseurs—is the Russian soup. This is quite true, and an example is supplied here, the sauerkraut soup known as *schchi* (why suffer?—it's pronounced chee), just the thing to warm you up after a hard day on the steppes of Russia. The famous Russian beet soup, *borscht,* is known all over the world.

*Cotletki pojarski* (chicken cutlets) are appreciated the world over; *koulebiaka,* a meat or fish pie, is another fine dish; these are merely highlights, for Russia's cuisine is extensive. An interesting feature of Russian cooking is the lavish use of sour cream. It must be remembered that refrigeration is a comparatively recent innovation, and without it cream spoils quickly. The sour taste has always appealed to the Russians, and it is used whenever possible: in almost all soups, in many of the meat dishes, and particularly on the many different kinds of pancakes that constitute a unique feature of Russian food. Cereals, particularly whole-grain types, are much appreciated in this cold land. *Kashoi,* or buckwheat groats, are exceptionally good and may be obtained in the United States in foreign groceries and specialty shops. Heavy, whole-grain breads are eaten by everyone; American-style white breads are unknown.

There are many unique features in the cuisine, characterized by an inordinate love of mushrooms and cucumbers, by a fondness for smoked fish, sauerkraut, dark breads, and sour milk and cream. Sturgeon, when it is available, is Russia's favorite fish.

Dinner is always an early meal in Russia, usually about 5 P.M. Recent industrialization, which entails changed working hours, has revised meal hours to a certain degree but not completely. Normally, and by choice, the

Russians like an early breakfast and prefer to lunch about noon. The favorite meal, for those who can manage it, is undoubtedly the late evening snack, served family style at about 10 P.M. This is the time for family and friends to gather, the time for conversation, and for eating the dainties that the Russians love so dearly. Tea is consumed in unbelievable quantities by our own one- or two-cup standards. A good Russian can drink a dozen glasses of tea; glasses, not cups, are used, reputedly because the people like to warm their hands on the hot glasses. To a Russian, tea never tastes so good as when the water is boiled in a samovar, a large brass or copper vessel made expressly for that purpose. Tea is not made in the samovar; water is boiled in it, and then the tea, which differs considerably from the varieties sold in this country, is steeped in a teapot.

## EGGPLANT CAVIAR

### RUBLNNYI BAKLAZHAN

1 large eggplant
1 small onion, sliced
2 tomatoes, peeled
3 tablespoons vinegar
1 slice white bread, trimmed

1½ teaspoons salt
½ teaspoon pepper
2 teaspoons sugar
4 tablespoons salad oil

Wash the eggplant and cut off the stem. Place the eggplant on a baking sheet or wrap it loosely in aluminum foil. Bake in a 325° oven for 1 hour. Cool for 30 minutes. Peel and set aside. Place the onion in a chopping bowl and chop fine. Add the tomatoes and eggplant and chop fine. Pour the vinegar on the bread, soaking it well. Add to the eggplant with the salt, pepper, sugar, and oil. Continue chopping until well blended. Correct seasoning; the mixture should be fairly spicy. Chill for at least 1 hour. Serve with slices of thin pumpernickel bread.

## SAUERKRAUT SOUP

### SCHCHI

3 pounds short ribs of beef
A few marrow bones, if available
3 cloves garlic, minced
2 onions, chopped
3 quarts water
1 No. 2 can tomatoes
1 large head cabbage
3 teaspoons salt

1 teaspoon pepper
¼ cup lemon juice
¼ cup sugar
2 tablespoons flour
2 tablespoons water
1 pound sauerkraut
½ cup sour cream

Wash the meat and bones and place in a deep pot. Add the garlic, onions, water, and tomatoes. Bring to a boil and skim the top of any foam. Shred the cabbage coarsely, discarding the core. Add to soup with salt and pepper. Cook for 1½ hours. Add the lemon juice and sugar. Cook 30 minutes. Mix the flour and water to a smooth paste and add to soup, stirring constantly. Add the sauerkraut and cook until meat is tender. Correct seasoning. The soup may need more sugar or lemon juice, depending on the tartness of the sauerkraut.

Serve in deep soup plates, garnished with sour cream. The meat may be served at the same time, on a separate platter. When served with *piroshki*, it is almost a complete meal.

## MEAT PASTRY

### PIROSHKI

1 cup flour
⅛ teaspoon salt
¼ pound butter
3 tablespoons sour cream
4 tablespoons melted butter

4 chicken livers or 1 slice calf's liver
½ cup sliced mushrooms
½ teaspoon salt
⅛ teaspoon pepper

Sift the flour and ⅛ teaspoon salt into a bowl. Add the butter and work together with the hand until well blended. Add the sour cream and mix again until smooth. Wrap in wax paper and chill at least 2 hours, overnight if possible.

Place the 4 tablespoons melted butter in a saucepan and add the livers, mushrooms, salt, and pepper. Cook over low heat for 10 minutes. Chop fine and cool for 15 minutes.

Roll out the dough ⅛ inch thick on a lightly floured board. Cut rounds with a cooky cutter. Place a heaping teaspoon of the liver mixture on each and fold over the dough, sealing the edges carefully. Place on a baking sheet. Bake in a 375° oven for 20 minutes. Serve hot. *Piroshki* are usually served with *schchi*. However, they may be served as hot hors d'oeuvres.

## ROAST CARP WITH PORRIDGE

### ZHARENNY CARP S KASHOI

2½ cups milk
  ½ pound buckwheat groats or
  cracked wheat cereal
3½ teaspoons salt

6 tablespoons butter
1 onion, chopped
5 pounds carp, whole fish or one piece
½ teaspoon pepper

Boil the milk in a saucepan. Gradually add the cereal, stirring constantly. Add 1½ teaspoons salt and 2 tablespoons butter. Cook over medium heat 30 minutes, stirring occasionally. Melt the remaining butter in a skillet. Add the onion and sauté for 5 minutes. Add to the cereal, mixing well.

Wash and dry the fish. Split it and open it flat. Sprinkle with the pepper and remaining salt. Place the cereal mixture in the fish and fasten the opening with thread or skewers. Place the fish in a buttered baking dish. Bake in a 450° oven for 15 minutes. Reduce heat to 375° and bake 45 minutes longer. Serve with the following sauce, if desired:

| | |
|---|---|
| 2 tablespoons butter | ½ teaspoon pepper |
| 1 onion, chopped | 1 tablespoon flour |
| 1 pound mushrooms, sliced | 1 pint sour cream |
| 1 teaspoon salt | |

Melt the butter in a saucepan. Add the onion and sauté for 5 minutes. Add the mushrooms, salt, and pepper. Cook over low heat for 10 minutes. Add the flour, stirring constantly. Cook 2 minutes. Add the sour cream. Heat but do not allow to boil. Serve in a separate sauceboat.

## FISH STEW

### SELIANKA

| | |
|---|---|
| 10 dried mushrooms | 1 teaspoon pepper |
| 2 pounds fresh-water fish, sliced, and head | 2 quarts water |
| | 3 tablespoons butter |
| 1 stalk celery, sliced | 1 onion, chopped |
| 2 carrots, peeled and sliced | 4 tablespoons tomato paste |
| 1 parsnip, peeled and sliced (optional) | 1 tablespoon capers, drained |
| 2 teaspoons salt | 10 ripe olives |

Soak the mushrooms in water to cover for 2 hours. Drain carefully. Rinse and slice.

Wash the fish and head. Place the head in a deep saucepan, reserving the fish itself. Add the celery, carrots, and parsnip, salt, pepper, and water. Boil for 45 minutes. Strain. Melt the butter in a large saucepan. Add the chopped onion and sauté for 10 minutes, stirring frequently. Add the fish and brown lightly on both sides. Add the tomato paste, capers, olives, and strained fish stock. Cook over medium heat for 40 minutes, or until fish is cooked. Correct seasoning. Serve in deep soup plates garnished with lemon slices and parsley.

## MEAT PIE

### KOULEBIAKA

| | |
|---|---|
| 1 cake or package yeast | 2 eggs, beaten |
| ½ cup warm milk | ½ teaspoon salt |
| 4 cups sifted flour | 1½ cups milk |
| 1 tablespoon butter | |

Place the yeast in a cup with the warm milk. Mix to a paste and allow to soak for 5 minutes. Add 1 cup of the flour and stir well. Place in a warm place, cover with a cloth, and allow to rise until double in size, about 1 hour. Add the butter, eggs, salt, milk, and the remaining flour. Knead into a dough. If necessary, add a little more flour to form the dough. Place in a bowl, cover with a cloth, and allow to rise in a warm place for 2 hours. While it is rising, prepare the filling:

| | |
|---|---|
| ¼ pound butter | 2 teaspoons salt |
| 2 onions, chopped | 1 teaspoon pepper |
| 2 pounds veal or beef, chopped | 4 tablespoons cream |
| ½ pound mushrooms, chopped | 1 egg yolk, beaten |
| 2 hard-cooked eggs, chopped | |

Melt the butter in a saucepan. Add the onions and sauté for 10 minutes, stirring frequently. Add the meat and mushrooms and cook for 20 minutes over medium heat, stirring occasionally. Add the chopped eggs, salt, pepper, and cream and mix well. Correct seasoning.

Roll out the dough about ½ inch thick on a lightly floured surface. Butter a 14-inch loaf pan thoroughly. Place the dough in the pan so that it extends over the sides. Place the meat mixture in the center and fold over the dough so that it meets in the middle. Allow to rise for 15 minutes. Preheat oven to 375°. Brush the top of the dough with the beaten egg yolk. Bake in a 375° oven for 35 minutes, or until browned on top. If desired, melted butter may be brushed across the top before serving. The loaf may be sliced in the pan or turned out onto a plate.

## CHICKEN CUTLETS

### COTLETKI POJARSKI

| | |
|---|---|
| 4 slices white bread | ½ pound mushrooms, sliced |
| ½ cup light cream | 1 tablespoon flour |
| 2 3-pound chickens | ¼ cup stock or ½ bouillon cube dissolved in ¼ cup boiling water |
| 1½ teaspoons salt | |
| ¼ teaspoon white pepper | 1½ tablespoons lemon juice |
| 1 pound butter | 3 egg yolks, beaten |
| 1 egg, beaten | Dash of cayenne pepper |
| ½ cup bread crumbs | |

Soak the bread in the cream. Remove the meat from the chickens (un-cooked) and grind in a food chopper as fine as possible. Add 1 teaspoon of the salt and the pepper. Melt 2 tablespoons of the butter and add with the bread. Chop the mixture until very smooth. Shape into 6 large or 12 small cutlets. Dip in the beaten egg and then in bread crumbs. Melt 4 tablespoons of butter in a skillet and fry the cutlets in it over low heat, until browned on both sides. Add more butter as necessary. Remove and keep warm.

Melt 2 tablespoons of butter in the same skillet. Add the mushrooms and sauté for 5 minutes. Sprinkle the flour on top, stirring until smooth. Gradually add the stock, stirring until the boiling point is reached. Cook over low heat for 5 minutes, stirring frequently. Set aside.

Divide the remaining butter into three pieces. Place one piece in the top of a double boiler; add the lemon juice and egg yolks. Place over hot, not boiling, water. Beat constantly with a wire whisk or wooden spoon. When the first piece of butter melts, add the second. When the mixture thickens, add the third piece, still beating constantly. Cook over low heat so that the water never boils. Continue cooking and beat-ing for 2 minutes after the last piece of butter melts. Remove from the heat. Add the remaining salt and the cayenne pepper. If the mixture curdles, add 1 tablespoon of heavy cream and beat vigorously. Add the mushrooms. Serve the sauce on top of the cutlets.


## SWEET PEPPER SALAD

SLADKY PEREZS

8 green peppers
2 cups water
2 teaspoons prepared mustard
2 teaspoons sugar

1 teaspoon salt
2 tablespoons vinegar
½ cup olive oil

Wash the peppers and cut into quarters, discarding the seeds and fibers. Place in a saucepan with the water. Boil for 20 minutes, or until tender. Drain, and cool in the refrigerator for 1 hour. Combine the mustard, sugar, salt, vinegar, and oil in a bowl and mix well. Pour over the peppers. Marinate for 2 hours. Serve cold.


## FRUIT JELLY DESSERT

KISSEL

1 pound sugar
1½ cups water

1 pound fresh or dried apricots
¼ cup potato flour

Combine the sugar and ½ cup of the water in a saucepan. Boil until the mixture is syrupy, about 15 minutes. Wash and pit the fresh apricots; if dried apricots are used, wash them and soak for 2 hours in water. Add to the syrup and cook until very soft. Force through a sieve. Combine the remaining 1 cup of water and the potato flour in a saucepan. Mix until smooth. Add the puréed apricots and cook until very thick over low heat, about 20 minutes. Pour into individual dishes. May be served either hot or cold, with heavy sweet cream.

## CHEESE PASTRIES

### VATROUSHKIS

2 cups sifted flour
½ pound salt butter
1 cup plus 2 tablespoons sour cream
1 pound cream cheese
2 eggs

2 tablespoons melted butter
½ teaspoon salt
1 teaspoon sugar
1 egg yolk, beaten

Sift the flour into a bowl. Cut the butter into the flour with a pastry blender or two knives. Add 2 tablespoons of the sour cream and mix together into a ball. Wrap in wax paper and place in the refrigerator overnight, or at least for 2 hours.

Cream the cheese until soft, add the eggs, and beat together until light and fluffy. Add the remaining sour cream, the melted butter, salt, and sugar. Mix well. Preheat oven to 375°. Roll out the dough ⅛ inch thick on a lightly floured surface. Cut out 3-inch circles. Place 2 teaspoons of the cheese mixture in the center of each circle of dough. Pinch the sides together but do not pinch the dough together in the center; the effect should be that of a cup. Brush each piece of pastry with the beaten egg yolk. Place on a baking sheet. Bake in a 375° oven for 20 minutes, or until delicately browned.

## WALNUT CAKE

### MAZOURKA

9 egg yolks
2 cups sugar
9 egg whites
3 cups flour

1 pound walnuts, ground
½ pound candied fruit peel, ground
2 tablespoons lemon juice

Beat the yolks in a bowl; add the sugar and beat well. Beat the whites in a separate bowl until stiff but not dry and fold into the yolk mixture carefully. Add the flour, walnuts, candied fruit, and lemon juice, mixing lightly. Preheat oven to 325°. Butter a flat pan, about 8 by 12 inches, and dust lightly with flour. Pour the mixture into it. Bake for 30 minutes in a 325° oven, or until a cake tester comes out clean. Dust with powdered sugar. The resulting cake will be about 1 inch high and should be served in long, thin slices.

*SCOTLAND*

Here is a region where the temperature seldom warms the visitor, but where the friendship and hospitality of the people make up for it. Scotland is hard and barren, and full of rugged scenery, but the people are not the dour folk that they have been made out to be; rather, they may be described as reserved in nature. Scotch hospitality comes as a surprise to those visitors who know Scotland only as the land of Scotch jokes. This section will contain no Scotch jokes whatsoever.

Scotland's contributions to the world of the gourmet may be limited in number, but those few are impressive in their importance. For example, the scotch whisky that has found acceptance the world over is produced here. No one knows whether it is the local water, the ingredients, or the method of manufacture, but it is certain that scotch whisky has never been successfully duplicated anywhere else in the world. While the people are justifiably fond of their own local product, there is very little scotch in Scotland. Most of it is exported, principally to the United States, in return for much-needed foreign credits.

Of the natural resources, Scotch salmon and trout are outstanding delicacies. Game birds are also exceptional, but not nearly so plentiful in numbers as they formerly were. Other local specialties include herring, Scotch bacon, locally grown mutton, and the staple food, porridge, or oatmeal as we call it. The porridge of Scotland is not the quick-cooking variety used by American housewives so that the family breadwinner can catch the 8:03. It is the slowly cooked, natural cereal that the Scots use, and their finished product is completely different from our anemic

American-style oatmeal. It takes much longer to make Scotch oatmeal, and in the kitchens of the country people it is customary to see a pot of porridge cooking over a low fire at any hour of the day. The raw oatmeal is also used for dipping and coating raw fish before cooking; fresh herring dipped in Scotch oatmeal is unusually good. To duplicate the recipes contained in this section, be sure to use the Scotch type of oatmeal, which may be had at many fine groceries or delicacy shops.

The one dish that typifies Scotland is haggis. Unfortunately most visitors do not care to eat it after learning that it is a kind of pudding prepared from the sheep's heart, liver, and lungs and cooked with oatmeal in the lining of the sheep's stomach. It is better than it sounds, but it still is not a dish for everyone. The recipe for pot haggis is much more to our taste.

Tea is a fine meal, because the Scotch are particularly adept at cakes and pastries. Scotland has produced its own shortbread, and of course there are the famous scones. As in England, most visitors enjoy breakfast and tea more than lunch and dinner. This need not be so if, instead of making fruitless attempts to find international food, the tourist will eat local specialties.

The Grosvenor Restaurant in Glasgow is one of the best-known restaurants in Scotland.


## HOT PINT

4 cups ale
1 egg, beaten

4 tablespoons sugar
½ cup scotch whisky

Heat the ale to the boiling point. Combine the egg, sugar, and scotch and mix well. Gradually add the boiling ale, stirring constantly to prevent curdling. Pour into mugs from a height, so as to create a froth. If the drink is poured into glasses, be sure to place a spoon in each glass. Drink immediately while the froth remains.


## TRADITIONAL CHICKEN AND LEEK SOUP

### COCKY-LEEKY

5-pound stewing chicken, disjointed
2½ quarts water
2 teaspoons salt
½ teaspoon pepper

12 fresh leeks or 18 scallions (green onions), sliced
1½ cups rice, half cooked

Wash the chicken carefully. Place in a saucepan with the water. Cook for 2 hours, or until tender. Add the salt and pepper at the end of the first hour of cooking. Remove the chicken and keep warm. Add the leeks and rice to the soup and cook for 25 minutes. Remove the chicken from the bones and add to the soup. Cook 5 minutes longer. This soup makes an excellent meal in one dish.

## FISH BALLER

2 fillets of sole
2 cups water
1 pound shrimp, shelled and cleaned
1 tablespoon chopped parsley
1¼ teaspoons salt
½ teaspoon pepper

¼ teaspoon thyme
1 egg
1½ cups bread crumbs
1 egg yolk, beaten
Fat for deep-fat frying

Combine the fillets and water in a saucepan. Bring to a boil and cook over medium heat for 10 minutes. Remove the fillets and set aside to cool. Place the shrimp in the same liquid in which the fish was cooked, and cook for 7 minutes. Drain and set aside to cool for 10 minutes. Grind the fillets and shrimp three times in a food chopper. Place in a bowl and add the parsley, salt, pepper, thyme, egg, and 1 cup of the bread crumbs. Beat the mixture until smooth and light, using an electric mixer if desired. Correct the seasoning. Shape into 1-inch balls. Dip them into the egg yolk and remaining bread crumbs. Heat the fat to 380°. Fry several of the fish balls at a time until they are golden brown, about 2 minutes. Drain. Serve hot.

## HAMBURGER, SCOTCH STYLE

### MINCE

3 tablespoons butter
2 pounds beef, ground
3 tablespoons boiling water

2 teaspoons salt
1 teaspoon pepper
2 onions

Melt the butter in a saucepan and add the meat, stirring constantly. Do not allow lumps of meat to form. When the meat is brown, add the water, salt, pepper, and onions. Cover and cook over very low heat for 35 minutes, stirring frequently. Serve with skirl in the pan (see recipe in this section).

## CHICKEN STOVIES

4 teaspoons salt
2 teaspoons pepper
6-pound chicken, disjointed
6 large potatoes, peeled and cut into sixths

4 onions, sliced
4 tablespoons butter
1½ cups stock or 1 can chicken consommé and ¼ cup water

Combine 2 teaspoons of the salt and 1 teaspoon of pepper and rub into the chicken thoroughly. Butter a casserole and arrange a layer of chicken on the bottom, followed by successive layers of potatoes and onions. Dot each layer with a little of the butter and sprinkle the remaining salt and pepper on the layer of potatoes. Pour the stock over the contents of the casserole. Cover. Bake in a 325° oven for 3 hours, or until tender. Serve hot, directly from the casserole.

## POT HAGGIS

| | |
|---|---|
| 1 pound liver | 1½ cups oatmeal (Scotch oatmeal, if |
| 3 cups water | possible) |
| 3 onions | 1½ teaspoons salt |
| ¼ pound raw beef fat | 1 teaspoon black pepper |

Combine the liver and water in a saucepan. Bring to a boil and cook over medium heat for 10 minutes. Add the onions and cook for 20 minutes. Remove the liver and onions, reserving the liquid. Grind the liver, onions, and beef fat together.

Place the oatmeal in a hot frying pan and stir continuously until lightly browned. Be sure the pan is completely dry, and be careful not to burn the oatmeal. Add the oatmeal to the liver mixture, together with the salt and pepper, and 1¾ cups of the reserved liquid. Mix well. Pour into a greased casserole. Cover the top, using a piece of aluminum foil if the cover does not fit tightly. Place in a deep pan of boiling water on top of the stove and steam for 2 hours.

*Note: The above recipe differs considerably from the Scotch method. The traditional recipe is to use the stomach bag of a sheep and fill it with the liver, heart, and other assorted parts of a sheep.*

## SKIRL IN THE PAN

| | |
|---|---|
| ⅓ cup butter | ½ cup boiling water |
| 2 onions, chopped fine | 2 teaspoons salt |
| ½ cup oatmeal (Scotch oatmeal, if | ⅛ teaspoon pepper |
| possible) | |

Melt the butter in a saucepan. Add the onions and sauté until brown, about 10 minutes, stirring frequently. Add the oatmeal, stirring constantly. Add the water, salt, and pepper and mix well. Cook over low heat for 20 minutes, or until soft. Serve with mince (see recipe in this section) or with other meats.

## CREAM SCONES

| | |
|---|---|
| 2 cups sifted flour | 3 tablespoons butter |
| ⅛ teaspoon salt | 1 egg |
| 1 teaspoon baking powder | 3 tablespoons cream |

Sift the flour, salt, and baking powder into a bowl. Cut in the butter with a pastry blender or two knives until the consistency of coarse sand. Beat the egg and cream together and add to the mixture, tossing lightly with a fork until a dough is formed. Roll the dough out about ¾ inch thick on a lightly floured surface. Do not roll more than once. Preheat oven to 400°. Butter a baking tin and dust lightly with flour. Place the dough on the tin and cut into 2-inch squares with a knife. Brush the top with a little milk. Bake in a 400° oven for 15 minutes. Recut the squares. Serve hot. Reheat before serving, if the scones are served again. They may be eaten plain or with butter.

## SCOTCH SHORTBREAD

| | |
|---|---|
| ½ pound sweet butter | 1 cup sifted cake flour |
| 1 cup confectioners' sugar | 2 tablespoons cornstarch |

Combine the butter and sugar together on a board. Blend together with the hands. Sift the flour and cornstarch together and gradually work it into the previous mixture until well blended. Preheat oven to 425°. Butter an 8-inch square pan and dust lightly with flour. Pat the dough into the pan with the hands, as this dough cannot be rolled. Prick the top with a fork in several places. Bake in a 425° oven for 5 minutes; then reduce the heat to 350° and bake 10 minutes longer, or until lightly browned. Cut into squares immediately.

*SPAIN*

Spain is a brilliant red cape, a hot, yellow sun; it is gay music and un-restrained flamenco dancing. These characteristics of the country and of the people are observable in the national cuisine, with its strong flavor combinations and unusual dishes. Just as the conservative British eat bland and colorless food, so the flaunting Spaniards prefer spicy and colorful fare. Gastronomically speaking, the two nations are a world apart, but just to confuse the issue, the contradictory English are extremely fond of Spanish sherry.

The food of Spain is based upon certain principal ingredients: olives and olive oil; the flavorings of garlic, saffron, and paprika; seafood, rice, beans, chick-peas, and smoked sausages. Fresh fruits and melons are often superb, and of course there are the renowned wines of the country.

Those who can afford it eat a light breakfast but make up for it with two enormous meals—lunch from 1 to 3 P.M., and dinner at ten in the evening, or even slightly later. The Spanish people love good food, and dining is a fine art. Tourists may have to adjust themselves to the late meal hours, but little adjustment is required to the delicious food. *Olla podrida* is the meat stew of the peasantry, but the tourist favorite is *paella valenciana,* a delicious combination of rice, chicken, lobster, and shrimp. *Angulas* (baby eels) may sound exotic, but they won't after you've tasted them. *Zarzuela de mariscos* (literally meaning a musical comedy of sea-food) is also very good, but neither of these two last preparations can readily be duplicated in this country.

With all their wonderful fresh fish, the Spaniards are inordinately fond of dishes made with sun-dried codfish. The usual meats are to be had, including goat and kid, but these are merely adequate and not equal to the seafood. *Gazpacho* is served either as a cold vegetable soup or as a salad, though a valid criticism might be that it is too dry for a soup and too wet for a salad.

131

The cocktail hour often starts here at 8:30 P.M. and even nine-thirty is not unusual! Red, white, and pink wines are produced in abundance almost everywhere in the nation, several of them being quite well known, particularly the Marqués de Riscal brand. The wine of Málaga, a sweet, dessert type, is justly accepted as a fine wine by the world. Interestingly enough, this wine is produced only by the third harvest of the vines, the first being used for drying into raisins, and the second for a white wine.

But it is the wine of Xeres de la Frontera region for which Spain is famous. Xeres is also Jerez, and the British anglicized their favorite drink into "sherris," and over the centuries it has become the familiar word "sherry." It is a unique wine, admittedly inimitable, dry or sweet, pale or dark, and suitable for use as an appetizer or as a dessert wine depending upon the type. The sweet, darker types usually have brandy added; the drier varieties are pale and unchanged. The principal divisions include the golden or sweet sherry, the *oloroso* or medium, and the finest of all, the dry *amontillado*. The Spanish people love the *manzanilla* wine produced in Andalusia, but its perfumed, aromatic flavor does not immediately receive everyone's approval.

In soft drinks, *horchata*, a cold, milky drink, is the warm-weather favorite. Hot chocolate for breakfast, and black coffee at other meals, are the other beverages of importance.

## COLD SOUP OR SALAD

### GAZPACHO

2 onions, chopped
2 cloves garlic, minced
4 green peppers, chopped
5 tomatoes, chopped
2 teaspoons salt
½ teaspoon pepper

2 teaspoons Spanish paprika
⅓ cup olive oil
⅓ cup wine vinegar
1½ cups water
1 cucumber, peeled and sliced very thin

Combine the onions, garlic, green peppers, and tomatoes. Force through a sieve or purée in an electric blender. Add the salt, pepper, and paprika. Add the olive oil gradually, beating steadily. Add the vinegar and water and stir well. Correct seasoning. Place in the refrigerator to chill for at least 2 hours, using a wooden or glass bowl; do not use a metal bowl. Add the cucumber slices before serving. If desired, slices of toast rubbed with garlic may be served with the *gazpacho*.

This dish may be served as either a cold soup or as a salad, though it will seem to be quite a wet salad. When *gazpacho* is served, no other soup or salad should be served.

## CHICK-PEA SOUP

### COCIDO MADRILEÑO

1 pound chick-peas (*garbanzos*)
3 quarts water
1½ pounds beef
2 marrow bones
1 pound smoked ham, cubed
¼ pound smoked sausage (Spanish sausage, if available), sliced

½ pound bacon strips, half cooked, and cut in half
2 carrots, sliced
1 onion, chopped
2 leeks, sliced
2 teaspoons salt
6 potatoes, peeled and cut in shoe-string lengths

Wash the chick-peas and discard any imperfect ones. Soak them over-night in water to cover. Drain and rinse. Boil the water in a large sauce-pan. Add the chick-peas and cook for 30 minutes. Add the beef and bones and cook over medium heat for 30 minutes. Add the ham, sausage, and bacon. Cover but allow the steam to escape, and cook over low heat for 1 hour. Add the carrots, onion, and leeks and cook for 30 minutes. Add the salt and potatoes and cook for 30 minutes. Correct seasoning. Strain the stock and serve. The meat and vegetables should be served on a separate plate.


## FISH PIE

### PASTEL DE PESCADO

3 tablespoons olive oil
½ cup ground almonds
2 cloves garlic, minced
4 onions, chopped
1 bay leaf
2 teaspoons salt

1 teaspoon pepper
5 tomatoes, peeled and chopped
5 fillets of sole or other white-meat fish
3 cups mashed potatoes, seasoned with salt and pepper

Heat the oil in a saucepan. Add the almonds and sauté for 5 minutes, stirring frequently. Remove the almonds and set aside. Place the garlic and onions in the saucepan and sauté for 10 minutes, stirring frequently. Add a little more olive oil if necessary. Add the bay leaf, salt, pepper, and tomatoes and cook over low heat for 10 minutes, stirring occasionally. Grind 1 of the fillets in a food chopper. Cut the remaining fillets in thirds. Reserve one-third of the tomato mixture as a sauce. Force the balance of the mixture through a sieve. Add the ground fish and the almonds. Cook over low heat for 10 minutes, stirring frequently.

Butter a 9-inch casserole. Line the bottom and sides carefully with the mashed potatoes but reserve some for the top of the casserole. Arrange layers of the tomato mixture and of the fish fillets until they are all used up. Cover the top with mashed potatoes. Bake in a 425° oven for 30 minutes. Serve directly from the casserole with the reserved tomato sauce, which should be heated.

## FISH CASSEROLE

SABETA

½ cup olive oil
3 cloves garlic, minced
3 tomatoes, peeled and chopped
3 onions, sliced
2 green peppers, cut into julienne strips
2 teaspoons Spanish paprika
¼ teaspoon saffron

6 slices mackerel or fresh tuna
2½ teaspoons salt
2 bay leaves
¼ teaspoon dried ground chili peppers
1½ cups white wine
1½ cups water
¾ cup rice

Heat ¼ cup of the oil in a saucepan. Add the garlic and tomatoes and sauté for 5 minutes, stirring frequently. Mash the tomatoes with a fork until smooth. Add the onions, green peppers, paprika, and saffron. Cook over low heat for 15 minutes, stirring frequently.

Heat the remaining oil in a casserole or saucepan. Add the fish and sauté until browned on both sides. Add the salt, bay leaves, chili peppers, wine, water, and the tomato mixture. Mix together gently. Bring to a boil and add the rice. Cover and cook over low heat for 25 minutes. Discard the bay leaf. Correct seasoning. Serve hot. A bottle of chilled white wine makes an excellent accompaniment.

## LOBSTER, CATALAN STYLE

LANGOSTA CATALANA

3 live lobsters, split
½ cup olive oil
5 onions, chopped
2 teaspoons salt
½ teaspoon dried ground chili peppers
½ cup brandy
2 tablespoons tomato paste
1½ cups stock or 1 can consommé and ½ can water

1 bay leaf
½ teaspoon orégano
¼ teaspoon thyme
½ cup chopped parsley
1 teaspoon saffron
2 cloves garlic, minced
½ ounce unsweetened chocolate

Remove the coral and liver from the lobsters and reserve. Heat the olive oil in a large casserole or Dutch oven. Add the onions and sauté for 15 minutes, stirring occasionally. Add the lobsters, salt, chili peppers, and brandy. Set the brandy aflame and cook over high heat until the brandy stops burning. Add the tomato paste, stock, bay leaf, orégano, thyme, and parsley. Mix. Bake in a 375° oven for 20 minutes.

Pound the saffron, garlic, chocolate, coral, and liver to a smooth paste. Add a little sauce from the casserole, mixing well. Return the mixture to the casserole and stir. Cook over low direct heat for 5 minutes. Correct seasoning and discard bay leaf. Place the lobsters on a platter. Pour the sauce over them and sprinkle with remaining parsley.

*Note: If the lobster is to be served as a main course for 6 people, double the recipe.*

## SPANISH NATIONAL STEW

OLLA PODRIDA

2 cups chick-peas (*garbanzos*)
3 quarts water
3 tablespoons olive oil
1 pound stewing beef, cubed
1 pound veal (breast preferably), cut into 2-inch strips
1 pound lamb, cubed
½ chicken, disjointed
1 pound smoked ham, cubed
4 smoked sausages (Spanish *chorizos*, if possible), sliced

2 onions, chopped
3 cloves garlic, minced
2 teaspoons salt
1 teaspoon pepper
2 cups shredded cabbage
1 pound fresh or ½ package frozen peas
½ pound fresh or ½ package frozen string beans
2 cucumbers, peeled and sliced
1 head lettuce, coarsely shredded

Soak the chick-peas overnight in water to cover. Drain. Place in a large saucepan with the water. Cook over medium heat for ½ hour. Heat the olive oil in a large frying pan. Sauté the beef, veal, lamb, and chicken in it until browned on all sides. Add the browned meats, ham, sausages, onions, garlic, salt, and pepper to the chick-peas. Cover and cook over low heat for 1½ hours, or until the meats are tender. Remove 2 cups of the stock and place it in a separate saucepan. Add the cabbage, peas, and string beans and cook for 10 minutes. Add the cucumbers and lettuce and cook 10 minutes longer.

Place the meat and chick-peas on a platter, reserving the stock. Drain the vegetables, again reserving the stock, and place on a separate platter. Combine the stocks. This constitutes a complete meal: soup, meat, and vegetables.

## SWEETBREADS IN SHERRY

MOLLEJAS DE TERNERA AL OLOROSO

| | |
|---|---|
| 3 pairs sweetbreads | ¼ pound butter |
| 1½ teaspoons salt | 3 onions, chopped |
| 1 tablespoon vinegar | 1 cup sweet sherry |
| 2 cups water | 6 shallots, if available |

Wash the sweetbreads. Combine in a saucepan with the salt, vinegar, and water. Bring to a boil, cover, and cook over low heat for 10 minutes. Drain. Cover with cold water. Allow to cool for 30 minutes. Drain and remove the membranes. Dice coarsely. Melt the butter in a saucepan. Add the sweetbreads and sauté for 5 minutes, stirring frequently. Add the onions and sauté for 10 minutes, stirring frequently. Add the sherry. Cook over low heat for 5 minutes, then add the shallots. Cook over low heat 5 minutes longer. Correct seasoning. Serve with buttered green peas. If served as a main course, double the number of sweetbreads.

## ROAST BEEF, SPANISH STYLE

CARNE ASADO

| | |
|---|---|
| 3 cloves garlic, minced | ¼ cup olive oil |
| 1 tablespoon salt | 2 green peppers, chopped |
| 1½ teaspoons pepper | 5 onions, chopped |
| 2 teaspoons Spanish paprika | 4 tomatoes, peeled and chopped |
| 6-pound rolled roast or 8-pound rib roast | 1 bay leaf |
| ½ cup red wine | ½ cup sliced mushrooms |
| ½ cup wine vinegar | ½ cup sliced, stuffed olives |

Combine the garlic, salt, pepper, and paprika. Rub into the meat well. Place the meat in a bowl. Combine the wine and vinegar and pour over the meat. Marinate in the refrigerator overnight. Baste frequently and turn the meat several times. Remove from the refrigerator 3 hours before roasting time.

Heat the olive oil in a roasting pan over direct heat. Drain the meat thoroughly, reserving the marinade. Brown the meat in the olive oil, turning frequently. Place the green peppers, onions, tomatoes, bay leaf, and mushrooms around the meat and pour the marinade over it. Roast in a 350° oven according to the weight of the meat, allowing 13 minutes for rare, 15 minutes for medium, and 18 minutes for well done, per pound. Baste frequently, adding water if the pan becomes dry. Discard the bay leaf. Force the vegetables and gravy through a sieve. Add the olives. Correct seasoning. Heat the gravy and serve separately.

## CHICKEN AND DUCK, VALENCIAN STYLE

POLLO VALENCIANA

1 cup olive oil
2 onions, chopped
2 cloves garlic, minced
3½-pound chicken, disjointed
4-pound duck, disjointed
½ pound pork, cubed
3 smoked sausages (Spanish type if possible), sliced
4 tomatoes, peeled and chopped
1 green pepper, sliced
6 cups stock or 2 cans consommé and 2½ cups water

2 teaspoons salt
1 teaspoon saffron
2 teaspoons Spanish paprika
1½ cups rice
¼ pound fresh or frozen string beans
½ pound green peas
1 cup cauliflower flowerets
12 shrimp, peeled and cleaned
1 lobster, cut into small pieces in the shell

Heat ½ cup of the olive oil in a frying pan. Add the onions and garlic and sauté for 15 minutes, stirring frequently. Remove them from the pan. Place the chicken, duck, pork, and sausage in the frying pan and brown well on all sides. Remove from the pan and place in a large casserole. To the casserole add the sautéed onions and garlic, the tomatoes, green pepper, stock, salt, saffron, and paprika. Cover and cook over low heat for 20 minutes. Heat the remaining ½ cup of olive oil in the frying pan. Add the rice and brown lightly, stirring frequently. Add to the casserole, together with the beans, peas, cauliflower, shrimp, and lobster. Cover. Bake in a 350° oven for 1 hour. Add more liquid in small amounts if casserole becomes too dry. Correct seasoning and serve.

## DUCK AND RICE

PATO Y ARROZ

¼ pound butter
2 4-pound ducks, disjointed
6 cups stock or 2 cans consommé and 2 cans water
4 tablespoons tomato paste
4 teaspoons salt
1½ teaspoons pepper
1 teaspoon Spanish paprika

1½ cups rice
1 cup cooked or canned green peas
¼ cup grated Gruyère cheese
½ cup sliced, sautéed mushrooms
⅛ pound ham, sliced in julienne strips
2 pimentos, sliced thin

Melt 3 tablespoons of the butter in a casserole or saucepan. Add the ducks and brown well on all sides. Add 1½ cups of the stock, 2 tablespoons of the tomato paste, 2 teaspoons of salt, 1 teaspoon of pepper, and the paprika. Cover and cook over low heat for 1¼ hours, or until the ducks are tender. Skim the fat from the gravy.

Melt the remaining butter in a saucepan. Add the rice and brown lightly. Add the remaining stock, tomato paste, salt, and pepper. Cover and cook over low heat for 20 minutes. Add the peas and cheese. Cook for 5 minutes. Correct seasoning. Add the mushrooms, ham, and pimentos. Mix lightly. Place the ducks in the center of a platter with the rice around it. Pour the gravy over the ducks. Serve with a chilled white wine.

## CAULIFLOWER

COLIFLOR

| | |
|---|---|
| 1 medium head cauliflower | 1 onion, chopped |
| 2 cups water | 2 cloves garlic, minced |
| 3 teaspoons salt | 2 tablespoons vinegar |
| 4 tablespoons olive oil or butter | ¼ teaspoon pepper |

Wash the cauliflower thoroughly, remove the leaves, and separate into pieces. Place in a saucepan with the water and 2 teaspoons of the salt. Boil for 10 minutes. Drain. Heat the oil in a saucepan. Add the onion and garlic and sauté for 5 minutes, stirring frequently. Add the vinegar, cauliflower, pepper, and remaining salt. Cover and cook over low heat for 10 minutes. Serve hot or cold.

## POTATO-ALMOND CASSEROLE

PATATAS EN CAZUELA

| | |
|---|---|
| 6 potatoes, peeled and sliced ¼ inch thick | ¼ cup milk |
| | 1 onion, chopped |
| 2 eggs, beaten | 2 cloves garlic, minced |
| 1½ teaspoons salt | ½ cup blanched ground almonds |
| ¾ cup sifted flour | 3 tablespoons chopped parsley |
| ⅓ cup olive oil | 1½ cups water |
| 2 slices white bread, trimmed | |

Dip the potato slices in the eggs. Mix the salt and flour together and dip the potato slices in it, coating them thoroughly. Heat the olive oil in a frying pan. Brown the potatoes in the oil quickly over fairly high heat. Remove and place in a buttered casserole.

Soak the bread in the milk for 5 minutes. Squeeze out all the liquid and crumble the bread. Place the bread, onion, garlic, and almonds in the same frying pan and sauté for 5 minutes, stirring frequently, until the mixture is quite smooth and lightly browned. If necessary, add a little more olive oil. Add the parsley and water and mix together. Pour the mixture over the potatoes. Bake in a 325° oven for 50 minutes. Serve hot, directly from the casserole.

## RICE SALAD

ENSALADA DE ARROZ

2 cups cooked rice
2 green peppers, sliced fine
2 pimentos, sliced fine
4 tomatoes, peeled and cubed
2 tablespoons chopped onion
2 tablespoons chopped parsley

¾ cup olive oil
¼ cup wine vinegar
1½ teaspoons salt
½ teaspoon pepper
1 clove garlic, minced

Combine the cooked rice, green peppers, pimentos, tomatoes, onion, and parsley in a bowl. Mix lightly with two forks. Beat together the olive oil, wine vinegar, salt, pepper, and garlic. Pour over the rice mixture and again toss lightly. Chill and serve very cold.

## WALNUT DESSERT PANCAKES

BALTASARES DE NUENCE

2 eggs
1 egg yolk
¼ cup sugar
2 teaspoons grated lemon rind
¾ cup ground walnuts

3 tablespoons sifted flour
3 tablespoons brandy
¼ pound butter
¼ cup sifted confectioners' sugar

Beat the eggs and egg yolk in a bowl. Add the sugar and beat until light. Add the lemon rind, walnuts, and flour and beat until well blended. Add the brandy. Mix. Melt half the butter and add to the walnut mixture, mixing lightly.

METHOD 1: Melt a small piece of the remaining butter in a 7-inch skillet. Pour a tablespoon of the mixture into it and turn the pan from side to side to coat the bottom. Make the pancakes as thin as possible. Bake over low heat until lightly browned on both sides; remove from pan and roll up immediately. Repeat until all the batter is used up. Sprinkle with confectioners' sugar.

METHOD 2: Melt the remaining butter in a baking pan. Pour into the pan by the tablespoon to form small circles. Bake in a 450° oven for 5

139

minutes. Turn each pancake and bake for 3 more minutes, or until browned. Remove from the pan and roll up immediately. Sprinkle with confectioners' sugar.

Serve hot or cold. The second method will produce a crisper pancake.

## BANANA CAKE

TORTA DE BANANA

4 tablespoons butter
½ cup sugar
2 eggs, beaten
1 cup sifted flour
½ teaspoon salt
1 teaspoon baking powder

3 bananas, peeled and halved lengthwise
2 tablespoons lemon juice
¼ cup dark brown sugar
¼ cup fresh or dried grated coconut
(optional)

Cream the butter. Add the sugar and beat until light and fluffy. Add the eggs and beat well. Sift the flour, salt, and baking powder together and add to the previous mixture, mixing well. Preheat oven to 350°. Butter an 8-inch square pan and dust lightly with flour. Pour the batter into the pan, spreading it as evenly as possible. Arrange the banana slices on top. Sprinkle with the lemon juice, brown sugar, and coconut. Bake for 30 minutes, or until a cake tester comes out clean. Remove from the oven and cool. Turn out carefully. Serve with whipped cream, if desired.

## SWEDEN

Sweden is still an almost undiscovered country from the tourist's point of view, for comparatively few tourists visit it in comparison with the vast numbers who see England and France. Yet Sweden offers much to the tourist—excellent accommodations, superb food, and unbelievable scenery. Someday Sweden will probably become a prime tourist center.

Here is the home of the *smörgåsbord,* the table loaded with dozens of plates filled with varying hors d'oeuvres. Often the choice involves not dozens but fifty or even a hundred different appetizing fish, meat, and cheese dishes. The etiquette of the *smörgåsbord* involves at least three visits to the table, in order not to mix the varying flavors of the different foods. The Swedes always start with the fish and herring, then go on to meat, hot dishes, and cheese. The amount of food consumed as a first course by many Swedish people would constitute a full meal for an average American, but the average Swede is a hearty eater and continues through a full dinner.

Cocktails and other alcoholic beverages are not normally served before dinner, but there is a considerable amount of skoaling, or toasting, which takes place during the dinner itself. It is considered extremely discourteous not to respond to a toast, but this works a great hardship on people who are not used to drinking. The usual drink with *smörgåsbord* is *snaps,* a type of brandy. *Snaps* is served ice cold, and is not tasted or sipped but swallowed in a gulp; it is very potent. The *snaps* bottle is often frozen into a small block of ice and brought to the table that way, an attractive way of serving it. Beer is extremely good and is considered essential, a normal conclusion in view of the large amount of salty fish dishes that the Swedish people love to eat. Wine is of limited importance except among the more sophisticated city inhabitants. The famous Swedish Christmas drink known as *glögg* has traveled all over the world and is almost as important a part of that holiday as the tree.

Meal hours follow the pattern that we are familiar with, except for a few slight variations. Upon arising coffee and rolls are served in one's hotel room; those who wish it may obtain a larger breakfast. Lunch and dinner are at normal hours, except that dinner is usually available from 5 P.M. The Swedes, in company with all Northern peoples, are hearty eaters and think much of good food. The finicky eater is not a part of the Swedish way of life, and ladies who eat heartily are more likely to get married than those who count calories.

Favorites of all the people are the rich, thick soups, of which the *vitkålsoppa,* or cabbage soup, is a typical example. With its large seacoast, Sweden depends heavily upon the sea to support itself, and fish dishes are unusually good. There are such things as fish puddings, herring salads, and of course the famous salmon dishes such as *lax med citronsås,* for which a recipe appears in the following section. The people like meat dishes, and lamb, beef, and pork are common foods. Probably the outstanding favorite of the meat dishes would be the *köttbuller* (meat balls made with sweet cream).

The Swedish people love coffee, and with it they must have their many different kinds of coffeecake. They cannot be challenged on this subject, for they are undoubtedly the world champions. Another great specialty of the country is the flat breads—crunchy, delicious, and particularly suited to the national custom of the *smörgåsbord*. The flat rye bread is *knäckebröd*, which the country people eat in almost unbelievable quantities.

Sweden has many famous restaurants, particularly in the capital city of Stockholm. These include such places as the famous fish restaurant known as Stureplan; the Gyllene Freden, a cellar spot of much atmosphere; Bacchi Wapen; Riche; and the Gillet.

## HERRING PUDDING

SILLPUDDING

| | |
|---|---|
| 6 fillets of salt herring | 2 eggs |
| 6 potatoes, peeled and sliced thin | 1½ cups milk |
| 4 onions, sliced thin | ¼ cup bread crumbs |
| 3 tablespoons chopped dill or parsley | 3 tablespoons melted butter |
| 1 teaspoon pepper | |

Soak the herring overnight in water to cover; change the water at least twice. Drain, then dry the herring. Cut into long, thin strips. In a buttered casserole arrange layers of potatoes, herring, and onions, sprinkling each layer with pepper and dill. Beat the eggs and milk together and add to the casserole. Sprinkle with the bread crumbs and dot with the butter. Bake in a 350° oven for 45 minutes. Serve hot as an appetizer or as a luncheon dish.

## COLD FRUIT SOUP

BLANDAD FRUKTSOPPA

| | |
|---|---|
| 1 pound assorted dried fruit (other than prunes) | 2 apples |
| ½ pound prunes | 1 cinnamon stick or 2 teaspoons powdered cinnamon |
| 8 cups water | 2 tablespoons cornstarch |
| ¾ cup sugar | 2 tablespoons cold water |

Wash the dried fruit and prunes thoroughly. Place in a saucepan with the water and sugar. Soak overnight. Peel and core the apples. Cut into eighths. Leaving the dried fruit in the same water in which it was soaked, place the saucepan over medium heat. Add the apples and cinnamon. Cook over medium heat for 45 minutes, or until the fruit is very soft. Remove the fruit and force through a sieve, discarding any pits. Return the fruit pulp to the soup and continue cooking over medium heat. Combine the cornstarch with the water in a cup and stir until smooth. Gradually add to the soup, stirring constantly until the boiling point is reached. Continue cooking for 5 minutes. Chill and serve ice cold.

*Note: This soup is quite sweet to American taste. It is therefore better suited to lunches or late suppers than as a part of large dinners. The cinnamon taste is very distinctive and may be reduced, if desired.*

## CABBAGE SOUP WITH DUMPLINGS

VITKÅLSOPPA MED KROPPKAKOR

4 tablespoons butter
3-pound head cabbage, coarsely
  shredded
2 tablespoons dark brown sugar

2 quarts stock or 3 cans chicken
  consommé and 5 cups water
2 teaspoons salt
½ teaspoon pepper

Melt the butter in a saucepan. Add the cabbage and sauté until brown, stirring frequently. Add the sugar and cook over medium heat for 3 minutes, stirring constantly. Add the stock, salt, and pepper. Cover and cook over low heat for 45 minutes. Correct seasoning. Serve with the following dumplings:

4 tablespoons butter
2 onions, chopped
¾ pound ham, diced
6 boiled potatoes, peeled

¾ cup sifted flour
1½ teaspoons salt
2 egg yolks, beaten

Melt the butter in a saucepan. Add the onion and sauté for 5 minutes, stirring frequently. Add the ham and sauté for 10 minutes. Set aside. Mash or rice the potatoes. Add the flour, salt, and egg yolks and mix together. Knead into a dough and shape into a long roll about 1 inch in diameter. Break off pieces of dough about the size of a golf ball and flatten with the hand on a lightly floured surface. Place a heaping teaspoon of the ham mixture on each and shape into dumplings, sealing the edges carefully. Drop into boiling, salted water and cook for 15 minutes. Drain. The dumplings may be placed in the cabbage soup or they may be served in a separate dish.

## SALMON WITH LEMON SAUCE

LAX MED CITRONSAS

3 onions, sliced
2 carrots, sliced
2 teaspoons salt
1 teaspoon white pepper
1 bay leaf

2 tablespoons white vinegar
4 tablespoons chopped dill
4 cups water
4 pounds fresh salmon (in one piece)
or 6 slices

Combine the onions, carrots, salt, pepper, bay leaf, vinegar, 2 tablespoons of the dill, and the water in a saucepan. Bring to a boil and add the salmon. Cover and cook over medium heat for 20 minutes. Remove cover and cook for 20 minutes. Remove the fish carefully and strain the stock. Sprinkle the fish with the remaining dill. Keep the salmon warm and prepare the following sauce:

3 tablespoons butter
2 tablespoons flour
¾ cup heavy cream, scalded
1 teaspoon salt

¼ teaspoon pepper
1 teaspoon sugar
3 tablespoons lemon juice
2 egg yolks

Melt the butter in a saucepan. Add the flour and mix to a smooth paste. Gradually add the cream and 1 cup of the reserved fish stock, stirring constantly until the boiling point is reached. Cook over low heat for 5 minutes. Add the salt, pepper, sugar, and lemon juice, and mix well. Beat the yolks in a bowl. Gradually add 1 cup of the sauce, beating constantly. Return this mixture to the saucepan and cook over low heat for 1 minute, stirring constantly. Do not allow to boil.

Serve the fish and the sauce separately. Tiny boiled and buttered potatoes are often served with the salmon. If desired, the salmon may be served cold. In that event the sauce should also be cold.

## SWEDISH MEATBALLS

KÖTTBULLER

¼ pound butter
1 onion, chopped
1 cup bread crumbs
1 cup light cream
1 pound beef, chopped
1 pound pork, chopped
½ pound veal, chopped

2 teaspoons salt
¾ teaspoon pepper
2 eggs, beaten
2 tablespoons chopped parsley
1 tablespoon flour
1½ cups heavy cream, scalded

Melt 3 tablespoons of the butter in a skillet. Add the onions and sauté for 10 minutes, stirring occasionally. Soak the bread crumbs in the cream.

Combine the beef, pork, and veal in a bowl. Add the sautéed onions, the bread crumbs, salt, pepper, eggs, and parsley. Mix well. Shape into 1-inch balls. Melt 3 tablespoons of the butter in a skillet and fry the balls in it until very brown, shaking the pan frequently. Be careful not to break the balls, and add butter as necessary. Remove the meat balls and keep warm.

Add the flour to the remaining butter in the skillet. Mix to a smooth paste. Gradually add the heavy cream, stirring constantly until the boiling point is reached. Cook over low heat for 5 minutes. Correct seasoning. Pour over the meat balls and serve.

## SWEDISH POT ROAST

### GRYTSTEK

| | |
|---|---|
| 3 teaspoons salt | 2 bay leaves |
| 2 teaspoons pepper | ½ teaspoon allspice |
| 5 pounds beef of cut suitable for pot roast | 3 carrots, sliced |
| | ¼ cup brandy |
| 4 tablespoons butter | 3 anchovy fillets |
| 3 onions, chopped | 1 tablespoon vinegar |
| 2 cups boiling water | 2 tablespoons flour |
| 4 tablespoons molasses | 1½ cups light cream |

Mix the salt and pepper together and rub into the meat thoroughly. Melt the butter in a large Dutch oven. Brown the meat on all sides. Add the onions and continue browning for 5 minutes. Add the water, molasses, bay leaves, allspice, carrots, and brandy and stir. Mash the anchovies in a small bowl and add the vinegar, mixing well. Add this mixture to the meat and stir well. Cover and cook over low heat for 2½ hours, or until tender.

Remove the meat from the Dutch oven and set it aside. Mix the flour and cream together until smooth and add to the gravy, stirring constantly until the boiling point is reached. Correct seasoning. Cook over low heat for 5 minutes. Remove the bay leaves. Carve the meat and serve with the gravy separately.

## ROAST LAMB IN THE SWEDISH MANNER

### STEKT LAMM

| | |
|---|---|
| 3 teaspoons salt | 1 cup hot double-strength coffee |
| 1 teaspoon pepper | ½ cup heavy cream |
| 1 leg of spring lamb | 1 tablespoon sugar |
| 3 onions, sliced | 2 tablespoons flour |
| 3 carrots, sliced | ¼ cup cold water |
| 1 cup stock or 1 cup canned consommé | |

Mix the salt and pepper together and rub into the leg of lamb thoroughly. Place it in a roasting pan with the sliced onions around the lamb. Roast in a 425° oven for 30 minutes. Reduce heat to 350° and add the carrots and stock. Roast for 30 minutes, then add the coffee, cream, and sugar. Roast for 22 minutes per pound (allowing for the hour the lamb has been roasting), or until the lamb is tender. Baste the meat frequently.

Remove the lamb from the pan. Force the gravy through a sieve. Mix the flour and water to a smooth paste in a saucepan. Gradually add the gravy, stirring constantly. Place over medium heat and cook until the mixture reaches the boiling point, stirring constantly. Correct seasoning, adding water if the gravy is too thick. Carve the meat and serve the gravy separately in a sauceboat.

## SEAFOOD SALAD

SALLAD JONAS

2 boiled lobsters
1 pound boiled shrimp
12 mussels (optional)
2 scallions (green onions), chopped, or 4 tablespoons chopped chives
3 tomatoes, cubed
1 tablespoon prepared mustard

¾ cup olive oil
¼ cup vinegar
2 tablespoons water
1 teaspoon salt
⅛ teaspoon pepper
1 head lettuce, finely shredded

Remove the lobster meat from the shells and cut into large pieces. Peel the shrimp and cut each one into four pieces. Combine the lobster meat, shrimp, mussels, onions, and tomatoes. Mix well. In a bowl mix the mustard and olive oil until smooth. Add the vinegar, water, salt, and pepper, and beat until well blended. Pour over the seafood mixture and mix carefully but thoroughly. Chill for 30 minutes. Arrange mounds of the seafood mixture on individual plates and cover with the shredded lettuce.

## SAFFRON COFFEECAKE

SAFFRANSBRÖD

1 cake or package yeast
¼ cup lukewarm water
½ teaspoon saffron
1 tablespoon brandy
⅛ teaspoon salt
4 cups sifted flour

1 cup sugar
1 cup milk
1 egg yolk, beaten
¼ pound butter, melted
1 egg, beaten
¼ cup ground almonds

Dissolve the yeast in the water and soak for 5 minutes. Dissolve the saffron in brandy and combine with the yeast mixture. Add salt and ½ cup of the flour. Mix well. Cover and set aside in a warm place for 1 hour. Mix ¾ cup of the sugar, the milk, egg yolk, and butter. Add the yeast mixture and remaining flour and mix well. Knead until smooth. Cover with a cloth and set aside in a warm place for 2 hours.

Knead on a lightly floured surface for 1 minute. Roll into eight strips about 1 foot in length. Take four of the strips, fasten them at one end, and braid them together. Repeat with the four remaining strips, making two loaves. If desired, the mixture may be divided in half (instead of making the eight strips) and shaped into two loaves.

Place in two buttered loaf pans. Cover and set aside in a warm place for 20 minutes. Preheat oven to 350°. Brush the tops of the loaves with the beaten egg and sprinkle with the remaining sugar and the almonds. Bake in a 350° oven for 25 minutes, or until lightly browned.


## APPLE CAKE WITH VANILLA SAUCE

ÄPPLEKAKA MED VANILJSÅS

| | |
|---|---|
| ¼ pound butter | 4 egg yolks |
| 3 cups stale spongecake crumbs or cracker crumbs | 4 tablespoons sugar |
| | 2 cups heavy cream |
| 2½ cups sweetened applesauce | 2½ teaspoons vanilla extract |
| 2 teaspoons cinnamon | |

Melt the butter in a skillet. Add the crumbs and cook over medium heat 5 minutes, stirring frequently. Butter an 8-inch square baking dish. Place a layer of crumbs on the bottom and add alternate layers of applesauce, cinnamon, and crumbs. Start and finish with the crumbs. Bake in a 350° oven for 30 minutes, or until set and delicately browned on top. Let cool, then turn out of the pan carefully.

Beat the egg yolks in the top of a double boiler. Add the sugar and beat well. Scald 1¼ cups of the cream and add it to the yolks, beating constantly. Place over hot water and cook until thick, stirring constantly. Remove from the hot water, add the vanilla, and let cool for 1 hour. Whip the remaining cream and fold it into the sauce. Cut the cake in squares and serve the sauce in a separate dish.

## TRADITIONAL SWEDISH CHRISTMAS DRINK

### GLÖGG

2 cups red wine (burgundy or claret)
2 cups port wine
1 tablespoon finely chopped orange or lemon peel
5 cardamom seeds
1 cinnamon stick (or 2 teaspoons powdered cinnamon)
5 cloves
¼ pound almonds, blanched
¼ pound seedless raisins
¼ pound cube sugar
2 cups brandy

A large copper kettle is the proper utensil for preparing *glögg*, but a large enamel or glass saucepan may be used. Combine the red wine and port in the saucepan over low heat. Take a piece of cheesecloth about 4 inches square and place in the center the orange peel, cardamom seeds, cinnamon, and cloves. Tie or sew the cheesecloth together securely, and place it in the wine mixture. Simmer for 20 minutes. Add the almonds and raisins and simmer for 10 minutes. Remove from the heat and discard the cheesecloth.

Place the cubes of sugar in a metal strainer and rest it on top of the saucepan if possible. Set the brandy aflame and pour it very gradually over the sugar. If there is any difficulty in lighting the brandy, warm it briefly. As the lighted brandy is poured over the sugar, it will caramelize. As an alternative, ½ cup of granulated sugar may be dissolved in the wine, and the brandy set aflame and poured into the wine. Serve hot in mugs.

## SWITZERLAND

This silent, majestic country known the world over for snow, winter sports, tourists, hotels, scenery, watches, and cheese, is comparatively little known for its cuisine. Since tourists flock to this land in tremendous numbers, the Swiss hotelkeepers have succumbed to pressure and serve the inevitable and apparently inescapable imitation-French hotel food known everywhere. The average tourist, too busy with his sight-seeing or skiing, leaves Switzerland under the impression that the Swiss people are the most hospitable in the world, are experts in putting holes in cheese, make the best watches in the world, but have practically nothing at all in the way of a national cuisine.

This is unfortunate because it is partially untrue. The Swiss do have their own food specialties, which may be tasted if the tourist will occasionally break away from the hotel *de luxe* and dine at a small village restaurant. There is much that will be of interest to the food-conscious visitor.

First, a brief explanation of Switzerland's background. It was formed principally from small segments of France, Italy, and Germany. These three languages are spoken to this day in Switzerland by a great number of persons. It is not surprising, therefore, to find that the cuisine has three distinct backgrounds—French in the west, Italian in the south, and German in the east and north.

Switzerland's contribution to the world of the gourmet consists largely of fine chocolates, cheese, wines, and liqueurs. The Swiss, like their neighbors the French, are very fond of wines and produce a substantial number of quite good types. The Neuchâtel and the Riesling-Sylvaner are probably the best known of these. The people prefer the dry white wines, and these are served as apéritifs, with food, and as refreshment any time during the day. Unfortunately many Swiss wines do not lend themselves to shipment, and may be fully enjoyed only in the country that produced them. Great favorites, too, are *kirsch*, a clear cherry brandy, and *marc*, a strong brandy made from the second pressing of the grape. Beer is well liked, particularly in the north and eastern portions of the country, which might be expected since those cantons are adjacent to Germany.

Although the Swiss cuisine is largely borrowed from its neighbors, the *fondue*, a melted cheese dish, may be said to be one of the truly national dishes. It is made with Swiss cheese, white wine, and *kirsch*. Etiquette decrees that pieces of toast be dipped into the *fondue*. *Râclette*, another national dish, is made by melting cheese before an open fire or stove, and is served with boiled potatoes. *Ramekins* are another cheese favorite.

Bern canton (province) has a local specialty in the *Berner Platte*, composed of assorted meats and sauerkraut; St. Gall canton boasts of a delicious veal sausage called *St. Galler Bratwurst;* Lucerne has a delicacy called *Kuegeli-Pastete*, a puff paste filled with sweetbreads, mushrooms, and other delicacies. The southern cantons feature Italian-style food.

Swiss chocolates are among the richest and smoothest in the world and are exported to the farthest corners of the earth.

## GRAVY SOUP

GERÖSTETE MEHLSUPPE

5 tablespoons butter or chicken fat
5 tablespoons flour
7 cups stock or 3 cans consommé and
2½ cans water

1 cup buttered croutons
¼ cup grated Swiss or Gruyère cheese

Melt the fat in a deep saucepan. Add the flour and stir well. Cook over low heat until a deep brown in color, stirring constantly to prevent burning. Gradually add the hot stock, stirring constantly until the boiling point is reached. Cover and cook over medium heat for 1½ hours, stirring occasionally. Correct seasoning. Serve with croutons on top and sprinkle grated cheese over each portion.

## SALMON, BASEL STYLE

LACHS, BASELER ART

6 slices fresh salmon
2 teaspoons salt
1 teaspoon pepper
4 tablespoons flour

¼ pound butter
2 onions, chopped
3 tablespoons stock or water

Sponge the salmon carefully but do not wash. Combine the salt, pepper, and flour and pat into the fish on all sides. Melt half of the butter in a skillet. Fry the salmon slices in it 5 to 8 minutes on each side or until golden brown. Place the fish on a heated platter and keep warm.

Melt the remaining butter in the same skillet. Sauté the onions over low heat for 15 minutes, stirring frequently, until they are soft and yellow but not browned. Pour the onions over the salmon. Place the stock or water in the same skillet, scraping any glaze or particles remaining in the pan. When the mixture boils, pour it over the fish. Sprinkle a little sweet paprika on the fish; chopped parsley may also be added. Serve with very thin slices of lemon. Although this is a comparatively simple dish, it is a great favorite of the Swiss.

## MEAT PLATTER, BERNE STYLE

BERNER PLATTE

1 smoked beef tongue
2 pounds ham or pork, or 1 pound of each
2 pounds short ribs of beef
3 pounds sauerkraut

¼ pound sliced bacon, half cooked and drained
½ pound smoked sausage (in one piece, if possible)

Place the tongue in a deep saucepan and cover with water. Bring to a boil and pour off the water. Cover with fresh boiling water. Cover and cook over medium heat for 1½ hours. Add the ham or pork and the short ribs of beef. Cover and cook for 2 hours, or until all the meats are tender. While the meats are cooking, combine the sauerkraut, bacon, and sausage in a saucepan. Cover and cook for 1½ hours. Slice the cooked meats and arrange on a platter with the sauerkraut in the center.

## ROAST BEEF, SOUTHERN STYLE

STUFFATO ALLA CHIASSESE

3 cloves garlic, minced
2 teaspoons salt
1 teaspoon pepper
4 tablespoons flour
6- to 8-pound rib roast of beef
2 tablespoons butter

2 onions, chopped
¼ pound sliced bacon, half cooked and drained
1 cup dry red wine
6 potatoes, peeled and quartered
3 tomatoes

Combine the garlic, salt, pepper, and flour and rub into the meat. Melt the butter in a large roasting pan on top of the stove. Add the onions and meat. Sear on all sides until well browned. Place the strips of bacon on top of the meat, fastening with toothpicks. Pour the wine over the meat.

Roast the meat in a 350° oven for 15 to 22 minutes per pound, depending on the degree of rareness desired. Baste occasionally. About 45 minutes before the meat is ready, add the potatoes and tomatoes. Small quantities of water may be added if required. Place the meat, potatoes, and tomatoes on a platter and serve hot.

## POTATO APPLES

FUNGGI

2 apples, pared and quartered
3 tablespoons sugar
3 cups water
3 tablespoons butter

1 onion, sliced
6 potatoes, peeled and cubed
1½ teaspoons salt
2 tablespoons cider

Combine the apples, sugar, and water in a saucepan. Bring to a boil and cook for 3 minutes.

Melt the butter in a large saucepan. Add the onion and sauté for 10 minutes, stirring frequently. Add the potatoes, salt, cider, and the apple mixture, including any liquid. Cover and cook for 30 minutes, or until very soft. Mix well. Serve hot in individual small dishes, together with meats or roasts.

## ONION SALAD

ZWIEBELN SALAT

4 tablespoons butter
4 large onions, sliced ½ inch thick
1 tablespoon flour

1 teaspoon salt
2 tablespoons vinegar

Melt the butter in a saucepan. Add the onions and sauté until light brown, stirring frequently. Sprinkle with the flour and cook for 3 minutes. Remove from the heat. Add the salt and vinegar and mix well. Serve hot or cold. The salad is particularly good when served with small, buttered, boiled potatoes as a separate course.

## THE SWISS NATIONAL CHEESE DISH

FONDUE

1 clove garlic
½ cup white wine
¼ pound Gruyère cheese, grated

2 teaspoons potato flour
2 tablespoons *kirsch* or dry sherry
12 slices toast

Rub an earthenware casserole or chafing dish with the garlic, then discard it. Pour the white wine into it and cook over medium heat for 2 minutes. Add the grated cheese and bring to the boiling point, stirring occasionally. In a cup, mix the potato flour and *kirsch* or sherry to a smooth paste and add to the cheese mixture, stirring constantly for 3 minutes, or until the mixture is thick. Cut the toast into 1-inch strips. Bring the casserole to the table and place the toast strips around it. Each guest spears a strip of toast with a fork and dips it into the *fondue*. This dish makes an excellent luncheon dish, or it may be served at a late supper.

## CHEESE TARTS

RAMEKINS

1 cup sifted flour
1 teaspoon salt
⅓ pound butter
⅓ cup heavy cream

½ pound Swiss cheese
1 tablespoon flour
4 eggs, beaten
Dash of pepper

Sift the flour and ½ teaspoon of the salt into a bowl. Add the butter, reserving 1 tablespoon. Work in the butter with the hand. Add 3 tablespoons of the cream and continue mixing until a ball of dough is formed. Wrap in wax paper and place in the refrigerator overnight, or for at least 2 hours. Roll out the dough ⅛ inch thick on a lightly floured surface. Line an unbuttered 9-inch pie plate or 6 small individual pie plates with the dough. Preheat oven to 375°.

Grate half of the cheese and cut the remaining half into tiny cubes. Combine the grated cheese, flour, remaining salt, remaining cream, eggs, and pepper in a bowl. Mix well and add the cubed cheese. Pour the mixture into the pie plate. Dot with the remaining butter. Bake in a 375° oven for 35 minutes if the 9-inch pie plate is used, or for 20 minutes if the smaller individual plates are used. Serve hot.

## HORSEHOOFS

STRÜZELS

| | |
|---|---|
| 2 cups sifted flour | ½ cup milk |
| 3 tablespoons sugar | 2 tablespoons seedless raisins |
| 2 tablespoons butter | 1½ teaspoons baking powder |
| 1 egg, beaten | Fat for deep-fat frying |

Sift the flour and sugar together into a bowl. Cut in the butter with a pastry blender or two knives. Add the egg and milk, mixing until well blended. Add the raisins and baking powder and again mix well. Shape a tablespoon of the mixture into a horseshoe. Heat fat in a deep saucepan to 360°. Drop the horseshoes into it and fry until golden brown. Drain and dust with powdered sugar. These pastries may be eaten either hot or cold.

## PEAR CAKE

BIRNENBROT

| | |
|---|---|
| 1 pound dried pears | 1 cup chopped walnuts |
| 1 cake or package yeast | ¼ cup seedless raisins |
| 1 cup milk, scalded and cooled | 1 cup sugar |
| ¼ cup melted butter | 2 tablespoons cinnamon |
| ¼ cup sugar | 1 tablespoon candied orange peel |
| 1 egg | 1 teaspoon grated lemon rind |
| 3¾ cups sifted flour | ½ cup *kirsch* or brandy |
| ½ teaspoon salt | |

Soak the pears in water to cover overnight. Combine the yeast and luke-warm milk in a bowl and mix until smooth. Set aside for 5 minutes. Add the butter, sugar, and egg and mix well. Sift the flour and salt together twice. Add to the yeast mixture gradually, mixing steadily. It may not be necessary to add all of the flour in order to make a dough. Knead the mixture until a stiff dough is formed. Cover and place in a warm place to rise until doubled in size, about 1½ hours. Punch the dough down and again allow to rise for 45 minutes.

Drain the pears well. Add fresh water and cook in a saucepan over medium heat until tender, about 30 minutes. Drain well and chop the pears finely. Combine the chopped pears, walnuts, raisins, sugar, cinnamon, orange peel, lemon rind, and *kirsch* or brandy and mix well.

Divide the dough into two parts, making one part half again as large as the other. Work the fruit and nut mixture into the smaller piece of dough. Roll out the larger piece of dough on a lightly floured surface so that it is sufficient to line and overlap a buttered 10-inch loaf pan. Place the dough-fruit mixture in the center of the pan and cover with the overlapping dough, sealing the edges well with a little water or egg white. Prick the top with a fork in several places. Preheat oven. Let rise for 20 minutes. Bake in a 375° oven for 45 minutes, or until lightly browned on top. The cake should keep well for more than a week. Serve hot or cold in slices. Although to American tastes this is suitable for serving as a cake, in Switzerland it is often used as a sweet bread.

*UKRAINE*

Although the U.S.S.R. is one political unit, it consists of numerous nations of which a principal one is the Ukraine, which has its own representative at the United Nations. Little Russia, the Ukrainians call their considerable area located just north of the Black Sea and immediately to the east of Poland. With a population of more than 30,000,000, whose capital city is located at Kiev, the Ukraine has a fine cuisine which differs considerably from that of Russia itself, though at the same time the two share many dishes in common.

Because the Ukraine is located on the Black Sea, fish is fairly important. Like the Russians, the Ukrainians also have a great liking for certain foods such as cucumbers, black breads, sour cream, and sauerkraut. Vodka, as in Russia, is the regional liquor. Tea is the beverage of the country, both winter and summer.

The type of food that is usually thought of as being Jewish-style was originally Ukrainian in origin. At one time the Ukraine had a very large Jewish population. About 1890 the Jews began to leave in large numbers and come to the United States to escape religious persecution. They brought with them the Ukrainian food customs, and these have been accepted as Jewish-style cooking, particularly in the New York City area. Such delicacies as *blintzes* and *varenikis* (little stuffed dough pockets) are now considered to be both Ukrainian and Jewish.

## TOMATO SOUP, UKRAINIAN STYLE

POMIDOROVA ZUPA

| | |
|---|---|
| 2 beef bones or ½ pound short ribs | 1 teaspoon sugar |
| 1 carrot, sliced | ¼ teaspoon pepper |
| 1 onion, chopped | 2 tablespoons flour |
| 1 cup shredded cabbage | ¾ cup sour cream |
| 7 cups water | 1 cup cooked rice |
| 2 pounds tomatoes, or 1 No. 2 can | 2 tablespoons chopped dill or parsley |
| 2 teaspoons salt | |

Place the bones, carrot, onion, cabbage, and water in a saucepan. Bring to a boil and skim the top carefully. Cook over low heat for 1 hour. Add the tomatoes, salt, sugar, and pepper. Cook over low heat for 45 minutes. Remove the bones and force the soup through a sieve.

Mix the flour and sour cream to a smooth paste. Add 1 cup of the soup, stirring constantly. Return this mixture to the balance of the soup, mixing well. Heat but do not allow it to boil. Place some rice in each soup plate, pour the hot soup over it, and sprinkle with dill.

## HERRING CROQUETTES

KOTLETI SLEDZIOWE

| | |
|---|---|
| 3 salt herring | 1 cup bread crumbs |
| ¼ pound butter | 1 egg, beaten |
| 1 onion, chopped | ⅛ teaspoon pepper |

Wash the herring thoroughly. Soak them overnight in water to cover, changing the water several times. Remove the skins and bones carefully.

155

Chop fine. Melt 3 tablespoons of the butter in a skillet. Add the onion and sauté for 10 minutes, stirring frequently. Add ½ cup of the bread crumbs. Cook for 15 minutes, stirring occasionally. Remove from heat. Add the egg, pepper, and chopped herring and mix well. Shape into croquettes of any desired size and dip in the remaining bread crumbs. Melt the remaining butter in a skillet. Fry the croquettes until brown on both sides. Serve with boiled potatoes.

## BAKED CHICKEN

PECHENE KURYATA

| | |
|---|---|
| 2 4-pound chickens, disjointed | 3 tablespoons water |
| 3 teaspoons salt | 1½ cups bread crumbs |
| 1 teaspoon pepper | ¼ pound butter |
| ¾ cup flour | 3 cups sour cream |
| 2 eggs | |

Wash and dry the chickens. Combine 2 teaspoons of the salt, ½ teaspoon of the pepper, and the flour, and lightly roll the chicken pieces in it. Beat the eggs and water together in a bowl. Dip the chicken in it, then roll in the bread crumbs. Melt half of the butter in a skillet and brown the chicken in it, adding more butter as needed. Arrange the chicken in a casserole or baking dish. Sprinkle with the remaining salt and pepper. Bake in a 375° oven for 25 minutes. Pour half the sour cream over the chicken. Bake 20 minutes longer, then add the rest of the sour cream. Bake until tender, about 30 minutes longer.

## BEETS AND APPLES

BURYAKE Z YABLOKAMY

| | |
|---|---|
| 4 large beets | ⅛ teaspoon pepper |
| 2 teaspoons cornstarch | 2 apples, peeled and grated |
| ¾ cup sour cream | 1 tablespoon lemon juice |
| 2 tablespoons butter | 2 teaspoons sugar |
| ½ teaspoon salt | |

Scrub the beets and cook in water to cover for 40 minutes. Drain. Peel and grate the beets. Mix the cornstarch and sour cream to a smooth paste in a saucepan. Add butter, salt, and pepper and mix well. Cook over low heat, stirring constantly until the boiling point is reached. Sprinkle the apples with lemon juice and sugar. Mix well and add to the sour cream mixture. Add the beets. Mix lightly. Cook over low heat for 3 minutes but do not allow to boil. Serve hot with roast fowl or roast meats.

## SAUERKRAUT SALAD
KVASHENA KAPUSTA SALAT

1½ pounds sauerkraut
  1 onion, chopped fine
  1 teaspoon sugar

½ teaspoon pepper
4 tablespoons salad oil
1 teaspoon caraway seeds

Wash the sauerkraut under cold water. If canned sauerkraut is used, it is advisable to wash it very thoroughly. Drain well. Chop fine. Add the onion, sugar, pepper, oil, and caraway seeds and mix well. Chill in the refrigerator for 30 minutes. Serve cold on lettuce leaves.

## CHEESE BLINTZES
BLINTZI Z SYROM

2 eggs
2 tablespoons salad oil
1 cup milk
¾ cup flour
½ teaspoon salt
4 tablespoons butter

¼ pound cream cheese
¼ pound cottage cheese
2 egg yolks
3 tablespoons sugar
1 teaspoon vanilla extract

Beat the eggs, oil, and milk together. Add the flour and salt and beat until smooth. Chill in the refrigerator for 30 minutes. The batter should be the consistency of cream. If too thick, add a little milk. Melt 1 teaspoon of the butter in a 7-inch frying pan. Pour a tablespoon of the batter into the pan, turning it quickly to cover the bottom of the pan. Fry for 1 minute on one side only. Remove from the pan and continue the process until the batter is used up. Stack the pancakes as they are made, with the fried side up.

Beat the cream cheese, cottage cheese, egg yolks, sugar, and vanilla until smooth. Place a tablespoon of the mixture on each pancake. Turn the two opposite sides in, then roll up carefully. Melt the remaining butter in a large frying pan and fry all the blintzes until they are lightly browned on both sides. Serve hot, with sour cream and a little sugar, if desired. They are also good cold.

## POPPY SEED AND HONEY PASTRY
LOMANCI Z MAKOM

1¼ cups flour
  ½ teaspoon salt
  ¼ pound butter
  4 tablespoons sour cream
  ¼ pound poppy seeds (about 1¼ cups)

¼ cup milk
1½ cups honey
½ cup nuts (filberts, walnuts, or almonds)
½ cup seedless raisins

157

Sift the flour and salt into a bowl. Work in the butter with the hand. Add the sour cream and continue mixing until a dough is formed. Chill for at least 3 hours. Preheat oven to 375°. Roll out the dough ⅛ inch thick on a lightly floured surface. Place it in a large pie plate or square pan. Prick the dough in several places with a fork. Bake in a 375° oven for 20 minutes, or until lightly browned. Remove from oven. Cool. Cut into ½-inch squares.

Grind the poppy seeds or have them ground in the store in which they were purchased. Combine the poppy seeds with the milk and soak for 10 minutes, or until the milk is absorbed. Place the honey in a saucepan and add the nuts, raisins, and poppy seeds. Cook over low heat for 5 minutes. Cool for 10 minutes. Pour the mixture into a serving bowl and gently add the pastry squares. Mix carefully. The mixture may be shaped into small balls and placed on a lightly floured plate. In the Ukraine the custom is to serve the entire dish, each guest helping himself with a spoon.

## BUCKWHEAT CREAM CAKE

LAKOMYNKAZ HRECHANYI MUKY

4 egg yolks
4 tablespoons sugar
4 tablespoons buckwheat flour
1 teaspoon baking powder
1 tablespoon grated lemon rind

4 egg whites
1 cup sour cream
3 tablespoons confectioners' sugar
1 cup sweetened cherries or strawberries (fresh, canned, or frozen), drained

Beat the yolks in a bowl. Add the sugar and beat until light. Add the buckwheat flour, baking powder, and lemon rind. Mix well. Beat the egg whites until stiff but not dry and fold them into the previous mixture gently. Preheat oven to 375°. Butter a 9-inch layer-cake pan and dust it lightly with bread crumbs. Pour the batter into it. Bake in a 375° oven for 20 minutes, or until a cake tester comes out clean. Cool and turn out onto a plate.

Whip the sour cream, add the sugar, and beat for a short additional period. Place the cream on top of the cake and arrange the fruit on top.

*YUGOSLAVIA*

Yugoslavia has many neighbors, its borders touching upon Italy, Austria, Hungary, Rumania, Bulgaria, Greece, and Albania. The Yugoslavs are rather antipathetic to the Italians, and the food of that country is not popular in Yugoslavia, but the others have contributed heavily to the local food customs. From Austria and Hungary the Yugoslavs have appropriated the many dishes flavored with paprika, such as *ribji guljaž*, a fish specialty made with paprika. In common with Rumania, the basic food of the peasant group is corn meal served in several different ways, but usually boiled and eaten as a porridge. As their neighbors, the Bulgarians, favor mutton, the Yugoslavs also appreciate lamb, often served with many different vegetables. The favorite of the Greeks, grape leaves stuffed with rice, veal, or lamb, is often seen in Yugoslav homes and restaurants. Even tiny Albania shares with her much larger neighbor to the north the custom of preparing vegetables in oil, as well as the frequent use of sour milk.

The people are simple and friendly, fond of good solid food and strong drink. The cuisine of the country has that great but swiftly disappearing virtue, simplicity. One cannot find here the intricate dishes of some of Yugoslavia's neighbors, but appetizing and wholesome food is usually available.

Plums grow particularly well in this agricultural land. In fact much of the national diet is based on plums, for they are used in many different ways. Some are dried, some are made into fine preserves. A favorite soft drink is a tablespoon of plum jam in a glass of ice-cold water. The people are also fond of prune brandies, known as both *šljiovica* and *slivovka*. There are endless varieties of prune brandy, but these are mostly consumed within the country itself. *Maraskino* is a liqueur of the highest quality. The country produces a wide variety of good red and white wines containing about twelve to sixteen per cent alcohol. There is good *pivo* (beer) to be had here, both light and dark.

159

The Yugoslavs are fond of onions, hot peppers, spicy pickles, and other relishes. A true Yugoslav can swallow hot red peppers one after the other without batting the proverbial eye. Visitors are well advised to approach the local "relishes" with a degree of caution.

A national favorite is the *ćevapčići*, a beef and veal sausage that is eaten by everyone. These are customarily roasted on open fires, as are most other meats. Another fine dish is *ćurka na podvarku* (turkey and sauerkraut). Rather simple desserts of fruit or cheese are eaten, although occasionally a rich confection filled with nuts and honey is prepared. Strong black coffee prepared in the Balkan style is the usual finish to a meal.

Cheese is a fine local product, characteristically excellent. In the Serbian portion of Yugoslavia there is *lipski*, somewhat similar to Port Salut. Croatia has *belo vrhnje*, a rich, delicious white cheese.


## BEAN SOUP

ČORBA OD PASULJA

2 cups dried white beans
1 pound ham, cut into 6 pieces
2 quarts water
3 tablespoons salad oil
3 onions, chopped

3 cloves garlic, minced
3 potatoes, peeled and diced
1 teaspoon sweet paprika
3 tablespoons chopped parsley

Soak the beans overnight in water to cover. Drain, and discard any imperfect beans. Cover with fresh water, bring to a boil, and drain. Add fresh water and cook for 1 hour, or until tender. In a separate saucepan cook the ham and the 2 quarts of water over medium heat for 1½ hours, or until tender. Heat the oil in a frying pan and add the onions, garlic, potatoes, paprika, and parsley. Sauté for 15 minutes, stirring frequently. Drain the beans and combine with the ham and water. Add the sautéed vegetable mixture. Cook over low heat for 15 minutes, mixing well. Serve hot.


## SPICY FISH, YUGOSLAV STYLE

RIBJI GULJAŽ

3 tablespoons olive oil
2 tablespoons chopped onion
2 teaspoons salt
1 teaspoon pepper
1 tablespoon sweet paprika
6 slices sea bass, fillet of sole, or
  similar fish

2 teaspoons tomato paste
2 tablespoons water
1 bay leaf
2 teaspoons vinegar
1 clove garlic, minced

Heat the olive oil in a large skillet. Add the onion and sauté for 5 minutes. Combine the salt, pepper, and paprika. Rub into each slice of fish. Place the fish in the skillet and brown on both sides. Add the tomato paste, water, bay leaf, vinegar, and garlic. Cook over low heat for 15 minutes, turning the fish once. Stir the sauce occasionally and baste the fish. Serve cold or hot.

## BEEF AND VEAL SAUSAGES

ČEVAPČIĆI

| | |
|---|---|
| 1 pound beef, ground | 2 teaspoons salt |
| 1 pound veal, ground | 1 teaspoon pepper |
| ⅛ pound beef fat, ground | 1 cup chopped onions (optional) |

Combine the ground beef, veal, and fat with the salt and pepper in a chopping bowl. Chop until well blended and fine in texture. Form into sausages about 2 inches long. Broil in a 500° oven fairly close to the heat. Turn frequently until the sausages are well browned. Serve with the chopped onions on the side. If served with the bean soup (see recipe in this section), it becomes a complete meal.

*Note: In Yugoslavia these sausages are usually broiled over an open fire. They make an excellent appetizer at a barbecue when prepared over a charcoal fire.*

## PRIEST'S LUNCH

POPINA JANJA YANJE

| | |
|---|---|
| 3 pounds brisket of beef, cut into 1-inch cubes | 3 cloves garlic, minced |
| 4 potatoes, peeled and diced | 1 teaspoon salt |
| 1 cup diced celery | 2 tablespoons paprika |
| 8 small white onions | 4 bay leaves |
| 3 tomatoes, quartered | 12 whole peppercorns |
| 4 tablespoons chopped parsley | 6 cups stock or 2 cans consommé and 2½ cans water |

Combine the beef, potatoes, celery, onions, tomatoes, parsley, garlic, salt, paprika, bay leaves, peppercorns, and stock in a deep casserole. Mix gently. Cover the casserole with a large piece of parchment paper or aluminum foil so that it slightly overhangs the outside edges of the casserole. Tie the paper with a string to make a tight seal. Place the casserole cover over the paper. Bake in a 350° oven for 2½ hours. Correct seasoning and serve directly from the casserole.

## ROAST TURKEY AND SAUERKRAUT

ČURKA NA PODVARKU

| | |
|---|---|
| 3 teaspoons pepper | 3 tablespoons chicken fat or butter |
| 3 teaspoons salt | 2 pounds sauerkraut |
| 1 teaspoon sweet paprika | 2 potatoes, grated |
| 12-pound turkey | 2 onions, grated |

Melt the fat in a saucepan. Add the sauerkraut, potatoes, onions, and 1 teaspoon of the pepper. Cook over high heat for 5 minutes, stirring constantly. Combine the remaining pepper, salt, and paprika and rub it into the turkey inside and out. If possible, this should be done the day before the turkey is to be cooked.

Place the sauerkraut mixture in a large roasting pan and put the turkey on top of it. Roast uncovered in a 350° oven. Allow 20 minutes per pound for roasting time. Turn the turkey several times during the roasting period, but end with the breast upward during the last 30 minutes. Baste frequently. Serve hot with the sauerkraut.

## HAZELNUT COOKIES

KOLAČI OD LJEŠNJAKA

| | |
|---|---|
| 3 eggs | 1 tablespoon zwieback crumbs or |
| ½ cup sugar | bread crumbs |
| 1 teaspoon vanilla extract | 2 cups ground hazelnuts (filberts) |
| 2 tablespoons brandy | ½ cup hazelnuts, halved |

Beat the eggs in a bowl until light. Add the sugar and continue beating. Add the vanilla, brandy, and crumbs. Mix well. Fold in the ground nuts carefully but thoroughly. Preheat oven to 300°. Shape a teaspoon of dough into a small ball. Place half of a hazelnut on each ball. If desired, the dough may be pressed flat. Bake in a 300° oven for 20 minutes, or until lightly browned.

## BUTTER CAKE

PUTICA

| | |
|---|---|
| 1 cake or package yeast | ¼ teaspoon salt |
| ⅓ cup lukewarm milk | 4 tablespoons butter |
| 3 cups sifted flour | 2 eggs, beaten |
| 1 cup sugar | |

Combine the yeast and milk in a cup. Set aside to soften for 5 minutes. Sift the flour, sugar, and salt together. Add the butter gradually, mixing well. Add the yeast mixture and mix well. Add the eggs. Mix until smooth and well blended. Cover with a cloth and allow to rise in a warm place for 2 hours. Meanwhile prepare the filling:

2 cups ground walnuts  
½ cup seedless raisins, chopped fine

2 tablespoons grated unsweetened chocolate  
⅔ cup honey

Mix the walnuts, raisins, chocolate, and honey together. Preheat oven to 375°. Roll out the dough ½ inch thick on a lightly floured surface. Spread the filling over the dough and roll up like a jelly roll. Place on a buttered baking sheet. Bake in a 375° oven for 25 minutes, or until lightly browned. Serve hot or cold. *Putica* is often served in the afternoon with coffee.

## WINE LIQUEUR

### VINSKI LIKER

1 quart red wine  
1¼ cups sugar

2 teaspoons vanilla extract  
2 cups brandy

Combine the wine and sugar in a saucepan. Bring to a boil and cook over medium heat for 10 minutes. Cool for 1 hour. Add the vanilla and brandy. Chill and serve cold.

# THE BALKANS, THE NEAR AND MIDDLE EAST

*Albania*

*Arabia, Iran, Iraq, and*

*Afghanistan*

*Bulgaria*

*Greece*

*Israel*

*Rumania*

*Syria, Lebanon, and Jordan*

*Turkey*

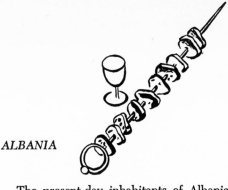

## ALBANIA

The present-day inhabitants of Albania are descended from hill tribes running back thousands of years. The people were once Christians but now are mostly of the Mohammedan faith. Since Mohammedans shun pork in any form, and inasmuch as few of the populace are Christians, the ham and other pork dishes of the Balkan countries to the north are seldom seen here. Under Turkish control for several centuries, the influence of that period has made itself strongly felt in the local culture and cuisine.

The nation's economy is largely agricultural, with a particular emphasis on dairy products, which are unusually high in quality. Yogurt and sour milk are probably more important in the country's diet than almost any other single item, and are consumed daily. A particular hot-weather favorite is a bowl of chopped raw vegetables filled with cold yogurt and sprinkled with some rough, coarse salt. It is similar in both appearance and taste to the Russian summertime specialty of sour cream (*smetana*) with chopped vegetables.

For some reason mint dishes appeal to the national palate to a rather surprising degree. Mint is quite popular all through the Near East and in the Arabic-speaking lands; the Albanians use mint in making meatballs, in lamb dishes, salads, and cold drinks.

The country is hardly a rich one, and progress is difficult because of poor road conditions, which hinder transportation. Filled with beautiful mountainous scenery and startling panoramas, the very things that have made the country beautiful have prevented its development. Good roads are always expensive, but good roads built on high mountains are clearly beyond the means of the country in the foreseeable future. The people therefore live from the soil and from the sea, taking full advantage of what nature has offered them. Actually they have little choice.

Vegetables and fruits grow in profusion, but the Albanian public has particular favorites such as okra, eggplant, peppers, and artichokes. These are usually prepared in the so-called Greek fashion, with plenty of olive oil and sometimes with the addition of tomatoes.

Chicken dishes are good, particularly when prepared in the Albanian fashion and stuffed with certain ingredients, varied according to what is available to the housewife. Lamb and mutton are naturally the meat favorites, as might be expected in a country located in the Near East and populated by Mohammedans. The cuisine is not complicated and the average Albanian peasant does not have a wide choice, but his food is almost always simple and good.

The drinks of the country include *raki,* the odd-flavored mulberry brandy known also in Turkey in a slightly different form. Since the countryside is laden with large, beautiful grapes during the harvest period, there is always plenty of wine of adequate quality, though seldom of exceptional or top rank. Black coffee, similar to the Turkish version, is also a favorite beverage.

Most of the meat dishes of the Near East are eaten in Albania, although they are handled somewhat differently than they would be, for example, in Turkey or Syria. The names, too, differ, but the lamb taste is almost always present.

## YOGURT SOUP

### TANABOUR

| | |
|---|---|
| ½ cup pearl barley | 2 cups yogurt |
| 4 cups stock or 2 cans consommé and 1 can water | 1 cup sour cream |
| 1 teaspoon salt | 1 egg |
| ½ teaspoon pepper | 4 tablespoons melted butter |
| | 2 tablespoons chopped parsley |

Soak the barley overnight in water to cover. Drain well. Combine with the stock, salt, and pepper in a saucepan. Cook over low heat for 2 hours, or until the barley is soft. Beat the yogurt, sour cream, and egg in a bowl. Gradually add 1 cup of the soup, beating constantly to prevent curdling. Return this mixture to the balance of the soup, beating well while adding. Add the butter and parsley, and stir well. Correct seasoning. Heat but do not allow to boil.

## LEEK AND COTTAGE CHEESE PIE

### BUREK ME PRESH

| | |
|---|---|
| 1¾ cups flour | ½ cup milk |
| 1¾ teaspoons salt | 1 pound cottage cheese |
| 1 cup water | 2 eggs |
| 1½ cups melted butter | ⅛ teaspoon pepper |
| 6 leeks or 12 scallions (white and green part), sliced thin | |

Sift the flour and 1 teaspoon of the salt together. Add the water and mix until a dough is formed. Knead gently. Roll the dough on a lightly floured surface as thin as possible. Brush half of the melted butter on the dough. Cut into squares approximately 3 by 3 inches; there should be about 12 in all. Place the squares on top of each other, 7 in one pile and 5 in the other. Set aside.

Melt 3 tablespoons of the butter in a saucepan. Add the leeks and sauté for 5 minutes, stirring frequently. Add the milk, stir, and cook over medium heat for 2 minutes. Beat the cottage cheese, eggs, pepper, and remaining salt together. Combine with the leeks and mix well. Preheat oven to 400°.

Roll and stretch the pile containing the 7 squares of dough, leaving them still in a pile, so that they cover a 9-inch buttered pie plate. Pour the cottage cheese mixture on top. Roll and stretch the other pile so that it is large enough to cover the top of the pie plate. Seal the edges carefully, pressing down with the edges of a fork. Pour the remaining butter on top. Bake in a 400° oven for 30 minutes. Reduce the heat to 325° and bake 15 minutes longer. Serve hot or cold, in pie-shaped wedges.

## ROAST STUFFED CHICKEN

PULE MEDROP

⅓ cup butter
2 cups bread crumbs
¼ cup seedless raisins
¼ cup currants
2 tablespoons chopped black walnuts
2 tablespoons chopped hazelnuts
2 tablespoons chopped pine nuts
2 tablespoons chopped almonds
¼ cup sugar
¼ cup stock or ½ bouillon cube dissolved in ¼ cup hot water
2 teaspoons salt
¼ teaspoon pepper
1 large roasting chicken

Melt 4 tablespoons of the butter in a saucepan and add the bread crumbs. Sauté for 5 minutes, stirring occasionally. Add the raisins, currants, nuts, sugar, and stock. Mix well. If mixture appears too dry, add a little more stock.

Mix salt and pepper together and rub into the chicken both inside and out. Stuff the chicken and close the opening carefully with thread or with skewers. Brush the chicken with the remaining butter. Roast in a 350° oven for 2½ hours, or until tender. Add ½ cup hot water after 1 hour and baste the chicken frequently with pan drippings during the roasting period.

## VEGETABLE CASSEROLE

GJELLE ME ZARZAVATA

6 potatoes, peeled and sliced thin
4 tomatoes, chopped
3 carrots, sliced thin
¼ cup chopped celery
2 onions, chopped fine
2 cloves garlic, minced

3 tablespoons chopped parsley
1½ teaspoons salt
½ teaspoon pepper
2 cups water
¼ cup olive oil

Place the potatoes in a shallow, buttered baking dish. Mix the tomatoes, carrots, celery, onions, garlic, parsley, salt, and pepper together. Spread over the potatoes and add the water. Bake in a 375° oven for 45 minutes. Pour the olive oil over the vegetables. Continue baking for 15 minutes. This dish may be served hot or cold.

## SWEET SESAME BISCUITS

ISMIR SIMIT

2 eggs
⅓ cup sugar
2 tablespoons milk
⅓ cup melted butter

1½ cups sifted flour
¾ teaspoon baking powder
¼ cup sesame seeds or ¼ cup ground
  blanched almonds

Beat 1 egg in a bowl. Add the sugar and beat until light. Add the milk and melted butter, and mix well. Sift the flour and baking powder together. Gradually add to the previous mixture, kneading until a dough is formed. If the dough is too soft, add a little more flour. Divide into about 18 small balls, or break off 18 pieces of dough. Roll each ball between the hands into a 9-inch strip. Fold each strip in thirds. Pinch the ends together. Place them on a buttered baking sheet. Preheat oven to 350°. Beat the remaining egg and brush some on each biscuit. Sprinkle with the sesame seeds or almonds. Bake in a 350° oven for 20 minutes, or until delicately browned.

## ALMOND PUFF PASTRY

EMATOR

1 cup water
¼ pound butter
1 cup sugar

1 teaspoon almond extract
2 cups sifted flour
¼ cup blanched almonds

Combine the water, butter, sugar, and almond extract in a saucepan.

168

Bring to a boil and cook until butter and sugar are completely melted. Add the flour all at once, beating vigorously. Cook over low heat for 5 minutes, beating constantly. Preheat oven to 325°. Spread the mixture on a greased jelly roll pan, about 10 by 15 inches, or use two 8-inch square pans. Cut into squares or diamonds with a sharp knife and place an almond in the center of each. Bake for 15 minutes, then place under the broiler for a minute to brown the top.

## ARABIA, IRAN, IRAQ, AND AFGHANISTAN

These countries are joined together in this section for several reasons: they are neighbors, they are Arabic-speaking, they share the same religion, but primarily they are combined because their cuisines follow a very close pattern. It is the purpose of this section to point out the similarities and differences that exist.

Arabia is a fabled land of sand, oases, palm trees, and sheiks, but a three-letter word already foretells the coming of civilization in the shape of cornflakes, air conditioning, chewing gum, modern plumbing, and Marilyn Monroe. The fact that underneath Arabia's sands are untold billions of gallons of o-i-l means that inevitably the sheiks of the future will be riding in purple Cadillac convertibles and eating Popsicles.

What was once biblical Mesopotamia is known today as Iraq. The famous city of Bagdad, curiously unaltered, still exists. The market places

169

are as facinating as they were two thousand years ago; only the ultra-critical will carp because Elizabeth Arden products have replaced the myrrh and incense of yesteryear, and the long-playing phonograph records on sale are more practical than lyres.

Fabulous Persia has been superseded by present-day Iran, but many of its former colorful ways and customs remain. Like a Fitzpatrick travel talk in color, the streets and market places are lively beyond our imagination.

Afghanistan is a place of mystery, almost inaccessible even today. Its scenery is of compelling grandeur often almost unbelievable. It is hardly a tourist land; there are no motels, and getting about the country is quite difficult since there are few roads, and Afghanistan has no railroad, at least at present.

Mohammedans are forbidden to drink wines, but in all the countries except Afghanistan some strong liquor is produced and even consumed. The explanation lies in the fact that Moslems are not specifically prohibited from drinking distilled liquors, since this process was not invented until after the death of the prophet, whereas wine was already known. The prohibition is therefore only against wine, according to religious scholars. At varying times many nations have attempted to prohibit the manufacture, sale, and consumption of alcoholic beverages. In our own country this attempt had an indifferent success. The one country that has succeeded in enforcing a strict prohibition is Afghanistan, where it has been one hundred per cent effective as to the local population. Erstwhile rum-runners are not advised to head for this country, for customers would be very scarce even if liquor could be smuggled into the country. Only the occasional traveler is permitted to bring in any alcoholic beverages.

The people of this region were historically nomads, almost always on the move with the exception of those in a few certain areas. Meat is usually prepared in the nomad fashion. Since pork is forbidden, lamb is almost always the meat of these countries—that is, when it is available. A prime favorite, even today, is a whole young lamb roasted over an open fire. A good trencherman can manage several pounds of meat at a time. The other usual treatment of lamb is the familiar *kebab*, or meat roasted on a skewer. Although *kebabs* may be made with fish or vegetables, lamb is preferred. Poultry and wild game, particularly in Afghanistan, are important to those lucky enough to afford such delicacies.

Certain regions have fish, but it is often out of reach of the general public because of the high price. Those who can afford it regard fish as a welcome change in their somewhat limited diet. In Iraq there is the fresh-water *chaboute*, similar to trout, and much of this comes from the Euphrates River. Shellfish are not highly regarded even where they are available.

With almost every dish there is rice, sometimes merely plain boiled, but often combined with spices, nuts, and other ingredients. The poor eat rice to stay their hunger, but the rich eat rice because they feel that no meal is complete without it. Semolina dishes are also appreciated here, notably the *couscous*, a recipe for which is in the section on Northern and Central Africa.

All fresh vegetables are in great demand, but eggplant evidently appeals to the local palate more than any other. Raw vegetables such as cucumbers, radishes, and green onions are made into cool salads to refresh those who have been out in the hot sun. In Iran the guest will find beautiful salads covered with dressings made of sugar and honey. Apparently sweet foods satisfy the taste of the people, for many dishes are unexpectedly found to be soaked in cloying sweetness, in contradistinction to the Western trend toward crisp, non-fattening foods.

Fruits and vegetables are often very good; in Afghanistan the melons, nuts, and grapes are worthy of their famous reputation. Of course figs and dates are of tremendous importance as foods throughout the region. Iraq is noted for its dates, the principal food of many peasants.

Cold drinks of all sorts are popular, particularly yogurt, the cultured milk, *doogh*, a buttermilk drink, and numerous fruit and ground nut drinks.

Almost everyone drinks tiny thimblefuls of sweet black coffee with the greatest frequency, but since the cups are so small, this is not too surprising. It is also interesting to report that tea is consumed on a large scale, often with the addition of mint.

## ARABIC STUFFED PEPPERS

### FLEIFELI MEHSHIA

| | |
|---|---|
| 12 green peppers, uniform size | 2 teaspoons salt |
| 1½ pounds beef, ground | ½ teaspoon pepper |
| 1 tomato, peeled and chopped | ¾ cup rice, half-cooked and drained |
| 2 onions, chopped | ½ cup canned tomato sauce |
| 3 tablespoons chopped parsley | 1 cup water |

Cut a ½-inch piece off the top of each pepper. Scoop out the seeds carefully. Mix the beef, tomato, onions, parsley, salt, pepper, and rice together. Stuff the peppers with this mixture. Place them in a baking dish. Pour the tomato sauce and water over them. Bake in a 350° oven for 1¼ hours, basting frequently. Add water to the pan if necessary.

*Note: If there is too much meat mixture for the peppers, form them into balls and place in the baking dish.*

**171**

## ARABIC LENTIL SOUP

### SHOURABAT ADAS

½ cup chick-peas
½ cup lentils (pink, if available)
½ cup *bourghol* (cracked wheat)
2 quarts water

3 tablespoons butter
2 onions, chopped
2 teaspoons salt
1 teaspoon pepper

Soak the chick-peas and lentils overnight in water to cover. Drain well. Place them in a saucepan with the *bourghol* and the water. Cover and cook over low heat for 1½ hours, or until the ingredients are tender. Melt the butter in a saucepan. Add the onions and sauté until brown, about 15 minutes, stirring frequently. Add to the soup, together with the salt and pepper. Cook for 10 minutes. Correct seasoning. To make a very smooth soup, run the mixture in an electric blender for 1 minute. Serve hot.

## STUFFED LAMB

### KABOURGA

3 tablespoons butter
1 cup rice, washed and drained
2 onions, chopped
1 green pepper, chopped
3 tablespoons chopped parsley
3 teaspoons salt
1½ teaspoons pepper

2 tablespoons chopped nuts or whole
    pine nuts
1 cup boiling water
2 cloves garlic, minced
4 pounds breast of lamb and ribs,
    with pocket for stuffing
1 can tomato sauce and 1 can water

Melt the butter in a saucepan. Add the rice, onions, and green pepper and sauté for 10 minutes, stirring frequently. Add the parsley, 1 teaspoon of the salt, ½ teaspoon of the pepper, the nuts, and the boiling water. Cover and cook over low heat for 10 minutes. Drain well.

Rub the lamb with the remaining salt and pepper and the garlic. Stuff the pocket with the rice mixture. Place the lamb in a roasting pan and pour the tomato sauce and water over it. Roast in a 350° oven for 2 hours, basting frequently.

## EGGPLANT STUFFED WITH LAMB AND NUTS

### SHEIKH EL-MIHSHIE

⅓ cup salad oil
3 eggplants, cut in half
2 pounds lamb, ground fine
2 teaspoons salt

1 teaspoon pepper
½ cup pine nuts or pistachios
1 can tomato soup
1 cup water

Heat 3 tablespoons of the oil in a skillet. Place the eggplants, unpeeled, in the oil and fry for 5 minutes on the cut side and for 10 minutes on the skin side. Heat the remaining oil in a separate skillet. Add the lamb, salt, and pepper and sauté for 10 minutes, stirring occasionally. Add the nuts and mix well.

Arrange the eggplants in a casserole. Slash each eggplant lengthwise in several places. Stuff the slashes with the lamb mixture. Combine the tomato soup and water and pour over the eggplants. Bake in a 350° oven for 1 hour. Serve hot.

## ROAST CHICKEN WITH SWEET STUFFING

DUGGAG MUHAMMAR

¼ pound butter
3 onions, chopped
Gizzard and livers of chicken
1½ cups rice, half-cooked
3 tablespoons chopped parsley
2 hard-cooked eggs, chopped

1 cup pistachio nuts
½ cup seedless raisins
1½ tablespoons salt
1½ teaspoons pepper
2 5-pound roasting chickens

Melt the butter in a saucepan. Add the onions and sauté for 10 minutes. Grind the gizzard and livers and add to the onions. Cook over low heat 10 minutes, stirring frequently. Add the rice, parsley, eggs, nuts, raisins, 2 teaspoons of the salt, and ½ teaspoon of the pepper. Mix well.

Combine the remaining salt and pepper and rub into the chickens, inside and out. Stuff the chickens with the previous mixture and fasten the openings with skewers or thread. Roast in a 350° oven for 2 hours, or until tender. Baste frequently with the pan juices.

## LENTILS AND RICE

MJDARA

2 cups dried lentils
3 cups boiling water
¾ cup rice
2 teaspoons salt

½ teaspoon pepper
½ cup olive oil
2 onions, chopped

Wash the lentils carefully and remove any imperfect ones. Soak overnight in water to cover. Drain well. Place them in a saucepan with the boiling water. Bring to a boil and cook over low heat for 1¼ hours. Add the rice, salt, and pepper and cook for 15 minutes, stirring occasionally. Add water if necessary. Heat the olive oil in a saucepan. Add the onions and sauté for 15 minutes, stirring occasionally. Add to the lentils and cook for 5 minutes. Correct seasoning.

## SQUASH CASSEROLE

MASBAHET ED-DARWEESH

| | |
|---|---|
| 2 pounds zucchini or yellow squash | 4 eggs, beaten |
| 2 teaspoons salt | ¾ cup bread crumbs |
| 1 cup grated American or Cheddar cheese | 3 tablespoons chopped parsley |
| ½ cup cottage cheese | ½ teaspoon pepper |
| | 3 tablespoons butter |

Grate the squash. Add the salt and set aside for 30 minutes. Squeeze all the liquid from the squash and discard. Mix the grated cheese and cottage cheese together. Add the squash, beaten eggs, bread crumbs, parsley, and pepper and mix well. Pour into a buttered baking dish and dot with butter. Bake in a 350° oven for 45 minutes.

## STRING BEANS WITH OLIVE OIL

LUBEY BE-ZEIT

| | |
|---|---|
| ½ cup olive oil | 1 cup tomato juice |
| 4 onions, chopped | 1 teaspoon salt |
| 2 pounds fresh or 2 packages frozen string beans | ½ teaspoon pepper |

Heat the olive oil in a saucepan. Add the onions and cook over low heat for 15 minutes, stirring frequently. Do not allow the onions to brown. Add the beans. Cover and cook over low heat for 15 minutes, stirring occasionally. Add the tomato juice, salt, and pepper. Cook over low heat for 15 minutes. Let cool. Serve cold.

## MIXED SALAD

FATTOUSH

| | |
|---|---|
| 3 tomatoes, cubed | 4 sprigs fresh mint, chopped, or 1 tablespoon dried mint |
| 2 cucumbers, peeled and diced | ½ cup olive oil |
| 1 green pepper, chopped | ¼ cup lemon juice |
| 8 scallions (green onions), sliced thin | 1 teaspoon salt |
| 4 tablespoons chopped parsley | 2 cups bread cubes, as small as possible |

Combine the tomatoes, cucumbers, green peppers, scallions, parsley, and mint in a bowl. Mix the olive oil, lemon juice, and salt together. Pour over the vegetables. Add the bread cubes and toss lightly. Chill for 1 hour before serving.

## STUFFED BAKED APPLES

TEFFAH BIL-FORN

¼ cup seedless raisins
6 large baking apples
1 cup sugar
½ cup cooked rice

¼ cup melted butter
1½ teaspoons cinnamon
2 cups water

Soak the raisins in hot water for 10 minutes. Cut a 1-inch-thick slice off the top of each apple and reserve the tops. Scoop out the centers of the apples carefully so as not to break the skin. Sprinkle 1 teaspoon of the sugar in each. Drain the raisins. Combine with the rice, butter, and ¼ cup of the sugar and mix well. Stuff the apples with the mixture and sprinkle each apple with the cinnamon. Replace the tops of the apples.

Place in a buttered baking dish. Sprinkle the remaining sugar over and around the apples. Add the water. Bake in a 325° oven for 45 minutes. Baste frequently. These may be served as a dessert, hot or cold. They may also be served with roast meats or poultry as a garnish.


## FARINA NUT DESSERT

IMRIG HELVA

1 cup milk
1 cup water
1 cup sugar

4 tablespoons butter
1 cup uncooked farina
¼ cup pine nuts or chopped almonds

Combine the milk, water, and sugar in a saucepan. Cook over low heat until the mixture boils. Remove from the heat. Melt the butter in a saucepan. Add the farina and nuts. Cook over low heat, stirring constantly, until the farina is light brown. Gradually pour the milk mixture over it, stirring constantly until the boiling point is reached. Cover and cook over low heat until the liquid is absorbed, stirring frequently.

When all the liquid is absorbed, remove from the heat and set aside for 15 minutes, covered. Serve warm but not hot. Cinnamon may be sprinkled on each portion.

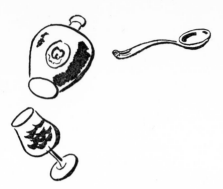

## BULGARIA

The food of Bulgaria bears considerable resemblance to that of its Balkan neighbors. This is not surprising in view of the troubled history of these nations during the past few centuries, during which the borders of the countries changed with great regularity. However, the diet of the Bulgarian peasant is more healthful than that of any other Balkan country if local chauvinists can be believed. According to proud Bulgarians, the average peasant eats raw onions and garlic, drinks fully of his beloved yogurt, and eats his bacon raw. This diet must be healthful, for it is apparently true that Bulgarians live longer than any other European group. Octogenarians are commonplace; to attract any attention in this land of sprightly oldsters you must be at least a centenarian.

Many people believe that yogurt is paramount in importance with regard to the health of the Bulgarians, for it is the one article in their diet that helps to explain their astonishing longevity. Yogurt, a cultured milk now quite common in the United States, probably originated in Bulgaria, though it is eaten in almost all the countries at the eastern end of the Mediterranean. The milk contains a beneficial bacillus which some experts think aids digestion and physical well-being. Certainly it must be admitted that Bulgarians consume fabulous quantities of this product, which resembles sour milk to a considerable extent. Yogurt appears at every meal, is used for almost every culinary purpose, and is apparently relished equally by the peasants and the city people.

The country is agricultural, and produces a large crop of grains of many different types. A rather poor nation in spite of its abundant soil, the people lean heavily on beans, lentils, rice, wheat, and other grains for the substantive basis of their food. The recipe for *fassoul yahnia* is typical of the bean dishes so popular in the nation.

Facing the Black Sea, the Bulgarians like the locally caught fruits of that sea and make some fine dishes of them, treating the fish in a manner similar to that employed by their neighbors. Raw salads are among the enthusiasms of the populace, and these, together with the local fondness for yogurt, support a nation of health faddists such as Gayelord Hauser might dream about. The recipe for *meshana salata,* or mixed salad with roast green peppers, is but one of many Bulgarian salads.

Meals end with dessert and black coffee. In season there will probably be fresh fruit; usually they serve dried fruit or fruit compote when fresh fruits are not available. The people also enjoy the rich, sticky, honey-laden dessert *baklawa,* which is a great favorite throughout the Near East.

Bulgarians drink freely of their local brandies, which are quite high in potency. Since the country is filled with vineyards, wines are a national pride. Most of these are good but not extraordinary, though a few vintages are exceptional. *Greyano vino,* a hot wine and spice drink, is much appreciated during cold weather.

## SOUP WITH MEAT BALLS

SOUPA SUS TOPCHETA

| | |
|---|---|
| 1 pound short ribs of beef and several bones | 1 teaspoon black pepper |
| | 1 pound chopped beef |
| 3 quarts water | 1 tablespoon vinegar |
| 2 onions | 2 tablespoons chopped parsley |
| 1 stalk celery | 3 eggs |
| 2 sprigs parsley | ½ cup flour |
| 1 turnip or parsnip | 1 cup uncooked rice |
| 1 carrot | 1 tablespoon butter |
| 1¼ tablespoons salt | 3 tablespoon lemon juice |

Combine the short ribs, bones, water, 1 onion, celery, parsley, turnip, and carrot in a saucepan. Bring to a boil and cook over medium heat for 3 hours. Strain the broth and add 3 teaspoons of the salt and ½ teaspoon of the pepper to it. Mix the chopped beef with the vinegar, chopped parsley, and remaining salt and pepper. Separate 1 egg and add the white to the meat mixture, reserving the yolk. Mix all together well. Shape into 1-inch balls and roll in the flour.

Bring the broth to the boiling point and add the rice. Cook for 10 minutes. Add the meat balls and cook 15 minutes longer. Chop the remaining onion. Melt the butter in a saucepan. Add the onion and sauté for 10 minutes, stirring frequently. Sprinkle 1 tablespoon of the flour on it, stirring constantly. Add 1 cup of the broth, again stirring constantly. Return this mixture to the balance of the broth. Cook over low heat for 10 minutes. Beat the eggs and the remaining yolk in a bowl. Add the lemon juice. Add 2 cups of the broth, stirring constantly. Return this mixture to the balance of the broth, mixing well. Correct seasoning. Serve hot. The reserved meat may be served in a separate dish with the soup or put aside for future use.

## FRIED BRAINS CROQUETTES

### KIUFTETA OT MOZAK

3 calves' brains
2 cups water
1 tablespoon vinegar
¼ pound butter
1 onion, chopped
1 slice white bread, trimmed
¼ cup milk

1 teaspoon salt
½ teaspoon pepper
2 tablespoons chopped parsley
3 eggs, beaten
¼ cup flour
½ cup bread crumbs

Wash the brains. Place in a saucepan with the water and vinegar. Bring to a boil and cook for 10 minutes. Drain. Plunge into cold water and set aside for 30 minutes. Drain. Remove the membrane and chop fine. Melt 2 tablespoons of the butter in a saucepan. Add the onion and sauté for 10 minutes, stirring frequently. Soak the bread in the milk for 5 minutes. Squeeze all the liquid out of it. Combine the brains, sautéed onion, bread, salt, pepper, and parsley together, and chop until smooth. Add 2 of the eggs, mixing until well blended. Shape into small croquettes. Dip in flour, then in the remaining egg, and finally in the bread crumbs. Melt the remaining butter in a saucepan and fry until brown on both sides. Serve at once.

## CHICKEN STEW

### PILE YAHNIA

¼ pound butter
2 4½-pound chickens, disjointed
3 onions, chopped
3 teaspoons salt
1 teaspoon paprika

2 tablespoons flour
2 tablespoons tomato paste
1½ cups water
1 pound uncooked chestnuts,
   peeled

Melt the butter in a saucepan. Add the chicken and brown on all sides. Add the onions. Cover and cook over medium heat until the onions begin to brown. Add the salt, paprika, and flour, mixing well. Mix the tomato paste and water together and add to the previous mixture, stirring well. Add the chestnuts. Cover and cook over low heat for 2 hours, or until the chicken is tender. Stir occasionally. Add water if the saucepan becomes dry. Serve hot.

## BEAN STEW

### FASSOUL YAHNIA

2 cups dried white beans
1 cup olive or salad oil
4 onions, chopped
2 teaspoons paprika

2 teaspoons salt
⅛ teaspoon thyme
½ cup vinegar

Soak the beans overnight in water to cover. Drain carefully. Add fresh water and boil for 1½ hours, or until tender. Drain. Heat the olive oil in a saucepan. Add the onions and sauté for 10 minutes, stirring frequently. Add the beans, paprika, salt, thyme, and vinegar. Cook over low heat for 15 minutes. Stir carefully a few times. Correct seasoning. Serve hot or cold.

## CHEESE POTATOES

### KARTOFI SUS SIRENE

8 potatoes, peeled and sliced thin
1 pound cottage cheese
1½ cups melted butter
2 teaspoons salt

1 teaspoon black pepper
2 eggs
1 cup yogurt

Place a layer of potatoes in a buttered casserole dish. Mix the cheese and butter together and spread a layer on top of the potatoes. Sprinkle with some of the salt and pepper. Continue with layers of potatoes, salt, pepper, and the cheese mixture until the ingredients are used up. Bake in a 375° oven for 30 minutes. Beat the eggs and yogurt together and pour over the top layer of the casserole. Bake 20 minutes longer, or until the egg mixture is set and lightly browned. Serve hot, directly from the casserole.

## MIXED SALAD WITH ROAST PEPPERS

### MESHANA SALATA

4 green peppers
3 tomatoes, sliced
2 onions, sliced
2 cucumbers, sliced

3 tablespoons vinegar
½ cup olive oil
1 teaspoon salt

Wash and dry the peppers. Place them on a fork, one at a time, and hold over a flame until the skin turns brown. Peel off the skin and cut the peppers in 1-inch strips. Chill for 1 hour. Combine the peppers, tomatoes, onions, and cucumbers in a salad bowl. Mix the vinegar, oil, and salt together and pour over the salad. Toss carefully and chill. Serve cold.

## BRANDIED FRUIT SALAD

FRUKTOVA SALATA

| | |
|---|---|
| 3 apples, peeled and sliced thin | 1 cup melon balls, fresh or frozen |
| 3 pears, peeled and sliced thin | ½ cup sugar |
| 2 oranges, peeled and sliced thin | 2 cups white wine |
| 1 cup pitted cherries, fresh or frozen | ½ cup brandy |

Combine the apples, pears, oranges, cherries, and melon balls. Sprinkle with the sugar. Mix the wine and brandy together. Pour over the fruit and mix gently but thoroughly. Chill for at least 3 hours. Serve very cold.

## HOT WINE AND SPICES

GREYANO VINO

| | |
|---|---|
| 6 cups red wine | 3 cloves |
| 3 apples, peeled and sliced thin | ¼ cup sugar |
| 2 teaspoons cinnamon | 1 teaspoon lemon juice |

Combine the wine, apples, cinnamon, cloves, sugar, and lemon juice in a saucepan. Bring to a boil and cook over low heat for 20 minutes. Strain. Return the strained mixture to the saucepan and reheat. Serve very hot.

*GREECE*

There is a great difference of opinion as to whether certain dishes are Greek, Turkish, or Armenian in origin. Since the borders of these countries have changed many times within the past century, it is impossible at this late date to determine the exact origin of any particular dish. Although certain dishes have become the particular favorites of a given country, this is not necessarily positive proof of the origin of the dish in question. This is especially true of the food of Greece and its neighbors, which in general is very similar. Each country, on the other hand, has a few items which are more or less confined to that country. Forgiveness is sought of those who feel that their national dishes have been misplaced.

Greece does not have an extensive cuisine, for it is still largely an agricultural country, undeveloped by Western industrial standards. The diet of its people, outside the big cities, is extremely limited. Many peasants exist principally by means of the olive trees which they grow, eating the olives for their meals and using the oil for cooking. By and large Greek food consists of fish, lamb, olives, fruits, and nuts. Fruits are of excellent quality.

The people are fond of fish dishes, customarily made with olive oil, garlic, and tomatoes. Shellfish is very popular, but usually the catch is not extensive. Octopus, squid, and mussels, in addition to the more usual varieties, are much appreciated by all the people. Rock lobsters are considered a great delicacy but are relatively scarce.

The favorite soups are fish stews, lentil soups, and what is probably the national soup, *soupa avgolemono*, a lemon-flavored chicken soup. This is a truly exceptional soup, popular far beyond the boundaries of the country.

Lamb is the principal meat, veal has some small importance, but beef is seldom seen. The recipe for *entrather* (lamb with artichokes) is typical of the lamb dishes of the country. Lamb is used for almost all meat dishes: broiled over an open coal fire, roasted, cut into pieces for tasty stews, and ground up into patties. *Moussaka* (eggplant stuffed with ground lamb) appears frequently at the table.

Greece produces beautiful, large, flavorful lemons, and the Greek housewife takes full advantage of them, using lemon juice on practically everything she serves. Preparing the salad is a ritual performed by the host himself at the table. Lemons are used in place of the customary vinegar, with pleasing and tart results.

Greek wines, many of which contain resin, are not palatable to our taste, but foreign residents in Greece find that a liking for this wine may be acquired. Greek brandy, on the other hand, though not quite up to French standards of excellence, is very fine and has been exported extensively. Metaxa is an especially well-known brand.

*Feta,* a white, goat-milk cheese, is not suitable for normal use by our standards, though the Greeks like to eat it plain with a crust of bread. A few pieces of *feta* cheese broken into a green salad give it a unique flavor.

## CAVIAR APPETIZER

### TARAMOSALATA

½ pound raw fish roe (pike, if possible)
1 teaspoon salt
1 onion, quartered
1 cup water
2 slices white bread, trimmed
1 cup olive or salad oil
1 egg yolk, beaten
½ cup lemon juice

Wash the roe carefully and drain. Place in a saucepan with the salt, onion, and water. Cook over medium heat for 30 minutes. Drain well and discard the onion. Set aside to cool for 30 minutes. Then place the roe in a wooden bowl and crush with a fork. Wet the bread and squeeze dry. Add to the roe, beating with a wooden spoon until well blended. Add the oil gradually, beating continuously until quite thick. Add the beaten egg yolk and the lemon juice, and mix well. Serve very cold, with French-style bread.

## BAKED FISH

### PSARIA PLAKI

½ cup olive oil
8 large onions, sliced
2 cloves garlic, minced
2 tablespoons butter
6 slices (½ inch thick) sea bass, haddock, or mackerel
2 teaspoons salt
1 teaspoon pepper
6 tomatoes, sliced
2 lemons, sliced
¼ cup water

Heat the olive oil in a skillet and sauté the onions and garlic until golden brown. Melt the butter in a large baking dish. Arrange the slices of fish in the dish, leaving some space between each slice. Sprinkle with the salt and pepper. Spread the onions over and around the fish slices. Place a slice of tomato on each piece of fish and top with a piece of lemon. Spread the remainder of the tomato and lemon slices around the dish. Add the water. Bake in a 375° oven for 30 minutes. Serve with the sauce remaining in the baking dish.

## LEMON SOUP

### SOUPA AVGOLEMONO

1 pound chicken parts (necks, backs, feet)
1 onion
1 stalk celery
1 carrot
3 quarts water
½ cup rice
2 egg yolks
2 tablespoons lemon juice
2 teaspoons salt

Wash the chicken parts well. Combine in a saucepan with the onion, celery, carrot, and water. Bring to a boil, then skim the top. Cook over medium heat for 2 hours. Strain and return to saucepan. Wash the rice in warm water and let soak for 15 minutes. Wash again and add to the stock. Cook over low heat for 15 minutes. Beat the egg yolks in a bowl. Add the lemon juice and salt. Gradually add the stock, beating constantly to prevent curdling. Return to saucepan, still beating constantly. Heat but do not allow to boil. Correct seasoning. Serve with a slice of lemon.

*Note: If desired, canned consommé may be substituted for the homemade stock.*

## LAMB AND ARTICHOKES

ENTRATHER

| | |
|---|---|
| ¼ pound butter | 1 bay leaf |
| 3 pounds lamb, cut into 1-inch cubes | 4 cups boiling water |
| 2 onions, chopped | 6 artichokes |
| 2 cloves garlic, minced | 3 eggs |
| 2 teaspoons salt | 2 tablespoons lemon juice |
| 1 teaspoon pepper | 12 ripe olives |

Melt the butter in a saucepan. Add the lamb and brown well on all sides. Add the onions, garlic, salt, pepper, bay leaf and boiling water. Cover and cook for 40 minutes, stirring occasionally.

Remove the largest outside leaves of the artichoke. Cut off and discard the top third of the artichoke. Cut the balance of the artichoke in half and add to the lamb mixture. Cover and cook over low heat for 45 minutes.

Beat eggs and lemon juice together in a bowl. Add 1 cup of the gravy from the saucepan very gradually to the contents of the bowl, beating steadily. Return this mixture to the saucepan, beating continuously. Add the olives. Cook over low heat for 5 minutes but do not allow to boil.

## ORÉGANO CHICKEN

KATES RIGANATI

| | |
|---|---|
| ½ cup olive oil | ¼ pound butter |
| 3 teaspoons salt | 2 cups canned tomatoes |
| 4 tablespoons lemon juice | 1 teaspoon pepper |
| 2 4½-pound roasting chickens | 2 teaspoons orégano |

Combine the olive oil, 2 teaspoons of the salt, and the lemon juice. Rub it into the chickens, inside and out. Place the chickens in a roasting pan. Roast in a 375° oven for 1 hour. Melt the butter in a saucepan. Add the tomatoes, remaining salt, pepper, and orégano. Cook over medium heat 5 minutes, stirring occasionally. Pour over the chickens and reduce the heat to 350°. Roast for 1 hour longer, or until tender, basting frequently.

## SPINACH ROLLS IN PASTRY

SPANAKOPETA

1¾ cups sifted flour
2 teaspoons salt
½ teaspoon pepper
1 cup water
¾ pound butter, melted
1 onion, chopped
10 scallions (green onions), sliced
4 tablespoons chopped dill

½ cup chopped parsley
2 pounds fresh or 1 package frozen spinach, cooked, drained, and chopped
3 eggs
½ pound *feta* cheese or cottage cheese
½ cup grated Parmesan cheese
3 tablespoons grated parsley

Sift the flour and 1 teaspoon of the salt into a bowl. Add the water, mixing well. Knead gently. Roll out on a lightly floured surface as thin as possible. Cut into four squares. Spread each with some melted butter. Stack the squares into layers. Set aside.

Combine ¼ cup melted butter and the onion in a skillet. Sauté for 10 minutes. Add the scallions, dill, and parsley. Sauté for 5 minutes. Add spinach, pepper, and remaining salt. Mix well. Cool for 10 minutes. Beat the eggs in a bowl. Add the *feta* or cottage cheese and Parmesan cheese. Mix until smooth. Add the spinach mixture, mixing until well blended. Correct seasoning. Preheat oven to 400°.

Roll the dough (still stacked) as thin as possible. Brush with half the remaining butter. Spread the spinach mixture over two thirds of the dough. Roll up as for a jelly roll. Place in a baking pan. Prick top in several places. Pour remaining butter over it. Bake in a 400° oven for 30 minutes, or until crisp and brown on top. Slice and serve hot.

## EGGPLANT CASSEROLE

MOUSSAKA MELITZANES

3 tablespoons olive oil
2 onions, chopped
1 large eggplant, peeled and cut into ½-inch cubes
2 tomatoes, chopped

2 teaspoons salt
1 teaspoon pepper
1 egg yolk, beaten
½ cup milk
½ cup cottage cheese

Heat the olive oil in a saucepan and add the chopped onions. Sauté for 5 minutes. Add the eggplant and continue cooking for an additional 10 minutes over low heat. Add the tomatoes, salt, and pepper, and cook for 10 minutes, stirring occasionally. Butter a 2-quart casserole and place the mixture in it. Combine the egg yolk, milk, and cottage cheese, and mix well. Pour over the eggplant. Bake in a 375° oven for 45 minutes.

## WALNUT CAKE WITH SYRUP

KARIDOPITA

| | |
|---|---|
| ¼ pound butter | ¾ cup ground walnuts |
| 1¼ cups sugar | ¼ cup milk |
| 4 eggs | 1 teaspoon vanilla |
| ¾ cup farina | 1 cup water |
| 2 teaspoons baking powder | 1 tablespoon lemon juice |
| Dash of salt | |

Cream the butter. Add ¾ cup of the sugar and continue creaming until light and fluffy. Add the eggs, one at a time, beating well after each addition. Add the farina, baking powder, salt, walnuts, milk, and vanilla, beating steadily. Pour into a buttered 10-inch loaf pan. Bake in a 350° oven for 35 minutes, or until a cake tester comes out clean. While the cake is baking, prepare the syrup.

Place the remaining ½ cup of sugar in a saucepan with the water and lemon juice. Bring to a boil and cook over low heat for 10 minutes or until thick and syrupy. Pour over the hot cake and serve from the pan. The cake may be served cold without the syrup if desired.

## ISRAEL

*Tzenna* (austerity) is the word for food in this young country. Many important foods are rationed, particularly meat, although tourists receive special consideration. Other commonplace ingredients are difficult to obtain, and the housewife must often struggle to lend variety to the daily meals.

Meat of any sort is in very short supply, and when it is available lamb is the overwhelming choice. Pork is forbidden to orthodox Jews in common with the Mohammedans of the surrounding countries, but only a moderate proportion of the Israeli population is both Jewish and orthodox. There are, of course, the familiar dishes of Jewish people all over the world, such as *gefulte fisch* (stuffed fish), *kugel* (a potato pudding), and *chulent* (a meat and lima bean casserole). Because Israel is located on the coast it has good fish dishes. Fish is almost always served on Friday night or Saturday as a part of the traditional sabbath meal.

Very important to the local diet are olives, eggplant, tomatoes, and okra, all of which are used in vegetables and salads. The Arab influence in Israeli food is strongly felt, for the dishes of the surrounding Moslem countries are commonly served throughout the nation. Practically any dish for which a recipe is given in the Near and Middle East countries could also be included in the Israeli section.

An example of a popular Israeli favorite of Arabic origin is *falafel*, considered as Israel's "hot dog" and sold on all street corners. Also of interest are *leben* and *lebenia*, both similar to yogurt, which probably originated in Bulgaria but are popular all through the Near East countries. *Leben* is made from skimmed milk, whereas *lebenia* is thicker and has the consistency of sour cream. They are used as all-purpose foods, for desserts, for refreshments, and are often combined with jams or syrups to make cold drinks. No mention of Israel could by-pass the egg bread of the country, *challah*, but the various flat breads, such as *kibbetz*, are equally well liked. Of the locally produced foods, such as dates, almonds, figs, raisins, and grapes, the biblical pomegranate is a particular favorite.

Israel has had a policy of almost unrestricted immigration, and the country is filled with refugees from Germany, Austria, and Poland. Each group has brought its familiar everyday recipes and its heritage of food and eating habits. On the other hand, there is also the *kosher* style of cooking, based upon centuries of religious observance. The three factors that have led to a clash in the Israeli cuisine are: European food, the standard *kosher* dishes, and the warm to hot climate of the country. Both the European and the traditional *kosher* Jewish food are German, Polish, and Russian in background or by modification. These are basically cold countries. Their substantial, heat-producing food is hardly required in the Mediterranean climate of Israel. For this reason Israel has adopted the cooling salads, fruits, sherbets, and refreshing beverages of their Arabic neighbors.

The cuisine of the country is in the process of changing, and this will undoubtedly continue for some time. The rigorous rationing of meat, the scarcity of ingredients that formerly made up the diet of the people, and the hot climate are all working toward a new set of food habits.

## ISRAELI "HOT DOGS"

FALAFEL

2 cups chick-peas
3 cloves garlic, minced
1½ teaspoons salt
¼ teaspoon dried ground chili peppers

1 egg, beaten
2 tablespoons water
½ cup flour
Fat for deep-fat frying

Wash the chick-peas in several changes of water. Drain. Soak overnight in water to cover. Drain. Grind twice in a food chopper. Add the garlic, salt, chili peppers, egg, and water and mix well. Use 1 tablespoon of the mixture to form a small croquette, and continue until all of the mixture is used up. Dip them lightly in the flour. Heat the fat to 370° in a deep saucepan. Fry the croquettes until brown on both sides, about 1 minute. Drain well and serve hot.

## LIMA BEAN AND MEAT CASSEROLE

CHULENT

1 cup dried lima beans
3 tablespoons rendered chicken fat or salad oil
3 onions, chopped
4 potatoes, peeled and quartered
½ cup barley

3 pounds short ribs of beef
1 tablespoon salt
1 teaspoon pepper
1 teaspoon paprika
1 tablespoon flour

Wash the lima beans thoroughly. Soak them in warm water to cover for 1 hour. Drain. Heat the chicken fat in a heavy saucepan. Add the onions and sauté for 10 minutes, stirring frequently. Add the beans, potatoes, and barley and stir. Place the meat in the center of the pot. Combine the salt, pepper, paprika, and flour and sprinkle on top. Add boiling water to cover ½ inch above the top of the ingredients. Cover and cook over very low heat for 5 hours. Check the pot frequently to see that it does not burn, adding a little water if necessary.

## COLD BEET SOUP

COLD BORSCHT

8 beets, washed and peeled
1 onion, chopped fine
2½ quarts water
1 tablespoon salt

⅓ cup lemon juice
3 tablespoons sugar
2 eggs
1 cup sour cream

Combine the beets, onion, water, and salt in a saucepan. Bring to a boil and cook over medium heat for 1 hour. Add the lemon juice and sugar and cook for 30 minutes. Correct seasoning; the soup may require a little more sugar or lemon juice, depending upon the sweetness of the beets.

Beat the eggs in a bowl. Gradually add 3 cups of the soup, beating constantly to prevent curdling. Return this mixture to the balance of the soup, beating steadily. Remove all of the beets from the soup. Grate 5 of the beets and return them to the soup. The remaining beets may be used in a cold salad. Chill the soup and serve very cold with a spoonful of sour cream in each plate.

*Note: If a very thick soup is desired, place the remaining beets in an electric blender with 2 cups of the soup and run the machine until the mixture is smooth. Add the mixture to the soup.*

## STUFFED FISH

### GEFULTE FISCH

| | |
|---|---|
| 5 pounds fillet of fresh water fish (pike, carp, whitefish) | 1 teaspoon sugar |
| Head, skin, and bones of the fish | ¼ cup cracker or matzo meal |
| 6 onions | 2 eggs, beaten |
| 4 teaspoons salt | ½ cup cold water |
| 2 teaspoons pepper | 6 cups boiling water |
| | 2 carrots, sliced |

Grind the fish and 2 of the onions in a food chopper. Place in a wooden bowl, add 2 teaspoons of the salt, 1 teaspoon of the pepper, the sugar, cracker meal, eggs, and cold water. Chop until fine in texture and well blended.

Place the fish head, skin, and bones in a deep saucepan. Slice the remaining onions and add with the boiling water, remaining salt and pepper, and the carrots. Bring to an active boil. Shape the fish mixture into 2-inch balls, between wet hands. Drop into the saucepan. Cover and cook over low heat for 1½ hours. Stir gently occasionally. Correct seasoning. Remove the fish balls from the saucepan carefully. Strain the fish stock into a separate bowl. Serve very cold. If a very stiff gravy is desired, add 1 teaspoon of softened gelatine to the hot fish stock before chilling.

## POTATO PUDDING

### KUGEL

| | |
|---|---|
| 3 egg yolks | ½ teaspoon pepper |
| 6 potatoes, peeled, grated, and drained | ¾ cup matzo or cracker meal |
| 3 tablespoons grated onion | ½ cup rendered chicken fat or melted butter |
| 1½ teaspoons salt | 3 egg whites |

Beat the egg yolks in a bowl. Add the potatoes, onion, salt, and pepper. Mix well. Add the matzo meal and the chicken fat. Mix thoroughly. Beat the egg whites until stiff but not dry. Fold into the potato mixture carefully but thoroughly. Preheat oven to 375°. Grease a 1½- or 2-quart baking dish with whatever kind of shortening was used in the recipe. Pour the mixture into it. Bake in a 375° oven for 40 minutes, or until browned on top and firm. Serve hot.

## EGG BREAD

CHALLAH

| | |
|---|---|
| 1 cake or package yeast | 1 teaspoon salt |
| ⅛ teaspoon saffron | 2 teaspoons sugar |
| 1 cup lukewarm water | 2 eggs, beaten |
| 4 cups sifted flour | 1 egg yolk, beaten |

Soak the yeast and saffron in the lukewarm water for 5 minutes. Sift the flour, salt, and sugar together. Add 1½ cups of the flour mixture to the yeast mixture, mixing until smooth. Cover the bowl with a cloth and allow to rise in a warm place until double in bulk, about 30 minutes. Add the eggs and mix well. Add the remaining flour and knead on a lightly floured surface until smooth and elastic. Place the dough in the bowl, dust the top with a little additional flour, and cover with the cloth. Allow to rise in a warm place until double in size, about 2 hours.

Knead the dough again for a few minutes. Divide it in three equal parts and roll with the hands into long, round strips. Fasten the three pieces at one end and braid them together. Place on a greased baking sheet and allow to rise again, covered, in a warm place for 1 hour. Preheat oven to 400°. Brush the top of the bread with the egg yolk. Bake in a 400° oven for 10 minutes. Reduce heat to 375° and bake 35 minutes longer, or until well browned on top.

## HONEY CAKE

LEKACH

| | |
|---|---|
| 2 eggs | ⅛ teaspoon salt |
| ½ cup sugar | ¾ teaspoon baking powder |
| ¼ cup freshly brewed coffee | ½ teaspoon baking soda |
| ½ cup honey | 1 cup coarsely chopped filberts, |
| 1 tablespoon salad oil | almonds, or walnuts |
| 1¾ cups sifted flour | 2 tablespoons brandy (optional) |

Beat the eggs in a bowl. Add the sugar and beat until light and fluffy. Mix the coffee, honey, and salad oil together and combine with the eggs.

Sift the flour, salt, baking powder, and baking soda together. Add the nuts and stir. Gradually add to the egg mixture, stirring constantly. Add the brandy and stir. Preheat oven to 325°. Oil a loaf pan and line it carefully with wax paper or aluminum foil. Pour the batter into it. Bake in a 325° oven for 45 minutes, or until a cake tester comes out clean. Remove cake from the oven and allow to cool thoroughly in the pan. Remove carefully.

## RUMANIA

Corn meal, often considered a typical early American food, is Rumania's favorite dish and in that country it is called *mamaliga*. This is a comparatively recent development in Rumania, for corn meal was brought to Europe from the New World only a few hundred years ago. It has taken hold of the public fancy to an astonishing degree, and people in all walks of life eat *mamaliga* practically every day; with the peasantry it is rare for any meal to go by without it. *Mamaliga* is eaten plain, hot or cold, and often with onions, garlic, sausages, sauerkraut, or whatever the cook has on hand.

*Ikra,* the Rumanian version of caviar, is a favorite and highly regarded appetizer. It is usual to serve it both with drinks and as the first course to a dinner. Herring and eggplant are other popular appetizers, very much to the taste of the Rumanian palate.

Soups are something of a cult here, but not the ordinary varieties made from meat, poultry, or vegetables. The national soups of the nation are called *tchorbas* (sour soups) and are based upon a fermentation agent, usually wheat bran, but often lemons, vine leaves, or sauerkraut juice. The recipe for *tchorba* given here is one made with veal, a typical variation.

Fish dishes are well liked, but the selection is somewhat narrow in choice. Carp, prepared in many different fashions, is served most often. Rumanian meat dishes are not complicated, for the national preference leans toward spicy sausages and the famous Rumanian broiled meat, for which no recipe is required. It consists merely of a wide assortment of meat, such as steak, lamb chops, sausage, sweetbreads, liver, pork chops, and almost any other available meat, broiled over charcoal simultaneously. These are served with a large number of spicy relishes, pickles, hot red peppers, and sauerkraut. Stews of all sorts, such as *tocana de cartofi* (potato stew), are prevalent.

*Ghivetch,* a medley of vegetables, is another national dish. Sometimes it is made of vegetables only, but often it is combined with fish or meat. The important point for the Rumanian cook to remember is that there must be as many different vegetables as possible, and that they should be the freshest and best available. Green vegetables for salad and also mushrooms are particular favorites of the country people.

Desserts are of several types. There are sweet pancake desserts, strudels, and tarts. Rumania's oriental heritage is indicated by a large group of desserts consisting of fruit and nut preserves and rose petals in thick syrup, known generally as *dulceata,* which are excessively sweet to our taste. The cottage cheese recipe given here, *alivenca,* will not be too cloying to our palates.

As in the Balkan countries, brandy of local manufacture is the favorite drink of the country. Brandy in Rumania means plum brandy, *tsuica,* a fine distilled liquor with a curious blossomlike aroma. Wines are produced in many areas, but the quality is not extraordinary by European standards.

The Rumanians are fond of cheese, and produce several excellent varieties. Both outstanding types, the *urda* and the *branza de burduf,* are made from sheep's milk. The latter is shipped to market in a container of pine or fir whose aroma permeates the cheese.

## CAVIAR, RUMANIAN STYLE

IKRA

1 pound pike roe
1 tablespoon salt
½ cup olive oil
2 tablespoons lemon juice

1 tablespoon ice water
1 onion, chopped fine
10 ripe olives, sliced thin

Wash the roe carefully and remove the veins. Place in a bowl and sprinkle with salt. Chill for at least 6 hours. Beat the roe with a fork for 1 minute. Gradually add the olive oil drop by drop, beating constantly. Add the lemon juice and ice water. Beat all together until the mixture is firm and each egg is separate. Sprinkle the onion and olives over the roe. The caviar should be served cold, as an appetizer, with quarters of lemon. Thin slices of dark bread are the usual accompaniment.

## SOUR SOUP

TCHORBA

1 tablespoon salad or olive oil
1 onion, chopped
1 carrot, diced
2 sprigs parsley
2 stalks celery
1 cup water
2 tablespoons rice
6 cups sauerkraut juice (if canned juice is used, 3 cups juice and 3 cups water)

¾ pound veal, ground
1 egg, beaten
1 slice bread, soaked in milk and crumbled
¾ teaspoon salt
½ teaspoon pepper
1 tablespoon chopped parsley

Heat the oil in a deep saucepan. Add the onion and carrot and sauté for 5 minutes, stirring occasionally. Add the sprigs of parsley, celery, and water. Bring to a boil, then add the rice. Cook for 10 minutes. Add the sauerkraut juice and boil for 10 minutes.

Combine the veal, egg, bread, salt, pepper, and chopped parsley in a bowl. Mix until smooth. Shape into walnut-sized balls and drop into the boiling soup. Cook over medium heat for 30 minutes. Serve hot.

## BAKED FISH WITH VEGETABLES

GHIVETCH

1 cup salad or olive oil
2 medium potatoes, diced
2 carrots, sliced
½ pound fresh or ¼ package frozen green peas
¼ pound fresh or ¼ package frozen string beans, cut into small pieces
½ small eggplant, peeled and diced
1 cup shredded cabbage
1 green pepper, sliced fine

2 onions, chopped
2 cloves garlic, minced
2 tomatoes, chopped
½ pound okra, sliced (optional)
⅛ teaspoon thyme
1 bay leaf
3 teaspoons salt
1½ teaspoons pepper
6 slices fish (carp preferably)

Pour the oil in a deep baking dish and bring to a boil. Preheat oven to 350°. Combine the potatoes, carrots, peas, beans, eggplant, cabbage, green pepper, onions, garlic, tomatoes, okra, thyme, bay leaf, 2 teaspoons of the salt, and 1 teaspoon of the pepper. Add to the oil in the casserole and stir well.

Bake in a 350° oven for 30 minutes. Place the fish on top of the vegetables and sprinkle with the remaining salt and pepper. Bake for 30 minutes, or until fish is done. Remove the bay leaf and serve directly from the baking dish.

## TONGUE WITH OLIVES

LIMBA CU MASLINE

1 beef tongue, fresh or pickled
3 tablespoons butter
2 onions, chopped
1 clove garlic, minced
2 tablespoons flour
½ cup canned tomato sauce

½ cup white wine
2 tablespoons vinegar
½ teaspoon pepper
1 bay leaf
½ teaspoon powdered ginger
1 cup ripe olives

Place the tongue in a deep saucepan with water to cover and boil for 3 hours, or until tender. Drain, reserving 1½ cups of the stock. Remove the skin carefully and slice the tongue into ¼-inch slices. Set aside.

Melt the butter in a saucepan and add the onions and garlic. Sauté for 5 minutes, stirring frequently. Add the flour and mix until smooth. Combine the reserved stock, tomato sauce, wine, and vinegar. Add to the onion mixture gradually, stirring constantly until the boiling point is reached. Add the pepper, bay leaf, ginger, olives, and the slices of tongue. Cook over low heat for 15 minutes. Correct seasoning, adding salt, if necessary. Serve hot with tiny boiled potatoes.

## STUFFED CABBAGE

SARMALE UMPLUTA

1 head cabbage
1½ pounds pork, ground
¾ pound beef, ground
1 slice bread, soaked in water and crumbled
1 onion, chopped
1 teaspoon salt

½ teaspoon pepper
1 slice uncooked bacon, chopped fine
1 pound sauerkraut
3 slices bacon, half cooked and drained
2 cups tomato juice
1 cup sour cream

Place the entire head of cabbage in a large bowl and pour boiling water over it. Drain the cabbage and separate each leaf carefully. Mix the ground pork and beef, crumbled bread, onion, salt, pepper, and chopped bacon together in a bowl. Place a tablespoon of this mixture in the center of each cabbage leaf and roll it up, turning in the ends carefully.

Place the sauerkraut on the bottom of an earthenware casserole or heavy pot. Arrange the cabbage rolls carefully on top of the sauerkraut. Cut each slice of bacon into 3 pieces and place them over the cabbage rolls. Pour the tomato juice over all. Cover and cook over medium heat for 2 hours. Uncover and bake in a 375° oven for 45 minutes, or until lightly browned. Add sour cream, mixing lightly. Heat on top of the stove for 5 minutes.

*Note: The flavor is improved by reheating, so prepare the cabbage the day before it is to be served, if possible.*

## BEANS, PEASANT STYLE

### FASOLE STIL TARANESC

1 pound dried white beans
3 cups water
¼ cup salad oil
1 onion, chopped
1 tablespoon flour
1 tablespoon tomato paste

1½ teaspoons salt
1 teaspoon pepper
3 tablespoons chopped parsley
3 tablespoons vinegar
12 small sausages (optional)

Wash the beans and place in a heavy saucepan with the water. Soak overnight. Cook in the same water until tender, about 2 hours, adding more water if necessary. Drain but reserve ½ cup of the liquid.

Heat the oil in a saucepan and add the chopped onion. Sauté for 10 minutes, stirring occasionally. Sprinkle with flour, add the tomato paste, salt, pepper, and parsley, and stir well. Add the reserved liquid and vinegar, mixing well. Add the beans and simmer for 15 minutes. Fry the sausages, drain, and add to the beans.

## POTATO STEW

### TOCANA DE CARTOFI

2 tablespoons chicken fat or butter
2 tablespoons flour
2 teaspoons salt
½ teaspoon pepper
¼ teaspoon sweet paprika

1 cup stock or 1 cup hot water and
1 bouillon cube
6 potatoes, peeled and cubed
¼ cup heavy cream

Melt the chicken fat in a deep saucepan, add the flour, salt, pepper, and paprika, and stir until smooth. Add the stock gradually, stirring constantly until the boiling point is reached. Add the potatoes and stir. Cover and cook over medium heat for 15 minutes. Add the cream and cook for 5 minutes. There should be only a small amount of sauce remaining. Serve hot with a little of the sauce poured over the potatoes.

## CORN MEAL, RUMANIAN STYLE

MAMALIGA

1 quart water
1½ teaspoons salt
1 cup yellow corn meal

¼ cup melted butter
¼ cup grated cheese (Swiss or
    Parmesan)

Bring the water and salt to a boil in a saucepan. Add the corn meal gradually, stirring constantly until thickened. Cook over medium heat for 20 minutes. Butter an 8-inch square pan and pour the corn meal into it. Chill until firm, about 2 hours. Turn out carefully onto a lightly floured surface. Cut into slices about ½ inch thick. Preheat oven to 375°.

Butter a baking dish thoroughly. Arrange the slices in layers, sprinkle the melted butter and grated cheese between each layer and on top. Bake in a 375° oven for 20 minutes, or until delicately browned.

*Note: Mamaliga is the great national dish of Rumania. It appears at practically every meal, and is often served in place of bread. It often accompanies ghivetch.*

## COTTAGE CHEESE DESSERT

ALIVENCA

2 pounds cottage cheese, drained
8 eggs, beaten
4 tablespoons corn meal
1 tablespoon cornstarch

½ teaspoon salt
2 tablespoons butter
1 cup sour cream
¼ cup sugar

Beat the cottage cheese in a bowl until smooth. Add the eggs and continue beating until well mixed. Add the corn meal, cornstarch, and salt and beat together. Preheat oven to 350°. Butter a 9-inch spring-form pan and pour the mixture into it. Dot with the butter. Bake in a 350° oven for 35 minutes, or until delicately browned. Remove the sides of the spring form. Serve hot, garnished with sour cream and sprinkled with sugar.

## PEAR COMPOTE

PERE ÎN COMPOT

8 large fresh pears, peeled and sliced
¾ cup bread crumbs
2 teaspoons cinnamon
4 cups water

⅓ cup sugar
3 tablespoons lemon juice
¼ cup white wine

Combine the pears, bread crumbs, cinnamon, and water in a saucepan. Cover and cook over low heat for 1 hour. Force through a sieve. Add the sugar, lemon juice, and wine and cook for 20 minutes. Chill. Serve cold, with a plain cake, such as spongecake.

## SYRIA, LEBANON, AND JORDAN

These three neighboring countries have so much in common in the way of language, religion, and background that it is only natural to find the people eating the same foods and following almost identical cuisines. The regions involved are historic ones, filled with many ruins of biblical times, and of great interest to the tourist. The Cedars of Lebanon, found in this area, are a rewarding sight and may be seen from the fine resort hotels in the region.

The diets of all three countries are quite similar. The basic foods are rice, lamb, eggplant, and yogurt. Meals are served in a colorful and interesting manner, particularly in private homes. Though the hotels and restaurants usually serve in the European fashion at normal tables and chairs, the local population prefers to eat at very low tables, barely two feet high, and thus, since ordinary chairs are useless, the guests must sit on the floor or upon cushions. Food is presented with considerable ceremony in the homes of the more prosperous, and although a meal may be simple or elaborate, depending upon the resources of the host, there is always an atmosphere of cordiality and hospitality toward any guest.

The only liquor served before a meal is *arrack*, the locally produced strong drink. Tourist hotels and restaurants serve the usual Western-style cocktails and drinks, but these do not appeal to the local population. Sometimes wine is served during the meal as a concession to Western visitors, but this custom is not always followed. The diner is more likely to be served with iced fruit drinks of great sweetness, or possibly with a soured milk beverage.

A typical native meal might consist of a thick lentil soup, stuffed eggplant prepared with plenty of olive oil, and a baked lamb dish. Rice is the basis of many dishes, and poor people literally exist on it. A favorite cooking style is the practice of wrapping mixtures of ground meat and rice in grape leaves and baking them, although this custom is followed throughout the region from the Balkans eastward to the oriental countries.

The *kebabs* (meats roasted on a skewer) are enormously popular with the people.

Figs, dates, and grapes are of the finest quality and many different varieties are available. Oversweet desserts are still the preference of most, and the usual rich pastries of commendable delicacy and lightness are unfortunately drenched in an overabundance of honey or fruit syrup. Calories do not interest the populace, for overweight is generally not considered to be important, and wives are often encouraged to gain and maintain excess poundage. Thus, more and more rich desserts are consumed.

The Turkish-style coffee, which is about one third sediment and two thirds thick liquid, is the choice of the people of the three countries. Men spend hours in the coffeehouses, business is transacted over coffee cups, and guests are always served coffee.

*Sambousiks,* or finger foods, much like our own hors d'oeuvres are served with *arrack. Arrack* is usually mixed with a little water, which makes it look like Grade C milk, but it is not recommended for milk shakes!

## CURRIED PASTRY

### SAMBOUSIKS

| | |
|---|---|
| 1¼ cups sifted flour | ¾ cup milk, scalded |
| 1 teaspoon salt | 1 tablespoon curry powder |
| ⅓ pound butter | 1½ cups chopped cooked chicken, beef, |
| 3 tablespoons ice water | or veal |

Sift the flour (reserving 1 tablespoon) and ½ teaspoon of the salt into a bowl. Cut in half the butter with a pastry blender or two knives. Add the ice water gradually, tossing lightly until a ball of dough is formed. Knead until smooth. Chill for 15 minutes. Roll out on a lightly floured surface. Flatten all but 1 tablespoon of the remaining butter and place it on the center of the dough. Fold the dough in half and then in quarters. Wrap in wax paper and chill for 1 hour.

Melt the remaining butter in a saucepan. Add the reserved flour and mix to a smooth paste. Gradually add the milk, stirring until the boiling point is reached. Add the curry and remaining salt and cook over low heat for 5 minutes, stirring occasionally. Add the chopped meat; mix lightly. Preheat oven to 375°.

Roll out the dough ⅛ inch thick on a lightly floured surface. Cut into circles with a cooky cutter. Place a tablespoon of the meat mixture in the center and fold over the dough, sealing the edges well. Place on a baking sheet. Bake in a 375° oven for 15 minutes or until brown. These hot pastries are excellent hot hors d'oeuvres.

## EGGPLANT APPETIZER

### BABA GANNOJ

| | |
|---|---|
| 1 eggplant | 2 tablespoons chopped parsley |
| 4 tablespoons butter | 2 cloves garlic, minced fine |
| 3 tablespoons sesame oil or olive oil | 1 green pepper, chopped fine |
| 3 tablespoons lemon juice | ½ cup yogurt or sour milk |

Peel the eggplant and cut it in half. Slice as thin as possible. Melt the butter in a frying pan and sauté the eggplant slices in it on both sides until tender, about 10 minutes. Set aside to cool for 1 hour. In a bowl combine the oil, lemon juice, parsley, garlic, green pepper, and yogurt. Mix well. Add the eggplant slices and baste them a few times. Chill. Serve with thin slices of bread.

## FISH AND RICE, DAMASCUS STYLE

### SAYADIET

| | |
|---|---|
| 6 fillets of fish | ½ teaspoon pepper |
| 3 tablespoons flour | 4 tablespoons butter |
| 1 teaspoon salt | |

Wash and dry the fillets. Combine the flour, salt, and pepper. Dip the fish fillets in it. Melt the butter in a frying pan or casserole. Brown the fish on both sides. Spread Arabic rice (see recipe in this section) over the fish. Cover and cook over low heat for 15 minutes. Serve hot.

## LAMB AND CRACKED WHEAT

### KIBBE

| | |
|---|---|
| 4 pounds lamb | 2 teaspoons salt |
| 2 pounds *bourghol* (cracked wheat) | ½ cup olive oil |
| 5 onions, chopped fine | ½ teaspoon cinnamon |
| 2 cloves garlic, minced | 2 cups coarsely chopped walnuts |

Grind the lamb in a food chopper 3 times. Soak the cracked wheat in warm water to cover for 5 minutes. Drain, then knead for 1 minute. Grind the cracked wheat in a food chopper together with 4 of the onions and the garlic. Combine this mixture with half of the ground lamb in a chopping bowl. Add 1 teaspoon of the salt and chop until very fine. Set aside.

Heat ¼ cup of the olive oil in a saucepan, add the remaining onion, lamb, salt, and the cinnamon. Sauté for 20 minutes, stirring occasionally. In a separate saucepan heat 2 tablespoons of the olive oil and add the walnuts. Sauté for 5 minutes, stirring frequently. Drain and add to the sautéed lamb mixture, mixing well.

Using 1 teaspoon of the olive oil, grease a round or square baking dish, about 12 inches across. Spread half of the lamb and cracked wheat mixture on the bottom, patting it down well. Place all of the lamb and walnut mixture on top, again patting it down. Cover with the remaining half of the lamb and wheat mixture, pressing down firmly. Sprinkle the remaining olive oil on top. Cut slices with a sharp knife, being sure to cut right down to the bottom of the dish. This must be done before baking, as a heavy crust forms and it is difficult to cut after baking. Bake in a 350° oven for 45 minutes.

## STUFFED CHICKEN, SYRIAN STYLE

DGAJ MUHSHY

⅓ cup olive oil
1 pound beef or lamb, ground
½ cup rice, half cooked
⅓ cup pine nuts
3 teaspoons salt
1 teaspoon pepper

¼ teaspoon nutmeg
Dash of thyme
6-pound roasting chicken
2 quarts water
1 onion
1 stalk celery

Heat 3 tablespoons of the olive oil in a skillet. Add the ground meat and sauté over medium heat for 10 minutes, stirring occasionally. Add the rice, pine nuts, 1 teaspoon of the salt, ½ teaspoon of the pepper, the nutmeg and thyme. Mix well. Stuff the chicken with the mixture, closing the opening carefully with thread or skewers. Place in a deep saucepan with the water, onion, celery, and remaining salt and pepper. Cover and cook over low heat for 2 hours.

Remove chicken from the saucepan and drain. Brush the chicken with the remaining olive oil. Roast in a 400° oven till brown and tender, about 30 minutes. Serve hot.

## CHICK-PEAS

HOMMOS

1 pound chick-peas
½ teaspoon baking soda
2 cloves garlic, minced

¼ cup sesame oil or salad oil
3 tablespoons lemon juice

Wash the chick-peas thoroughly and remove any imperfect ones. Soak in water to cover overnight. Drain well and rinse. Place in a saucepan with water to cover and add the baking soda. Boil until soft, about 1½ hours. Drain thoroughly. Place the chick-peas in a bowl and chop fine. Add the garlic and mix well. Gradually add the oil, chopping steadily. Sprinkle the lemon juice on top of the mixture. Serve cold.

## OKRA STEW

BAMIYEH

¼ pound butter
2 3-pound chickens, disjointed
2 cloves garlic, minced
½ teaspoon coriander
2 pounds okra, stems removed

2 cups tomato juice
2 cups water
1 teaspoon salt
½ teaspoon pepper

Melt the butter in a saucepan, reserving 2 tablespoons. Add the chicken pieces and brown well on all sides. Add the garlic and coriander and mix well. Cover and cook over low heat for 30 minutes.

In a separate saucepan melt the remaining butter, add the okra, and fry for 5 minutes. Add to the chicken with the tomato juice, water, salt, and pepper and stir. Cover and simmer over low heat for 45 minutes. Stir carefully so as not to break the okra. Correct seasoning. Serve hot, being careful to lift the okra out of the saucepan gently.

## ARABIC RICE

RIZ MAFALFEL

2 cups rice
5 cups boiling water
2 teaspoons salt

¼ pound butter
¼ cup nuts (pine nuts or pignolias if available)

Wash the rice in several changes of water. Place in a bowl and add half the boiling water. Soak for 2 hours. Rinse with cold water. Drain well. Bring the remaining water to an active boil. Add the rice, salt, and all but 2 tablespoons of the butter. Cover and cook until the water is absorbed. Melt the remaining butter in a skillet. Add the nuts. (If large nuts are used instead of the pine nuts or pignolias, chop them.) Sauté until lightly browned and sprinkle over the rice.

## SALAD, DAMASCUS STYLE

TABOOLI

½ pound *bourghol* (cracked wheat)
4 tomatoes, cubed
8 scallions (green onions), sliced
6 sprigs parsley, chopped

3 tablespoons olive oil
¼ cup lemon juice
½ teaspoon salt
Lettuce leaves

Soak the cracked wheat in hot water to cover for 2 hours. Drain thoroughly. Combine the tomatoes, scallions, parsley, olive oil, lemon juice, and salt in a bowl. Toss together lightly. Add the cracked wheat and again toss lightly. Arrange beds of lettuce leaves on individual plates. Sprinkle a few drops of olive oil on each portion. Divide the mixture into even portions. Serve cold.

*Note: In Lebanon a little minced garlic is added to the above ingredients. The vegetables are chopped very fine on a chopping board, combined with the other ingredients, then chilled. The salad is served in a bowl surrounded by individual scoops of crisp romaine lettuce leaves, and everyone helps himself. Served in this fashion, it makes a good cocktail accompaniment. In the absence of romaine lettuce, use potato chips.*

## YOGURT PANCAKES

### FATAYER BIL-LEBAN

3 egg yolks
2 tablespoons corn syrup
2 cups yogurt or sour milk
1 teaspoon baking soda

1½ cups sifted flour
2 teaspoons baking powder
¼ cup melted butter
3 egg whites

Beat the yolks in a bowl and add the corn syrup, yogurt, and baking soda. Beat well. Sift the flour and baking powder together and add to the previous mixture, mixing well. Add the melted butter, beating steadily. Beat the egg whites until stiff but not dry and fold them into the previous mixture carefully. Bake on a lightly greased griddle or frying pan until browned on both sides. Serve with honey.

## FARINA DESSERT

### HREEST AL LOWZ

1 cup sugar
½ cup water
¼ cup butter

3 cups cooked farina or cream of wheat
½ cup honey
½ cup chopped walnuts

Boil the sugar and water in a saucepan until thick and syrupy, about 15 minutes. Add the butter and farina and stir well until completely blended. The mixture should be quite thick. Pour into individual serving dishes. Sprinkle the honey and walnuts on top. Serve hot.

*TURKEY*

No longer a country of mystery, veiled women, and E. Phillips Oppen-heim international-spy stories, Turkey has progressed immeasurably in recent years. It is rich in thousands of years of history, and the Byzantine architecture of Istanbul always delights visitors.

Eating is an important matter here; the gourmet is regarded with reverence, and homage is accorded his opinions. Shopping for food is a delight to the eye and nose, because not only is the market colorful but the air is always filled with the aroma of freshly brewed coffee and rare spices.

Fish is in great demand, for there is a great variety of it, and appar-ently the waters surrounding the country abound in some of the world's finest seafood. Swordfish, fresh or smoked in the local fashion, is excellent. *Hamsi,* best described as a sort of sprat or anchovy, is considered a great delicacy, particularly by the coastal residents. Caviar from the roe of the locally caught sturgeon is expensive but greatly prized, and used fre-quently by those who can afford it.

Scarcely a dinner begins without soup, of which the Turks have a wide variety, both hot and cold. The recipe for the traditional *düğün chorbasi* (wedding soup) is hardly typical but it is of classic stature.

The people are very fond of starchy foods, such as lentils, rice (which is made into *pilafs*), chick-peas, and dried beans. Even Italian spaghettis and macaronis are frequently served, and most dinners contain one course in this category. The most popular vegetables are eggplant and okra, which are prepared with great regularity and in many different fashions.

Lamb and beef are the national meats, and *shish kebab* (broiled meat on a skewer) probably originated with the Turks, though there is some doubt expressed by their neighboring countries regarding this, despite the fact that the words themselves are Turkish. Pork is eaten only by non-Moslems, who are in the minority. Poultry of all sorts, including some wild game birds, appear frequently on the menu.

A great local specialty is the *börek*, a fine pastrylike dough wrapped around cheese or meat and fried crisp. It is an excellent cocktail appetizer when made in a small version.

Desserts are immensely popular here, and all sorts of confections are prepared and eaten with great relish. Possibly only Vienna equals Istanbul in the love of desserts. Fresh fruits, particularly figs, cherries, grapes, and peaches, are of superb quality. Melons are very good, and there is a wide selection. Cheeses are extremely popular, but there are only a few of meritorious quality.

*Raki,* a grape distillation tasting of anise, is the strong drink of the nation. It is not appreciated at first taste, and beginners are advised to dilute it half and half with water. Many after-dinner liqueurs are prepared in an assortment of fruit flavors. Wines are improving steadily in quality, and there is a wide selection available in red and white, sweet and dry, still and sparkling types. As yet, however, these have not become generally available for export.

## LAMB AND EGG SOUP

DÜĞÜN CHORBASI

| | |
|---|---|
| 3 pounds lamb and bones | 4 tablespoons butter |
| 1 onion | 4 tablespoons flour |
| 1 carrot, peeled | 3 egg yolks |
| 2 teaspoons salt | 3 tablespoons lemon juice |
| Dash of cayenne pepper | ⅓ cup melted butter |
| 2½ quarts water | ½ teaspoon paprika |

Combine the lamb, bones, onion, carrot, salt, cayenne pepper, and water in a saucepan. Bring to a boil; cover and cook over low heat for 3 hours. Strain the soup, reserving the meat. Mince the meat and return to the soup. Melt the butter in a separate saucepan. Add the flour and mix to a smooth paste. Gradually add the soup, stirring constantly until the boiling point is reached. Cook over low heat for 15 minutes. Beat the egg yolks and lemon juice in a bowl. Gradually add 2 cups of the soup, stirring constantly. Return to the balance of the soup, stirring constantly. Do not allow soup to boil after the eggs are added. Add 1 tablespoon of butter to each portion and sprinkle with paprika.

*Note: This is the traditional "wedding soup" of Turkey.*

## SWORDFISH ON SKEWERS

### KINCH SHISHTE

| | |
|---|---|
| 1½ pounds swordfish | 1 teaspoon salt |
| 2 tablespoons olive oil | 1 tablespoon lemon juice |
| ¼ teaspoon paprika | 10 bay leaves |
| 2 tablespoons finely grated onion | |

Wash and dry the fish. Remove the skin carefully and cut into 1½-inch cubes. Combine in a bowl the olive oil, paprika, onion, salt, lemon juice, and bay leaves. Stir well. Place the cubes of fish in it and see that each piece of fish is coated with the mixture. Marinate in the refrigerator for at least 5 hours, overnight if possible. Divide the fish in six parts and place pieces carefully on skewers. Broil in a 450° oven for 6 minutes on each side. Serve with the following sauce:

| | |
|---|---|
| 6 tablespoons lemon juice | ½ teaspoon salt |
| 4 tablespoons olive oil | 1 tablespoon chopped parsley |

Combine the lemon juice, olive oil, salt, and chopped parsley. Stir all together. Serve at room temperature in a sauceboat.

*Note: If swordfish is unobtainable, fresh tuna or halibut may be substituted.*


## MEAT PASTRY

### KIYMAH BÖREK

| | |
|---|---|
| 2¾ cups sifted flour | 1 pound beef, chopped |
| 1¾ teaspoons salt | 3 onions, chopped |
| 4 eggs, beaten | ½ teaspoon pepper |
| 3 tablespoons water | ½ cup melted butter |
| 4 tablespoons salad or olive oil | ½ cup milk |

Sift the flour and ½ teaspoon of the salt into a bowl. Combine the eggs and water and add, mixing well. Knead until the dough is smooth and elastic; it should be soft. If necessary, add water or flour to make the dough soft and pliable. Cover with a wet cloth while preparing the filling. Heat the oil in a skillet. Add the beef, onions, pepper, and remaining salt. Sauté over low heat 15 minutes, stirring occasionally. Cool 15 minutes.

Divide the dough into eight balls, seven of which should be of equal size and one half again as large. Roll out the smaller balls 9 inches in diameter, stacking them with wax paper between each layer. Roll the larger ball to fit a 9-inch pie plate but allow it to overhang the edge. Preheat oven to 375°. Place three layers of the dough in the lined pie plate, brushing each with melted butter and milk. Place the meat mixture over the layers and cover with the remaining layers, again brushing each one with melted butter and milk. Fold over the overhanging dough and press the edges together. Bake in a 375° oven for 35 minutes or until brown on top. Turn out onto a plate and cut pie-shaped wedges.

## MEAT AND CABBAGE CASSEROLE

LAHANA BASDI KELAM

2 pounds lamb or beef, cut into ½-inch cubes
3-pound cabbage, cut into 12 sections
3 onions, chopped

3 teaspoons salt
Dash of cayenne pepper
3 cups stock or 1 can consommé and 1 can water
3 tomatoes, chopped

Place a layer of meat on the bottom of a casserole. Sprinkle with a little of the salt and cayenne pepper. Add a layer of cabbage and sprinkle with a little of the salt and cayenne. Add the onions on top and again sprinkle with the balance of salt and cayenne pepper. Pour the stock over it. Place the tomatoes on top. Cook over medium heat for 2 hours, or until the meat is tender. If possible, prepare this dish earlier in the day and reheat slowly before serving.

## RICE WITH TOMATOES

DOMATESLI PILAF

2 cups rice
4 tablespoons butter
3 tomatoes, peeled and chopped

3½ cups stock or 1 can consommé and 1½ cans water
1 teaspoon salt

Wash the rice in several changes of water. Place in a bowl and cover with boiling water. Soak for 15 minutes. Drain. Melt the butter in a saucepan. Add the tomatoes and cook over low heat 10 minutes. Mash the tomatoes. Add the stock and salt. Bring to a boil and add the rice, stirring steadily. Cook over medium heat until the stock is absorbed. Reduce heat to very low and cook 15 minutes, stirring occasionally. Correct seasoning.

## CUCUMBER SALAD

JAJIK

4 cucumbers
1 teaspoon salt
1 tablespoon vinegar
1 clove garlic, sliced

1 teaspoon chopped dill
2 cups yogurt
3 tablespoons olive oil
1 tablespoon chopped mint leaves

Peel the cucumbers and cut in quarters lengthwise. Slice fine, about ⅛ inch thick. Place in a bowl and sprinkle with the salt. Place the vinegar and garlic in a cup and soak for 10 minutes. Strain. In a separate bowl place the dill and yogurt and add the strained vinegar. Mix until smooth. Pour over the cucumbers and mix well. Sprinkle the olive oil and chopped mint leaves on top of the salad. Serve cool, but do not refrigerate.

## TURKISH FRUIT SALAD

MEYVE SALATA

| | |
|---|---|
| 2 teaspoons powdered ginger | 1 cup fresh or canned pineapple, |
| ½ cup brandy | cubed |
| 2 oranges, peeled and sliced thin | 1 cup strawberries, halved |

Dissolve the ginger in the brandy. Combine the oranges, pineapple, and strawberries in a bowl. Pour the brandy over the fruits, basting them for a few moments. Cover the bowl and chill for 3 hours. Arrange the salad on lettuce leaves and serve.

*Note: Any combination of three fruits may be used with the ginger-brandy dressing for an unusual fruit salad.*

## SHREDDED WHEAT PIE

TEL KADAYIF

| | |
|---|---|
| 1 package shredded wheat | 2 cups coarsely chopped walnuts |
| 3 cups boiling water | 2 cups milk |
| ½ pound butter, melted | 1¾ cups sugar |

Dip the shredded wheat in the boiling water. Drain well. Wrap in aluminum foil or several layers of heavy wax paper and place in the refrigerator overnight or for at least 4 hours. Preheat oven to 375°. Spread 3 tablespoons of the butter on the bottom and sides of an 11-inch pie plate. Cut the biscuits in half lengthwise and arrange half of them on the bottom of the pie plate. Spread with the walnuts and cover with the remaining biscuits. Pour the remaining butter over the top. Press down firmly with a plate, then remove the plate. Bake in a 375° oven for 25 minutes, or until brown.

Prepare the syrup while the pie is baking. Combine the milk and sugar in a saucepan. Bring it to a boil, mix well, and cook until syrupy. Pour the syrup over the pie as soon as it is baked. Cover with a plate and set aside to cool for at least 2 hours. Turn out onto a plate.

# AFRICA

*Egypt*
*North and Central Africa*
*Union of South Africa*

*EGYPT*

Lying in the northeastern part of Africa, Egypt is a tremendous land of which the western half is almost entirely an uninhabited desert. Since only a tiny portion of its land is available for cultivation (a reasonable approximation being about three per cent), the nation is practically supported by the area surrounding the Nile River. The great stream of fabulous history overflows its banks about early September of each year and carries with it the thick silt of the river bed. As the water drains away, the life-sustaining soil remains, permitting the raising of crops which would otherwise be impossible.

Egyptians are famous for their heavy breakfasts and for their exotic choice of foods at this first meal of the day. What makes this surprising is that none of the other Mediterranean or Near Eastern peoples begin the day with a heavy meal. Dinner, usually enjoyed in the evening cool after the great heat of the day has abated somewhat, is likewise an important meal. Between breakfast and dinner, the people do not exactly starve, for in addition to lunch they nibble on little delicacies, such as nuts, fruits, dates, figs, and other oddments. The Egyptians love cool, refreshing soft drinks and there are numbers from which to choose. Both tea and coffee are popular here.

Some fish is eaten, but poultry and meat are more appreciated by the average person. In Egypt "meat" usually means mutton, which is preferred to the younger and more delicate meat of the sheep which we call lamb. The fat of the full-grown sheep is quite strong in flavor and most Westerners find it unappetizing, though it must be admitted that in Australia and New Zealand there is little objection to mutton. Egyptians prefer their meat practically swimming in fat, and this, too, is hardly to our taste. The hotels and restaurants that cater to tourists have learned to avoid an overabundance of grease in their cooking; authentic French cuisine is the rule.

Bread is of the flat type, usually a rather large, spongy, whole wheat mixture which takes the place of cutlery for the *fellah,* or peasant, who sops up his food with it. Most people cannot afford fancy fare, and filling food such as beans, chick-peas, and rice are preferred by the majority. *Couscous,* though probably Algerian in origin, is a great favorite here. It is a meat or poultry dish based on a coarse cereal and is very satisfying.

The sweet desserts beloved of all people of the Near East are in evidence here. Wheat flour, thick fruit syrups, and honey are combined with calorific pastries to form desserts far too sweet for our tastes. Candies, too, are of such sweetness and richness that one piece will cloy the palate.

Water—yes, water—is the national drink of Egypt since it is a Moslem country; after water comes Turkish-style sweet, muddy coffee. Beer and alcoholic drinks are available but are generally unimportant. At Mariout, wines are being grown with reasonable success, and the Clos Mariout, a white wine, is well received by wine drinkers. In addition several satisfactory red wines are in production.

## BEANS, EGYPTIAN STYLE

FOOL MUDAMMAS

| | |
|---|---|
| 1½ cups white beans | ½ cup olive oil |
| 2 teaspoons salt | ¼ cup lemon juice |
| 2 cloves garlic, minced | 3 scallions (green onions), sliced fine |

Wash the beans thoroughly and soak in water to cover overnight. Drain, and cover with fresh water. Cook until the skins split, about 2 hours. Drain well and cool. Place the beans in a bowl. Add the salt, garlic, olive oil, and lemon juice, and mix well. Chill in the refrigerator. Serve with the scallions on top as an appetizer. If desired, the beans may be served as a salad on a bed of romaine lettuce.

## FISH AND LAMB MOLD

BAMIA AU GOMBOS

| | |
|---|---|
| 3 tablespoons olive oil | 2 teaspoons salt |
| 2 onions, chopped | ½ teaspoon pepper |
| 1 pound lamb, ground | 1 cup sherry |
| 3 tomatoes, chopped | 6 fillets of sole |

Heat the olive oil in a frying pan. Add the onions, lamb, tomatoes, salt, and pepper. Sauté for 15 minutes, stirring frequently. Add the sherry and stir well. Cook over low heat for 15 minutes. Butter a 7- to 9-inch casserole or mold. Arrange the fillets so that they cover the bottom and sides of the casserole. Pour in the lamb mixture. If the fillets extend over the outside edge of the casserole, turn them inward to cover the lamb mixture. Bake in a 275° oven for 2 hours.

## CHICKEN AND GREENS

MLOOKHIA

| | |
|---|---|
| 5-pound chicken, quartered | 1 teaspoon ground coriander |
| 1 onion | 3 cloves garlic, minced |
| 1 carrot | 2 teaspoons salt |
| 2½ quarts water | ¼ pound butter |
| 2 pounds spinach, kale, or chard | |

Combine the chicken, onion, carrot, and water in a saucepan. Cook over medium heat for 2 hours, or until chicken is tender. Wash the spinach carefully. Drain well and dry thoroughly. Chop coarsely. Pound the coriander, garlic, and salt to a smooth paste. Melt the butter in a saucepan. Add the paste and chicken. Sauté for 10 minutes. Add the spinach. Cook over medium heat for 10 minutes. Correct seasoning. Serve with boiled rice. The chicken broth may be served separately.

*Note: Mlookhia is a unique and very popular Egyptian vegetable. The green vegetables substituted are similar in flavor, though not so bitter.*

## MEAT CROQUETTES

KUFTA

| | |
|---|---|
| 1 pound beef, chopped | ¼ teaspoon cayenne pepper |
| 1 pound lamb, chopped | ¼ teaspoon orégano |
| 1 onion, chopped fine | 3 tablespoons chopped parsley |
| 2 eggs, beaten | 1½ cups bread crumbs |
| ½ cup milk | ¼ pound butter |
| 1½ teaspoons salt | |

Mix the beef, lamb, onions, eggs, milk, salt, cayenne pepper, orégano, parsley, and 1 cup of the bread crumbs together. Form into large croquettes and dip in the remaining crumbs. Melt half the butter in a frying pan. Fry the croquettes in it slowly over low heat until browned on both sides, about 20 minutes. Add butter as required.

## EGGPLANT AND LAMB CASSEROLE

BEDINGANE ABIAD

½ cup sesame oil or salad oil
1 eggplant, peeled and sliced ¼ inch
   thick
2 onions, chopped fine
2 pounds lean lamb, ground

2 teaspoons salt
1 teaspoon pepper
1½ teaspoons cinnamon
2 cups cooked rice

Heat ¼ cup of the oil in a skillet. Brown the eggplant slices in it on both sides. Remove the eggplant and set aside. Add the remaining ¼ cup of oil to the skillet and heat. Add the onions, lamb, salt, pepper, and cinnamon. Sauté for 10 minutes, stirring frequently.

Butter or oil a casserole. Arrange a layer of rice on the bottom. Cover with about one third of the lamb mixture. Add layer of eggplant and successive layers of rice, lamb and eggplant until the ingredients are used up, ending with rice on top. Bake in a 375° oven for 35 minutes, or until browned on top. Serve directly from the casserole.

## CHICKEN AND CRACKED WHEAT

HAREESIE

5-pound chicken, disjointed
2 onions, chopped fine
8 cups water
2 cups *bourghol* (cracked wheat)
2 teaspoons salt

½ teaspoon pepper
1 teaspoon cinnamon
⅛ teaspoon ground cloves
¼ pound butter

Combine the chicken, onions, and water in a saucepan. Bring to a boil and skim the top carefully. Cook over low heat for 30 minutes. Meanwhile, soak the *bourghol* in water to cover for 20 minutes. Drain the *bourghol* and add to the chicken, together with the salt. Cover and cook over low heat for 2 hours, or until the chicken is tender and the liquid thickens.

Remove the chicken meat from the bones, cut into small pieces, and return to the saucepan. Add the pepper, cinnamon, cloves, and butter. Cook over low heat for 15 minutes. Mix well. Correct seasoning. Serve each portion in a large soup plate. The consistency of the dish should be that of a porridge.

## RICE FLOUR PUDDING

MEHALLABIA

½ cup seedless raisins
1½ cups sugar
1 tablespoon cornstarch
⅓ cup rice flour

4 cups milk
1 tablespoon rose water, orange
    flower water, or vanilla extract

Soak the raisins in water to cover for 15 minutes. Combine the sugar, cornstarch, and rice flour in a saucepan. Gradually add the milk, stirring constantly until smooth. Cook over medium heat, stirring constantly until the boiling point is reached. Cook for 10 minutes, stirring occasionally. Reduce to low heat and cook, without stirring, until the mixture caramelizes on the bottom of the pot. Add the flavoring. Drain the raisins thoroughly and add, stirring gently. Pour the mixture into a serving dish or into 6 individual dishes. Chill at least 4 hours.

## NORTH AND CENTRAL AFRICA

Any discussion of the food habits, diet, and customs of millions of people living in thousands of square miles of territory can be treated only in general terms. In defense of this, it must be admitted that although the area has its high points of local food they cannot, with few exceptions, be called culinary specialties. For the most part, what makes them unique is the use of locally produced ingredients—wild game, fruits, and other produce.

The north coast of Africa consists principally of French and Spanish Morocco, Algeria, Tunisia, Libya, and Egypt (which is discussed separately). Spain has Spanish Morocco, France has French Morocco, Algeria, and Tunis, and Libya is Italian, but underlying the culture of the colonizers is the way of life of the Mohammedan people. Thus in each area there are three conflicting and modifying influences upon the food of the region: the Islamic background of a large part of the population, the respective mother countries, and the kinds of native foodstuffs available.

The one point of agreement throughout the north coast region is *couscous*, a filling semolina dish. Although its exact origin is somewhat doubtful, it is usually attributed to Algeria; in any event it is that country's most important dish. There are many recipes for *couscous*, usually quite spicy, but it may be made with sweet ingredients, such as fruits, or with nuts. Another similarity in the food of this region is the extensive use of fish along the coastal area. Some of the local soups and stews are quite good.

Strong liquors are of no great consequence here because of the Moslem rules on the subject; the possible exception is *lagmi*, a palm wine, which is the only wine permitted by the Koran. Wines are very important in Algeria, where the wine-conscious Frenchmen live. Though certain of the wines produced here must be classified as *vin ordinaire*, others are highly regarded. When a Frenchman is willing to admit that a wine made outside *la belle France* is entitled to serious consideration, it is news indeed. Both reds and whites are produced, but the red burgundylike qualities of the Mascara, Bône, and Bouïra regions are probably the best. Also worth mentioning is the very sweet raisin and fig liqueur called *boura*, and of course the ever present milk drink *leben*, or yogurt.

Senegal is a fairly prosperous country, at least by African standards. Fish dishes are great local favorites, but otherwise the usual chicken, rice, nuts, and fruits are the staple foods.

Throughout the central part of the dark continent game is often plentiful. First-time visitors to Africa may be surprised to learn that game can also be very scarce, owing to varying factors such as rainfall, terrain, and the supply of available food for the game to feed upon. The natives eat all types of wild beasts, including many that are considered palatable by Western standards. Many other creatures of the jungle, which we consider inedible, are enjoyed here. Among these are monkeys, buffaloes, porcupines, elephants, crocodiles, lizards, serpents, ants, grasshoppers, slugs . . . but need we continue?

More to our taste are such things as pawpaw soup, cassava croquettes, and groundnut stew, all of which can be reasonably approximated in our own homes. Most of these dishes are common throughout French West Africa, Nigeria, and French Equatorial Africa. *Jolov*, a rice dish of the area, is a particular household favorite in Liberia. A potatolike tuber, the *mattambala*, is a familiar item of the local diet.

Of Ethiopa (Abyssinia) it can be said that the food is spicy, spicier, spiciest. Hot pepper, ginger, and other inflammable condiments are apparently required in almost every dish to satisfy the local palate. Coffee is highly regarded, and there is also a barley beer, *talla.*

In the Belgian Congo the one native dish of importance is *moamba,* known to the English-speaking residents as palm oil chop. It is quite similar to groundnut stew, for which a recipe is given. A Ugandan specialty is cream of peanut soup, a very nourishing and satisfying dish. Most of the other food is strictly non-habit-forming.

Concerning the culinary style of the cannibals who remain today in Africa, it is believed that little purpose would be served by furnishing their recipes. However, there are people who enjoy such exotic food as snails, squirrels, and frogs' legs, and those who wish may try the following recipe furnished by a local chieftain: "Take one very large pot, with a capacity of about 75 quarts, and fill it with water. When it begins boiling, add ½ pound of salt, and . . ."

The large region that constitutes the Union of South Africa is discussed separately. The island of Madagascar, located southeast of the continent, is well supplied with oysters, shrimp, squid, and all sorts of fish, common and rare. Everything tastes different here; chicken has the flavor of duck, pork has its own variation, and even beef is hardly recognizable. Since chicken tastes like duck, how is the taste of duck to be described? It is believed that the water supply and the aromatic plants and vegetation of the region upon which the animals feed have altered their flavor. This makes it quite simple for the tourist in Madagascar who wishes to eat chicken, pork, or beef: merely order something else. Possibly a good choice for the startled traveler would be the local rum, *tokanem.*

## CREAM OF PEANUT SOUP

**UGANDA**

2 tablespoons cornstarch
3 cups milk
3 cups hot chicken stock or 1 can consommé and 1¼ cans water

2 cups ground peanuts
2 tablespoons grated onion
2 teaspoons salt
⅛ teaspoon cayenne pepper

Place the cornstarch in a deep saucepan. Slowly add the milk, stirring until smooth. Add the stock, peanuts, onion, salt, and cayenne pepper, stirring constantly. Bring to a boil and cook over medium heat for 5 minutes. Beat with a rotary beater for 1 minute. Strain. Serve hot.

## PAWPAW SOUP

WEST COAST OF AFRICA

2 tablespoons butter
1 onion, sliced thin
1 large papaya, peeled and cut into
   small pieces
2 sprigs parsley
3 cups water

1½ teaspoons salt
½ teaspoon pepper
   Dash of mace
1 tablespoon cornstarch
3 cups milk

Melt the butter in a saucepan, add the onion, and sauté for 5 minutes, stirring occasionally. Add the papaya, parsley, water, and salt. Cook over low heat for 1½ hours. Force through a sieve, then return to the saucepan. Add the pepper and mace. Mix the cornstarch and milk until smooth and add to the soup, stirring constantly. Cook for 10 minutes over low heat but do not allow to boil. Serve with croutons.

*Note: Although papayas are not generally available in this country, the recipe is included because it it so typical of this region of Africa. Papayas are obtainable in Florida and certain other areas. Other varieties of melons may be substituted for the papaya.*

## FISH STEW

MAÏKA, NORTH COAST OF AFRICA

¼ cup olive oil
3 onions, chopped
2 tablespoons flour
4 cloves garlic, minced
2½ teaspoons salt
1 teaspoon pepper
½ teaspoon dried ground chili peppers
¼ teaspoon ground coriander

7 cups milk
2 pounds sliced, assorted fish
   (3 different varieties)
½ pound shrimp, shelled and cleaned
2 lobsters, in the shell, chopped into
   small pieces
6 slices toast (French bread, if possible)
3 tablespoons grated lemon rind

Heat the olive oil in a large saucepan. Add the onions and sauté for 15 minutes, stirring frequently. Sprinkle with the flour and mix until smooth. Add the garlic, salt, pepper, chili peppers, and coriander. Gradually add the milk, stirring constantly until the boiling point is reached. Add the fish, shrimp, and lobster and cook over low heat for 25 minutes. Correct seasoning. Place a slice of toast in each soup bowl. Sprinkle with the lemon rind and pour the soup over it. Arrange the fish on a separate platter and serve.

## AFRICAN GUINEA HEN

½ pound butter
2 small guinea hens or 2½-pound
  chickens, disjointed
1 onion, chopped
1 clove garlic, minced
1 tablespoon flour
¾ cup white wine

1 cup water
2 teaspoons salt
½ teaspoon pepper
1 bay leaf
3 tomatoes, chopped
3 sweet potatoes, peeled and cubed
5 firm bananas, sliced 1 inch thick

Melt all but 3 tablespoons of the butter in a saucepan or casserole. Add the poultry, onion, and garlic and sauté until brown, stirring frequently. Sprinkle with the flour and add the wine, water, salt, pepper, bay leaf, and tomatoes. Mix well. Cover and cook over low heat for 20 minutes. Add the sweet potatoes and cook over low heat for 35 minutes, or until the poultry and potatoes are tender. Correct seasoning.

Melt the remaining butter in a skillet. Add the banana slices and sauté lightly. Arrange the poultry in the center of a platter and place the potatoes and bananas around it. Skim the fat off the remaining gravy and serve separately.

## ALGERIAN COUSCOUS

1 cup dried or 2 cups canned,
  drained chick-peas
2 cups *faufal* (see Note)
2 cups water
1½ tablespoons salt
½ pound butter
3 onions, chopped
5-pound chicken, disjointed
2 pounds lamb, cubed
3 tomatoes, cubed

2 green peppers, sliced
2 carrots, sliced
1 teaspoon pepper
¼ teaspoon cayenne pepper
1 pound fresh or ½ package frozen
  green peas
1 cup yellow squash, cubed
6 canned or fresh artichoke hearts
  (optional)

If dried chick-peas are used, soak in water to cover overnight. Place the *faufal* in a bowl. Add the water and 1 teaspoon of the salt and stir. Rub the *faufal* between the hands about 1 foot above the bowl, allowing it to drop into the bowl. Repeat the process several times. Do not allow any lumps to form. Soak the *faufal* until all the water is absorbed.

Melt half of the butter in a large saucepan. Add the onions, chicken, and lamb and brown well. Add barely enough water to cover. Drain the chick-peas, and add, together with the tomatoes, green peppers, carrots, pepper, cayenne pepper, and remaining salt. (If canned chick-peas are used, do not add until the green peas are added.)

Place the *faufal* in a large strainer or colander over the saucepan. Cover as well as possible and cook over low heat for 1½ hours. Add the green peas, squash, and artichokes to the chicken mixture, cover again, and continue cooking over low heat for 45 minutes, or until the chicken is tender. Add the remaining butter to the *faufal*, stirring with a fork. Place the *faufal* in the center of a platter and arrange the chicken and vegetables around it.

*Note:* Faufal *consists of tiny pellets of wheat obtainable in Near Eastern or oriental food stores. Cracked wheat or wheat semolina or even farina may be used, but none of these substitutes will duplicate the* faufal. *The amount of cayenne pepper may be increased slightly for those who wish a more authentic* couscous.

## GROUNDNUT STEW

MOAMBA, WEST COAST OF AFRICA

| | |
|---|---|
| 2 4-pound chickens, disjointed | 2 sweet potatoes, peeled and quartered |
| 6 cups water | tered |
| 1½ cups ground peanuts | 2 teaspoons salt |
| 2 onions, chopped fine | 6 hard-cooked eggs, shelled |
| | 4 cups hot cooked rice |

Clean the chickens carefully and place in a deep saucepan with the water. Bring to a boil and cook over medium heat for 30 minutes. Add the peanuts and stir well. Add the onions, sweet potatoes, and salt. Cook for 1½ hours, or until chicken is tender. Correct seasoning. Place a whole egg on each plate and cover with some of the rice. Place the chicken and sauce on top. Serve with side dishes of sliced cucumbers, chutney, and sliced bananas.

## LIBERIAN RICE AND CHICKEN

JOLOV

| | |
|---|---|
| 2 3-pound chickens, disjointed | 3 green peppers, minced |
| 4 teaspoons salt | 2 cans tomato paste |
| ¼ pound butter | 2 cups water |
| 3 tablespoons salad oil | 2 cups rice |
| 4 onions, chopped | |

Wash and dry the chicken pieces. Sprinkle with 2 teaspoons of the salt. Melt the butter in a saucepan. Add the chicken and brown well on all sides over high heat. Cover and cook over low heat until tender.

Heat the oil in a separate saucepan. Add the onion and green peppers and sauté for 10 minutes, or until lightly browned, stirring occasionally.

Add the tomato paste, water, and remaining salt. Mix well and bring to a boil. Wash the rice in several changes of water and add to the tomato mixture. Cover and cook over low heat for 20 minutes, or until rice is tender. Add small additional amounts of water, if necessary. Correct seasoning. Combine the rice with the chicken and stir. If desired, press the rice into molds or cups, then unmold and arrange the chicken around the mounds of rice.

## CASSAVA CROQUETTES

WEST COAST OF AFRICA

2 cups grated cassava or potatoes
3 eggs
2 tablespoons grated lemon rind
⅛ teaspoon nutmeg
⅛ teaspoon pepper
¾ teaspoon salt
2 tablespoons chopped parsley
½ cup bread crumbs

Wet the cassava with water, then squeeze it dry in the hands. Add 2 eggs, the lemon rind, nutmeg, pepper, salt, and parsley. Mix well. Beat the remaining egg in a bowl. Shape the mixture into croquettes or pancakes and dip in the beaten egg, then in the bread crumbs. Fry in butter or shortening over low heat until browned on both sides, about 10 minutes.

*Note: Cassava is obtainable in certain cities with large Spanish-speaking populations, such as New York City. It is a large, starchy root and the use of white potatoes will somewhat approximate the taste of it. An even closer resemblance may be obtained by adding 1 tablespoon of either farina or instant tapioca to the grated potato.*

## LIBERIAN RICE CAKE

½ pound butter
1 cup sugar
4 eggs, beaten
2 cups rice flour
2 teaspoons cream of tartar
1 teaspoon baking soda
1 cup milk
½ teaspoon nutmeg
1 teaspoon vanilla extract

Cream the butter and add the sugar gradually. Beat until light and fluffy. Add the eggs and beat well. Preheat oven to 325°. Sift the rice flour, cream of tartar, and baking soda together. Add to the egg mixture alternately with the milk. Beat constantly. Add the nutmeg and vanilla. Beat well. Pour into a 12-inch buttered loaf pan. Bake in a 325° oven for 35 minutes, or until a cake tester comes out clean.

## UNION OF SOUTH AFRICA

The word "Africa" usually brings to mind vast plains and wild animals, and while this is true to a certain extent, Capetown and Johannesburg (called Joburg by its inhabitants) are extremely modern cities filled with fine buildings and not a few skyscrapers. The visitor is always surprised by the pace and tempo of these cities.

Four principal groups in addition to numerous minorities are represented here: the Dutch, British, Indian, and native populations. The Dutch (Boers) were the earliest settlers of this land, and brought with them their own style of cooking, names of dishes, and eating habits. *Melksnysels* (ribbons of dough in milk soup) is a typical Dutch dish. The British, as they have the world over, brought a little bit of England with them in their hearts, and they prefer English food and the English way of life, typified by elaborate teas and formal dinners. The Indians came originally to labor under the hot African sun but have become shop-keepers. They, too, brought their food customs with them. The Bantu, the principal group of aborigines, have few dishes of interest to us, except those based on the wild game of the region.

Unfortunately for the curious gourmet, hotels and restaurants limit themselves to the hotel-style food known the world over as "international," which customarily means taking little or no advantage of the area's fine foodstuffs. To enjoy an *Afrikander* dinner, it would probably be necessary to secure an invitation to the home of a long-time resident, as these dishes are seldom seen on menus in public dining places.

The native groups are particularly fond of their home brew, known as Kaffir beer, but comparatively few tourists ever get around to tasting it. South Africa produces in a moderate-sized area numerous wines of good quality, particularly sweet types. Both still and sparkling wines are available, though they are not yet of export standard, except for the local sherry-type wine. Local brandies are quite satisfactory. Of course the usual imported liquors may be had. In passing, it may be noted that the cocktail party is the most popular of all social events.

Until recently the great shellfish specialty of South Africa was unknown to the rest of the world. However, since the advent of frozen foods, the *langouste,* marketed as the South African lobster tail, has been well received. These are eaten broiled, boiled, sautéed in butter, served on noodles, and in many other fashions. Rock oysters and salmon are also unusually fine.

Lamb is raised extensively in the region and is the basis for many local dishes. The young lamb is appreciated by visitors, but the older specimens appeal only to those who have eaten mutton all their lives. Among the old standbys of the country are *babottee* (a meat pie) and bean *bredee* (a stew). The local preference is for dishes of this nature.

The fruits—melons and berries—are astonishing. The variety is apparently limitless, but their quality is also very high. Not only are there all the familiar fruits, there are also the rare, the exotic, and the romantic.

## PICKLED SALMON

12 thin slices salmon, cut in half
4 teaspoons salt
1 teaspoon pepper
¼ cup olive or salad oil
6 large onions, sliced in thin rings
3 tablespoons curry powder

½ teaspoon dried ground chili peppers
1 cup seedless raisins
2 tablespoons sugar
1 teaspoon turmeric
3 cups vinegar

Wash and dry the salmon. Mix 1 teaspoon of the salt with the pepper and sprinkle the fish with it. Heat the oil in a skillet and brown the fish in it on both sides. Remove the fish and let cool. Add 4 onions to the oil remaining in the pan and fry until brown.

Combine 2 tablespoons of the curry powder, the chili peppers, raisins, sugar, and turmeric. Add 3 tablespoons of the vinegar and mix well. Arrange several successive layers of fish, fried onions, and the spice mixture in a bowl or jar. Combine the remaining onions, vinegar, salt, and curry powder in a saucepan. Boil for 15 minutes. Pour over the layers of fish and allow to cool for 1 hour. Cover and keep in the refrigerator for at least 2 days before using. Prepared this way, the fish will keep about 2 weeks. Serve cold as an appetizer.

## CURRIED POTATO SOUP

3 tablespoons butter
1 pound stewing beef, cut into ¼-inch cubes
3 onions, chopped
8 cups water

2 teaspoons salt
2 tablespoons curry powder
2 bay leaves
3 potatoes, sliced
1 tablespoon vinegar

Melt the butter in a deep saucepan. Add the beef and onions and fry until brown. Add the water, salt, curry powder, and bay leaves. Cook over medium heat for 45 minutes. Add the potatoes and vinegar. Cook for 30 minutes, or until the meat and potatoes are tender. Correct seasoning. Discard bay leaves. Serve hot in deep soup plates.

## MILK SOUP WITH RIBBONS

**MELKSNYSELS**

1⅛ cups sifted flour
¼ teaspoon salt
½ teaspoon baking powder
2 quarts milk

3 egg yolks
¼ cup sugar
½ teaspoon cinnamon
3 egg whites

Sift 1 cup of the flour, the salt and baking powder into a bowl. Add gradually about ½ cup of the milk, using just enough to make a stiff dough. Knead until the dough is elastic and springy. Roll out as thin as possible on a lightly floured surface. Allow to remain for 15 minutes. Sprinkle with the remaining flour and roll up lightly like a jelly roll. Cut evenly into ¼-inch slices. Bring the remaining milk to an active boil in a deep sauce-pan. Drop the noodle ribbons into it and cook until they come to the top. Drain, reserving the milk, and keep warm.

Beat the yolks, sugar, and cinnamon in a bowl. Gradually add 1 cup of the hot milk, beating constantly to prevent curdling. Return the con-tents of the bowl to the balance of the milk, stirring constantly. Heat but do not allow to boil. Beat the egg whites until stiff but not dry. Pour the milk mixture over them, mixing gently. Place the noodles in bowls or soup plates and pour the milk mixture over them. Serve hot.

## AFRIKANDER LAMB CHOPS

⅔ cup tomato sauce
⅔ cup vinegar
½ cup Worcestershire sauce
1 onion, grated

1 teaspoon dry mustard
1 teaspoon salt
12 lamb chops

Combine the tomato sauce, vinegar, Worcestershire sauce, onion, mustard, and salt in a bowl. Mix well. Marinate the chops at room temperature for 1 hour. Drain, reserving the sauce. Pan-fry the chops. Turn frequently until done. Heat the sauce in a separate saucepan and pour over the chops.

## MEAT STEW, CAPE MALAY STYLE

CURRIED BEAN BREDEE

1½ cups dried white beans
2 tablespoons salad oil or butter
4 pounds mutton or lamb, cut into 2-inch cubes
3 onions, chopped
8 tomatoes, peeled and chopped
2 teaspoons salt

¼ teaspoon dried ground chili peppers
2 tablespoons curry powder
1 tablespoon sugar
¼ cup water
2 tablespoons vinegar
1 cup chopped sour apples
½ cup seedless raisins

Place the beans in a saucepan with water to cover and soak overnight. Drain, cover with water again, and boil for 1 hour.

Heat the oil in a heavy saucepan that has a tight fitting lid. Add the onions and sauté for 5 minutes. Add the meat and brown well on all sides. Add the tomatoes, salt, and chili peppers. Cover and cook over very low heat for 30 minutes. Mix the curry powder, sugar, water, and vinegar together until smooth. Add to the meat and stir well. Drain the beans and add, together with the apples and raisins, again stirring well. Cover and cook over very low heat for 2½ hours, or until meat is very tender. Small amounts of water may be added if required.

The resulting stew should be quite thick and rich. Best results will be obtained if the saucepan is tightly covered and the meat cooked slowly. Serve with boiled rice.

## STEAK AND MACARONI CASSEROLE

2 pounds steak
3 teaspoons salt
1 teaspoon pepper
1 cup grated cheese

1 cup bread crumbs
2 eggs, beaten
Oil or shortening for deep-fat frying
4 cups cooked macaroni

Cut the steak into 1-inch squares. Sprinkle with 1½ teaspoons of the salt and ½ teaspoon of the pepper. Reserve half the cheese and dip the steak pieces in the remaining half. Then dip the pieces in the bread crumbs, eggs, and once again in the bread crumbs. Heat the oil to 375° in a deep saucepan. Drop several pieces of the meat into the fat at a time, and fry for 1 minute. Drain.

Place the macaroni in a buttered casserole. Sprinkle with the remaining salt, pepper, and cheese. Place the steak pieces on top. Bake in a 450° oven for 10 minutes, or until browned on top. This dish is often served with broiled tomatoes.

## GROUND BEEF PIE

BABOTTEE

| | |
|---|---|
| 3 tablespoons butter | 2 tablespoons curry powder |
| 3 onions, chopped | 1 teaspoon salt |
| 2 slices white bread | 2 tablespoons plum jam |
| 1 cup milk | 3 tablespoons lemon juice |
| 3 pounds beef, ground 3 times | ¼ cup ground almonds |
| 2 eggs | 3 bay leaves |

Melt the butter in a saucepan. Add the onions and sauté for 10 minutes, stirring occasionally. Soak the bread in the milk and squeeze dry, reserving the milk. Mash the bread fine. In a bowl combine the beef, sautéed onions, bread, 1 egg, curry powder, salt, plum jam, lemon juice, and almonds. Mix well. Place the bay leaves on the bottom of a buttered baking dish and place the meat mixture over them. Beat the remaining egg with the reserved milk and pour it over the meat. Bake in a 350° oven for 1¼ hours. Serve hot from the dish.

## OAT BREAD

| | |
|---|---|
| 2 tablespoons sugar | 1½ cups oatmeal |
| 1 cup water | 1½ cups sifted flour |
| ½ cake or package yeast | ⅛ teaspoon salt |

Dissolve the sugar in the water. Add the yeast and 2 tablespoons of the oatmeal, stirring until smooth. Combine the remaining oatmeal, the flour, and salt in a bowl. Make a well or depression in the center and pour in the yeast mixture. Cover with a towel and set aside in a warm place for 20 minutes. Blend the oatmeal mixture into the yeast with the hand until a stiff dough is formed. Add slightly more flour if necessary. Cover and allow to rise for 1 hour. Preheat oven to 375°. Form the dough into 2 small loaves or 1 large one and place in a buttered loaf pan. Bake in a 375° oven for 20 minutes, or until browned.

## FRIED CAKES

KOEK SISTERS

| | |
|---|---|
| 2 cups sifted flour | Oil or fat for deep-fat frying |
| ⅛ teaspoon salt | 1½ cups sugar |
| 1 teaspoon cream of tartar | ⅓ cup water |
| 3 tablespoons butter | ½ teaspoon cinnamon |
| 1 egg, beaten | |

Sift the flour, salt, and cream of tartar together into a bowl. Cut in the butter with a pastry blender or two knives until the consistency of coarse sand. Add the egg and toss lightly with a fork until the mixture forms a ball of dough. Roll out ¼ inch thick on a lightly floured surface. Cut into circles and roll up in the shape of cornucopias, so that one end is closed and the other open.

Heat the fat to 385° in a deep saucepan. Drop a few cornucopias at a time into the fat. Fry until they rise to the surface. Remove immediately and drain. Combine 1 cup of the sugar, the water and cinnamon in a saucepan. Boil until syrupy, about 5 minutes. Dip each cake into the syrup, then roll in the remaining sugar.

# ASIA

*Burma*
*China*
*Hong Kong*
*India and Ceylon*
*Indonesia*
*Japan*
*Korea*
*Pakistan*
*Singapore and Malaya*
*Thailand* (*Siam*)

## BURMA

Tourists who are disappointed to find that Venice and Rio de Janeiro are more touristy than foreign will not be likely to complain about Burma. It is indeed an exotic place to an occidental. While it is true that the Burmese are much taken with American ways and American products, the local way of life is most appealing. No amount of chromium, neon lights, and blaring radios can change Burma.

Tourists folders often describe a country as being populated with smiling people, and the traveler will find this trite description to be true of Burma. The people actually smile. Very few countries can make that statement. They really seem happy, and are apparently satisfied with their lives. Of course they are a simple, trusting people who are unaware of ulcers, the stock market, high blood pressure, 3-D, inflation, and the other benefits of civilization. Foolishly, they go on their way, wearing the colorful *lungyi*, something like a skirt, indulging themselves in their delightful festivals, little dreaming of the more important (?) things of life, such as social security, taxes, and unemployment insurance.

From the moment the Pan American plane puts down at modern Mingaladon Airport, you will be able to re-create Kipling's Burma, although it will have to be in your mind. It was on the road to Mandalay that his British soldier saw the Burma girl smoking a cheroot. (The dictionary says that a cheroot is a cigar with a truncated end. A truncated end is . . .)

The land itself is a good one, heavily irrigated by the rivers which rise almost fifty feet during the rainy season. This flooding of the adjacent fields makes them particularly suitable for the growing of rice, sugar cane, and the local tobacco, which is made into cigars with truncated ends called cheroots, which in turn are smoked by Burma girls, or are we confused and is it the other way round? Speaking of women, it is only in

Burma, of all the Asian countries, that those of female persuasion are held in high esteem by the male contingent. The respect and deference to their opinions are unique in the Orient.

On rising, there is coffee or tea with bread. At about 9 A.M., a breakfast of rice, soup, and curry. The midday meal, called tiffin in the British fashion, is a fairly simple meal of meat, bread, and fruit. Dinnertime is usually 6 P.M. The meal often begins with soup, although all the dishes are placed on the table at the same time. Soups are of two kinds: the regular type, *hingyo*, and the acid soup, *chin-ye-hin*. Everyone in the family helps himself from the various bowls according to his appetite and preferences. Except on special occasions, cakes and other sweet desserts are not served. Fresh or preserved fruits are the rule, and these often end the meal.

The Burmese cuisine is similar to those of India and Indonesia. Curries are standbys, and curry powder itself is the favorite seasoning. Pickles and relishes of all kinds are well liked by the people, and a great favorite is the garlic-laden pickled cabbage. Noodle dishes, such as fried vermicelli and *panthay khowse* (noodles and chicken), are popular. Most of this descriptive material as to the food habits of the people applies only to those who can afford it; there are many who must be satisfied with a bowl of rice flavored with a little *nga-pi-gyet*, a garlic and shrimp sauce that may reasonably be described as noxious. In all fairness it must be allowed that it is possible to learn to like this Burmese favorite; the Burmese are tolerant about our fondness for our smelly cheese, which they abhor.

Although coffee is well liked, this is a tea-growing country. The Burmese prefer their tea with an orange blossom or jasmine fragrance; in addition, they like to thicken it with grains or cereals until it has a gumbo-like consistency, whereupon it ceases to taste like tea. On second thought, perhaps they don't like tea as much as we first believed.

## CABBAGE SOUP

MON LA HINGYO

2 tablespoons sesame or peanut oil
1 tablespoon anchovy or shrimp paste
2 onions, chopped fine
3 cloves garlic, minced
1 teaspoon plum jam
1 teaspoon lemon juice
2 fresh chili peppers, chopped fine,
or ½ teaspoon dried ground chili peppers
2 tomatoes, chopped
3 cups shredded cabbage
6 cups beef stock or 3 cans consommé and 2 cans water
1½ teaspoons salt
¼ teaspoon pepper

Combine the oil, anchovy or shrimp paste, onions, garlic, jam, lemon juice, chili peppers, tomatoes, and cabbage in a deep saucepan. Cover and cook over low heat for 20 minutes. Add the stock, salt, and pepper. Bring to a boil. Cook uncovered over low heat for 20 minutes. Correct seasoning and serve.

*Note: Plum jam and lemon juice are used in this recipe as a substitute for the usually unavailable tamarind.*

## CURRIED FISH BALLS

### NGA SOK HIN

2 pounds fillets of any white-meat fish
½ cup sesame oil or peanut oil
2 fresh chili peppers, ground, or ½ teaspoon dried ground chili peppers
3 onions, chopped fine

4 cloves garlic, minced
1 teaspoon grated lemon rind
1 teaspoon turmeric
2 teaspoons salt
¼ cup flour
3 tomatoes, chopped

Wash the fish thoroughly and remove any bones. Grind it twice in a food chopper, or chop very fine. Heat ¼ cup of the oil in a skillet. Add the chili peppers, onions, garlic, lemon rind, turmeric, and salt. Sauté for 10 minutes, stirring frequently. Remove one third of this mixture and add to the ground fish. Chop together until smooth. Form the fish mixture into walnut-size balls. Roll lightly in the flour.

Add the remaining oil to the mixture in the skillet and heat. Add the fish balls and brown on all sides, stirring frequently. Add the tomatoes and cook over low heat for 25 minutes. Serve hot with boiled rice.

## GINGER BEEF

### AHME HNAT HIN

5 onions, chopped fine
4 cloves garlic, minced
2 teaspoons turmeric
2 fresh chili peppers, chopped, or ½ teaspoon dried ground chili peppers
1-inch piece fresh ginger, chopped, or 2 teaspoons powdered ginger

2 teaspoons salt
3 pounds beef, cut into 1½-inch cubes
½ cup sesame oil or peanut oil
8 tomatoes, chopped, or 1 No. 2 can
2 cups stock or 1 can consommé and ½ cup water

Combine the onions, garlic, turmeric, chili peppers, ginger, and salt. Chop or pound together until very fine. Place the beef in a bowl and add the spice mixture. Coat the meat as well as possible. Leave in the bowl for 3 hours, turning frequently. Heat the oil until it bubbles, using a deep saucepan. Add the beef and spices and brown well. Add the tomatoes and cook over medium heat for 10 minutes. Add the stock. Cover and cook over low heat for 1 hour, or until the meat is tender.

## NOODLES AND CHICKEN, BURMESE STYLE

PANTHAY KHOWSE

3 cups fresh or dried grated coconut
4 cups milk
½ cup sesame oil or peanut oil
3 onions, chopped fine
6 cloves garlic, minced
1-inch piece of fresh ginger, chopped fine, or 2 teaspoons powdered ginger
1 tablespoon curry powder
2 4-pound chickens, boned and cut into small cubes
1 cup boiling water
2 teaspoons salt
¼ cup cornstarch or potato flour
¼ cup cold water
3 8-ounce packages broad noodles, boiled
2 fresh chili peppers, chopped fine, or ½ teaspoon dried ground chili peppers
4 hard-cooked eggs, chopped
6 scallions (green onions), sliced thin

Combine the coconut and the milk in a saucepan. Bring to a boil, remove from the heat, and soak for 30 minutes. Press all the liquid from the coconut and discard the pulp.

Heat the oil in a saucepan. Add the onions, garlic, and ginger and sauté for 10 minutes, stirring frequently. Add the curry powder; stir, and cook 2 minutes longer. Add the chicken and sauté for 15 minutes, stirring occasionally. Add 2 cups of the previously prepared coconut milk, the boiling water, and the salt. Stir well and cover. Cook over low heat for 30 minutes, or until the chicken is tender. Mix the cornstarch and water to a smooth paste in a cup. Add to the chicken mixture, stirring constantly until the boiling point is reached. Cook over medium heat for 10 minutes, stirring frequently. Add the remaining coconut milk and stir. Heat but do not allow the mixture to boil.

Arrange the boiled noodles on a large platter or divide into individual portions. Sprinkle the chili peppers, eggs, and scallions over them. Pour the chicken mixture on top.

## COCONUT RICE, BURMA STYLE

OHN HTAMIN

3 cups fresh or dried grated coconut
4 cups milk
2 tablespoons sesame oil or peanut oil
3 onions, sliced
3 cups rice
2 teaspoons salt

Combine the coconut and milk in a saucepan. Bring to a boil, remove from the heat, and soak for 30 minutes. Press all the liquid from the coconut and discard the pulp.

Heat the oil in a deep saucepan. Add the onions and sauté for 15 minutes, stirring frequently. Wash the rice in several changes of water.

Drain well. Add to the onions and cook over high heat until lightly browned, stirring constantly. Add the coconut milk and salt and stir. Add enough water, if necessary, to cover the rice by ½ inch. Cover and cook over low heat until rice is tender, about 15 minutes. Stir the rice from the bottom at least several times during this period. The rice is ready when all of the liquid has been absorbed, but do not allow the rice to become dry.

## COCONUT CAKE

OWN THEE MOANT

| | |
|---|---|
| ¼ pound butter | 1 teaspoon baking powder |
| 1 cup sugar | 1½ cups fresh or dried grated coconut |
| 4 egg yolks | 1 teaspoon vanilla extract |
| ¾ cup farina | 4 egg whites |
| ½ cup sifted flour | |

Cream the butter; add the sugar and beat until light and fluffy. Add the egg yolks and beat again. Sift the farina, flour, and baking powder together and add to the butter mixture, beating well. Chop the coconut very fine and add with the vanilla. Mix well. Preheat oven to 350°. Beat the egg whites until stiff but not dry and fold into the coconut mixture carefully. Pour into two buttered 8-inch layer-cake pans. Bake in a 350° oven for 20 minutes or until a cake tester comes out clean.

*Note: In Burma the cake is served plain. It may be iced or decorated with whipped cream and grated coconut if desired.*

## CHINA

Probably the largest and most popular group of foreign restaurants in this country is Chinese. However, the majority of these specialize in dishes that are seldom representative of the cuisine of their country. So widespread is this practice that many Chinese restaurants advertise themselves only by the flashing neon sign *Chop Suey*. This dish does not even exist in China! The exact manner in which a non-existent dish became a part of the English language is lost in conflicting folklore, but it is certain that *chop suey* is practically unknown in China. *Chow mein,* on the other hand, is an authentic Chinese item and merely means fried noodles.

Most Americans limit themselves to a few simple things such as egg rolls, egg drop soup, and similar dishes. They miss a world of culinary adventure by doing so. It has been said that there are four great cuisines in the world—French, German, Italian, and Chinese—and the Chinese is probably not the least of these. Just as we have our own local styles of preparing American food, so may Chinese cooking be divided into Canton, Peking, Szechuan, Fukien, and Shanghai styles. The majority of Chinese immigrants to the United States had their origins in Canton or Peking, and naturally these two styles are the most popular here.

Many normally curious people hesitate to try anything other than the few Chinese dishes with which they are familiar. They have heard of such rare and unpleasant-sounding ingredients as sharks' fins, birds' nests, and ancient eggs. But these are exotic and expensive, and certainly not necessarily representative of Chinese food. It is more important to understand the theory of the Chinese cuisine, which is founded upon economy, complexity, and subtlety. Few people in China are prosperous enough to think in terms of a whole duck or a whole roast beef. Rather, their dishes are based on staple foods such as rice or noodles, to which are added vegetables and a sauce, the whole flavored with the addition of an ounce or two of meat or poultry. Having a long history of developing culinary arts, but lacking ingredients on a sufficient scale, the cooks of China have devised complex flavor patterns. Most of the recipes in this section contain meat or poultry in amounts which would ordinarily be reserved for holidays in China. Fish is often used in more generous quantities, but only along the coastline.

Chinese dinners are quite unlike those of the Western world. A primary difference is the fact that men and women do not dine together; men eat first, followed by the women, who must content themselves with what is left over. Naturally one wonders whether the women cooks who prepare the dinner remove the choicest morsels before serving the men. Chinese women have thus quietly instituted their own code of equality. Instead of serving separate courses, all the food is placed on the table at the same time, Asiatic style. For this reason Chinese serving dishes containing hot foods are always covered. Desserts are of comparatively little importance and usually consist of nothing more than preserved fruit or a simple cooky.

The Chinese have many favorite locally made wines and liquors, but these have little appeal to our Westernized palates. Possibly the one exception is the hot rice wine, which many persons of European or American background have learned to appreciate. Tea, of course, is the national drink. But it is not the commercial tea with which we are familiar. Rather, it is the so-called "China" tea, comparatively little known in this country, where the Pekoe and Orange Pekoe varieties have captured the market. Chinese of all classes drink large quantities of hot, unsweetened tea from tiny cups without handles. If you plan to serve a Chinese dinner, buy some Chinese tea and steep it in a teapot. It should be served throughout the entire meal.

There are fine Chinese dishes, almost without number. Those included here represent a small sampling of the world of Chinese cookery. If you will examine the ingredients called for in the recipe, you will find that few of them are exotic. Rather, it is the method of preparation that is unusual. Vegetables are cooked briefly and are incorporated directly into the main dish; they are seldom served separately. Try to obtain the items required for a recipe instead of omitting them. Often it is a seemingly unimportant ingredient that gives a dish its unique flavor. Do not overcook Chinese food; serve it promptly when it is ready.

Chinese cooks use monosodium glutamate extensively. This vegetable derivative, marketed in this country under various trade names, actually does improve the flavor of most cooked dishes.

## BARBECUED SPARERIBS

SHEW PYE GULT

6 tablespoons honey
6 tablespoons vinegar
1 tablespoon sugar
6 tablespoons soy sauce
2 cloves garlic, minced

⅛ teaspoon powdered ginger
1½ cups stock or 2 bouillon cubes dissolved in 1½ cups boiling water
2 tablespoons sherry
3 pounds spareribs

Combine in a bowl the honey, vinegar, sugar, soy sauce, garlic, ginger, stock, and sherry. Mix well. Cut the spareribs into individual ribs and place them in the bowl. Spoon the sauce over the ribs for at least 3 minutes. Marinate at room temperature for at least 3 hours, basting frequently. If possible, marinate overnight in the refrigerator. Remove the ribs from the marinade and place them on a flat roasting pan. Roast in a 350° oven for 1 hour. Pour off the fat as it accumulates on the bottom of the pan, at least four times during the roasting period. At the same time, baste the ribs with the marinade. When properly roasted the ribs should be crisp but not dried out.

One 3-pound rack of spareribs is enough for 6 people as an appetizer. If it is to be served as a main course, use 2 racks of spareribs and serve with rice. The quantity of marinade in this recipe will be sufficient for 2 racks.

# FRIED MEAT BALLS AND CRAB MEAT

## CHAN FAR YOOK KUN

1½ pounds pork, ground
¼ pound cooked or canned crab meat
½ cup chopped mushrooms
½ cup chopped canned water chestnuts (optional)
2 teaspoons salt
½ teaspoon pepper
1 teaspoon sugar
1 cup cornstarch
2 eggs, beaten
2 tablespoons water
Fat for deep-fat frying

Combine the pork, crab meat, mushrooms, water chestnuts, salt, pepper, and sugar in a chopping bowl. Chop until well blended and very fine in texture. Shape into 1-inch balls. Dip each ball in cornstarch and coat well. Combine the eggs and water and dip each ball in the mixture. Heat the fat to 360° and drop the balls into it. Fry for 15 minutes. Drain well. Serve with sliced cucumbers. These little balls are excellent as hors d'oeuvres; spear each one with a toothpick and a thin slice of cucumber.

# STUFFED POCKETS OF DOUGH

## WON TON

2 cups sifted flour
1½ teaspoons salt
2 eggs
⅛ cup water
1½ cups cooked chopped beef, pork, or chicken
2 teaspoons soy sauce
¼ teaspoon pepper
2 scallions (green onions), sliced fine
1 quart salted, boiling water
6 cups chicken stock or 2 cans chicken consommé and 2½ cans water
1 cup cooked sliced beef, pork, or chicken
½ pound raw spinach, shredded

Sift the flour and salt together twice. Beat the eggs and combine them with the water. Add to the flour and mix until well blended. Place on a lightly floured board and knead until smooth. Set aside while preparing the filling.

Mix the chopped meat, soy sauce, pepper, and scallions until well blended. Roll out the dough as thin as possible. Cut into 4-inch squares. Place a heaping teaspoonful of the meat mixture in the center of each square and fold over diagonally. Press the edges together, using a little water. Bring the quart of salted water to the boiling point and drop the *won ton* into it. Boil for 12 minutes. Drain.

Heat the stock and add the sliced meat and the spinach. Cook for only 2 minutes. Place 3 *won ton* in each soup plate and pour the soup over them. If desired, the *won ton* may be served without soup. After boiling them, drain well and fry in hot fat. Serve hot.

## SOUR AND SWEET FISH

CHO LOW YU

6 slices fish or 2 whole sea bass or carp (about 2 pounds each)
3 egg yolks, beaten
5½ tablespoons cornstarch
½ teaspoon salt
4 tablespoons sherry
¼ cup flour
¼ cup finely ground bread crumbs

1 cup shortening for frying
4 tablespoons peanut or salad oil
3 tablespoons sugar
6 tablespoons vinegar
2 tablespoons honey
1 teaspoon powdered ginger
¼ cup pickled tiny onions, drained
½ cup cold water

Wash and dry the fish. If whole fish are used, with a sharp knife make several gashes to the bone of the fish on each side. If pieces of fish are used, it is better if the skin remains on during the cooking process to hold the fish together. The authentic Chinese style is to use whole fish. Beat the yolks until light, add 4 tablespoons of the cornstarch, the salt and sherry, and mix well. Dip the fish in this mixture, turning many times to make sure that it is well coated. Combine the flour and bread crumbs and dip the fish in it, again being careful to coat all sides. Heat the shortening until it smokes, then reduce the heat to medium. Place the fish in it carefully and cook for 5 minutes on each side if slices are used; allow 8 minutes on each side for whole fish. Remove from heat and drain.

Heat the oil in a saucepan. Add the sugar, vinegar, honey, ginger, and onions. Cook over low heat for 2 minutes. Mix the remaining cornstarch and water to a smooth paste and add gradually, stirring constantly until smooth and thick. Pour the sauce over the fish and serve.

## FRIED RICE WITH SHRIMP

HAR CHOW FON

1½ cups rice
2½ cups water
4 tablespoons peanut or salad oil
3 eggs
1 teaspoon salt
½ teaspoon pepper

1 pound shrimp, shelled, cleaned, and coarsely chopped
3 onions, chopped
¼ pound mushrooms, sliced
3 tablespoons soy sauce
1 teaspoon sugar

Wash the rice thoroughly. Soak in warm water for 15 minutes. Drain and rinse again. Combine in a saucepan with the water. Cover and bring to a boil. Cook over low heat for 12 minutes, or until the water is absorbed. Heat the oil in a large heavy skillet. Break the eggs into it. Fry until firm, then turn over and fry 1 minute. Remove the pan from the heat and cut the eggs into very thin shreds, while still in the pan. Return the pan to the heat. Add the salt, pepper, shrimp, onions, and mushrooms. Cook over low heat for 5 minutes, stirring frequently. Add the rice, soy sauce, and sugar. Cook over medium heat for 5 minutes, stirring almost constantly.

## BEEF AND PEPPERS

LOT JU KAIR NGOW

1 tablespoon cornstarch
¼ cup cold water
3 pounds beef (top round or sirloin), cut into thin strips
3 cloves garlic, minced
1 teaspoon powdered ginger
¾ cup peanut or salad oil
2 tomatoes, cut into small wedges

2 green peppers, cut into julienne strips
2 onions, chopped
1 cup chicken stock or 1 bouillon cube dissolved in 1 cup hot water
1 teaspoon sugar
1 teaspoon salt
¼ teaspoon pepper
4 tablespoons sherry

Mix the cornstarch and water to a smooth paste. Combine this mixture with the strips of meat, garlic, and ginger. Heat the oil in a heavy skillet and add the meat mixture. Cook for 5 minutes over high heat, stirring constantly. Remove the meat but leave the oil in the skillet.

Reduce the heat to medium and add the tomatoes, green peppers, and onions. Cook for 2 minutes, stirring frequently. Do not overcook; the vegetables must be crisp. Add the stock, sugar, salt, pepper, and sherry, stirring constantly, and cook for 3 minutes. Add the meat and cook for 2 minutes, stirring constantly. It is important that the cooking times specified be followed exactly and that the dish be served immediately when it is ready. Serve with boiled rice.

## BEEF AND STRING BEANS

DOW JAY, NGOW YOK SOONG

3 tablespoons peanut or salad oil
1 clove garlic, minced
½ teaspoon powdered ginger
½ pound beef or pork, ground
3 onions, sliced
1 pound fresh or 1 package frozen string beans

1 cup stock or 1 bouillon cube dissolved in 1 cup hot water
2 tablespoons soy sauce
2 sprigs parsley
1 bay leaf
1 teaspoon salt
½ teaspoon pepper

Heat the oil in a saucepan. Add the garlic, ginger, meat, and onions. Cook over high heat for 3 minutes, stirring constantly. Reduce the heat. Add the string beans, stock, soy sauce, parsley, bay leaf, salt, and pepper. Cook over low heat for 30 minutes, stirring occasionally. Discard the bay leaf. Correct seasoning. Serve with boiled rice.

## FRAGRANT DUCK

NGHONG AUCK

| | |
|---|---|
| 1½ cups dark brown sugar | 1 tablespoon salt |
| 3 teaspoons cinnamon | 1 6-pound duck, washed and dried |
| 2 cloves | 2 teaspoons soy sauce |
| 1 cup water | 2 teaspoons powdered ginger |

Place the sugar in a saucepan and cook over low heat until it melts. Add half the cinnamon, the cloves, and the water. Cook until syrupy. Combine the salt and remaining cinnamon and rub into the duck thoroughly, inside and out. Place the duck on a roasting pan. Combine the syrup with the soy sauce and ginger and mix well. Pour over the duck.

Roast in a 425° oven until golden in color, basting frequently. Reduce the heat to 350° and roast until tender, about 2½ hours altogether, including the browning time. Add additional water if the pan becomes too dry, and baste frequently. Cut the duck into small pieces and serve. The Chinese serve the duck with a sauce made by mixing ½ cup of vinegar and 3 cloves of garlic, minced. The duck bits are dipped into this sauce.

## PEKING DUST

LUT TZE DAN GO

| | |
|---|---|
| 1 pound chestnuts | 8 preserved kumquats |
| 2 tablespoons sugar | ¼ cup sugared or glazed walnuts |
| ⅛ teaspoon salt | 1 orange, peeled and sliced |
| 1½ cups heavy cream | |

Make a crisscross cut on the top of each chestnut. Cover with water and boil for 45 minutes, or until soft. Shell the chestnuts, then mash very fine. Add the sugar and salt and stir. Cool for 15 minutes. Whip the cream. Fold ½ cup of the whipped cream into the chestnut mixture. Press gently into a bowl, then turn out onto a platter. Chill for 1 hour. Garnish with the remaining whipped cream, kumquats, walnuts, and orange slices.

*HONG KONG*

Hong Kong is one of the most fascinating ports in the world. Although it is a British Crown Colony, it is a "crossroads of the world," as they like to say in 1934 television movies, for here are representatives of most of the peoples of the globe. Since it is practically a free port, shopping is a great adventure, although exceptional values are obtained only after bargaining. The most important shopping streets in the city, called "ladder streets," are narrow flights of stairs with shops on both sides. The trick here is to start at the top and walk down, but this is not always possible.

Hong Kong has become a great refugee city, particularly in the past few years. All styles of Chinese cooking have come to the crown colony, and an exceptional cuisine has gradually evolved. Travelers look forward to Hong Kong and its fine restaurants. In addition to the Hong Kong Hotel, good food may be had at Kam Ling, Café de Chine, and the Golden Dragon restaurants.

The two-meal-a-day custom is still observed by most of the Chinese residents. These meals are usually served about eleven in the morning and shortly after 5 P.M. Breakfast is usually nothing but a little *congee*, or water in which a small amount of rice has been boiled. The Chinese are fond of between-meal snacks, and frequently eat little delicacies called *dim sim*. A favorite time for serving these dainties is about 1 P.M., when large quantities of them are eaten, usually accompanied by many small cups of unsweetened, perfumed China tea. Those with good appetites and those who stay up late in the evening usually have a large bowl of rice or possibly noodles before retiring. On the other hand, the Western idea of eggs, toast, and coffee for breakfast, followed by lunch and dinner, has been making itself felt in Hong Kong. The young people in particular, strongly influenced by American motion pictures and magazines to the dismay of the British residents, are the strongest advocates of Westernized food habits; the older people still stand loyally by the food and customs of their ancestors.

Chinese liquors are popular here. Among the best known are Ng Gar Pei, Gay Gook, and Ching Moy.

It is thought that Chinese food reaches a particularly high point in

237

Hong Kong. Bearing in mind the premise that the Chinese cuisine is a great one, and that the Chinese have had to improvise dishes based on tiny cut-up pieces of meat or poultry, we now find this great cuisine operating, with variations, on an island where food is fairly plentiful. Dishes which were good are now improved, since the refugee Chinese cooks are no longer limited to a few ounces of meat.

## HONG KONG GIMLET

3 tablespoons powdered sugar      Juice of 5 lemons
6 jiggers gin

Place the powdered sugar, gin, and lemon juice in a cocktail shaker with plenty of cracked ice. Shake well. Strain and pour into cocktail glasses, about two thirds full. Fill each glass with carbonated water. Serve ice cold.

*Note: This drink is popular with the foreign colony only; the Chinese seldom drink gin.*

## MEAT CAKE SOUP

TSU YUK BENG TONG

1½ pounds pork, ground
  6 scallions (green onions), chopped fine
  1 teaspoon salt
  1 teaspoon soy sauce
¼ teaspoon pepper
3 eggs, beaten
6 cups stock or 2 cans consommé and 2½ cans water

Combine the pork, scallions, salt, soy sauce, pepper, and eggs in a bowl. Mix well. Shape into 2-inch balls. Place the stock in the top of a double boiler over hot water, or use a saucepan over an asbestos pad. Add the meat balls. Cover and cook for 1 hour. Parsley may be sprinkled on top before serving.

## SHRIMP AND GREEN PEAS

CHING DAO HA YAN

2 pounds shrimp
3 tablespoons peanut or salad oil
3 scallions (green onions), sliced thin
1-inch piece of fresh ginger, chopped, or 1½ teaspoons powdered ginger
2 cloves garlic, minced
1½ cups canned tiny green peas, drained
2 teaspoons cornstarch
1 teaspoon salt
1 teaspoon sugar
1 teaspoon soy sauce
3 tablespoons cold water

Shell the shrimp and remove the veins. Wash thoroughly and pat dry with a towel. Heat the oil in a skillet until it bubbles. Add the shrimp and brown quickly on both sides. Add the scallions, ginger, garlic, and peas. Combine the cornstarch, salt, and sugar in a cup or bowl. Add the soy sauce and water and mix to a smooth paste. Add to the shrimp gradually, stirring constantly until the boiling point is reached. Serve immediately.

## STEAMED BUNS

### CHA SIU BAO

2½ cups sifted flour
½ cup confectioners' sugar
2 tablespoons baking powder
⅓ cup shortening
½ cup cold water

2 teaspoons vinegar
2 cups coarsely chopped cooked pork
2 tablespoons soy sauce
2 tablespoons chopped scallions
  (green onions)

Sift the flour, confectioners' sugar, and baking powder into a bowl. Add the shortening and mix with the hand until well blended. Add the water and vinegar. Knead for 5 minutes. Roll with the hand into a long roll. Break off 2-inch balls. Flatten each piece as thin as possible.

Combine the pork, soy sauce, and scallions, mixing well. Place a tablespoon of the mixture in the center of each piece of dough. Pinch the edges together to form little dumplings. Place each dumpling on a 3-inch square of wax paper. Place the dumplings on a trivet over rapidly boiling water in a saucepan. (An asparagus cooker is excellent for this purpose.) Cover the pan and steam for 30 minutes, or until the dough is cooked. Serve on the paper. Each person removes the paper before the dumpling is eaten.

*Note: These dumplings are examples of the traditional dim sim, favorites for luncheon or teatime. The fillings may be varied to include chicken, beef, etc.*

## WALNUT CHICKEN

### HOP PO GAI DING

2½- to 3-pound chicken
1 teaspoon salt
2 teaspoons sugar
3 tablespoons sherry
1 tablespoon soy sauce
3 tablespoons cornstarch
1 egg, beaten
⅓ cup peanut or salad oil

½-inch piece of fresh ginger, chopped,
  or 1 teaspoon powdered ginger
1 cup blanched walnuts
2 cloves garlic, minced
¾ cup boiling water
1 teaspoon monosodium glutamate
1 cup canned bamboo shoots, sliced
  thin

Cut the uncooked chicken off the bones in small cubes. Combine the salt, 1 teaspoon of the sugar, the sherry and soy sauce in a bowl. Place the chicken cubes in it and spoon the mixture over them. Marinate for 15 minutes. Remove the chicken from the marinade and place on wax paper, reserving half the marinade. Sprinkle the cornstarch over the chicken, coating it well. Dip each piece in the egg.

Heat the oil in a skillet until it bubbles; add the walnuts and sauté until brown. Remove the walnuts and set aside. Add the ginger, garlic, and chicken to the oil remaining in the skillet. Brown well. Add the boiling water, monosodium glutamate, the remaining sugar, and the marinade. Cover and cook over low heat for 20 minutes, or until chicken is tender, stirring occasionally. In a separate saucepan, cook the bamboo shoots in their own liquid for 10 minutes. Drain well. Add the bamboo shoots and walnuts to the chicken. Cook over medium heat for 5 minutes. Serve with boiled rice.

## FRIED NOODLES, HONG KONG STYLE

YUK SHI CHOW MEIN

3 quarts water
2 teaspoons salt
1 8-ounce package fine noodles
⅓ cup peanut or salad oil
½ pound lean pork, cut into strips
4 tablespoons cornstarch
½ pound mushrooms, peeled and sliced

1 cup canned bean sprouts
1 teaspoon monosodium glutamate
2 tablespoons soy sauce
2 cups stock or 1 can consommé and ½ can water
2 tablespoons chopped chives or scallions (green onions)

Bring the water to a boil in a saucepan. Add the salt and noodles; boil for 8 minutes. Drain and rinse with cold water. Drain well. Place in a flat bowl and chill for 3 hours.

Heat 2 tablespoons of the oil in a skillet until it bubbles. Add the pork and brown lightly. Sprinkle the cornstarch on top and mix well. Add the mushrooms; cook until the liquid evaporates. Add the bean sprouts. Combine the monosodium glutamate, soy sauce, and stock and add, stirring constantly until the boiling point is reached. Cook over low heat for 20 minutes, or until the pork is tender. Correct seasoning.

Heat the remaining oil in a skillet until it smokes. Turn the noodles into it. Press down with a plate to form a pancake. Turn carefully and brown on the other side. Place the noodles on a platter and pour the pork mixture over it. Sprinkle with the chives and serve hot.

## STEAMED SPONGECAKE

KAI TAN KO

3 egg yolks
¾ cup sugar
3 egg whites

¾ cup sifted cake flour
½ teaspoon baking powder

Beat the yolks until thick. Add the sugar and continue beating until light and foamy. Beat the egg whites until stiff but not dry. Add to the yolk mixture and beat well with a rotary mixer, about 5 minutes. Sift the flour and baking powder together three times. Add to the previous mixture and blend well.

Butter 12 custard cups or individual baking cups, or a muffin tin. Fill each cup about half full. Preheat oven to 325°. Place the container in a pan of hot water. Cover the pan carefully, using either aluminum foil or a pot cover, and bake in a 325° oven for 35 minutes. Serve hot.

## INDIA AND CEYLON

The cuisine of India is historic, surrounded by religious rituals and customs, and it is likely that centuries ago the inhabitants ate food prepared in much the same fashion as it is today. But this does not mean that all Indians eat the same type of food. India is not a completely unified nation, either politically or religiously, for it is populated by differing and conflicting groups of Brahmins, Moslems, Buddhists, Sikhs, Parsis, and Hindus. One group will eat beef but not pork, another is completely vegetarian, and a third group will eat pork but not beef, looking upon all cattle as holy.

To a person who approaches the food without any restrictions, the cuisine of India is delightful and unusual. Many Americans who spend a short time in India become so fond of the curries and other specialties that these dishes become lifetime favorites. More than likely, any curries you may have had outside India were not authentic. Curries do not necessarily have to be hot and spicy, and many of them are very light and delicate in flavor. Almost completely unknown to Americans are the great dishes of India, such as chicken korma, the delectable *copra kana* (coconut rice), and many excellent desserts.

Indians have distinctive food customs. Since there are no particular names for the various meals, guests are invited to dine at a given hour, rather than for lunch or dinner. In general, only one substantial meal is eaten each day. As might be imagined in the land where tea grows, it is a national favorite. Indians do not drink wines or liquors; however, most visitors have found that beer is an excellent adjunct to a curry.

Many tourists are surprised at the local fondness for hot curries, in view of the high temperatures of India. This raises the question as to whether a person is better or worse off eating spicy foods during warm weather. The Indian theory is that spicy foods heat the body, thus making the surrounding air seem cooler. This is in accordance with the Russian idea of drinking boiling-hot tea during summer weather.

Calcutta hotels, particularly the Great Eastern and Spence's, have very good restaurants. Also well known and highly regarded are Neera's and Firpo's. When you walk down Calcutta's colorful Chowringhee Road, you'll be tempted by the food vendors, selling *chupatties* (unleavened wheat cakes) and *rosso gotta* (sweet cakes).

Ceylon, located almost directly south of India, is an island of about twenty-five thousand square miles with food customs much like those of her immense neighbor to the north. Fish, vegetables, coconuts, and rice are the staple foods, but no matter how they are combined, they inevitably taste like curry. The island is still largely forested and is filled with wild game of all sorts; nonetheless, the local diet is primarily vegetarian.

Ceylon's world-famous tea and its cinnamon and cocoa are the principal exports in the food category. Colombo, the capital city, is the center of activities for the entire country. Ceylon offers much to the tourist who is seeking nature in its unspoiled state, but accommodations could be improved.

## LENTIL SOUP

PURPOO MULLIGATUNNY

½ cup dried lentils
7 cups water
2 tablespoons butter
3 tablespoons chopped onions
1 clove garlic, minced

¼ teaspoon dried ground chili peppers
2 teaspoons Indian curry powder
1 teaspoon lemon or lime juice
1 teaspoon salt

Wash the lentils and discard any imperfect ones. Soak in water to cover overnight. Drain well. Boil the 6 cups of water in a saucepan and add the lentils. Cook until soft, about 1 hour. Melt the butter in a separate sauce-pan. Add the onions, garlic, chili peppers, and curry powder. Mix well and sauté for 3 minutes over low heat, stirring constantly. Add this mixture to the lentils. Add the lemon juice and salt and stir well. Cook for 15 minutes. If desired, the lentils may be forced through a sieve or puréed in an electric blender.

## FISH ROLLS, BENGAL STYLE

BENGAL MUCHLEE.

8 fillets of fish
3 teaspoons salt
1 teaspoon pepper
1 cup water
1 clove garlic, minced
2 onions, chopped
3 tomatoes, chopped

½ teaspoon cinnamon
½ teaspoon powdered ginger
2 cardamom seeds, ground
2 eggs
1 cup bread crumbs
Fat for deep-fat frying

Combine 2 of the fillets, 1 teaspoon of the salt, ½ teaspoon of the pepper, and the water in a saucepan. Bring to a boil and cook for 10 minutes. Drain. Chop the fish very fine. Add the garlic, onions, tomatoes, cinnamon, ginger, cardamom seeds, 1 teaspoon of the salt, and the remaining pepper. Mix well. Spread an equal amount of the mixture on each of the 6 remaining fillets. Roll up carefully and fasten with toothpicks or tie with string.

Beat the eggs in a bowl with the remaining salt. Dip the fish rolls in the eggs, then in the bread crumbs. Heat the fat to 360° in a deep saucepan. Drop the fish rolls in carefully. Fry until brown, about 10 minutes. Drain and serve hot.

## FISH AND RICE KEDGEREE

KEDGEREE

1 pound halibut or other white-meat fish
1 onion, sliced
2½ teaspoons salt
½ teaspoon pepper
¾ cup rice
2 cups water
4 tablespoons butter
2 onions, chopped

2 cloves garlic, minced
1 teaspoon ground turmeric
½ teaspoon salt
2 hard-cooked eggs, sliced
1 green chili pepper, sliced thin, or ¼ teaspoon dried ground chili peppers
1 canned pimento, sliced thin

Wash the fish and place in a saucepan with water to cover. Add the sliced onion, 1 teaspoon of the salt, and ¼ teaspoon pepper. Bring to a boil and cook over low heat for 20 minutes. Drain well and discard the onion. Flake the fish and set it aside.

Wash the rice thoroughly in several changes of water. Bring the 2 cups of water to a boil, add 1 teaspoon of the salt and the rice. Cover and cook over medium heat for 15 minutes, or until the water is absorbed. Melt the butter in a skillet and add the chopped onions and the garlic. Sauté over low heat for 5 minutes but do not allow the onions to brown. Add the turmeric and cook for 2 minutes. Add the flaked fish, rice, remaining salt and pepper and mix all together lightly. Cook over low heat for 2 minutes. Garnish with the eggs, chili pepper, and pimento.

## CHICKEN, KASHMIRI STYLE

CHICKEN KUNDOU

¼ pound butter
4 onions, sliced
1-inch piece fresh ginger, chopped,
  or 1 teaspoon powdered ginger
2 cloves garlic, minced
¼ teaspoon dried ground chili
  peppers

1½ cups sour milk or buttermilk
2 tomatoes, chopped
¼ cup ground almonds
¼ cup ground cashew nuts
2 3½-pound chickens, disjointed
2 teaspoons salt
½ cup heavy cream

Melt the butter in a large saucepan. Add the onions and sauté for 10 minutes, stirring frequently. Add the ginger, garlic, and chili peppers. Cook over low heat for 5 minutes, stirring occasionally. Add the sour milk and tomatoes and cook over low heat for 10 minutes. Add the almonds, cashew nuts, chickens, and salt and cook over low heat for 1 hour, or until the chickens are tender. Add a little more sour milk if they become too dry. When the chickens are tender, correct seasoning. Pour the cream over them and stir well. Serve immediately.

## CHICKEN KORMA

MORGEE KORMA

2 3½-pound frying chickens, disjointed
1 cup buttermilk or yogurt
4 cloves garlic, minced
4 tablespoons butter

2 onions, chopped fine
½ teaspoon powdered ginger
2 cloves
1½ teaspoons salt

Clean the chicken parts carefully and place in a large bowl. Mix the buttermilk or yogurt with half the garlic and pour over the chicken. Marinate at room temperature for 2 hours, basting frequently. Melt the butter in a casserole or heavy saucepan. Add the onions, remaining garlic, the ginger, cloves, and salt. Sauté over low heat for 5 minutes, stirring frequently. Prepare either of the following mixtures. The Indian *korma* mixture will give a superior flavor.

INDIAN KORMA MIXTURE
2 teaspoons ground coriander
2 teaspoons ground almonds
¾ teaspoon ground turmeric
¼ teaspoon ground cumin seed
⅛ teaspoon pepper
⅛ teaspoon dried ground chili
  peppers

SIMPLE KORMA MIXTURE
1 tablespoon imported Indian curry powder
1 teaspoon ground almonds

Add either mixture to the onions and stir well. Cook for 5 minutes, stirring frequently. Add the chicken and its marinade. Cover and cook over low heat for 1½ to 2 hours, or until chicken is tender, stirring occasionally. Serve with boiled rice.

## SPICY COCONUT RICE

COPRA KANA

1 cup fresh or dried grated coconut
2 cups milk
2 cups water
¼ pound butter

3 tablespoons chopped onion
1½ tablespoons Indian curry powder
2 cups rice

Combine the coconut, milk, and water in a saucepan. Bring to a boil, remove from the heat, and soak for 15 minutes. Press all the liquid from the coconut and discard the pulp. Melt the butter in a saucepan. Add the onion and curry powder. Sauté over very low heat for 5 minutes, stirring occasionally. Wash the rice in several changes of water. Add the rice to the onion. Cook over medium heat for 3 minutes, stirring constantly. Bring the coconut milk to a boil and add to the rice. Cover and cook over low heat until all the liquid is absorbed. Stir frequently, as the milk is apt to burn.

## EGGPLANT, CEYLON STYLE

BRINJALS

1 clove garlic, peeled
2 eggplants, peeled
¾ cup bread crumbs
3 tablespoons grated onion
3 tablespoons chopped parsley

⅛ teaspoon powdered ginger
⅛ teaspoon turmeric
2 teaspoons salt
1 teaspoon pepper
¼ cup melted butter

Rub a casserole with the garlic. Slice the eggplant lengthwise in ½-inch slices and arrange several slices on the bottom. Combine in a bowl the bread crumbs, onion, parsley, ginger, turmeric, salt, and pepper. Sprinkle some of this mixture over the eggplant slices. Arrange another layer of eggplant, sprinkle with the bread-crumb mixture, and continue until all the eggplant and bread-crumb mixture are used up. Pour the melted butter over it. Bake in a 350° oven for 45 minutes.

## LENTIL AND EGG CURRY

### DHALL CURRY

1 cup dried lentils
3 tablespoons butter
2 onions, sliced
1 tablespoon curry powder

¾ cup water
1 teaspoon salt
6 hard-cooked eggs, sliced

Soak the lentils overnight in water to cover. Drain well. Melt the butter in a saucepan. Add the onions and curry powder and sauté for 10 minutes, stirring frequently. Add the water and lentils. Cover and cook over low heat for 45 minutes, or until the lentils are tender. Add the salt and sliced eggs and mix gently. Correct seasoning. Cook over low heat for 5 minutes. Serve hot.

## STEWED TOMATOES, INDIAN STYLE

### THUCAHLEY FOOGATHS

4 tablespoons butter
1 onion, chopped
2 cloves garlic, minced
¼ teaspoon powdered ginger
¼ teaspoon dried ground chili peppers

4 tomatoes, peeled and chopped
1 teaspoon salt
1 tablespoon fresh or dried grated coconut

Melt the butter in a skillet. Add the onion, garlic, ginger, and chili peppers. Sauté for 5 minutes, stirring occasionally. Add the tomatoes, salt, and coconut. Cook over low heat for 15 minutes, or until the liquid is absorbed. Serve as a vegetable.

## CUCUMBER BOORTHA

### BOORTHA

3 medium cucumbers
1 cup water
1 onion
1 clove garlic
½ green pepper
½ teaspoon powdered ginger

⅛ teaspoon dried ground chili peppers
½ teaspoon salt
2 tablespoons olive oil
2 tablespoons lemon juice

Peel the cucumbers, and cut into thick slices. Place in the water and cook for about 10 minutes, or until soft. Drain thoroughly. Chop the onion, garlic, and green pepper as fine as possible. Add the cucumber and continue chopping. Add the ginger, chili peppers, salt, olive oil, and lemon juice. Mix well. Chill for at least 2 hours. Serve as a salad or relish.

## VEGETABLE RELISH

### SAMBAL

3 tablespoons butter
2 onions, chopped
2 cloves garlic, minced
¼ teaspoon dried ground chili peppers

½ teaspoon powdered ginger
1 teaspoon turmeric
¼ teaspoon ground cumin seed
2 cucumbers, sliced thin
2 tomatoes, sliced thin

Melt the butter in a saucepan. Add the onions, garlic, chili peppers, ginger, turmeric, and cumin seed. Sauté over low heat for 10 minutes, stirring frequently. Divide the mixture in half and place in two bowls. Add the cucumber to one bowl and the tomatoes to the other. Mix gently. Allow to stand for 1 hour before serving. Serve at room temperature. *Sambals* are served with curries.

## VERMICELLI DESSERT

### PAYASAM

1 tablespoon seedless raisins
½ cup water
4 tablespoons butter
¼ cup cashew nuts

½ pound vermicelli
2 cups milk
1¼ cups sugar
1 teaspoon vanilla extract

Soak the raisins in water for 20 minutes. Drain well. Melt the butter in a saucepan. Add the nuts and raisins and sauté for 5 minutes, stirring frequently. Remove the nuts and raisins and set aside.

Place the vermicelli in the saucepan and brown lightly. If necessary, break the vermicelli in half. Add the milk and bring to a boil. Cook over low heat for 8 minutes. Add the sugar and vanilla, and cook 2 minutes longer. Add the nuts and raisins. Serve hot.

## SWEET BANANA PUFFS

### MEETA KAYLA PUSTHOLES

2 cups sifted cake flour
Dash of salt
¼ pound butter
¼ cup buttermilk or sour milk

3 ripe bananas
4 tablespoons fresh or dried grated coconut
Fat for deep-fat frying

247

Sift the flour and salt into a bowl. Cut in the butter with a pastry blender or two knives. Add the buttermilk and mix well. Knead together. Roll out the dough ¼ inch thick on a lightly floured surface. Cut with a round cooky cutter.

Mash the bananas, add the coconut, and mix well. Place a spoonful of this mixture in the center of each round of dough. Fold over and seal the edges, using a little water. Heat the fat to 360° and drop the pastries into it carefully. Fry until golden brown. Drain well. Serve hot or cold. If desired, the pastries may be baked on a buttered baking sheet in a 400° oven for 20 minutes.

INDONESIA

The Republic of Indonesia consists principally of Java, Bali, Borneo, Sumatra, and various other beautiful small islands, most of which were formerly a part of the Dutch East Indies. Gastronomically speaking, the most interesting of these is undoubtedly Java.

Rice is the principal food and overshadowing any other dish is the world-renowned rice table, or *rijsttafel*. This was originally a Javanese dish, but the Dutch colonists took to it with such gusto that they have adopted it for their own, somewhat modifying its preparation. It is a great experience and one that almost everyone enjoys. Many local residents who have lived for years in the islands eat *rijsttafel* every day of the year, and declare that they look forward to eating it the next day.

*Rijsttafel* is a little hard to describe, for it consists of many different foods composed upon a bed of boiled rice. Each person is served with a large soup plate filled with rice. In the better hotels of the islands and on formal occasions, a dozen or more waiters line up, each carrying a single dish from which the diner helps himself. In your own home a buffet-style dinner may be served, each person helping himself to the various side dishes. There are usually combinations of fish, shrimp, chicken, or beef, as well as an occasional vegetable dish. Many of these are quite spicy and should be cautiously tested by those unacquainted with *rijsttafel*. Each helping from the side dishes is carefully placed upon the mound of boiled rice and eaten separately. It is not cricket to mix everything together.

To temper the spicy food, it is customary to serve tiny side dishes of palate refreshers, such as sliced cucumbers, grated coconut, chopped peanuts, and the like. The only beverage served with *rijsttafel* is cool beer, but resident Europeans usually begin with a drink or two of Holland dry gin (*jenever*). In this section will be found one of the favorite *rijsttafel* recipes, *nasi goreng*. For those who might wonder why the Javanese should have reason to honor the tragicomic figure of World War II, it might be in order to point out that *nasi* means boiled rice.

Since the local cuisine is built so solidly around the rice table and its accompaniments, it is natural that soups and other unnecessary dishes should be unimportant, although soups are served on occasion. Desserts, which are seldom served, are usually fresh fruit or based on fruit. Of increasing importance in the islands are the Chinese, who have taken over control of much of the commerce and industry; similarly, the Chinese influence on cookery is being felt, for the islanders enjoy Chinese dishes, particularly those containing noodles, a great local favorite.

Of course the many peasants and villagers live very simply on rice, with the possible addition of fish, coconuts, or vegetables and with an occasional treat of chicken or meat. No matter how poor or primitive the people are, the food is usually well prepared, seasoned with the high spicing that the people enjoy, and appetizingly served.

The word "Java" itself has become a part of the English—or is it the American?—language to signify coffee, and Java does produce much fine coffee. This is always served black and drunk with plenty of sugar. Alcoholic beverages are unimportant, for most Javanese are Mohammedans. Tea is also an important local drink.

## EAST INDIES COCKTAIL

1 cup brandy
1 tablespoon curaçao
1 tablespoon pineapple juice

2 teaspoons maraschino, or cherry
   brandy
1 teaspoon bitters
6 slices lemon peel

Combine the brandy, curaçao, pineapple juice, maraschino or cherry brandy, and bitters in a cocktail shaker. Add cracked ice and stir well. Pour into chilled cocktail or champagne glasses and place a twist of lemon peel in each.

*Note: This recipe is not regionally authentic but was very popular with the foreign colony.*

## CHICKEN-GINGER SOUP

### SOTO AJAM

5-pound chicken
2 stalks celery
1 carrot, peeled
2½ quarts water
2½ teaspoons salt
1-inch piece fresh or preserved ginger, sliced fine, or 1 teaspoon powdered ginger

3 tablespoons salad oil
3 onions, sliced
1 cup bean sprouts, drained
3 hard-cooked eggs, sliced
6 slices lemon

Wash the chicken thoroughly. Place in a saucepan with the celery, carrot, and water. Bring to a boil; skim the top. Cook over medium heat for 2½ hours, or until chicken is tender. Add salt after the first hour. Strain the stock, add the ginger, and set aside. Cut the chicken into slivers. Heat the oil in a skillet. Add the onions and sauté for 15 minutes. Add the bean sprouts and cook over low heat for 5 minutes. Place onions, bean sprouts, sliced eggs, and chicken in a bowl. Serve the soup in individual plates, with a slice of lemon on top. It is customary for each person to help himself from the bowl of chicken.

## INDONESIAN CHICKEN, SHRIMP, AND RICE

### NASI GORENG

4-pound chicken
7 cups water
2 leeks
1 bay leaf
2 sprigs parsley
3 teaspoons salt
2 cups rice
⅔ cup peanut or salad oil
4 onions, chopped
2 cloves garlic, minced

1½ cups chopped, cooked shrimp
1 cup cooked or canned crab meat
1 cup cubed ham
2 teaspoons ground coriander
1 teaspoon ground cumin seed
½ teaspoon dried ground chili peppers
¼ teaspoon mace
4 tablespoons peanut butter

Clean the chicken carefully. Place it in a deep saucepan with the water, leeks, bay leaf, parsley, and 2 teaspoons of the salt. Bring to a boil and cook over medium heat for 1½ hours, or until the chicken is tender. Strain the stock and reserve. Remove all the meat from the bones and cut into strips. Wash the rice in several changes of water. Combine the rice, the remaining salt, and 3½ cups of the reserved stock in a deep saucepan. Cover and cook over low heat for 20 minutes, or until the rice is tender. If any liquid remains, drain it. Heat the oil in a large skillet or casserole. Add the onions and garlic and sauté for 10 minutes, stirring frequently.

Add the rice and cook until it browns, stirring frequently. Add the chicken, shrimp, crab meat, ham, coriander, cumin seed, chili peppers, mace, and peanut butter. Mix thoroughly. Cook over low heat for 10 minutes, stirring gently. Serve with several side dishes, such as slices of chilled cucumber, chutney, finely chopped peanuts, and slices of banana.

*Note: In Indonesia the rice is cooked the day before it is to be used so that it will be dry.*

## BAKED SPICY FISH

### IEKAN BANDANG PANGGANG

| | |
|---|---|
| 1 teaspoon salt | ½ cup melted butter |
| ¼ teaspoon pepper | 3 tablespoons lemon juice |
| 2 cloves garlic, minced | ¼ cup soy sauce |
| 4-pound shad or other fat fish, split and boned | ¼ teaspoon ground dried chili peppers |

Mix the salt, pepper, and garlic to a smooth paste. Rub into the fish, inside and out. Place the fish in a buttered baking dish. Bake in a 375° oven for 10 minutes. Meanwhile, combine in a bowl the butter, lemon juice, soy sauce, and chili peppers and mix well. At the end of 10 minutes of baking time, pour one third of the sauce over the fish. Baste and turn the fish several times while baking for an additional 25 minutes. Heat the remaining sauce. Place the fish on a platter and pour the sauce over it. Serve with boiled rice.

## LAMB, JAVANESE STYLE

### SATE KAMBING

| | |
|---|---|
| 2 teaspoons ground coriander | 2 teaspoons salt |
| ½ teaspoon dried ground chili peppers | 3 pounds boneless lamb, cut into ½-inch cubes |
| 1 teaspoon cumin seed, pounded | 1 cup vinegar |
| ½ teaspoon saffron | 4 tablespoons peanut or salad oil |
| 1 teaspoon powdered ginger | ½ cup water |
| 2 cloves garlic, minced | |

Pound together the coriander, chili peppers, cumin seed, saffron, ginger, garlic, and salt. Roll the pieces of lamb in the mixture. Place the lamb in a bowl and pour the vinegar over it. Marinate for 1 hour. Drain the meat and discard the vinegar. Heat the oil in a saucepan. Add the meat and brown on all sides. Add the water and cover. Cook over low heat for 30 minutes, or until tender. Serve hot.

## JAVANESE CHICKEN LIVERS

### SAMBAL HATI HATI

1 cup fresh or dried grated coconut
1 cup milk
4 tablespoons butter
1 onion, chopped
3 cloves garlic, minced
2 chili peppers, sliced thin, or ½ teaspoon dried ground chili peppers
1½ pounds chicken livers, coarsely
chopped

¼ cup ground almonds
2 tablespoons grated lemon rind
2 tablespoons orange juice
1 tablespoon lemon juice
1 tablespoon plum jam
1 teaspoon sugar
1 teaspoon salt

Combine the coconut and milk in a saucepan. Bring to a boil, remove from heat, and soak for 15 minutes. Press all the liquid from the coconut and discard the pulp.

Melt the butter in a saucepan. Add the onion, garlic, and chili peppers. Sauté for 5 minutes, stirring frequently. Add the chicken livers and sauté for 10 minutes, stirring occasionally. Add the coconut milk, almonds, lemon rind, orange juice, lemon juice, plum jam, sugar, and salt. Cook over low heat for 10 minutes, stirring occasionally. Serve hot with boiled rice.

*Note: Lemon juice and plum jam are used as a substitute for tamarind, usually unavailable.*

## CARAMEL PUDDING

### KUWE SIRKAJA

1½ cups sugar
2 tablespoons butter
4 tablespoons sifted flour
6 egg yolks, beaten

1¼ cups milk
2 tablespoons grated orange rind
1 teaspoon vanilla extract
6 egg whites

Melt ¾ cup of the sugar in a heavy saucepan. Cook over low heat until browned and caramelized. Divide the mixture among 6 individual, buttered ovenproof dishes. Set aside.

Cream the butter. Add the remaining sugar and beat well. Add the flour and beat again. Add the egg yolks and beat until light and fluffy. Add the milk, orange rind, and vanilla, mixing well. Preheat oven to 350°. Beat the egg whites until stiff but not dry. Fold into the milk mixture gently. Divide among the prepared dishes. Place the dishes carefully in a pan of hot water. Bake in a 350° oven for 45 minutes, or until the puddings are set. Remove and allow to cool, then chill for at least 6 hours. Serve directly in the dish or run a knife around the edges of each dish and turn out onto a plate.

*JAPAN*

A great many mistaken ideas regarding Japanese food have become a part of the American credo. These are based primarily upon that bit of American mythology which firmly holds that the Japanese eat raw fish, seaweed, and rice exclusively. As to the raw fish, it is a fact that most of us eat raw oysters and clams; and the raw fish dish of Peru, *seviche,* is quite similar in preparation to the *sashimi* of Japan. Soup made from seaweed does not taste substantially different from our own clam broth; and there certainly is nothing very exotic about eating rice.

The Japanese are great perfectionists in the fine art of preparing and serving a meal. While the cuisine is not extensive—is even somewhat limited from the Western point of view—the attractive appearance of Japanese food goes a long way toward equalizing any possible deficit in that regard. Every dish is presented to the best possible advantage and is pleasing to the eye as well as the palate. With this in mind, the food is carefully arranged in colorful, dainty dishes, small portions are artistically arranged, and receptacles are carefully selected to blend and harmonize with the particular food being served.

Japanese food may be divided into the following rough groups: soups, including both *suimono* (clear soup) and *miso-shiru* (soup made with a fermented malt); *nimono* (boiled food), of which an example might be a boiled chicken dish; *yakimono* (broiled food), such as the great favorite *kabayaki* (broiled eels); *agemono* (fried food), the best known being *tempura,* deep-fat-fried shrimps; *mushimono* (steamed food), of which there are many steamed egg dishes; and the most renowned of all, *nabemono* (open frying-pan food), especially the famous *sukiyaki,* which

253

is particularly attractive to watch while it is being made at your table. In addition, there are various other types of dishes, but rice is the common denominator of all Japanese food.

The use of certain flavorings gives Japanese food much of its unique character. Among these are *shoyu* (soy sauce), which more or less eliminates the need for salt; *miso*, a type of fermented paste made from malt; *mirin*, a rather sweet variety of rice wine; and *ajinomoto*, already well known in this country as monosodium glutamate, used to bring out the flavoring in various foods.

The favorite beverages of the nation are beer and *sake*. Japanese beers are very much like the European types and are exceptionally good. *Sake*, the so-called rice wine, is actually as much a beer as it is a wine. Golden yellow in color, it is usually made from white rice but occasionally from other grain, and tastes something like Spanish sherry. The Japanese prefer to drink it hot for reasons known only to themselves. The recent production of Japanese Western-style whisky is worthy of mention, and is in accordance with the well-known Japanese ability to mimic. Of course Japan is the land of tea, in this case green tea, which is the basis for a ritualistic ceremony, partly religious and partly symbolic, called *tscha-no-yu*.

The cuisine is built upon a few basic items such as rice, green tea, seafood, *shoyu* sauce, and the colorful local vegetables. Most visitors to Japan usually find themselves drawn to two dishes, the *tempura* (fried shrimp) and *sukiyaki*.

Just one fascinating bit of nonsense about the impact of the Western world upon the imperturbable Japanese. Into a formal and stately language has come a new Japanese word meaning appetizers. That word is, and we hesitate to use it, *o'dobre*. Oh, Admiral Perry, little did you know what you were doing to Japan when you opened her to trade with the Western world!

## SHRIMP TOAST

### HA DO SHI

2 tablespoons peanut or salad oil
1 onion, chopped fine
1 pound shrimp, peeled, cleaned, and chopped fine
1 teaspoon salt
½ teaspoon sugar
½ teaspoon pepper
½-inch piece fresh ginger, chopped fine or 1 teaspoon powdered ginger

1 egg white
12 slices stale bread, trimmed and cut in triangles
2 eggs, beaten
1 cup bread crumbs
Peanut or salad oil for deep-fat frying

Heat the 2 tablespoons of oil in a skillet and add the onion. Sauté for 10 minutes, stirring frequently. Combine the sautéed onion, shrimp, salt, sugar, pepper, and ginger in a bowl. Beat the egg white until it begins to stiffen and fold it into the shrimp mixture.

Dip the bread triangles into the beaten eggs. Spread the bread with the shrimp mixture and dip these into the beaten eggs again, then into the bread crumbs, coating all sides well. Heat the oil in a deep saucepan to 360°. Drop each bread triangle carefully into the fat. Fry until golden brown. Drain and serve hot.


## JAPANESE EGG ROLL

### TAMAGO-YAKI

| | |
|---|---|
| ⅓ pound halibut or white-meat fish | 4 tablespoons water |
| 3 tablespoons sugar | 2 tablespoons soy sauce |
| ½ teaspoon salt | 3 tablespoons sherry |
| 6 eggs, beaten | 1 tablespoon salad oil |

Remove the skin and bones from the fish carefully. Grind or chop it very fine. Add the sugar and salt and mix well. Beat the eggs, water, soy sauce, and sherry together. Combine with the fish mixture and mix well. Heat half of the olive oil in an 8-inch square pan, or use an oblong pan of similar size (not a round one). Pour half of the mixture into it. Fry until lightly browned on both sides, turning it over carefully. Turn out onto a piece of wax paper, aluminum foil, or a napkin, and roll up like a jelly roll. If desired, fasten the ends with toothpicks. Repeat this procedure with the balance of the ingredients. Set aside for 30 minutes. Cut into slices about ½ inch thick. These are very good as hors d'oeuvres.


## VEGETABLE SOUP

### YASAI-SUIMONO

| | |
|---|---|
| ¼ cup dried mushrooms | ¼ cup canned bamboo shoots, sliced thin, or ¼ cup diced celery |
| 6 cups stock or 3 cans consommé and 2 cans water | 1 tablespoon soy sauce |
| ½ pound pork, cut into julienne strips | 1 cup chopped spinach |
| 1 carrot, cut into julienne strips | 1 teaspoon powdered ginger |

Wash the mushrooms carefully. Soak them in cold water for 1 hour. Drain well and slice thin. Heat the stock in a saucepan. Add the pork and mushrooms. Bring to a boil and cook over low heat for 10 minutes. Add the carrot, bamboo shoots, and soy sauce and cook for 5 minutes. Add the spinach and ginger, and cook for 1 minute. Serve hot.

# LOBSTER, TEMPURA STYLE

### ISE-EBI TEMPURA

1 cup stock or 1 bouillon cube dissolved in 1 cup hot water
4 tablespoons soy sauce
4 tablespoons sherry
1 teaspoon powdered ginger
1 cup sifted flour

4 eggs, beaten
¼ cup water
3 fresh lobster bodies or 3 frozen lobster tails, split, in the shells
Fat for deep-fat frying
½ cup grated radish or turnip

Combine the stock, soy sauce, sherry, and ginger in a saucepan. Bring to a boil. Set aside to cool. Combine the flour, eggs, and water in a bowl. Mix lightly. If fresh lobsters are used, remove the claws and use for lobster salad or other purpose. Split the bodies in half, using a half for each person. If frozen lobster tails are used, split each tail lengthwise when it has thawed. Make several cuts in the meat of either type of lobster used, and dip into the flour and egg mixture, coating the lobster and its shell completely. Heat the fat in a deep saucepan to 350°. Fry the lobster in it, not more than two at a time, until well browned. Drain.

Pour the cooled soy sauce mixture into 6 small individual saucers or serving dishes. Place a heaping mound of grated radish in the center of each. Serve the lobsters and sauce together. Some boiled rice may accompany this dish. Dip pieces of the lobster in the sauce, in the Japanese fashion.

# BEEF AND SOY SAUCE

### SUKIYAKI

4 tablespoons sesame oil or salad oil
2 pounds sirloin steak, cut into strips, ½ inch by 2 inches
½ cup stock or ½ bouillon cube dissolved in ½ cup boiling water
¾ cup soy sauce
¼ cup sugar
1 tablespoon sherry

3 onions, sliced thin
1 cup sliced celery
1 cup sliced, canned bamboo shoots
½ pound mushrooms, sliced thin
1 cup shredded spinach
4 scallions (green onions), sliced
1 pound vermicelli, boiled and drained

Heat the oil in a large frying pan. Add the meat and brown on all sides. Combine the stock, soy sauce, sugar, and sherry in a bowl. Add half of this mixture to the meat, reserving the balance. Push the meat to one side of the frying pan. Add the onions and celery and cook over low heat for 3 minutes. Add the remaining stock mixture, bamboo shoots, mushrooms, and spinach. Cook over low heat for 3 minutes. Add the scallions and cook for 1 minute. Place the vermicelli on one side of a platter and the sukiyaki on the other side and serve immediately.

*Note: In Japan, this dish is made at the table. This custom may be duplicated by preparing the sukiyaki in a chafing dish. It is very important to follow the cooking times as specified, as the vegetables should be very crisp at the time they are served.*

## CHICKEN AND SHRIMP

### YAKI-TORI TO KO-EBI

¼ cup dried mushrooms
12 shrimp, peeled and cleaned
2 cups stock or 1 can consommé and ½ can water
1 teaspoon salt

4 tablespoons sugar
3 tablespoons soy sauce
2-pound chicken, cut into cubes
⅓ cup sherry
6 spears canned white asparagus

Wash the mushrooms thoroughly. Soak them in cold water for 1 hour. Drain. Combine the shrimp, stock, salt, sugar, and soy sauce in a saucepan. Bring to a boil and cook over medium heat for 7 minutes. Remove the shrimp and keep warm. Add the chicken cubes, sherry, and mushrooms to the stock mixture and cook over medium heat for 10 minutes, or until chicken is tender. Do not overcook. Remove the chicken and mushrooms and keep warm. Place the asparagus in the stock and cook for 2 minutes only. Arrange the shrimp, chicken, mushrooms, and asparagus in separate mounds on a platter. Pour the sauce over it and serve. The sauce should be moderately thick; if it is not, boil it rapidly, uncovered, for a few minutes in order to thicken it.

## STEAMED CHICKEN AND EGG

### CHAWAN MUSHI

8 dried mushrooms
3-pound chicken
3 tablespoons peanut or salad oil
20 chestnuts, cooked and shelled (optional)
1 onion, sliced thin
3 scallions (green onions), sliced

2 cups stock or 1 can consommé and ½ can water
3 tablespoons soy sauce
1 tablespoon sherry
12 spinach leaves
4 eggs, beaten
6 thin slices lemon

Wash the mushrooms thoroughly. Soak them in cold water for 1 hour. Drain. Slice thin. Remove all the meat from the uncooked chicken and cut into narrow strips. Heat the oil in a skillet. Add the chicken and cook over low heat for 5 minutes, stirring frequently. Add the chestnuts, onion, scallions, 4 tablespoons of the stock, soy sauce, sherry, and mushrooms. Bring to a boil and cook over low heat for 2 minutes. Do not overcook.

Divide the mixture among 6 individual custard cups or place in a large bowl. Beat the eggs together with the remaining stock. Pour over the chicken mixture. Cover with spinach leaves. Place the cups or bowl in a pan of hot water and cover the pan. Steam for 25 minutes, or until the egg mixture is set. Serve hot with slices of lemon.

## GELATINE DESSERT

#### AWAYUKIKAN

2 tablespoons gelatine
½ cup cold water
1½ cups boiling water
2 cups sugar

2 tablespoons raspberry or cherry jelly
1 egg white

Soak the gelatine in the cold water for 5 minutes. Combine the boiling water, sugar, and jelly and cook over medium heat until the mixture is syrupy, about 5 minutes. Add to the gelatine mixture, stirring until dissolved. Let cool for 30 minutes. Beat the egg white until stiff. Fold into the previous mixture. Pour into a lightly greased 8-inch square pan. Chill for at least 3 hours. Cut into strips and serve.

## JAPANESE HONEY CAKE

#### KASUTERA

5 eggs
¾ cup sugar
¼ cup honey

½ cup sifted flour
2 tablespoons confectioners' sugar

Beat the eggs, sugar, and honey in a bowl until very thick. Add the flour, beating well. Preheat oven to 350°. Pour the batter into a greased oblong pan, about 9 by 12 inches. Bake in a 350° oven for 45 minutes, but *stir* the cake with a spoon after the first 15 minutes of baking time. Continue baking in the ordinary manner thereafter. Allow the cake to cool in the pan. Dust with confectioners' sugar, cut into strips, and serve.

*Note: The baking instructions are unusual; in Japan the cake is stirred every 15 minutes. A modification has been made for convenience and appearance. This is not part of the ancient authentic cuisine, as it has been a part of Japanese cooking for only four hundred years.*

A few years ago the majority of people would have found it difficult to locate Korea with any degree of accuracy. Recent events have focused world attention upon Korea and its name has become a household word. It is unlikely that the world will soon forget Korea, just as it is improbable that the impact of foreign nations on the Korean people will be overlooked.

Until quite recently the Koreans lived their own lives, and ate the rice, barley, wheat, and soy of their fields, and caught the abundant fish of the surrounding waters. The coming of the Japanese many years ago also changed Korean life substantially; not the least of the changes was the introduction of dairy products and many Japanese foodstuffs. Peculiarly enough, Korean food resembles Chinese food as much as it does Japanese, though there are certain distinguishing features which make it differ from either of them.

Korean food has this in common with Chinese: it is usually prepared in cut-up form so that it may be readily handled with chopsticks; flavoring is often reminiscent of Chinese sauces, particularly those containing soy sauce and ginger; and rice is the basic staple. A Japanese custom of letting each diner prepare his own food on small, individual charcoal burners at the table is also a part of the Korean food style, and Koreans like several dishes that are favorites with the Japanese.

The people are extremely fond of *kooks* (soups), which are prepared in many different fashions. They are all so rich and hearty that they would make a meal for many people. The peninsular of Korea juts into waters teeming with fish, and peacetime fisheries are of great importance. Clams and other seafood are greatly appreciated by the inhabitants, and the people living along the coast take full advantage of the large catches of fish.

As previously mentioned, the many meat dishes of Korea are both different and yet similar to their Chinese equivalents. Koreans are particularly fond of mixtures of pork and chicken, or of fish and meat; they also like food in which there are distinctive and sharply different flavors. Few Chinese dishes are spicy, but many Korean preparations are very highly seasoned with pepper and garlic. The recipe for broiled pork (*ton yuk kui*) is a fine Korean dish containing sesame seeds. These seeds are a national favorite. Rice and beans (*pah jook*) is a dish that may appear at almost any Korean meal.

A unique feature of Korean food is *keem chee,* probably the most commonly seen dish. It is a sort of pickle, usually made of Chinese cabbage but often prepared with turnips, cucumbers, celery, or whatever is available at the particular season of the year. Most Koreans consider that they have not eaten a meal unless *keem chee* appears at the table. It is practically a standard food, and its peculiar odor greets(?) the person who approaches a Korean village even before he sees the people.

*Cha* (strong tea), taken plain, is the drink of the country.

## BEAN SPROUT SOUP

### KONG NA MOOL KOOK

1 tablespoon peanut or salad oil
½ pound beef, coarsely chopped
1 onion, chopped
1 clove garlic, minced
1 teaspoon salt
⅛ teaspoon pepper

2 teaspoons sesame seeds
1 cup canned bean sprouts
2 tablespoons soy sauce
7 cups stock or 3 cans consommé and 2 cups water
2 scallions (green onions), chopped

Heat the oil in a deep saucepan. Add the chopped beef, onion, garlic, salt, and pepper. Cook over high heat, stirring constantly, for 5 minutes. Add the sesame seeds and stir. Drain the bean sprouts thoroughly and add to the meat, stirring well. Add the soy sauce and stock. Cook over medium heat for 30 minutes. Add the chopped scallions and cook for 5 minutes. Serve hot.

## BOILED FISH WITH VEGETABLES

### SANG SUHN JIM

6 fillets of white-meat fish
½ pound beef, ground
2 tablespoons sugar
5 tablespoons soy sauce
3 scallions (green onions), chopped
2 cloves garlic, minced
3 tablespoons peanut or salad oil
½ cup sliced mushrooms
2 onions, sliced

2 carrots, peeled and sliced
2 stalks celery, sliced
¼ teaspoon dried ground chili pepper
½ teaspoon powdered ginger
2 teaspoons salt
1 teaspoon pepper
2 cups water
1 fried egg

Wash the fish and cut into 2-inch pieces. Drain well. Combine the beef, sugar, 2 tablespoons of the soy sauce, scallions, and garlic in a bowl. Mix well. Heat the oil in a casserole or heavy saucepan. Spread half the meat mixture on the bottom. Add half the fish. Combine the mushrooms, onions, carrots, celery, chili peppers, ginger, salt, and pepper. Spread half the mixture over the fish in the casserole. Repeat the layers in the same order. Add the water and remaining soy sauce. Cover and cook over low heat for 1 hour. Shred the fried egg and sprinkle on top before serving.


## BROILED PORK

TON YUK KUI

½ cup soy sauce
3 tablespoons sugar
2 scallions, chopped
2 cloves garlic, minced
½ teaspoon pepper
½ teaspoon powdered ginger

1 tablespoon sesame seeds
2 pounds pork tenderloin (other cuts may be used, but tenderloin is desirable)
1 tablespoon peanut oil

Combine the soy sauce, sugar, scallions, garlic, pepper, ginger, and sesame seeds in a bowl. Stir well. Cut the pork into ¼-inch slices and place in the bowl. Marinate at room temperature for at least 1 hour. Baste the meat frequently. Remove the meat from the marinade and place it on a lightly oiled broiling pan. Broil for about 5 minutes on each side, or until well browned. Place the marinade in a saucepan and heat to the boiling point while the meat is broiling. Serve it as a sauce with the pork.


## RICE AND BEANS

PAH JOOK

1 cup red beans
1 cup rice
7 cups water
2 teaspoons salt

3 cups stock or 3 bouillon cubes dissolved in 3 cups boiling water
½ cup flour, sifted
¾ teaspoon baking powder
3 tablespoons cold water

Wash the beans thoroughly and discard any imperfect ones. Place in a saucepan, add 5 cups of water, and soak overnight. Cook in the same water for 2 hours. Force through a sieve. Wash the rice thoroughly. Soak for 15 minutes, drain, and wash again. Place in a saucepan and add 2 cups of water and the salt. Cover and bring to a boil. Cook over low heat for 20 minutes. Add the bean purée to the rice. Also add the stock and cook over low heat for 20 minutes, stirring occasionally.

Mix the sifted flour and baking powder together. Add the cold water and knead to a soft dough. Roll into balls the size of marbles. Add to the rice and bean mixture and stir well. Cook for 15 more minutes. Serve very hot.

## CUCUMBER PICKLE

O-I KEEM CHEE

6 cucumbers
2 tablespoons salt
2 scallions (green onions)
1 clove garlic, minced
⅛ teaspoon dried ground chili peppers

⅛ teaspoon powdered ginger
½ teaspoon chopped candied ginger (optional)
⅔ cup water

Scrub the cucumbers thoroughly. Cut in half lengthwise, then cut into pieces ½ inch thick. Sprinkle with 1 tablespoon of the salt and set aside for 10 minutes. Wash and drain the cucumbers. Chop the scallions coarsely. Add the garlic, chili peppers, ginger, and remaining salt. Combine these ingredients with the cucumbers and place in a bowl. Add the water and stir.

Cover and place in a warm spot. Marinate for at least 48 hours, although if the weather is cool it will sometimes take several days longer to become pickled. In order to prevent the pickle odor from spreading, either place in a secluded spot or cover well with several layers of cloth. Chill and serve cold as a relish.

## FLOWER CAKES

HWA JUHN

1 cup sifted flour
½ teaspoon salt
1 teaspoon baking powder
3 tablespoons sugar

¼ cup ice water
6 dates, chopped fine
½ cup peanut or salad oil, for frying

Sift the flour, salt, baking powder, and sugar together. Add the ice water and mix well. If the mixture is too dry to handle, add a very little additional ice water. The dough should be fairly firm, however. Roll out very thin on a lightly floured board. Cut with a cooky cutter and press some chopped dates into each piece of dough. Heat the oil until it begins to bubble and place the cut-out pieces of dough in it. Reduce the heat somewhat so the oil does not get too hot. Turn over the cakes when they are browned on one side. Drain and serve hot. Sprinkle with powdered sugar before serving. This dessert somewhat resembles a pancake, and is not in accordance with our usual idea of a dessert.

PAKISTAN

A newly formed country, Pakistan consists of two parts: the smaller portion, located east of India, and the larger area, about a thousand miles to the west. Gastronomically speaking, the nation is subject to two principal influences. In the low, lush region of the east adjacent to Burma, there is a decided emphasis on such foods of that region as curries and spices. The western portion has the geographic and climatic variety of California, although this statement is made without the consent of the respective Chambers of Commerce, to whom explanations and apologies are extended in advance. West Pakistan thus has a wider variety of food and produce from which to select. Aside from these local variations, Pakistani cuisine is largely similar to that of neighboring India.

The people eat all sorts of meat except pork, which is forbidden to them by their religion. Also, they are not often given to vegetarianism as are many Indians. Lamb and chicken dishes are appreciated here, and they appear frequently in the diet. An example of the influence of the Near and Middle East on West Pakistan is *murgh-i-musallam* (spicy baked chicken), which is the type of dish often found in neighboring Iran. *Huzoor pasand pulao,* made from lamb, fruit, and rice, also fits this description. Incidentally, the *pulao* dishes of this area have become a standard part of the cuisine of the world; in our country, *pulao* has become pilau, the herbs and seasoning have been changed, but the basic idea of the dish is the same.

Spicy food is the rule in Pakistan: chili peppers, dry mustard, ginger, and other spices form a part of almost every dish. Coconuts, raisins, nuts, and fruits of all sorts, and especially the delicious melons, help to round out the cuisine. However, these are all superstructure and trimmings resting upon the firm base of rice and wheat, the primary foods of the multitudes. And Pakistan is a land of multitudes, with more than eighty million people, the fifth largest population of any country in the world; Karachi, the capital, is a city of more than a million.

Fruits are the subject of great local pride. They are delightful for breakfast, for dessert, or at any time of the day. Many drinks, both alcoholic and non-alcoholic, are made from these fruits but most Pakistanis would rather drink tea. The national preference is for iced, sweet soft drinks; beers and wines are unimportant. Western-style liquors are available, but the majority of the people never touch alcohol and much prefer a glass of cold milk in the best tradition of the health-food stores of our own country. Ahoy there, Bernarr Macfadden!

In Karachi, fine food may be had at the restaurants in the Palace, Metropole, and Beach Luxury hotels. The Shezan, Manhattan, and Firpo's restaurants tend to emphasize local cooking, whereas the hotels lean toward international menus.

One pleasant point to remember about visiting Karachi is that there is practically no rainfall; the weather is almost always pleasant, but November to March are the very best months for a visit. Carved articles made of ivory are outstanding values here.

## FISH IN KASHMIR STYLE

BECKTI KASHMIRI

2 cloves garlic, minced
1 teaspoon salt
½ teaspoon black pepper
¼ teaspoon dried ground chili pepper
⅛ teaspoon ground cumin seed

6 fillets of sole
4 tablespoons butter
½ cup sour milk or buttermilk
2 teaspoons lemon juice

Mix the garlic, salt, pepper, chili peppers, and cumin seed together. Rub into the fish carefully and thoroughly. Melt the butter in a skillet. Add the fillets and brown well on both sides. Add the milk and lemon juice. Cook over low heat until the milk is absorbed. Serve hot.

## FISH AND RICE

MAHI BIRIANI

2 cups rice
1 cup sour milk, buttermilk, or yogurt
1 teaspoon cumin seed
½-inch piece fresh ginger, chopped, or 1 teaspoon powdered ginger
2½ teaspoons salt

2 cloves garlic, minced
2 pounds halibut or cod, in one piece
½ teaspoon saffron
¾ cup boiling water
3 tablespoons butter
1 onion, chopped fine

Wash the rice thoroughly in several changes of water. Soak in cold water to cover for 15 minutes. Bring to a boil in the same water and cook for 10 minutes. Drain. Combine the milk or yogurt, cumin seed, ginger, salt, and garlic in a bowl. Add the fish and turn it several times in the mixture. Marinate for 30 minutes. Soak the saffron in the boiling water for 10 minutes.

Melt the butter in a large saucepan. Add the onion and sauté for 10 minutes, stirring frequently. Remove the onion and set aside. Place the fish and the marinade in the saucepan. Spread the rice over it. Spread the onion on top and sprinkle with the saffron water. Bring to a boil, cover, and cook over low heat for 35 minutes.

## LAMB AND FRUIT

### HUZOOR PASAND PULAO

3 cups rice
¼ pound butter
3 pounds boneless lamb, cut into 1-inch cubes
3 onions, sliced thin
4 cups sour milk, buttermilk, or yogurt
2 cloves garlic, minced
1 teaspoon coriander
1-inch piece fresh ginger, chopped, or 2 teaspoons powdered ginger
½ teaspoon pepper

2 cloves
3 cardamom seeds
1 tablespoon salt
1 teaspoon saffron
2 tablespoons boiling water
½ cup sliced, mixed nuts (almonds, pistachios, etc.)
2 oranges, peeled, segmented, and pitted
½ cup seedless grapes (remove seeds if grapes are not seedless)

Wash the rice thoroughly in several changes of water. Soak in cold water for 15 minutes. Drain well. Melt the butter in a saucepan. Add the lamb and onions; brown well on all sides. Add the milk or yogurt, garlic, coriander, ginger, pepper, cloves, cardamom seeds, and salt and stir well. Place the rice over it. Dissolve the saffron in the boiling water and add to the saucepan, stirring well. Arrange the sliced nuts, oranges, and grapes on top. Cover and cook over medium heat for 10 minutes. Reduce heat to low and cook for 25 minutes, or until the lamb and rice are tender.

## LENTILS

### DAL

2 cups lentils (red, if available)
3 cups water
¼ teaspoon dried ground chili peppers
2 teaspoons salt

½ teaspoon turmeric
4 tablespoons butter
1 onion, chopped
1 clove garlic, minced

Wash the lentils carefully and soak them overnight in water to cover. (This step will not be necessary if presoaked lentils are used.) Drain. Add the 3 cups of water, chili peppers, salt, and turmeric. Cook over low heat for 2 hours, or until the lentils are soft and the water is absorbed. Stir frequently. Correct seasoning. Melt the butter in a saucepan. Add the onion and garlic and sauté for 15 minutes, stirring occasionally. Pour over the lentils and serve hot.

## SPICY BAKED CHICKEN

MURGH-I-MUSALLAM

2 3½-pound chickens
6 cloves garlic, minced
2 onions, chopped
½ teaspoon dried ground chili peppers
½ teaspoon ground cloves
1½ teaspoons salt
1 teaspoon black pepper

2 cardamom seeds, ground
¼-inch piece fresh or dried ginger, crushed fine, or ½ teaspoon powdered ginger
½ cup ground blanched almonds
4 tablespoons melted butter
2 tablespoons water

Carefully remove all of the skin from the whole chickens. Prick the chickens all over with a fork. Mix the garlic, onions, chili peppers, cloves, salt, pepper, cardamom seeds, ginger, almonds, butter, and water into a paste. Spread over the chickens and rub a little on the inside. Be sure to cover the chickens thoroughly with the mixture. Place in a buttered baking dish or a roasting pan. Roast in a 350° oven for 1½ hours, or until tender. Add a little water if necessary to prevent the chickens from burning. Carve the chickens and serve hot.

## POTATOES AND RICE, PAKISTANI STYLE

ALU-KI-TARI

2 cups rice
¼ pound butter
2 onions, sliced thin
4 potatoes, peeled and quartered
2 teaspoons salt
1 teaspoon turmeric

1 teaspoon coriander
2 cloves garlic, minced
½-inch piece fresh ginger, chopped, or 1 teaspoon powdered ginger
Dash of cayenne pepper
4 cups boiling water

Wash the rice thoroughly in several changes of water. Soak in cold water for 30 minutes. Drain well. Melt the butter in a saucepan. Add the onions and sauté for 15 minutes, stirring frequently. Add the rice, potatoes, salt, turmeric, coriander, garlic, ginger, cayenne, and boiling water and stir.

Bring to a boil. Cover and cook over low heat for 30 minutes, or until the potatoes are tender.

## NUT CANDY

### HALVA

½ pound butter
2 cups farina or semolina
2 cups confectioners' sugar
½ cup ground almonds

½ cup ground pistachio nuts
½ teaspoon ground cardamom seeds
4 tablespoons light cream

Melt the butter in a saucepan. Add the farina or semolina, stirring constantly with a wooden spoon until lightly browned. Remove from the heat. Add the sugar, almonds, pistachio nuts, and cardamom and mix well. Add the cream and cook over low heat, stirring constantly, until the mixture forms a ball and leaves the sides of the saucepan.

Butter an oblong baking dish. Pour the mixture into it and spread evenly. Cut into desired shapes and allow to cool. When cool, cut out the shapes completely. This dessert will keep very well in the refrigerator for more than a week.

## SINGAPORE AND MALAYA

Singapore and the Christmas and Cocos islands make up a tiny part of the British Empire and are governed as a British Crown Colony. The Federation of Malaya, directly to the north, came into existence in 1948. Singapore is a very modern city, with a large and cosmopolitan population consisting of British, Indian, Chinese, Japanese, and Malayans, in addition to small groups representing many other races and nationalities.

The British residents often attempt to live as if they were still in England, and meals are planned as though they were living seventy-seven miles north of Eastbourne and not seventy-seven miles north of the equator. It would be easier to be sympathetic to the British point of view in wishing to retain their familiar dishes if these were well prepared. Unfortunately the contrary is true, for even though surrounded by unusual and often excellent native produce the British residents tenaciously prepare their heavy, dull fare. The other groups take considerably more advantage of the local produce than do the English.

Since Singapore is in the tropics and practically at sea level, the climate may not be disregarded with impunity. Business must be transacted early in the day, before the lunch hour and before the heat becomes unbearable. Most people stay indoors during the middle of the day, particularly during the hot months from June to September—except mad dogs and certain foreign residents. Activity commences once again at teatime, which in turn leads to a rather late dinner hour. There is a considerable amount of drinking, particularly of scotch whisky, by the foreign residents rather than by the local population. The Singapore gin sling originated here, of course.

The two principal food styles of Singapore and Malaya are the Chinese and the Malay fashions. Both are excellent and unusual, and may be prepared in Western kitchens with no particular difficulty. The Chinese dishes of the area differ somewhat from the customary Chinese fare; they are local adaptations of recipes brought by these emigrants from their homeland.

The Malayans are small people as a rule, and their capacity for food is somewhat limited, but they are extremely fond of dishes seasoned with their own selections of spices and herbs. The basis of most Malay dishes is rice, which is a mainstay at almost every meal. Sometimes it is served plain but usually it is the foundation for a meat or fish dish. Two favorite spicing agents are ginger (both fresh baby shoots and the dried variety) and red chili peppers. These are used for flavor and color. Other frequently used spices include turmeric (which lends a yellow color), cloves, coriander (for its spicy aroma), garlic (no comment), tamarind, and fenugreek.

Malays do not drink alcoholic beverages as a general rule, although some of the younger people are breaking away from the old customs. Plain water is considered a very satisfactory drink, and Malayans seldom drink anything else before or during a meal.

Unquestionably the best desserts are the many fresh fruits of this region, some of which are familiar to us. The more unusual ones include many rare types of bananas, the mangosteens, and an evil-smelling but delicious fruit known as *durian,* or jack fruit.

## SINGAPORE GIN SLING

2 tablespoons powdered sugar
6 jiggers gin
1 jigger cherry brandy

Juice of 2 lemons
6 maraschino cherries
6 finger-length slices fresh pineapple

Mix the powdered sugar, gin, cherry brandy, and lemon juice together in a cocktail shaker. Half fill 6 tall highball glasses with cracked ice. Place a cherry and a slice of pineapple in each glass. Add the liquor and fill each glass with carbonated water. Serve ice cold. Add a fresh strawberry or paper-thin slices of lemon or orange, if available.

## CHICKEN LIVER AND PEA SOUP

CHENG TAU, HU CHI

1 pound pork and several pork bones
  (see Note)
2 teaspoons salt
2 quarts water
½ pound chicken livers

½ cup chopped mushrooms
1 teaspoon powdered ginger
1 No. 1 can green peas, drained
1 tablespoon soy sauce
½ teaspoon pepper

Combine the pork, bones, salt, and water in a saucepan. Bring to a boil and cook over medium heat for 2 hours. Strain the stock and reserve it. Chop the livers coarsely. Place them in a saucepan with the mushrooms, stock, ginger, and green peas. Cook over low heat for 10 minutes. Add the soy sauce and pepper. Bring to a boil and remove from heat. Serve very hot. The pork may be used for another dish, or may be served separately.

*Note: If desired, 2 cans of beef or chicken consommé and 3 cans of water may be used instead of making a pork stock.*

## FISH AND STRING BEANS

IKAN MASAK ASAM

1 teaspoon turmeric
1-inch piece of fresh ginger, chopped,
  or 1 teaspoon powdered ginger
½ teaspoon dried ground chili peppers
6 cooked shrimp, peeled and chopped fine
5 onions, chopped

4 tablespoons butter
½ pound fresh or ½ package frozen
  (defrosted) string beans
2 cups water
3 tablespoons lemon juice
2 tablespoons plum jam
4 fillets of mackerel
2 teaspoons salt

Combine the turmeric, ginger, chili peppers, shrimp, and onions. Chop or pound the ingredients to a smooth paste. Melt the butter in a large saucepan. Add the previous mixture and sauté for 5 minutes, stirring frequently. Add the beans and sauté for 3 minutes. Add the water. Mix the lemon juice and plum jam together, and add, stirring well. Cook over medium heat for 5 minutes. Add the mackerel and salt and cook over low heat for 20 minutes. Correct seasoning. Serve hot, over boiled rice.

*Note: Lemon juice and plum jam are used as a substitute for tamarind, which is not readily available.*

## SPICY STEAK BITS

### DONDENG

½ teaspoon dried ground chili peppers

10 almonds, coarsely chopped

3 tablespoons grated lemon rind

1-inch piece fresh ginger, ground, or 1 teaspoon powdered ginger

3 onions, chopped

4 cloves garlic, minced

3 pounds steak (about ½ inch thick), cut into strips 1 x 2 inches

¼ pound butter

2 cups boiling water

1 teaspoon sugar

2 teaspoons salt

4 tablespoons lemon juice

3 tablespoons plum jam

Combine the chili peppers, almonds, lemon rind, onions, and garlic and mix well. Roll the steak pieces lightly in the mixture. Melt the butter in a saucepan. Add the meat and cook over high heat for 5 minutes, stirring constantly.

Combine the water, sugar, salt, lemon juice, and plum jam and add to the meat, mixing well. Cook over low heat for 15 minutes, or until the meat is tender. Stir occasionally. Correct seasoning. Serve with boiled rice and pour the sauce over the rice and meat.

## FISH, STRAITS CHINESE FASHION

### OTAK OTAK

1½ cups fresh or dried grated coconut

1 cup milk

2 tablespoons butter

2 pounds fish fillets

¼ cup ground almonds

3 tablespoons grated lemon rind

1-inch piece fresh ginger, grated, or 1½ teaspoons powdered ginger

1 teaspoon turmeric

½ teaspoon basil

1 teaspoon salt

3 onions, chopped fine

2 cloves garlic

2 eggs, beaten

Combine 1 cup of the coconut and the milk in a saucepan. Bring to a boil, remove from the heat, and soak for 30 minutes. Press all the liquid from the coconut and discard the pulp. Melt the butter in a skillet; add the remaining coconut and sauté until lightly browned, stirring constantly. Grind the fish in a food chopper or chop it. Add the almonds, lemon rind, ginger, turmeric, basil, salt, onions, garlic, and eggs; mix well. Add the sautéed coconut and the coconut milk. Mix well.

Cut squares (about 6–8 inches) of aluminum foil or parchment paper and butter them lightly. Place 2 tablespoons of the mixture on each square and fold the edges of the paper over carefully to keep the liquid from leaking out. Place on a buttered baking sheet. Bake in a 375° oven for 35 minutes. Serve the fish in its wrapping and have each person open his at the table.

*Note: A smaller version may be used as a hot hors d'oeuvre.*

## SINGAPORE LOBSTER CURRY

3 cups milk
2 cups fresh or dried grated coconut
¼ pound butter
5 onions, chopped
2 cloves garlic, minced
⅛ teaspoon cumin seed
2 teaspoons powdered ginger
Dash of cayenne pepper
2 teaspoons salt

2 tablespoons curry powder
2 tomatoes, chopped
2 tablespoons flour
1 cucumber, peeled and cubed
Meat from 2 boiled lobsters
or 1 pound lobster meat, cubed
2 tablespoons lemon juice
1 tablespoon plum jam

Combine the milk and coconut in a saucepan. Bring to a boil, remove from the heat, and soak for 30 minutes. Press all the milk from the coconut and discard the pulp.

Melt the butter in a saucepan and add the onions and garlic. Sauté for 10 minutes, stirring frequently. Add the cumin seed, ginger, cayenne pepper, salt, curry powder, and tomatoes. Cover and cook over low heat for 10 minutes, stirring frequently. Add the flour, stirring constantly. Add the coconut milk slowly, stirring steadily until the boiling point is reached. Add the cucumber and lobster meat and cook over low heat for 15 minutes. Mix the lemon juice and jam together and add to the lobster mixture. Correct seasoning. Mix well. Serve hot, with boiled rice.

*Note: Singapore is famous for the fieriness of its curries. Additional curry powder may be added if desired.*

## COCONUT-GINGER CHICKEN

RENDAN SANTAN

2 cups fresh or dried grated coconut
1½ cups light cream
2 tablespoons butter
1 tablespoon ground coriander
1 teaspoon ground anise
½ teaspoon saffron
1-inch piece fresh ginger, ground, or 1 teaspoon powdered ginger
2 cloves garlic, minced
2 tablespoons grated lemon rind
1 fresh chili pepper, sliced fine, or ½ teaspoon dried ground chili peppers
3 tablespoons lemon juice
1 tablespoon plum jam
1 teaspoon sugar
1 teaspoon salt
3 onions, sliced
3½-pound chicken, disjointed

Combine 1½ cups of the coconut and the cream in a saucepan. Bring to a boil, remove from the heat, and soak for 30 minutes. Press all the liquid from the coconut and discard the pulp. Melt the butter in a saucepan. Add the remaining coconut and fry until brown. Combine the coriander, anise, saffron, ginger, garlic, lemon rind, chili peppers, lemon juice, plum jam, sugar, and salt. Mix well. Add the sliced onions and browned coconut.

Remove the chicken meat from the bones and cut into small pieces. Place the chicken, the spice mixture, and the coconut cream in a saucepan. Place over high heat and cook, stirring constantly, until the mixture boils actively. Reduce the heat and cook for 10 minutes, or until chicken is tender. Serve hot with boiled noodles or rice. Pour the sauce over the chicken and noodles.

## COCONUT CUSTARD

SARIKAUJA

1½ cups fresh or dried grated coconut
1½ cups milk
4 eggs
1½ cups sugar

Combine the coconut and milk in a saucepan. Bring to a boil, remove from the heat, and soak for 20 minutes. Press all the milk from the coconut. Strain, and discard the pulp. Beat the eggs well. Add the sugar and beat until light and fluffy. Add the coconut milk and beat well. Preheat oven to 350°. Pour into 6 individual buttered custard cups. Place them in a pan of water and cover each cup. Bake for 20 minutes in a 350° oven, or until the custard is set. Sprinkle a little grated coconut on top of each portion.

*THAILAND (SIAM)*

Formerly known as Siam, and presently as the locale of the recent Broadway hit *The King and I,* Thailand is one country which tourists acclaim as the ultimate in local color. Surely a large portion of its charm must be attributed to its people, smiling, cheerful, and polite, to whom the modern civilized world, as it is laughingly called, seems a sort of never-never land. In the same manner, although in reverse, Thailand is equally unbelievable to Westerners.

Bangkok, the throbbing, teeming capital city, is on the general order of Venice, for it is crisscrossed by a network of canals and waterways. But whereas Venice has fourteenth-century buildings facing onto the canals, here one finds tropical foliage and the moist air of the jungle. People of the rivers live their entire lives on their boats, and a trip through the canals will not be soon forgotten. There is even a floating market, though this is seen at its best rather early in the morning.

Thailand's food is influenced by its neighbors, China and India, and both styles of cooking are practiced in addition to the local cuisine. Seafood is a basic part of Thailand's diet. Particularly good are the prawns, which are used to make *hae kün* (shrimp rolls). There is also a rather large fish, the *plakapon,* that has a fine flavor. *Namplā* is an enormously popular smelly seasoning, in the form of a sauce made from salted shrimp or fish.

Indian influence may be noted in the popularity of curries, often thought by local connoisseurs to be among the best in the world, although this claim is frequently made in Southeast Asia. The curries (*kaeng phed*) are quite hot and should be approached with caution and considerable respect. *Kaeng chüd* (soup) is served at the same time as the other dishes making up the meal. Rice is the staple food of the nation, eaten by rich and poor alike, for the locally grown rice is of the highest quality.

Vegetables of all sorts are great favorites, and are often served with *nam prik* sauce, which is made of varying ingredients but usually includes garlic, pounded dried shrimp, and chili peppers. It is a startling (!) taste (!!) sensation (!!!) to most tourists. Salads (*yams*) are popular and are made from almost any growing thing: green plants, vine leaves, shrubs, and even the tender shoots of young fruit trees. Fruits grow in superabundance and are often magnificent in both taste and eye appeal; there are not only familiar species but, as might be expected in this exotic country, many uncommon types as well. A novel end to a meal is the so-called liquid dessert, a sweet syrup made from coconut milk, tapioca, bananas, rice, flowers, and many other ingredients. *Saton* (the wood apple) is often used for this purpose. The more usual desserts are sweet confections based on rice or cassava flour, palm sugar, mung beans, taro, or tapioca, in addition to fresh fruits.

Tea is truly the beverage of the country. Almost everyone drinks it frequently throughout the day. Often it is made with the addition of orange, lemon, or jasmine flavoring. A host would be derelict in his duty if he did not offer a guest some tea as soon as he arrived. *Arak*, made from the sap of palm trees or fermented rice, and *mekong*, a local rice whisky, are both popular strong drinks.

## SHRIMP SOUP

### KAENG CHÜD

3 cups heavy cream
4 cups milk
3 cups fresh or dried grated coconut
2 fresh chili peppers, sliced, or ½ teaspoon dried ground chili peppers
4 cloves garlic, minced
3 shallots or 1 onion, minced
1 tablespoon sugar

1 tablespoon shrimp or anchovy paste
1 tablespoon soy sauce
1 tablespoon grated lemon rind
4 peppercorns
6 coriander seeds
2 pounds shrimp, peeled and cleaned

Combine the cream, milk, and coconut in a saucepan. Bring to a boil, remove from the heat, and soak for 30 minutes. Press all the liquid from the coconut and discard the pulp. Cook the coconut cream over low heat for 10 minutes. Combine the chili peppers, garlic, shallots, sugar, shrimp paste, soy sauce, and lemon rind in a bowl. Pound until very smooth. Add the mixture to the coconut cream, stirring well. Add the peppercorns, coriander seeds, and shrimp. Cook over low heat for 6 minutes. Correct seasoning. Serve hot.

## FRIED FISH IN SPICY SAUCE

TRA PLA TURD

8 dried mushrooms (Chinese type, if possible)
1 cup flour
1 tablespoon olive oil
1 cup water
1 teaspoon salt
6 slices fish
   Fat for deep-fat frying
6 tablespoons vinegar

2 scallions (green onions), coarsely chopped
4 tablespoons sugar
1 tablespoon soy sauce
4 tablespoons minced preserved ginger
2 tablespoons powdered ginger
1 tablespoon cornstarch
3 tablespoons chopped parsley

Soak the mushrooms in water to cover for 30 minutes. Mix the flour, olive oil, ½ cup of the water, and the salt to a smooth paste. Dip the fish in the mixture on both sides. Heat the fat to 360° and fry the fish in it until brown.

Drain the mushrooms and chop fine. Combine the mushrooms, vinegar, scallions, sugar, soy sauce, preserved and powdered ginger in a saucepan. Bring the mixture to a boil and cook over low heat for 5 minutes. Mix the cornstarch with the remaining water until smooth, and add, stirring constantly until the boiling point is reached. Cook over low heat for 5 minutes, stirring occasionally. Arrange the fish on a platter and sprinkle with the parsley. Pour the sauce over it and serve.

## SHRIMP SALAD

YAM KOONG

1 cup milk
1 cup fresh or dried grated coconut
2 pounds shrimp, peeled and cleaned
2 cups water
2 teaspoons salt
1 bay leaf
1 tablespoon olive oil

2 cloves garlic, minced
2 shallots, minced, or ½ onion, grated
2 green peppers, chopped
2 tablespoons soy sauce
1 apple, peeled and grated
3 tablespoons chopped peanuts

Combine the milk and coconut in a saucepan. Bring to a boil, remove from the heat, and soak for 30 minutes. Press all the milk from the coconut and discard the pulp. Combine the shrimp, water, salt, and bay leaf in a saucepan. Boil for 8 minutes. Drain, and split the shrimp lengthwise. Chill for 1 hour.

Heat the olive oil in a saucepan. Add the garlic and shallots and sauté for 2 minutes, stirring frequently. Remove from the heat. Add the green peppers, soy sauce, grated apple, and peanuts and mix well. Combine this mixture with the coconut milk and chill for at least 1 hour. Arrange the shrimp on a platter, pour the sauce over them, and serve cold.

## COCONUT CHICKEN

KAI P'ANAENG

2 cups heavy cream
1½ cups fresh or dried grated coconut
6 chicken breasts
3 cloves garlic, minced
2 shallots, minced, or ½ onion, grated
½ teaspoon dried ground chili peppers

3 tablespoons ground peanuts
1 tablespoon grated lemon rind
6 coriander seeds
1 teaspoon sugar
1 tablespoon mushroom essence or soy sauce

Combine the cream and coconut in a saucepan. Bring to a boil, remove from the heat, and soak for 30 minutes. Press all the liquid from the coconut and discard the pulp. Combine the coconut cream and the chicken breasts in a saucepan. Cover and cook over medium heat for 30 minutes. Add the garlic, shallots, chili peppers, peanuts, lemon rind, coriander seeds, sugar, and mushroom essence. Stir until well mixed. Cook for 15 minutes or until chicken is tender. Turn the chicken frequently to coat with the sauce. Correct seasoning. If soy sauce is used, probably no salt will be required; if mushroom essence is used, it may be necessary to add about 2 teaspoons of salt. Serve with boiled rice.

## SQUAB WITH SWEET AND PUNGENT SAUCE

NAM CHIM PRIA WAN

¼ cup peanut oil
2 cloves garlic, minced
3 squabs, cut in quarters
2 onions, sliced thin
3 tomatoes, cut in eighths
3 green peppers, diced
1 cucumber, peeled and diced
4 coriander seeds

1 tablespoon flour
3 tablespoons confectioners' sugar
½ cup vinegar
¼ cup water
2 tablespoons soy sauce
1 teaspoon salt
½ teaspoon pepper

Heat the oil in a saucepan. Add the garlic and sauté for 1 minute, stirring constantly. Add the squabs and brown well on all sides. Cover and cook over low heat for 20 minutes. Add the onions, tomatoes, green peppers, cucumber, and coriander seeds. Mix the flour, sugar, and vinegar to a smooth paste. Add the water, soy sauce, salt, and pepper and stir. Add to the saucepan, stirring constantly. Cook over medium heat for 5 minutes longer, or until the squabs are tender. Stir frequently. Serve with boiled rice.

## SIAMESE CRULLERS

KHANŎM SAI KAI

½ teaspoon saffron
1 tablespoon boiling water
2 cups sugar
1½ cups water

1¼ cups sifted flour
1 teaspoon baking powder
⅛ teaspoon salt
Fat for deep-fat frying

Soak the saffron in boiling water for 5 minutes. Combine the sugar and 1 cup of the water in a saucepan and cook until thick and syrupy.

Sift the flour, baking powder, and salt into a bowl. Add ½ cup of water and the saffron mixture, mixing until very smooth. Heat the fat to 370° in a heavy saucepan. Pour the batter through a narrow funnel into the fat in 2-inch lengths. After a little practice it will be possible always to pour the correct amount. Make only a few of the crullers at a time. Drain them, then place in the sugar and water mixture. Turn them a few times and remove to a platter to cool.

# THE
# PACIFIC

*Australia*

*Fiji Islands*

*Hawaii and the Polynesian Islands*

*New Zealand*

*The Philippines*

## AUSTRALIA

The land "down under" has many surprises for visitors. They are always astounded at the vast distances—often hundreds of miles—between communities, most of which are located along the east coast. It should be remembered that Australia is the only country in the world that occupies an entire continent. Australian back country today is very much like the western United States of two hundred years ago, with one important exception. The airplane is that exception; it has cut the traveling time between habitations from weary days to short hours.

The Australians are hearty eaters; they like large, substantial meals. The meal-hour pattern follows our own, except that dinner may be served a little earlier than we are accustomed to. Most of Australia's cuisine has come by way of England and has been adopted by the people. A typical example is toad-in-the-hole, originally an English item and now an everyday dish in Australia. Meat, of course, is greatly favored, as might be anticipated in this land of hundreds of thousands of grazing acres. Lamb is the first choice, but beef is almost equally popular. Since Australia is surrounded by the sea, fish dishes are almost always of high quality and well prepared. Fruits are very good, and there are many fruit desserts. No meal is complete without tea, for here, too, the tea habit is as strong as in England.

Australians are fairly heavy drinkers, particularly of the locally produced beer. This is a meritorious product and has a higher alcoholic content than our usual brews. Beer drinking has been described as the national pastime, and beer parties are common. Liquor laws are puzzling to the stranger, and many places serve liquor only at particular hours. Australian wines are growing in importance, and deservedly so, for they are of top quality. The very best local wines are apparently the pink champagne and the sparkling burgundy.

Sydney has most of the country's better restaurants, although Melbourne has its fair share. The capital is Canberra, a rather small city of about 15,000, but most of the life of the country is elsewhere. The visitor to Australia will find much to interest him, including the tremendous area of

279

undeveloped open country and the Great Barrier Reef, a thousand miles of nature showing herself to best advantage.

Australians are firm believers in the English breakfast: fruit or juice, cereals, eggs, and bacon. Lunch and dinner are much on the British style, and almost any British dish is likely to be served here, though on a much more generous scale than in England. Australians are vigorous outdoor people; a delicate appetite is regarded with suspicion. In this democratic country an invitation to have something to eat or drink is sincerely meant; a refusal is often regarded as an insult.

Actually the Australian cuisine is a healthy one, for it is based on raw fruits and vegetables, green salads (usually too sweet), delicious seafood, grilled meats, and fine dairy products. Oh, those Americans! Here, too, are the milk shakes, malteds, and ice creams of our nation which few countries have resisted.

## PUMPKIN SOUP

2 pounds pumpkin
2 onions, chopped
6 cups stock or 2 cans consommé and 2½ cans water
1 teaspoon salt

½ teaspoon pepper
1 tablespoon flour
¼ cup cold water
1 cup light cream

Peel the pumpkin, discard the seeds and fiber, and cut into ½-inch cubes. Place in a deep saucepan with the onions, stock, salt, and pepper. Cook over low heat for 1 hour, or until the pumpkin is very soft. Force the pumpkin through a sieve and return it to the saucepan. Place the flour and cold water in a cup and stir until very smooth. Add to the soup, stirring constantly until the boiling point is reached. Add the cream, mixing well. Correct seasoning. Serve with toasted croutons.

## TOAD-IN-THE-HOLE

1½ cups sifted flour
½ teaspoon baking powder
2 teaspoons salt
1 egg, beaten
2 cups milk

3 cups sliced cooked chicken or 6 slices cooked roast beef
3 tablespoons chopped parsley
½ teaspoon pepper

Sift the flour, baking powder, and 1 teaspoon of the salt into a bowl. Add the egg and milk and beat until smooth. Preheat oven to 350°. Place the chicken or meat in a buttered casserole. Sprinkle with parsley, pepper, and salt. Pour the batter over it. Bake in a 350° oven for 1 hour.

*Note: Although this recipe originated in England, it is a well-accepted part of the Australian cuisine and is popular throughout the entire country.*

## LAMB PIE

1 cup sifted flour
2½ teaspoons salt
⅓ cup shortening
3 tablespoons ice water
1 teaspoon pepper
6 boned loin lamb chops
3 tablespoons butter

1 onion, chopped
½ cup chopped mushrooms
2 carrots, grated
2 cups stock or 1 can consommé and
½ can water
3 tablespoons chopped parsley

Sift the flour and ½ teaspoon of the salt into a bowl. Cut in the shortening with a pastry blender or two knives until the consistency of coarse sand. Add water, tossing lightly until a ball of dough is formed. Wrap in wax paper and chill while preparing the lamb.

Combine the remaining salt and the pepper and sprinkle over the chops. Melt the butter in a skillet and brown the chops on both sides. Add the onion, mushrooms, carrots, and stock. Cover and cook over medium heat for 10 minutes. Add parsley and stir. Correct seasoning.

Arrange the chops in a buttered baking dish. Pour the vegetables and gravy over them. Preheat oven to 375°. Roll out the dough to fit the top of the baking dish. Seal the edges carefully. Prick the dough in several places. Bake in a 375° oven for 45 minutes, or until browned on top. Serve directly from the dish.

## OATMEAL BREAD

AUSTRALIAN JACK

¼ pound butter
⅓ cup dark brown sugar
¼ teaspoon baking soda

2 teaspoons water
1½ cups oatmeal
1 teaspoon powdered ginger

Cream the butter; add the sugar and beat until light and fluffy. Dissolve the baking soda in the water and add, stirring well. Add the oatmeal and ginger, mixing well. The mixture should be fairly firm. If necessary, add a little more oatmeal. Knead lightly on a floured surface. Preheat oven to 300°. Press the mixture into a buttered baking dish, about 8 by 12 inches. The dough should be about ½ inch thick. Bake in a 300° oven for 35 minutes, or until brown on top. Cut into squares while hot.

## CHEESE-CURRY BISCUITS

¾ cup flour
½ teaspoon baking powder
2 teaspoons curry powder
4 tablespoons butter
⅔ cup grated cheese

1 egg yolk
2 tablespoons milk
⅛ teaspoon dry English mustard
¼ teaspoon salt
Dash of cayenne pepper

281

Mix the flour, baking powder, and curry powder together. Cut in the butter with a pastry blender or two knives. Add the cheese and continue mixing. Combine the egg yolk, milk, mustard, salt, and cayenne pepper. Add to the mixture, stirring with a fork until a dough is formed. Preheat oven to 400°. Roll out ⅛ inch thick on a lightly floured surface. Cut in any desired shape. Place on a buttered baking pan. Bake in a 400° oven for 7 minutes.

## NUT SPONGECAKE

WIENCO TOOTE

| | |
|---|---|
| 3 tablespoons butter | ⅔ cup sifted flour |
| ⅓ cup confectioners' sugar | 1 teaspoon baking soda |
| 4 egg yolks | 2 teaspoons cream of tartar |
| ⅓ cup ground nuts | 4 egg whites |

Cream the butter well. Add the sugar gradually, creaming until light and fluffy. Add the egg yolks and nuts and beat well. Sift the flour, baking soda, and cream of tartar together. Beat the egg whites in a bowl until stiff but not dry. Fold the flour and the egg whites into the sugar mixture alternately. Preheat oven to 350°.

Butter two 8-inch layer tins and dust lightly with flour. Pour half of the batter into each. Bake in a 350° oven for 20 minutes, or until a cake tester comes out clean. When cool, spread raspberry jam between the layers. Now prepare the following icing:

| | |
|---|---|
| 4 tablespoons butter | 2 ounces unsweetened chocolate |
| 2 cups sugar | 1 teaspoon vanilla extract |
| ½ cup milk | |

Melt the butter in a saucepan. Add the sugar and milk. Bring to a boil, stirring constantly, and cook over low heat for 10 minutes. Melt the chocolate over hot water and add gradually to the previous mixture, stirring well. Remove from the heat and beat with a rotary beater until the mixture thickens. Add the vanilla. Ice the top and sides of the cake as evenly as possible. If the icing hardens, it may be softened by placing it over hot water.

*FIJI ISLANDS*

Although there are almost three hundred islands in this British Crown Colony, the only one that most tourists see is Viti Levu. Suva, the capital, is on the eastern portion of the island and one of the standard tourist sights is the local police force, colorful and unique.

Here is the land of bushy-haired natives, the bluest ocean in the world pounding on the whitest beach, luxuriant tropical growth, and, of course, the calm, reserved British officials who govern the islands. Here, too, are the East Indians who now outnumber the native Fiji population and are gradually taking over the business life of the colony.

Fruits and vegetables grow to enormous size here; there are many both familiar and unfamiliar, such as the granadilla, mandarin, soursop, breadfruit, taro, and, of course, the Fiji asparagus, the *duruka*.

The food is somewhat primitive, although a tourist stopping at such a place as the Grand Pacific Hotel would hardly realize it. Nonetheless, the islands have several fine native dishes that are much appreciated by visitors. Naturally, many of the more interesting fruits and vegetables are unobtainable in our part of the world, but several recipes representative of the local food style have been selected. For example, the yam fish balls, shrimp in coconut, and the spinach in coconut milk may all be made in our own country. Meals usually conclude with fresh fruit, particularly the fine pineapple grown on the islands.

Tea is a favorite with everyone, and this, too, is locally grown. The natives also drink a homemade firewater, *yaqona*, or *kava*, as it is more popularly called. It is prepared from the pounded or grated *yaqona* root and mixed with water. The Fijians serve it at all important festivals and ceremonials, and it is drunk in extreme quantities on these occasions. Although this beverage is supposed to have curative properties, this fact has yet to be proven. To date, the only recorded cures have been of the local thirsts. Most visitors do not find it to their liking, preferring their own customary drinks, which offer no cures whatsoever.

## BANANA CUP

½ cup tomato sauce
3 tablespoons lemon juice
2 tablespoons finely chopped celery

3 teaspoons Worcestershire sauce
6 small bananas, diced

Combine the tomato sauce, lemon juice, celery, and Worcestershire sauce. Mix well. Peel and dice the bananas. Pour the sauce over them and chill for at least 30 minutes. Serve as an appetizer.

## YAM FISH BALLS

2 pounds fish fillets
1 cup water
1 onion, sliced
2 teaspoons salt
1 teaspoon pepper

1 pound yams or sweet potatoes
½ cup hot milk
1 egg, beaten
½ cup flour
Shortening for deep-fat frying

Wash the fish and place it in a saucepan with the water, onion, salt, and pepper. Cook for 20 minutes, or until fish is flaky. Cool for 30 minutes.

Peel the yams and cut into quarters. Place in a saucepan with water to cover. Cook until soft, about 30 minutes. Drain well and mash until smooth. Add the hot milk and beat until very light and fluffy. Flake the fish into shreds and add it to the yam mixture. Add the beaten egg and stir. Correct seasoning. Roll the mixture into 2-inch balls. Dip each ball into flour. Heat shortening to 375° and fry the balls until lightly browned on all sides.

## MOCK TURTLE SOUP

### BAIGAN SOUP

2 large eggplants
1 quart milk
3 cups stock or 1 can consommé and
1 can water
2 tablespoons flour
2 tablespoons water

1 tablespoon anchovy paste
2 tablespoons butter
½ teaspoon salt
¼ teaspoon pepper
3 tablespoons chopped parsley

Peel the eggplants and cut into 1-inch cubes. Place in a saucepan with the milk and stock and bring to a boil. Cook over low heat for 45 minutes, or until the eggplant is very soft. Mix the flour and water to a smooth paste and add it to the eggplant mixture, stirring constantly. Cook for 5 minutes, stirring frequently. Remove the eggplant from the saucepan, force it through a sieve, then return it to the saucepan. Add the anchovy paste, butter, salt, and pepper. Correct seasoning. Heat again but do not allow to boil. Serve with the chopped parsley.

## SHRIMP IN COCONUT

¾ cup water
2 cups fresh or dried grated coconut
2 pounds shrimp, shelled and cleaned
2 onions, chopped fine
¼ teaspoon dried ground chili peppers
1 teaspoon salt
½ cup heavy cream

Combine the water and coconut in a saucepan. Bring to a boil, remove from the heat, and soak for 30 minutes. Press all the liquid from the coconut and discard the pulp. Place the shrimp in a saucepan. Add the coconut milk, onions, chili peppers, salt, and cream. Cook over low heat for 20 minutes. Correct seasoning. Serve hot.

*Note: If a fresh coconut has been used, the shrimp mixture may be served in the scooped-out shell.*

## FIJI BAKED FISH

2 cups fresh or dried grated coconut
1½ cups heavy cream
3-pound sea bass, pompano, or snapper or 6 slices of any white-meat fish
2 teaspoons salt

Combine the coconut and cream in a saucepan. Bring to a boil, remove from the heat, and soak for 30 minutes. Press all the liquid from the coconut and discard the pulp. Wash, clean, and dry the fish. Sprinkle thoroughly with the salt. Arrange the fish in a buttered baking dish. Pour the coconut liquid over the fish. Bake in a 350° oven for 50 minutes.

## SPINACH IN COCONUT MILK

1 cup fresh or dried grated coconut
1 cup milk
2 pounds or 1 package frozen spinach
1 teaspoon lemon juice
1 teaspoon salt
½ teaspoon pepper
1 onion, sliced thin

Combine the coconut and milk in a saucepan. Bring to a boil, remove from the heat, and soak for 30 minutes. Press all the liquid from the coconut and discard the pulp. Wash the spinach thoroughly and drain well. Combine the spinach, lemon juice, salt, pepper, onion, and coconut milk in a saucepan. Cover and cook over low heat for 20 minutes. Serve hot.

## HAWAII AND THE POLYNESIAN ISLANDS

Among the last remaining escapist outposts are the several Hawaiian Islands. Since they are so easily reached by Pan American planes from Seattle, San Francisco, and Los Angeles, the increasing popularity of Hawaii may be readily understood. Unfortunately many tourists find Honolulu something less than they expected; instead of tropical, languorous native villages, they find an island metropolis, humming, buzzing, vibrant, and about as exotic as South Norwalk, Connecticut. To those who are taken aback, a word of advice is offered, for all is not lost. The Hawaiian Islands are more than Waikiki Beach, hot dogs, and commercialized hula dancers. There are the other islands, easily reached by plane, such places as Maui, Kauai, and the most primitive of all, Molokai Island. On these islands flowers seem to have worked out a special arrangement with nature, for seldom does one see such magnificent giant ferns, torch ginger, the great favorite, silversword, which apparently grows only in Hawaiian volcano craters, and of course the famous local orchids.

The staple food of the islanders is *poi,* a pasty substance made from taro root that has a fascinatingly repulsive taste. It has somewhat unfairly been said that *poi* tastes like sour mucilage; but this is a gross canard. Actually it tastes much more like white library paste. *Poi* is so bad, many people say, that they have to keep on tasting it over and over again to see if it is really as bad as they first thought. It is. Peculiarly enough, many people grow to like it eventually. Etiquette requires that it be eaten with the fingers only, apparently on the theory that if you suffer enough you might learn to appreciate it. There is two-finger or three-finger *poi,* indicating the consistency of this delicacy and the number of fingers required for its manipulation. Other staple island foods include yams, coconuts, the local fish (some very good, others insipid), breadfruit, and, inevitably, pineapples. Usually fresh pineapple is eaten by the islanders, to the surprise of visitors nurtured on the canned fruit.

Surely pineapple is Hawaii's contribution to the world of good eating; the word "Hawaiian," appearing on any menu, means "served with pineapple" anywhere in the world from Tallahassee to Tanganyika.

To appreciate the flavor of island food, it is necessary to eat at a *luau*, a festive dinner usually combined with some entertainment. *Lomi*, the favorite salmon dish, makes a good appetizer. *Laulau*, which combines meat and fish in the same dish, may sound exotic, but it is no more unusual than the classic Italian combination of veal and tuna fish. The shellfish specialties, particularly the local crabs, are worth while. Of course to most islanders a barbecued roast suckling pig is the high point in the art of good living. Desserts are usually quite simple. The melons are delicious; and the pomegranates, lichees, and other local fruits are not to be overlooked. Macadamia nuts are very popular and have an excellent flavor.

Tourists usually find that the hotels and restaurants serve unusual and elaborate drinks, such as those served in scooped-out pineapples or coconuts, foot-high rum drinks, or bowls of mixed liquors with gardenias floating in them. These concoctions are very pretty and usually harmless except to the final figures on the dinner check and to the state of mind of susceptible misses from the mainland. The islanders look with tolerance upon these foibles of their eccentric but welcome visitors, although they prefer their own homemade *okolehao*, a firewater of authority.

In addition to Hawaii, in the Polynesian group there are the Marshall, Gilbert, Caroline, Tonga, and Samoan islands, which are inhabited by people of similar ethnic origins. The inhabitants of these many and varying islands are dependent for their food chiefly upon natural resources. There is a great similarity in the diets of the people. Seafood is most important, for it is customarily available in large supply. Much of the warm-water fish has little flavor, but the shellfish is almost always excellent. Chickens are appreciated; beef and lamb are of little importance. For some reason, islanders all over the globe love pork, particularly piglets, preferably roasted over an open fire or wrapped in green leaves and placed over hot stones.

The staple foods are taro, breadfruit, yams, and bananas, which can usually be counted on even when the fishing fails, as it does on occasion.

Meals are habitually two in number: breakfast, consisting of fresh fruit, and a more substantial meal in the late afternoon or early evening.

Polynesian drinks vary according to the locality. Some make liquor from sugar cane, whereas others distill palm-tree nuts or fibers, or prepare alcoholic coconut beverages. The fabled drink of the islands is *kava*, made by chewing kava fibers (thus mixing it with the saliva) and spitting it into a bowl containing water. This is all told to you in the interests of your greater knowledge; it is an example of pure science at work. The concoction ferments quickly, and, although non-alcoholic, becomes extremely intoxicating in several hours. *Kava*, anyone?

## HAWAIIAN SALMON

### KAMANO LOMI

| | |
|---|---|
| 1 pound smoked salmon | ½ teaspoon salt |
| 12 scallions (green onions) | 4 tomatoes, peeled and chopped |
| ¼ cup ice water | |

Soak the salmon in cold water for 3 hours. Change the water at least once. Drain well. Remove any skin and small bones. Shred the salmon finely. Chop the scallions as fine as possible, until they are almost a paste. Add the ice water and salt. Combine the salmon and tomatoes. Crush with a fork or a pestle and mortar until very smooth. Add the scallions and mix well. Chill. Serve in a deep bowl as an hors d'oeuvre.

## HAWAIIAN LOBSTER AND COCONUT

| | |
|---|---|
| 2 cups milk | 3 1¼-pound boiled lobsters or 1½ |
| 2 cups light cream | pounds lobster meat |
| 3 cups fresh or dried grated coconut | |

Combine the milk, cream, and coconut in a saucepan. Bring to a boil, remove from the heat, and soak for 30 minutes. Press all the liquid from the coconut and discard the pulp. Cut the lobster meat into 1-inch pieces and combine with the coconut milk. Heat but do not allow to boil. Serve hot or cold in bowls.

## SALMON AND PORK, HAWAIIAN STYLE

### LAULAU

| | |
|---|---|
| ½ pound smoked salmon, sliced thin | 2 pounds fresh spinach (large |
| 2 pounds fat pork, cut into slices 1 | leaves) |
| inch thick | |

Soak the salmon in ice water for 3 hours. Cut the slices into 1-inch strips. Remove any bones. Cut the pork into 2-inch squares. Wash the spinach leaves thoroughly in running water until all traces of sand are gone. Separate the leaves, using only the largest, and remove the stems.

Prepare sheets of aluminum foil, about 6 inches square. Place several overlapping spinach leaves on the aluminum foil, so that it is completely covered. Place a piece of pork in the center of the spinach leaves, and a piece of salmon in the center of the pork. Fold over carefully, so that the pork and salmon are covered by the aluminum foil. Tie the foil with thread, so that it cannot come apart. Drop into boiling water. Cover and cook for 3½ hours, being careful not to let the water evaporate. Serve with hot sweet potatoes.

*Note: This is an outdoor Hawaiian dish, made with taro leaves, which are not available here. The spinach leaves are used as a substitute for these.*

## MARINATED STEAKS ON SKEWERS

### TARIYAKI

| | |
|---|---|
| 1 cup soy sauce | 1 clove garlic |
| ⅓ cup *sake* or sherry | 18 pieces sirloin steak, ½ inch thick |
| 1-inch piece fresh or 1 teaspoon powdered ginger | 12 cubes canned pineapple |
| | 12 mushroom caps, sautéed |
| 4 tablespoons dark brown sugar | 1 tablespoon cornstarch |
| 3 tablespoons grated onion | 2 tablespoons water |

Combine the soy sauce, *sake* or sherry, ginger, brown sugar, onion, and garlic in a bowl. Mix well. Cut the steak into 1-inch squares and marinate in the sauce for 2 hours. Drain the steak, strain the marinade and reserve. Broil the steak in a very hot oven for 2 minutes on each side.

Alternate the steak, pineapple, and mushrooms on 6 skewers, starting and ending with the steak. Set aside. Mix the cornstarch and water to a smooth paste in a saucepan. Add the marinade gradually. Cook over low heat, stirring constantly, until smooth and thick. The *tariyaki* may be served cold or reheated in the broiler. Serve the sauce hot in any event.

*Note: Tariyaki is a Hawaiian specialty brought to the islands by the Japanese. Pan American World Airways serves this dish on Pacific flights.*

## CHICKEN AND COCONUT

### MOA LUAU
### A ME WAI NIU

| | |
|---|---|
| 1 cup fresh or dried grated coconut | 2 teaspoons salt |
| 1 cup milk | ½ cup water |
| 2 tablespoons salad oil | 1½ pounds fresh or 1 package frozen spinach |
| 2- to 2½-pound chicken, boned and cubed | 3 tablespoons butter |

Combine the coconut and milk in a saucepan. Bring to a boil, remove from the heat, and soak for 30 minutes. Press all the liquid from the coconut and discard the pulp. Heat the oil in a saucepan. Add the chicken and brown well on all sides. Add 1½ teaspoons of the salt and the water. Cover and cook over low heat for 20 minutes, or until the chicken is tender.

Wash the spinach carefully in many changes of water, if fresh spinach is used. Remove any stems or tough fibers. Melt the butter in a saucepan and add the spinach and the remaining salt. Cover and cook over very low heat for 20 minutes. Drain well. Drain the chicken. Combine with the spinach and coconut milk. Bring to a boil over low heat, stirring occasionally, and serve.

## SWEET POTATO PUDDING

### KOELE PALAO

2½ cups fresh or dried grated coconut    4 tablespoons sugar
2 cups light cream    2 tablespoons butter
4 sweet potatoes

Combine 2 cups of the coconut and the cream in a saucepan. Bring to a boil, remove from the heat, and soak for 30 minutes. Press all the liquid from the coconut and discard the pulp. Boil the sweet potatoes, unpeeled, until they are soft. Peel and mash them. Add the coconut cream and the sugar. Beat until light and fluffy. Pour the mixture into a buttered, shallow baking dish. Bake in a 400° oven for 15 minutes. Melt the butter in a frying pan. Add the remaining coconut and sauté for 2 minutes, stirring constantly, or until the coconut is lightly browned. Sprinkle the sautéed coconut on top of the pudding. Serve hot or cold.

## COCONUT PUDDING

### HAUPIA

3 cups fresh or dried grated coconut    ⅓ cup cornstarch
3 cups milk    ⅓ cup sugar

Combine the coconut and milk in a saucepan. Bring to a boil, remove from the heat, and soak for 30 minutes. Press all the liquid from the coconut and discard the pulp. Combine the cornstarch and sugar in a saucepan. Gradually add the coconut milk, mixing until smooth. Cook over low heat, stirring constantly, until thick. Pour into an 8-inch buttered pan and cool. Place in the refrigerator until firm. Cut into squares and serve.

*NEW ZEALAND*

These islands, members of the British Commonwealth, are made of the stuff fishermen dream about, for the big ones usually get caught here.

That rule holds equally true for the deep-sea varieties and the fresh-water trout and salmon. New Zealanders are very fond of sports, and outdoor life heads their list of pleasures.

Since this is the case, game and seafood dishes are in the foreground of the national cuisine. There is a variety of green clam, the *toheroa,* which is undoubtedly the giant of all edible clams. It forms the basis of many fine dishes which unfortunately cannot be duplicated since the *toheroa* is not available and there is no adequate substitute. Although it is canned, few export shipments are made. Also unusual are the *pipis,* a shellfish, and the *pauas,* a type of abalone. There are also oysters, crayfish, whitebait, and many others, familiar and unfamiliar. An island recipe for lemon fish is included in this section.

As in Australia, mutton dishes are popular. However, beef and pork are also appreciated. Since New Zealand is practically one enormous game preserve, pheasants, wild duck, and red deer are used in many fine regional specialties. Barbecued wild pig is a local dish, but since wild pig is seldom available to us, the recipe for it has been modified; the resulting dish will be excellent nonetheless.

*Kumeras,* a type of sweet potato, is a satisfying item when roasted; *kumi kumi* is something like pumpkin; and a fine salad is made from *rauriki,* a green leaf of the milkweed family.

With their English heritage, New Zealanders naturally prefer beer and ale, and drink it in fairly large quantities. Wines are appreciated, but beer is undoubtedly the national beverage. The martini is a popular cocktail, but in general straight drinks are preferred.

One meal on which emphasis is placed is tea. Morning tea is usually just a simple cup of tea, but afternoon tea is an event, usually accompanied by cakes, particularly scones, for which a recipe is supplied. When guests are invited for tea, it often turns out to be a substantial meal.

New Zealand is the land of the kiwi, the famous bird that cannot fly, which has become the national emblem. Another national bird, almost as interesting, is the mutton bird, which lives on cliffs alongside the sea and dines exclusively on fish. Since it is such a seafood addict, the mutton bird tastes like fish and is extremely oily. Before being prepared, the bird must be boiled in three or more changes of water to remove a fraction of its fishiness, but some fishy taste always remains. The Maoris, the native population of New Zealand, are particularly fond of this bird, and usually omit the three water changes because they like the oily flavor.

The restaurants of the country are not outstanding for their food, but the hotels are. In Wellington, fine food is available at the St. George Hotel.

## LEMON FISH

3 pounds flounder, halibut, or other white-meat fish, cut into 6 thick slices
2 teaspoons salt
3 tablespoons butter
2 onions, sliced fine
½ teaspoon pepper
½ teaspoon powdered ginger
Dash of mace
2 cups water
⅓ cup lemon juice
2 tablespoons grated lemon rind
2 eggs
2 tablespoons flour
½ teaspoon saffron
2 tablespoons chopped parsley

Wash and dry the fish. Sprinkle with salt. Melt the butter in a saucepan. Add the onions and sauté for 5 minutes. Add the fish slices and brown slightly. Add the pepper, ginger, mace, and water. Cover and cook over low heat for 30 minutes. Add the lemon juice and rind and stir.

Beat the eggs in a bowl and add the flour, saffron, and parsley, beating well. Add ½ cup of the fish stock, beating constantly. Return the contents of the bowl to the saucepan, again stirring constantly. Cook over very low heat, stirring constantly, until thick. Do not allow the mixture to boil. Place the fish on a platter and pour the sauce over it. Serve with boiled potatoes and green peas.

## PORK ON A SKEWER

3 pounds boneless pork, loin or leg
3 teaspoons salt
¾ teaspoon pepper
½ teaspoon sage
4 apples
4 tomatoes
1½ teaspoons dry mustard
1 teaspoon paprika
1 teaspoon sugar
¼ cup vinegar
⅓ cup olive oil
3 tablespoons chopped olives
1 tablespoon grated onion

Cut the pork into pieces ¾ inch thick and 2 inches square. Combine 2 teaspoons of the salt, ½ teaspoon of the pepper, and the sage, and rub into the pork thoroughly. Peel and slice the apples ½ inch thick. Cut the tomatoes into ½-inch-thick slices. Using individual skewers, thread pieces of pork, apple, and tomato one after the other until all are used up.

Combine the mustard, paprika, sugar, and remaining salt and pepper in a saucepan. Add the vinegar and stir well. Add the oil, olives, and onion. Place over low heat and bring to a boil. Simmer for 2 minutes.

Broil the pork in a 350° oven for 45 minutes, turning the skewers occasionally so that the pork is well browned on all sides. Using a charcoal fire to barbecue the pork will give even more satisfactory results. During the last 10 minutes of broiling, baste the meat with a little of the sauce. Serve the sauce separately in a sauceboat. This dish may be served with boiled rice or small boiled potatoes.

## STUFFED STEAK, NEW ZEALAND STYLE

| | |
|---|---|
| 6 thin, boneless steaks | 6 tablespoons ketchup |
| 2 teaspoons salt | 1½ cups stock or 1½ cups hot water |
| 1 teaspoon pepper | and 2 bouillon cubes |
| 2 onions, chopped | 3 tablespoons flour |
| 4 slices bacon, half cooked, chopped fine | 3 tablespoons water |
| ⅛ cup bread crumbs | 3 tablespoons butter |

Pound the steak with a mallet or the flat side of a knife until very thin. Sprinkle with the salt and pepper. Combine the onions, bacon, bread crumbs, and ketchup in a bowl. Mix well. Place equal amounts of the mixture on each of the steaks. Roll up each steak and fasten with string or skewers. Place in a buttered casserole. Pour the stock over the steaks and cover the casserole. Bake in a 350° oven for 35 minutes. Mix the flour and water together to form a smooth paste. Add to the casserole, mixing well. Dot the steaks with the butter. Correct seasoning. Leaving the casserole uncovered, bake for 10 minutes longer. Serve hot, together with the sauce.

## BAKED LETTUCE

| | |
|---|---|
| 4 heads lettuce | 1 teaspoon salt |
| 4 tablespoons butter | Dash of cayenne pepper |
| 3 tablespoons flour | ½ cup bread crumbs |
| 1¼ cups milk, scalded | ½ cup coarsely chopped nuts |

Wash the lettuce thoroughly and remove any imperfect leaves. Do not cut, but break each head into quarters with the hands. Pour boiling water over the lettuce and drain well. Cover with fresh water in a saucepan and boil for 5 minutes, or until tender. Drain, and press all excess moisture from the lettuce.

Melt 2 tablespoons of the butter in a saucepan and add the flour, stirring until smooth. Gradually add the milk, stirring constantly until the boiling point is reached. Add the salt and cayenne pepper. Cook over low heat for 5 minutes, stirring occasionally.

Place the lettuce in a buttered casserole. Pour the cream sauce over it. Sprinkle with the bread crumbs and nuts. Dot with the remaining butter. Bake in a 425° oven for 15 minutes, or until browned.

## DROP SCONES

| | |
|---|---|
| 1 egg | 1 teaspoon baking powder |
| 1 cup milk | Butter for frying |
| ½ cup sifted flour | |

Beat the egg and milk together in a bowl. Sift the flour and baking powder together and add to the previous mixture, mixing until smooth. The batter should be the consistency of thin cream. Add more flour if necessary. Grease a griddle or large frying pan lightly. Drop the batter by tablespoons, and bake over low heat until lightly browned on both sides. Serve with plenty of butter, and jelly if desired. This is a favorite teatime specialty.

*Note: Although the drop scone originated in Scotland, the New Zealanders consider it a local specialty, owing to the large number of persons of Scottish descent living there.*

## BANANA OMELET

| | |
|---|---|
| 1¼ cups bread crumbs | 2 tablespoons sugar |
| 1 cup milk | 3 ripe bananas, chopped fine |
| 4 egg yolks, beaten | 4 egg whites |
| ½ teaspoon salt | 4 tablespoons butter |
| 1 teaspoon vanilla extract | |

Soak the bread crumbs and milk in a bowl for 5 minutes. Add the egg yolks, salt, vanilla, and sugar and mix well. Add the bananas and stir gently. Beat the egg whites until stiff but not dry and fold into the previous mixture carefully but thoroughly. Melt 2 tablespoons of the butter in an omelet pan and pour half of the mixture into it. Cook until browned on both sides. Keep warm while preparing the other omelet. Cut into individual portions, sprinkle with sugar, and serve hot with whipped cream, if desired.

## APRICOT AND ALMOND PASTRY

### KOROMIKO FLAN

| | |
|---|---|
| 1¼ cups sifted cake flour | ¼ pound butter |
| ¼ teaspoon salt | ½ cup sugar |
| ¾ cup shortening | ¼ cup cooky or cake crumbs |
| 3 eggs | ¼ cup ground almonds |
| 1 cup apricot jam | |

Sift the flour and salt into a bowl. Cut in the shortening with a pastry blender or two knives, until the consistency of coarse sand. Beat one egg and add to the flour mixture, tossing lightly until a ball of dough is formed. Wrap in wax paper and chill for 1 hour. Roll out the dough ¼ inch thick on a lightly floured surface and line a 9-inch pie plate with it. Spread the apricot jam over it. Preheat oven to 350°. Cream the butter and add the sugar, beating until light and fluffy. Add the remaining eggs and beat well. Add the crumbs and nuts, beating well. Pour into the prepared pie plate. Bake in a 350° oven for 30 minutes, or until delicately browned on top.

## ORANGEADE, NEW ZEALAND STYLE

| | |
|---|---|
| 1 large lemon | ¼ teaspoon powdered ginger |
| 5 oranges | ¼ teaspoon cinnamon |
| 1 cup honey | 2 cloves |

Wash the lemon and oranges. Grate the lemon and one of the oranges. Squeeze the juice from the lemon and oranges and place in a saucepan with the grated rind. Add the honey. Bring to a boil and add the ginger, cinnamon, and cloves. Boil for about 5 minutes, or until the mixture is reduced by half. Force the mixture through a very fine sieve, pour into a bottle or other covered container, and cool. Place in the refrigerator.

Place a tablespoon of the orange mixture in a tall glass and fill with cracked ice and water. If desired, carbonated water may be used. Decorate the glass with a maraschino cherry and with slices of orange and lemon.

## THE PHILIPPINES

During the war the G.I.s were very much taken with Philippine beer, which they pronounced uniformly excellent. Whether or not the climate of the islands helps to improve the taste of the beer is difficult to determine, for the temperature in the Philippines makes frequent cold drinks almost a necessity. It seldom gets cool in Manila, which is a definite understatement, and most of the time it is quite hot; the cool season is during January and February, when the *average* temperature is about seventy-five degrees, which should give you a general idea. The favorite drink of the native population is *tuba*, a potent, fermented beverage made from the sap of palm trees. Although some wine is consumed, by and large it is not too important.

The cuisine of the islands is exceptionally interesting, because four different cultural forces are at work. They are the American, native, Spanish, and Chinese. The American influence is obvious since, though it is now a republic, the country was formerly a dependency of the United States and still has a pronounced degree of attachment for things American. The native feeling in cooking is also apparent, since the people are quite loyal to the old ways of doing things. With a Spanish colonial history, the Iberian cuisine has left a definite impression on the food of the islands. Finally, the Philippines are close to China, and large numbers of Chinese live here, many of them having become nationalized. Chinese food is particularly popular, and there are Chinese restaurants everywhere. Noodle dishes are greatly appreciated, and are really staples in the local diet.

Breakfast is a very large meal even by our standards; it usually consists of rice, with the addition of fish (fresh or dried) and possibly a meat dish, plus hot coffee or thick hot chocolate. Some people eat another breakfast later in the morning, but the American toast-and-coffee influence is making itself felt, particularly in the cities. Lunch and dinner are very similar, both in size and with regard to the type of food eaten. Soup is often served as a separate course, but it is frequently combined with the main dish. The *merienda* (teatime) custom is still carefully observed, particularly by the ladies of the islands, and it constitutes an informal but important social hour.

Philippine food requires an understanding of the terms involved. If a dish has the word *manok* in it, it contains chicken; *isda* means fish; *baboy* is pork; *carne* is beef. Since a *tortillang* is an omelet, a *baboy tortillang* would be an omelet with pork, and so forth.

The undoubted favorite of the people is pork. *Lechon*, a whole barbecued pig, is a national dish, as is *adobo*, a mixture of chicken and pork regularly served in the majority of Filipino homes, although the recipe given is just one of dozens of variations on this dish. When made with pork only it is known as *adobo baboy*. Rice is the staple food and is served with practically any dish.

The people of the islands are very fond of odd snacks which they eat between regular meal hours. Some of these tidbits would be considered quite odd to anyone who has never lived there, but in a little while they become commonplace. The visitor soon finds himself eating food that would have seemed exotic a few short weeks before.

MANILA COCKTAIL

½ cup canned, sweetened pineapple juice
3 jiggers sweet vermouth

6 jiggers gin
6 egg whites
2 tablespoons cherry brandy

Boil the pineapple juice in a saucepan rapidly until only 2 tablespoons of juice remain. Cool for 3 minutes. In a cocktail shaker place the pineapple juice, vermouth, gin, egg whites, and cherry brandy. Add plenty of ice. Shake vigorously for at least 1 minute. Pour into chilled cocktail glasses. Decorate with a maraschino cherry.

## MEAT SOUP

### PICADILLO

| | |
|---|---|
| 3 tablespoons salad oil | 4 potatoes, peeled and cubed |
| 3 cloves garlic, minced | 2 quarts water |
| 4 onions, chopped | 1 cup stock or 1 cup consommé |
| 1½ pounds beef, ground | 1 tablespoon salt |
| 3 tomatoes, coarsely chopped | 1 teaspoon pepper |

Heat the oil in a saucepan. Add the garlic and onions and sauté for 10 minutes, stirring frequently. Add the beef and cook over high heat for 5 minutes, stirring frequently. Add the tomatoes and potatoes and continue browning for an additional 5 minutes. Add the water, stock, salt, and pepper. Reduce heat to medium and cook for 25 minutes. Correct seasoning. Serve hot.

## FISH WITH EGG SAUCE

### PESCADO CON SALSA DE HUEVOS

| | |
|---|---|
| 6 slices fish (sea bass, mackerel, snapper, etc.) | 3 tomatoes, chopped |
| | 1 onion, sliced thin |
| 1 cup water | 4 hard-cooked eggs |
| 6 tablespoons olive oil | 4 scallions (green onions), sliced thin |
| 4 tablespoons vinegar | |
| 1½ teaspoons salt | 2 pimentos, chopped |
| 1 teaspoon pepper | |

Combine the fish, water, 2 tablespoons of the olive oil, 2 tablespoons of the vinegar, 1 teaspoon of the salt, ½ teaspoon of the pepper, 2 tomatoes, and the onion in a saucepan. Bring to a boil and cook over low heat for 30 minutes. Remove fish to a platter and reserve ½ cup of the stock.

Mash the yolks of the eggs but reserve the whites. Add the remaining oil, vinegar, salt, and pepper and mix to a smooth paste. Chop the egg whites and add to the mixture. Add the scallions and pimentos. Combine with the reserved stock. Bring to a boil. Pour the sauce over the fish and serve with the remaining tomato, cut in wedges.

## MIXED MEAT ROLL

MORCÓN

½ pound ham, ground
½ pound pork, ground
4 tablespoons grated cheese (Gruyère or American)
¼ cup chopped sweet pickles
¼ cup chopped black olives
3 teaspoons soy sauce
2 tablespoons lemon juice
4 teaspoons salt
2 teaspoons pepper
1 egg

3 pounds boneless sirloin, cut ¼ inch thick (in one piece, if possible)
3 hard-cooked eggs, quartered
2 cups water
¼ cup vinegar
½ cup tomato sauce
1 onion, sliced
3 cloves garlic, minced
1 bay leaf
2 tablespoons flour

Combine the ham, pork, cheese, pickles, olives, 1 teaspoon of the soy sauce, lemon juice, 2 teaspoons of the salt, 1 teaspoon of the pepper, and the egg. Mix well. Place the steak on a flat surface and spread with the mixture. If several steaks are used, divide the mixture evenly. Arrange the quartered eggs on the mixture. Roll up the steak carefully and fasten in several places with thread.

Place the meat roll in a deep saucepan. Add the water, vinegar, tomato sauce, onion, garlic, bay leaf, and remaining soy sauce, salt, and pepper. Cover and cook over medium heat for 1 hour, or until tender. Mix the flour with an equal amount of cold water and add to the gravy, stirring until smooth. Cook over low heat for 5 minutes. Remove the meat roll carefully from the gravy and place on a platter. Cut the threads and remove them. Slice the meat at an angle and serve with the sauce.

## CHICKEN AND PORK CASSEROLE

ADOBO

1 cup fresh or dried grated coconut
1 cup water
3½-pound chicken (see Note)
¼ cup olive oil
3 pounds boneless pork, cut into ½-inch cubes
6 cloves garlic, minced

1 tablespoon salt
1 teaspoon pepper
4 whole peppercorns
2 bay leaves
½ cup stock or ½ can consommé
½ cup wine vinegar

Combine the coconut and water in a saucepan. Bring to a boil, remove from the heat, and soak for 30 minutes. Press all the liquid from the coconut and discard the pulp.

Wash and dry the chicken pieces. Heat the olive oil in a saucepan or casserole. Add the chicken and pork and sauté until brown on all sides. Add the garlic, salt, pepper, peppercorns, bay leaves, stock, and vinegar. Cover and cook over low heat for 1 hour, or until the chicken and pork are tender, stirring frequently. Add the coconut milk and cook for 10 minutes. Correct seasoning. Serve with boiled rice.

*Note: A whole chicken should be chopped up into 2-inch pieces, by the butcher if possible. The pieces should be both bone and meat, not separated. If this is not possible, cut the raw chicken into pieces as small as possible.*

## STUFFED DUCK

### RELLENADO DE PATO

2 4-pound ducks
2 cloves garlic, minced
4 teaspoons salt
2 teaspoons pepper
¼ cup lemon juice
1 tablespoon honey
1 pound smoked ham, ground

1 pound sausage meat or Spanish-style sausage
½ pound beef, ground
3 eggs, beaten
¼ cup capers, drained
2 tablespoons seedless raisins
1 onion, chopped fine

Wash and dry the ducks thoroughly. Combine the garlic, salt, pepper, lemon juice, and honey, and rub into the ducks at least 2 hours before roasting them.

Combine the ham, sausage (if Spanish-style sausage is used, remove the casings), beef, eggs, capers, raisins, and onion, and mix well. Correct seasoning, depending on the type of sausage used. Stuff the ducks with the mixture, fastening the openings with skewers or with thread. Place in a roasting pan. Roast in a 425° oven for 20 minutes, then remove the fat from the pan. Reduce heat to 325° and roast 2 hours longer, removing the fat from time to time as it accumulates. The duck should be crisp and brown. Serve immediately.

## RICE, LUZON FASHION

### ARROZ À LA LUZONIA

¼ cup oil
3 cloves garlic, minced
1 onion, chopped
½ pound pork, cut into strips the size of matchsticks
8 shrimp, peeled and cut in half
2 teaspoons salt
1 teaspoon pepper

1 teaspoon Spanish paprika
2 cups boiled rice
4 eggs, beaten
3 pimentos, sliced thin
2 hard-cooked eggs, sliced thin
3 tablespoons butter
6 bananas, sliced

Heat the oil in a frying pan. Add the garlic, onion, and pork and sauté for 20 minutes, stirring frequently. Add the shrimp and sauté for 5 minutes. Add the salt, pepper, paprika, and rice and mix well. Cook for 15 minutes. Add the eggs and stir. Correct seasoning.

Butter or oil a mold or casserole generously. Arrange pimentos and egg slices on the bottom. Place the rice mixture on top. Cover with a piece of aluminum foil and tie it securely around the edges. Place the mold or casserole in a pan of water. Cook for 40 minutes.

Meanwhile, melt the butter in a skillet. Sauté the banana slices in it until lightly browned. Unmold the rice carefully onto a platter. Arrange the banana slices around it. Serve immediately.

## FILIPINO CUSTARD

### LECHE FLAN

| | |
|---|---|
| 2 cups fresh or dried grated coconut | 4 eggs |
| 2 cups light cream | 2 egg yolks |
| 1 cup dark brown sugar | 1 cup white sugar |
| 3 tablespoons water | 2 teaspoons grated lemon rind |

Combine the coconut and cream in a saucepan. Bring to a boil, remove from the heat, and soak for 30 minutes. Press all the liquid from the coconut and discard the pulp.

Combine the brown sugar and water in a saucepan. Cook over medium heat until a thick syrup is formed. Spread three fourths of the mixture on the bottom of a buttered mold, soufflé dish, or cake tin. Mix the remaining syrup with the coconut cream. Cook over low heat, stirring constantly, until the syrup is dissolved. Beat the eggs and egg yolks in a bowl. Add the sugar and lemon rind, beating well. Gradually add the cream mixture, beating constantly. Pour into the mold. Place the mold in a pan of water. Cook over very low heat for 1½ hours, or until the custard is firm. Do not allow the water in the pan to boil. Place the custard under the broiler for 1 minute to brown the top. Serve hot or cold.

# NORTH AMERICA

*Alaska*

*and the Eskimo Regions*

*Canada*

*Central America*

*Mexico*

*United States*

## ALASKA
## AND THE ESKIMO REGIONS

There are many misapprehensions about Alaska, particularly with reference to its population and climate. There are about 125,000 white residents, and roughly about 35,000 of the native population, including the Eskimos, Aleuts, and Indians. Alaska is growing at a tremendous pace and there are few apparent signs of any slackening in this direction. Certainly there is room for all this growth and even a little more, at least with regard to space, for Alaska alone is equal to one fifth of the total land area of the United States. The climate is not as severe as most people think, particularly near Juneau, the capital. The summers are usually quite delightful, and flowers, vegetables, and fruit often attain tremendous size during the short growing season.

With a background of old-fashioned movies, most of us think of Alaska as a land filled with golden-hearted dance-hall girls, hard drinkers, bottles on the bars of saloons, and all the usual stereotyped paraphernalia of the Far North. While Alaska has not yet swung over completely to the milk shake, there are definite signs in that direction. Smile when you drink that chocolate malted, pardner! Coffee undoubtedly surpasses hard liquor as the favorite drink, and is consumed steadily by the population from morning to night. Coffee is the standard greeting to a guest, and few Alaskan households fail to keep a coffeepot going most of the day; this hospitality cannot be criticized, but few coffee drinkers would subscribe to the practice of boiling coffee.

It cannot be denied that Alaska's cuisine is based largely upon that of the United States, but certain distinctions must be drawn. The people rely on their local foods, particularly the fish of Alaskan waters. Cod, halibut, herring, and salmon are the largest catches, but salmon is the great favorite as well as the most important catch dollarwise. Fine salmon dishes appear frequently on Alaskan menus, and the fish is a treat when merely broiled with butter. Baked salmon is popular, and the salmon doughnut recipe is an unusual variation. Alaska crab, a giant among crustaceans, is becoming quite important economically; considerable shipments of this delicacy have been made to the States.

Everyone has heard of the Alaskan "sourdoughs," the gold prospectors of the early days. Since this hardy breed had no bread nor any store where bread could be bought when on the trail, it was the custom to make a batch of sour dough and keep it going from day to day. Although there are few prospectors left, many people in Alaska still make sour dough pancakes and breads. In fact all kinds of breads, pastries, and cakes are popular here, probably because the crisp weather intensifies the desire for starches and sweets. Doughnuts are special favorites, and the recipe for potato doughnuts is a good example.

Alaska has many oddities in the food line. Bulb kelp, a type of seaweed found along the shore, is made into pickles and jellies. Cranberries and blueberries are somewhat different from the varieties to which we are accustomed, and are used in many unusual ways: for relishes, puddings, and even a cranberry ketchup. Wild strawberries are found in the fields even near the snow line. There are many other berries, such as the salmonberry, a seeded yellow or red berry used for jellies; black and red huckleberries; black and purple gooseberries; yellow cloudberries; and juneberries, which are used for preserves.

Wild game is still available in Alaska, and the people make the most of their opportunity. There are wild ducks, geese, and ptarmigan (the last a particular favorite of the Eskimos), mountain goats and rabbits, and even beaver. Bear meat, caribou, moose, and reindeer are not rare and are used for steaks, chops, rib roasts, burgers, meat loaves, and pot roasts in the same way that an American housewife might use beef. A "mooseburger" or barbecued venison dinner is typical of the Alaskan approach to game cookery.

The Eskimos have shown a great appreciation for the material goods of the white man and are slowly abandoning their old way of life. Canned fruits, wheat flour, and sugar have made a strong impression upon them. While they still cling to their principal diet of raw fish, seal meat, and hot tea, the younger generation shows signs of preferring the diet of the whites.

The feet of bears, seal livers, white whale meat, ducks, and ptarmigan are considered good eating by the Eskimos. One of the great favorites is Eskimo ice cream, made as follows: Reindeer fat is rubbed or grated as fine as possible. Seal oil is added gradually to the reindeer fat, and a little water added for consistency. The mixture becomes very pale in color and foamy in texture. Eskimo gourmets then add blueberries or other wild berries for flavor. It is a great delicacy—at least Eskimo children find it so. It is not likely to become a popular favorite along the highways of the United States.

## SALMON DOUGHNUTS

2 7-ounce cans salmon, drained and
flaked
1 tablespoon lemon juice
1 teaspoon salt
½ teaspoon pepper

2 tablespoons grated onion
½ cup mashed potatoes
1 egg, beaten
1 cup bread crumbs
Fat for deep-fat frying

Combine the salmon, lemon juice, salt, pepper, onion, potatoes, and egg in a bowl. Blend well and chill for 1 hour. Remove from refrigerator and place on a lightly floured surface. Pat the mixture flat until it is about ½ inch thick. Cut out with a doughnut cutter. Heat the fat in a deep saucepan to 375°. Place the doughnuts in the fat and fry until golden brown, about 5 minutes. Drain and serve hot. Miniature doughnuts make excellent hot hors d'oeuvres.

## BAKED ALASKA SALMON

4 pounds fresh salmon (either the
whole fish or in one slice)
2 cups bread crumbs
2 tablespoons finely chopped onion
1 tablespoon chopped parsley
2 teaspoons salt

½ teaspoon pepper
1 teaspoon sage
4 tablespoons melted butter
1 cup stock or 1 bouillon cube dissolved in 1 cup hot water
6 strips bacon

Wash and dry the salmon. Split the fish open, leaving the skin intact. In a bowl combine the bread crumbs, onion, parsley, salt, pepper, and sage. Mix well. Add the melted butter and the stock and mix. Stuff the fish with the mixture carefully; do not pack down, or the filling will become heavy. Fasten the edges with skewers or thread.

Place the fish in a large buttered baking dish. Arrange the slices of bacon across the top of the fish. Bake in a 350° oven for 1 to 1½ hours, depending upon whether the whole fish or sliced fish is used.

## POTATO DOUGHNUTS

1 cup hot mashed potatoes
1 cup sugar
½ teaspoon salt
2 eggs, beaten
3 tablespoons melted butter

½ cup milk
1¾ cups sifted flour
2½ teaspoons baking powder
½ teaspoon nutmeg
Fat for frying

Combine the mashed potatoes, sugar, and salt in a bowl. Mix well. Add the eggs, melted butter, and milk, beating until very light and fluffy. Sift the flour, baking powder, and nutmeg together. Add to the potato mixture. Knead into a dough. Roll out ⅛ inch thick on a lightly floured surface. Cut out with a doughnut cutter. Heat the fat to 360°. Drop the doughnuts into it carefully. Do not fry too many at once. Fry until lightly browned on both sides. Drain. Dust with sugar before serving. These are especially good hot.

## SOUR DOUGH PANCAKES

2 potatoes, peeled and cut into small cubes
1 cup water
½ cake or package yeast
½ cup warm water
2 tablespoons sugar

1 cup sifted flour
1 egg, beaten
2 tablespoons melted shortening
½ teaspoon baking soda
1 tablespoon hot water

Boil the potatoes and water in a saucepan for 25 minutes. Mash the potatoes in their water until it becomes a smooth, thick liquid. Cool until lukewarm. Place the yeast in the ½ cup warm water and mix to a smooth paste. Combine with the potato water, add the sugar, and mix. Place in a bowl, cover, and let stand in a warm place for 24 hours. The mixture will ferment overnight. Add the flour, mix well, cover, and again put in a warm place overnight. (It is not possible to make the dough in less than 2 days.)

Add the egg, shortening, and baking soda dissolved in the hot water. Mix well. Pour out desired size of pancakes on a lightly greased frying pan. Brown on both sides. Serve with ham or bacon and syrup.

*Note: This is a slight modification of the famous sour dough pancakes of the early days of the Yukon. The acid taste of the pancakes may not appeal to everyone, but the miners of those days swore by them. The practice was to keep a pot of sour dough going all the time. They would remove a cup or two of the mixture, add flour, and make their pancakes. To the balance of the old mixture they would add more potato water and sugar, and thus have more sour dough the following day.*

## CRANBERRY RELISH

6 apples
1 cup raw cranberries

1 orange
1 cup sugar

Wash and core the apples. Cut into small pieces, unpeeled. Wash and drain the cranberries. Wash the orange; do not remove the peel but cut into small pieces, removing any seeds and membranes. Grind all the pieces of apple, the cranberries, and the pieces of orange, using a food chopper or mill. Place in a saucepan with the sugar and bring to a boil. Place in a bowl or jar and refrigerate for 24 hours before serving.

## CANADA

Canada is an immense country stretching from ocean to ocean and having two principal cultures: English and French. There are also several important minority groups which have strongly influenced Canada and its customs, principally the Scots, Italians, and Ukrainians. In most of the country English is spoken; in the Province of Quebec the language is French, although it is considerably different from that spoken in Paris.

As to Canadian cuisine, English-style food is eaten over most of the country, except in Quebec, where the French influence still holds sway. There are variations, of course, as in the maritime province of Nova Scotia, where there is an unmistakable Scottish touch.

Along the western coast line and on the eastern seaboard, in Nova Scotia, Prince Edward Island, and Newfoundland, fish and the products of the sea are vitally important. From the ice-cold waters of the three eastern provinces are taken the excellent lobsters proclaimed by gourmets as the finest in the world. In the east the salmon are the Gaspé and the famous Atlantic salmon from the rivers of New Brunswick. The west coast swears by the coho salmon.

The basic items of Canadian diet are few and simple: potatoes, homemade bread, and maple syrup. Canadians are exceedingly fond of potatoes, and they eat enormous quantities of them prepared in countless ways. Dainty, thin slices of pale white bread would not be appreciated in this hardy country; instead there is a demand for large loaves of home-style bread, hot and delicious. Even city dwellers will not accept anything but the country-style bread. The national sweet tooth inclines toward maple syrup and large amounts of it are used for sweetening practically everything. But there is much more to Canadian food: such specialties as the famous Canadian pea soup, the locally made cheeses and ales, *tourtière* (the national meat pie), and *grand-pères* (a maple syrup dessert). In the western part of the nation, game, such as venison, rabbit, bear, duck, and geese, plays an important part in the diet.

On the whole, the people of Canada lead energetic outdoor lives and consequently meals must be fairly substantial in bulk and contain large amounts of calories in the form of sweets.

Any brief discussion of a country that stretches from the Atlantic to the Pacific Ocean can deal only in generalities. Certainly what is true of the apartment dweller of Montreal does not hold equally true for a wheat farmer in Manitoba. Although the nation has not developed a truly unique style of cooking, having borrowed most of it from the British, it cannot be denied that this young and vigorous country has several original dishes worth investigating.

A unique Canadian product is the Canadian bacon, well accepted all over the world, but particularly in the United States. Canada produces a fair amount of wine, but since none of it is unusual, it is almost never exported. Canadian beers and ales and the "Canadian whisky" are the preferred alcoholic drinks. Both coffee and tea are popular with the Canadian public.

## CHEDDAR CHEESE SOUP

4 tablespoons butter
1 tablespoon grated onion
4 tablespoons flour
4 cups stock or 2 cans consommé and
 2½ cans water

2 cups milk, scalded
2 cups grated Cheddar cheese
½ teaspoon salt
½ teaspoon pepper

Melt the butter in a saucepan; add the onion and sauté for 5 minutes. Add the flour and stir until smooth. Gradually add the stock, stirring constantly until the boiling point is reached. Add the milk, cheese, salt, and pepper. Mix well. Cook over low heat until the cheese is thoroughly melted and the soup bubbles. Stir occasionally. Correct seasoning. Serve very hot.

## CANADIAN PEA SOUP

SOUPE AUX POIS CANADIENNE

2 cups dried yellow peas
8 cups water
2 onions, chopped
4 slices bacon, cut into 1-inch pieces

2 teaspoons salt
½ teaspoon pepper
⅛ teaspoon sage
2 tablespoons chopped parsley

Wash the peas thoroughly and discard any imperfect ones. Soak them in the water overnight. Cook the peas in a large saucepan, in the water in which they were soaked. Add the onions, bacon, salt, pepper, and sage. Cover and cook over low heat for 4 hours. Add more water if necessary, but the soup should be fairly thick. Correct seasoning. Add parsley and serve.

## LOBSTER, PICTOU STYLE

6 boiled lobsters
¼ pound butter
½ cup cider vinegar
2 teaspoons sugar
1½ teaspoons salt

⅛ teaspoon pepper
¼ teaspoon nutmeg
Dash of cayenne pepper
1½ cups heavy cream
6 slices toast

Remove the lobster meat from the shell and cut into small cubes. Melt the butter in a saucepan. Add the lobster meat and cook over low heat for 5 minutes, stirring occasionally. Add the vinegar, sugar, salt, pepper, nutmeg, and cayenne pepper. Cook over very low heat for 5 minutes but do not allow the mixture to boil. Remove from the heat. Add the cream gradually, stirring constantly. Correct seasoning. Place a slice of toast in each soup plate and pour some of the lobster mixture over it.

## FISH SALAD

1 pound cod, haddock, or any other
   salt-water, white-meat fish
1½ cups water
1 onion
1 teaspoon salt
2 apples, peeled and diced
½ cup peeled, diced cucumbers

½ cup diced celery
2 teaspoons parsley
½ teaspoon Worcestershire sauce
½ teaspoon grated onion
3 tablespoons mayonnaise
2 hard-cooked eggs

Wash the fish and place in a saucepan with the water, onion, and salt. Bring to a boil and cook over medium heat for 20 minutes. Drain well, flake, and let cool in the refrigerator for 2 hours.

   Place the fish in a large bowl. Add the apples, cucumbers, and celery and mix well. Add the parsley, Worcestershire sauce, grated onion, and mayonnaise. Toss the ingredients together lightly. Arrange the portions on individual beds of lettuce leaves. Chop the yolks of the eggs fine, and sprinkle on top of each serving.

## CLAM PIE

1 cup sifted flour
¼ pound salt butter
3 tablespoons ice water
¼ pound salt pork, cubed
3 onions, chopped
4 carrots, diced fine
½ cup white wine
2 cups fresh or canned clam juice

4 potatoes, peeled and diced
3 tablespoons chopped parsley
1 clove garlic, minced
2 bay leaves
2½ dozen clams, coarsely chopped
½ teaspoons pepper
1 tablespoon cornstarch

Sift the flour into a bowl. Cut in the butter with a pastry blender or two knives. Add the water and toss lightly until a dough is formed. Chill for 1 hour.

Combine the pork, onions, and carrots in a saucepan. Cook over medium heat for 10 minutes, stirring frequently. Add the wine, clam juice, and potatoes and cook over low heat for 15 minutes. Add the parsley, garlic, bay leaves, clams, and pepper. Mix the cornstarch with a little water to a smooth paste and add, stirring steadily until the boiling point is reached. Correct seasoning and remove the bay leaves. Pour into a buttered casserole or baking dish. Preheat oven to 375°.

Roll out the dough on a lightly floured surface to fit the top of the casserole. Place the dough on top of the casserole and seal the edges well. Prick the dough with a fork in several places. Bake in a 375° oven for 30 minutes. Serve hot directly from the casserole.

## PORK PIE

### TOURTIÈRE

3 cups sifted flour
1 teaspoon salt
¾ cup shortening (butter or lard)
1 egg, beaten
4 tablespoons cold milk
3 pounds pork or 1½ pounds pork and 1½ pounds veal
3 slices bacon

2 onions
1 clove garlic, minced
½ cup boiling water
1½ teaspoons salt
½ teaspoon pepper
Pinch of sage
3 tablespoons chopped parsley

Sift the flour and salt together. Cut in the shortening with a pastry blender or two knives until the consistency of corn meal. Combine the beaten egg and the milk and add to the flour mixture. Toss lightly with a fork until a ball of dough is formed. Wrap in wax paper and chill for at least 1 hour.

If possible, use both pork and veal, as the dish will have a better flavor. Grind the meat, bacon, and onions. Add the garlic and mix. Place in a heavy ungreased saucepan, and cook over medium heat for 5 minutes, stirring constantly. Add the water, salt, pepper, sage, and parsley. Cover and cook for 20 minutes. The mixture should not be allowed to become too dry, and small quantities of boiling water should be added if required. Cool for 15 minutes.

Remove the dough from the refrigerator and divide into four pieces, two of which should be slightly larger than the other two pieces. Preheat oven to 450°. Roll out the four pieces of dough on a lightly floured surface. Line two 8-inch pie plates with the larger pieces of dough. Fill them equally with the meat mixture. Cover each pie with the smaller pieces of dough. Make a few slits across the top of each pie. Bake in a 450° oven for 10 minutes. Reduce heat to 350° and bake for 25 minutes, or until well browned.

## CANADIAN BOILED DINNER

### BOUILLI

3 tablespoons butter
5-pound stewing chicken, disjointed
1 pound lean beef, cubed
½ pound lamb, cubed
½ pound salt pork, cubed
1 turnip, peeled
2 cloves
2 onions
8 cups boiling water

1 tablespoon salt
1 teaspoon pepper
¼ teaspoon thyme
2 bay leaves
6 carrots, peeled
1 head cabbage, quartered
6 potatoes, peeled and quartered
1 pound fresh string beans, tied in
  6 individual bunches with thread

Melt the butter in a large saucepan. Add the chicken, beef, and lamb and brown well on all sides over high heat. Add the salt pork and turnip. Place a clove in each onion and add, together with the boiling water, salt, pepper, thyme, and bay leaves. Cover and cook over low heat for 2¼ hours. Add the carrots, cabbage, potatoes, and string beans and cook 45 minutes longer. Correct seasoning. Arrange the meats in the center of a platter and place the vegetables around it. The soup should be served separately.

## DUMPLINGS IN MAPLE SYRUP

### GRAND-PÈRES

2 cups sifted cake flour
1 tablespoon baking powder
½ teaspoon salt
3 tablespoons butter

¾ cup milk
2 cups maple syrup
2 cups water

Sift the flour, baking powder, and salt together at least three times. Cut in the butter with two knives or with a pastry cutter. Add the milk and mix well. Combine the maple syrup and water in a saucepan and bring to a boil. Drop a tablespoon of the dough into the syrup mixture, and continue, tablespoon by tablespoon, until the dough is used up. Cover immediately.

Since the dumplings must steam, it is essential that the cover should not be removed until they have cooked for 25 minutes over medium heat. Serve very hot, together with the syrup in which the dumplings were cooked.

## CENTRAL AMERICA—GUATEMALA, HONDURAS, EL SALVADOR, NICARAGUA, COSTA RICA, AND PANAMA

Guatemala has one of the most colorful Indian populations of any country in the Western Hemisphere, and has in addition a delightful year-round climate in the highlands. Tourists are invariably (and we use the word advisedly) thrilled with Chichicastenango, the Indian village located in the mountains: Chichi (the familiar name) is one of those rare places that is more exciting than the travel folder.

The country has many dishes in common with its neighbor to the north, Mexico, although Guatemala uses fewer spices and seasonings. There are the usual Mexican preparations, but these are handled with a somewhat more delicate hand; this is merely a generalization, it must be admitted. Bean dishes such as *boquitas de frijoles* are favorites. The *Guatemaltecos*, as they like to call themselves, celebrate All Saints' Day with a special meat dish that requires considerable advance preparation but is as much a part of the holiday as turkey is of Thanksgiving.

Coffee and hot chocolate are the national beverages, although they are prepared somewhat differently than in the United States. Guatemalan coffee is among the world's finest, since it grows in the highlands at carefully selected altitudes. When your Pan American plane lands at La Aurora, the Guatemala City airport, the government greets you with cups of hot coffee (prepared from a concentrate), as the country's most typical product. Unfortunately, this fine coffee is usually served with hot water and milk. A keen student of the subject may recognize the resulting mixture as coffee, but any resemblance to freshly brewed coffee is purely coincidental.

Meal hours follow our customary pattern, except that lunch is a more substantial meal than its American equivalent. An unusual Guatemalan custom is that of stacking all of the dishes to be used for a meal in front of each diner. On top of the stack is the soup plate, as soup usually begins the meal.

Beer is good here, and wines are liked, but these last are imported and consumed only by the city folk. The general population much prefer their own rum, which is coarse, crude, and not subject to argument.

Honduras is quite another story, politically, historically, and in most other ways. Gastronomically speaking, the country resembles Mexico rather strongly, but with American and European variations. Most of the local food is based on the Mexican staple dishes: beans, rice, *tortillas*, *tamales*, and the like.

American influence is becoming steadily more important, since most of the canned goods and prepared products come from the United States. Eating is not the amusement in Honduras that it is in Costa Ríca, and Hondurans eat regular meals very much in the ordinary, three-meal-a-day pattern. In the agricultural section of the country the food is very simple and the diet often quite limited.

El Salvador, on the other hand, likes to serve its big meal at midday, and it often consists of seemingly endless courses, at least to visiting Americans accustomed to an appetizer, main course, and dessert. The best food in San Salvador, the capital, is at the Hotel Astoria. *Chicha*, the national strong drink, is very popular with all classes of people. It is served straight, mixed into cocktails, and even used in cookery in the manner shown in the recipe for *gallo en chicha* (chicken in cider—hard, that is).

The people are fond of eating at odd times and places, and one is always tempted by between-meal snacks. In this vein there are many different and original cocktail appetizers. The nation produces some fair wine, of which *nancito* wine is the most interesting. It is made from a native fruit, *nance*, and is generally unavailable outside of El Salvador.

Nicaragua, the largest of the Central American republics, is swiftly losing its sleepy, banana-country atmosphere; improvements are being made at a rapid pace. The country's cuisine is closely akin to its neighbors', but with certain differences. The *sopa de mondongo* (tripe soup) is an unusual variation on a theme, and *maduro en gloria*, fascinatingly named "heavenly bananas," is likely to become your family favorite.

Having a large corn crop, the nation uses all the standard Mexican-style corn dishes. However, the local *tamales*, here called *nacatamales*, are a chicken- and pork-filled variety, a little too difficult to try at home. There are also *tamales* of shrimp, turkey, olives, and fish, and practically any other possible (or impossible) combination.

The country has several good soft drinks, such as *champola*, made from *guanábana*, a remarkable tropical fruit, and the enormously favored *tiste*, made of roast dried corn, pulverized cocoa, cold water, sugar, and cracked ice. *Tiste* is very palatable and refreshing in hot weather. Beer, locally made, is good, and there is also *aguardiente,* a crude type of brandy.

Costa Rica is a peaceful place, the people generally relaxed and easygoing. The countryside is filled with flowers and growing things, and although the nation is not rich, no one seems to mind. Frequent and unhurried dining is the rule here, with meals and refreshments seldom more than three hours apart. The city businessman of our own country, with his hastily gulped coffee for breakfast and a chicken sandwich for lunch, finds no counterpart in pleasure-loving Costa Rica.

A great favorite is *elote* (green corn boiled in the husks), which is a welcome change from the ever present rice. American influence is quite strong here, and American canned products, prepared breakfast cereals, and other foods are well received.

Panama is divided into two parts by the Panama Canal. A tremendous international traffic in ships and men traverses the canal with great regularity, for Panama, like Singapore, is truly that cliché, the "crossroads of the world." Whereas Panama's neighbor to the north, Costa Rica, has an easygoing, *mañana* attitude, the Panamanians must be infected by that American virus, the urge to collect dollars; in any event, life in the cities of Panama moves at a swifter, more hustling pace than in any other Central American city.

Food is therefore much more cosmopolitan, since so many foreigners reach Panama's shores. Meals are Spanish, American, French, slightly international, and occasionally even Panamanian. The one favorite dish is the *sancocho,* the renowned soup-stew of all the Latin countries. Panama features liquors extensively in its restaurants and hotels, since it caters to large numbers of seafaring visitors, who are seldom known to spend their shore leaves attending symphony concerts.

Panama City and Colón are great shopping spots, with some phenomenal values in French perfumes, imported china and crystal, liquors and wines from all over the world, plus a considerable amount of useless gimcracks at fancy prices.

## NANCITO COCKTAIL

| | |
|---|---|
| 6 jiggers *nancito* wine or Dubonnet | Cracked ice |
| ½ teaspoon bitters | Ginger ale |
| 2 tablespoons lemon juice | |

Chill 6 tall glasses in the refrigerator for at least 1 hour. Combine the wine with the bitters and lemon juice and stir. Fill the glasses with cracked ice and divide the mixture evenly among the glasses. Fill with ginger ale, stir, and serve.

313

## CLAM APPETIZER

PICANTE DE ALMEJAS

1 green pepper
1 onion
2 tomatoes, peeled

12 fresh clams, minced, or 1 can
minced clams, drained
2 teaspoons Worcestershire sauce

Remove the stem and seeds of the pepper. Chop in a bowl with the onion. Add the tomatoes and continue chopping until very fine. Add the clams and Worcestershire sauce. Chop until well blended. Correct seasoning. Serve cold, as a cocktail dip, or heap it on toast.

## BLACK BEAN APPETIZER

BOQUITAS DE FRIJOLES

1 cup black beans
4 cups water
2 onions
3 cloves garlic
1 teaspoon salt

3 tablespoons olive oil
Fat for frying
6 slices toast, trimmed
¼ cup grated Parmesan cheese

Wash the beans thoroughly and discard any imperfect ones. Soak overnight in water to cover. Drain, and wash the beans again. Combine the beans, water, 1 onion, and the garlic in a saucepan and cook over medium heat until the beans are soft, about 2 hours. Force through a sieve. Add the salt and mix. Chop the remaining onion. Heat the olive oil in a saucepan, add the chopped onion and the bean pulp, stirring constantly until the mixture is thick, about 5 minutes. Correct seasoning.

Heat fat to 375°; the fat should be fairly deep. Drop tablespoons of the mixture into the fat and fry until they rise to the surface, about 2 to 3 minutes. Drain. Serve on individual slices of toast and sprinkle with grated cheese. In Guatemala, the *boquitas* are served on fried *tortillas,* a crisp, flat corn cake.

## SALVADORAN SEAFOOD SOUP

SOPA DE MARISCOS

¼ pound butter
1 stalk celery, sliced
3 onions, chopped
3 potatoes, cubed
2 quarts water
2 teaspoons salt

¼ teaspoon dried ground chili peppers
1 pound shrimp, shelled
1 dozen fresh clams, coarsely cut, or 1 can clams, drained
¼ pound crab meat

Melt the butter in a large saucepan and add the celery and onions. Sauté over low heat for 10 minutes but do not allow to brown. Add the potatoes, water, salt, and chili peppers. Cook for 10 minutes, stirring occasionally. Add the shrimp and clams and cook for 15 minutes. Add the crab meat and continue cooking for 5 minutes. Correct the seasoning. Serve with a very thin slice of lemon in each plate.

## TRIPE SOUP

SOPA DE MONDONGO

4 pounds tripe
½ cup vinegar
1 calf's foot or 2 beef bones
4 quarts water
2 cloves garlic
3 onions, chopped
1 green pepper, sliced
2 cups cubed squash
3 ears of corn, cut into 1-inch pieces

2 sweet potatoes, peeled and cut into 1-inch cubes
2 white potatoes, peeled and cut into 1-inch cubes
2 cups coarsely shredded cabbage
⅛ cup rice
3 teaspoons salt
1 teaspoon pepper

Soak the tripe in vinegar, with water to cover, for 2 hours. Drain well, then rinse. Place the tripe, calf's foot, and 4 quarts of water in a saucepan. Bring to a boil and skim the top carefully of all foam. Cook over low heat for 4 hours. Strain the stock. Cut the tripe in small pieces and set aside.

Measure the stock into a saucepan, adding enough water to make 8 cups of liquid. Add the garlic, onions, green pepper, squash, corn, sweet potatoes, potatoes, cabbage, rice, salt, and pepper. Cook over medium heat for 45 minutes. Add the tripe and cook for 10 minutes. Correct seasoning. This soup is substantial enough to constitute a main course.

## RED SNAPPER, CUSCATLECA STYLE

HUACHINANGO CUSCATLECA

5 tablespoons butter
3 tablespoons olive oil
3 medium onions, sliced
2 cloves garlic, minced
1 teaspoon salt

6 small snappers or 6 individual portions of snappers or 6 butterfish
1 tablespoon wine vinegar
½ cup white wine
½ teaspoon pepper

Heat the butter and olive oil in a large frying pan. Sauté the onions and garlic for 5 minutes over low heat, add the salt, and stir. Place the fish in the pan and brown well on both sides. Add the vinegar, wine, and pepper and cook over low heat for 15 minutes, turning the fish once. Serve hot with tiny boiled potatoes.

## MEAT AND VEGETABLE STEW

### SANCOCHO

2 onions, chopped
3 cloves garlic, minced
4 tablespoons chopped parsley
3 coriander seeds
1 bay leaf
3 tablespoons lemon or lime juice
1 tablespoon salt
1 teaspoon pepper
2 pounds pork, cut into 1-inch cubes

1 pound beef, cut into 1-inch cubes
2 ounces ham, cut into small cubes
1 tomato, chopped
3 potatoes, peeled and cubed
1½ cups cubed squash or pumpkin
1 Spanish-style sausage (*chorizo*), sliced ¼ inch thick
2 green bananas, sliced ½ inch thick

Place the onions, garlic, parsley, coriander seeds, and bay leaf in a bowl. Pound until very fine in texture. Add the lemon juice, salt, and pepper and mix to a smooth paste. Place the pork, beef, and ham in a saucepan and add water to cover. Add the onion mixture and stir well. Cover and cook over low heat for 1½ hours. Add the potatoes, squash, and sausage, and cook for 20 minutes. Add the banana slices and cook for 15 minutes. Correct seasoning. Serve in deep soup plates.

## COLD MEATS

### FIAMBRE, TODOS SANTOS

2 pounds fresh, or 1 package frozen green peas
12 carrots, cut into strips
1 head cauliflower, broken into tiny flowerets
12 small white onions

1 pound fresh, or ½ package frozen string beans, cut into strips
6 medium potatoes, peeled and cut into ½-inch cubes
1 cup vinegar

Cook the peas, carrots, cauliflower, onions, string beans, and potatoes *separately* in salted water to cover. They should be cooked until almost tender but still slightly undercooked and quite firm. Cool for 1 hour. Combine the vegetables in a large bowl and stir them together gently. Pour the vinegar over them. Marinate in the refrigerator for 2 or 3 days, basting occasionally. At least 24 hours before the dish is to be served, prepare the following:

½ pound sliced cooked corned beef
¼ pound sliced cooked tongue
6 cooked sausages
6 spicy sausages (Spanish style, if available)

1 cup vinegar
3 tablespoons sugar
½ teaspoon salt
½ teaspoon pepper

Add the corned beef, tongue, both varieties of sausages, vinegar, sugar, salt, and pepper to the previously prepared vegetables. Mix well, but gently, so as not to break the ingredients. Return the mixture to the refrigerator until actually ready to be served on the following day. Prepare:

| | |
|---|---|
| 1 head lettuce, washed and drained | 6 canned pimentos |
| 6 slices cold cooked chicken | ½ cup gherkins, drained |
| 6 slices bologna or salami | ½ cup ripe olives |
| 1 can sardines, drained | ⅛ cup capers, drained |
| 3 hard-cooked eggs, sliced | 3 tablespoons grated Parmesan |
| 1 3-ounce package cream cheese, cut into 6 pieces | cheese |

Arrange the lettuce leaves as uniformly as possible on a very large platter. Place the chicken and bologna slices in the front center of the platter. Remove the vegetable and meat mixture from the refrigerator and drain thoroughly. Fill a cup with the mixture and unmold onto the center of the platter; repeat 6 times or until the vegetables are used up, placing the mounds around the first cup of vegetables. Place the sardines alongside the bologna; place egg slices on the lettuce; place the cream cheese and pimentos on the platter. Form mounds of the gherkins and olives. Sprinkle the capers and cheese over the entire platter.

*Special Note: This dish must be started about 4 or 5 days before it is to be served. It is the traditional holiday dish of Guatemala and is served on November 1, All Saints' Day* (Todos Santos). *Colorful ceremonies accompany this important holiday.*

## ROAST YOUNG PIG

### ASADO DE TEPESCUINTLE

| | |
|---|---|
| 3 cloves garlic, minced | 3 onions, chopped |
| 2 teaspoons salt | 1½ cups red wine |
| 1 teaspoon pepper | ½ cup olive oil |
| ½ teaspoon thyme | 2 tablespoons flour |
| 6 pounds young loin of pork or 1 very small suckling pig | 3 tablespoons butter |
| | 3 bananas, sliced |

The day before the dish is to be served, combine the garlic, salt, pepper, and thyme. Rub into the pork very well. Place the pork in a bowl, or use a roasting pan for the suckling pig. Add the onions and 1 cup of the wine and place in the refrigerator overnight, basting as frequently as possible. Heat the olive oil in a roasting pan. Place the pork and marinade in it. Roast for 25 minutes per pound, basting frequently.

Remove the pan juices and place in a saucepan. Add the flour and stir until smooth. Add the remaining wine, stirring constantly until the boiling point is reached. Cook over low heat for 10 minutes, stirring occasionally. Force through a sieve. Melt the butter in a skillet and fry the bananas in it lightly. Carve the pork into desired portions and arrange on a platter, with the bananas around it. Pour the gravy over the meat and serve.

## BRAISED RABBIT

CONEJO PINTADO

2 teaspoons salt
1 teaspoon pepper
2 cloves garlic, minced
3 onions, chopped
2 tomatoes, chopped
½ teaspoon thyme
2 bay leaves

½ cup wine vinegar
Dash of tabasco sauce
2 small rabbits, disjointed
4 tablespoons olive oil
1 cup stock or 1 bouillon cube dissolved in 1 cup hot water
¼ cup sherry

Combine the salt, pepper, garlic, onions, tomatoes, thyme, bay leaves, vinegar, and tabasco sauce in a bowl. Mix well. Add the rabbit, turning the pieces several times to coat them. Marinate in the refrigerator overnight.

Remove the rabbits from the marinade and reserve the marinade. Heat the oil in a saucepan and add the rabbits. Brown well on all sides over high heat. Add the marinade and stock and mix. Cover and cook over low heat for 1¼ hours, or until the rabbits are tender. Add the sherry and correct seasoning. Cook over low heat for 10 minutes. Serve hot.

## CHICKEN IN CIDER

GALLO EN CHICHA

¼ pound butter
3 onions, chopped fine
2 teaspoons salt
1 teaspoon pepper
2 4-pound chickens, disjointed
2 cloves garlic, minced
2 green peppers, sliced fine
¼ teaspoon dried ground chili peppers
2 cups hard cider, or 1 cup apple brandy and 1 cup cider

3 tablespoons vinegar
12 prunes, presoaked
12 stuffed olives
3 tablespoons capers, drained
12 small white onions
4 potatoes, peeled and cut into 1-inch cubes
6 sausages (Spanish style, if possible)

Melt the butter in an earthenware casserole or a heavy pot. Add the chopped onions and sauté until brown, stirring frequently. Remove the onions and set aside. Combine the salt and pepper and rub into the chicken pieces. Place in the casserole and brown on all sides. Add the sautéed onions, garlic, green peppers, chili peppers, cider, and vinegar. Cover and cook over low heat for 1 hour, or until chicken is almost tender. Add the prunes, olives, capers, and white onions and cook for 10 minutes. Cut the sausages into small pieces and fry in a separate saucepan for 5 minutes. Drain and add to the chicken. Cook for 10 more minutes, or until chicken is tender.

## SQUASH IN BUTTER SAUCE

### CALABAZA EN MANTEQUILLA

3 small yellow squash
1 tablespoon salt

¼ pound cream cheese
½ cup melted butter

Peel the squash and cut in half lengthwise. Be sure to use very small, young squash. Place them in a saucepan with water to cover and add the salt. Boil for 15 minutes and drain well.

Spread the cream cheese on each piece, then put them together again. Place the squash in a buttered baking dish. Pour the melted butter over them, turning to coat the squash on all sides. Bake in a 375° oven until lightly browned, about 20 minutes. Cut each squash in half at right angles to the previous cut. Serve hot.

## TAMALE, COSTA RICAN MANNER

### TAMALE TICOS

2 pounds pork, cubed
2 cups water
¼ pound butter
4 onions, chopped
5 cloves garlic, minced
1 cup rice
1½ cups boiling water
2 cups canned tomatoes
2 green peppers, diced
4 teaspoons salt

2 teaspoons pepper
3 boiled potatoes, peeled
4 slices fried bacon
2 cups corn kernels, drained
1 cup canned chick-peas, drained
1 cup canned small green peas, drained
¼ cup seedless raisins
3 pimentos, sliced thin

Combine the pork and water in a saucepan. Cook over medium heat for 1 hour. Melt half of the butter in a saucepan. Add half of the onions and garlic and sauté for 10 minutes, stirring frequently. Add the rice and cook over low heat for 5 minutes, stirring constantly. Add the boiling water, tomatoes, green peppers, 2 teaspoons of the salt, 1 teaspoon of the pepper, and the remaining butter. Cover and cook over low heat for 45 minutes.

Drain the pork and reserve the stock. Grind the pork, potatoes, bacon, and corn. Add the remaining onions, garlic, salt, and pepper. Add the reserved stock and mix well. Place in a saucepan and cook over low heat for 10 minutes, stirring almost constantly.

Add the chick-peas, peas, and raisins to the rice mixture and mix carefully. In a large buttered casserole or baking dish arrange successive layers of the pork mixture, followed by the rice mixture, until they are all used up. Arrange the pimentos on top. Cover the casserole. If the cover is not tight-fitting, cover with a piece of aluminum foil and then put the casserole cover on top. If a baking dish is used, tie a piece of aluminum foil over the top to make a tight seal. Place in a pan of hot water and bake in a 350° oven for 45 minutes. Serve hot.

*Note: In Costa Rica tamales are made individually in plaintain or banana leaves. If desired, wrap small quantities of the two mixtures in aluminum foil. Boil in salted water for about 30 minutes. A corn-meal dough similar to the hallacas of Venezuela may be used as a base, as well.*

## STRING BEANS WITH EGG

EJOTES ENVUELTOS EN HUEVO

2 pounds fresh string beans
2 cups water
1½ teaspoons salt

2 eggs, separated
Fat for deep-fat frying

Wash the string beans and cut off the ends, but leave them whole. Combine with the water and salt in a saucepan. Bring to a boil and cook over medium heat for 10 minutes, or until almost tender. Drain. Divide the beans into 6 bunches and tie each bunch together with white sewing thread.

Beat the egg yolks well. In another bowl, beat the egg whites until stiff but not dry and fold them into the yolks gently but thoroughly. Dip the bunches of string beans into the egg mixture, coating them on all sides. Heat fat in a deep saucepan to 375°. Drop the beans into the fat. Fry until light brown, about 2 minutes. Drain. Serve hot.

## NICARAGUAN TROPICAL SALAD

ENSALADA TROPICAL

1 cup fresh or dried grated coconut
2 cups finely shredded cabbage

1 cup fresh pineapple cubes
1 cup mayonnaise

If dried coconut is used, soak it in cold water for 15 minutes before using. Drain well. Combine the coconut, cabbage, pineapple cubes, and mayonnaise. Mix well. Chill. Serve on lettuce leaves.

## HEAVENLY BANANAS

MADURO EN GLORIA

4 tablespoons butter
6 firm bananas
¼ pound cream cheese

4 tablespoons sugar
1 teaspoon cinnamon
1 cup heavy cream

Melt the butter in a skillet. Peel the bananas and slice each one lengthwise. Brown quickly in the butter over high heat. Place half of the banana slices on the bottom of a buttered pie plate. Cream the cream cheese until very soft. Add the sugar and cinnamon, beating until light and smooth. Spread half of the mixture on the bananas. Place the remaining banana slices on top, then spread with the remainder of the cream cheese mixture. Pour the cream over the top.

Bake in a 375° oven for 20 minutes, or until almost all the cream is absorbed and the top is lightly browned. Do not allow all the cream to be absorbed, or the bananas will be too dry. Serve hot. If desired, some whipped cream may be served with the bananas.

## ALMOND TART

TARTA DE ALMENDRAS

2 cups sifted flour
½ teaspoon salt
1 cup shortening
3 eggs
2 tablespoons ice water
¼ cup apricot or raspberry jam
4 tablespoons butter

4 tablespoons sugar
1 tablespoon cornstarch
⅓ cup ground almonds
1 teaspoon grated lemon rind
½ teaspoon almond extract
2 tablespoons brandy

Sift the flour and salt into a bowl. Cut in the shortening with a pastry blender or two knives. Beat 1 of the eggs and the ice water together, and add to the previous mixture, tossing lightly with a fork until a ball of dough is formed. Chill for at least 1 hour. Roll two-thirds of the dough about ¼ inch thick on a lightly floured surface. Place in a 9-inch pie plate. Spread with the jam.

Cream the butter. Add the sugar and cornstarch, beating until light and fluffy. Add the remaining eggs, beating well. Add the almonds, lemon rind, almond extract, and brandy and mix well. Pour into the pie plate. Preheat oven to 425°. Roll out the remaining dough. Cut into strips and arrange evenly on top of the pie. Bake in a 425° oven for 10 minutes. Reduce the oven temperature to 350° and bake 20 minutes longer, or until a cake tester comes out clean. Serve cold.

## NICARAGUAN EGGNOG

ROMPOPE

2 egg yolks
1 quart milk
1 cup sugar
1 tablespoon corn meal
½ cup rum or brandy

½ stick cinnamon or ½ teaspoon powdered cinnamon
1 teaspoon grated lemon rind
1 teaspoon vanilla extract

Beat the egg yolks in a saucepan until light. Add the milk, sugar, and corn meal. Cook over low heat, stirring constantly, until the mixture is syrupy. Remove from the fire and beat until cool, about 10 minutes. In a bowl combine the rum, cinnamon, lemon rind, and vanilla and mix together. Set both mixtures aside for 3 hours. Strain the rum mixture. Combine with the milk mixture and chill. Serve ice cold.

*MEXICO*

Our good neighbor to the south has three rather unusual liquors—*pulque, mezcal,* and *tequila.* Interestingly enough, all three drinks are made from a cactus plant, the maguey. *Pulque,* truly the national strong drink, is a partially fermented beverage consumed in tremendous quantities by everyone. Most visitors do not appreciate its yeasty taste. Nonetheless, saloons are called *pulquerías. Mezcal* is a potent, distilled beverage. *Tequila* is the drink most liked by visitors. There is a ritual attached to drinking *tequila* that is still followed. The drink is swallowed by throwing it quickly to the back of the throat, a quartered lemon is sucked, and finally one licks at a mound of coarse salt previously placed on the back of the hand; there are those heretics who execute the process in reverse. It is not known whether this is done to improve the taste or to prevent the throat from catching on fire.

Mexico has a strong Indian heritage, and this is clearly indicated in the national cuisine. If we think of bread as a staple, consider Mexico, where *tortillas* (pancakes made of ground corn) form the basic item of practically every meal for almost the entire nation. When *tortillas* are deep-fat-fried they are called *tostados;* a *taco* is a *tortilla* filled with beans or meat and other spicy ingredients, and so on. Corn *tortillas* are a little too difficult to make at home, but they are often available in Mexican stores in the larger cities, and they may be purchased in cans in U.S. specialty food shops. Mexico is also the land of *frijoles* (beans), served in endless variations, hot and cold.

One of the high points of the cuisine is the famous *mole de guajolote* (turkey in a *mole* sauce). This dish contains many ingredients, but the most surprising one is chocolate! After you have tried it, you will understand why it has acquired a national character. Those who say that they couldn't possibly eat turkey with chocolate sauce are respectfully requested to sample this dish.

Many people do not realize that chocolate is native to Mexico and is enormously popular even today, although coffee has made strong inroads. Mexican chocolate, stirred to a froth with a specially designed wooden paddle, is quite different than our usual hot chocolate. There are many other soft drinks which are everyday affairs with the people, for they are fond of the habit of taking frequent refreshment. Beer of excellent quality is also important in Mexico.

Mexico City, a delightful capital with a wonderful climate, has many fine restaurants where food is served at reasonable prices. It must be admitted that few of them specialize in Mexican food, although there are exceptions. There are always Mexican dishes on the menu at the luxurious Reforma Intercontinental hotel. The Tacuba Restaurant is renowned for its authentic Mexican dishes.

Breakfast depends upon where you eat it; in Mexico City it is usually coffee and a roll, but the peasants like a substantial meal of beans and whatever else is available. The largest repast of the day is lunch, from 1:30 P.M. until about three-thirty or sometimes later. Dinner, often a smaller meal, practically never starts earlier than 8:30 P.M. and is in full swing in the better restaurants as late as ten-thirty! A familiar sight is that of a hungry American tourist in search of something to eat at about seven-thirty in the evening.

Not all of Mexico consists of Mexico City, Taxco, and Cuernavaca, though these are well worth seeing. Most Americans find Acapulco tremendously interesting, even though it is often quite hot. Yucatán, fascinating to those who like the unusual, is highly recommended but not necessarily to everyone.

## AVOCADO MIX

GUACAMOLE

| | |
|---|---|
| 1 small onion | 2 teaspoons chili powder |
| 1 tomato, peeled | 1 teaspoon salt |
| 2 avocados | 2 teaspoons vinegar |

Chop the onion and tomato very fine. Mash the avocados with a wooden spoon, and add to the onion-tomato mixture. Add the chili powder, salt, and vinegar. Mix lightly until well blended. Serve on lettuce leaves as a salad. *Guacamole* may also be served in a bowl, with crackers, potato chips, or *tortillas*, as a cocktail dip.

## PICKLED SHRIMP

### ESCABECHE DE CAMARONES

¾ cup olive oil
3 cloves garlic
2 onions, coarsely chopped
2 pounds shrimp, peeled and cleaned
2 onions, sliced thin
½ cup vinegar

1½ teaspoons salt
¼ teaspoon dry mustard
½ teaspoon pepper
¼ teaspoon dried ground chili peppers or 2 pickled chili peppers (*jalapeños*), cut into strips

Heat ¼ cup of the oil in a saucepan. Add the garlic and chopped onions and sauté for 10 minutes, stirring frequently. Add the shrimp and sauté for 7 minutes, stirring occasionally. Remove from heat and let cool for 15 minutes. Combine the sliced onions, remaining olive oil, vinegar, salt, mustard, pepper, and chili peppers in a bowl. Add the shrimp and baste. Marinate for 24 hours, basting several times. Serve cold as an appetizer.

## RICE SOUP

### SOPA DE ARROZ

3 tablespoons olive oil
1 cup rice
2 onions, chopped
2 cloves garlic, minced
1 green pepper, chopped fine

2½ quarts stock or 4 cans consommé and 3 cans water
4 tomatoes, peeled and cubed
2 teaspoons salt
¼ teaspoon dried ground chili peppers

Heat the olive oil in a deep saucepan. Add the rice, onions, garlic, and green pepper. Cook over high heat for 10 minutes, stirring frequently. Add the stock, tomatoes, salt, and chili peppers and stir well. Cover and cook over low heat for 40 minutes. Correct seasoning and serve.

## COCONUT SOUP

### SOPA DE COCO

2 cups shredded fresh or dried coconut
2 cups milk

4 cups chicken stock or 2 cans chicken consommé and 1 can water
2 egg yolks
¼ cup heavy cream

Combine the coconut and milk in a saucepan. Bring to a boil, remove from the heat, and soak for 30 minutes. Strain and combine the coconut milk with the stock. Cook over very low heat for 20 minutes. Beat the egg yolks and the cream in a bowl. Gradually add 2 cups of the soup, beating constantly to prevent curdling. Return to the balance of the soup and beat well. Continue cooking for 5 minutes over low heat but do not allow to boil.

## STUFFED GREEN PEPPERS

### CHILES RELLENOS

¼ cup olive oil
¾ pound beef, ground
3 tablespoons tomato paste
2 cloves garlic, minced
2 teaspoons chili powder
1 teaspoon salt

3 tablespoons ground almonds or peanuts
6 large green peppers
¼ cup flour
2 eggs, beaten
1 cup fine bread crumbs
Shortening for deep-fat frying

Heat the oil in a skillet and add the beef, tomato paste, garlic, chili powder, salt, and ground nuts. Sauté over low heat for 5 minutes, stirring constantly. Correct seasoning. Set aside. Remove the stems and seeds of the peppers, leaving an opening large enough to stuff. Place the peppers in a saucepan with water to cover. Bring to a boil and immediately drain the water. Set the peppers aside to cool for 5 minutes.

Stuff the peppers with the previously prepared meat mixture. Sprinkle the flour on the tops of the peppers at the open ends. Dip each pepper in the beaten eggs, so that it is completely moistened. Then dip in the bread crumbs, once again in the eggs, and again in the bread crumbs. Heat the shortening in a heavy, deep saucepan to 375°. Place one or two peppers in the fat at a time. Fry until browned, then drain. Serve hot.

## PORK LOIN IN PEPPER SAUCE

### LOMO DE PUERCO EN SALSA RAJA

5 tablespoons olive oil
3 cloves garlic
3 small sausages (Spanish or Italian, if possible)
4 pounds loin of pork
3 onions, chopped
2 tomatoes, peeled and chopped

2 cups stock or 1 can consommé and ½ can water
2 teaspoons salt
1 teaspoon pepper
6 green peppers, sliced thin
3 tomatoes, cut into wedges

Heat 3 tablespoons of the oil in a saucepan; add the garlic and the sausages, cut into small pieces. Fry for 5 minutes, stirring frequently.

Remove the sausages and set aside. Place the pork in the saucepan and brown on all sides. Add half of the onions, the chopped tomatoes, stock, salt, and the sausages. Cover and cook over medium heat for 2½ hours.

In a skillet heat the remaining olive oil. Add the remaining chopped onions and the sliced green peppers. Sauté for 10 minutes, or until brown, stirring frequently. Remove the pork and slice it. Arrange on a platter and pour the pan gravy on the pork. Spread the sautéed peppers and onions on top. Garnish with the tomato wedges.

*Note: If desired, the pork may be roasted in 350° oven in a covered pan for the same length of time.*

## STUFFED CHICKEN PANCAKES

ENCHILADAS DE POLLO

| | |
|---|---|
| 1 cup salad oil | 1 tablespoon chopped seedless raisins |
| 6 tomatoes, peeled and chopped | |
| 1 onion, chopped | 3 tablespoons chopped green olives |
| 2 green peppers, chopped | 12 *tortillas*, fresh or canned, or 12 |
| 1 teaspoon salt | pancakes (see recipe below) |
| ½ teaspoon pepper | 2 eggs, beaten |
| 1 cup chopped cooked chicken | |

Heat 3 tablespoons of the oil in a saucepan. Add the tomatoes, onion, peppers, salt, and pepper. Cook over low heat for 20 minutes, stirring occasionally.

Combine the chicken, raisins, and olives in a bowl and mix well. Dip the *tortillas* or pancakes in the beaten eggs. Place a tablespoon of the chicken mixture in the center of each. Roll up and fasten with a toothpick. Place the balance of the salad oil in a saucepan and heat to 375°. Fry the *tortillas* for 3 minutes. Drain. Place them on a plate and cover with the tomato mixture. This dish may be garnished with finely sliced onions, minced lettuce, radishes, and avocado slices.

PANCAKES:

| | |
|---|---|
| 6 eggs | 2 tablespoons corn meal |
| 4 tablespoons cold water | ⅛ teaspoon salt |
| ¼ cup sifted flour | Butter for frying |

Beat the eggs and water in a bowl. Add the flour, corn meal, and salt, beating well until very creamy. Heat a teaspoon of the butter in a 7-inch frying pan until it bubbles. Pour a generous tablespoon of the batter into it and rotate the pan quickly so as to cover the bottom evenly. Fry over medium heat for 1 minute on each side. Stack the pancakes on top of each other until ready to use.

## TURKEY WITH *MOLE* SAUCE

MOLE DE GUAJOLOTE

6- to 8-pound turkey, cut into serving
    pieces
2 teaspoons salt
½ cup olive oil
3 green peppers
2 tablespoons sesame seeds
6 cloves garlic
1 slice dry white toast

½ cup almonds
8 tomatoes
½ teaspoon cinnamon
¼ teaspoon pepper
2 tablespoons chili powder
2 ounces unsweetened chocolate,
    grated

Cook the turkey pieces in water to cover, together with 1 teaspoon of the salt. Cook until almost tender, about 1½ hours. Drain, reserving 2 cups of stock. Dry the turkey. Heat ¼ cup of the olive oil in a frying pan. Add the turkey and brown well on all sides. Remove the turkey and place in a casserole.

Grind together the green peppers, sesame seeds, garlic, toast, almonds, and tomatoes. Add the cinnamon, remaining salt, pepper, chili powder, and chocolate and mix well. Heat the remaining oil and add the mixture. Cook over low heat for 5 minutes, stirring constantly. Place the casserole over low heat and pour the stock over the turkey. Spread the chocolate mixture over the turkey. Cover and cook for 2 hours. Stir occasionally. Serve hot with boiled rice, and pour some of the sauce on the rice.

## EGGS, RANCH STYLE

HUEVOS RANCHEROS

2 onions, chopped
3 green peppers, chopped
½ cup tomato sauce
½ cup grated American cheese
½ teaspoon salt
¼ teaspoon pepper

½ cup salad oil
6 *tortillas* or 6 slices toast, trimmed
6 eggs, fried
3 sausages, cut in 1-inch pieces, fried,
    and drained

Combine the onions, green peppers, tomato sauce, cheese, salt, and pepper. Mix well. Heat the oil in a saucepan and fry the *tortillas* or toast until brown on both sides. Drain well. Place a fried egg on each *tortilla* or slice of toast.

The tomato sauce is served cold in Mexico, but it may be heated if desired. Pour the tomato mixture over the eggs. Arrange slices of sausage around each portion. Serve immediately.

## CORN CAKES

TORTILLAS

¾ cup cornstarch
1 cup milk
2 eggs

½ teaspoon salt
⅓ cup corn meal
2 tablespoons melted butter

Mix the cornstarch and milk to a smooth paste. Beat the eggs and salt in a bowl. Add the corn meal and mix well. Add the melted butter and the cornstarch-milk mixture and beat well. Pour a scant tablespoon of the mixture into a hot greased 7-inch skillet. Turn the pan quickly to coat the bottom with the mixture. The *tortillas* should be as thin as possible. Bake until brown on both sides. Stack the *tortillas* as they are made. Serve hot, with butter and coarse salt.

*Note: This recipe is not authentic, as it is extremely difficult to make* tortillas *at home. However, the above recipe gives an approximation of the taste and texture of the true* tortillas, *which are made from freshly ground corn.*

## BAKED DOUGHNUTS

PUCHAS

6 egg yolks
¼ cup sifted sugar
1¾ cups sifted flour

¼ cup brandy
2 egg whites
2 tablespoons confectioners' sugar

Beat the egg yolks in a bowl until lemon-colored. Add the sugar and again beat well. Gradually add the flour and brandy alternately. Mix well. Roll the dough into a long thin strip and break off 3-inch pieces. Form each piece into a ring. Place on a greased baking sheet. Bake in a 350° oven for 20 minutes, or until lightly browned.

While the doughnuts are baking, beat the egg whites in a bowl until stiff but not dry. Fold in the confectioners' sugar gently. When the doughnuts are lightly browned, spread the egg-white mixture over the top of each doughnut. Bake 3 minutes longer.

## UNITED STATES

It is not a simple matter to explain the food of this country to a person who has never visited our shores. Most foreigners, particularly Europeans, complain exceedingly about the monotony of our meals, the lack of original dishes, the limited menus in our homes, and the few good restaurants where satisfactory meals may be obtained. Perhaps they are partially correct, because it is true that the average restaurant does not turn out inspired food and most menus stay close to the steak, chops, and chicken routine. Perhaps these visitors are also somewhat wrong, because there are many specialties in this country that are unexcelled anywhere in the world.

The cuisine of the United States may be divided into many different subdivisions, but a reasonable, albeit arbitrary, grouping might be: Eastern, Southern, New Orleans Creole, Southwestern, and Western. Naturally a substantial argument may be advanced by those who would, for example, extol the virtues of cooking in the style of Maine, the Pennsylvania Dutch, and the Middle West.

In the East, there are many fine specialties, such as clam fritters, clam chowder, blueberry pancakes, Philadelphia ice cream, Boston baked beans and brown bread, Indian pudding, New England boiled dinner, apple and mince pies, and cranberry sauce. Concerning clam chowder, a few words of explanation are undoubtedly in order. Apparently there is a long-stand-ing war between the devotees of two different schools of thought—the Maine and the Manhattan styles. In Maine clam chowder is made with milk or cream, plus potatoes and salt pork. In New York it is prepared with tomatoes and usually without milk or cream. It is feared that the two warring factions will never be reconciled, although Maine has not seceded from the Union on this account, as was once reported.

In the South, advantage is taken of the natural resources of the sea and the soil. In Maryland and the Tidelands many delicious preparations are made of crabs, such as crab bisques, crab stews, crab cakes, and so forth. In Virginia the local peanut-fed hams and bacon play an important part in the diet of the people. Aged country hams are a specialty of North Carolina. It is somewhat farther south that one finds the famous Southern dishes—fried chicken, hominy, black-eyed peas, spoon bread, corn dodgers, pecan pie, Brunswick stew, corn pone, and old-fashioned shortcake.

The Creole food of New Orleans is unlike anything else in the country. It is here that European visitors to our country more often than not find food to their liking, if indeed they ever do find any. New Orleans dishes bear little or no resemblance to those of any other part of the United States. Somehow this style of food survives in the state of Louisiana, with its headquarters in New Orleans. For those to whom the early history of the United States is hazy, it may be appropriate to recall that France once owned and settled what is now Louisiana; the food, customs, and language of France have survived to the present day. Good use is made of the local seafood, including shrimp, crabs, and oysters. This is the only place in the world where authentic gumbos, *filés*, and jambalayas are to be had, although these dishes have spread throughout the Caribbean. There are about a half dozen famous restaurants in New Orleans where Creole food may be enjoyed in the perfection of fresh ingredients and authentic spices, prepared by cooks who know what to do with them.

The southwestern part of the United States has a proud history. Texas, particularly, has contributed heavily to this country in many ways, and its cuisine has made almost as deep an impression on the nation as a whole as has its citizenry. Texas was once part of Mexico, and its food has been strongly influenced by this early Mexican heritage. However, chili con carne, generally thought to be Mexican in origin, is really a Texas dish, and is practically unknown in Mexico, except in border towns catering to food-conscious American tourists in search of authentic Mexican food. Arizona and New Mexico, too, have contributed to our national cuisine.

On the west coast, outdoor living has dictated the food customs of these healthy, vigorous people. Because of the general excellence of the climate (all hail, California Chambers of Commerce!) and the increasingly popular American custom of dining outdoors, great local emphasis is placed on fresh vegetables, fruits, melons, and charcoal-broiled steaks and chops. Equally as important as the barbecued meats are the local salads, one of which, the Caesar salad, has been nationally accepted. In California it is customary to serve the salad before the main course; thus it actually becomes an appetizer, which inevitably startles all foreign visitors who have just become reconciled to potato chips and cheeseburgers.

In the northwestern part of the country the giant crabs are highly regarded as a delicacy and are now being exported to the rest of the nation. The renowned money-shell, razor, and giant geoduck clams are truly excellent.

But all of the above omits the Middle West, which has contributed substantially to the national diet. The region has good fish from the Great Lakes. Particularly important are dishes based on corn, for it is here that corn is grown by the thousands of acres. Strangers to our country are astonished at corn on the cob, since in most countries corn is looked upon as food for cattle. Attention, all French skeptics: if the corn is very young and freshly picked, and boiled briefly in milk with a little sugar, it will be found to be a true gourmet's delight, so help us Brillat-Savarin.

This discussion has concerned itself thus far with what is good and right with our food. What of those visitors to our country who find things wrong with our food, our meals, and our restaurants? The usual complaints concern our factory-made white breads, which they find tasteless; possibly this complaint is justified, but there is certainly an increase in the number of whole-grain breads, and better-quality white breads. Another point usually mentioned is that our beef is excellent but our lamb and veal inferior. This position is probably well taken. Beef *is* better here; but our lamb and veal do not usually match the foreign cuts, mainly because of our laws regarding the age at which cattle may be slaughtered.

Our food is at its worst when it attempts to imitate French food; it is at its best when it is based on our own local specialties. Most foreign visitors look for French food and are inevitably disappointed except in a very few New York City restaurants. Most of our French restaurants are about as French as Paris, Kentucky. Foreigners would do better not to criticize our food until after they have tried our truly native dishes. Some few visiting gourmets have pronounced our specialties excellent, but they have nothing but scorn for the national habits of putting mayonnaise on everything cold and a floury white sauce on anything hot.

Not too long ago children were being told that it was impolite to discuss food; this was at a time when children in Europe were listening to endless dissertations on the arts of dining and the table. Times have changed in our country, and probably in this regard, for the better. It is now considered proper to discuss food, and there is a tremendous tidal wave of interest in food and its preparation. This awakening has not been limited to the big cities, for it is just as strong in the small communities that dot the nation.

Our meal habits are quite different from those of most of the rest of the world, and therefore call for a little discussion. In Europe and South America the average breakfast is merely coffee and a piece of bread. In the United States breakfast is often a substantial meal consisting of fruit juice, hot or cold cereal, eggs and bacon, toast, and coffee. But of late, particularly in the larger cities on the two coasts, breakfast has been simplified, on the order of the European breakfast, with the addition of fruit juice. Possibly the smallness of this meal has been responsible for the development of what is known as the "coffee break," now a widespread custom of many business houses at 11 A.M.

Lunch in the larger towns and cities is usually a sandwich and a cup of coffee, with the possible addition of ice cream or pie for dessert. The custom of eating a large meal in the middle of the day still survives in certain parts of the country; where this is so, the evening meal is referred to as supper. The so-called "cocktail hour" has spread all over the world, so that no further discussion of this custom is required. Dinner, the evening meal, comes anywhere from about 6 P.M. to 8:30 P.M.; in general, earlier in the smaller communities and later in the more populous ones.

A fairly large quantity of hard liquor is consumed before meals, straight or in cocktails; after dinner it is taken in the form of highballs. While scotch whisky is a popular drink on the east coast, the rest of the nation apparently prefers rye or bourbon, both of which contain considerable alcohol; the principal difference between them is that rye is made from wheat, whereas bourbon is derived from corn.

Wines are growing steadily in importance in this country and are produced in abundance in the states of California, Ohio, and New York. Formerly the wine producers had the unfortunate habit of calling their products "New York State sauterne," "California burgundy," etc., which was unfair both to the sauterne and burgundy of Europe and to the unique products of our own vineyards. At the present time most wine producers and their customers have become educated to the fact that the wines of this country do not duplicate those of Europe but are often new and original wine creations in their own right. In general, however, it must be admitted that wine is not yet an everyday household item. Beer, on the other hand, is widely appreciated and well received throughout the land.

No description of food in the United States should omit those two products of our roadside stands—the "hot dog" and the hamburger. These popular snacks are consumed by the million in our smallest hamlets and our most sophisticated communities. They are truly a bit of Americana.

If the national drink of our country is not a glass of cold milk or a chocolate malted, then it must inevitably be a cup of coffee. Served with cream and sugar, in defiance of experts the world over who advocate only unsweetened, black coffee, it is the one beverage that almost everyone drinks for breakfast, lunch, and dinner. To end on a note of complete confusion calculated to send our theoretical French gourmet screaming into the streets, in the Boston and New England area generally, coffee is served with the main course! Naturally no gourmet would permit such a mixture of flavors in his native France.

## OLD-FASHIONED COCKTAIL

EASTERN

| | |
|---|---|
| 6 lumps sugar | 6 slices orange |
| 6 dashes bitters | 6 maraschino cherries |
| 12 cubes ice | 6 large jiggers rye or bourbon |
| 6 pieces lemon peel | |

Use the 5- or 6-ounce glass commonly known as an old-fashioned glass. Place a lump of sugar in each and splash the bitters on the sugar. Mash the sugar with a spoon. If desired, add a tablespoon of cold water to each glass; this will aid in mashing the sugar. Place 2 ice cubes in each glass. Add the lemon peel, orange, and cherry. Pour in the rye or bourbon and serve with a muddler or stirring rod. If desired, a stick of fresh pineapple may be added.

## NEW ENGLAND CLAM CHOWDER

EASTERN

| | |
|---|---|
| 1 quart hard clams or 2 No. 1 cans minced clams | 3 potatoes, peeled and diced fine |
| ½ pound bacon, diced | ½ teaspoon pepper |
| 3 onions, chopped fine | 3 cups milk |
| 2 cups boiling water | 2 cups heavy cream |

Wash, scrub, and open the clams, reserving all the juice. Grind the clams in a food chopper, again reserving the juice. Fry the bacon in a large saucepan until half cooked; pour off most of the fat. Add the onions and sauté until brown. Add the boiling water, potatoes, pepper, and clam juice. Cover and cook over medium heat for 20 minutes. Add the clams, milk, and cream, mixing gently. Cook over low heat for 15 minutes but do not allow the soup to boil. Correct seasoning. No salt is provided in the recipe, as clams are usually salty.


## MANHATTAN CLAM CHOWDER

EASTERN

| | |
|---|---|
| 1 quart hard clams | ¾ cup coarsely chopped celery |
| ¼ pound salt pork, diced | 4 tablespoons chopped parsley |
| 4 onions, chopped | 2 bay leaves |
| 2 cups diced tomatoes or 2 cups canned tomatoes | ½ teaspoon thyme |
| | 2 small potatoes, peeled and diced |
| 2 quarts water | 1 teaspoon pepper |

Scrub the clams thoroughly and open them, reserving all the juice. Grind the clams, again saving all the juice. Place the salt pork in a large saucepan and cook until well browned. Discard the pieces of pork. Add the onions to the pork fat and sauté for 10 minutes. Add the tomatoes, water, celery, parsley, bay leaves, and thyme. Cover and cook for 2 hours. Add the clam juice and potatoes and cook for 30 minutes. Add the clams and pepper. Cook for 15 minutes. Correct seasoning. No salt is included in this recipe, as clams are usually salty.


## BOSTON BAKED BEANS

EASTERN

| | |
|---|---|
| 3 cups pea beans | ¾ teaspoon dry mustard |
| 1 pound fat salt pork, sliced | 3 tablespoons dark brown sugar |
| 1 teaspoon salt | 2 tablespoons molasses |

Wash the beans in several waters and discard any imperfect ones. Place in a deep saucepan and soak in water to cover overnight. Drain and cover with fresh water. Cook over low heat for 45 minutes. Drain well.

Pour boiling water over the pork and drain. Place a layer of pork on the bottom of a deep pot, preferably earthenware. Pour half the beans over the pork and place the rest of the pork on top. Add the remaining beans. Mix the salt, mustard, brown sugar, and molasses together with a little hot water. Pour the mixture over the beans and add enough water to cover the beans. Cover the pot. Bake in a 275° oven for 8 hours, removing the cover for the last hour of baking time. If beans appear to be too dry, add a little more water.

## GRIDDLECAKES

EASTERN

2 cups sifted flour
3 tablespoons baking powder
1 teaspoon salt
1 tablespoon sugar

2 eggs, beaten
1½ cups milk
4 tablespoons butter, melted

Sift the flour, baking powder, salt, and sugar together. Beat the eggs and milk and add to the flour mixture. Beat until very smooth. Add the melted butter and beat again.

Heat an unbuttered griddle or, if a griddle is not available, use a lightly buttered frying pan. Pour small amounts of the batter onto the griddle and cook until brown on the bottom and air spaces begin to form on the top. Turn the griddlecake over only once, and cook until done on the other side. Serve hot, with plenty of butter and maple syrup.

## INDIAN BREAD

EASTERN

½ cup sifted flour
1½ cups corn meal
½ teaspoon salt
4 tablespoons sugar

2 eggs, beaten
1 cup sour cream
1 teaspoon baking soda
1½ cups milk

Sift the flour, corn meal, salt, and sugar into a bowl. Add the eggs and sour cream and beat until very smooth. Preheat oven to 400°. Dissolve the baking soda in the milk. Add to the previous mixture and stir well. Pour into a buttered 12-inch loaf pan. Bake in a 400° oven for 25 minutes, or until a cake tester comes out clean and the bread is lightly browned.

## CHEESECAKE, NEW YORK STYLE

EASTERN

½ pound butter
1 cup sifted flour
Dash of salt

¼ cup sugar
1 egg yolk

Place the butter in a bowl. Add the flour, salt, and sugar. Blend together, using one hand. Add the egg yolk and continue mixing with the hand until well blended. Wrap in wax paper and place in the refrigerator for 1 hour. Preheat oven to 400°. Roll out one third of the dough on a lightly floured surface, to form a 9-inch circle. Place on the bottom of a 9-inch spring-form pan. Bake in a 400° oven for 10 minutes.

Remove from the oven. Butter the sides of the spring form and fasten it in place over the base. Roll the remaining dough in long strips to fit the sides and press into place, joining the bottom edges. Preheat oven to 475°. Now prepare the filling:

| | |
|---|---|
| 2½ pounds cream cheese | 1 teaspoon vanilla extract |
| 1¾ cups sugar | 6 eggs |
| 2 tablespoons flour | ½ cup heavy cream |
| ¼ teaspoon salt | |

Beat the cheese with a rotary beater until light and fluffy, using an electric mixer if available. Add the sugar, flour, salt, and vanilla gradually, beating well. Add the eggs one at a time, beating well after each addition. Add the cream and blend well. Pour into the prepared pan. Bake in a 475° oven for 10 minutes. At the end of 10 minutes, reduce oven temperature to 225° and bake 1 hour longer.

Turn off the oven and open the door. It is not advisable to have windows open in the vicinity of the stove, as they may create drafts and affect the cake. Allow to remain in the oven for 5 minutes. Remove from the oven carefully and allow to cool in a place completely free of drafts. The cake will take about 2 to 3 hours to cool completely. When cooled, run a knife around the edge carefully and remove the sides of the spring form. Do not remove the bottom.

This cake is extremely rich, and small portions may be served. It is often served with coffee late in the evening. It is too heavy for dessert with a dinner, unless the meal has been a very light one.


MINT JULEP

SOUTHERN

| | |
|---|---|
| 12 sprigs fresh mint | Cracked ice |
| 6 lumps sugar | 12 jiggers bourbon |
| 6 tablespoons water | |

Use a 12- or 16-ounce silver goblet or a tall glass for each individual drink. Crush a sprig of mint against each glass or goblet, then discard the mint. Dissolve a lump of sugar in a tablespoon of water in each glass. Half fill each glass with cracked ice. Add 2 jiggers of bourbon and stir gently.

Garnish each glass with a sprig of fresh mint.

*Note: Apparently no two people agree on the proper method of making a mint julep. However, the recipe above is a popular one.*

## OYSTER STEW

SOUTHERN

3 tablespoons butter
2 tablespoons flour
4 cups milk, scalded
1 cup heavy cream, scalded

1 teaspoon salt
¼ teaspoon pepper
1½ quarts shelled oysters

In the top of a double boiler melt the butter and flour over direct heat, stirring constantly until the mixture is smooth. Gradually add the milk and cream, stirring constantly until the boiling point is reached. Add the salt and pepper and stir. Remove from the heat. Drain the oysters and add the liquid to the milk mixture, mixing well. Place over hot water and cook for 15 minutes. Add the oysters, stir, and continue cooking until the oysters curl at the edges. Place a lump of butter in each individual soup plate and pour in the stew, dividing the oysters as evenly as possible.

## BAKED HAM, SOUTHERN STYLE

SOUTHERN

10-pound ham
2 tablespoons whole cloves
1 stick cinnamon or 2 teaspoons powdered cinnamon
1 cup sugar
1¼ cups vinegar

2 cloves garlic (optional)
1 onion
1 cup dark brown sugar
2 teaspoons dry mustard
¾ cup water

Wash the ham carefully and place in a large saucepan with water to cover. Add 1 tablespoon of the cloves, the cinnamon, sugar, 1 cup of the vinegar, the garlic, and onion. Bring to a boil, reduce to medium heat, and simmer for 2½ hours. Remove from heat and let cool for 3 hours.

Remove the skin from the ham and then dry the ham. Place the remaining cloves in the ham at more or less regular intervals. Combine the brown sugar and dry mustard and rub into the ham well. Place in a baking pan and add the remaining vinegar and the water. Bake in a 350° oven for 1 hour, basting frequently after the first 30 minutes.

## SOUTHERN FRIED CHICKEN

SOUTHERN

2 3-pound frying chickens, disjointed
2 eggs
1 cup milk
2 teaspoons salt

½ teaspoon pepper
1 cup flour
Shortening or oil for deep-fat frying

Clean the chickens carefully. Beat the eggs well, add the milk, salt, and pepper, and mix well. Place the chicken pieces in the mixture, making

337

sure that each individual piece is coated. Allow to stand for 10 minutes in the mixture. Remove the chicken and roll in the flour. Heat the shortening or oil to 360°. Place a few pieces of chicken in a frying basket and lower it into the fat. Fry until golden brown on all sides. As the pieces are removed, keep them hot until all of the chicken is fried. Serve with a cream gravy prepared as follows:

2 tablespoons of the fat in which the chicken was fried

1 tablespoon flour
1 cup light cream, scalded

Place the fat in a saucepan. Add the flour and stir until smooth. Very gradually add the scalded cream, stirring constantly until the boiling point is reached. Correct the seasoning. Serve on top of the pieces of chicken.

## BRUNSWICK STEW

SOUTHERN

5-pound stewing chicken, disjointed
1 pound beef, cut into 1-inch cubes
2 quarts water
3 large onions, chopped
1 teaspoon salt
½ pound fresh or 1 cup frozen lima beans
¼ pound fresh or frozen okra
3 potatoes, peeled and cubed

2 tablespoons catsup
2 stalks celery
2 fresh tomatoes, chopped
1 cup canned corn kernels, drained
4 tablespoons butter
4 tablespoons sugar
2 tablespoons vinegar
Dash of cayenne pepper

Clean the chicken carefully. Place in a large saucepan with the beef, water, onions, and salt. Cook over medium heat for 2½ hours. Remove the chicken and meat. Cut the chicken from the bones and set aside.

Add the lima beans, okra, potatoes, catsup, celery, tomatoes, corn kernels, and butter to the soup. Cook for 30 minutes, stirring occasionally. Return the meat and chicken to the soup and cook until most, but not all, of the liquid is absorbed. Add the sugar, vinegar, and cayenne pepper and cook 5 minutes longer, stirring frequently. Serve in deep dishes.

## SPOON BREAD

SOUTHERN

1¼ cups white or yellow corn meal
1¼ teaspoons salt
1 teaspoon sugar
1½ cups boiling water
5 tablespoons butter

1½ cups milk
½ cup light cream
4 eggs
1 tablespoon baking powder

Combine the corn meal, salt, and sugar. Bring the water to an active boil in a saucepan and add the corn meal mixture slowly and gradually, stirring constantly. Remove from the heat. Add the butter, milk, and cream and stir well. Beat the eggs until light in color and add, again stirring steadily. Add the baking powder and mix well. Preheat oven to 350°. Butter an ovenproof dish and pour the mixture into it. The dish should not be more than two thirds full, to allow for expansion. Bake in a 350° oven for 35 minutes. Serve in place of potatoes.

## PECAN PIE

SOUTHERN

| | |
|---|---|
| 1¼ cups sifted flour | ⅔ cup brown sugar |
| ¼ teaspoon salt | ¾ cup dark corn syrup |
| ⅓ cup shortening | 3 eggs, beaten |
| 3 tablespoons ice water | 1 teaspoon vanilla extract |
| ¼ cup butter | 1 cup shelled pecan halves |

Sift the flour and salt together. Cut in the shortening with a pastry blender or two knives until the consistency of coarse corn meal. Add the ice water and stir together lightly. Shape into a ball, wrap in wax paper, and chill for at least 1 hour. Roll out the dough to fit an 8-inch pie plate. Place in the pie plate and flute the edges.

Preheat oven to 400°. Cream the butter and sugar together until light and fluffy. Add the corn syrup, eggs, and vanilla and beat well. Add the pecans and stir. Pour the mixture into the prepared pie plate. Bake in a 400° oven for 10 minutes. Reduce the heat to 350° and bake 30 minutes longer, or until a knife comes out clean. Cool. Serve with whipped cream, if desired.

## POUNDCAKE

SOUTHERN

| | |
|---|---|
| 1 pound butter | ½ teaspoon salt |
| 1 pound sugar | 1 teaspoon baking powder |
| 10 eggs, separated | 1 teaspoon vanilla extract |
| 4 cups sifted flour | ½ teaspoon mace (optional) |

Cream the butter and gradually add the sugar, continuing to cream the mixture until light and fluffy. Beat the egg yolks and add, beating steadily while adding them. Sift the flour, salt, and baking powder together 4 times. Add gradually to the butter mixture, mixing well. Add the vanilla and mace. Beat well, using an electric mixer if possible. Preheat oven to 300°. Beat the egg whites until stiff but not dry and fold gently and lightly into the previous mixture.

Butter two 12-inch loaf pans and dust with flour. Pour half the mixture into each pan. Bake in a 300° oven for 1 to 1¼ hours or until a toothpick or cake tester comes out clean.

## SAZERAC COCKTAIL

NEW ORLEANS

| | |
|---|---|
| 1 tablespoon Herbsaint (absinthe substitute) | ¼ teaspoon bitters |
| | 12 cubes ice |
| 4 tablespoons water | 6 jiggers bourbon |
| 6 lumps sugar | 6 twists of lemon peel |

Using old-fashioned glasses, place a little of the Herbsaint in each one. Revolve each glass so that it is coated as much as possible. Pour out any liquid. Place ½ teaspoon of water and 1 lump of sugar in each glass, and mash the sugar with a muddler or spoon until the sugar is dissolved. Add a little of the bitters to each glass. Add 2 ice cubes and 1 jigger of whisky to each glass and stir well. Place a twist of lemon peel in each. If desired, the glasses may be iced in the refrigerator before preparing the drink.

## SHRIMP REMOULADE

NEW ORLEANS

| | |
|---|---|
| 2 pounds shrimp | 6 tablespoons olive oil |
| 3 onions, sliced | 3 tablespoons lemon juice |
| 3 cloves garlic, minced | 1 tablespoon chili sauce |
| 1 teaspoon salt | 3 tablespoons catsup |
| ½ teaspoon pepper | 1 tablespoon horseradish |
| 1 bay leaf | 1 tablespoon prepared mustard |
| 1 stalk celery | ½ teaspoon paprika |
| 3 cups water | Dash of cayenne pepper |
| 2 scallions (green onions), chopped fine | |

Shell and clean the shrimp, reserving a few shells. Wash and drain well. Combine the shells, onions, 2 cloves garlic, salt, pepper, bay leaf, celery, and water in a saucepan. Cook over medium heat for 30 minutes. Add the shrimp and cook over low heat for 5 minutes. Allow the shrimp to cool in the liquid. Drain well.

Combine the scallions, olive oil, lemon juice, chili sauce, catsup, horseradish, mustard, paprika, cayenne pepper, and remaining garlic in a bowl. Beat well and pour over the shrimp. Marinate the shrimp for at least 3 hours, overnight if possible.

## SOLE AMANDINE

NEW ORLEANS

| | |
|---|---|
| 1 teaspoon salt | 4 tablespoons white wine or vermouth |
| ¼ teaspoon pepper | |
| ⅓ cup flour | ½ cup sliced blanched almonds |
| ½ pound butter | 1 tablespoon minced parsley |
| 6 fillets of sole | |

Mix the salt, pepper, and flour together. Dip the fillets in it lightly. Melt half the butter in a skillet until bubbles form. Place the fillets in it carefully. Sauté for 5 minutes on each side. Add the wine and cook 2 minutes longer.

In a separate skillet heat the remaining butter. Add the almonds and sauté until brown, stirring frequently. Add the parsley and stir. Place the fillets on a serving dish and pour the almonds and sauce over them. Serve with a thin slice of lemon on each fillet.

*Note: This was originally a French dish but it has become a part of the New Orleans cuisine.*

## GUMBO FILÉ

NEW ORLEANS

| | |
|---|---|
| 5-pound chicken, disjointed | ½ teaspoon thyme |
| 2½ teaspoons salt | ½ teaspoon rosemary |
| 1 teaspoon pepper | ¼ teaspoon dried ground chili peppers |
| 1 clove garlic, minced | |
| 3 tablespoons butter | 1 cup canned tomatoes |
| 2 onions, chopped | 1 cup okra |
| ½ pound boiled ham, cut into strips | 24 oysters |
| 3 quarts water | 1 tablespoon filé powder |

Clean the chicken carefully. Combine the salt, pepper, and garlic and rub into the chicken. Melt the butter in a large saucepan. Add the onions and chicken. Brown well. Add the ham, water, thyme, rosemary, chili peppers, and tomatoes. Cover and cook over low heat for 1½ hours. Add the okra and cook for 1 hour. Add the oysters, bring the mixture to a boil, and cook for 3 minutes.

Remove the saucepan from the heat and immediately add the filé powder. Mix well. Serve at once. Do not return the gumbo to the heat once the filé powder is added, or it will become stringy. Serve in soup plates with boiled rice.

## CREOLE JAMBALAYA

NEW ORLEANS

1½ cups rice
1½ quarts water
2 teaspoons salt
2 tablespoons butter
½ pound uncooked ham, cut into small pieces
1 clove garlic, minced
½ pound spicy sausage, sliced thin

2 onions, chopped
2 green peppers, chopped
4 tomatoes, chopped, or 1 cup drained, canned tomatoes
2 cups stock or 2 bouillon cubes dissolved in 2 cups boiling water
2 cups cooked shrimp, chicken, or turkey, sliced

Wash the rice carefully. Place in a large saucepan with the water and salt. Cover and cook over low heat until the boiling point is reached. Cook 5 minutes longer. Drain, and rinse with cold water. Drain again.

In a separate saucepan, melt the butter and add the ham, garlic, sausage, onions, and green peppers. Cook over medium heat for 10 minutes, stirring frequently. Reduce to low heat and add the tomatoes and stock. Add rice. Cook until almost all the liquid is absorbed.

Since there are many types of jambalaya, they may be made with either shrimp, chicken, or turkey. Add the desired ingredient. Correct the seasoning, bearing in mind that the dish is normally quite spicy. Heat thoroughly and stir gently.

This dish, followed by a salad, makes an excellent lunch.

## LEG OF LAMB, CREOLE

NEW ORLEANS

6 tablespoons chili sauce
2 tablespoons vinegar
½ cup red wine
2 tablespoons olive oil
1 teaspoon salt
½ teaspoon pepper
1 tablespoon sugar

2 onions, chopped fine
2 cloves garlic, minced
1 bay leaf
1 cup beef stock or 1 bouillon cube dissolved in 1 cup boiling water
6-pound leg of lamb

In a bowl combine the chili sauce, vinegar, wine, olive oil, salt, pepper, sugar, onions, garlic, bay leaf, and beef stock. Stir well. Trim as much fat as possible from the leg of lamb. Pour the marinade over the lamb. Marinate for at least 6 hours, overnight if possible. Baste frequently.

Place the lamb and marinade in a roasting pan and roast in a 400° oven for 15 minutes. Then reduce heat to 350° and roast for 20 minutes per pound of weight. Baste frequently during the roasting process. Should the liquid evaporate too rapidly, add small quantities of boiling water to the pan. Skim any fat from the gravy and serve in a sauceboat with the lamb.

## CAFÉ BRÛLOT

NEW ORLEANS

1 tablespoon whole allspice
1 lemon rind, cut into thin strips
1 orange rind, cut into thin strips
1 whole stick cinnamon

4 lumps sugar
¼ cup brandy
3 cups extra-strength coffee, hot

In the top of a chafing dish place the allspice, lemon rind, orange rind, and cinnamon. Place the sugar and brandy in a ladle or bowl and heat. Set the brandy afire and pour it over the spice mixture. Light the flame under the chafing dish and, using the ladle or a large spoon, keep pouring the brandy over the other ingredients until the sugar dissolves. When dissolved, immediately add the coffee, which should be freshly made and about fifty per cent stronger than usual. Keep ladling for a few moments to mix the coffee, then serve in demitasse cups.

## BARBECUED SPARERIBS

SOUTHWESTERN

3 tablespoons butter
1 cup vinegar
1 cup water
2 tablespoons Worcestershire sauce
1 teaspoon tabasco sauce
¼ teaspoon cayenne pepper
½ teaspoon dry mustard

2 teaspoons sugar
1 teaspoon paprika
½ cup chili sauce
2 cloves garlic, minced
2 onions, chopped fine
3 racks of small spareribs, cracked

Combine in a saucepan the butter, vinegar, water, Worcestershire sauce, tabasco sauce, cayenne pepper, mustard, sugar, paprika, chili sauce, garlic, and onions. Bring the mixture to a boil. Place the spareribs in a bowl and pour the vinegar mixture over them. Marinate at room temperature for at least 2 hours, basting frequently. Place the spareribs on a baking sheet and roast in a 350° oven for 1 hour. Baste frequently with 1 cup of the marinade.

## CHILI CON CARNE

SOUTHWESTERN

2 cups red beans, dried, or 2 cups canned chili beans
3 tablespoons salad or olive oil
2 onions, chopped
3 tablespoons chili powder
3 cloves garlic, minced

2 pounds lean beef, cut in ¼-inch cubes
2 tablespoons flour
3 cups canned tomatoes
2 tablespoons salt

If dried beans are used, wash carefully and discard any imperfect ones. Place in a saucepan, with water to cover, and soak overnight. Wash thoroughly again and cover the beans with fresh water. Cook over low heat until the beans are tender, about 3 hours. Drain well.

Heat the oil in a separate saucepan and add the onions, chili powder, garlic, and beef. Cook over high heat until the meat is very brown on all sides. Reduce heat to low. Add flour, stirring constantly until well blended. Add the tomatoes. Cover and cook for 1½ hours. Add the salt and beans. Cook for 45 minutes. Correct seasoning. The chili will have a better flavor if prepared a day in advance.

## SWEET POTATO PIE

### SOUTHWESTERN

1 cup sifted flour
⅛ teaspoon baking powder
¼ teaspoon salt
⅓ cup shortening
3 tablespoons ice water
¾ cup butter

¾ cup sugar
1½ cups grated sweet potatoes
⅓ cup milk
¾ teaspoon ground ginger
2 tablespoons grated orange rind

Sift the flour, baking powder, and salt into a bowl. Add the shortening and cut it into the flour with a pastry blender or two knives, until the consistency of coarse sand. Add the water, drop by drop, tossing lightly with a fork until a ball of dough is formed. Chill for at least 1 hour. Roll out the dough on a lightly floured surface and line an unbuttered 11-inch pie plate with it. Place the pie plate in the refrigerator while preparing the filling. Preheat oven to 300°.

Cream the butter, add the sugar, and continue creaming until light and fluffy. Gradually add the sweet potatoes and milk alternately, beating well. Add the ginger and orange rind and again beat well. Pour into the prepared pie plate. Bake in a 300° oven until delicately browned, about 45 minutes. Serve hot, with whipped cream on the side.

## WESTERN OMELET

### WESTERN

8 eggs
¾ teaspoon salt
¼ teaspoon pepper
6 tablespoons cold water

1 cup diced bacon
½ cup chopped onions
1 large green pepper, diced

Beat the eggs with the salt, pepper, and water until well blended. Place the bacon in a large skillet, and fry for 5 minutes. Pour off most of the grease and add the onions and green pepper. Cook for 10 minutes. Add

0

the eggs and cook over very low heat, lifting the mixture with a spatula as it cooks on the bottom, and tipping the pan to allow the uncooked mixture to run under. Do not cut through the mixture; keep it in one large piece.

## CIOPPINO

WESTERN

½ cup dried mushrooms
½ cup olive oil
2 onions, chopped
2 cloves garlic, minced
1 green pepper, chopped
3 tablespoons chopped parsley
1½ cups canned tomatoes
1½ cups dry red wine

2 bay leaves
2 teaspoons salt
⅛ teaspoon cayenne pepper
3-pound striped bass, cut into slices
1 lobster or 1 Dungeness crab, cut in small pieces
1 cup shrimp, shelled and cleaned
2 cups shelled clams

Soak the mushrooms in water to cover for 3 hours. Drain and slice fine. Heat the oil in a deep, heavy saucepan. Add the onions, garlic, green pepper, parsley, and mushrooms. Sauté for 10 minutes, stirring occasionally. Add the tomatoes, wine, and bay leaves. Cover and cook over low heat for 1½ hours. Add the salt, cayenne pepper, striped bass, lobster, and shrimp and cook 20 minutes. Add the clams and cook 5 minutes. Correct seasoning. Serve in soup plates, with toast or toasted French bread.

## CAESAR SALAD

WESTERN

1 cup olive oil
6 slices white bread, trimmed and cubed
3 cloves garlic, minced
3 heads romaine lettuce, washed, drained, and chilled
6 anchovies, minced

½ teaspoon dry mustard
½ teaspoon coarsely ground black pepper
1 teaspoon salt
⅓ cup wine vinegar
1 egg, boiled 1 minute
¾ cup grated Parmesan cheese

Heat ½ cup of the oil in a skillet. Add the croutons and garlic. Sauté until brown. Set aside. Break the lettuce into 2-inch pieces, discarding any discolored or tough pieces. Place in a large bowl. Add the anchovies, mustard, pepper, salt, and the remaining oil. Toss with two spoons until the lettuce is well coated. Add the vinegar and toss. Break the egg over the salad and toss. Add the cheese and toss. Add the croutons before serving.

*Note: Caesar salad is served as a first course.*

# THE ATLANTIC
# AND THE
# CARIBBEAN

*Bermuda*

*Bahamas*

*The Greater Antilles*

  *Cuba*

  *Jamaica*

  *Haiti*

  *Dominican Republic*

  *Puerto Rico*

*The Lesser Antilles*

## BERMUDA

Not a British crown colony, not a commonwealth nor yet a dominion, Bermuda occupies a unique position in the British Empire, for it is correctly known as the "British Colony of Bermuda." Although there are about three hundred islands (if tiny coral islets are included), the total land area is barely twenty square miles. Because of Bermuda's great physical beauty and its famous springlike climate, it has become a favorite resort and vacation spot.

Bermuda is plentifully supplied with de luxe hotels which, like luxury hotels the world over, serve the so-called "international cuisine." Not only in Bermuda, although the situation is acute there, but everywhere in the world there has been a gradual deterioration of interest in serving unusual dishes on the part of chefs and owners of luxury hotels. Instead guests are served "international" food, which by its very name indicates that it is not the national food of any particular country. It means thick, floury cream sauces, innocuous soups, steaks and chops with green peas dyed a horrible green color, ice cream for dessert, the complete avoidance of spices and herbs, and the appearance on the menu of only those dishes which are completely familiar to the diner.

Unfortunately most hotels claim that they are only giving their guests what they want. Apparently myths die slowly, particularly among hotel clans. Some few places in Bermuda do serve native dishes, but on the whole they are obtainable only in private homes.

Beer and wines are of comparatively little importance here, although they are generally available. Imported scotch and rye whiskies are commonplace. Rum drinks, on the other hand, are outstanding favorites, and the swizzle is probably the most usual type of rum drink. The recipe for the Bermuda swizzle cup is only one version of the many different swizzles made in the islands.

Bermuda imports the vast majority of its food, but fish is the great exception, for the surrounding waters are filled with a wide assortment of both commercial and game fish. Fish chowders, Bermuda lobsters, and even shark are typical local fish dishes. The renowned Bermuda codfish breakfast is becoming a rarity, but it is an interesting recipe.

Cassava, a heavy, whitish root similar to the potato, is used to make a crust for chicken or meat pie. Another local specialty is the Bermuda onion, probably the most delicately flavored of all onions, which is used in many ways. The recipe for baked Bermuda onions is a fine example of old-fashioned Bermuda cookery. Almost every bit of meat is imported and there are no unusual recipes in this category other than the previously mentioned cassava pie. Desserts are of the usual American or British variety, except that there are some old-fashioned cooky and fruitcake recipes.

A plea to Bermuda hotel owners: Why not try to revive the old Bermuda style of cooking, at least on one day per week? Or why not serve one native dish every evening?


## BERMUDA SWIZZLE CUP

| | |
|---|---|
| 2 whole eggs | 3 teaspoons bitters |
| 4 tablespoons sugar | 6 jiggers light rum |

Place the eggs, sugar, and bitters in a tall glass and mix with a swizzle stick. Divide among 6 tall glasses. Add 1 jigger of rum to each glass, fill with cracked ice, and stir until the ingredients are well mixed.


## HAMILTON FISH CHOWDER

| | |
|---|---|
| ¼ pound salt pork or bacon, diced small | 3 quarts water |
| | ⅛ teaspoon thyme |
| 1 onion, sliced | 1 tablespoon chopped parsley |
| 1 pound halibut, sole, or other white meat fish, cut into 1-inch pieces | 2 tablespoons butter |
| | 4 tablespoons flour |
| 3 fish heads | ½ cup sherry |

Place the salt pork in a deep saucepan. Cook until there are about 3 tablespoons of fat in the saucepan. Add the onion and fish. Cook over high heat until the fish is browned, stirring occasionally. Reduce to low heat. Add the fish heads, water, thyme, and parsley. Cover and cook for 3 hours. Remove the fish heads and any bones.

Melt the butter in a separate saucepan. Add the flour and stir constantly until the mixture is smooth and brown. Gradually add a cup of the fish stock, stirring constantly. Add to the balance of the fish stock, stirring constantly. Correct seasoning. Add the sherry immediately before serving, and stir well.

## BERMUDA CODFISH BREAKFAST

2 pounds salt cod
6 potatoes, peeled
2 tablespoons chopped parsley
⅓ cup butter or olive oil
½ teaspoon tabasco sauce

1 teaspoon prepared mustard
1 hard-cooked egg, chopped fine
3 bananas, sliced
1 avocado, peeled and sliced

Soak the codfish overnight in water to cover. Drain and rinse thoroughly. Place in a saucepan with water to cover and cook over medium heat for 2 hours. Drain, remove skin and bones, and return fish to the saucepan. Add fresh water to cover and the whole potatoes. Cook over medium heat for 30 minutes, or until potatoes are tender. Drain well. Keep warm. Combine the butter, tabasco sauce, mustard, and egg in a saucepan. Bring to a boil and remove from the heat. Arrange the fish and potatoes on a platter, and place the bananas and avocado around the outside. Pour the sauce over all and serve.

## BAKED BERMUDA ONIONS

4 large, sweet Bermuda onions
3 slices buttered toast
1 cup grated cheese
3 eggs

1 cup milk
½ teaspoon salt
3 tablespoons butter

Peel the onions and place in a saucepan. Cover with water and bring to a boil. Cook for 5 minutes. Drain well and cool for 10 minutes. Slice the onions ½ inch thick. Cut the toast in half diagonally, so as to form triangles. Place the buttered side of the toast face down in a large, deep pie plate or casserole. Arrange the onion slices over the toast. Sprinkle the grated cheese on top.

In a separate bowl beat the eggs well and add the milk and salt. Again beat well, then pour the mixture over the onions. Dot with butter. Bake in a 350° oven for 30 minutes, or until the egg mixture is firm.

## CASSAVA PIE

1½ pounds pork, cubed
4-pound chicken, cut into pieces
1½ teaspoons salt
½ teaspoon thyme
4 cups water

2 pounds cassava or white potatoes,
   grated
½ cup dark brown sugar
4 eggs, beaten
¼ cup melted butter
¾ teaspoon baking powder

Combine the pork, chicken, salt, thyme, and water in a saucepan. Cook over medium heat for 1½ hours. Correct seasoning. Drain, reserving the liquid. Carefully remove the chicken from the bones. Combine the chicken meat with the pork and set aside.

Peel the cassava, removing the inner yellow skin. Grate on a fine grater. Wet the grated cassava, then wring it dry with the hands. Place in a bowl, add the sugar, eggs, and melted butter, and mix well. Add the baking powder and mix well again. Line the bottom and sides of a deep, buttered casserole with the cassava mixture, reserving enough to cover the top of the casserole. Fill the center with the pork and chicken, and pour 1½ cups of the previously reserved stock over it. Spread the remaining cassava mixture on top. Bake in a 325° oven for 2 hours, basting occasionally with ½ cup of the stock. Serve hot.

*Note: Cassava is not generally obtainable in the United States except in cities having large Spanish-speaking groups, such as New York City. However, the taste may be imitated by using white potatoes, with the addition, for this recipe, of 2 tablespoons of either farina or instant tapioca.*

## BERMUDA FRUITCAKE

¼ pound butter
1 cup dark brown sugar
2 cups sifted flour
1½ cups buttermilk or sour milk
½ cup chopped candied lemon peel

1 cup seedless raisins
2 teaspoons ground cinnamon
1 teaspoon ground nutmeg
¼ teaspoon allspice
2 teaspoons baking soda

Cream the butter and add the sugar, beating well. Add the flour (reserving 2 tablespoons) and the buttermilk alternately, spoon by spoon, stirring steadily. Beat well. Dust the lemon peel and raisins with the reserved flour and add to the mixture. Add the cinnamon, nutmeg, allspice, and baking soda and beat together. Preheat oven to 375°. Butter a 12-inch loaf pan generously. Dust with a little flour. Pour the mixture into the pan. Bake in a 375° oven for 1 hour, or until a cake tester comes out clean.

## OLD-FASHIONED BERMUDA COOKIES

6 tablespoons butter
4 tablespoons vegetable shortening
    or lard
8 tablespoons sugar
1 egg, beaten

2 cups sifted flour
⅛ teaspoon salt
1 teaspoon nutmeg
⅛ teaspoon baking soda
1 tablespoon brandy

Cream the butter and shortening together. Add the sugar and beat until well blended. Add the egg and continue beating. Sift the flour, salt, and nutmeg together and add to the butter mixture. Blend well. Dissolve the soda in the brandy and add to the mixture, stirring well. Preheat oven to 375°.

Dust the hands well with flour and form small balls of dough. Press flat with the hands and place on an unbuttered baking sheet. Designs may be made on top of each cooky, if desired, or a pastry wheel may be run around the edges. Bake in a 375° oven for 15 minutes, or until brown. These cookies are quite rich. They will expand while baking, so use only small amounts of dough for each cooky.

*BAHAMAS*

Many hundreds of tiny bits of land, reefs, and soil form the British Bahama Islands. Many of these islands are uninhabited, some have a very few natives living on them, but others are comparatively well settled. To the majority of tourists, the Bahamas mean just one spot—the capital city of Nassau on New Providence Island. To another specialized breed, deep-sea fishermen, the Bahamas mean the famous Bimini Island, located adjacent to the Gulf Stream, and the scene of the annual tuna competitions. Eleuthera and Harbour islands are somewhat off the beaten track but offer excellent vacations to those who wish to dispense with night clubs, television, and other trappings of civilization.

Nassau is filled with hotels, guesthouses, and other places offering accommodations to visitors, most of whom come from the States. The islands are nevertheless distinctly British in flavor and tempo, and extremely conservative. The food is more likely to be American style than British, in honor of the large number of tourists, or possibly in the international style beloved by hotelmen. Local food is hard to find except in private homes.

British drinking habits are followed to a certain extent, although the American-style cocktail hour (or hours) is a recognized part of the local scene. Social life is at a high point during the winter season, with a considerable amount of formal entertaining. All liquors are available in Nassau at comparatively low prices, but rum mixtures and whisky and soda are the local choices.

The islands find it difficult to produce enough food for the inhabitants plus the tourists, and thus a great deal of it is imported, mostly from the States. Actually the only foods available locally are vegetables, fish, and some fruit, with a few exceptions. Fish of all deep-sea species are plentiful, and the local people make various chowders and stews of the many varieties available. Nassau fish chowder is a local specialty, but this is merely one example. Conchs (pronounced conks) are large shellfish common in the area, used for soup, chowders, and the conch fritters for which a recipe is given. Crabs are particularly good here, and often very plentiful. If he can find it, no visitor to Nassau should leave without trying turtle pie, an interesting food specialty of the islands.

Meat is imported, and there are practically no unique meat dishes of importance. On the other hand, chicken dishes are well prepared, as are such game birds as the wild pigeons and ducks of the region. The famous song about "Mama don't want no peas an' rice an' coconut oil" describes in reverse the local passion for peas and rice, probably the favorite native dish.

Almost all the hotels serve good meals, though local dishes are seldom encountered. In addition to the hotels, the Buena Vista and Cumberland guesthouses are well known for their food; otherwise there are few suitable places to dine except for the Garden Club and Grand Central restaurants.

## NASSAU FISH CHOWDER

| | |
|---|---|
| 3 pounds assorted fish | ½ teaspoon thyme |
| 1 teaspoon salt | 2 bay leaves |
| 3 tablespoons lemon juice | 2 sprigs parsley |
| ¼ pound salt pork | 1 teaspoon peppercorns |
| 3 onions, chopped | 4 cups boiling water |
| 1 No. 2 can tomatoes, strained | 2 tablespoons Worcestershire sauce |
| 4 potatoes, peeled and cubed | ¼ cup sherry |
| 12 pilot crackers | |

Wash and dry the fish. Cut it into 2-inch cubes, removing all the skin and bones. Sprinkle with the salt and lemon juice. Place the salt pork in a saucepan and fry until brown. Discard the pork. Add the onions and sauté for 10 minutes, stirring occasionally. Add the tomatoes and cook over low heat for 25 minutes.

In a heavy saucepan or Dutch oven arrange layers of the tomato mixture, fish, potatoes, and pilot crackers until all the ingredients are used up. Add the thyme, bay leaves, parsley, pepper, and boiling water. Cover and cook over medium heat for 40 minutes. Add the Worcestershire sauce and sherry. Cook 20 minutes longer. Serve hot.

## CONCH FRITTERS

| | |
|---|---|
| 3 cups ground conch or clams, drained | ½ teaspoon salt |
| 1 cup sifted flour | ½ teaspoon pepper |
| 1 teaspoon baking powder | 1 egg, beaten |
| 2 tablespoons chopped onion | 2 tablespoons water |
| | Fat for deep-fat frying |

Combine the ground conch or clams, flour, baking powder, onion, salt, pepper, egg, and water. Mix well. Form into walnut-size balls. Heat the fat to 375°. Fry a few balls at a time until browned on all sides. Drain well. Serve hot, on toothpicks, as an appetizer.

*Note: Conch is a large shellfish of the Florida and West Indies region. Although clams do not taste exactly like conch, the texture is similar.*

## TURTLE PIE

| | |
|---|---|
| 2 cups sifted flour | 3 onions, chopped |
| 1½ teaspoons salt | 1 tablespoon cornstarch |
| ½ cup shortening | ½ cup tomato sauce |
| 2 eggs | 1 tablespoon melted butter |
| 2 teaspoons cold water | 2 egg yolks |
| 3 pounds turtle meat (see Note) | ¼ teaspoon pepper |
| ¾ teaspoon thyme | ½ cup bread crumbs |
| ½ teaspoon marjoram | 4 tablespoons fat |
| 2 cups hot water | 1 cup sherry |
| 4 tablespoons butter | |

Sift the flour and ½ teaspoon salt into a bowl. Cut in the shortening with a pastry blender or two knives until the consistency of coarse sand. Beat 1 egg and the cold water together and add, tossing lightly until a ball of dough is formed. Wrap in wax paper and place in the refrigerator while preparing the filling.

Divide the meat in half; cube one half and grind the other. Place the cubed meat in a saucepan and cover with water. Bring to a boil, drain, and rinse with cold water. Combine in the saucepan with the thyme, marjoram, and hot water. Cook over low heat for 45 minutes. Drain, reserving the stock. Set the cubed meat aside. Melt the butter in a saucepan; add 2 onions. Sauté for 10 minutes. Add the cornstarch, stirring well. Add the tomato sauce and the reserved stock and mix well. Cook over low heat for 30 minutes. Strain and combine with the cubed meat. Correct seasoning.

Combine the ground meat with the remaining onion. Add the melted butter, egg yolks, pepper, and remaining salt. Mix well. Shape into 2-inch balls. Beat the remaining egg and dip the balls in it, then into the bread crumbs. Heat the fat in a skillet and fry the balls in it until brown on all sides.

Pour the cubed meat mixture into a deep casserole. Place the balls on top and pour the sherry over it. Preheat oven to 350°. Roll out the dough on a lightly floured surface to fit the top of the casserole. Place on top of the casserole, sealing the edges well. Brush the top with a little beaten egg or milk. Bake in a 350° oven for 35 minutes.

*Note: Although turtle meat is available, either fresh or in cans, veal may be substituted. Veal doesn't taste like turtle, but it's texture and appearance are similar enough to justify its use.*

## BAHAMIAN ROAST CHICKEN

| | |
|---|---|
| 1 large roasting chicken, whole | 2 onions, chopped fine |
| 3 teaspoons salt | 3 tablespoons melted butter |
| 1 teaspoon pepper | 2 cups water |
| 4 tablespoons butter | 3 tomatoes, chopped |
| 3 cups bread crumbs | 3 potatoes, peeled and halved |
| ⅛ teaspoon thyme | 6 carrots, peeled |

Wash and dry the chicken. Make a paste of 2 teaspoons of the salt, ½ teaspoon of the pepper, and 4 tablespoons butter. Rub it into the chicken, inside and out. Combine the bread crumbs and the remaining salt and pepper, the thyme, onions, and melted butter. Mix well. Reserve 1 cup of the mixture and stuff the chicken loosely with the balance. Fasten the opening with skewers or with toothpicks. Place the chicken in a roasting pan. Spread the reserved bread-crumb mixture around the chicken. Add the water and tomatoes.

Roast in a 350° oven for 1¼ hours, basting occasionally. Add the potatoes and carrots and roast 45 minutes longer, or until the chicken is tender. Serve with boiled rice. The sauce remaining in the roasting pan should be poured over the chicken and rice.

## PEAS AND RICE, BAHAMA STYLE

| | |
|---|---|
| 2 cups dried pigeon peas | 3 cups boiling water |
| 3 tablespoons salad oil | 2 teaspoons salt |
| 1 onion, chopped | ¾ teaspoon pepper |
| 3 tomatoes, chopped | 1 cup rice, washed and drained |

Soak the peas overnight in water to cover. Drain, add fresh water, and boil for 1 hour, or until soft. Drain and force through a strainer. Heat the oil in a saucepan and add the onion. Sauté for 10 minutes, stirring frequently. Add the tomatoes and cook over low heat for 5 minutes. Add the water, the bean purée, salt, and pepper. Bring to a boil. Add the rice and mix together lightly. Cover and cook for 25 minutes, or until rice is tender. Watch the liquid carefully, adding small additional quantities of boiling water if necessary to prevent burning.

*Note: Canned cooked pigeon peas are available. If used, omit cooking and proceed as directed.*

## BANANA PUDDING

10 ripe bananas
⅓ cup flour
1 cup sugar

1 tablespoon melted butter
1 teaspoon nutmeg

Mash the bananas. Add the flour, sugar, butter, and nutmeg. Pour into a buttered 8-inch square pan. Bake in a 325° oven for 30 minutes, or until delicately browned on top. Cut into squares and serve hot or cold, dusted with powdered sugar. If desired, whipped cream may be placed on each portion.

*CUBA*

Cuba is so close to the United States, only about an hour from Miami to Havana by Pan American plane, that tremendous numbers of American tourists have visited it over the past years. In view of its excellent year-round climate, this is not surprising, and most people are favorably impressed by what they see. The Cubans reciprocate by visiting Miami themselves during the summer months.

There are tourists who stay up all night touring the dozens of bars and night clubs that dot Havana, and they report solemnly to the folks at home that Cubans do nothing but dance the rhumba, preferably from midnight on. Even the more curious tourists are likely to visit only Havana and beautiful Varadero Beach, missing the rest of the country.

The misunderstanding of Cuba by Americans is matched only by the Cuban failure to comprehend their welcome visitors. They fail to understand why we limit ourselves to one city and one beach, and they persist

355

in that stubbornly held belief, apparently subscribed to with implicit faith by restaurant owners, that Americans will only eat American food. If this were once true (and there is considerable doubt on that score) it is true no longer. The Nacional Hotel, an Intercontinental hotel, combines on its menus the best features of American and Cuban cuisine. If you so desired, you could have corned beef hash and *arroz con pollo* in the same meal! Reasonably authentic Cuban food is served at Havana's excellent but unfortunately expensive restaurants. La Zaragozana is a seafood restaurant, where one may dine on Moro crabs, among the world's outstanding shellfish delicacies, prepared in many different styles. The Ambos Mundos is located in downtown Havana, and the Miami, Paris, Florida, and La Reguladora restaurants are all worth visiting. Lunch is at a normal hour, but dinner is from 9 P.M. on.

Certain ingredients dominate all Cuban food, which in turn has a Spanish background. Beans, coconuts, pork, seafood, and saffron are the basic items, and the majority of popular dishes contain one or more of these ingredients. Of course the locally caught fruits of the sea are superb but visitors are recommended particularly to the *langostinos* (fresh-water prawns). Meat dishes are likely to have a European background, with the possible exception of roast suckling pig, the great holiday favorite. Rice, the staple starchy food, is used with poultry, meat, or seafood, usually combined with saffron. The one dessert that always appeals to Americans, ice cream fanciers to a man, is fresh coconut ice cream, customarily served in half a coconut shell. The fact that each shell contains about a pint or more of ice cream apparently does not deter anyone from finishing his portion. That is, anyone worthy of being called a red-blooded American!

Cuba is a sugar island, and rum is made from the pressings of the sugar cane. Probably the best known of all rums is the Bacardi rum, but numerous other fine brands are available. Of course bacardi and daiquiri cocktails are local specialties. Rum and cola, the renowned *Cuba libre,* may or may not have originated here; no one knows, but it is known that tourists order it regularly and with authority on the assumption that it is a Cuban specialty. Beer, on the other hand, while not so well publicized as rum, is also a national drink, and may be of greater importance to the Cubans than rum. And whisper the following very softly: many Cubans like water, fruit drinks, and Coke better than anything else.

BACARDI COCKTAIL

6 jiggers Bacardi rum
2 teaspoons grenadine

Juice of 2 lemons or limes

Place the rum, grenadine, and lemon or lime juice in a cocktail shaker with cracked ice. Shake well. Strain into chilled cocktail glasses.

## BLACK BEAN SOUP

SOPA DE JUDÍAS COLORADAS

2 cups black beans
3 quarts water
½ pound ham, cubed
2 tablespoons olive oil
2 onions, chopped
2 cloves garlic, minced
¼ cup chopped celery
1 carrot, sliced
1 green pepper, chopped
2 tomatoes, chopped

1 bay leaf
2 teaspoons salt
¼ teaspoon dried ground chili peppers
1 teaspoon Spanish paprika
2 tablespoons butter
2 tablespoons flour
3 tablespoons rum
3 hard-cooked eggs, sliced
6 slices lemon

Wash the beans thoroughly. Soak in water to cover overnight. Drain completely and rinse again. Combine in a saucepan with the 3 quarts of water and the ham. Bring to a boil. Cover and cook over low heat for 3 hours.

Heat the olive oil in a frying pan. Add the onions, garlic, celery, carrot, and green pepper. Sauté for 15 minutes, stirring frequently. Add to the beans, together with the tomatoes, bay leaf, salt, chili peppers, and paprika. Cover and cook over low heat for 1 hour. Force the mixture through a sieve and return to the saucepan. Knead the butter and flour together until it forms a ball. Add to the soup, stirring constantly until the boiling point is reached. Correct seasoning. Add the rum. Serve the soup garnished with slices of egg and lemon.

## BAKED FISH WITH ALMONDS

PESCADO HORNEADO CON ALMENDRAS

3 tablespoons olive oil
2 onions, chopped fine
1 clove garlic, minced
1 cup ground almonds
3 tablespoons chopped parsley
1 tablespoon beef extract
2 tablespoons lemon juice

1 teaspoon salt
½ teaspoon pepper
6 fillets of pompano, snapper, or sole
4 tablespoons butter
2 onions, sliced
½ teaspoon thyme

Heat the olive oil in a saucepan. Add the chopped onions and garlic. Sauté for 10 minutes, stirring frequently. Add the almonds and parsley and sauté for 5 minutes, stirring almost constantly. Add the beef extract and mix well. Cook over low heat for 5 minutes, stirring occasionally.

Combine the lemon juice, salt, and pepper in a cup. Rub into the fish thoroughly. Melt the butter in an ovenproof baking dish and place the onion slices in it. Sprinkle with the thyme. Arrange the fish fillets over the onions. Bake in a 375° oven for 15 minutes. Pour the sauce over the fish. Bake 20 minutes longer. Serve with lemon or lime wedges.

## FRIED STEAKS

### VACA FRITA

| | |
|---|---|
| 4 tablespoons olive oil | 2 cloves |
| 3 onions, chopped | 2 teaspoons salt |
| 3 cloves garlic, minced | ¼ teaspoon dried ground chili peppers |
| 1 green pepper, chopped | |
| 1 carrot, diced | 1 teaspoon Spanish paprika |
| 6 tomatoes, chopped, or 2 cups canned tomatoes, drained | ¾ cup bread crumbs |
| | 6 individual steaks |
| 2 slices half-cooked bacon, minced | 3 canned pimentos, sliced |
| 1 bay leaf | 4 tablespoons chopped parsley |

Heat the olive oil in a saucepan. Add the onions and garlic and sauté for 10 minutes, stirring frequently. Add the green pepper, carrot, tomatoes, bacon, bay leaf, cloves, salt, chili peppers, and paprika. Cover and cook over low heat for 30 minutes, stirring frequently. Add the bread crumbs, mixing well. Correct seasoning. Cook over the lowest possible heat while preparing the steaks. Discard bay leaf.

Heat a skillet. Add the steaks and fry over high heat for 3 minutes on each side, or until the steaks are done. Place the steaks on a platter and pour the sauce over them. Arrange the pimentos on top and sprinkle with the parsley. Serve immediately.

## CHICKEN WITH RICE

### ARROZ CON POLLO

| | |
|---|---|
| 1 cup olive oil | 2 teaspoons saffron |
| 2 3-pound chickens, disjointed | 1 tablespoon salt |
| 3 onions, chopped | ½ teaspoon pepper |
| 3 cloves garlic, minced | 1 fresh chili pepper, sliced, or ¼ teaspoon dried ground chili peppers |
| 2 cups rice | |
| 1½ cups canned tomatoes | 1 cup canned tiny green peas |
| 3 fresh tomatoes, chopped | 3 canned pimentos, sliced |
| 2 cups stock or 1 can consommé and ½ can water | |

Heat ½ cup olive oil in a large casserole or saucepan. Add the chicken and brown well on all sides. Remove the chicken. Sauté the onions and garlic in the same casserole for 10 minutes. Remove. Add the remaining oil to the casserole. Brown the rice in it lightly, stirring constantly. Replace the chicken, onions, and garlic. Add the canned and fresh tomatoes, stock, saffron, salt, pepper, and chili peppers. Mix carefully. Cover.

Bake in a 325° oven for 1½ hours. Add the peas and pimentos, and a little water if the rice is dry. Bake for 20 minutes, or until chicken is tender. Serve hot, right from the casserole. A dry white wine is recommended for this classic dish.

## CUBAN CHICKEN STEW

GUISADO DE POLLO

3 cloves garlic, minced
2 teaspoons salt
1 teaspoon pepper
2 teaspoons Spanish paprika
2 3-pound chickens, disjointed
¼ cup olive oil
3 onions, chopped

1 bay leaf
½ cup white wine
3 potatoes, peeled and cubed
1 No. 1 can French-style green peas
½ cup sliced green olives
½ cup sliced canned pimentos

Mix the garlic, salt, pepper, and paprika to a paste. Rub into the chickens thoroughly, inside and out. If possible, season the chickens the day before they are to be used.

Heat the olive oil in a saucepan or casserole. Add the onions and sauté for 15 minutes, stirring frequently. Remove the onions and set aside. Add the chickens and brown well on all sides. Return the onions to the saucepan. Add the bay leaf and white wine. Cover and cook over low heat for 1 hour. Add small additional amounts of water if needed. Add the potatoes and stir gently. Cover and cook over low heat for 20 minutes. Correct seasoning. Add the peas, olives, and pimentos and cook over low heat for 10 minutes.

*Note: The flavor will be greatly improved if the stew is prepared early in the day and reheated before serving.*

## AVOCADOS STUFFED WITH VEGETABLES

AGUACATES RELLENO

½ cup olive oil
2 tablespoons vinegar
1 teaspoon salt
½ teaspoon pepper
1 clove garlic, minced
1 cup diced boiled potatoe.
½ cup sliced cooked carrots

½ cup canned or cooked green peas
6 canned or cooked asparagus spears, sliced
¼ cup canned or cooked diced beets
3 avocados, cut in half
1 cup mayonnaise
2 hard-cooked eggs, chopped

359

Combine the olive oil, vinegar, salt, pepper, and garlic in a bowl. Beat until well blended. Combine the potatoes, carrots, peas, asparagus, and beets in a bowl. Pour the dressing over the vegetables and mix well. Marinate for 30 minutes, mixing frequently.

Divide the mixture evenly and stuff the avocados. Mask the stuffing completely with mayonnaise. Sprinkle with the chopped egg. If desired, decorate with lettuce leaves or pimentos. Chill for 1 hour. Serve cold.

## DOUBLE YOLK DESSERT

### YEMA DOBLE

| | |
|---|---|
| 2 cups sugar | 2 egg whites |
| 1 cup water | 1½ tablespoons flour |
| 6 egg yolks | 2 tablespoons sherry |

Combine the sugar and water in a saucepan. Cook until thick and syrupy. Remove half of the mixture and set it aside. In a bowl, beat the egg yolks until light in color. In a separate bowl, beat the egg whites until stiff but not dry. Sift the flour over the whites and fold in carefully. Fold in the egg yolks carefully.

Bring the syrup in the saucepan to a boil. Drop the egg mixture into it by tablespoons, but do not have more than 3 tablespoons of the mixture cooking at one time. When the little "omelet" floats on the top, fold it in half with two forks and remove it to a platter. Continue until all of the egg mixture is cooked. Should more syrup be required, add some from the reserved half. Add the sherry to the reserved syrup and heat it. Pour over the little omelets.

## SPONGECAKE

### PANATELA

| | |
|---|---|
| 1⅛ cups sifted flour | 1½ cups sifted sugar |
| 1 teaspoon cream of tartar | 7 eggs, separated |
| ¼ teaspoon salt | 2 tablespoons brandy |
| 1⅛ cups water | |

Sift together the flour, cream of tartar, and salt 4 times. Set aside. Combine the water and sugar in a saucepan. Cook over low heat until a thread forms when a fork is lifted from the syrup. Beat the egg whites until stiff but not dry. Add the syrup very gradually, beating constantly until the mixture cools. Beat the egg yolks until thick. Add the brandy and stir. Fold into the egg-white mixture. Preheat oven to 325°. Fold the flour mixture into the egg mixture gently but thoroughly.

Butter an angel-cake pan and dust lightly with flour. Pour the batter into it carefully. Bake in a 325° oven for 1 hour, or until a cake tester comes out clean. Invert the pan and allow to cool in that position. Remove from the pan and sprinkle with powdered sugar, if desired.

*DOMINICAN REPUBLIC*

Even the poorest scholar cannot leave school without remembering one historic date, that of 1492, the year in which Columbus discovered America. That intrepid explorer actually landed on the island of Hispaniola, little realizing that his fate was inescapably linked with it, for Columbus' body lies today in Ciudad Trujillo, the capital of the country.

The island of Hispaniola is shared by two dissimilar nations, Haiti and the Dominican Republic. The French overtones of Haitian cuisine are not evident in the Dominican portion of the island; the emphasis is upon local foodstuffs, although certain dishes have a generally Spanish background.

This is a country of fruits and vegetables, all easily grown in a warm land of considerable sunshine and fertile soil. Sugar cane, sweet potatoes, squash, coffee, bananas, and mangos are plentiful and are mainstays in the local diet. Lobsters and shrimp are available along the comparatively long coast line, and they are incorporated into the diet to good effect; *sopa hamaca*, a fish soup with vegetables, is an interesting example of making the most of what is available.

Roast pork in any form is considered the most delectable of all meats, a truism of all the islands of the West Indies. *Carne de cerdo* (browned pork strips) is a recognized Dominican specialty; of even greater popularity is roast suckling pig, preferably cooked outdoors over an open fire. The wonderful soup-stew of the Latin countries, *sancocho*, is undoubtedly the people's choice for a national dish. Although *sancocho* is often made with two dozen different ingredients, the Dominicans have a *sancocho de siete carnes*, made with seven different meats in addition to the usual items, which is undoubtedly the champion *sancocho* of all. To scare off any possible rival claimants, it is made with bitter orange juice and all

361

sorts of odd ingredients, such as *longaniza, yucca, yautia, mapuey, rulos, platanos,* and other foods unavailable to us. A more readily duplicated recipe for *sancocho* is listed in the section on Central America.

Beans and rice, the staple foods of the peasantry, are eaten at least once almost every day, and often several times daily. The people are very fond of sweet desserts, principally based on coconuts, bananas, and pineapple.

Santo Domingo coffee is not only the normal end to a meal, it is also the standard refreshment offered to guests, both business and social. The number of cups of coffee consumed per person is probably surpassed only in Brazil, and even that statement might be the subject of a poll by Dr. Gallup.

A fair amount of rum of reasonable quality, although not outstanding enough for exportation, is produced locally. The local people do not quibble on this point but consume it straight and in mixed drinks. Possibly the beer is better than the rum; certainly everyone seems to drink it.

The country has very good weather the year around. It can be quite warm during the summer months, though not unpleasantly so. Actually the best season to visit the Dominican Republic is from November to March inclusively. The Hotel Jaragua in Ciudad Trujillo is extremely luxurious and serves good food, albeit of the routine international variety usually. Local food specialties can be ordered if desired.


## FISH, SANTO DOMINGO STYLE

PESCADO, SANTO DOMINGO

| | |
|---|---|
| 6 slices sea bass, mackerel, or similar fish | 2 tablespoons olive oil |
| ¾ cup flour | 2 onions, sliced thin |
| 3 teaspoons salt | 1 clove garlic, minced |
| 1½ teaspoons pepper | 3 tomatoes, cubed |
| ½ cup salad oil | 1 tablespoon tomato paste |
| | 2 tablespoons vinegar |

Wash and dry the fish. Sprinkle with the lemon juice. Mix the flour, 2 teaspoons of the salt, and 1 teaspoon of the pepper together. Dip the fish slices into the mixture, coating them well. Heat the salad oil in a frying pan. Add the fish and fry until well browned on both sides, about 20 minutes. Remove the fish from the pan and place in a shallow bowl.

Heat the olive oil in a skillet. Add the onions and garlic and sauté for 5 minutes, stirring frequently. Add the tomatoes, tomato paste, vinegar, and remaining salt and pepper. Cook over low heat for 5 minutes. Pour the sauce over the fish and cover the bowl. Place in the refrigerator for 24 hours before serving. Serve as an appetizer on a bed of lettuce leaves.

## FISH AND VEGETABLE SOUP

SOPA HAMACA

½ cup olive oil
2 onions, chopped
2 cloves garlic, minced
2 pounds fish, cubed
1 lobster, removed from shell and cut into pieces
1 cup rice
4 potatoes, peeled and cubed

2 tomatoes, chopped
2 cups coarsely shredded cabbage
2 tablespoons tomato paste
2½ quarts boiling water
3 pimentos, sliced thin
2 teaspoons salt
½ teaspoon pepper
½ teaspoon orégano

Heat the olive oil in a large saucepan. Add the onions and garlic and sauté for 5 minutes, stirring frequently. Add the fish, lobster, and rice and cook over high heat for 5 minutes, stirring constantly. Add the potatoes, tomatoes, cabbage, tomato paste, boiling water, pimentos, salt, pepper, and orégano. Stir well and cook over medium heat for 30 minutes. Correct seasoning. Serve hot.

## MARINATED CHICKEN

CARNE DE AVES

3 1½-pound broilers, quartered
½ cup vinegar
2 green peppers, chopped
4 tomatoes, chopped
3 onions, chopped
2 cloves garlic, minced

2 teaspoons salt
1 teaspoon pepper
1 teaspoon orégano
½ cup olive oil
2 tablespoons tomato paste
1 cup sliced stuffed green olives

Wash and dry the chickens. Sponge with the vinegar and place in a bowl. Add the green peppers, tomatoes, onions, garlic, salt, pepper, and orégano. Mix well. Cover and marinate for 2 hours. Remove the chicken from the marinade, reserving the marinade. Heat the olive oil in a large skillet. Brown the chicken on all sides. Add the reserved marinade, tomato paste, and olives. Cover and cook over low heat for 30 minutes, or until the chicken is tender. Correct seasoning.

## BROWNED PORK STRIPS

CARNE DE CERDO GUISADA

4 tomatoes, chopped
3 onions, chopped
2 cloves garlic, minced
2 teaspoons salt
½ teaspoon pepper

4 pounds boneless pork, cut into pieces ½ by 2 inches, ½ inch thick
¼ cup olive oil
¾ cup water

Combine the tomatoes, onions, garlic, salt, and pepper in a bowl. Mix well. Add the pork strips and stir well. Cover and set aside for 1 hour. Remove the pork from the bowl, reserving the vegetables.

Heat the olive oil in a saucepan until it smokes. Add the pork strips and cook over high heat without stirring for 5 minutes. Then cook over high heat for 5 minutes, stirring occasionally. Combine the reserved vegetables with the water. Add slowly to the pork, stirring constantly. Cover and cook over low heat for 45 minutes. Correct seasoning. Serve with boiled or fried rice.

## COCONUT CHEESE TART

TORTA DE COCO

| | |
|---|---|
| 1¼ cups sifted flour | ¼ cup sugar |
| ⅛ teaspoon salt | 1 cup milk, scalded |
| ⅔ cup shortening | ½ cup heavy cream, scalded |
| 3 eggs | ½ cup cottage cheese, drained |
| 1 tablespoon cold water | ½ cup fresh or dried grated coconut |

Sift the flour and salt into a bowl. Cut in the shortening with a pastry blender or two knives until the consistency of coarse sand. Beat 1 of the eggs with the water and add, tossing lightly until a ball of dough is formed. Chill for 1 hour.

Beat the remaining eggs in a bowl. Add the sugar and mix. Gradually add the milk and cream, beating steadily. Add the cottage cheese and mix until smooth. Add the coconut and again mix well. Preheat oven to 350°. Roll out the dough ⅛ inch thick on a lightly floured surface. Line a 9-inch pie plate with the dough. Pour the mixture into it. Bake in a 350° oven for 45 minutes, or until a cake tester comes out clean. Serve hot or cold.

## JAMAICA

South of Cuba and west of Haiti is Jamaica, the largest of all the islands that make up the British West Indies. It is a British colony, and combines

Britain and the tropics in a rather engaging fashion. Kingston, the capital city, is a busy and thriving community. The island is famous as a resort, and many excellent places to stay are scattered over the island. Among these might be mentioned the traditionally famous Myrtle Bank, the Shaw Park, Jamaica Inn, and the Tower Isle. Montego Bay, situated so beautifully in the northwestern portion of the island, has become a great meeting place for Americans, and there are many first-class hotels.

The climate is usually tropical, but a regular trade wind blows almost constantly. With weather such as this, the vegetation is lush and thick, and parts of the island have a junglelike quality. A perfect place to examine the island's plant life is at the Hope Botanical Gardens, a few miles from Kingston. The produce of the island consists principally of beans, corn, ginger, sugar, coffee, and fruit. At one time sugar cane was almost the only crop, but now there is a fair amount of diversification.

The waters surrounding Jamaica are filled with many kinds of seafood, and fish dishes are a daily part of the diet. In addition, the rivers and streams supply several types of fresh-water mullet, some of which are excellent. There are shellfish, and of these, the lobster is the most highly esteemed. The recipe for stuffed lobster is a good example of the local method of handling this delicacy.

Meat is of considerably less importance than fish in the everyday life of the people. On the other hand, pork, beef, and lamb are well liked, although possibly lamb is the island favorite. Of course it must be understood that the hotels and restaurants serve food of the type and style that have become standardized in luxury establishments the world over. Thus the preference for fish is primarily on the part of the people of the island. Jamaica pepperpot is an interesting local soup specialty.

Vegetables grow abundantly and are used regularly, although the islanders have certain favorites. Dried beans and peas are so overwhelmingly popular that they almost inevitably appear at every native meal in one style or another. Red peas are particularly important to the Jamaicans; these are used in making the famous red pea soup and also in the preparation of beef and red peas.

The best desserts are the fruits, either in their natural state or in ice creams and puddings. Baked bananas are a typical dessert.

The drink of the island is the local rum, which is quite different from the Martinique, Haiti, Barbados, Virgin Islands, and Cuban types. Rum is somewhat of a staple article, frequently used in cooking. The renowned Planter's Punch is the drink of the island, or at least the tourists like to believe that it is. This belief assists the sale of rum, which in turn pleases the producers of rum, thus making everyone happy.

## PLANTER'S PUNCH

Cracked ice
6 dashes aromatic bitters
Juice of 3 limes or lemons
6 teaspoons sugar

9 ounces light Jamaica rum (1⅛ cups)
6 half slices orange
6 maraschino cherries

Fill 6 tall highball glasses with finely cracked ice. Add a dash of bitters to each glass. Add the lemon juice, sugar, and rum and shake or stir until cold. Garnish each glass with an orange slice and a cherry. Serve with a straw.

## STAMP AND GO

1 pound salt cod
1 onion, chopped fine
½ tomato, chopped
1 clove garlic, minced

3 eggs, beaten
¼ cup flour
3 tablespoons butter

Soak the cod in cold water overnight, or at least 3 hours. Drain completely. Place in a saucepan with water to cover and cook for 40 minutes. Additional water may be required. When cooked, remove the bones carefully. Mince fine with a fork. Add the onion, tomato, and garlic and mix. Beat the eggs and add. Mix well. Form into small fritters.

Dip each fritter in flour. Heat the butter in a frying pan and fry the fritters until golden brown on both sides. In Jamaica, this dish is served with boiled green bananas or with fried plantains. However, it may be accompanied by French fried potatoes. Small fritters make very good hot hors d'oeuvres.

## JAMAICA PEPPERPOT

2 pounds kale or cabbage
2 pounds beef, cut into 1-inch cubes
½ pound chipped beef
1 cup fresh or dried grated coconut
12 okra, stems removed
2 onions, coarsely chopped

1 quart water
½ teaspoon salt
⅛ teaspoon cayenne pepper
½ teaspoon thyme
2 scallions (green onions), sliced

Wash the kale or cabbage thoroughly and cut away any discolored or tough portions. Cut into large pieces and place in a saucepan with the cubed beef, chipped beef, coconut, okra, chopped onions, and water. Bring to a boil and cook over low heat for 1 hour. Remove the kale or cabbage and okra from the saucepan; force them through a sieve and return the pulp to the saucepan. Add the salt, cayenne pepper, thyme, and scallions. Cook for 15 minutes, or until meat is tender. Correct seasoning, bearing in mind that the soup is fairly hot and spicy.

## STUFFED LOBSTER, JAMAICA STYLE

6 lobsters, split
¼ pound butter
2 onions, chopped
¼ pound mushrooms, chopped
1 tablespoon flour
½ cup stock

1 teaspoon salt
¼ teaspoon pepper
Dash of cayenne pepper
½ cup bread crumbs
½ cup grated cheese

Remove the meat from the lobsters and cut in small pieces. Reserve the shells. Set aside. Melt 3 tablespoons of the butter in a saucepan. Add the onions and mushrooms and sauté for 15 minutes. Add the flour, stirring constantly. Add the stock, continuing to stir until the mixture boils. Add the lobster meat, salt, pepper, and cayenne pepper. Cook for 15 minutes. Correct seasoning and mix gently.

Place the lobster mixture in the shells. Sprinkle with the bread crumbs and cheese. Dot with the remaining butter. Place on a baking sheet. Bake in a 350° oven for 15 minutes, or until lightly browned on top. Serve with lime or lemon wedges.

## BEEF AND RED PEAS

2 cups dried red peas
2 pounds chipped beef
½ teaspoon pepper
⅛ teaspoon dried ground chili peppers
¼ teaspoon thyme
½ cup stock or ½ bouillon cube dissolved in ½ cup hot water

2 scallions (green onions), sliced
¼ pound butter
3 eggs
½ teaspoon salt
¾ cup sifted flour
¾ cup milk

Soak the peas in water to cover overnight. Soak the chipped beef in water to cover for 4 hours. Drain the peas, rinse, and cover with fresh water. Cook over medium heat 1 hour. Drain. Drain the chipped beef, add fresh water, and cook over medium heat for 30 minutes. Drain. Combine the peas and beef in a saucepan and add the pepper, chili peppers, thyme, stock, and scallions. Cover and cook over low heat for 30 minutes.

Cream 3 tablespoons of the butter. Add the eggs and salt, beating well. Add the flour and milk alternately, beating well. Add the remaining butter to the bean mixture, mixing gently. Drop the batter into the saucepan by the tablespoon. Cover and cook 15 minutes.

## IRIS SALAD

1 clove garlic, minced
¼ cup vinegar
¼ teaspoon salt
⅛ teaspoon pepper
¼ teaspoon paprika
¾ cup salad or olive oil
1 tablespoon chopped green pepper
1 tablespoon chopped pimento

1 tablespoon chopped green olives
1 tablespoon chopped sweet pickles
2 heads romaine lettuce
3 tomatoes, peeled and sliced ½ inch thick
3 hard-cooked eggs, sliced
¼ cup chopped blanched almonds
2 bananas, diced

Place the garlic in the vinegar and allow to remain for 30 minutes. Strain, discarding the garlic. Combine the salt, pepper, paprika, oil, and vinegar in a bowl. Mix all the ingredients thoroughly. Add the green pepper, pimento, olives, and pickles. Mix well and chill.

Wash and dry the lettuce thoroughly. Arrange the leaves on individual plates. Place 2 slices of tomato on each plate, and place egg slices on the tomatoes. Sprinkle some almonds on each. Add the diced bananas to each portion. Pour the salad dressing over each salad and serve.

## BAKED BANANAS WITH COCONUT CREAM

1 cup heavy cream
1 cup fresh or dried grated coconut
6 large firm bananas
4 tablespoons melted butter

1 tablespoon cinnamon
½ cup sugar
½ cup lime or lemon juice

Combine the cream and coconut in a bowl, place in the refrigerator, and soak for 30 minutes. Peel the bananas and place in a buttered baking dish. Mix the butter, cinnamon, sugar, and lime juice together and pour over the bananas. Bake in a 350° oven for 25 minutes, basting occasionally. Strain the cream, squeezing all the liquid from the coconut. Whip the cream and serve with the hot bananas.

*HAITI*

Although most people think of Spanish as the language of the Caribbean, this does not hold true for Haiti, where French is the official language. Official or not, the actual means of communication for most Haitians is Creole, which may be roughly described as a strange mixture of French, English, Spanish, and African.

There is something definitely foreign about Haiti: the language, the people, the perfumed air (although this sounds as if it were stolen from a travel folder, it is correct in this case). Even the food is off the beaten path, although there are French overtones (or undertones?) to many dishes.

Rum, known as *rhum* in Haiti, is the national alcoholic drink; it is prepared from the locally grown sugar cane. There are numerous varieties, and the best of them is indeed a fine product. Barbancourt is the great name among the *rhums*. Rum is served straight or in mixed drinks and is inexpensive. Many restaurants serve sugar, ice, and limes with the rum, permitting the diner to mix the proportions to suit himself.

If there is one simple dish that typifies the food of the peasants, it is probably the rice and beans or peas of the country folk. It is eaten at almost every meal and as a separate course. Haiti is surrounded by the sea, and fish dishes are often outstanding. The recipe for *huîtres marinées* (pickled oysters) is typical of the unusual ways fish is prepared. There are numerous good beef, pork, and poultry dishes to supplement the seafood, which nevertheless forms the basis of much of Haiti's cuisine.

Desserts are great specialties here, for the people are fond of sweet foods. Ice creams made from locally grown fruit are of particular importance. The coconut ice cream is often unbelievably rich, far surpassing

369

the commercial product to which we have become accustomed. Sweet potatoes, cheap and nourishing, are eaten everywhere in the country and are often combined with sugar and syrup to make puddings and pies.

Haitian fruits are among the finest in the world; however, it is not an exotic fruit that is the favorite, for the people's choice is the familiar orange. The recipe for an orange soufflé in this section is not a dish of the country people but an example of high cuisine in the larger cities. Every meal in Haiti ends with small cups of the nation's fine coffee, served black and very sweet.

Having enjoyed a tremendous tourist boom, the island has large numbers of fine, modern hotels, serving good and often superb food. While the hotels occasionally prepare some native food, this is more easily obtained in the towns and villages. Local specialties are available in Port-au-Prince at a restaurant called Aux Cosaques, and also at Le Picardie in Pétionville.

There are people who enjoy a vacation only in a foreign country. For them, Haiti is ideal, for it has a degree of the exotic that is difficult to define. Put it this way: you never for a moment feel as if you're in Brooklyn or your own home town. In addition, it is quite close to the United States, so you have the maximum of foreignness and the minimum of traveling expense.

## HAITIAN RHUM PUNCH

3 teaspoons sugar
3 tablespoons lemon juice
1 tablespoon nutmeg

Cracked ice
3 cups rum
Mint leaves

Combine the sugar, lemon juice, and nutmeg. Stir until the sugar is completely dissolved. Add cracked ice and fill each glass with the rum. Stir. Garnish with several fresh mint leaves or use a few drops of mint flavoring.

## PICKLED OYSTERS

### HUÎTRES MARINÉES

2 cups vinegar
12 small white onions
3 chili peppers, sliced, or ¾ teaspoon dried ground chili peppers

2 teaspoons salt
6 peppercorns
36 oysters

Combine the vinegar, onions, chili, salt, and peppercorns in a large jar or container with a tight-fitting cover. Place the oysters in a bowl and pour boiling water over them. Leave in the water for 3 minutes. Drain well. Place the oysters in the vinegar mixture. Cover and place in the refrigerator for at least 3 days. Serve cold as an appetizer or cocktail accompaniment.

## SHRIMP AND AVOCADO, VINAIGRETTE

CREVETTES ET AVOCATS, VINAIGRETTE

1 pound cooked shrimp
3 avocados
¼ teaspoon dry mustard
½ teaspoon salt
¼ teaspoon black pepper

⅓ cup olive oil
3 tablespoons wine vinegar
1 onion, chopped
1 clove garlic, minced

Shell the shrimp and cut into small pieces. Cut the avocados in half and carefully scoop out the meat, reserving the shells. Cut the avocado meat into small cubes and combine with the shrimp. Mix the mustard, salt, and pepper in a bowl. Gradually add the oil, mixing carefully until the spices are dissolved. Add the vinegar, onion, and garlic and beat well. Pour over the shrimp and avocado mixture and mix carefully. Fill the shells with the mixture. Serve as an appetizer or salad.

## CHICKEN SOUP, HAITIAN STYLE

SOUPE AU POULET

1 tablespoon salt
½ teaspoon black pepper
4-pound chicken, disjointed
3 tablespoons butter
½ pound ham or a ham bone
3 quarts water
1 chili pepper, sliced, or ¼ teaspoon dried ground chili peppers

2 onions, chopped
1 stalk celery
3 potatoes, peeled and cut into quarters
2 sweet potatoes, peeled and cut into small cubes
2 tablespoons flour
2 tablespoons tomato sauce

Combine the salt and pepper and rub it into the chicken thoroughly. Melt the butter in a large saucepan and brown the chicken in it on all sides. Add the ham, water, chili peppers, onions, and celery. Bring to a boil and skim the top. Cover and cook over medium heat for 1 hour. Add the potatoes, carrots, and sweet potatoes. Cover and cook for 1½ hours. Mix the flour and tomato sauce to a smooth paste. Add 1 cup of the soup, mixing constantly. Return this mixture to the balance of the soup, mixing well. Bring to a boil and cook over low heat for 10 minutes. Correct seasoning. Serve hot. If desired as a one-course meal, use 2 chickens.

## FLAMING LOBSTER

### HOMARD FLAMBÉ

| | |
|---|---|
| 2 tablespoons olive oil | 1 teaspoon black pepper |
| ½ cup chili sauce | 3 boiled lobsters, split in half |
| ½ cup wine vinegar | ½ cup rum, heated |

Heat the olive oil, chili sauce, vinegar, and pepper in a saucepan. Remove the lobster meat carefully and cut into large pieces, reserving the shells of the body. Add the lobster meat to the sauce and cook over low heat for 5 minutes. Correct seasoning. Fill the shells with the mixture. Place a half lobster on each plate and pour the rum over it. Set aflame immediately before serving.

## VEAL WITH CASHEW NUT SAUCE

### ESCALOPE AUX NOIX

| | |
|---|---|
| 2 teaspoons salt | 3 tablespoons tomato sauce |
| 1 teaspoon black pepper | 1½ cups water |
| 2 cloves garlic, minced | 2 onions, chopped |
| 3 pounds veal, cut into 1-inch cubes | 1 teaspoon flour |
| 4 tablespoons butter | 1 teaspoon Worcestershire sauce |
| 2 cups cashew nuts | |

Mix the salt, pepper, and garlic to a smooth paste. Roll the veal in it. Melt the butter in a casserole or Dutch oven; brown the veal in it. Add the nuts, tomato sauce, water, and onions. Cover and cook over low heat for 1 hour. Mix the flour and Worcestershire sauce together and add to the gravy, stirring constantly. Cook, uncovered, for 30 minutes, or until veal is very tender. Correct seasoning. Serve with boiled rice.

## ORANGE SOUFFLÉ

### SOUFFLÉ AUX ORANGES

| | |
|---|---|
| 4 tablespoons butter | 5 egg yolks |
| 4 tablespoons flour | 5 tablespoons sugar |
| 1½ cups light cream, scalded | 1 orange, peeled and sliced thin |
| 3 tablespoons grated orange rind | 2 tablespoons confectioners' sugar |
| 2 teaspoons orange extract | 6 egg whites |
| 2 tablespoons curaçao or brandy | |

Melt the butter in a saucepan. Add the flour and mix until smooth. Gradually add the cream, stirring constantly until the boiling point is reached. Cook over low heat for 5 minutes, stirring occasionally. Add the orange rind, orange extract, and the liquor. Remove from heat and cool for 10 minutes. Beat the egg yolks and sugar in a bowl. Gradually add the cream mixture, beating constantly to prevent curdling. Cool for 20 minutes.

Butter a 2-quart soufflé dish (or other ovenproof dish, preferably one with straight-edge sides) and dust with sugar. Place the orange slices on the bottom of the dish and sprinkle with the confectioners' sugar. Preheat oven to 350°. Beat the egg whites in a bowl until stiff but not dry and fold them into the orange mixture gently and carefully. Pour into the soufflé dish. Bake for 30 minutes in a 350° oven, or until lightly browned. Do not open the oven under any circumstances until at least 20 minutes have passed. The soufflé should be fairly well set, otherwise the center will be too moist. Serve immediately when ready, or the soufflé will fall.

## PUERTO RICO

The island of Puerto Rico is about five hours' flying time southeast of Miami, and may be said to be situated roughly between the Caribbean Sea and the Atlantic Ocean. U.S. visitors to this sunny land, where there is some sunshine about 355 days out of every year, never fail to notice that although the atmosphere is Spanish, there is definitely a feeling of being at home because of the considerable amount of English spoken.

In addition to boasting of their weather, Puerto Ricans are entitled to be proud of their wonderful seafood. Deep-sea fishing is unusually good here, and fine catches are made regularly, both by sportsmen and by commercial fishermen. Lobsters are good, and the local waters are filled with a wide variety of fish of all sorts. But although fresh fish is plentiful, it must be admitted that most people prefer to eat the dried salt cod imported from Newfoundland and Spain. The shrimp (often of unbelievable size) and crabs are more than good; they have been acclaimed by gourmets as among the finest in the world. Many excellent local dishes are prepared from these delicately flavored crustaceans. *Asopao,* really "soupy rice," is an important dish made of rice and either seafood or chicken. The shrimp version of *asopao* is considerably more interesting to the enterprising gourmet than the chicken *asopao*.

Rum is the favorite drink of the islands, and is inexpensive and high in quality. It is the custom to prepare your own drink by mixing the desired portions of rum, ice, limes, and sugar to suit the individual taste.

The island is becoming industrialized at a fast pace but generally may still be classified as an agricultural area. Sugar, tobacco, coffee, and all sorts of fruits and vegetables are grown in abundance. At one time sugar constituted almost the sole crop; at the present time a reasonable amount of diversification exists although not enough to satisfy certain critics.

There is definitely a Spanish quality to the food and tastes of the people, but certain American touches have been noted. In general, however, the people prefer such old favorites as *arroz con pollo* (chicken and rice but with local modifications). Roast suckling pig is probably the favorite dish of everyone, although it is usually reserved for holiday occasions.

Desserts are not unusual here, being limited largely to a few familiar standbys such as fresh fruit, ice cream, and guava jelly. There are a few coconut and banana desserts, and of course the tourist hotels serve American-style desserts. The Puerto Ricans prefer to eat their candies as dessert; these are sold at all street corners and are probably better than the usual desserts. Black coffee, usually served quite strong, is the typical end to a fine dinner. At breakfast, however, it is always prepared half and half with hot milk (*cafe con leche*). Puerto Rican coffee is of good quality but has not yet found its true level in the world's coffee markets.

An interesting habit of the Puerto Ricans is their love of little snacks purchased at street corners throughout the day; of these, the leading favorite is pork cracklings, possibly not too sanitary but very delicious.

## FROZEN DAIQUIRI, PUERTO RICAN STYLE

| | |
|---|---|
| 2 tablespoons powdered sugar | 6 large jiggers pale rum (Puerto |
| 5 tablespoons lime or lemon juice | Rican type) |
| | Cracked ice |

Place cocktail or champagne glasses in the refrigerator about 30 minutes before they are needed. Put the sugar, lime juice, and rum in an electric blender. Crack the ice very fine and add to the blender. Run the blender for about 2 minutes. Pour into the chilled glasses and serve immediately. Small straws may be served with this drink if desired.

*Note: Although the daiquiri probably originated in Cuba, the frozen style has become a Puerto Rican specialty.*

## ONION SOUP

SOPA DE CEBOLLA

3 tablespoons butter
5 onions, chopped
1½ cups blanched almonds

8 cups stock or 3 cans consommé and
3 cans water
6 slices toast
1 cup grated Gruyère cheese

Melt the butter in a large saucepan. Add the onions and sauté for 20 minutes, stirring frequently. Grind the almonds as fine as possible. Add to the onions, together with the stock. Cover and cook over low heat for 30 minutes. Correct seasoning. Place a slice of toast on the bottom of each soup plate. Sprinkle some of the grated cheese on each slice. Pour the soup over it and serve. If desired, the soup may be strained.

## ROAST PORK

CERDO ASADO

2 tablespoons lard or butter
2 cups orange juice
1 tablespoon grated orange rind
2 cloves garlic, minced
3 teaspoons salt

1 teaspoon pepper
Dash of cayenne pepper
⅛ teaspoon orégano
6 pounds loin of pork

Melt the fat in a saucepan. Add the orange juice and rind, garlic, 1 teaspoon of the salt, ½ teaspoon of the pepper, the cayenne pepper, and orégano. Mix together. Rub the remaining salt and pepper into the pork. Place the piece of pork in a roasting pan and pour the orange mixture over it. Baste several times.

Roast in a 350° oven for 3 hours, or until the pork is well browned. Baste frequently during the roasting period. Serve thick slices of the pork. Any remaining juice in the pan may be served with the meat.

## FISH STEW

PESCADO GUISADO

½ cup olive oil
2 onions, coarsely chopped
1 carrot, peeled and sliced thin
2 leeks, sliced
2 cloves garlic, minced
2 tablespoons chopped parsley
2 pounds white-meat fish, cut into cubes (use 2 or 3 varieties, if possible)

1 bay leaf
2 teaspoons salt
½ teaspoon pepper
2 tomatoes, cut into small cubes
1 cup water
1 pound shrimp, shelled and cleaned
¼ pound scallops (or conch meat)
½ teaspoon saffron

Heat the olive oil in a deep saucepan. Add the onions, carrot, leeks, garlic, and parsley and sauté for 10 minutes, stirring frequently. Add the fish, bay leaf, salt, pepper, tomatoes, and water and cook for 20 minutes. Add the shrimp, scallops, and saffron, and cook for 10 minutes. Serve in deep soup plates, with lime or lemon wedges on the side. If desired, rub garlic on toast and serve 1 slice with each portion.

*Note: In Puerto Rico this dish is made with the meat of the conch, a large shellfish of the West Indies. Scallops have been substituted, but conch is available in certain parts of the southeastern United States, either fresh or in cans.*

## EGGS AND CORN

HUEVOS DE MAÍZ

3 tablespoons butter
2 onions, sliced
2 green peppers, coarsely chopped
1 cup chopped tomatoes
2 teaspoons salt
½ teaspoon pepper

½ teaspoon chili powder
1 cup canned corn kernels, drained
2 tablespoons olive oil
6 or 12 eggs (use 12 eggs if served as a main course)

Melt the butter in a saucepan. Add the onions and green peppers and sauté for 10 minutes, stirring frequently. Add the tomatoes, 1 teaspoon of the salt, ¼ teaspoon of the pepper, and the chili powder. Cover and cook over low heat for 2 minutes. Correct seasoning.

Spread the mixture on the bottom of a baking dish or divide among 6 individual baking dishes. Spread the corn evenly over the tomato mixture and sprinkle with the olive oil. Break the eggs carefully on top of the corn, as for poached eggs. Sprinkle with the remaining salt and pepper. Bake in a 375° oven for 10 minutes, or until the eggs are set. Serve directly from the baking dish.

## CUCUMBERS WITH ORANGE SAUCE

COHOMBROS CON SALSA DE NARANJA

6 cucumbers
2 tablespoons cornstarch
1½ cups orange juice
3 tablespoons butter

1 teaspoon salt
⅛ teaspoon pepper
2 tablespoons grated orange rind

Wash the cucumbers and scrape lightly, leaving a little peel on them. Cut each cucumber in four. Place in a saucepan with water to cover and cook for 15 minutes. Drain. Mix the cornstarch and orange juice in a saucepan until very smooth. Add the butter and cook over low heat, stirring constantly until the boiling point is reached. Add salt, pepper, and orange rind and cook for 5 minutes, stirring frequently.

## SOUPY RICE, PUERTO RICAN STYLE

ASOPAO

2 onions
1 green pepper
¼ pound bacon
¼ pound salt pork
1 8-ounce can tomato sauce
1 bay leaf
¼ cup olive oil
2 3-pound chickens, with meat removed from bones and cut into small pieces

8 cups stock or 3 cans consommé and 3 cans water
1 teaspoon salt
1 teaspoon pepper
2 cups rice
½ cup capers, drained
½ cup sliced stuffed olives
2 pimentos, sliced
12 fresh or canned asparagus tips
1 cup small canned peas

Chop the onions, green pepper, bacon, and salt pork very fine. Place in a saucepan and cook over low heat for 15 minutes, stirring frequently. Add the tomato sauce and bay leaf and cook 15 minutes longer.

Heat the olive oil in a large saucepan or casserole. Add the chicken and brown lightly on all sides. Add the onion mixture, stock, salt, and pepper. Cover and cook over low heat for 10 minutes. Add the rice and cook over low heat for 30 minutes, stirring frequently; add more liquid if required. Add the capers, olives, and pimentos and cook 5 minutes longer. As the dish should be quite soupy and liquid, add more stock if rice becomes dry.

Heat the asparagus tips and peas separately. Arrange the rice mixture in deep soup plates with all of the liquid, and place the asparagus and peas on top of each portion.

## COCONUT RICE

ARROZ CON COCO

1 cup fresh or dried grated coconut
1½ cups light cream
2 cups rice, washed and drained
1½ quarts milk

¾ cup sugar
2 egg yolks, beaten
1 teaspoon cinnamon

Combine the coconut and cream in a saucepan. Bring to a boil. Remove from the heat and cool for 20 minutes. Press all the liquid from the coconut and discard the pulp.

Place the rice in a saucepan with water to cover and bring it to a boil. Drain immediately. Boil the milk in a large saucepan. Add the rice. Cover and cook over low heat for 20 minutes. Add the coconut cream, sugar, egg yolks, and cinnamon, beating well. Cook for 1 minute only and remove from the heat. Pour into a bowl and chill. Serve ice cold. A little whipped cream may be placed on top if desired.

## ALMOND PUDDING

PUDÍN DE ALMENDRAS

| | |
|---|---|
| ½ cup seedless raisins | 1 cup heavy cream |
| ½ cup white wine | 1 cup bread crumbs |
| 2 eggs | 1 cup finely ground almonds |
| 1 cup sugar | 2 teaspoons cinnamon |
| 1 cup milk | 1 teaspoon nutmeg |

Soak the raisins in the wine for 15 minutes. Drain. Beat the eggs in a bowl. Add the sugar, beating well. Add the milk and cream and mix well. Add the bread crumbs, almonds, cinnamon, nutmeg, and raisins and mix well. Preheat oven to 350°. Butter 6 individual custard cups or other individual dishes. Pour the mixture into it. Place the dishes in a pan of water. Bake in a 350° oven for 25 minutes, or until delicately browned on top and moderately firm. Serve hot or cold. Whipped cream may be placed on each portion.

## THE LESSER ANTILLES

The Greater Antilles are composed of Cuba, Jamaica, Haiti, the Dominican Republic, and Puerto Rico. The Lesser Antilles are those delightful islands curving in a semicircle directly to the southeast of Puerto Rico and then southwest, stretching to the coast of South America. Without exception, the islands are all affiliated to a greater or lesser degree with either the United States, Britain, France, or the Netherlands.

The Virgin Islands were once Danish, but they now form a welcome part of the United States. Since this is a free port, good values are often obtainable, though prices are usually not quite so reasonable as in Curaçao and Panama. The islands were once forgotten by everyone but conscientious State Department clerks. They were once known to barbershop patrons of the nineties as the source of supply of bay rum. The Yankee dollar has caused quite a few changes here—certainly enough to confound the solid and sensible Danish officials who once governed the islands. Luxury hotels, deep-sea fishing yachts, glass-bottom boats, and good bathing attract increasing numbers of visitors. The islands have not been hurt by the local law which permits a divorce after six weeks of residence; thus it is possible to combine the proverbial business with pleasure.

Fruits are important in the local diet and are used in fruit cocktails, salads, and desserts. *Fungi* (corn meal balls) are served with *mauffay* (a salt-pork dish) and are typical examples of the local food. The islanders have an interesting custom of calling breakfast "tea" and of referring to the noonday meal as "breakfast."

In a southeasterly direction from the Virgins (as they are familiarly called) is Saba, an island without a harbor. Since ships cannot come alongside a pier, getting ashore is a difficult operation, particularly when the sea is running. Visitors are brought fairly close to shore in small boats and then carried to dry land by the islanders.

Nevis is a British Crown Colony seldom visited by tourists. It should be more popular with Americans, for it is the birthplace of Alexander Hamilton. Also overlooked is Antigua, noted for its bathing beaches.

Guadeloupe and Martinique, separated by about eighty miles, are unique among the islands of the West Indies. They, and several additional small islands, are all that remain today of the French West Indian colonial empire. Here is a small but charming bit of France. Guadeloupe, while interesting, does not offer as much to the visitor as does Martinique, which has achieved the status of a French province, roughly equivalent to statehood in our own country. They are properly known as the "fortunate islands," as they undoubtedly are.

The food is French but with local touches, emphasis being placed on what is available, mostly fish and fruit, since almost all other foodstuffs have to be imported. *Acra l'en mori* (codfish balls) is an example of a local dish in the French-Martinique manner. The wines and liquors of France are available here at reasonable prices. A local pride is Martinique *rhum*, quite different from the other West Indian products.

Dominica lies between Guadeloupe and Martinique, and is British and very quiet, particularly when compared to the Gallic excitability of its neighbors. It is known for its many rivers, of which there are several hundred.

Saint Lucia has comparatively few accommodations for tourists, for the island is not a regular tourist haunt. Wonderful and enormous lobsters are caught in the surrounding waters, and these are prepared in a variety of ways. No matter how they are prepared, they will be found to be a treat. Fruits, too, are often of exceptional quality.

Saint Vincent, a British colony, has a colorful capital in Kingstown. The fame of the island is directly connected with the notorious Captain Bligh, who commanded the good ship *Bounty*, with orders to obtain breadfruit plants in Tahiti and bring them to Saint Vincent, which was in need of a low-cost food. Charles Laughton was so stubborn—that is, Captain Bligh was so stubborn—that after the mutiny he obtained another ship and subsequently completed his assignment by actually bringing the breadfruit to Saint Vincent in 1793, about six years after the mutiny. Mr. Christian, indeed!

Barbados is one of the few islands of the West Indies that produces green vegetables, but of course sugar cane is the principal crop. Barbados rum is good and bargain-priced. In the way of food, there is nothing unusual except flying fish, which are very good eating.

Grenada is the famous "spice island" of the West Indies. The delightful aroma of nutmeg and clove is everywhere, often noticeable at a considerable distance offshore. Grenada has very few restaurants, but the hotels offer good and sometimes fine meals.

Tobago is likely to become an important tourist spot someday. It has beautiful beaches, excellent hotels often serving wonderful meals, and many other creature comforts.

Trinidad offers the exotic, for it has a polyglot population, loads of color, and much excitement. This is the home of the calypso and also of the steel band. Calypso competitions are held in January and are worth attending.

Very small oysters, a Trinidadian specialty, are noteworthy, as are the shellfish in general. Trinidad has a large East Indian population, and Indian food is an accepted part of the island fare. Chicken *pelau*, not pilau (U.S.) or *pulao* (Pakistan), is a transplanted dish from the homeland. Pepperpot, a spicy meat dish, is a great local favorite; many people keep the pepperpot going steadily, merely adding fresh meat as required.

Trinidad produces rum in substantial volume; its retail price is extremely low, both by the bottle and by the drink. Angostura bitters originated and still is manufactured here.

No discussion of these islands could possibly omit Curaçao and Aruba, the principal islands of the Dutch West Indies. These islands, however, are not part of the Lesser Antilles and are more correctly referred to as the Netherlands Antilles. However formal the correct and official designation, the islands are still the same friendly places. Most tourists see only Curaçao, famous as one of the best shopping ports in the world, particularly for perfumes, watches, linens, and liquors. The local food is quite good and varied, with dishes from many different lands available.

The famous liqueur, curaçao, is made here from the peel of locally grown oranges. This product is fairly good, but not up to the standard of the Dutch product, which is made from local orange peel, shipped to the mother country, and processed there. The Dutch product is then returned to the island of Curaçao and sold to tourists who happily believe that they have purchased a regionally produced liquor.

## FISH CAKES

ACRA L'EN MORI

| | |
|---|---|
| ½ pound fish fillets | 1 cake or package yeast |
| ½ onion | 1½ cups lukewarm water |
| 2 cloves garlic, minced | 2 cups sifted flour |
| ½ teaspoon thyme | 1½ teaspoons salt |
| ¼ teaspoon pepper | Fat for deep-fat frying |

Grind the fish and onion in a food mill or chopper. Add the garlic, thyme, and pepper and mix well. Combine the yeast and ½ cup of the lukewarm water. Soak for 5 minutes. Mix until smooth. Combine with the balance of the lukewarm water. Sift the flour and salt into a bowl. Add the yeast mixture, stirring until a soft batter is formed. Add more water or flour if necessary to have a batter of pouring consistency. Add the fish mixture, beating well until very smooth. Cover and set aside in a warm place for 2 hours.

Heat the fat in a deep saucepan to 360°. Drop the mixture into the fat by tablespoons, but do not fry more than a few at a time. Fry until the fish cakes are browned. Drain well. Serve hot. A smaller version of these fish cakes makes an excellent hors d'oeuvre.

## TRINIDAD RUM PUNCH

| | |
|---|---|
| ⅓ cup water | ⅓ cup lime or lemon juice |
| ⅓ cup sugar | 1⅛ cups Trinidad rum |
| 1 cup cracked ice | 6 pieces lime or lemon rind |
| ⅛ teaspoon bitters | |

Combine the water and sugar in a saucepan. Bring to a boil and cook over low heat for 15 minutes. Set aside to cool for 1 hour. Place the cracked ice in a mixing glass or pitcher. Add the bitters, lime juice, rum, and sugar syrup. Mix well. Strain into 6 chilled glasses and decorate each with a twist of lime or lemon rind.

## CREOLE PEA SOUP

½ cup split peas
3 tablespoons butter
1½ pounds beef, cubed small
1 onion, chopped
2 quarts water
1 carrot
2 teaspoons salt

¼ teaspoon pepper
2 sprigs parsley
½ teaspoon thyme
⅛ teaspoon nutmeg
2 white potatoes, peeled and cubed
2 sweet potatoes, peeled and cubed
½ cup chopped spinach

Wash the peas and discard any imperfect ones. Soak overnight in water to cover, if the presoaked variety is not used. Drain well. Melt the butter in a large saucepan. Add the beef cubes and onion and sauté until brown. Add the split peas, water, carrot, salt, pepper, parsley, thyme, and nutmeg. Cover and cook for 1 hour. Add the white and sweet potatoes and the spinach. Cover and cook for 30 minutes, or until the beef and vegetables are tender.

## CRAB GUMBO

2 onions, chopped
4 tomatoes, chopped, or 1 cup
   canned tomatoes
7 cups water
10 okra, sliced
2 bay leaves
3 sprigs parsley

1½ teaspoons salt
½ teaspoon thyme
¼ teaspoon dried ground chili peppers
4 tablespoons butter
1 pound fresh or canned lump crab meat

Combine the onions, tomatoes, water, okra, bay leaves, parsley, salt, thyme, and chili peppers in a saucepan. Cover and cook over medium heat for 30 minutes, stirring occasionally. Melt the butter in a frying pan. Add the crab meat and sauté lightly until delicately brown, stirring frequently. Add to the tomato mixture. Cover and cook over low heat for 30 minutes. Correct seasoning. Serve with boiled rice.

## FISH PUDDING

2 onions
1 clove garlic
1 green pepper
1 stalk celery
¼ pound butter
½ cup tomato sauce

2½ pounds fillets of bluefish, mackerel, or other similar fish
½ cup cracker meal
4 eggs, well beaten
¾ cup milk
2 teaspoons salt
½ teaspoon pepper
½ teaspoon mace

Place the onions, garlic, green pepper, and celery together in a chopping bowl. Chop very fine. Melt the butter in a saucepan. Add the onion mixture and sauté for 10 minutes, stirring frequently. Add the tomato sauce and cook over low heat for 10 minutes. Remove from the heat and set aside.

Grind the fish in a food chopper or chop it fine. Add the tomato mixture, and also the cracker meal, eggs, milk, salt, pepper, and mace. Mix all the ingredients together until well blended and smooth. Preheat oven to 350°. Pour the mixture into a buttered baking dish or casserole. Sprinkle the top with cracker meal or bread crumbs, if desired. Bake in a 350° oven for 35 minutes, or until firm and browned on top.

## VIRGIN ISLANDS POT ROAST

### DAUBE MEAT

4 pounds beef (top round or top sirloin), cut 1½ inches thick
2 teaspoons salt
1 teaspoon pepper
2 cloves garlic, minced
½ teaspoon thyme
½ teaspoon mace

½ teaspoon nutmeg
2 tablespoons chopped parsley
3 onions, sliced
2 tomatoes, chopped
¼ cup vinegar
2 tablespoons butter
½ cup boiling water

Wash and dry the meat. Combine the salt, pepper, garlic, thyme, mace, and nutmeg. Rub into the meat thoroughly. Place the meat in a bowl and add the parsley, onions, tomatoes, and vinegar; mix well. Cover and marinate for 2 hours. Remove the meat, reserving the marinade. Melt the butter in a saucepan. Brown the meat well over high heat. Reduce heat and add the boiling water and the reserved marinade. Cover and cook over low heat for 1 hour, or until the meat is tender.

## TRINIDAD PEPPERPOT

4-pound chicken, disjointed
2 pounds pork, cubed
1 pound corned beef, cubed, or 2
pounds pickled spareribs, with ribs
cut apart
2 cups water
3 onions, sliced

1 clove garlic, minced
½ teaspoon dried ground chili peppers
½ teaspoon thyme
2 tablespoons dark brown sugar
2 tablespoons Worcestershire sauce
½ teaspoon pepper

Combine the chicken, pork, corned beef, and water in a saucepan. Cover and cook over medium heat for 2 hours. Add the onions, garlic, chili peppers, thyme, brown sugar, Worcestershire sauce, and pepper and mix together. Cover and cook over low heat for 1 hour, or until meats are tender. Correct seasoning. Serve hot.

## VIRGIN ISLANDS PORK AND FISH

MAUFFAY

½ pound salt pork, cubed
3 onions, chopped
1 pound pork, cut into 1-inch cubes
1 pound beef, cut into 1-inch cubes
7 cups water

2 fillets of fish (snapper, sole, bluefish), cut into 1-inch pieces
1 teaspoon salt
½ teaspoon pepper
¾ teaspoon thyme
3 tomatoes, chopped
½ cup corn meal

Place the salt pork in a saucepan. Cook over low heat until some of the fat is melted. Add the onions, pork, and beef and brown well. Add the water and cook over medium heat for 30 minutes. Add the fish, salt, pepper, thyme, and tomatoes. Add the corn meal gradually, stirring constantly to prevent lumps. Cook over low heat for 30 minutes. Correct seasoning. Serve with *fungi* (see recipe in this section).

## CHICKEN AND PORK, GUADELOUPE STYLE

COLOMBO CREOLE

½ cup olive or salad oil
2 onions, chopped
3-pound chicken, disjointed
1½ pounds boneless pork, cubed
2 cloves garlic, minced
3 cups diced eggplant
6 carrots, sliced

6 potatoes, peeled and cubed
2 teaspoons salt
½ teaspoon pepper
¼ teaspoon dried ground chili peppers
½ teaspoon thyme
1 tablespoon curry powder
2 cups water

Heat the oil in a saucepan. Add the onions and sauté for 10 minutes, stirring frequently. Remove the onions and set them aside. Add the chicken and pork and brown on all sides. Return the onions to the saucepan. Cover and cook over low heat for 25 minutes, stirring frequently.

Add the garlic, eggplant, carrots, potatoes, salt, pepper, chili peppers, thyme, curry powder, and water. Mix gently. Cover and cook over low heat for 45 minutes, or until the chicken is tender. Correct seasoning. Serve hot.

*Note: This dish is an adaptation of an Indian curry, with local variations, and is an example of two different cuisines combined in one dish.*

## TRINIDAD CHICKEN PELAU

¼ cup flour
4 teaspoons salt
½ teaspoon pepper
2 3-pound chickens, disjointed
½ cup olive oil
2 onions, chopped
2 tomatoes, peeled and cubed

2 teaspoons sugar
½ teaspoon thyme
3 cups stock or 1 can consommé
 and 1½ cans water
1½ cups rice
¼ cup chopped ripe olives

Combine the flour, 2 teaspoons of the salt, and 1 teaspoon of the pepper. Roll the chicken parts in it. Heat ¼ cup of the olive oil in a heavy saucepan or casserole. Add the chicken and brown well on all sides. Remove the chicken and set aside. Add the remaining olive oil and the onions and cook over medium heat for 5 minutes, stirring frequently.

Add the tomatoes, sugar, thyme, and the remaining salt and pepper and cook over medium heat for 5 minutes. Return the chicken to the saucepan and add the stock. Cover and cook over low heat for 45 minutes. Add the rice and mix gently. Cover and cook over low heat for 25 minutes, or until the chicken and rice are tender, adding a little more water if necessary. When cooked, there should be no liquid remaining but the rice should be moist. Correct seasoning. Sprinkle the olives on top and serve.

## CORN MEAL BALLS

FUNGI

1 cup corn meal
1 cup cold water
2 cups boiling water

1½ teaspoons salt
3 tablespoons butter

Mix the corn meal and cold water to a smooth paste. Have the boiling water and salt in a saucepan. Add the corn meal paste gradually, stirring constantly until thick. Add the butter and cook over low heat for 20 minutes, stirring frequently. Grease a teacup thoroughly. Using a tablespoon of corn meal at a time, shape into balls in the cup, and turn out. Serve hot with *mauffay* (see recipe in this section).

## CORN CAKES

¼ pound butter
½ cup sugar
¾ cup sifted flour
½ cup corn meal
2 teaspoons baking powder

¼ teaspoon cinnamon
¼ teaspoon nutmeg
2 eggs
½ cup milk

Cream the butter until smooth. Add the sugar, beating until light and fluffy. Sift the flour, corn meal, baking powder, cinnamon, and nutmeg together. Add to the butter mixture, beating well. Add the eggs and milk, again beating well. Preheat oven to 350°. Pour into buttered muffin pans. Bake in a 350° oven for 20 minutes, or until a cake tester comes out clean. Serve hot or cold. The corn cakes may be served as a dessert or as a sweet bread.

## GROUNDNUT MACAROONS

2 egg whites
½ cup sugar

⅔ cup ground peanuts
1 teaspoon vanilla extract

Beat the egg whites until stiff but not dry. Add the sugar gradually, beating steadily. Add the peanuts and vanilla, mixing lightly. Preheat oven to 300°. Butter a baking sheet well. Force the previous mixture through a pastry tube or drop by the tablespoon onto the baking sheet. Do not place the macaroons too close together. Bake in a 300° oven for 20 minutes, or until firm.

## CONKIES

¼ pound butter
¼ cup sugar
3 eggs

½ cup cooked or canned pumpkin
½ cup milk
2 cups corn meal

Cream the butter until smooth. Add the sugar and beat together until light. Add the eggs and beat well. Add the pumpkin, milk, and corn meal and mix well until smooth in texture.

Form into 2-inch balls. Wrap each one in aluminum foil or parchment paper. If parchment paper is used, tie each one securely with white thread; this will not be necessary if aluminum foil is used. Drop into boiling water and cook for 1 hour. Drain well. Serve hot in the paper in which they were cooked. They make an unusual dessert.

## PEANUT PIE

1½ cups sifted flour
½ teaspoon salt
½ cup shortening
4 tablespoons cold water
2 eggs

½ cup sugar
½ cup milk
½ cup molasses
¾ cup coarsely chopped peanuts
½ teaspoon vanilla extract

Sift the flour (reserving 1 tablespoon) and salt into a bowl. Cut in the shortening with a pastry blender or two knives. Add the water, tossing lightly until a ball of dough is formed. Roll out on a lightly floured surface to fit a 9-inch pie plate. Fit into the plate and flute the edges. Preheat oven to 425°.

Beat the eggs in a bowl. Add the sugar and remaining flour and beat until light and fluffy. Add the milk and molasses and beat well. Add the peanuts and vanilla. Mix lightly. Pour into the lined pie plate. Bake in a 425° oven for 10 minutes; reduce heat to 350° and bake for 25 minutes longer, or until a knife comes out clean. Serve hot or cold, with whipped cream if desired.

## ARROWROOT AND APPLE CUSTARD

| | |
|---|---|
| 3 tablespoons butter | 2 eggs, beaten |
| 4 apples, peeled and sliced | ⅓ cup sugar |
| 1 tablespoon arrowroot | 2 tablespoons seedless raisins |
| 2 cups milk | ½ cup crushed cornflakes |

Melt the butter in a saucepan. Add the apples and cook over low heat for 10 minutes, stirring occasionally. Mix the arrowroot and 3 tablespoons of the milk to a smooth paste. Add the eggs and sugar and mix well. Place the remaining milk in a saucepan and bring to a boil. Pour gradually into the arrowroot and egg mixture, stirring constantly. Return to the saucepan. Cook over low heat, stirring constantly until the mixture is thickened, about 2 minutes. Add the apples and the raisins and mix well. Preheat oven to 350°.

Pour into a buttered pie plate and sprinkle with the cornflakes. Bake in a 350° oven for 20 minutes. Serve hot or cold, with whipped cream, if desired.

# SOUTH AMERICA

*Argentina*
*Bolivia*
*Brazil*
*Chile*
*Colombia*
*Ecuador*
*The Guianas*
*Paraguay*
*Peru*
*Uruguay*
*Venezuela*

*ARGENTINA*

Air travelers to Buenos Aires are surprised to find the world's largest airport, the Ministro Pistarini, serving that great metropolis. But their surprise continues to mount as they find Buenos Aires to be an amazingly sophisticated city, having a great deal in common with Paris in both appearance and atmosphere. The city has a population of more than 3,000,000 but greater Buenos Aires totals about 4,500,000.

Tourists must likewise adjust to the mealtimes. Although Argentinians conform to the general South American custom of the late dinner hour, the lateness of the hour reaches its extreme in Buenos Aires. Breakfast is a simple meal, inevitably served in your room. Lunch comes early, about noon, and is an extremely substantial meal of many courses. Food is quite cheap here, and the Argentinians love to eat well. Tea is served about 5 P.M. or so, and is usually much more satisfying than merely tea and cake; meat is often served at teatime! Dinner is not eaten until 10 P.M. and often much later than that, particularly in the smarter restaurants and hotels. The dinner rush hour in Buenos Aires is about 11 P.M., and possibly as late as midnight.

As everyone has probably heard, Argentina is the land of the steak. Everyone eats, and in tremendous quantities, the excellent native beef. Until fairly recently a steak was automatically served with every meal whether it was ordered or not, and without additional charge, so cheap and plentiful was the local meat. Although Argentinians prefer steaks broiled over charcoal, there are some unusual steak recipes, one of which is furnished in this section.

389

Most tourists are surprised at the frequency with which Italian dishes appear on the menus, but this is because of the large number of Italian immigrants. Argentinian favorites include the *puchero,* a meat and vegetable soup something on the order of a New England boiled dinner, but with more meat; beef stews, such as the *carbonada;* and sweet desserts, of which the *dulce de leche* is a typical example.

Beer is a fine local product, but Argentina is primarily a country of wine drinkers. Both red and white wines are produced here, among which the best known are Casa de Piedra and Bianchi Cabernet. Champagnes are relatively cheap and of high quality.

Shopping for leather and suede articles on Buenos Aires' famous, narrow Calle Florida can be great fun, particularly in view of the bargains offered. When you get hungry, you'll find a great many of the city's best restaurants and hotels nearby. The Hotels Plaza and Alvear Palace have exceptional restaurants. Tourists seem to be extremely fond of La Cabaña, where diners select their own steaks before sitting down to dinner. In addition there are such places as the Shorthorn Grill, La Estancia, and many others. All meat-and-potatoes men are immediately referred to Buenos Aires and to Argentina; however, it will be only a matter of time before they are sated and start looking for a fish dinner and a green salad.

The real, native, and most widespread drink of all is *maté,* the so-called Paraguayan tea. *Maté* is prepared from the very young leaves of an evergreen tree, and the resulting infusion tastes much like tea but somewhat less astringent in flavor. Although efforts have been made to introduce the beverage in the United States, they have not been too successful, since most people do not like it until they become better acquainted with it.

## ROSITA COCKTAIL

| | |
|---|---|
| 6 jiggers gin | 1 jigger Crème de Rose (optional) |
| 2 jiggers brandy | 6 maraschino cherries |
| 2 teaspoons grenadine | 6 pieces lemon peel |
| 1 teaspoon lemon juice | |

Place the gin, brandy, grenadine, lemon juice, and Crème de Rose in a cocktail shaker with about 8 ice cubes. Shake well for at least 1 minute and pour into chilled cocktail glasses. Garnish each glass with a maraschino cherry and a slim twist of lemon peel.

*Note: Crème de Rose is a French cordial made from rose petals and is difficult to obtain in the United States, although quite common in South America. It merely gives the drink an aroma. As a substitute, place a gardenia or rose petal in each glass.*

## PICKLED SQUABS

POLLITO EN ESCABECHE

4 onions, sliced thin
3 small squabs, pigeons, or partridges, cut in half
2 cloves garlic, minced
2 pimentos, sliced thin
3 tablespoons chopped parsley
1 stalk celery, chopped
4 bay leaves

½ cup tarragon vinegar
½ cup white wine
1 cup olive oil
½ teaspoon black pepper
⅛ teaspoon dried ground chili peppers
2 teaspoons salt

Place half the onions in an earthenware casserole. Arrange the squabs on top and cover with the remaining onions, the garlic, pimentos, parsley, celery, and bay leaves. In a bowl combine the vinegar, wine, olive oil, pepper, chili peppers, and salt. Pour over the contents of the casserole. Cover the casserole and cook over low heat for 45 minutes, or until tender.

Remove the squabs and continue boiling the sauce until it is reduced to about half of the original quantity. Pour over the squabs and place in a refrigerator until cold. Serve cold, together with the sauce. This dish makes an excellent appetizer for a dinner. It may also be served as a luncheon dish.

*Note: This dish is usually made with partridges. However, breast of chicken, squabs, or any game birds may be used.*

## ARGENTINE BOILED DINNER

PUCHERO CRIOLLO

1 cup dried or 2 cups canned, drained chick-peas
2 pounds short ribs of beef
½ pound lean salt pork, sliced
3½-pound chicken, disjointed
3 spicy sausages (Spanish, if possible)
6 carrots, peeled
6 onions

6 cloves garlic, minced
1 small squash, peeled and sliced
6 tomatoes
1 cabbage, cut into eighths
1 green pepper, chopped
6 potatoes, peeled
6 leeks or scallions (green onions)
2 tablespoons chopped parsley

If dried chick-peas are used, soak overnight in water to cover. Drain. Measure 4 quarts of water into a large saucepan. Add the soaked chick-peas. (If canned chick-peas are being used, do not add until the vegetables are added.) Bring the water to a boil. Add the beef, pork, and chicken. Cover and cook over medium heat for 1½ hours. Add the sausages and carrots. Cook for 30 minutes. Add the onions, garlic, squash, tomatoes, cabbage, green pepper, potatoes, leeks, and parsley. Cook for 30 minutes, or until potatoes are tender. Correct seasoning. (No salt is provided in the recipe, because of the salt pork and sausage.)

Remove the meats and arrange on a platter. Place the vegetables around the meat. Serve the soup in individual plates at the same time.

## FRIED STEAKS

### CHURRASCO REBOSADO

| | |
|---|---|
| 4 egg yolks | ½ teaspoon marjoram |
| 1½ cups sifted flour | 4 egg whites, stiffly beaten |
| ½ cup milk | 6 fillets of beef or 6 individual bone- |
| 1 clove garlic, minced | less sirloin steaks |
| 1½ teaspoons salt | 1 cup oil |
| ½ teaspoon pepper | |

Beat the yolks in a bowl. Add the flour, beating until smooth. Add the milk, garlic, salt, pepper, and marjoram and beat again until smooth. Fold in the egg whites carefully. Dip the steaks in the batter, coating them well. Heat the oil in a frying pan until it smokes. Fry the steaks in it for 2 minutes on each side. Serve with boiled rice and a crisp green salad.

## FILLET OF BEEF, MAR DEL PLATA STYLE

### LOMO, MAR DEL PLATA

| | |
|---|---|
| 3 tablespoons butter | ½ cup stock |
| 3-pound fillet of beef (in 1 piece) | 1 onion, chopped |
| 4 slices bacon | 1 bay leaf |
| 2 hard-cooked egg yolks, chopped | 3 peppercorns |
| ½ cup chopped mushrooms | ¼ teaspoon thyme |
| 2 tablespoons chopped parsley | 2 tablespoons flour |
| 2 tablespoons olive oil | 2 tablespoons water |
| 1 cup white wine | ¼ cup bread crumbs |
| | ¼ cup grated Parmesan cheese |

Melt the butter in a skillet. Brown the fillet in it on all sides. Place the bacon on the bottom of a casserole or roasting pan, with the fillet over it. Mix the egg yolks, mushrooms, parsley, and olive oil together and spread it on the fillet. Add wine, stock, onion, bay leaf, peppercorns and thyme.

Roast in a 350° oven for 30 minutes. Turn the fillet over and continue roasting for 40 minutes. Remove the meat and keep warm. Mix the flour and water to a smooth paste and add to the gravy in the casserole. Place over direct heat and cook for 5 minutes, stirring constantly. Discard the bay leaf.

Slice the fillet ½ inch thick. Mix the bread crumbs and Parmesan cheese together and sprinkle it on the sliced fillet. Return the meat to the casserole, crumb side up, and brown under the broiler for 3 minutes.

## CORN PIE

PASTELITO DE CHOCLO

⅓ cup butter
2 onions, chopped
3 green peppers, cut into thin julienne strips
3 tomatoes, chopped
1½ pounds ground beef
⅓ cup sugar
1½ teaspoons salt
⅛ teaspoon pepper
½ cup currants
3 hard-cooked eggs, chopped
3 cups corn kernels, drained and ground
1 cup flour
1 cup milk
7 eggs, beaten

Melt 3 tablespoons of the butter in a saucepan. Add the onions and green peppers and sauté for 10 minutes, stirring frequently. Add the tomatoes and cook over medium heat for 5 minutes. Add the meat, 2 tablespoons of the sugar, 1 teaspoon of the salt, and the pepper. Cook over medium heat for 15 minutes, stirring occasionally. Add the currants and eggs and mix well. Remove from the heat and set aside.

In a separate saucepan, melt the remaining butter. Add the corn and stir. Mix the flour, milk, and remaining sugar and salt to a smooth paste in a bowl. Add to the corn, stirring constantly. Cook over low heat for 10 minutes, stirring occasionally. Set aside to cool for 5 minutes. Add the eggs, beating well. Pour half of the corn mixture into a buttered casserole. Pour the meat mixture on top and cover with the remaining corn mixture. Bake in a 375° oven for 30 minutes. Serve hot, directly from the casserole.

## BUTTER COOKIES

ALFAJORES

⅓ pound butter
1 cup sugar
1 egg
2 egg yolks
1 teaspoon vanilla extract
2 teaspoons grated lemon rind
1½ cups cornstarch
½ cup flour
1 teaspoon baking powder
1 tablespoon brandy

Cream the butter, add the sugar, and continue creaming. Add the egg and egg yolks, beating until light and frothy. Add the vanilla extract and lemon rind. Sift the cornstarch, flour, and baking powder together and add

393

to the butter mixture, mixing well. Add the brandy and knead until smooth. Set aside for 10 minutes. Preheat oven to 325°.

Roll out ½ inch thick on a lightly floured board. Cut rounds with a cooky cutter. Place on a buttered baking sheet.

Bake in a 325° oven for 20 minutes, or until lightly browned. Set aside to cool. Fill each pair of cookies with *dulce de leche* (see recipe in this section).

## SWEET MILK DESSERT

DULCE DE LECHE

2 cups milk
¾ cup sugar
1 teaspoon vanilla extract

Dash of baking soda
1 cup fresh or dried grated coconut

Combine the milk, sugar, vanilla, and baking soda in a saucepan. Bring to a boil. Cook over very low heat 2½ hours, or until the mixture forms a soft ball when a small amount is dropped into cold water. Mix occasionally. Test the mixture once or twice to see whether the desired stage has been reached. Spread the *dulce de leche* between 2 *alfajores* (see recipe in this section). Sprinkle the coconut on a piece of wax paper and roll each cooky on its side so as to pick up the coconut.

*Note: If desired, the Argentine custom may be followed, which is to use condensed milk, instead of regular milk and sugar. Shake 2 cans of condensed milk very well. Place in a saucepan and cover completely with water. Boil rapidly for 1½ hours, making sure that the cans are always covered with water. Cool under cold water. It is not necessary to add sugar, vanilla, or baking soda. Merely spread the alfajores with the contents of the can.*

## *BOLIVIA*

Your Panagra plane (Pan American's affiliate) lands at the El Alto de la Paz Airport some 13,500 feet above sea level in extremely rarefied atmosphere. La Paz, the *de facto* capital of the country, is located at about 12,000 feet, and is therefore *below* the airport. Its only rival to the title of the highest capital in the world is Lhasa, Tibet, but La Paz is certainly the highest capital customarily reached by tourists.

Bolivia is not too far from the equator, and most people think of it as a tropical country; this is certainly true of the nation's lowlands, the Yungas, which are subtropical. In these narrow, steep valleys grow the delicious fruits of the country including the avocados, bananas, cherimoyas, and—particularly worthy of note—the local pineapples. La Paz itself is an amazing city, with an unbelievably colorful Indian population and sights that are sure to startle the tourist who believes that he has seen everything. Its altitude limits your movements for the first few days until some adjustment has been made to the great height, but after that it is possible to ski nearby at a mere 17,000 feet if that is your desire, and assuming that you know how to ski. The weather is extremely variable, and it is warm only in the middle of the day even during the summer.

Possibly because of the high altitude or the chilly weather, the Bolivians are fond of spicy foods, such as *picantes* (tiny pieces of chicken or other ingredients served in a very hot sauce). *Ají de carne* (actually a pepper meat) is a favorite treatment of beef and pork. The food eaten here is similar to that of Chile and Peru, but whereas in those countries red peppers are treated with a moderate amount of respect, in Bolivia all caution is cast aside.

Dinner is usually eaten when the temperature hovers in the low thirties, and hot, thick soups are justifiably popular. An interesting example is the *valdiviano con huevos* (a soup with eggs). Spaghettis and starchy foods of all sorts have become regular parts of the local diet, as heat-producing foods are much needed. *Parilladas* (meat roasted over open fires) are also greatly appreciated. Fresh fish is an unexpected treat in these high altitudes, since it comes from the world's highest navigable lake, Titicaca. A trip across this shallow lake is an unforgettable and very cold experience.

The Bolivians have a particular favorite in *chuño*, the frozen potato beloved of the Indian population. Owing to the altitude, local potatoes are fairly small at the beginning but then they are frozen, thawed, and frozen again. The process may be repeated several additional times, often ending with a potato the size of a golf ball. The net result is that almost all the moisture is removed from the poor little potato, leaving a small ball of practically pure starch. *Chuño* is then used in many different ways, often in Bolivian stews, but also with eggs or fish, to which it adds a rather unique, cheeselike flavor.

There are quite a few good restaurants in La Paz, including Victor's, Daiquiri, and the La Paz Club restaurant. Although local wines and beer are available, the tourist is well advised to use them sparingly during the first few days of a visit because of the extreme altitude. The very best wine, it is agreed, comes from the Cochabamba region, the *muyurina*. Bolivian beer is indeed among the best in South America, if not the very best, as local chauvinists like to claim. Until a little adjustment has been made to the chilly evenings and the high altitude, most tourists are content to do without icy-cold beer, no matter how good it may be.


## SOUP WITH EGGS

### VALDIVIANO CON HUEVOS

½ cup olive or salad oil
5 onions, chopped
3 cloves garlic, minced
½ teaspoon achiote (optional)
½ pound dried beef, shredded

2 quarts stock or 3 cans consommé
  and 3 cans water
½ teaspoon marjoram
6 eggs
4 tablespoons chopped parsley
⅛ teaspoon cayenne pepper

Heat the oil in a saucepan. Add the onions, garlic, and achiote and sauté for 15 minutes, stirring frequently. Add the beef, stock, and marjoram and cook over low heat for 30 minutes. Correct seasoning. Break the eggs carefully into the soup. Cook for 3 minutes over medium heat. Place an egg in each soup plate. Pour the soup over the eggs. Sprinkle with the parsley and cayenne pepper. Serve immediately.


## BAKED FISH FILLETS

### PESCADO AL HORNO

½ pound butter
2 onions, chopped
3 cups bread crumbs
4 egg yolks, beaten
2 tablespoons heavy cream
½ cup sherry

3 teaspoons salt
1 teaspoon pepper
¼ teaspoon nutmeg
6 fillets of sole, snapper, or other
  similar fish

Melt half the butter in a frying pan. Add the onions and sauté for 10 minutes, stirring frequently. Add the bread crumbs and cook over low heat for 2 minutes, stirring constantly. Remove the pan from the heat. Add the egg yolks, mixing constantly. Add the cream, ¼ cup of the sherry, 1½ teaspoons of the salt, ½ teaspoon of the pepper, and the nutmeg. Mix well.

Divide the mixture evenly among the 6 fillets and roll each one up, fastening them with toothpicks. Melt the remaining butter in a baking dish. Place the fillets in it. Sprinkle with the remaining sherry, salt, and pepper. Bake in a 400° oven for 30 minutes, basting frequently. Serve with boiled potatoes and a dry white wine.

## PEPPER PORK

AJÍ DE CARNE

½ cup olive oil
5 onions, chopped
3 cloves garlic, minced
3 tablespoons rice
3 pounds pork or beef, cut into
½-inch cubes
4 tomatoes, chopped
¼ teaspoon saffron
2 teaspoons salt
½ teaspoon pepper
¼ teaspoon dried ground chili peppers

1 clove
¼ teaspoon cinnamon
2 cups stock or 1 can consommé and
½ can water
6 potatoes, peeled and quartered
2 green bananas, peeled and quartered
½ cup ground peanuts
½ cup heavy cream
1 tablespoon molasses

Heat the olive oil in a large saucepan. Add the onions and garlic and sauté for 5 minutes, stirring frequently. Add the rice and meat and cook over high heat until the meat is brown. Add the tomatoes, saffron, salt, pepper, chili peppers, clove, cinnamon, and stock. Cover and cook over low heat for 30 minutes.

Add the potatoes and bananas and cook 15 minutes longer. Add the peanuts, cream, and molasses. Cook for 15 minutes, or until the meat and potatoes are tender. Correct seasoning. Serve hot.

*Note: This is a fairly spicy dish, and the Bolivians use considerably more chili peppers than called for in this recipe.*

## DUCK "DELICIOUS"

PATO DELICIOSO

2 4-pound ducks, disjointed
2 quarts water
5 carrots, sliced
3 stalks celery, sliced
3 cloves garlic, minced
5 leeks, sliced, or 2 onions, sliced thin
1 green pepper, sliced thin

1 tablespoon salt
1 teaspoon pepper
6 potatoes, peeled
3 tablespoons butter
2 cups bread crumbs
3 hard-cooked eggs, sliced

Remove as much fat as possible from the uncooked ducks. Combine the ducks in a large saucepan with the water, carrots, celery, garlic, leeks, green pepper, salt, and pepper. Bring to a boil and skim the top carefully. Cover and cook over medium heat for 45 minutes. Add the potatoes and cook for 30 minutes, or until the ducks and potatoes are tender. Remove the ducks and set aside. Strain the stock and reserve the stock and vegetables separately.

397

Melt the butter in a saucepan. Add the bread crumbs and mix well. Add 2 cups of the reserved stock. Cook over low heat for 5 minutes, stirring frequently. Correct seasoning. Place the ducks on a platter, with the vegetables on top. Pour the bread-crumb mixture over and around the duck. Serve hot.

## ALMOND COOKIES

### ALFAJORES DE ALMENDRAS

½ pound butter
1 cup sugar
3 eggs, beaten
3 tablespoons grated lemon rind
1 tablespoon brandy

⅛ teaspoon almond extract
1 cup sifted flour
2½ cups ground blanched almonds
1 egg white

Cream the butter. Add the sugar and cream until light and fluffy. Add the eggs, beating well. Add the lemon rind, brandy, almond extract, flour, and 2 cups of the ground almonds, again mixing well. Form the mixture into a ball, wrap in wax paper, and chill for at least 3 hours. Preheat oven to 375°.

Roll out the dough about ⅛ inch thick on a lightly floured surface. Cut into any desired shape, such as circles, strips, or squares. Brush with the egg white and sprinkle with the remaining almonds. Place on a buttered cooky sheet. Bake in a 375° oven for 12 minutes, or until lightly browned.

## COCONUT TARTS

### PASTELITOS DE COCO

2 cups sifted flour
½ teaspoon baking powder
1 teaspoon salt
½ cup shortening
4 tablespoons ice water
⅔ cup sugar

1½ cups fresh or dried grated coconut
¾ cup light cream
3 egg yolks, beaten
3 tablespoons butter

Reserve 1 tablespoon of the flour and sift the balance into a bowl with the baking powder and salt. Cut in the shortening with a pastry blender or two knives. Add the water, tossing lightly until a ball of dough is formed. Wrap in wax paper and place in the refrigerator while preparing the filling.

Mix the reserved tablespoon of flour with the sugar, coconut, and cream in a saucepan. Cook over low heat, stirring constantly, until the mixture is thick. Add 2 of the beaten egg yolks gradually, mixing constantly. Add the butter and cook over low heat for 3 minutes. Remove from the heat and set aside.

Roll out the dough about ⅛ inch thick on a lightly floured surface. Cut into 3-inch squares or circles. Place 1 tablespoon of the coconut mixture on half the pieces and cover with the remaining pieces, pressing the edges together carefully with a fork. Preheat oven to 425°. Place on a baking sheet and brush the tops with the remaining egg yolk. Bake in a 425° oven for 12 minutes, or until lightly browned.

*BRAZIL*

World travelers often debate as to which city has the most beautiful setting, and the winner is inevitably Rio de Janeiro. Since words have always failed those who attempt to describe the beauties of nature, no attempt will be made to describe Rio except to say that it must be seen in person. One of the greatest experiences of a lifetime is coming into Rio on a Pan American plane with the sea and the mountains as a background. São Paulo, the industrial city south of Rio de Janeiro, is growing so fast that no one can foresee the end of its phenomenal growth. As the Brazilians say, Rio for pleasure, São Paulo for work.

When you mention Brazil to a gourmet, his first thought is of coffee, and of course this is truly the land of coffee. But Brazil has many fine native dishes, many unique food creations, any number of rare fruits and, of course, fine seafood. The shrimp are particularly good, and you'll want to try them prepared in the local styles, particularly barbecued on a spit and the little shrimp pies (*empadinhas de camarões*) served as appetizers. Possibly "hash" is a horrible word to you, but that is because you have never eaten *picadinho*, the Brazilian version of hash, and probably the world's best. *Pato com môlho de laranja* (duck with orange sauce) is well worth searching for. Brazilians like meats broiled over coals, which they call *churrasco;* the meats are always sprinkled with a starchy flour called *mandioca,* which is made from the ground cassava roots found in Brazil.

If you asked a Brazilian what one dish typifies the country, he would probably select the *feijoada,* a bean dish made in different ways but usually containing meat, rice, and spices. Beans in any form are popular here and are served with practically any dish you might select.

Brazilians, in accordance with South American custom, have only coffee, usually served half and half with hot milk, for breakfast. During the rest of the day they drink ten, fifteen, twenty, or even more tiny thimblefuls of coffee, usually black and sweet, at one of the tiny coffee stands scattered throughout the city. Lunch is a large meal and so is dinner, which is eaten about 9 P.M. Teashops are very popular with everyone and are usually crowded in the afternoon, when the people stop for *chá*—that is, to drink their fourteenth, no, twenty-fourth cup of coffee.

One Brazilian specialty that has made its way around the world (in cans) is that great delicacy *palmitos,* or hearts of palm. They are obtained from the hearts of palm trees and have an exquisite flavor. Brazilians like them in salads, but they often appear surprisingly in many other dishes.

Other than coffee and *maté* (discussed in the sections on Paraguay and Uruguay), the Brazilians like their own *cachaça,* a raw rum that is pale only in color, for its effect is far from colorless. Most tourists do not approve of its unrefined taste, and prefer to drink the local beer, which is probably among the best in the world. Almost any given brand will be found to be excellent. While some wine is produced and imported, it cannot be said that wine drinking has assumed much importance in the land. There are many excellent bottled soft drinks, of which the best is probably *guaraná,* a popular favorite.

Oh yes, B----l nuts grow in Brazil. They are rather difficult to obtain in Rio de Janeiro, because most of them are shipped north to the United States, from Belém, in Pará. While in that colorful city you could hardly do better than dine at the Hotel Grande.

## BATIDA

| | |
|---|---|
| 6 jiggers rum or brandy | 1 tablespoon honey |
| 1 cup grapefruit juice | 1 tablespoon fresh or dried grated |
| 1 cup pineapple juice | coconut |
| 1 ripe banana, cut into small pieces | 1 teaspoon almond extract |
| 1 teaspoon grenadine | 1 cup finely cracked ice |
| 1 tablespoon lemon or lime juice | |

Place the rum, grapefruit and pineapple juice, banana, grenadine, lemon or lime juice, honey, coconut, almond extract, and cracked ice in an electric blender. Mix for at least 1 minute. Strain into chilled glasses. Decorate with a marschino cherry or a fresh mint leaf.

*Note: In Brazil, this drink is often made with* cachaça, *a pale, under-aged rum. It is not available in the United States.*

## INDIVIDUAL SHRIMP PIES

### EMPADINHAS DE CAMARÕES

1½ cups sifted flour
2 teaspoons salt
¾ cup shortening
1 egg, beaten
¼ cup ice water
2 tablespoons olive oil
1 onion, chopped

5 tomatoes, chopped, or 1½ cups
   canned tomatoes, drained
1½ cups coarsely chopped cooked
   shrimp
½ teaspoon pepper
¼ cup chopped ripe olives
1 hard-cooked egg, chopped
3 tablespoons chopped parsley

Sift the flour and 1 teaspoon of the salt into a bowl. Cut in the shortening with a pastry blender or two knives until the consistency of coarse sand. Combine the egg and water and add, tossing lightly until a ball of dough is formed. Wrap in wax paper and place in the refrigerator for 2 hours.

Heat the olive oil in a saucepan. Add the onion and sauté for 10 minutes. Add the tomatoes and cook over low heat for 10 minutes. Add the shrimp, pepper, and remaining salt. Cook over low heat for 10 minutes. Add the olives, chopped egg, and parsley. Correct seasoning. Cool for 15 minutes. Preheat oven to 400°.

Roll out the dough ¼ inch thick on a lightly floured surface. The dough may be cut to fit muffin pans or cut into 5-inch circles. If muffin pans are used, line each one with dough and fill with the shrimp mixture. Place a little round of dough on top of each one. If the circles are used, place a tablespoon of the shrimp mixture in the center of each circle and fold over the dough, sealing the edges well. Place on a baking sheet. Bake either variety in a 400° oven for 20 minutes. Serve hot.

## BAKED CRAB MEAT

### CASQUINHO DE CARANGUEJO

½ cup olive oil
2 onions, chopped fine
2 tomatoes, chopped fine
2 green peppers, chopped fine
1 clove garlic, minced
3 tablespoons chopped parsley

1 pound cooked or canned crab
   meat
1½ teaspoons salt
½ teaspoon pepper
2 eggs, beaten
1 cup bread crumbs
6 stuffed green olives, sliced

Heat olive oil in a saucepan. Add the onions and sauté for 10 minutes, stirring occasionally. Add the tomatoes, green peppers, garlic, and parsley and cook over low heat for 15 minutes. Add the crab meat, salt, and pepper and mix carefully. Cook over low heat for 5 minutes, stirring occasionally. Pour the eggs over the mixture and cook for 2 minutes, stirring constantly. Correct seasoning. Divide the mixture among 6 individual buttered ramekins or casseroles. Sprinkle heavily with bread crumbs and arrange olive slices on top. Bake in a 375° oven for 15 minutes, or until lightly browned on top. Serve hot.

## BLACK BEANS, BRAZILIAN STYLE

FEIJOADA A BRASILEIRA

3 cups dried black beans
1 pound dried beef or uncooked corned beef, cut into small pieces
1 pound Spanish-style sausage
¼ pound bacon, half cooked
2 pounds pork, cut into 2-inch cubes
1 cup orange juice
1 cup red wine
2 tablespoons olive oil
1 onion, chopped
2 cloves garlic, minced
½ teaspoon dried ground chili peppers or 1 fresh chili pepper, chopped fine
3 oranges, sliced
3 baked acorn squash, peeled and cut into 2-inch squares
3 cups boiled rice

Soak the beans overnight in water to cover. Soak the dried beef separately in water to cover; if corned beef is used, overnight soaking is not necessary. Drain the beans, add fresh water to cover, and cook over low heat for 2 hours. Meanwhile prepare the meats. Drain the beef. Place in a saucepan with water to cover and bring to a boil. Drain well. Add fresh water to cover, and also add the sausage (reserving a few pieces), bacon, and pork. Cook over medium heat for 2 hours.

Combine the beans and the meat and cook over very low heat 2 hours longer, or until the beans are very soft. Add the orange juice and wine and mix well. Add salt if necessary. Cook 20 minutes longer. Remove 1½ cups of the beans and force them through a sieve or purée them in an electric blender.

Heat the olive oil in a saucepan. Add the onion and garlic and sauté for 10 minutes, stirring frequently. Mash the reserved pieces of sausage and add them. Also add the chili peppers and bean purée. Add enough liquid from the beans to make the sauce the consistency of a thick gravy. Cook over low heat for 15 minutes. Correct seasoning. Add half of this sauce to the beans and meat and stir well.

Place the rice in a large, deep dish and pour the beans over it. Slice the sausages and arrange them on top of the beans together with the other meats. Pour the remaining half of the sauce over the dish. Arrange the orange slices around the edges of the dish and serve with baked acorn squash.

*Note: This is practically the national dish of Brazil and is much appreciated, although its preparation requires considerable time. The dish will*

*be all the better if additional smoked meats, such as tongue, ham, or other
various pork products, are included.*

## DUCK IN ORANGE SAUCE

PATO COM MÔLHO DE LARANJA

| | |
|---|---|
| 2 ducks | 2 bay leaves |
| ¼ cup lemon or lime juice | ¼ cup rum |
| 3 teaspoons salt | 2 tablespoons flour |
| 1 teaspoon pepper | 2 tablespoons water |
| 3 cups orange juice | ¼ cup ground Brazil nuts |
| 3 tablespoons grated orange rind | ¼ cup curaçao |
| 4 bananas, cut into 1-inch pieces | 1 cup currant jelly, cut into small cubes |

Clean the ducks carefully and singe the skin over a flame. Wash and dry.
Sprinkle with the lemon or lime juice, then rub in the salt and pepper
thoroughly. Place the ducks in a roasting pan and roast in a 425° oven for
20 minutes. Drain the fat. Reduce the heat to 350° and roast 50 minutes
longer. Drain the fat again. Pour the orange juice over the ducks and
sprinkle the orange rind over them. Add the bananas, bay leaves, and
rum, and continue roasting for 1 hour, basting frequently. The ducks may
require a short additional roasting time.

Remove the ducks and bananas from the pan and set aside. Skim the
fat from the gravy and discard. Strain the remaining gravy. Mix the flour
and water together to a smooth paste in a saucepan. Add the strained
gravy, stirring constantly until the boiling point is reached. Add the
Brazil nuts and curaçao and cook over low heat for 5 minutes, stirring
occasionally. Carve the ducks and arrange them on a platter with the
bananas and currant jelly around it. Pour a little gravy over the ducks and
serve the remainder in a sauceboat.

## TURKEY, BRAZILIAN STYLE

PERÚ A BRASILEIRA

| | |
|---|---|
| 1 turkey | 4 green peppers, chopped |
| 1½ tablespoons salt | ½ cup chopped parsley |
| 2 teaspoons pepper | 1½ cups vinegar |
| 3 cloves garlic, minced | 1 pound thinly sliced smoked ham |
| 1 cup olive oil | (Prosciutto or Parma type) |
| 4 tomatoes, cubed | |

The turkey should be seasoned the day before it is used. Mix the salt,
pepper, and garlic together to a paste. Rub into the turkey thoroughly,

both inside and out. Place the turkey in a roasting pan. Combine the olive oil, tomatoes, green peppers, parsley, and vinegar. Pour over the turkey. Place overnight in the refrigerator, basting occasionally.

Remove the turkey from the refrigerator 4 hours before it is to be roasted. Baste frequently during this 4-hour period. Place in a 350° oven and roast for 20 minutes per pound, basting quite frequently. Carve the turkey into slices and arrange on a platter, alternating with a slice of ham after every third slice of turkey. Force the gravy through a sieve and serve separately in a sauceboat.

## AVOCADO SALAD

SALADA DE ABACATE

1 clove garlic, minced
2 tablespoons grated onion
2 tablespoons finely chopped capers
1 tablespoon chopped parsley
1 teaspoon chopped chives
½ teaspoon sugar
½ cup olive oil

2 tablespoons tarragon vinegar
1 teaspoon salt
½ teaspoon pepper
2 heads romaine lettuce, washed and chilled
1 endive, washed and chilled
1 avocado, peeled and sliced thin

Combine the garlic, onion, capers, parsley, chives, sugar, olive oil, vinegar, salt, and pepper in a salad bowl. Mix well. Tear the lettuce leaves into thirds and add to the dressing. Separate the endive and add, together with the avocado. Toss lightly and chill for 1 hour. Toss again before serving.

## BRAZIL NUT CAKE

TORTA DE CASTANHA-DO-PARÁ

10 egg yolks
1¾ cups powdered sugar
3 cups ground Brazil nuts
⅛ teaspoon salt
2 tablespoons brandy

2 tablespoons bread crumbs
10 egg whites
1½ cups heavy cream
2 tablespoons coffee essence
3 tablespoons confectioners' sugar

Beat the egg yolks in a bowl. Gradually add the powdered sugar, beating until thick. Add the nuts, salt, brandy, and bread crumbs, mixing well. Preheat oven to 350°. Beat the egg whites until stiff but not dry and fold into the nut mixture.

Butter a 10-inch spring-form pan and dust lightly with bread crumbs. Pour the batter into it. Bake in a 350° oven for 45 minutes or until a cake tester comes out clean. Leave the cake in the oven with the heat off and the door open for 5 minutes after it is finished baking. Cool for 2 hours. Remove from the form. Split the cake.

Whip the cream and add the coffee essence and confectioners' sugar, mixing lightly. Spread some of the cream between the halves and place the rest on top. Chill. Some sliced or chopped Brazil nuts may be sprinkled on top if desired.

*CHILE*

Probably the most food-conscious nation of the South American countries is Chile, the (2900-mile) long land located on the southwestern portion of the continent. But while the shape of the nation is long and lean, a great deal of fat living is available there, particularly for those who enjoy seafood, game, fruits, and wines. Although the physical contours of Chile are like those of an anemic fashion model, with Chile's fine food, it is remarkable that any woman can remain slim.

It is advisable to eat only the typical breakfast of coffee and a bit of pastry or bread, for the meals that follow will make up for it. Lunch is always a substantial meal, and tea is a "must," a meal at which tea itself often plays an unimportant part, for it is actually a complete light meal usually served about 5:30 P.M. Custom decrees a brief pause, and then the "vermouth" hour begins at about six-thirty or so; it is so called because originally everyone drank a glass of vermouth, which has now been, to some extent, replaced by cocktails. Then everyone goes to see the latest motion picture at a performance advertised as the "Vermouth Showing," followed by a large dinner at ten in the evening.

The people are fond of thick, rich soups filled with meat and chicken, and these are important in the national diet. Corn, beans, and sausage are also in great demand and are used in numerous different fashions in cooking.

With its tremendous coast line facing the Pacific, Chile can fish in its own back yard for food, and out of the sea come many delicious and unusual fish. Running alongside the coast is that mysterious movement of water known as the Humboldt Current, a cold stream in the ocean moving northward from the Antarctic and carrying with it both fish and the food the fish live on. There are *congrio, corbina,* and swordfish—all extraordinarily fine-tasting. Chile has such unique shellfish as the *erizos* (a sea urchin often served in a green sauce), *locos* (best described as a cross between an abalone and a scallop), *chorros* (giant clams), as well as oysters, shrimp, mussels, and many others. *Jaibas* (crabs) are excellent. The favorite treatment for shellfish is to prepare it as a *chupe,* or seafood chowder, sometimes mild but often very spicy. Seaweed found along the shore, *luche,* is used frequently. The pride of all Chilean seafood is probably the *langosta,* a delicately flavored lobster caught principally in the waters surrounding the Juan Fernández Islands off the coast of Chile. It is so good that it is usually just served boiled and cold with a little mayonnaise.

Game of all sorts is plentiful, and the Chileans make the most of their partridges, pigeons, plover, quail, and wild duck. Grilled meat is popular, but the national meat dish is a type of boiled dinner with many different vegetables. Fruits and vegetables are very fine, and the *paltas* (avocados) are of extraordinary richness. Desserts are usually of fruit, but *empanaditas de crema* (tiny cream pies) are seen everywhere.

The wines of Chile are unimpeachable and are often exported to the United States. The vineyards of Chile are considered the finest in South America and produce reds and whites, with a wide range of quality. The excellent local champagne costs a fraction of the price of an equivalent French wine. *Chacolí* (a fermented grape cider) is a customary refreshment.

Santiago, the capital city, has a delightful climate and a world-famous hotel, the Carrera, which serves fine food. The local Chilean specialties may be had at the hotel restaurant and at a few other places in the city.


CHAMPAGNE-FRUIT COCKTAIL

CAZUELA EN CHAMPAÑA

½ cup chopped fresh pineapple
1 orange, peeled and sliced
½ cup strawberries

3 tablespoons sugar
¾ cup cognac
1 bottle champagne, well chilled

Chop together the pineapple, orange, and berries until very fine. Sprinkle with the sugar and pour the cognac over the mixture. Chill for at least 1 hour. Divide the mixture among 6 chilled champagne glasses. Fill with the champagne and serve immediately.

## SHRIMP AND SCALLOP STEW

CHUPE DE MARISCOS

1 pound shrimp, peeled and cleaned
1 pound scallops
½ cup water
½ cup white wine
1½ cups bread crumbs
1 cup milk
¼ pound butter
4 onions, chopped

1 teaspoon Spanish paprika
1 cup cream
2 teaspoons salt
½ teaspoon pepper
⅛ teaspoon dried ground chili peppers
3 hard-cooked eggs, quartered
½ cup grated Parmesan cheese

Combine the shrimp, scallops, water, and wine in a saucepan. Bring to a boil and cook over low heat for 6 minutes. Strain, reserving the stock. Reserve 3 shrimp and 3 scallops, and chop the remainder coarsely.

Soak the bread crumbs in the milk. Melt the butter in a saucepan. Add the onions and paprika and sauté for 10 minutes, stirring frequently. Squeeze the excess milk from the bread crumbs and discard. Add the bread crumbs to the onions. Add the reserved stock, mixing well. Add the chopped shrimp and scallops, cream, salt, pepper, and chili peppers. Cook over low heat for 10 minutes, stirring frequently. The *chupe* should be placed in individual earthenware or casserole dishes, garnished with the eggs, and sprinkled with cheese. Cut the reserved shrimp and scallops in half and place some on each portion.

*Note: In Chile this dish is preferred in a spicy form, often extremely hot. For those who wish to duplicate the Chilean style, double the amount of chili peppers.*

## CHILEAN FISH SOUP

CALDILLO DE PESCADO

1 cup olive oil
4 onions, chopped
2 cloves garlic, minced
1 teaspoon marjoram
3 pounds fish, cut into 1-inch pieces
6 cups water
2 teaspoons salt

½ teaspoon pepper
4 potatoes, cubed
1 cup sherry
4 tomatoes, peeled and sliced
3 egg yolks
4 tablespoons chopped parsley

Heat the olive oil in a saucepan. Add the onions and garlic and sauté for 15 minutes, stirring frequently. Add the marjoram, fish, water, salt, and pepper. Cover and cook over medium heat for 30 minutes. Add the potatoes and sherry. Cover and cook over medium heat for 20 minutes. Add the tomatoes and cook 10 minutes longer. Correct seasoning.

Beat the egg yolks and parsley in a bowl. Gradually add 1 cup of the soup, beating constantly. Return the mixture to the balance of the soup, beating steadily. Heat but do not allow the soup to boil. Serve hot.

## SQUABS STUFFED WITH NOODLES

POLLITA DE GRANO MENDEZ VIGO

| | |
|---|---|
| 1 pair sweetbreads | ½ pound butter |
| 1 cup water | 1 onion, chopped |
| 1 tablespoon vinegar | 1 cup chopped mushrooms |
| 3 teaspoons salt | 2 cups medium-fine egg noodles, |
| 1½ teaspoons pepper | boiled |
| 2 cloves garlic, minced | 1 cup cream |
| 6 squabs, with livers and gizzards | ¾ cup sherry |

Wash the sweetbreads in cold water. Place in a saucepan with the cup of water and the vinegar. Bring to a boil and cook over low heat for 10 minutes. Drain. Cover with cold water and set aside for 20 minutes. Drain. Remove the membrane and cut the sweetbreads into small cubes. Mix 2 teaspoons of the salt, 1 teaspoon of the pepper, and the garlic to a smooth paste. Rub into the squabs. Grind the livers and gizzards in a food chopper.

Melt half the butter in a frying pan. Add the onion and mushrooms and sauté for 5 minutes, stirring frequently. Add the noodles, sweetbreads, cream, sherry, and remaining salt and pepper. Mix carefully. Correct seasoning. Stuff the squabs with the mixture. Fasten the openings with skewers or with thread. Melt the remaining butter in a casserole or baking dish. Brown the squabs on all sides. Roast in a 375° oven for 35 minutes, or until tender. Baste frequently.

## BEEF STEW, CHILEAN STYLE

CARBONADA

| | |
|---|---|
| 4 tablespoons butter | ¼ cup rice |
| 4 pounds top sirloin, cubed | 1 cup diced pumpkin or squash |
| 1 onion, chopped | ½ cup green peas |
| 2 teaspoons paprika | ½ cup corn kernels |
| 4 potatoes, peeled and cubed | 3 cups boiling water |
| 2 teaspoons salt | 2 egg yolks, beaten |
| ½ teaspoon pepper | |

Melt the butter in a large saucepan. Add the meat, onion, and paprika. Cook over high heat until the meat is browned on all sides. Add the potatoes and continue browning for 10 minutes, stirring occasionally. Add the rice, pumpkin or squash, peas, corn, and water. Cook over low heat for

1 hour, or until meat is tender. Stir occasionally. Correct seasoning. Place the beaten egg yolks in a deep serving dish or tureen. Pour the stew over it gradually, stirring well. Serve immediately.

## PEASANT SALAD

ENSALADA CAMPESINA

1 cup dried chick-peas or 2 cups canned, drained garbanzos
½ pound cream cheese, diced
2 onions, sliced thin
½ cup olive oil

¼ cup lemon juice
1 teaspoon salt
½ teaspoon ground coriander
3 hard-cooked eggs, quartered

Soak the chick-peas overnight in water to cover. Drain well. Add fresh water and cook for 2 hours, or until tender. (If canned chick-peas are used, omit these steps.) Drain well. Chill for 2 hours. Combine the chick-peas, cheese, and onions in a bowl. Mix the olive oil, lemon juice, salt, and coriander together. Pour over the previous mixture. Toss lightly. Place on lettuce leaves and garnish with the eggs. Serve very cold.

## CHICKEN AND CORN SALAD

BOCADO PRIMAVERA DE AVE

3 cups diced boiled chicken
2 cups cooked or canned corn kernels
6 tomatoes, cubed
3 green peppers, minced

3 cups mayonnaise
1 teaspoon salt
½ teaspoon pepper
Lettuce leaves
3 hard-cooked eggs, quartered

Combine the chicken, corn, tomatoes, green peppers, 1 cup of the mayonnaise, salt, and pepper. Mix gently but thoroughly. Arrange the lettuce leaves on a platter or individual plates. Heap the chicken mixture on it and smooth out as evenly as possible. Cover with the remaining mayonnaise, coating the salad mixture so that only the mayonnaise may be seen. Arrange the quartered eggs around it. If desired, radishes and olives may be placed around the salad. Chill and serve very cold.

## TINY CREAM PIES

EMPANADITAS DE CREMA

2¾ cups milk
1 cup sugar
1 teaspoon vanilla extract
7 egg yolks

3 cups sifted flour
¼ pound butter
Fat for deep-fat frying
½ cup confectioners' sugar

Scald 2 cups of the milk and add the sugar, reserving 2 tablespoons. Add the vanilla. Beat 5 of the egg yolks in a saucepan. Add 1 cup of the flour, mixing until smooth. Gradually add the milk mixture, stirring constantly. Cook over low heat until smooth and thick, about 5 minutes, stirring constantly. Add the butter and stir well. Set aside to cool while preparing the dough.

Sift the remaining flour into a bowl. Add the remaining egg yolks, 2 tablespoons sugar, and ¾ cup milk. Mix until a soft dough is formed. Roll the dough about ⅛ inch thick on a lightly floured surface. Cut into 4-inch circles, using a cooky cutter or cup. Place a tablespoon of the cream mixture on each. Fold over the dough, sealing the edges carefully with a fork. Heat the fat to 360°. Drop the little pies into the fat carefully. Fry until browned, about 6 minutes. Drain well. Sprinkle with confectioners' sugar. Serve hot or cold.

## COLOMBIA

Colombia has changed considerably in the past few decades and has become a much more prosperous and industrialized country. Accommodations for travelers, which were formerly only adequate, are now excellent. What hasn't changed about Colombia are the orchids, which apparently grow by the millions, and the world's finest emeralds, which, judging by their astronomical prices, do not grow with equal profusion.

But you can't eat emeralds or orchids, except for the pod of the *Vanilla planifolia* orchid, which produces the edible vanilla bean. You *can* enjoy Colombia's fine coffee and extraordinary fruits. A visit to a native market will disclose many fruits you have never seen before, in addition to the familiar tropical species. You'll want to try them all, particularly the *curubas* and the *guanábanas*.

Colombians are fond of high seasoning, and spicy dishes are to be expected, although occasionally a bland one will surprise you just when your palate has become accustomed to sharply spiced foods. Soups such as *cuchuco* (a wheat soup) and many more, almost all very filling and calorific, are great favorites. Seafood is very worth while here, since Colombia has two coast lines, one facing the Caribbean and the other fronting on the Pacific Ocean. The recipe for *arroz con pescado* (fish and rice) is simple but good.

Chicken dishes are well prepared and often contain fruits, corn, and various cereals. *Piquete*, almost always served outdoors, picnic fashion, contains chicken, pork, corn, and both white and sweet potatoes, and is typical of the country. *Ajiaco* (a pork and vegetable stew) is also important with both city and country people.

The food has Spanish overtones, but there is much in it that is purely local in character. The country is excessively fond of high seasoning, and beer is the favorite drink for neutralizing the spiciness of the food. Wines are of little importance, but the same cannot be said for the local fire-water, *aguardiente*, which has almost no taste but considerable effect.

Of desserts there is little to say, other than that the very best are the country's fine fresh fruits, or ice creams made from them. No discussion of Colombia and its eating habits could afford to overlook the famous Sunday breakfast, which has assumed the importance of a great tradition. *Tamales* are the great Sunday morning treat, and it is a rare Colombian indeed who will forgo his *tamal*, usually accompanied by hot chocolate, bread, and the locally produced cheese.

Visitors to this lovely land find it easy to become adjusted to almost anything but the extremely late dinner hour. Ten o'clock is a normal dinnertime, but eleven or even midnight is not too extraordinary, particularly for a dinner party with many guests. Bogotá, the capital, is located up in the mountains, and before the coming of commercial aviation was quite inaccessible. It still retains a certain Shangri-La atmosphere, and the people like to think of their proud city as the Athens of the continent. Many citizens have cards printed which indicate their name and occupation, such as "Pedro Gomez, poet." Bogotá's pride for luxury and fine food is the new Hotel Tequendama. Native specialties are served at the Casa Marina and the Restaurante Temel.

## EGG AND AVOCADO APPETIZER
PICANTE DE HUEVOS

6 hard-cooked eggs, chopped
2 avocados, chopped fine
1 fresh chili pepper, chopped fine, or ¼ teaspoon dried ground chili peppers

1 onion, chopped fine
3 tablespoons chopped parsley
2 tablespoons vinegar
1½ teaspoons salt

Combine the eggs, avocados, chili pepper, onion, parsley, vinegar, and salt. Mix well and chop until very smooth and well blended. Chill. Serve as an hors d'oeuvre on toast, or on lettuce leaves, as an appetizer.

## WHEAT SOUP

CUCHUCO

| | |
|---|---|
| 1 pound stewing beef | ½ cup cracked wheat (cereal) |
| 1 large beef bone | 1 tablespoon salt |
| 2½ quarts water | 2 potatoes, peeled and cubed |
| 1 onion | 1 cup fresh or frozen green peas |
| 1 clove garlic, minced | |

Combine the beef, bone, water, onion, and garlic in a deep saucepan. Bring to a boil and skim the top carefully. Cook over medium heat for 1 hour. Add the cracked wheat, stirring constantly. Cook over low heat 30 minutes longer. Add the salt, potatoes, and peas. Cook for 20 minutes, or until the potatoes are tender. The meat should be cut into small pieces and served in the soup.

*Note: This is a very substantial and filling dish, and should be followed ordinarily by a light main course.*

## FISH WITH RICE

ARROZ CON PESCADO

| | |
|---|---|
| 3 cups water | 2 onions, chopped |
| 3 teaspoons salt | 1 clove garlic, minced |
| 1½ cups rice | 3 fillets of sole, shredded |
| 4 tablespoons butter | ½ teaspoon pepper |
| 2 tablespoons olive oil | |

Combine the water and 2 teaspoons of the salt in a saucepan. Bring it to a boil and add the rice. Cover and cook over medium heat for 15 minutes. Drain. Combine the butter and olive oil in a large skillet. Add the onions and garlic and sauté for 10 minutes, stirring frequently. Add the fish, pepper, and remaining salt; sauté 5 minutes. Add the rice and cook over high heat for 5 minutes, stirring frequently to prevent burning. Correct seasoning. Serve with a chilled dry white wine.

## CHICKEN, HUNTER'S STYLE

POLLO AL CAZADOR

| | |
|---|---|
| ¼ cup dried chick-peas or ½ cup canned chick-peas, drained | 3 tomatoes, peeled and chopped |
| 2½ teaspoons salt | 1½ cups sliced mushrooms |
| ½ teaspoon pepper | 2 green peppers, sliced |
| ¼ cup flour | 1½ cups red wine |
| 2 3-pound chickens, disjointed | ¼ teaspoon dried ground chili peppers |
| ⅓ cup olive oil | ¼ teaspoon orégano |
| 3 onions, quartered | 1 bay leaf |

Wash and soak the chick-peas overnight in water to cover. Drain well. Cook in water to cover for 1 hour. Drain well. (If canned chick-peas are used, omit these steps.) Combine the salt, pepper, and flour. Roll the chicken parts in it lightly. Heat the olive oil in a heavy saucepan. Add the chicken and brown well on all sides. Add the chick-peas, onions, tomatoes, mushrooms, green peppers, wine, chili peppers, orégano, and bay leaf. Cover and cook over low heat for 1 hour, or until the chicken is tender. Remove bay leaf and correct seasoning.

## PORK AND CHICKEN, COLOMBIAN STYLE

### PIQUETE

| | |
|---|---|
| 3 onions, chopped fine | 3½-pound chicken, disjointed |
| 2 cloves garlic, minced | 2 quarts water |
| 3 tablespoons chopped parsley | 6 white potatoes, unpeeled |
| 2 teaspoons salt | 3 sweet potatoes, peeled |
| ½ teaspoon dried ground chili peppers | 3 ears sweet corn, cut in half |
| 1 teaspoon ground cumin seed | 6 pork chops |

Combine the onions, garlic, parsley, salt, chili peppers, and cumin seed in a bowl. Pound together until quite smooth. Add the chicken, turning it for several minutes in the mixture until it is well coated. Cover and marinate overnight in the refrigerator. Place the chicken, spice mixture, and water in a saucepan. Bring to a boil, cover, and cook over medium heat for 1 hour or until chicken is tender. Remove the chicken, reserving the stock. Place the chicken in a buttered baking dish. Preheat oven to 450°. Bake in a 450° oven for 15 minutes, or until the chicken is brown.

Add the unpeeled white potatoes and the peeled sweet potatoes to the stock. Boil for 15 minutes. Add the corn and cook 15 minutes longer, or until the potatoes are tender. Place the pork chops in a hot skillet and fry for 15 minutes on each side, or until the pork is tender. Arrange the meats on one platter and the vegetables on another. It is customary to serve the following sauce with this dish:

| | |
|---|---|
| ½ cup bread crumbs | 2 tomatoes, chopped |
| ½ cup milk | ½ cup grated Gruyère or American |
| 2 tablespoons olive or salad oil | cheese |
| 2 onions, chopped | 1 teaspoon salt |

Soak the bread crumbs in the milk. Heat the oil in a skillet. Add the onions and sauté for 5 minutes. Add the tomatoes and cook over low heat for 10 minutes, stirring frequently. Add the bread-crumb and milk mixture. If the sauce is too thick, add a little additional milk. Cook over low heat for 2 minutes, stirring constantly. Add the grated cheese and salt. Cook, stirring constantly, until the cheese melts. Serve separately in a sauceboat.

## BANANA OMELET

TORTILLA DE BANANA

4 tablespoons butter
4 bananas, sliced
6 egg yolks
1 teaspoon salt

¼ cup milk
6 egg whites
2 tablespoons chopped parsley
Dash of cayenne pepper

Melt the butter in a skillet. Add the bananas and sauté for 5 minutes, stirring frequently. Set aside. Beat the egg yolks, salt, and milk together in a bowl. Preheat oven to 350°. Beat the egg whites in a bowl until stiff but not dry. Fold into the yolk mixture carefully. Pour into a buttered baking dish and arrange the bananas on top. Bake in a 350° oven for 20 minutes, or until the omelet is set and delicately browned on top. Remove the omelet from the baking dish and fold it in half. Sprinkle with the parsley and cayenne pepper. Slice and serve.

## VEGETABLE SALAD

ENSALADA DE LEGUMBRES

3 Italian- or Spanish-style sausages, sliced thin, or ¼ pound salami, in small pieces
½ cup cooked string beans
½ cup canned corn kernels
2 tomatoes, peeled and sliced
1 head of lettuce, *broken* into small pieces

¼ cup olive oil
⅓ cup wine vinegar
1 tablespoon chopped scallions (green onions)
1 tablespoon chopped parsley
1 clove garlic, minced
1 teaspoon salt
½ teaspoon pepper

Fry the sausages until lightly browned. Drain well and let cool. Combine the string beans, corn, tomatoes, lettuce, and sausages in a salad bowl. Mix together in a bowl the olive oil, vinegar, scallions, parsley, garlic, salt, and pepper. Pour over the salad. Toss lightly. Chill. Serve very cold.

## TINY COCOA CAKES

PASTELES DE CACAO

¼ pound butter
1½ cups sugar
3 eggs
¾ cup cocoa powder

1½ cups sifted flour
3 teaspoons baking powder
⅔ cup milk
1 teaspoon vanilla extract

Cream the butter until soft. Add the sugar gradually, beating until light and fluffy. Add the eggs, beating well. Sift the cocoa, flour, and baking powder together. Add to the butter mixture alternately with the milk, beating steadily. Add the vanilla and mix well. Preheat oven to 375°. Butter two muffin or cupcake pans and dust lightly with flour. Fill two thirds full. (The average pan has 8 cups.) Bake in a 375° oven for 20 minutes, or until a tester comes out clean. Serve hot or cold.

*ECUADOR*

If those restless souls of several centuries ago in search of a land of perpetual spring had found Ecuador, their search would have been terminated. Few places in this world are blessed with so magnificent a climate as are the highlands of this country. Although the word "Ecuador" means equator, and although people automatically assume that any country located on the equator must be hot and humid, it must also be remembered that most of Ecuador is situated on the slopes of the towering Andes. The coastline, including the seaport city of Guayaquil, is usually tropical and steaming, but the beautiful mountain towns of Ambato and Baños have a gardenlike atmosphere. Not to be missed by any visitor is the unusual and colorful Indian market held for centuries at Otavalo. Quito has about 9000 feet of altitude to contend with, but most people aren't disturbed by it, and the city and the natives are captivating in a way that is difficult to explain.

Ecuador is rich in fruits of all sorts, many of which are completely unfamiliar to us. There are dozens of varieties of bananas, ranging from the very tiny ones to tremendous species. The *chirimoya,* with its green exterior and snowy-white interior, is particularly delicious. Possibly the most interesting fruit of all is the *naranjilla,* which may be described as a type of orange with a bright green interior and a luscious, tropical taste. Ecuador doesn't know what it is in for, when color television hits this country—imagine commercials advertising green orange juice! Ice cream made from *naranjillas* is truly among the ultimate in taste thrills. Special today at your favorite soda fountain—green *naranjilla* ice cream.

While enjoying the unusual combination of palm trees set against snow-capped mountains, you may also enjoy the distinctive specialties of the nation. *Locro,* a great favorite, is a thick soup made from potatoes or from kernels of corn of an enormous size, as much as ten times the size of our usual varieties. In addition there are such things as *ají de pollo* (chicken with chili peppers) and *camarones con almendras* (shrimp with an almond sauce). The people are extraordinarily fond of sweet desserts and eat fairly large amounts of jam, jellies, and preserves. A unique sweet is *mazamorra morada,* a red and purple corn dessert which unfortunately cannot be duplicated here.

Breakfast may be small but lunch is a large meal. Afternoon tea, a great institution, is served about 6 P.M., almost the exact time the sun sets in Quito every day of the year. Naturally, after such a late tea, dinner is even later, certainly not before 9 P.M., and usually much later. The people are hearty eaters, and large meals are the rule.

*Chicha,* a potent, locally made beverage, is drunk by many of the inhabitants, but its ill-mannered taste does not usually appeal to visitors. However, that is hardly the case with the local beers. These are excellent and highly regarded. Two soft drinks the small fry enjoy are *rosero,* made of corn and fruit juices, and *fresco de arroz,* made of rice and fruit juices.

Color-camera fans will be very happy in Ecuador. Of course there are the most wonderful opportunities to get shots of the Indians and their colorful costumes, but the countryside offers much more. The most perfect color picture of Ecuador must certainly be the green palm trees of the country set against the snow-capped mountains, with a sky of Technicolor blue. It's corny, but we love it.

## ECUADORIAN TAMALES

CHOCLOTANDAS

| | |
|---|---|
| 4 tablespoons butter | 4 egg whites, stiffly beaten |
| ¼ pound cream cheese | 1 cup ground, cooked corn kernels |
| 4 egg yolks, beaten | (canned corn may be used) |
| 1 teaspoon salt | |

Cream the butter and cream cheese together until smooth. Add the egg yolks and salt and beat well. Add the egg whites, mixing thoroughly. Add the ground corn and mix well.

Cut parchment paper or aluminum foil into 5-inch squares. Place a heaping tablespoon of the mixture in the center of each and form into thin strips, about 3 inches long and ½ inch wide. Fold over the paper and tie with a string. If aluminum foil is used, the string is unnecessary. Drop into rapidly boiling, salted water and boil for 30 minutes. Serve in the papers in which they were boiled. These tamales make excellent hot hors d'oeuvres.

## POTATO SOUP

AJIACO

4 tablespoons butter
3 onions, chopped fine
2 tablespoons flour
3 cups stock or 1 can consommé and 1¼ cans water
4 potatoes, diced
⅛ teaspoon saffron

1½ teaspoons salt
Dash of cayenne pepper
3 cups milk, scalded
½ cup cooked green peas
3 eggs
¼ pound cream cheese
1 avocado, peeled and sliced

Melt the butter in a deep saucepan. Add the onions and sauté for 10 minutes. Add the flour and mix until smooth. Gradually add the stock, stirring constantly until the boiling point is reached. Add the potatoes, saffron, salt, and cayenne pepper. Cook over low heat for 20 minutes. Add the milk and peas and cook over low heat 5 minutes longer.

Beat the eggs and cream cheese together in a bowl. Gradually add 2 cups of the hot soup, beating constantly to prevent curdling. Return the contents of the bowl to the saucepan, stirring steadily. Correct seasoning. Place a few slices of avocado in each soup plate and pour the soup over it. Serve hot.

## SHRIMP WITH ALMOND SAUCE

CAMARONES CON SALSA DE ALMENDRAS

2 pounds shrimp
2 teaspoons salt
1½ cups water
1 stalk celery
½ teaspoon pickling spice
5 slices white bread, trimmed
1½ cups milk
4 tablespoons butter

2 onions, chopped fine
2 cloves garlic, minced
½ teaspoon black pepper
1 teaspoon Spanish paprika
¼ teaspoon dried ground chili peppers
½ cup olive oil
1 cup ground almonds

Wash the shrimp well. Combine in a saucepan with 1 teaspoon salt, the water, celery, and pickling spice. Bring to a boil and cook over medium heat for 5 minutes. Allow to cool in the stock for 15 minutes. Drain, reserving 1 cup of the stock. Peel the shrimp and remove the black vein. Set aside. Soak the bread in the milk for 5 minutes. Mash it until smooth. Melt the butter in a skillet. Add the onions, garlic, pepper, paprika, chili peppers, and remaining salt. Sauté for 15 minutes, stirring occasionally. Add the bread and sauté for 5 minutes, stirring frequently. Add the olive oil very gradually, stirring steadily. Add the almonds, again mixing well. Add the shrimp and stock. Cook over low heat for 5 minutes. Serve hot.

## PORK ROAST

### PUERCO HORNEADO

1 teaspoon salt
1 teaspoon saffron
½ teaspoon marjoram
½ teaspoon basil
½ teaspoon ground cumin seed
1 teaspoon pepper
3 cloves garlic, minced
1 fillet of pork (4 pounds) or loin of pork (6 pounds)

1 cup boiling water
3 tablespoons grated onion
2 tablespoons wine vinegar
¼ teaspoon dried ground chili peppers
2 tablespoons chopped parsley
½ cup cold water

Combine the salt, saffron, marjoram, basil, cumin seed, pepper, and garlic. Mix into a paste and rub into the pork. Wrap in wax paper and place in the refrigerator overnight. Place the pork in a roasting pan and roast in a 400° oven for 30 minutes. Reduce the heat to 350°, pour the boiling water over the pork, and roast 25 minutes a pound. Baste frequently.

Remove ¼ cup of the pan gravy and combine in a saucepan with the onion, vinegar, chili peppers, parsley, and cold water. Bring to a boil and cook over low heat for 2 minutes. Carve the pork and serve the sauce in a separate sauceboat. The pork is equally good when served cold.

## CHICKEN IN PEPPER SAUCE

### AJÍ DE POLLO

½ cup olive oil
2 onions, sliced
2 cloves garlic, minced
2 3½-pound chickens, disjointed
3 teaspoons salt
½ teaspoon pepper
2 cups stock or 1 can consommé and ½ can water
5 tomatoes, peeled and chopped, or 1½ cups canned tomatoes

2 onions, chopped fine
4 potatoes, peeled and diced
1 red or green pepper, cut into julienne strips
½ teaspoon dried ground chili peppers
½ teaspoon marjoram
1 cup bread crumbs
4 hard-cooked eggs, quartered
12 ripe olives

Heat ¼ cup of the olive oil in a large saucepan. Add the sliced onions and garlic and sauté for 5 minutes, stirring frequently. Add the chicken and brown on all sides over high heat. Add 2 teaspoons of the salt, the pepper, and 1 cup of the stock. Cover, reduce the heat, and cook for 1 hour, or until tender.

Heat the remaining oil in a separate saucepan. Add the tomatoes, chopped onions, potatoes, pepper, chili peppers, marjoram, and remaining salt. Cook over high heat for 5 minutes, stirring constantly. Add the remaining stock. Cover and cook over low heat for 20 minutes. Add the bread crumbs and mix. Add to the chicken. Stir well and correct seasoning. Serve garnished with the hard-cooked eggs and the olives.

*Note: This dish is quite spicy. If desired, reduce the quantity of ground chili peppers to cut down on the spiciness.*

## VEGETABLE STEW

LOCRO

2 tablespoons butter
2 onions, chopped
2 cloves garlic, minced
½ cup canned tomato sauce
½ cup water
1 cup fresh or canned corn kernels
1 cup fresh or frozen green peas
1 teaspoon salt

½ teaspoon pepper
4 potatoes, peeled and quartered
2 cups cooked or canned pumpkin
  purée
¾ cup grated American or Gruyère
  cheese
1 cup milk

Melt the butter in a large saucepan. Add the onions and garlic and sauté for 10 minutes, stirring frequently. Add the tomato sauce, water, corn, peas, salt, and pepper. Cover and cook over low heat for 10 minutes. Add the potatoes and pumpkin. Cover and cook for 20 minutes, or until the potatoes are tender. Add the grated cheese and milk and stir carefully but thoroughly. Cook 5 minutes longer. Serve with boiled rice on the side. This makes an excellent luncheon dish.

## SWEET FRITTERS

BUÑUELOS

2 tablespoons butter
½ cup sugar
2 tablespoons grated lemon rind
1 cup water

⅞ cup sifted flour
3 eggs
  Fat for deep-fat frying

Combine the butter, sugar, lemon rind, and water in a saucepan. Bring to a boil, stirring occasionally. Add the flour all at once, beating hard. Cook until the dough leaves the sides of the pan. Remove from the heat. Add 1 egg at a time, beating hard after each addition, and until the dough is smooth and shiny. Heat the fat to 375° in a very deep saucepan. Drop the batter by the teaspoon into the fat. Fry until light brown, approximately 5 minutes. Drain. Prepare the following sauce:

1 cup dark brown sugar
3 tablespoons flour
1 cup water

2 tablespoons heavy cream
1 tablespoon butter
½ teaspoon vanilla extract

Combine the sugar and flour in a saucepan. Add the water, stirring to a smooth paste. Cook over medium heat until the mixture becomes thick, stirring occasionally. Add the cream, butter, and vanilla, mixing well. Pour over the fritters and serve either hot or cold.

## COLD RICE DRINK

FRESCO DE ARROZ

½ cup rice
2 quarts boiling water
1½ cups sugar
1 cup orange juice
¼ cup lemon juice
1 cup canned or fresh pineapple juice

1 cup canned or fresh pineapple, cut into ¼-inch cubes
¼ teaspoon cinnamon
4 cloves
3 tablespoons grated orange rind

Wash the rice in several changes of water. Have the water boiling in a saucepan and add the rice. Cook for 35 minutes, or until extremely soft. Force the rice and liquid through a sieve, or purée in an electric blender. Combine the sugar, orange juice, lemon juice, and pineapple juice in a saucepan. Cook until syrupy, about 10 minutes. Add the strained rice, pineapple cubes, cinnamon, cloves, and orange rind. Bring to a boil and remove the cloves. Chill and serve very cold. Sliced strawberries may be added immediately before serving.

## THE GUIANAS

The three Guianas are located in the northeastern part of the South American continent, and many of the present-day boundary lines were settled only during the past half century. The Guianas consist of three parts, the British, the Dutch (who also call their territory Surinam), and the French territories.

Georgetown, the capital of British Guiana, has a rather unusual personality of its own. Possibly this is owing to the population, which consists of a mixture of Chinese, Indonesians, Negroes, Europeans, and natives. The outstanding spot from a tourist's point of view is Kaieteur Falls, roughly five times higher than our own Niagara.

British Guiana produces rice, coffee, coconuts, molasses, and sugar in the food line. There are not too many local food specialties, but *callalu* soup is good, and *broas,* a local cooky, is a favorite. Breadnuts are standard here, and a good soup is made from it. Crabs are exceptional, and a local fish known as *queriman* is cooked in the usual styles of fish cookery. Worthy of mention are such things as *eddoe,* the edible taro leaves, and *casareep,* a liquid seasoning made from cassava. Guavas and soursops are tasty local fruits.

A liquor produced from the juice of the sugar cane is called "shrub." The true liquor specialty of this region is the local Demerara rum, a rum of merely 151 proof! If it ever got that cold in British Guiana, it could be used as an anti-freeze for automobiles.

Dutch Guiana, or Surinam, has Paramaribo as its capital. The country itself is a racial mélange consisting of Europeans, Indonesians, Indians, Negroes, natives, and assorted mixtures of these different groups. Like Dutch people the world over, they are happiest when surrounded by the food and liquors of their own country, and Holland beers and liquors are the ones most frequently seen. Tourist accommodations could be improved, but the Palace and Riverview hotels are the best available.

Among the local food items of interest are such things as *kwie-kwie* (a swamp fish), *taja,* which resembles a potato, and *paksoi* and *amsoi* (green, leafy vegetables). Otherwise, Dutch food is what the people prefer.

Cayenne is the capital of the French part of the Guianas. French Guiana is actually the worst off of the three parts on all counts. It has the lowest population, the smallest land area, is the poorest in natural resources, and is also undoubtedly the least developed of all.

Incidentally, French Guiana was the location of the formerly notorious penal camp, Devil's Island, whose most famous prisoner was Dreyfus. The Ile du Diable is just a small, rocky island located immediately off the coast of French Guiana, and was almost but not quite escape-proof. Numerous heroic movie actors, particularly in the day of the silent film, made good their escape from the island.

The preferred food and liquor of this portion of the Guianas are naturally as French as the people can afford.

## GEORGETOWN RUM SWIZZLE

2 cups finely cracked ice
6 jiggers Demerara rum
½ cup lemon or lime juice
1 cup fresh grapefruit juice
2 tablespoons grenadine
2 tablespoons cherry brandy
½ teaspoon bitters

6 slices fresh pineapple
6 maraschino cherries
6 slices orange
6 slices lemon
6 sprigs mint or 1 teaspoon liquid
mint flavoring

In a large pitcher—*not* in a cocktail shaker—place the cracked ice, rum, lemon or lime juice, grapefruit juice, grenadine, cherry brandy, and bitters. Using a long swizzle stick between the palms of the hands, agitate the mixture until the pitcher becomes ice cold. In tall highball glasses arrange a pineapple slice, maraschino cherry, orange slice, lemon slice, and a sprig of mint. (If fresh mint is not available, add the liquid mint to the pitcher.) Fill each glass about three fourths full of the liquor and add carbonated water.

*Note: Demerara rum is produced locally in British Guiana. It is extremely potent, being about 151 proof.*

## STUFFED CRABS

1 pound fresh cooked or canned crab
meat and crab shells, if available
1 cup bread crumbs
½ cup melted butter
1 teaspoon salt

¼ teaspoon pepper
Dash of mace
2 tablespoons lime or lemon juice
2 pimentos, chopped
2 tablespoons butter

Place the crab meat in a bowl and shred it gently with a fork. Add ¾ cup of the bread crumbs, the melted butter, salt, pepper, mace, lime or lemon juice, and pimentos. Mix well together. Preheat oven to 375°. Clean the crab shells carefully or butter 6 individual ramekins. Place the mixture in the shells or ramekins. Sprinkle with the remaining bread crumbs and dot with the butter. Bake in a 375° oven for 20 minutes, or until delicately browned.

## PEANUT SOUP, PARAMARIBO

4 tablespoons butter
½ cup flour
8 cups chicken stock or 3 cans consommé and 3 cans water

1½ cups peanut butter
1 teaspoon pepper

Melt the butter in a saucepan. Add the flour and mix until smooth. Gradually add 6 cups of the stock, stirring constantly until the boiling point is reached. Mix the remaining stock and the peanut butter together in a bowl until smooth. Add to the soup and stir. Add the pepper and mix well. Cook over low heat for 10 minutes, stirring occasionally. Correct seasoning. If there is any leftover cooked chicken available, it may be cut up into small pieces or shreds and sprinkled on top of the soup. Serve hot.

## CALLALU SOUP

2 pounds fresh or 1 package frozen spinach
1 onion, chopped
½-pound slice of smoked ham (1 piece)
2 quarts water

12 okra, stems removed
12 shrimp, shelled and cleaned
12 shallots (if available)
½ teaspoon black pepper
⅛ teaspoon thyme

Wash the spinach carefully in many changes of water and remove the stems. Combine the spinach, onion, ham, and water in a saucepan. Cook over medium heat for 20 minutes. Add the okra, shrimp, shallots, pepper, and thyme. Cook 20 minutes longer. Correct seasoning. Remove the ham and cut into small cubes. Return ham to the soup and serve hot.

## PORK CASSEROLE

### HOT POT

12 small pork chops
6 potatoes, peeled and sliced
6 onions, sliced
3½ teaspoons salt
½ teaspoon pepper

2 cups boiling water
1 cup sifted flour
½ cup shortening
1 egg, beaten
2 tablespoons ice water

In a heavy casserole arrange alternate layers of the pork chops, potatoes, and onions, sprinkled with 3 teaspoons salt and the pepper. Use half the ingredients for each layer. Add the boiling water. Cover and bake in a 325° oven for 2½ hours.

While the casserole is baking prepare the crust. Sift the flour and remaining salt into a bowl. Cut in the shortening with a pastry blender or two knives. Combine the egg and ice water and add, tossing lightly until a ball of dough is formed. Wrap in wax paper and place in the refrigerator for 45 minutes.

Roll out the dough on a lightly floured surface to fit the top of the casserole. Remove the cover of the casserole and place the dough on top, carefully sealing the edges. Prick the top. Increase the oven temperature to 375° and bake for 25 minutes, or until the top is brown.

*Note: The recipe is of Dutch origin but has become a part of the cuisine of Dutch Guiana.*

423

## CHICKEN AND POTATO CASSEROLE

POM

½ pound butter
2 3½-pound chickens, disjointed
3 onions, chopped
2 cups canned tomatoes
3 celery stalks, sliced

1 tablespoon salt
2 teaspoons pepper
2 teaspoons nutmeg
6 potatoes, peeled and grated
½ cup fresh orange juice

Melt the butter in a large saucepan. Add the chicken and brown well on all sides. Add the onions and sauté for 5 minutes. Add the tomatoes, celery, salt, pepper, and nutmeg. Cover and cook over low heat for 1 hour or until the chicken is tender. Remove the chicken and cut the meat from the bones, reserving the sauce.

Mix ¾ cup of the reserved sauce, the grated potatoes, and orange juice together. Line a buttered casserole dish with two thirds of this mixture and place the cut-up chicken meat on top. Pour the remainder of the sauce over it. Cover the top with the remaining third of the potato mixture. Bake in a 350° oven for 1¼ hours. Serve directly from the casserole.

## CHICKEN PILAU

2 4-pound chickens, cut into halves
1½ cups rice
1 tablespoon salt
1½ cups seedless raisins

1 cup light cream
¼ teaspoon nutmeg
3 tablespoons butter

Clean the chickens carefully, place in a large saucepan with water to almost but not quite cover. Cover the saucepan and cook over medium heat while preparing the rice. Wash the rice in several changes of water and place in a separate saucepan with water to cover. Bring to a boil, turn off heat, let soak for 5 minutes, and drain well.

Add the rice and salt to the chicken. Cover and cook over medium heat for 45 minutes. Add the raisins and cook until chicken is tender. Remove the chicken from the saucepan; place it on a heated platter and keep warm. Add the cream, nutmeg, and butter to the rice and stir well. Pack the rice into small cups or molds and turn out onto the platter surrounding the chicken.

## COOKIES, BRITISH GUIANA STYLE

BROAS

¼ pound butter
1 cup sugar
2 cups sifted flour
1 teaspoon baking powder

1 teaspoon cinnamon
2 teaspoons grated lemon or lime rind
2 eggs

Cream the butter in a bowl until soft; add the sugar, beating until light and fluffy. Sift the flour, baking powder, and cinnamon together. Add to the butter mixture, beating until well blended. Add the grated rind and stir. Add 1 egg at a time, beating well after each addition. Continue mixing until a ball of dough is formed. Roll teaspoonfuls of the dough into balls, and place on a well-buttered baking sheet, allowing about 1 inch between each ball of dough. Bake in a 350° oven for 20 minutes, or until lightly browned.

## PARAGUAY

One of the two countries in South America without a coast line (to save you the trouble of looking it up on a map, the other is Bolivia), Paraguay's development has been hindered by a lack of transportation, although the airplane has helped the situation along to a certain degree. It is a semimythical land to most of us, for it is off the regular tourist path and visited by comparatively few people. For example, the city of Asunción, capital of the republic, does not have running water, although a few hotels and homes have private installations.

This is a country where the people enjoy eating huge quantities of food, and at very frequent intervals. On arising, most Paraguayans have a cup of *maté*, or Paraguayan tea. This drink closely resembles tea but has a rather bitter taste. Nevertheless, most visitors eventually learn to like the drink and enjoy it as much as coffee. The popularity of *maté* has spread throughout the neighboring countries and is particularly important in Argentina and Uruguay. The morning cup of *maté* is followed by a substantial breakfast later in the morning. Lunch is at the customary time, dinner is served between eight and nine in the evening, and both are meals of many different courses. In the larger communities the ladies gather for afternoon tea, which consists of a few cakes and much local gossip.

Paraguay is not a country for the average tourist looking for luxury accommodations and the comforts and conveniences of civilization. Many people have found this inland country fascinating for countless other

425

reasons, such as the unbelievably soft air, the colorful dress of the people, and the unhurried tempo of life. The country is a great producer of oranges and the atmosphere is always laden with the odor of orange blossoms as though weddings were constantly in progress. Bachelors lead nervous lives here, always frightened by the smell of orange blossoms. Oranges are so plentiful that almost no market exists for them and, since it is almost impossible to ship them out of the country owing to the lack of transportation, they are fed to the cattle. It is difficult, almost requiring a real effort of the will, to starve in Paraguay because of the tropical fruits and lush vegetation.

There are many good *Paraguayo* dishes, since the people are particularly fond of fine food. Meat stews are a national tradition, and dishes on the order of the *puchero* are made frequently (for a recipe, see the section on Argentina). An excellent local specialty is *costillas de cerdo en vinagre* (pickled and fried spareribs). All sorts of spaghetti and noodle preparations are appreciated here, and *tallarines con salsa de hongos* (noodles and mushroom sauce) is not too far removed from the Italian version. Corn is a regular part of the diet, used in many fashions, such as in the delicious cheese bread (*chepa*). In addition, there are many foods of *Guaraní* (native Indian) origin.

In Asunción good meals are obtainable at the hotels and in a few local restaurants. Most tourists approve of the Richmond Terraza, which serves many of the *Paraguayo* dishes.

Some adequate local wines are produced, although the best drink of the country is the *caña*, a light rum. It is used in making all sorts of mixed drinks, accompanied by various local fruits.

Are you happy? Would you like to be sad at the same time? Follow our advice: first, go to Paraguay; second, order a drink made with *caña;* and third, listen to the melancholy songs of the plains, the *Paraguayo* music.

## STUFFED FISH

### PESCADO RELLENO

4 tablespoons butter
3 white onions, chopped
1 cup mushrooms, sliced
¼ pound ham, minced
12 pitted ripe olives, minced
½ cup white wine
2 slices white bread, trimmed
½ cup milk
1 egg, beaten
2 hard-cooked eggs, chopped

3 teaspoons salt
1½ teaspoons pepper
1 whole fish (about 4 pounds), snapper, whitefish, pompano or mackerel
1 teaspoon Spanish paprika
3 tablespoons lemon juice
4 tablespoons olive oil
¾ cup bread crumbs

Melt the butter in a saucepan. Add the onions and mushrooms and sauté for 10 minutes, stirring frequently. Add the ham and olives and sauté for 5 minutes. Add the wine. Cover and cook over low heat for 15 minutes. Remove from heat and let cool for 10 minutes. Soak the bread in the milk for 5 minutes. Squeeze out all the liquid. Mash the bread with a fork and add to the previous mixture. Add the egg, chopped eggs, 1 teaspoon of the salt, and ½ teaspoon of the pepper, and mix well.

Have the fish split but not cut apart, so that it may be stuffed. Remove the central bones. Sprinkle the fish with the remaining salt and pepper, paprika, lemon juice, and olive oil. Stuff the fish with the mixture and fasten the opening carefully with skewers, toothpicks, or thread. Preheat oven to 375°. Place in a buttered baking dish. Sprinkle with the bread crumbs and dot with butter. Bake in a 375° oven for 40 minutes, or until the fish is browned and flaky. Sprinkle a little parsley on the fish and place on a platter. Serve hot or cold.

## PICKLED AND FRIED SPARERIBS

COSTILLAS DE CERDO EN VINAGRE

| | |
|---|---|
| 1 cup vinegar | 5 eggs |
| 2 teaspoons salt | 2 tablespoons flour |
| 1 teaspoon pepper | ½ cup bread crumbs |
| 1 teaspoon Spanish paprika | 2 tablespoons chopped parsley |
| ½ teaspoon marjoram | Fat for deep-fat frying |
| 2 racks of spareribs, cut into ribs | |

Mix the vinegar, 1 teaspoon of the salt, the pepper, paprika, and marjoram in a bowl. Place the spareribs in it and marinate at room temperature for 2 hours, basting frequently. Remove from the marinade and place on a roasting pan. Roast in a 400° oven for 10 minutes. Remove and let cool for 20 minutes.

Mix the eggs, flour, bread crumbs, parsley, and remaining salt in a bowl. Dip the ribs in the mixture, coating each one well. Heat the fat to 370° in a deep saucepan. Fry the ribs in the fat until brown, about 10 minutes. Drain well. Serve hot.

## RICE AND MEAT

ARROZ CON CARNE

| | |
|---|---|
| 4 tablespoons olive oil | ½ teaspoon pepper |
| 3 onions, chopped | 1 teaspoon Spanish paprika |
| 1 clove garlic, minced | 3 cups boiling water |
| 3 pounds beef (cross rib, bottom round, or similar cut), cubed | 1 Spanish-style sausage, sliced |
| 2 green peppers, sliced | 1 cup rice |
| 2 teaspoons salt | 3 tablespoons chopped parsley |
| | ½ cup sliced stuffed olives |

Heat the olive oil in a heavy saucepan. Add the onions, garlic, beef, and green peppers. Cook over high heat until the meat is browned on all sides. Add the salt, pepper, paprika, and water. Cover and cook over low heat for 2 hours.

Add the sausage slices and rice. Mix together gently. Cook over low heat for 30 minutes, stirring occasionally. The rice should be moist but no gravy should remain. Add the parsley and olives and mix together lightly. Correct seasoning and serve.

## NOODLES WITH MUSHROOM SAUCE

TALLARINES CON SALSA DE HONGOS

2 tablespoons olive oil
2 onions, chopped
1 cup tomato sauce
1 tomato, chopped
1 teaspoon salt
½ teaspoon pepper
3 slices bacon, chopped
¼ pound ham, cut into julienne strips
2 sausages (Spanish style, if possible), sliced thin
1 cup chopped mushrooms
1 cup stock or 1 bouillon cube dissolved in 1 cup hot water
¾ pound medium noodles, boiled in salted water
1 cup grated American, Cheddar, or Parmesan cheese

Heat the olive oil in a saucepan. Add the onions and sauté for 10 minutes, stirring frequently. Add the tomato sauce, tomato, salt, pepper, bacon, ham, and sausages and stir. Cover and cook over low heat for 20 minutes. Mix the mushrooms and stock together and add. Cover and cook over low heat for 15 minutes. Correct seasoning.

Arrange successive layers of cooked noodles, grated cheese, and the sauce in a buttered baking dish. Arrange as many layers as possible, but the top layer should consist of the sauce. Bake in a 375° oven for 25 minutes, or until delicately browned on top. Serve hot, directly from the dish.

## CHEESE BREAD

CHEPA

⅔ cup shortening
2 eggs
1½ cups grated American or Cheddar cheese
2¼ cups corn meal
¼ teaspoon salt
⅓ cup milk

Cream the shortening. Add the eggs, beating well. Add the cheese and mix until smooth. Combine the corn meal and salt. Add to the cheese mixture, alternately with the milk, mixing steadily. Knead together with the hands until well blended. Preheat oven to 375°. Place the dough in a buttered 9-inch loaf pan. Cover the top with a piece of aluminum foil. Bake in a 375° oven for 35 minutes, or until firm.

## RAISIN CAKE

TORTA DE PASA

| | |
|---|---|
| 1 tablespoon cornstarch | 2 eggs, beaten |
| ½ cup water | 2 cups sifted flour |
| ¾ cup sugar | 1½ teaspoons cream of tartar |
| 1¼ cups seedless raisins | 1½ teaspoons baking soda |
| ½ cup chopped nuts | ½ cup milk |
| ¼ pound butter | 1 teaspoon vanilla extract |
| ½ cup dark brown sugar | |

Mix the cornstarch and water in a saucepan until smooth. Add ½ cup of the sugar and cook over low heat, stirring constantly until thick, about 5 minutes. Add the raisins and nuts. Mix lightly and set aside while preparing the batter.

Cream the butter. Add the brown sugar and the remaining white sugar, creaming until light and fluffy. Add the eggs, beating well. Sift the flour, cream of tartar, and baking soda together and add alternately with the milk. Add vanilla. Mix well. Preheat oven to 375°. Pour half the batter into a buttered 8-inch square pan. Spread the raisin mixture over it and cover with the remaining batter. Bake in a 375° oven for 25 minutes or until a cake tester comes out clean. Cool, then turn out of the pan. Cut in squares.

*PERU*

In the middle of South America's west coast is this land of powerful contrasts. Here is a country of extremes—barren, icy highlands; fresh, flower-laden towns with temperate climate; and savage jungles, thick and impenetrable. Peru is served by Panagra, a part of Pan American World Airways System. For those who enjoy lost cities, there is the fabulous Inca city of Machu Picchu high up in the Andes, definitely a highlight of any trip to South America. Nearby is Cuzco, a city more than 10,000 feet

429

above sea level, the ancient capital of the Incas. The life of the Indians in the area is not substantially different from that of their great ancestors of centuries ago.

Peru is curiously rich and curiously poor. Partly developed but largely agricultural, it lives in hope of what the future will bring. But the people are friendly, though formal in manner, and they enjoy good living and good food. The cuisine is not unlimited, but there are at least a dozen excellent local specialties.

Everyone in Peru is fond of pickled food, and *seviche* is a great favorite. It is made from raw fish, but the finished dish has a cooked taste and is not nearly so exotic as it sounds; and as previously remarked, even cautious people eat raw oysters and clams. Peru may safely claim distinction in regard to its soups, for these have been developed to a greater extent than in almost any other Latin-American country. Most people eat a thick soup made of vegetables and meat almost every day. Much more unusual from the American point of view are the *chupes* (soups made of shrimp, fish, or other ingredients); a recipe for *chupe de camarones* is supplied. No mention of the food of Peru could possibly overlook the national snack, *anticuchos* (pieces of beef heart dipped in a spicy sauce and roasted over a charcoal fire). A tremendous favorite is the *huancaina* sauce, somewhat spicy but very delicious, which the Peruvians put over meats, vegetables, and practically anything else.

Partridges and other small game are imaginatively prepared. The country has some delicious fruit, particularly the *cherimoya,* which is most enjoyable when eaten fresh and cold, or with sweet cream. Owing to a large Chinese population, Lima, the capital city, has a fair number of Chinese restaurants known as *chifas* which serve Chinese food with a Peruvian twist. Life can be complicated, particularly when selecting Chinese food from a Spanish menu.

There are some fairly good wines in Peru, but the beer is of the very highest quality. The cheap, popular drink is *chicha,* a superpowerful distillation generally advisable for supermen only. The unusual drink of the nation is *pisco,* a cross between gin and brandy that is entitled to consideration as a novel drink in the world of alcoholic beverages. *Pisco* is made into many different drinks, but the *pisco* sour has been almost unanimously (and justifiably) acclaimed as the national mixed drink. If your stomach is strong, we may now consider what might be called, if we wanted to be polite, an alcoholic potion. This—this—this *creation* is known as *aguardiente anisado.* Its basic ingredient is a crude, unpleasant-tasting alcohol; you'll note that we are proceeding cautiously, so that those who wish to may avoid what is coming. Next is added anise flavoring and then goats' milk for vitamin content! The final product is so delicious that we had better talk about something else.

## PISCO SOUR

| | |
|---|---|
| 6 jiggers *pisco* | ½ teaspoon bitters |
| 1 jigger sugar syrup or honey | 1 egg white |
| 3 tablespoons lemon juice | Cracked ice |

Stir together in a cocktail shaker the *pisco*, sugar syrup or honey, lemon juice, and bitters. When well mixed, add the egg white and cracked ice. Shake well. Serve immediately, ice cold.

*Note: Pisco is a very pale grape brandy, approximately 100 proof. There are a very few places in this country where it is obtainable; however it may be imitated by using the lightest possible grape brandy in place of the Peruvian pisco. A California grape brandy is a reasonable substitute.*

## TINY CHEESE PIES

### EMPANADITAS DE QUESO

| | |
|---|---|
| 1 cup sifted flour | 4 tablespoons cream cheese |
| 1 teaspoon baking powder | ½ teaspoon salt |
| 2 tablespoons butter | 1 teaspoon chili powder |
| 2 egg yolks, beaten | 1 egg white |
| 2 tablespoons water | Fat for deep-fat frying |
| 4 tablespoons cottage cheese | |

Sift the flour and baking powder into a bowl. Cut in the butter with a pastry blender or two knives. Add the egg yolks and water and toss lightly with a fork until a soft dough is formed. Add more water if necessary. Combine the cottage cheese, cream cheese, salt, and chili powder, mixing until smooth. Beat the egg white until stiff but not dry and fold into the cheese carefully.

Roll out the dough as thin as possible on a lightly floured surface. Cut into rounds with a cooky cutter. Place a teaspoon of the cheese mixture on each round and fold over the dough, sealing the edges carefully with a little water. Press the edges with the tines of a fork, if desired. Heat the fat to 385° and fry until lightly browned. Drain well. These tiny pies are served as cocktail snacks.

## PICKLED RAW FISH

### SEVICHE

| | |
|---|---|
| 6 fillets white-meat fish | ½ cup vinegar |
| 1 cup white wine | 2 chili peppers, crushed, or ¼ tea- |
| 1 cup lemon juice | spoon dried ground chili peppers |
| 3 onions, sliced thin | ¼ teaspoon pepper |
| 2 teaspoons salt | 3 cooked sweet potatoes |
| 1 cup water | Lettuce leaves |

Wash the fish carefully, removing any remaining skin or bones. Cut the fish into thin strips, julienne fashion. Place in a bowl. Add the wine and lemon juice and marinate at room temperature for 3 hours.

Place the onions in a separate bowl. Add 1 teaspoon of the salt and the water and soak for 20 minutes. Pour off the water and squeeze the onions between the hands to remove any remaining moisture. Wash the onions with fresh water and drain completely. Replace the onions in the bowl and add the vinegar. Soak for 1 hour, then drain. Add the chili peppers, pepper, and remaining salt. Mix well and add to the previously prepared fish. Mix the ingredients together carefully and marinate 2 hours longer. Place in the refrigerator. Serve cold. Garnish with sliced cold sweet potato and lettuce leaves.

## SHRIMP SOUP

CHUPE DE CAMARONES

2 tablespoons olive oil
2 onions, chopped
2 cloves garlic
3 tablespoons canned tomato sauce
6 cups boiling water
½ cup green peas
½ cup corn kernels
5 potatoes, peeled and cubed
2 teaspoons salt
¼ teaspoon dried ground chili peppers
¼ teaspoon marjoram
¼ pound cream cheese
2 cups milk
24 shrimp, shelled and cleaned
4 eggs
6 small pieces fried fish (optional)

Heat the olive oil in a deep saucepan and add the onions and garlic. Sauté until brown, about 10 minutes, stirring frequently. Remove the garlic cloves. Add the tomato sauce, water, peas, corn, potatoes, salt, chili peppers, and marjoram. Cook for 20 minutes. Mash the cream cheese to a smooth paste and add to the soup. Add the shrimp. Cook for 10 minutes.

Beat the eggs in a bowl. Gradually add 2 cups of the hot soup, stirring constantly to prevent curdling. Return to the soup in the saucepan, stirring well. Reheat the soup but do not allow it to boil. Place a piece of fried fish in each soup plate, if desired. Serve hot.

*Note: This soup is served in varying degrees of spiciness, depending upon the locality, the cook, and various other factors. If a less spicy soup is desired, substitute ¼ teaspoon of black pepper for the ground chili peppers. If a hot, spicy soup is wanted, increase the chili peppers to ½ teaspoon.*

## BARBECUED MEAT

ANTICUCHOS

2 pounds steak or 1 beef heart
1 cup tarragon vinegar
2 fresh chili peppers or ½ teaspoon
   dried ground chili peppers
¼ teaspoon saffron

3 cloves garlic, minced
12 peppercorns
1 teaspoon salt
½ cup water
3 tablespoons olive oil

Cut the steak into 1-inch cubes; if a beef heart is used, wash it very well, remove the skin, dry, and cut into 1-inch cubes. Combine in a bowl the vinegar, chili peppers, saffron, garlic, peppercorns, salt, and water. Add the meat cubes and marinate overnight.

Place the cubes on skewers and brush with olive oil. Broil until tender, turning frequently, and basting occasionally with the marinade. Serve with corn on the cob or roasted sweet potatoes.

Note: Anticuchos are always prepared with beef heart in Peru, where their relative popularity is identical with frankfurters here. As a concession to popular taste, steak may be used instead of beef heart. The curious and courageous are urged to try beef heart; the results are rewarding.

## SAUTÉED BEEF, HOTEL BOLIVAR FASHION

LOMITO SALTADO, HOTEL BOLIVAR

3 tablespoons butter
4 potatoes, peeled and cubed
4 tablespoons olive oil
3 pounds sirloin steak, cut into 1-inch
   strips
3 onions, chopped

4 tomatoes, chopped
2 teaspoons salt
½ teaspoon pepper
¼ teaspoon dried ground chili peppers
2 tablespoons vinegar
½ cup fresh or canned peas

Melt the butter and add the potatoes. Fry them for 10 minutes, browning on all sides. Heat the oil in a separate skillet. Place the meat in it and cook over high heat for 3 minutes, shaking the pan frequently. Turn the meat over to sear it on all sides. Remove the steak from the pan and keep warm.

Place the onions in the same skillet; sauté for 5 minutes. Add the tomatoes, salt, pepper, and chili peppers and cook over medium heat for 5 minutes, stirring frequently. Add the steak and potatoes and mix gently. Add the vinegar and stir carefully. Add the peas and cook over low heat for 10 minutes, stirring occasionally. Serve hot.

# STEAK WITH *HUANCAINA* SAUCE

LOMO A LA HUANCAINA

¼ pound cream cheese
4 hard-cooked egg yolks, chopped
2 fresh chili peppers, ground, or ½
teaspoon dried ground chili peppers
1 teaspoon salt
½ cup olive oil

¾ cup heavy cream
⅛ teaspoon lemon juice
2 onions, chopped fine
6 individual steaks
12 ripe olives
3 hard-cooked eggs, quartered

Beat the cheese until smooth. Add the chopped egg yolks, chili peppers, and salt and beat with a wooden spoon. Add the olive oil drop by drop, beating steadily with the wooden spoon. Add the cream, lemon juice, and onions, mixing well. Heat the mixture in a saucepan. Broil the steaks to the desired degree of rareness and place on a large serving platter. Pour the sauce over them and garnish with the olives and hard-cooked eggs. This sauce is quite spicy but is an unusual combination of flavors.

# PERUVIAN CRULLERS

PICARONES

1 cake or package yeast
½ cup lukewarm water
½ cup fresh or canned sweet potatoes,
puréed
¼ teaspoon salt

1¾ cups sifted flour
¼ teaspoon mace
2 eggs, beaten
3 tablespoons brandy
Fat for deep-fat frying

Combine the yeast and water in a cup and allow to soften for 5 minutes. Mix until smooth. Place the sweet potatoes in a bowl. Add the yeast mixture, salt, flour, and mace and mix well. Add the eggs and brandy, beating well until smooth and creamy. Cover the bowl with a cloth and put in a warm place for 2 hours, or until double in bulk. Heat the fat to 370° in a deep saucepan. Drop the batter into it by the teaspoonful. Fry for 5 minutes, or until browned on both sides. Sprinkle with powdered sugar and serve with syrup or jelly.

*URUGUAY*

This comparatively small republic is one of the most progressive countries in the world. Because of its extremely solvent financial position, it has one of the soundest currencies in the world. A good deal of nervous capital has made its way to Uruguay. It has a remarkable climate with a rather small variation in temperature, although the winter months of July and August (their seasons are reversed) are often gray, damp, and cloudy. Montevideo, the capital, is located on the coast and has an impressive bathing beach that runs for many miles. It was near Montevideo that the German warship *Graf Spee* was scuttled. Punta del Este is a resort town with a tremendous future, for it is the center for vacationists from all over South America, and cruise ships from the United States have often made special stops there in recent years.

The country is a heavy producer of fruit (grapes in particular), grains, olives, and cattle. The national economy is built to a substantial degree on meat; a great deal of it is consumed and also exported as frozen beef, particularly to meat-hungry Great Britain. The *gauchos,* the local cowboys, consume beef in quantities that would amaze anyone, possibly including the *gauchos* themselves. For that matter the per capita consumption of beef in Uruguay is extremely high.

Meal hours and customs follow the usual South American pattern. Teatime is a special ritual, cheerfully honored by the populace who make a point of consuming large numbers of irresistible pastries every afternoon at about 5 P.M. Dinner is usually a meal of many courses, elaborate and substantial, almost never served before nine-thirty in the evening, and often much later.

With its high grape production, it is not surprising to find a serious effort in the direction of wine making. The country produces some white wine, but the reds are superior though not quite up to Chilean standards.

Uruguayans are hearty eaters and appreciate fine food, as their diet indicates. Good soups, on the order of the *pavesa*, for which a recipe is given, are typical. Fish of all sorts are liked, and with its coastline on the south Atlantic, a fair supply is available. The population contains a high percentage of Italian immigrants who have brought their own food habits with them; this accounts for the large number of Italian dishes frequently served here. A good many of Uruguay's restaurants are Italian-owned and -operated, and spaghettis and other *pastas* are standard on every menu.

But beef is *the* dish, prepared as *carbonada criolla, puchero,* or the cowboy specialty, beef barbecued in its own hide (*asado con cuero*). The *gauchos* often exist on only two foods, roast meat and *maté,* the national drink of the country, and for weeks on end during the grazing season eat nothing else. Apparently the beef and the *maté* supply all the needed vitamins, for the cowboys are very healthy specimens. *Maté* closely resembles tea and is made from the leaves of the *Ilex paraguayensis* tree. Although it may be served in a cup, the native fashion is to drink it from a gourd, in which the leaves are steeped in hot water; it is then sipped through a silver tube with a strainer at the lower end. It may be taken *maté amargo* (without sugar) or *maté dulce* (with sugar), and sometimes with orange peelings to add a little extra flavor.

Very fine food may be had in Monte (please forgive the familiarity) at the new Victoria Plaza Hotel; also at Cassoni's, El Aguila, and Morini's restaurants.


## EGG AND SPINACH HORS D'OEUVRES

TORTA PASCUALINA

| | |
|---|---|
| 2 cups sifted flour | ¾ teaspoon black pepper |
| 3 egg yolks | ¼ teaspoon nutmeg |
| ⅓ cup olive oil | ¼ cup grated Parmesan cheese |
| ½ cup lukewarm water | 6 eggs |
| 2 cups cooked spinach, drained | 2 teaspoons salt |

Sift the flour onto a board; make a well in the center. Place the egg yolks and 3 tablespoons of the olive oil in the center. Gradually work the flour into it, adding enough of the lukewarm water to make a stiff dough. Knead the dough until smooth and elastic. Cover with a cloth and set aside for 10 minutes. Roll out the dough as thin as possible on a lightly floured surface and brush with some of the oil. Cut the dough into four pieces, each large enough to fit an oblong baking dish measuring about 8 by 15 inches. Grease the dish and place two layers on the bottom.

Combine the spinach, pepper, nutmeg, and cheese. Mix well and place evenly over the dough. Make six evenly spaced depressions in the spinach mixture, using the back of soup spoon. Break an egg into each depression and sprinkle with the salt. Cover with the remaining two layers of dough, sealing the edges carefully. Run a pastry wheel or the handle of a knife over the dough, so as to divide it into six equal portions with an egg in each. Bake in a 375° oven for 35 minutes, or until lightly browned on top. Serve hot or cold.

## BEEF BROTH

### PAVESA

2 pounds short ribs of beef
Several beef bones
8 cups water
1 onion
1 stalk celery
1 carrot
2 sprigs parsley

3 teaspoons salt
1 teaspoon pepper
6 eggs
6 slices buttered toast (made from French-style bread, if possible)
¼ cup grated Parmesan cheese

Combine the beef, bones, water, onion, celery, carrot, parsley, salt, and pepper in a deep saucepan. Bring to a boil and skim the top. Cook over medium heat for 2 hours. Strain the soup. Pour 2 cups of the strained soup into a saucepan and poach the eggs in it carefully. Place an egg in each soup plate and return the 2 cups of soup to the balance. Pour the soup over the eggs. Sprinkle the toast with the cheese and place a slice in each soup plate. The meat may be eaten separately.

## BAKED FISH IN CASSEROLE

### CAZUELA DE PESCADO

½ cup olive oil
2 onions, sliced thin
3 tomatoes, peeled and chopped
½ cup water
½ teaspoon saffron
2 teaspoons salt
½ teaspoon pepper

1 bay leaf
6 fish fillets
1 cup boiled potato balls
2 green peppers, sliced thin
½ cup fresh or frozen green peas
3 canned pimentos, sliced thin

Heat the olive oil in a saucepan. Add the onions and sauté for 10 minutes, stirring frequently. Add the tomatoes, water, saffron, salt, pepper, and bay leaf. Cook over low heat for 15 minutes. Place the fillets in a buttered casserole. Arrange the potato balls, green peppers, and peas around the fish. Pour the tomato sauce over the fish and place the sliced pimentos on top. Cover. Bake in a 375° oven for 40 minutes. Serve directly from the casserole.

## VEAL AND FRUIT STEW

### CARBONADA CRIOLLA

3 tablespoons olive oil
2 tablespoons butter
3 onions, cut into eighths
3 pounds veal, cut into ½-inch cubes
½ cup white wine
1 tablespoon tomato paste
1 bay leaf
2 sprigs parsley
1 stalk celery
½ teaspoon thyme
2 teaspoons salt
½ teaspoon pepper

3 cups stock or 1 can consommé and
  1 can water
2 potatoes, peeled and cut into small
  cubes
1 small squash, cubed
2 sweet potatoes, peeled and cut into
  small cubes
2 apples peeled and cut into small
  cubes
2 pears, peeled and cut into small
  cubes
2 tablespoons seedless raisins
2 tablespoons chopped parsley

Heat the oil and butter in a casserole. Add onions and sauté for 15 minutes, stirring frequently. Remove the onions and set aside. Add the meat and brown on all sides over high heat. Return the onions to the casserole and add the wine and tomato paste. Tie the bay leaf, parsley, and celery together with some white thread and add to the casserole, together with the thyme, salt, pepper, and stock. Cover and cook over medium heat for 50 minutes.

Add the potatoes, squash, and sweet potatoes. Cover and cook over low heat for 30 minutes, or until the veal is tender. Add the apples, pears, and raisins and cook for 10 minutes. Correct seasoning. Sprinkle the parsley on top and stir. Remove the bay leaf, parsley, and celery and discard. Serve with boiled rice.

## TURKEY CASSEROLE

### CACEROLA DE PAVO

1 tablespoon salt
1 teaspoon pepper
1 teaspoon Spanish paprika
3 cloves garlic, minced
8-pound turkey, disjointed
¾ cup vinegar
2 bay leaves
¼ cup olive oil

3 tablespoons butter
2 onions, chopped
1 cup stock or 1 bouillon cube
  dissolved in 1 cup hot water
2 pimentos, sliced
12 green olives, sliced
½ cup capers, drained

Combine the salt, pepper, paprika, and garlic. Rub into the turkey pieces thoroughly. Place the turkey in a bowl and pour the vinegar over it. Add the bay leaves and allow the turkey to marinate for 2 hours. Drain.

Heat the olive oil and butter in an earthenware casserole or heavy saucepan. Add the turkey and onions. Cook over high heat until the turkey is well browned on all sides, stirring frequently. Add the stock. Cover and cook over low heat for 1¾ hours, or until the turkey is tender. Add the pimentos, olives, and capers and stir well. Correct seasoning. Serve directly from the casserole.

## CORN BREAD PUDDING

### PAN DE MAÍZ

| | |
|---|---|
| 3 tablespoons olive oil | 2 cups sifted corn meal |
| 3 onions, chopped | 1 teaspoon baking powder |
| 3 tomatoes, chopped | ½ pound cottage cheese |
| ¾ cup stock or 1 bouillon cube dissolved in ¾ cup water | 3 tablespoons melted butter |
| | 1½ cups milk |
| 1 teaspoon salt | |

Heat the olive oil in a saucepan. Add the onions and sauté for 5 minutes, stirring frequently. Add the tomatoes and sauté for 10 minutes, again stirring frequently. Add the stock and salt and cook over medium heat for 10 minutes. Preheat oven to 350°.

Sift the corn meal and baking powder into a bowl. Add the cottage cheese and butter and mix well. Add the milk and beat well. Combine with the tomato mixture. Pour into a buttered 8-inch square pan. Bake in a 350° oven for 1 hour, or until lightly set. Turn out onto a platter and serve at once in 1-inch slices.

## MERINGUE DESSERT

### POSTRE CHAJA

| | |
|---|---|
| 4 egg whites | 5 egg yolks |
| ⅛ teaspoon salt | ½ pound sweet butter |
| ½ teaspoon vinegar | 1 tablespoon brandy |
| 1¾ cups sugar | 6 slices spongecake or 12 lady fingers |
| 1 teaspoon vanilla extract | gers |
| ¼ cup water | 1 cup strawberries |
| ⅛ teaspoon cream of tartar | 2 cups whipped cream |

Beat the whites and salt until stiff but not dry. Add the vinegar and gradually add 1 cup of the sugar, spoon by spoon, beating constantly until ¾ cup of the sugar is used; fold in the remaining ¼ cup, and the vanilla. Drop by tablespoons onto a buttered baking sheet, or use a pastry bag. Bake in a 250° oven for 30 minutes, or until delicately browned. Remove from the pan immediately with a spatula and set aside to cool.

Combine the remaining ¾ cup of sugar, the water and cream of tartar in a saucepan. Boil until very syrupy. If a spoon of the mixture is lifted out of the syrup, a thread should form. Beat the egg yolks in a bowl and gradually add the syrup, beating constantly until the mixture is cool and thick. Cream the butter until fluffy and soft and add gradually to the syrup mixture. Add the brandy and mix together.

Place a meringue on each plate and top with a slice of spongecake or 2 lady fingers. Arrange a few strawberries on the spongecake and cover with whipped cream. Place a meringue on top and cover completely with the previously prepared butter cream. Some crumbled meringue may be sprinkled on top.

## VENEZUELA

Venezuela consists of two principal parts—the tropical, unexplored jungles of the interior and the more modern region bordering the coastline. Far back in the *savannas* (the plains) there are hundreds of miles of territory where no white man has yet been, and where the trees are filled with orchids, and parrots and monkeys scream from the treetops. This description may sound like a Hollywood trailer for a color film about Africa, but then even Hollywood can be right. In the small communities surrounding the wild *savannas* the people eat simple and tasty local dishes based upon what is produced and available in their area, for transportation is poor. Corn forms the basic part of their diet; it is boiled or made into a variety of homemade bread. *Aresancocho,* a meat stew containing many unusual ingredients, is a Venezuelan favorite, and is quite similar to *sancocho,* a recipe for which appears in the Central American section. *Mondongos* are soup-stews on the order of Argentinian *pucheros.*

Nature has been very kind to Venezuela, and the country owns large natural resources of what is known as black gold, or oil. This wealth has permitted the nation to prosper at an amazing pace, and as a result many visitors are surprised to find the capital city, Caracas, a truly modern city with fine homes, hotels, and restaurants. As is true of all big cities, prices of everything are *extremely* high even by our own standards.

Naturally the city folk do not eat the same fare as their country cousins, and their diet is closer to that of other foreign city dwellers than to the diet of their own peasantry.

A good breakfast is eaten almost everywhere in the country—an exception to the usual South American custom. Eggs, homemade bread, and either hot chocolate or coffee start the day. Lunch and dinner are both quite substantial meals of numerous courses. Dinner is often eaten quite late in the evening, extremely late by comparison with our habits.

Beans, root vegetables, stews, corn, and starchy potato tubers (like *apio*, for example) form the basic items of the local diet. If one dish were to be selected as representative of the country, it would have to be *hallacas*, a sort of tamale stuffed with meat. It may be eaten as an hors d'oeuvre or as a main course. In general, fish is available only near the coast line and in the major cities; red snapper is the great favorite.

The outstanding cheese is *queso de mano*, or hand cheese, so called because it is kneaded by hand until the desired elastic quality is obtained. It is much used in Venezuela and deserves to be exported, but owing to the high prices that already obtain in Venezuela, it would have to sell at unwarrantedly high prices here.

As to liquors, a considerable amount of hard liquor is made from corn and sugar cane: there is also *cocuy*, a brandy made from cactus which is not for sissies, or for strong men either, for that matter. Beer is good and is consumed in large quantities, and home brew made from palm trees is popular. Imported wines and liquors are available at very high prices but are not important to the majority of Venezuelans. An exception must be noted in favor of French brandies, for which the country has an extreme fondness. At those prices, too!

Travelers to Maracaibo will want to stay and dine at the Hotel del Lago; it's famous for its excellent kitchen.

## PICKLED FISH
### PESCADO EN ESCABECHE

8 fillets of sole, snapper, or other white-meat fish
3 tablespoons lemon juice
2 tablespoons salt
1 teaspoon pepper
¼ cup sifted flour
1½ cups olive or salad oil
3 cups cider vinegar
1 cup water
1 tablespoon sugar
4 onions, sliced
4 green or red peppers, cut into julienne strips
3 tablespoons capers, drained
2 tablespoons mustard pickles
2 tablespoons bread crumbs

Cut the fillets in half and sprinkle with the lemon juice. Combine the salt, pepper, and flour and roll the fish in it. Heat ½ cup of the oil in a skillet and fry the fish in it until well browned on both sides. Place the fish in a deep bowl.

Combine the vinegar, water, sugar, onions, peppers, and remaining oil in a saucepan. Bring to a boil and cook over medium heat for 5 minutes. Add the capers, pickles, and bread crumbs, mixing lightly. Pour over the fish and marinate overnight. Garnish the fish with ripe olives. The fish will keep a week in the refrigerator.

## FISH AND ALMOND SOUP

### SOPA DE PESCADO Y ALMENDRAS

| | |
|---|---|
| 2 tablespoons butter | ½ cup rice |
| 1 onion, chopped | 1 cup ground blanched almonds |
| 1 pound fillet of sole | 1 teaspoon salt |
| 1 pound shrimp, shelled and cleaned | ½ teaspoon pepper |
| ¼ pound ham, chopped fine | 1 teaspoon saffron |
| 2 quarts stock or 4 cans consommé | 3 hard-cooked egg yolks, chopped |
| and 3 cans water | 3 tablespoons chopped parsley |

Melt the butter in a saucepan. Add the onion and cook over low heat until soft, but do not allow the onion to brown. Cut the fillet of sole and the shrimp into small pieces. Add to the onion. Add the ham and stock and bring to a boil. Add the rice, almonds, salt, pepper, and saffron and stir. Cook over low heat for 30 minutes. Before serving, add the chopped egg yolks and parsley. Serve with French-style bread.

## VENEZUELAN NATIONAL CORN MEAL DISH

### HALLACAS

| | |
|---|---|
| 1½ pounds beef, diced | 4 tablespoons chopped parsley |
| 1½ pounds pork, diced | 4 teaspoons salt |
| 2 cups water | 3 tablespoons vinegar |
| 4 cloves garlic, minced | 1 teaspoon sugar |
| 1 cup canned chick-peas | 2 teaspoon capers |
| 3 tablespoons olive oil | ½ cup seedless raisins |
| 4 tomatoes, chopped | ½ cup sliced stuffed olives |
| 4 onions, chopped | 3 cups corn meal |
| 2 green peppers, chopped | 4 cups boiling water |
| ½ teaspoon dried ground chili peppers | ⅓ cup butter |
| pers | 2 eggs, beaten |

Combine the beef, pork, water, and garlic in a saucepan. Bring to a boil and cook over medium heat for 45 minutes. Drain and chop coarsely. Add the chick-peas, mixing lightly. Heat the oil in a large skillet. Add the tomatoes, onions, green peppers, chili peppers, parsley, 2 teaspoons of the salt, vinegar, sugar, and the meat mixture. Cook over low heat for 15 minutes, stirring occasionally. Add the capers, raisins, and olives. Mix lightly. Set aside.

Mix the corn meal with a little cold water. Add to the boiling water in a saucepan, stirring constantly. Add the butter and remaining salt. Cook over low heat for 15 minutes. Remove from the heat and add the eggs, beating until a smooth dough is formed. Butter a large (3-quart) round or square baking dish. Line it with two thirds of the corn-meal mixture and pour the meat mixture into it. Spread the remaining corn meal on top. Cover the dish with a piece of aluminum foil and tie it. Place in a pan of water. Bake in a 350° oven for 1 hour.

In Venezuela the dish is prepared in the form of *tamales*. Banana leaves are used for wrapping the *hallacas,* but aluminum foil or parchment paper will serve as a substitute. Cut 10-inch squares of either paper. Spread about 4 tablespoons of the corn-meal dough in the center and press as thin as possible. Place 2 tablespoons of the meat mixture on the dough and fold over, sealing the edges as well as possible. If the dough breaks, patch it with a little more dough. Fold the paper around the *hallacas* carefully and tie it securely. (If aluminum foil is used, it is not necessary to tie it.) Boil in a large saucepan of salted water for 1½ hours. Serve in the papers.


## STUFFED CHICKEN CASSEROLE

### CACEROLA DE GALLINA RELLENA

¼ pound lean pork
4 onions
6 tomatoes
3 teaspoons salt
1 teaspoon pepper
¼ cup chopped mustard pickles
1 tablespoon minced capers
½ cup bread crumbs

2 eggs, beaten
5- to 6-pound roasting chicken
2 tablespoons butter
2 tablespoons olive oil
1 bay leaf
3 potatoes, cubed
8 carrots, peeled and halved
¼ cup sherry

Grind the pork, 2 onions, and 2 tomatoes in a food chopper. Add 1 teaspoon salt, ½ teaspoon pepper, the pickles, capers, bread crumbs, and eggs. Mix well. Wash and dry the chicken. Sprinkle with remaining salt and pepper. Stuff with the pork mixture and close the opening with thread or skewers.

Heat the butter and oil in a casserole or Dutch oven. Brown the chicken in it on all sides. Slice the remaining onions and add. Cook over high heat for 5 minutes. Quarter the remaining tomatoes and add with the bay leaf. Cover and cook over low heat for 2½ hours, basting occasionally.

Add the potatoes, carrots, and a little water, if necessary. Cook for 20 minutes.

Place the chicken on a platter with the potatoes around it. Keep warm. Discard the bay leaf. Force the gravy through a sieve and combine in a saucepan with the sherry. Bring to a boil, correct seasoning, and serve in a separate sauceboat.

## NOODLES AND CHEESE OMELET

### TORTILLA DE TALLARINES Y QUESO

6 eggs  
1 cup grated Parmesan cheese  
1 teaspoon salt  
¼ teaspoon pepper

3 cups cooked noodles or spaghetti, broken into very small pieces  
4 tablespoons butter

Beat the eggs in a bowl. Add the cheese, salt, pepper, and noodles. Mix well. Melt 2 tablespoons of the butter in a skillet. Pour 2 tablespoons of the mixture into it and fry until brown on both sides. Continue until all of the mixture is used up. Add more butter as required. Keep the little omelets in a warm place until they are all ready to be served. Serve hot.

## AVOCADO-SPINACH SALAD

### ENSALADA DE ESPINACA Y AGUACATE

½ pound spinach  
2 cups boiling water  
2 tablespoons olive or salad oil  
2 onions, sliced  
½ teaspoon salt

1 avocado, peeled and sliced  
1 hard-cooked egg  
Lettuce leaves  
½ cup mayonnaise

Wash the spinach until free of sand. Place in a bowl and pour the boiling water over it. Soak for 5 minutes. Drain. Heat the oil in a skillet. Add the onions and salt. Sauté for 5 minutes, stirring occasionally. Place in a chopping bowl. Add the spinach, avocado, and egg. Chop until the mixture is well blended and smooth. Chill for 1 hour. Place the lettuce on individual plates and spoon the avocado mixture over it. Place a tablespoon of mayonnaise on top.

## RICE AND COCONUT PUDDING

### ARROZ CON COCO

1 cup rice  
3 cups water  
1 teaspoon salt  
1 cup sugar

¼ cup fresh or dried grated coconut  
1 cup milk  
2 teaspoons grated lemon rind  
2 teaspoons cinnamon

Wash the rice in several waters. Combine the water and salt in a saucepan and bring to a boil. Add the rice gradually and boil for 15 minutes. Drain. Return the rice to the saucepan and add the sugar, coconut, and milk. Mix well and cook over low heat until creamy and thick, about 15 minutes. Add the lemon rind. Mix lightly. Serve hot or cold, sprinkled with cinnamon.

WELCOME HOME—

*we hope your trip was enjoyable and that you have enjoyed trying these new dishes.*

# COOKING HINTS

## HELPFUL TIPS

*Avocados*  To keep avocados from turning dark when peeled, place the pit in the center of the dish.

*Baking*  Always have ingredients at room temperature. Butter is creamed more easily; sudden changes in temperature affect baking results.

*Coconut Milk*  To extract the liquid from coconut pulp when making coconut milk or cream, squeeze the liquid and coconut through cheesecloth until the pulp is dry.

*Dairy Products*  Use sweet butter whenever possible.

*Deep-Fat Frying*  Don't crowd the frying basket or kettle; don't use butter, as it burns too quickly.

*Dried Fruits*  To chop raisins and other sticky fruits, heat the knife or food chopper before using.

*Fish*  Remove fish from refrigerator 30 minutes before using.

*Herbs*  Keep herbs and spices well covered, and replace frequently. The flavor of dried herbs may be brought out by soaking for a few moments in hot water, then in cold.

*Knives*  Always use the sharpest possible knives for the cutting and preparation of foods.

*Meats*  Remove from the refrigerator 1 hour before cooking.

*Nuts*  To blanch nuts, cover with cold water, bring to a boil, let soak until skins wrinkle, drain, cover with cold water, and slip the skins off between the fingers. Use a special nut chopper or Mouli grater for grinding nuts, or roll on a board with a rolling pin.

*Poultry*  Season poultry the day before it is to be cooked, if possible. Remove from the refrigerator 1 hour before cooking.

*Salad Greens*  Tear lettuce and other greens into pieces instead of cutting.

*Sour Milk*  If not available, sour milk can be made by adding 2 teaspoons of lemon juice or vinegar to a cup of milk; cook over low heat until milk curdles. Cool and use.

*Stock*  Canned consommé, or bouillon cubes dissolved in hot water, may be substituted for stock. When large quantities are called for, use the canned consommé, as bouillon cubes have a strong flavor when used in quantity.

*Yeast*  Yeast is sold fresh (compressed) or dry in 1-ounce packages.

## USEFUL KITCHEN EQUIPMENT *other than normal essentials*

Cake tester
Colander
Cookie cutters
Electric mixer or
   blender
Food chopper
Garlic press

Meat cleaver or
   pounder
Mortar and pestle
Nut grinder or
   Mouli grater
Pastry blender
Pastry brush

Pastry tube
Poultry shears
Rotary egg beater
Skewers
Wire whisk
Wooden spoon, for
   mixing

## TEMPERATURE GUIDE, *Fahrenheit*

| | |
|---|---|
| Very slow oven | 225° |
| Slow oven | 250° to 300° |
| Moderate oven | 325° to 375° |
| Hot oven | 400° to 450° |
| Very hot oven | 475° and over |

## DEEP-FAT FRYING TEMPERATURES, *Fahrenheit*

| | |
|---|---|
| 360° to 375° | Uncooked mixtures; doughnuts, fritters, or shellfish |
| 375° to 385° | Cooked mixtures with coatings; croquettes, etc. |
| 385° to 395° | French-fried potatoes, vegetables, etc. |

## COOKING MEASUREMENTS

| | | |
|---|---|---|
| Dash | = | Less than ⅛ teaspoon |
| 3 teaspoons | = | 1 tablespoon |
| 2 liquid tablespoons | = | 1 ounce |
| 4 tablespoons | = | ¼ cup |
| 16 tablespoons | = | 1 cup |
| 1 cup | = | ½ pint |
| 2 liquid cups | = | 1 pound |
| 16 ounces | = | 1 pound |
| 4 cups | = | 1 quart |

## TABLE OF EQUIVALENT WEIGHTS AND MEASURES

| | | | |
|---|---|---|---|
| Baking powder | 1 ounce | = | 3½ tablespoons |
| Beans, dried | ½ pound | = | 1 cup |
| Bread crumbs | 3 ounces (approx.) | = | 1 cup |
| Butter and solid fats | 1 pound | = | 2 cups |
| Butter and solid fats | ¼ pound | = | 8 tablespoons |
| Butter and solid fats | ¼ pound | = | ½ cup |
| Cheese, cottage | ½ pound | = | 1 cup |
| Cheese, cream | ½ pound | = | 1 cup |
| Cheese, grated | ¼ pound | = | 1 cup |
| Chocolate | 1 ounce | = | 1 square |
| Cinnamon | 1 ounce | = | 4½ tablespoons |
| Coconut, grated dried | ¼ pound | = | 1 cup, packed |
| Consommé | 1 can | = | 10½ ounces |
| Corn meal | 1 pound | = | 3 cups |
| Cornstarch | 4½ ounces | = | 1 cup |
| Cream | ½ pint | = | 1 cup |
| Dates, pitted | ½ pound | = | 1¼ cups |
| Eggs | 2 ounces | = | 1 egg |
| Egg whites | 8 to 10 | = | 1 cup |
| Flour | 1 pound | = | 4 cups, sifted |
| Flour | ¼ ounce | = | 1 tablespoon |
| Honey | 12 ounces | = | 1 cup |
| Lemon juice | 1 lemon | = | 2 to 3 tablespoons |
| Lemon rind, grated | 1 lemon | = | 2 to 3 teaspoons |
| Nuts, ground | ¼ pound | = | 1 cup |
| Oil | 7½ ounces | = | 1 cup |
| Peanut butter | 1 pound | = | 1¾ cups |
| Potatoes | 1 pound | = | 3 average |
| Raisins | 1 pound | = | 3 cups |
| Rice, uncooked | 1 pound | = | 2 cups |
| Rice, uncooked | 1 cup | = | 3 cups, cooked |
| Sugar, brown | 1 pound | = | 2¼ cups, packed |
| Sugar, confectioners' | 1 pound | = | 3½ to 4 cups, sifted |
| Sugar, granulated | 1 pound | = | 2 cups |
| Tomatoes, fresh | 1 pound | = | 3 average |
| Tomato sauce (1 can) | 7¾–8 ounces | = | 1 cup |

*Aspic* Clear jelly, variously prepared, used to garnish fancy dishes.

*Bake* To cook by means of dry heat, usually in an oven.

*Barbecue* Has many different meanings but generally refers to food roasted outdoors over an open fire; a spicy, smoky sauce.

*Baste* To brush or spoon liquid over a food while marinating or cooking.

*Batter* Any combination that includes flour, water, milk, butter, eggs, or the like, used for dipping, coating, or for pancakes, cake, etc.

*Beat* To mix, using a fork, wire whisk, electric or rotary beater.

*Blanch* To place in cold water, then bring to a boil. Nuts are blanched by the same method, then placed in cold water and the skin slipped off between the fingers.

*Blend* To combine several ingredients; to mix together until smooth.

*Boil* To heat a mixture or liquid until bubbles appear on the surface and vapor rises; also to continue the process thereafter.

*Boiling Point* The temperature at which a liquid begins to bubble around the edge.

*Bouillon* Clear soup, usually made from bones, poultry, meat, or fish.

*Bouillon Cube* Cube containing various solids, usually salted, and to which liquid may be added to produce a bouillonlike liquid.

*Braise* To brown in a little fat, then cook over low heat in very little liquid in a covered pan.

*Broil* To cook by direct heat close to the fire or other source of heat.

*Brush* To spread seasoning, butter, or other coating.

*Caramelize* To melt sugar slowly over low heat until brown and of a sticky consistency.

*Chill* To cool foods by placing in the refrigerator.

*Chop* To cut food into small pieces.

*Combine* To join two or more ingredients together.

*Cream* To soften ingredients by beating with a spoon, rotary or electric beater until soft and of creamy texture.

*Cube* To cut foods into pieces with 6 approximately equal sides; to cut in cubes.

*Cut In Shortening* To mix shortening with flour by using a pastry blender or two knives until shortening is distributed evenly.

*Devilled* Seasoned highly.

*Dissolve* To melt, break up, or liquefy.

*Dredge* To coat a food well, usually with flour or sugar.

*Drippings* Fat or juices that cook out of foods.

*Dust* To sprinkle lightly with a dry coating such as bread crumbs, flour, or sugar.

*Flake* To separate foods gently with a fork.

*Fold In* To use a spoon in a gently rolling circular action as a means of combining ingredients.

*Fry* To cook foods in hot oil or other fat.

*Garnish* To decorate foods.

*Grate* To rub food into small pieces on a grater.

*Grill* To broil foods near open, direct heat.

*Grind* To put food through a food chopper or mill; to reduce or crush into small pieces, flakes, or powder.

*Knead* To manipulate or work with the hands, usually a dough, using a folding-back and pressing-forward motion, until of the desired consistency.

*Lard* To insert strips of fat under the skin or into the meat with a larding needle or other pointed instrument, or to cover a food with strips of fat.

449

*Marinade* Liquid used for pickling or seasoning by soaking; usually contains vinegar or wine, spices, herbs, and oil.

*Marinate* To soak in vinegar, wine, or other liquid, usually containing spices, herbs, and oil.

*Melt* To heat until the ingredient is changed from solid to liquid.

*Mince* To chop as fine as possible.

*Mix* To stir ingredients together.

*Mortar and Pestle* A mortar is a bowl or container in which foods may be ground or crushed; the pestle is a club-shaped utensil used to assist in this process.

*Pan Broil* To cook in a hot skillet with little or no fat.

*Pan Fry* To cook foods in a frying pan over direct heat, using some oil or other fat.

*Parboil* To cook foods partially in water or other liquids.

*Pare* To remove the outside skin or peel of fruits, vegetables, etc.

*Poach* To cook in a liquid just below the boiling point.

*Preheat* To turn on the oven to a selected temperature 10 minutes before it is needed.

*Purée* Food, usually cooked, forced through a sieve to produce a smooth mixture; to force through a sieve.

*Render* To melt solid fat away from connective tissue; to clarify fats by melting.

*Roast* To cook in an oven.

*Roll* To place on a flat surface and spread thin with a rolling pin.

*Roux* A smooth mixture of fat and flour, used as a thickening agent.

*Sauté* To cook or brown over low heat in a little fat, oil, or butter.

*Scald* To pour boiling liquid over a food; to heat almost to boiling.

*Score* To cut narrow gashes on the surface of a food.

*Sear* To brown the surface of a food at high heat.

*Sieve* A utensil with a perforated bottom used to separate coarse pieces from fine, and as a strainer of liquids.

*Sift* To separate coarse pieces from fine by shaking through a sieve, thus removing lumps and foreign particles.

*Simmer* To cook over low heat just below the boiling point.

*Skewer* To fasten with a wood or metal pin, to hold something in place while cooking; a long wood or metal pin.

*Soak* To cover a food with liquid until very wet.

*Spatula* Broad, flexible knife suitable for lifting foods.

*Stalk* An individual piece; in celery, for example, the various stalks make up a bunch.

*Steam* To cook by contact with live steam in a covered container or in a perforated container placed over hot water.

*Steep* To soak in hot liquid below the boiling point.

*Stir* To mix ingredients together within a container; usually by means of a spoon.

*Stock* Broth in which meat, poultry, bones, or fish have been cooked, used as base for gravies, sauces, and soups. Substitutes: bouillon cubes dissolved in water; canned consommé; meat extracts. (Where a large quantity is required, canned consommé is preferable to bouillon cubes.)

*Truss* To secure the body of fowl in such a fashion that it will not move during the cooking process.

*Whip* To beat a liquid to a froth; to increase the volume of a liquid by beating air into it.

*Abaisse* A thin, flaky pastry (French).

*Abats* French term for so-called variety meats: liver, kidneys, lungs, etc.

*Abendmahl* Supper (German).

*Abricotine* Apricot brandy (French).

*Achaja* A Greek wine.

*Achiote* See Annatto.

*Adet* A brandy.

*Advocaat* An apéritif, made with brandy; has a characteristic yellow color.

*Aemono* Fish and vegetables, Japanese style.

*Agar-agar* Jellylike substance obtained from seaweed; used as a thickening agent in various foods.

*Agaric* Variety of mushroom.

*Agave* Mexican cactus plant used in the making of certain Mexican liquors.

*Agemono* Fried vegetables or fish, Japanese style.

*Agnellotti* Italian dumplings stuffed with meat and spices.

*Aiguillette* A long, thin cut of cooked food, such as meat or poultry.

*Aillade* Sauce containing garlic.

*Akala* Dark-colored Hawaiian berry.

*Aku Malou* Air-dried tuna fish.

*À la* In the manner of (French); used to describe the fashion in which dishes are prepared.

*À la carte* Prepared to order (French); food not served on a dinner at a fixed price.

*Al Dente* Italian expression for slightly underdone spaghetti or other similar foods.

*Albacore* Type of tuna fish.

*Ale* Beverage resembling beer, but usually somewhat stronger or darker; contains about 4% alcohol.

*Alewife* Variety of fish particularly known in England.

*Alligator Pear* An avocado.

*Allspice* Spice prepared from the dried berry of the pimento tree.

*Almond Paste* Prepared baking mixture made of sugar, dried eggs, and ground almonds.

*Amer Picon* Apéritif wine of France.

*Amontillado* Dry sherry of Spain.

*Amoroso* Medium sherry of Spain.

*Ananas, Crème d'* Crème of pineapple, French cordial.

*Anchovy* Small fish, commonly salted, dried, or packed in oil; used as an appetizer, in cooking, etc.

*Anchovy Pear* Fruit of a West Indies tree; eaten, pickled, as a relish.

*Andouille* Sausage or pudding made of pork; popular in parts of France.

*Angelica* Plant used in flavoring various liqueurs; also candied, and eaten plain or used in baking.

*Anglaise, à l'* Boiled in plain water.

*Angostura* Bitters, prepared in the West Indies.

*Anise* Seeds or oil obtained from a plant and used as a flavoring; also aniseed or aniseed oil.

*Anisette* French liqueur made from aniseed.

*Anjan* Siamese food coloring.

*Annatto* Red, natural dye used for coloring foods, particularly popular on the west coast of South America; also known as achiote.

*Antipasto* Italian term for the typical appetizer served before a dinner; usually miscellaneous vegetables, fish, cold meats, etc.

*Apéritif* Appetizer drink, very popular in France.

*Apio* South American tuber.

*Apple Brandy* Cider, with considerable water removed by distillation.

*Apple Gin* Greenish-yellow gin, flavored with apple.

*Apricot Brandy* Yellowish brandy flavored with apricots.

*Aqua d'Orott* Italian cordial made with rose petals.

*Aquavit* Clear liquor with caraway seed flavor; popular in Scandinavian countries.

*Arabica* Colombian coffee.

*Arancini* Meat and rice dish popular in Sicily.

*Areca* Betel nut of Asia.

*Aromatics* Old term for herbs, spices, and seasoning.

*Arrack* Strong liquor of the Near East.

*Arrowroot* Natural starch obtained from a West Indies root plant.

*Artichoke, Globe* Green vegetable, only moderately popular; head composed of individual leaves, part of each leaf being edible.

*Artichoke, Jerusalem* Tuber resembling the common potato; not readily prepared since it is irregular and knobby.

*Asado* Roast meat dish popular in Uruguay and Argentina.

*Assam* An Indian tea.

*Atka Fish* Small Pacific Ocean fish.

*Attorta* Italian almond pastry.

*Aubergine* Eggplant.

*Au Beurre* French term for foods served with plain melted butter.

*Au Bleu* French designation for a fish dish prepared quickly in white wine or water; the fish must be alive immediately before the dish is prepared.

*Au Gratin* Usually applied to a scalloped dish with a crust of bread crumbs, sometimes mixed with cheese or butter.

*Au Jus* Any dish containing only its own natural juices.

*Au Naturel* French term for food served uncooked or otherwise unaltered.

*Aurum* Italian orange liqueur.

*Avocado* Green fruit with a thick skin and an oily, rich yellow interior; alligator pear.

*Baba* Light, buttery yeast cake.

*Babassu Nut Oil* Oil obtained from the babassu palm; greatly resembles coconut oil.

*Bacalao* Dried codfish, Spanish style.

*Bacardi* Well-known Cuban rum.

*Bagna Cauda* Italian sauce of truffles, garlic, olives, and anchovies.

*Bagoong* Dried shrimp used in the Philippines.

*Baicoli* Italian-style sweet pastry.

*Bain-Marie* French cooking utensil similar to a double boiler in principle, used for cooking food slowly, or for keeping it warm, by surrounding it with hot water.

*Baissière* Sediment in wine.

*Baking Powder* Combination of several chemical ingredients used to increase the size of dough and lighten its texture; usually contains cream of tartar and sodium bicarbonate.

*Ballotine* French term for small balls of meat or poultry used in French-style cookery.

*Bannock* Flat type of Scotch cake.

*Bap* Floury, Scotch breakfast roll.

*Barcelonas* Nuts similar to hazelnuts.

*Bar-le-duc* French currant jelly.

*Baron of Beef* Twin sirloins of beef cooked together.

*Barquette* Boat-shaped pastry.

*Barsac* A French white wine.

*Bavette* Type of Italian macaroni that is particularly light and frothy.

*Bay Leaf* Medium-sized green leaf, often dried, and used for flavoring foods.

*Bay Salt* Rough salt.

*Bean Curd* Soft cakes made from soybeans, used in oriental dishes.

*Bean Sprouts* Young bean shoots.

*Béarnaise* Rich sauce, often served with roast meats.

*Beaujolais* A favorite French red wine.

*Béchamel* One of the most important French sauces.

*Bêche-de-Mer* Sea slug, considered a great delicacy by various oriental peoples.

*Beignet* Any type of fritter.

*Bel Paese* Medium-soft Italian cheese quite popular in Italy and the United States.

*Bēlachan* Siamese shrimp paste.

*Benedictine* Famous French cordial.

*Benzoate of Soda* Commonly used food preservative.

*Bergamot* Herb, formerly much used for flavoring.

*Betel Nut* Obtained from the betel palm tree; a favorite of the people of Indo-China.

*Beurre Fondue* Melted butter. (French).

*Beurre Noir* Literally, black butter; usually refers to a brown butter.

*Bifteck* French for beefsteak.

*Bitters* Liquid containing some alcohol and one or more bitter flavoring ingredients, such as quinine, angostura, etc.

*Blackstrap Molasses* Poorest grade of molasses.

*Blaeberry* Edible northern berry.

*Blancmange* General term used to describe a variety of white puddings.

*Blimbing* Acidulous fruit of Asia.

*Blinis* Thin buckwheat pancakes, of Russian origin.

*Bloater* Smoked herring.

*Blue Points* Large, excellent variety of oysters.

*Blue Rose* A southern rice.

*Bluefin* Type of tuna fish.

*Bombay Duck* Dried bummalo fish; popular in India with curried food.

*Bonbon* General term, but usually refers to small candies, particularly those with icing.

*Bonito* Similar to but not exactly like tuna fish.

*Bordelaise* Sauce that presumably originated near Bordeaux, France; made with wine.

*Boudin* Main-course pudding, usually made with meat or poultry.

*Bouillabaisse* Famous fish soup or stew of the south of France.

*Bouquet Garni* French term for a small bundle of herbs fastened together during cooking, to prevent separation and facilitate subsequent removal.

*Bourbon* Whisky distilled from a mash containing no less than 51% corn grain.

*Bourgeoise* Family, or home-style, food.

*Bourghol* Cracked wheat.

*Bourride* Fish soup or stew, popular in France.

*Brazil Nut* Extremely oily, rich nut obtained from Brazil; has three angles.

*Breadnut* A fruit, usually eaten in the West Indies as a substitute for bread.

*Bream* Type of fish.

*Bree* Scotch term for soup or stock.

*Bressans* A cheese, usually made with goat milk.

*Brigidini* Italian biscuits flavored with aniseed.

*Brillat-Savarin* Famous writer on food and a gourmet of high repute.

*Brinjal* Eggplant (India).

*Brioche* Famous breakfast bread popular in France; made with yeast in a characteristic shape.

*Brochan* Scotch word for porridge.

*Broche, à la* Broiled over direct heat on a skewer.

*Brochette, en* Small pieces of meat, fish, or vegetables roasted on a skewer.

*Brodetto* Meat, or occasionally fish, served with a considerable amount of sauce or gravy (Italian).

*Brose* Scotch milk and oatmeal dish.

*Brûlé* Burned, a French cooking term.

*Buccellato* An Italian cake.

*Buckwheat* Herb, commonly used as a food after processing into flour.

*Bullace* A wild plum.

*Burdwan* Curried dish popular in India.

*Burgol* Cracked wheat.

*Burgundy* Wines produced in the general Burgundy area of France.

*Buridda* Fish stew of the Italian Riviera; closely resembles the *bourride* of southern France.

*Buttermilk* Liquid left after butter has been removed during churning.

*Byrrh* Apéritif popular in France.

*Cacciatora* Italian term for foods prepared quite simply, "Hunter's

Style"; usually a chicken dish with tomatoes and onions.

*Cacciucco*  Italian fish soup.

*Caciocavallo*  Italian cheese of fairly firm consistency, somewhat like *provolone*.

*Café*  Restaurant or bar specializing in drinks; coffee (French).

*Café au Lait*  Coffee and hot milk, half and half.

*Caffè Espresso*  Italian style of coffee-making, involving forcing steam through finely ground coffee; produces a very strong, black coffee.

*Café Noir*  Black coffee (French); usually a demitasse.

*Calamondin*  A citrus fruit.

*Calavo*  Avocados grown in California under a trade name.

*Calimyrna*  Variety of fig.

*Calvados*  French apple brandy.

*Calzone*  Macaroni dish prepared with cheese and meat.

*Cambur*  Variety of banana.

*Camembert*  One of the great cheeses of France.

*Camote*  Sweet potato.

*Canapé*  Small piece of bread with varying ingredients, served as an hors d'oeuvre.

*Cannelloni*  An important Italian macaroni dish; usually a very large macaroni resembling a pipe.

*Cannoli*  Italian dessert made in the shape of a cornucopia.

*Capellini d'Angelo*  Very thin type of Italian macaroni.

*Capers*  Flower buds, pickled and used as a relish or for flavoring.

*Capon*  Castrated male chicken; flavor somewhat superior to that of ordinary chicken.

*Caponatina*  Italian appetizer, usually made with assorted pickled vegetables.

*Cappelletti*  Type of Italian macaroni.

*Capsicum*  Genus of peppers; includes many different types.

*Carambola*  An Asiatic fruit.

*Caraway*  Seeds, used as a spice.

*Caraway Oil*  Obtained from the caraway plant; used as a flavoring agent in liqueurs, bread, cheese, etc.

*Cardamom*  Seasoning ingredient popular in East Indian countries.

*Carrageen*  Edible Irish seaweed.

*Casareep*  West Indian flavoring syrup.

*Cashew Nut*  Grown principally in India; used extensively as a food.

*Cassata*  Italian type of ice cream, usually extremely rich.

*Cassis*  French currant liqueur.

*Cassola*  Fish soup, Italian style.

*Caviar*  Roe of certain varieties of sturgeon; eggs may be black, gray, or gold.

*Cayenne*  Extremely spicy variety of capsicum, the red pepper plant; used as a seasoning.

*Celeriac*  Celery root.

*Celery Oil*  Yellowish oil produced from celery seeds and used as a flavoring.

*Celery Salt*  Celery plant seeds, ground fine and used as a flavoring.

*Cèpe*  Variety of mushroom popular in France.

*Ceriman*  Fruit with a pineapple and banana flavor.

*Ceylon Spinach*  Climbing vegetable plant with thick leaves.

*Chablis*  White Burgundy wine of France.

*Champagne*  Sparkling white wine of the Champagne region of France.

*Char*  Type of fresh-water trout.

*Charcuterie*  Any cold, prepared, cooked meats.

*Chartreuse*  French liqueur; both yellow and green varieties are made.

*Chaudfroid*  Cold meat or poultry covered with a glazed, cold sauce.

*Chawanmushi*  Japanese steamed egg dish, usually with other ingredients added.

*Chayote*  A vegetable, particularly appreciated in Latin and South American countries.

*Cheddar*  A classic English cheese.

*Cherimoya*  Important fruit, particularly in South America, with a white interior and a green exterior.

*Cherry Whisky* Red liquor.

*Chervil* Herb with a parsley flavor, commonly used for flavoring.

*Cheshire* Hard type of English cheese; comes in both red and white.

*Chevalier, à la* Batter-fried food.

*Chianti* An Italian wine.

*Chick-pea* Starchy pea, much used for food in the Near and Middle East.

*Chico* A fruit of the Philippines.

*Chicory* Green plant whose bitter leaves are used in salads; dried root used to flavor coffee.

*Chili Peppers* Various types of hot red peppers of the capsicum group; may be used fresh, dried, or ground.

*Chine* Term for two unseparated pork loins.

*Chinese Radish* Large radishlike vegetable; tastes much like turnip.

*Chipolata* Small sausages of various types.

*Chitterlings* Cooked animal intestines, popular in parts of the southern U.S.

*Chive* Grasslike herb with a mild onion flavor.

*Choucroute* Sauerkraut (French).

*Choux* Rich cooked paste made of eggs, butter, and flour.

*Choux de Bruxelles* Brussels sprouts.

*Chowl* Indian term for rice.

*Chub* Variety of fresh-water fish.

*Chufa* Underground nut resembling a peanut or almond.

*Chupatty* East Indian wheat cake, used as a bread.

*Chutney* Spicy Indian relish made from various combinations, but usually containing mangoes, spices, and sugar.

*Cider* Apple juice, used as a beverage.

*Cinnamon* A favorite spice available in several styles: whole pieces in stick form, ground, etc.

*Cinnamon Oil* Oil usually made from cinnamon leaves, used as a flavoring agent.

*Citrange* Variety of bitter orange.

*Citric Acid* Acid commonly present in citrus fruits.

*Citron* Fruit of the citron tree; rind often preserved with sugar.

*Claret* Another name for the Bordeaux wines of France.

*Cloudberry* Arctic berry.

*Clove* Dark red-brown bud used as a spice.

*Clove Oil* Distilled from the flower buds of the plant, used for flavoring purposes.

*Cobnut* Type of filbert.

*Cockle* A shellfish.

*Cocoa* Chocolate with much of the fat removed in a cooking process; used as a beverage.

*Cocotte* Individual serving dish, usually ovenproof.

*Cognac* Brandy manufactured in the Cognac region of France; other brandies may not be called cognac.

*Cohune* A nut from which an edible oil is obtained.

*Cointreau* Clear orange-flavored after-dinner liqueur.

*Collops* Term for small slices of prepared meats, usually sautéed.

*Compote* Cooked fruits in sweet syrup; use of term limited to fruits that retain their shape in cooking.

*Consommé* Any clear soup, but usually broth made from meat or poultry.

*Coppa* Italian variety of salami, usually made with pork products.

*Coquille* Shell (French); seafood dish served in a shell.

*Coriander* Seed with a pleasant odor, used for flavoring.

*Corn Meal* Flour obtained by grinding corn; used for cooking and baking.

*Corn Oil* Oil obtained by crushing corn; principally used for mayonnaise and salad dressing.

*Corn Syrup* Obtained by processing crude cornstarch.

*Corn Whisky* Whisky distilled from

455

a mash containing between 80% and 90% corn.

Cornstarch Starch obtained by a complex process from corn; used for brewing, food, etc.

Coteghino Italian salami containing various starchy legumes, such as beans, etc.; also cotechino.

Cottonseed Oil Yellow oil obtained from cottonseed; has many uses for food, canning, etc.

Court Bouillon Liquid in which fish is cooked; usually contains spices, wine, water, etc.

Crawfish A shellfish without claws, but much resembling lobster.

Crayfish A fresh-water shellfish resembling the lobster, but quite small.

Crème de Menthe After-dinner liqueur with a mint flavor.

Creole, à la Term describing foods served with rice and various spices.

Crêpe Thin pancake (French).

Cress Mustard greens.

Croquette Any ground or finely minced mixture, dipped in crumbs or batter and fried.

Croustade Piece of bread fried in butter or oil.

Croûtons Small cubes of fried bread, used to garnish soup or salads.

Cuisson Meat, fish, or poultry stock.

Cumin Seed Imported spice largely used in meat products; also cumin.

Curaçao Orange-flavored liqueur made in the Dutch West Indies and in Holland.

Curry Powder Mixture of various spices used in the making of curry, the favorite dish of the East Indies.

Cuscusu Italian variation of couscous, made with fish.

Custard Apple A tropical fruit.

Dab Variety of fish.

Damascene Small type of plum.

Damson Variety of plum; customarily used in making jam.

Darjeeling An Indian tea.

Darne A fish slice.

Dato Reddish, tropical fruit obtained from a cactus.

Demitasse A half cup (French); any small cup, but usually refers to after-dinner coffee.

Devonshire Cream Cream prepared by scalding; very rich and thick.

Dewberry Variety of blackberry.

Dhall East Indian lentil.

Diable, à la Food served with a spicy sauce.

Dibs Sweet wine of the Near East.

Dill Green herb used for flavoring; popular in Scandinavian countries.

Dolichos Similar to the string bean, popular in Malaya.

Dop Secondary type of brandy, usually made by expressing grape-skins.

Drambuie A scotch-whisky cordial flavored with honey.

Drawn Butter Melted butter.

Drupe Fruit with a hard pit or stone, such as peach, cherry, etc.

Dubonnet French apéritif wine.

Duku Fruit popular in Malaya.

Dulse Edible seaweed.

Durian Fine Indo-Chinese fruit with an objectionable odor.

Dushab Near East syrupy drink made from date wine.

Earthnut Peanut.

Eau de Vie French term for brandy in general.

Edam Famous Dutch cheese, usually made in the shape of a ball.

Elderberry Berry used principally for making wine.

Elver Baby eel; when very young and transparent, considered a great delicacy in Mediterranean countries.

Emincé Food cut into small pieces, or sometimes chopped fine.

Endive Chicory plant leaves, used principally in salads.

Escabeche Pickled dish containing fish, meat, or poultry; popular in Latin countries.

Escoffier Great French chef; creator of numerous original dishes.

Estouffade Usually a meat dish prepared in a casserole with a sauce.

Etuvée Thick stew, French style.

**Faggot** Bunch of herbs, such as celery, parsley, etc., tied together for use in cooking.

**Fagottino** An Italian pastry.

**Farci** French term for a dish such as poultry, etc., stuffed with a prepared mixture.

**Farina** General term used to describe any flour.

**Farina Dolce** Italian flour made from ground chestnuts.

**Fennel** Herb with a delightful flavor and aroma; particularly used in fish cookery.

**Fennel Oil** Yellowish oil used principally to flavor gin or other liquors.

**Fennel Seed** Brownish seed used largely for flavoring.

**Fenugreek** Herb often used in curry powders.

**Fidelini** An Italian noodle.

**Filbert** Similar to but not identical with the hazelnut.

**Fine Champagne** Type of French brandy.

**Fines Herbes** Finely chopped herbs.

**Finnan Haddie** Smoked haddock; also called *Findon haddock,* after Findon, the Scotch village where it is smoked.

**Flageolet** A French kidney bean.

**Flamande, à la** Food served in the Flemish manner.

**Flambé** Aflame; refers to any dish in the preparation of which a liquor is set afire.

**Flan** Custard dessert popular with Latin people.

**Flensjes** Dutch pancake dessert.

**Florence Oil** A better-quality olive oil.

**Flummery** Cold oatmeal dessert.

**Fondant** Cooked, white sugar icing used to decorate cakes.

**Fondue** Melted-cheese dish of Swiss origin.

**Fontina** An Italian cheese.

**Foratina** Variety of macaroni.

**Forbidden Fruit** A cordial, a liqueur.

**Forcemeat** Any ground or finely chopped stuffing.

**Fra Diavolo** Italian term customarily used to describe a lobster dish having a tomato base; "Brother Devil," the Italian bandit.

**Fraisia** Sweet strawberry liqueur made in France.

**Framboise** Raspberry (French).

**Frappé** Iced, or partly frozen.

**Friandise** Small, dainty fruit or dessert cake or candy.

**Fricandeau** Large piece or slice of veal larded with fat.

**Fricandelle** Chopped meat mixture similar to hamburger.

**Frit** Any fried food (French).

**Fritto Misto** Mixed fry.

**Fumet** Strong essence obtained from cooked fish, meat, or poultry.

**Galantine** Rolled meat or poultry, usually covered with aspic.

**Galette** Food shaped into a small patty.

**Galuska** Finger-size dumplings of Hungarian origin.

**Game** General term used to describe all edible, wild birds and animals not usually raised for food.

**Garbure** Thick French soup, usually made with vegetables and various other ingredients.

**Garni** French term for stuffed or decorated food.

**Gaufrette** Flat, sweet wafer popular in France.

**Gelato** Any Italian ice cream.

**Genipap** Acid, tropical fruit.

**Gerome** A French cheese.

**Gervais** A rich French cheese.

**Ghee** Clarified butter; butter with as much water removed as possible.

**Gherkin** Midget cucumber, used as a relish.

**Gin** A strong liquor, usually flavored with juniper berries, but may also be made with various other flavoring ingredients.

**Ginger** Tropical plant whose root is used for flavoring; also candied or preserved.

**Ginger Beer** English drink with a distinct ginger flavor.

**Glacé de Viande** Meat or fish concentrate used in cooking; prepared by cooking the foods rapidly so as to remove as much moisture as possible.

*Glaze* Concentrate of fish or meat stock; also, to cover foods with melted jam or other sweetening.

*Gnocchi* Small boiled or baked Italian dumplings, made from potatoes, semolina, corn meal, or combinations thereof.

*Goldwasser* Gold water, a German liqueur actually containing gold flakes.

*Gorgonzola* Italian cheese closely resembling Roquefort.

*Granada* Tropical fruit somewhat resembling pomegranate.

*Granadilla* A tropical fruit.

*Grappa* A potent Italian liquor made from grape pressings.

*Gras-double* Tripe (French).

*Graves* Wine of moderate quality produced in a particular part of France.

*Grissino* Italian breadstick.

*Groats* Oats with the husks removed.

*Groundnut* Peanut.

*Gruyère* A cheese made in Switzerland or imitated elsewhere; has a characteristic taste and is filled with holes.

*Guarana* Popular Brazilian soft drink.

*Guava* Tropical fruit, principally used for making preserves, pastes, or jelly.

*Guayaba* Tropical fruit best used in preserves.

*Gudgeon* Favorite French fish.

*Guisada* A national dish of Spain, usually containing meat and vegetables.

*Gula Malacca* Sugar made from the coconut palm.

*Haggis* Scotch national dish; made of a sheep's pluck, and cooked in the lining of a sheep's stomach.

*Hallowis* Type of edible date.

*Herb* Any plant whose leaves, roots, or stems are used as a food or for flavoring.

*Hock* General term for Rhine wines.

*Hollandaise* Classic sauce made of eggs, butter, and lemon juice.

*Holland Gin* Famous dry gin manufactured in Holland.

*Hominy* Finely ground, parched corn. There is also a "Big Hominy."

*Hops* Blossoms of hop vines grown for beer brewing.

*Hors d'oeuvre* General term for an appetizer.

*Horseradish* Herb used as a condiment; often combined with sugar, vinegar, or beets.

*Hyssop* Flowering shrub, generally used near beehives to flavor honey; also a tea.

*Imbu* A tropical fruit.

*Jack Fruit* Large fruit of southwestern Asia; largely used as a native food.

*Jaggery* Palm-tree sugar.

*Jantong* Flower of the banana.

*Jardinière* Any dish containing vegetables.

*Jereboam* Wine bottle holding equivalent of four ordinary bottles.

*Jigger* Measure of liquor, usually 1½ ounces.

*Jimmies* Hard crabs.

*Jojoto* Tropical corn.

*Jujube* Tropical fruit usually made into jelly or used as a relish.

*Julienne* Term for various foods cut into thin strips like matches.

*Juniper Berry* Evergreen plant; berries used for flavoring purposes; commonly used in gin.

*Kadanga* Flower of southeastern Asia used in desserts.

*Kadota* Type of fig.

*Kaffir* African tree producing a starchy food; South African native food.

*Kapi* Siamese shrimp paste.

*Kava* Intoxicating beverage made by South Pacific natives.

*Kebob* Food cooked on a skewer.

*Kedgeree* Dish containing a combination of rice, eggs, fish, spices, etc.

*Kĕladi* Tuber popular in Malaya.

*Kelp* Dehydrated seaweed, often used for food.

*Kipper* Split, smoked herring.

*Kirsch* Clear, cherry-flavored brandy.

*Kola Nut* Bitter nut of trees grown in Brazil, the West Indies, and Africa; used in preparation of kola (or cola) drinks.

*Kosher* Food prepared according to Orthodox Jewish rules.

*Kumiss* Fermented milk drink of Asiatic origin.

*Kümmel* Liqueur made with caraway seeds and flavored with cumin seeds.

*Kumquat* Small citrus fruit usually preserved or candied.

*Kvass* Russian beer.

*Lactic Acid* Fermented acid, used in pickles, beer, sauerkraut, etc.

*Ladies' Fingers* Another name for okra.

*Lager* Any light beer.

*Lamprey* Edible eel.

*Lard* Fat obtained from hogs.

*Larding Needle* Utensil designed to permit the insertion of fat in lean meats.

*Lardoon* Long, thin piece of bacon or other fat used in the larding process.

*Lasagne* One of the largest of all the Italian macaroni products.

*Lechosa* Tropical form of melon, with a perfumed taste.

*Leek* Edible onionlike plant with flat leaves; flavor comparatively mild.

*Legume* Starchy vegetable, such as beans, peas, etc.

*Lemon Grass* Herb used for flavoring.

*Lentils* Seeds of the lentil plant; a favorite starchy food.

*Limburger* A German cheese.

*Lime* Fruit of the lime tree; similar to lemon, but often has a characteristic taste.

*Lime Oil* Oil obtained from limes; used principally for flavoring.

*Limequat* A citrus fruit; cross between a lime and a kumquat.

*Limu* Edible Hawaiian seaweed.

*Liqueur* Beverage with a high alcoholic content, usually sweet.

*Liqueur Brandies* Old, thick brandies.

*Locksoi* Chinese macaroni.

*Lodigiano* An Italian cheese.

*Loganberry* Berry obtained by crossing blackberry and raspberry.

*Loquat* Citrus fruit of little commercial importance.

*Love Apple* Common tomato.

*Lucullus, à la* Any dish containing rich ingredients.

*Luganica* Spicy Italian sausage.

*Macaroni* General term for most Italian dough products, such as spaghetti, lasagne, etc.

*Mace* Edible outer covering of nutmeg; used as spice.

*Macédoine* Mixture of cut-up vegetables or fruit.

*Madeleine* Molded cake.

*Magnum* Wine bottle holding the equivalent of two ordinary bottles.

*Maitrank* German festival wine of May Day.

*Maize* Another name for corn.

*Majorca* Type of almond.

*Makrut* Siamese citrus fruit.

*Malmsey* Type of sweet Madeira wine.

*Maloreddus* Italian dumpling colored with saffron.

*Malt* Germinated, moist barley, used in brewing.

*Malt Whisky* Whisky distilled from a mash containing not less than 51% malted rye or barley.

*Mammee* A tropical fruit; often used for ice cream.

*Mango* Excellent tropical fruit grown in many parts of the world; has many different tropical fruit flavors.

*Mangosteen* Fine sour-sweet tropical fruit.

*Manicotti* An Italian macaroni; usually a large noodle stuffed with cheese.

*Manju* Japanese bean-paste buns.

*Manzanilla* Light-colored Spanish wine held in high esteem.

*Manzano* Type of South American banana.

*Maraschino* Cherry liqueur.

*Marble* Fat streaks in meat.

*Marinara* Italian term meaning "sailor fashion"; used to describe various Italian sauces.

*Marrons* Chestnuts (French).

*Marsala* Sweet, fairly rich dessert wine produced in Sicily.

*Marzipan* Crushed almonds combined with sugar; used in baking.

*Maté* South American beverage resembling tea; of great importance in Argentina, Paraguay, and Uruguay.

*Matzoth* Unleavened Passover bread of Orthodox Jews.

*Methuselah* Wine bottle holding the equivalent of eight ordinary bottles.

*Meunière* Sauce, usually containing butter, lemon juice, and parsley.

*Mille-feuille* French term for very thin, flaky pastry.

*Milt* Fish roe.

*Minestrone* Rich, Italian version of vegetable soup, usually containing some macaroni.

*Mirabelle* Small French plum with a good flavor.

*Mirepoix* Vegetables and ham or bacon, diced very small and cooked together in a sauce.

*Mirin* Japanese wine somewhat resembling sherry.

*Miso* Japanese flavoring ingredient.

*Morel* Type of cherry; variety mushroom popular in France.

*Mornay* Sauce whose principal flavor is that of cheese.

*Mortadèlla* Large Italian-style salami.

*Moselle* Type of German wine.

*Mostacciòlo* Sweet Italian cake.

*Mousse* Cold dish of a frothy nature, usually containing beaten egg whites or whipped cream.

*Mousseline* Frothy sauce based upon *hollandaise*, but including beaten egg whites or whipped cream.

*Mozzarella* Soft type of Italian cheese.

*Mulberry* Edible berry.

*Mullet* Increasingly important food fish; largest catches made in Florida waters.

*Muscat* Type of raisin.

*Mushimono* General Japanese term for steamed foods.

*Must* Young wine immediately before fermentation.

*Mustard* Spicy condiment prepared from mustard seeds.

*Namplā* Siamese sauce made from salted shrimp.

*Namprik* Siamese mixed spice.

*Nartje* African citrus fruit.

*Nebuchadnezzar* The largest of all champagne bottles; holds the equivalent of twenty ordinary bottles.

*Nectarine* Peach with a smooth, plumlike skin.

*Nepal* Type of Indian pepper.

*Neufchâtel* French cheese of a rather soft consistency.

*Noggin* One quarter pint of alcoholic spirits.

*Nori* Edible seaweed used in Japanese cookery.

*Nutmeg* Fruit of a tropical tree used as a spice; *see* Mace.

*Olives* Fruit of the olive tree; principal types are green (unripe) and black (ripe), with dozens of varieties.

*Oloroso* Type of Spanish sherry.

*Orange Flower Water* Liquid containing some essence of distilled orange blossoms; used for flavoring.

*Orégano* Wild marjoram.

*Orgeat* Almond- and orange-flavored syrup.

*Ortolan* Game bird.

*Ovar* Type of Hungarian cheese.

*Palm Kernel Oil* Made from palm trees and used in confectionery products and margarine.

*Palma* Rather dry sherry.

*Panade* Mixture consisting of bread boiled or soaked in a liquid such as milk, stock; etc.; *panada.*

*Panettone* An Italian cake.

*Panforte* An Italian cake containing nuts and candied fruits.

*Papain* Dehydrated juice of the papaya tree; largely used to tenderize meats.

*Papelon* Crude, raw sugar.

*Papillote, en* Foods cooked in paper or parchment to retain juices during cooking process.

*Paprika* Spice of two principal types: Hungarian, strong and sweet; and Spanish, fairly mild.

*Parisian Spice* Mixture of various spices, usually used in conjunction with salt.

*Parmigiana* Italian term for a dish made with cheese.

*Partan* A large crab (Scotland).

*Passion Fruit* Well-flavored fruit grown in various places; makes an excellent beverage.

*Pasta* General Italian word for macaroni; *pasta asciutta* is used for dry macaroni products.

*Pasta e Fagiola* Italian term for a dish of beans and macaroni.

*Pasticceria* Italian word for bakeries and their products.

*Pastiera* Italian type of sweet pastry, usually eaten at Easter.

*Pastina* Very small variety of Italian macaroni, customarily used in soup.

*Pâté de Foie Gras* Smooth paste made of goose livers.

*Pawpaw* Papaya.

*Peanut Oil* Oil obtained by crushing peanuts; generally classified as a vegetable oil.

*Pectin* White substance found in certain plants; used to thicken jellies.

*Pekoe* Variety of Chinese tea.

*Pelardon* A French cheese.

*Pennoni* Type of Italian macaroni.

*Peppercorn* Whole pepper seed.

*Perilla* Oriental herb closely resembling mint in flavor.

*Periwinkle* A shellfish.

*Perry* Alcoholic beverage prepared from pears.

*Persimmon* Yellow- to orange-colored fruit, with an extremely distinctive flavor.

*Pesto* Favorite Genoese flavoring; contains garlic, cheese, nuts, and olive oil.

*Petite Marmite* Classic French soup.

*Petits Fours* French term for small, decorated, glazed cakes.

*Piccalili* Chopped vegetable relish.

*Pigmeo* Venezuelan banana.

*Pignolias* Edible seed of the nut pine.

*Pilchard* West Coast sardine.

*Pimento* Mild pepper; also spelled *pimiento.*

*Pimento Oil* Produced in Jamaica, B.W.I.; has the odor of cloves and nutmeg; also known as *allspice oil.*

*Pinza* Italian dessert, usually a type of cake.

*Pizze* Italian word for any flat, baked dough product; type of pie made with tomato sauce, with or without the addition of cheese, salami, etc.; also known as *pizza.*

*Plaice* Fish resembling sole.

*Plaintain* Large variety of banana, usually inedible before cooking.

*Pluck* Liver and various other organs of an animal.

*Poêlé* Dish roasted with butter.

*Poi* Hawaiian staple food made from taro.

*Polenta* Italian dish based on corn meal.

*Pont l'Evêque* Fairly mild French cheese.

*Poppy Seeds* Edible flower seeds used for flavoring.

*Porter* Type of English beer.

*Potted* Any food preserved in a jar, usually in pounded or ground form.

*Printanier* Dish or soup made with cut-up spring vegetables.

*Prosciutto* Italian type of ham particularly suited for an appetizer or hors d'oeuvre; salted and dried.

**461**

*Provençal* Food cooked in the southern French style and containing oil, garlic, onions, etc.

*Provola* Soft type of Italian cheese.

*Provolone* Medium to hard type of Italian cheese with a rather smoky taste.

*Pulque* Alcoholic drink of Mexico made from a cactus plant.

*Pumpernickel* Dark Germanic bread of heavy texture.

*Quenelles* Fish or meat ground smooth and formed into balls.

*Racahout* Sweet drink popular in the Near East.

*Ragoût* French term for a thick stew.

*Rakia* Hungarian liqueur.

*Rambutan* Fruit of southeast Asia.

*Raspings* Grated bread crusts; often applied to bread crumbs.

*Ratafia* Bitter almond extract; also a liqueur.

*Ravioli* Italian specialty; little pockets of dough stuffed with varying ingredients; usually served with a sauce.

*Reggiano* An Italian cheese.

*Rehoboam* Wine bottle holding the equivalent of six ordinary bottles.

*Rennet* Stomach lining of various animals; used largely in cheese making, milk curdling, etc.

*Rice, Wild* Greenish grain grown in Wisconsin and the Southern states; much appreciated by gourmets.

*Ricotta* Type of Italian cheese similar to cottage cheese; often used for stuffing macaroni.

*Rigatoni* Rather large type of Italian macaroni.

*Rio* Type of Brazilian coffee.

*Risotto* Italian rice dish; may be served with or without the addition of seafood, etc.

*Rissole* Ground or chopped meat, fish, or poultry wrapped in pastry, or having a crust.

*Rocambole* Similar to garlic but slightly milder.

*Rosefish* A fish, usually caught off the New England coast

*Rosell* Tart berry found in Asia and Australia.

*Rum* Alcoholic drink made from sugar cane.

*Rusks* Twice-toasted bread or semisweet cake.

*Rye Whisky* Whisky distilled from a mash which contains not less than 51% rye grain.

*Sage* Gray- to green-colored herb.

*Sake* Japanese rice wine, but actually similar to beer.

*Salami* General term for any of various beef, pork, or similar products usually prepared in the familiar long shape.

*Salmanasar* Wine bottle holding the equivalent of twelve regular bottles.

*Salmi* Poultry mixture or hash.

*Salpicon* Various meats or vegetables diced fairly small and used for stuffing or in sauce.

*Saltimbocca* Classic Italian dish of veal and ham.

*Samp* Hulled corn.

*Sangaree* West Indies wine punch.

*Sanguinaccio* Type of Italian blood sausage.

*Santan* Coconut milk.

*Sarsaparilla* Flavoring obtained from smilax roots.

*Sassafras* Bark and leaves of tree in laurel family used for tea, etc.

*Sassafras Oil* Distilled oil used for flavoring.

*Sauerkraut* Fermented cabbage product, usually obtained by action of lactic acid.

*Savory* Also *savoury;* British preparation usually served after dessert and before coffee, often a spicy or cheese mixture.

*Sawi* Chinese cabbage.

*Sayers* Variety of dates.

*Scallion* Young green onion that has either developed no bulb or a quite small one.

*Scaloppine* Italian term for thin slices of meat (usually veal) prepared in varying fashions.

*Scamozza* Type of Italian cheese.

*Scampi* Type of shellfish similar to large shrimp, usually found only in the Adriatic Sea.

*Scungilli* Large Italian shellfish, often prepared with various sauces.

*Scuppernong* Variety of grapes suitable for making wine.

*Semolina* Hardest part of the wheat, which is left after the removal of the flour; principally used for making macaroni products.

*Sesame Seeds* Oily seeds frequently used in cooking and baking; popular in Near Eastern countries.

*Sherbet* In the United States, a semi-soft frozen confection of water, flavoring, sugar, etc.; in the Near East, a very sweet, cold drink.

*Sherry* Unique Spanish wine.

*Shortening* Any of a wide variety of edible fats.

*Skillet* Frying pan.

*Sling* Cold alcoholic drink, usually made with cracked ice, sugar, liquor, and flavorings.

*Sloe Gin* Gin flavored with the wild, purple berries of the blackthorn shrub.

*Smolt* Salmon, about two years old.

*Smörgåsbord* Swedish hors d'oeuvres.

*Smørrebrød* Danish open-faced sandwiches.

*Soba* Japanese noodles.

*Sodium Benzoate* Food preservative.

*Sorbet* Water ice.

*Sorgo Syrup* Very sweet, edible product widely used.

*Soubise* Sauce which is predominantly onion-flavored.

*Soufflé* Light, frothy dish that increases in size during baking owing to use of egg whites, if a hot soufflé; whipped cream is usually added to a cold soufflé.

*Soursop* Tart-flavored tropical fruit.

*Soy Sauce* Favorite Japanese seasoning sauce made from fermented soybeans.

*Soybean Oil* Edible oil obtained from soybeans.

*Spaghetti* Most popular type of Italian macaroni; usually the thinner type.

*Spaghettini* Very thin type of spaghetti.

*Sprat* Small fish, usually dried; particular favorite of Scandinavian people.

*Spring-form Pan* Round pan with a removable frame held in place with a spring.

*Spumante* Descriptive of Italian sparkling wines.

*Spumoni* Variety of rich, Italian-style ice cream.

*Sterlet* Young sturgeon.

*Stirabout* An Irish porridge.

*Stracchino* Variety of Italian cheese, usually quite soft.

*Strega* Yellowish Italian liqueur.

*Strufoli* Italian-style cake.

*Sturgeon* One of the most prized of all fish; the roe is caviar.

*Sunflower Oil* Prepared from sunflower seeds; used for shortening, edible oils, etc.

*Suribachi* Japanese mortar much used in cookery.

*Sushi* Japanese rice with vinegar and other flavorings.

*Sword Bean* Type of edible broad bean.

*Sybo* Green onion or scallion in Scotch usage; also *cibol.*

*Tagliarini* Narrow Italian noodle.

*Tamara* Italian mixed spice, usually containing cinnamon, fennel, etc.

*Tansy* Herb used for flavoring.

*Tapioca* Starchy food obtained from the cassava plant.

*Tarragon* Aromatic herb used principally in flavoring vinegar.

*Tartaric Acid* Natural acid, particularly noticeable in grapes; used in baking powder, various foods, drinks, etc.

*Tattie* Familiar term for a potato in Scotland.

*Tempura* Shellfish or vegetables deep-fat fried in the Japanese manner.

*Terrapin* Edible turtle used for soups, stews, etc.

*Thyme* Herb commonly used for flavoring.

*Timbale* Dish containing meat or poultry combined with custard.

*Tokay* Hungarian wine.

*Tomalley* Matter in the body of a lobster; also known as *liver of lobster.*

*Tomato Paste* Paste with a concentrated tomato flavor, usually produced by dehydration.

*Torrone* Italian nougat-type candy.

*Tortellini* Variety of Italian macaroni.

*Tortilla* Flat corn cake; staple food of Mexico.

*Tournedos* Rather small, thin slices of tenderloin steak.

*Travancore* An Indian tea.

*Treacle* Molasses.

*Truffle* An edible substance, possibly either a fungus or a tuber, which grows underground and has a strong, aromatic effect on food; particularly esteemed in France.

*Tufoli* Type of Italian macaroni.

*Tuna* Green tropical fruit obtained from a cactus plant; also the seafood.

*Turbot* Fish highly regarded by European chefs.

*Udon* Japanese noodle made of corn flour.

*Usquebaugh* Spicy Irish whisky or brandy.

*Valencia* Type of almond.

*Vanilla Bean* Edible bean of an orchid plant; a very important flavoring source.

*Vanillin* Active element of the vanilla bean; provides characteristic odor and flavor.

*Velouté* Creamy, white, thick sauce.

*Vermicelli* Thinnest of all spaghettis.

*Vermouth* Apéritif wine, usually prepared with wormwood and other herbs.

*Victoria* A Brazilian coffee.

*Vin Blanc* White wine; also any white wine sauce.

*Vlattero* Greek currant liqueur.

*Vodka* National alcoholic drink of Russia.

*Vol-au-Vent* Pastry shell filled with any mixture.

*Wasabi* Japanese herb with a sharp, spicy flavor.

*Water Chestnut* Small tuber, with the texture and general shape of a chestnut; popular in oriental cookery.

*Wensleydale* A British cheese.

*Whelk* Variety of shellfish.

*Widgeon* Game bird of the duck family.

*Wine* Any fermented product obtained from grape juice.

*Wintergreen Oil* Natural or synthetic product used for flavoring.

*Woodruff* Leaves of a plant commonly used for flavoring; used to perfume German "May Wine."

*Wormwood* A bitter herb; formerly used in the manufacture of absinthe.

*Yellowtail* Type of tuna fish.

*Yogurt* Cultured milk food of custard-smooth consistency, made from fresh, pasteurized cow's milk to which the yogurt cultures are added; when yogurt is cooked, the action of the cultures is inhibited.

*Yokan* A Japanese candy.

*Zabaglione* Also *zabaione;* rich, foamy Italian dessert made with eggs and wine.

*Zakuska* Russian term for hors d'oeuvres.

*Zest* Glossy outside skin of an orange or other citrus fruit.

*Ziti* Rather large type of Italian macaroni.

*Zizania* Another name for wild rice.

*Zuppa Inglese* A rich Italian dessert often prepared with liquor.

# SOURCES OF FOREIGN INGREDIENTS

*FOODS*

The following list is for your guidance. These stores are representative of fine food shops throughout the country which carry imported ingredients. It is always best to visit them in person if possible. If not, write to them, specifying your needs. Many department stores also carry a wide variety of foreign foods.

CALIFORNIA: *Vendome-Martha Smith Caterers,* 327 North Beverly Drive, Beverly Hills; *Jurgensen's Grocery Company,* 842 East California Street, Pasadena; *City of Paris,* Geary and Stockton Avenue, San Francisco

CONNECTICUT: *Patsy Totaro,* 36 Elm Street, New Canaan

DISTRICT OF COLUMBIA: *Larimer's, Inc.,* 1727 Connecticut Avenue, Washington

ILLINOIS: *O'Donnell's,* 1051 North Rush Street, Chicago

LOUISIANA: *Solari, Ltd.,* 201 Royale Street, New Orleans

MAINE: *Model Market,* 89 Middle Street, Portland

MASSACHUSETTS: *S. S. Pierce Company,* 133 Brookline Avenue, Boston

MINNESOTA: *Crystal's,* 18 East Superior Street, Duluth; *J. D. Holtzermann,* 415 Cedar Avenue, Minneapolis

NEW YORK: *Vendome Table Delicacies,* 415 Madison Avenue, New York City; Bloomingdale Brothers, Lexington Avenue, 59th Street, New York City; Hammacher Schlemmer & Co., Inc., 145 E. 57th Street, New York City; Macy's Department Store, Herald Square, New York City

NORTH CAROLINA: *Bocock-Stroud Company,* Fourth at Spruce Street, Winston-Salem

PENNSYLVANIA: *Gourmet's Bazaar,* Mechanic Street, New Hope; *Thomas C. Fluke Company,* 1732 Chestnut Street, Philadelphia; *Union Supply Company,* 1509 Muriel Street, Pittsburgh

RHODE ISLAND: *William B. Chase, Inc.,* 802 Hope Street, Providence

TEXAS: *Simon David,* 4311 Oak Lawn Avenue, Dallas; *European Import Corporation,* Preston at Main Street, Houston

*SPECIALISTS*

The following group specialize in utensils, particular foods, or those of a given region. Very often they also carry other fine foods.

CARIBBEAN: *Marcus Matza,* Stand 461, N.Y.C. Public Market, 114th Street and Park Avenue, New York City

CHEESE: *Phil Alpert,* 181 East Houston Street, New York City

COOKING UTENSILS: *Bazar Français,* 666 Sixth Avenue, New York City; *Lewis & Conger,* 45th & Avenue of Americas, New York City

FRANCE: *Vendome Table Delicacies,* 415 Madison Avenue, New York City

GREECE AND THE BALKANS: *M. G. Couphopoulos,* 306 West Fortieth Street, New York City

HAWAII: *Orchids of Hawaii, Inc.,* 54 West Fifty-sixth Street, New York City

INDONESIA AND MALAYA: *Edward Jurrjens,* R.F.D. 1 Box 409, Farmingdale, N.J.

ITALY: *Manganaro Foods,* 488 Ninth Avenue, New York City

MEATS AND GAME: *E. Joseph, Inc.,* Washington Market, New York City; *S. Schweitzer & Sons,* 421 East Fourteenth Street, New York City

MEXICO: *Ashley's, Inc.,* El Paso, Texas

MIDDLE EUROPE (Hungary, Austria, etc.): *Atlas Importing Company,* 1109 Second Avenue, New York City

NEAR AND MIDDLE EAST: *Trinacria Importing Company,* 415 Third Avenue, New York City; *A. Sahadi & Co., Inc.,* 195 Washington Street, New York City

ORIENT (Japan, China, etc.): *Oriental Food Shop,* 2791 Broadway, New York City; *Katagiri & Company, Inc.,* 224 East Fifty-ninth Street, New York City

SCANDINAVIA: *Lund's Mail Order House,* 5314 Eighth Avenue, Brooklyn, N.Y.; *Nordic House,* 3233 Market Street, Oakland, Calif.

SPANISH AND LATIN AMERICA: *Joseph Victori & Company, Inc.,* 164 Pearl Street, New York City

SPICES AND HERBS: *Twin Tree Gardens, Inc.,* Lynbrook, L.I., N.Y. (information only); *TelBurn of New York,* 335 East Fifty-fifth Street, New York City

TRUFFLES: *Paul A. Urbani,* 113 Tyler Street, Trenton, N.J.

## WINES AND LIQUORS

CALIFORNIA: *Llords & Elwood,* 8847 Beverly Boulevard, Beverly Hills

CONNECTICUT: *Sherry Wine & Spirits Company,* 183 Bedford Avenue, Stamford

FLORIDA: *Weinkles,* 1711 Alton Road, Miami Beach

LOUISIANA: *Fernandez Wine Cellar,* 801 Decatur Street, New Orleans

MASSACHUSETTS: *S. S. Pierce Company,* 133 Brookline Avenue, Boston

MINNESOTA: *Benny Haskell,* 2760 Dean Boulevard, Minneapolis

MISSOURI: *Berbiglia's,* 208 Westport Road, Kansas City; *European Import Corporation,* 23 North Bemiston Avenue, Clayton

NEW JERSEY: *Montclair Food Company,* 517 Bloomfield Avenue, Montclair

NEW YORK: *Sherry Wine & Spirits Co., Inc.,* 679 Madison Avenue, New York City

TEXAS: *Centennial Liquor Store,* 4224 Live Oak Street, Dallas

*Turn page for Conversion Table for use outside of the United States.*

*CONVERSION TABLE for use outside of the United States
(all equivalents are approximate)*

## WEIGHT

| | |
|---|---|
| 15 grams | = ½ ounce |
| 30 grams | = 1 ounce |
| 50 grams | = 1¾ ounces |
| 75 grams | = 2½ ounces |
| 100 grams | = 3½ ounces |
| 500 grams | = 17 ounces (1 pound, 1½ ounces) |
| 1 kilogram | = 35 ounces (2 pounds, 3 ounces) |

## LIQUID

| | |
|---|---|
| 1 declitre | = 3½ ounces |
| 1 demilitre | = ⅞ pint |
| 1 litre | = 1¾ pints (35 ounces) |
| 1 American pint | = 16 fluid ounces |
| 1 American cup | = 8 fluid ounces |
| 1 American cup | = 16 fluid ounces |
| 1 teaspoon | = 4.9 cubic centimeters |
| 1 tablespoon | = 14.8 cubic centimeters |
| 1 cup | = 236.6 cubic centimeters |

## SAMPLE COMPARISONS

| | | |
|---|---|---|
| Butter (solid fats) | 230 grams | = 1 American cup = ½ pound |
| Flour | 115 grams | = 1 American cup = ¼ pound |
| Sugar, granulated | 230 grams | = 1 American cup = ½ pound |

*For other equivalents, see page 448*

## AMERICAN CAN SIZES

| | |
|---|---|
| 8 oz. | = 1 cup |
| #1 Picnic | = 1¼ cups |
| #1 | = 1½ cups |
| #300 | = 2 cups |
| #303 | = 2 cups |
| #2 | = 2½ cups |
| #2¼ | = 3½ cups |
| #1 square | = 1 pound |

ASIA

Indian
Ocean

AUSTRALIA

Pacific
Ocean